Group Policy

Fundamentals, Security, and the Managed Desktop

Group Policy

Fundamentals, Security, and the Managed Desktop

Jeremy Moskowitz

WILEY

Wiley Publishing, Inc.

Acquisitions Editor: Agatha Kim
Development Editor: Sara Barry
Technical Editor: Thorbjörn Sjövold
Production Editors: Elizabeth Campbell, Christine O'Connor
Copy Editor: Liz Welch
Editorial Manager: Pete Gaughan
Production Manager: Tim Tate
Vice President and Executive Group Publisher: Richard Swadley
Vice President and Publisher: Neil Edde
Book Designers: Judy Fung and Bill Gibson
Compositor: Craig Woods, Happenstance Type-O-Rama
Proofreaders: Sheilah Ledwidge, Paul Sagan
Indexer: Nancy Guenther
Project Coordinator, Cover: Lynsey Stanford
Cover Designer: Ryan Sneed
Cover Image: © Polka Dot Images / JupiterImages

Dear Reader,

Thank you for choosing *Group Policy: Fundamentals, Security, and the Managed Desktop*. This book is part of a family of premium-quality Sybex books, all of which are written by outstanding authors who combine practical experience with a gift for teaching.

Sybex was founded in 1976. More than 30 years later, we're still committed to producing consistently exceptional books. With each of our titles, we're working hard to set a new standard for the industry. From the paper we print on, to the authors we work with, our goal is to bring you the best books available.

I hope you see all that reflected in these pages. I'd be very interested to hear your comments and get your feedback on how we're doing. Feel free to let me know what you think about this or any other Sybex book by sending me an email at nedde@wiley.com. If you think you've found a technical error in this book, please visit http://sybex.custhelp.com. Customer feedback is critical to our efforts at Sybex.

Best regards,

Neil Edde
Vice President and Publisher
Sybex, an Imprint of Wiley

To my wife, Laura, who always gives me the support I need.
—Jeremy

Acknowledgments

First, I want to thank my assistant Diane Tkacs for doing the good, bad, and downright ugly jobs here at "Group Policy Central." I seriously don't know how I could do half the stuff I do without you clearing the path necessary for me to write this book. You always do a great job, with a smile, and I'm happy to have you as my right arm. Thank you.

Next, I want to thank Thorbjörn Sjövold for taking on the not-so-glamorous job of Technical Editor. You're "scary smart" and I'm really glad you helped me clean up the little messes I made during the writing process. Note: if there are still any technical problems with the book, blame me, not him. Thorbjörn was awesome.

I want to thank Sara Barry for taking my initial chapters and kneading them from a wad of dough into tasty pizza. And to Elizabeth Campbell who has worked with me through every major project to completion for almost 10 years now. We joke that she's "...been making Jeremy sound like Jeremy since 2001." And it's mostly true. Thank you.

Special thanks to my Sybex and Wiley compatriots: Agatha Kim, Jay Lessandrini, and Neil Edde. Once again, your dedication to my book's success means so much to me. You take everything I create and deal with it so personally, and I really know that. Thank you, very sincerely.

Thanks to Jeff Hicks, PowerShell MVP, who helped me write the new downloadable bonus chapter on Group Policy and PowerShell. Jeff, you did a smashing job, thank you.

Thank you to Microsoft Group Policy team and the Group Policy MVPs who support me directly and indirectly and help me out whenever they can.

Thank you, Mark Minasi, for being a trusted friend, and a great inspiration to me personally and professionally.

Finally, I want to thank all the readers of the previous editions who believed in Group Policy and have used it daily to make their administration experiences even better. And a heartier thanks to those folks on GPAnswers.com who ask questions, help others, and help me make this book the best it can be.

About the Contributors

Jeffery Hicks (MCSE, MCSA, MCT) is a Microsoft MVP and an IT veteran with almost 20 years of experience, much of it spent as an IT consultant specializing in Windows Server technologies. He works today as an independent author, trainer, and consultant. Jeff is a columnist for Redmond Magazine and MCPMag.com. He has co-authored or authored several books, courseware, and training videos on administrative scripting and automation. His latest book is *Windows PowerShell 2.0: TFM* (SAPIEN Press, 2010), coauthored with Don Jones. Jeff is a moderator at ScriptingAnswers.com, a subject matter expert at TheExpertsCommunity.com, and a frequent contributor to many scripting-related forums. You can follow Jeff at jdhitsolutions.com/blog and twitter.com/jeffhicks.

Thorbjörn Sjövold is the CTO and founder of Specops Software (www.specopssoft.com), a provider of Group Policy–based systems management and security extension products. Reach him at thorbjorn.sjovold@specopssoft.com.

Contents at a Glance

Contents

Introduction

Turns out, this Group Policy thing is popular.

Even though we've renamed the book (again), you could think of this book as the "6th edition" of my original *Group Policy, Profiles, and IntelliMirror* book—from way back in 2001.

That's an amazing run for one technology. What other technology has been around for almost 10 years and is still *gaining* in popularity? Its increased popularity and widespread use has grown, year after year. And the underlying technology—both at its core and what it controls—has received an infusion of new technologies to keep it not only still relevant, but indeed, *central* to any Active Directory administrator's tool belt of required knowledge.

Group Policy and Active Directory go hand in hand. If you have Active Directory, you get Group Policy.

And Group Policy has one goal: to make your administrative life easier. Instead of running around from machine to machine, tweaking a setting here or installing some software there, you'll have ultimate control from on high.

Like Zeus himself, controlling the many aspects of the mortal world below, you will have the ability, via Group Policy, to dictate specific settings pertaining to how you want your users and computers to operate. You'll be able to shape your network's destiny. You'll have the power. But you need to know how to tap into this power and what can be powered.

In this introduction and throughout the first several chapters, I'll describe just what Group Policy is all about and give you an idea of its tremendous power. Then, as your skills grow, chapter by chapter, we'll build on what you've already learned, and help you do more with Group Policy, troubleshoot it, and implement some of its most powerful features.

Group Policy Defined

If we take a step back and try to analyze the term *Group Policy*, it's easy to become confused. When I first heard the term, I didn't know what to make of it.

I asked myself, "Are we applying 'policy' to 'groups'? Is this some sort of old-school NT 4 System Policy applied to Active Directory groups?"

Turns out, "Group Policy" as a name isn't, well, excellent. That's because, at cocktail parties, I have a hard time telling the person next to me what I teach and write about.

If I said something like "I teach databases," he would cheerfully go back to his scotch and soda and leave me alone. But because I say, "I teach Group Policy to smart people looking to get smarter," he (unfortunately) wants to know more. He'll say something like "What does that mean? I've never heard of Group Policy before." And while I love talking about Group Policy to you, the friendly IT geeks, at a cocktail party full of stuffed shirts, I just want to get another canapé.

So, the name "Group Policy" can be kind of confusing, but it's also intriguing. Microsoft's perspective is that the name "Group Policy" is derived from the fact that you are "grouping together policy settings." Group Policy is, in essence, rules that are applied and enforced at multiple levels of Active Directory. Policy settings you dictate must be adhered to by your users and computers. This provides great power and efficiency when manipulating client systems.

Instead of running around from machine to machine, you're in charge (not your users).

When going through the examples in this book, you will play the various parts of the end user, the OU administrator, the domain administrator, and the enterprise administrator. Your mission is to create and define Group Policy using Active Directory and witness it being automatically enforced. What you say goes! With Group Policy, you can set policies that dictate that users quit messing with their machines. You can dictate what software will be deployed. You can determine how much disk space users can use. You can do pretty much whatever you want—it is up to you. With Group Policy, you hold all the power. That's the good news.

And this magical power only works on Windows 2000 or later machines. That includes Windows 2000, Windows XP, Windows Server 2003 (as a client), Windows Vista, Windows Server 2008 and 2008 R2 (as a client), and, of course, Windows 7.

This shouldn't be a problem, since you've expunged all the Windows 95, Windows 98, or Windows NT workstations or servers. Hey, it is 2010, after all!

I'll likely say this again in multiple places, but I want to get one "big ol' misconception" out of the way right here, right in the introduction. The Group Policy infrastructure does not care what mode your domain is in. If you have only one type of Domain Controller, or a mixture of Domain Controllers, 100 percent of everything we cover in this book is valid.

Said another way, even if your domain level is the "old and crusty" Windows 2000 mixed mode, you're still 100-percent covered here. Group Policy is all about the client (the target) operating system, and not the Domain Controllers or domain modes.

If the range of control scares you—don't be afraid! It just means more power to hold over your environment. You'll quickly learn how to wisely use this newfound power to reign over your subjects, er, users.

Group Policy vs. Group Policy Objects vs. Group Policy Preferences

Before we go headlong into Group Policy theory, let's get some terminology and vocabulary out of the way:

- *Group Policy* is the concept that, from on high, you can do all this "stuff" to your client machines.

- A *policy setting* is just one individual setting that you can use to perform some specific action.

- *Group Policy Objects (GPOs)* are the "nuts and bolts" contained within Active Directory Domain Controllers, and each can contain anywhere from one to a zillion individual policy settings.

- The *Group Policy Preferences* is a newer add-on to the existing set of the "original" Group Policy many have come to know and love. Group Policy Preferences (sometimes shortened to GPPrefs, or GPP) don't act quite the same as their original cousins. We'll cover the Group Policy Preferences in detail in Chapter 5.

- *Preference item* is a way to describe one "Group Policy Preferences directive." It's like a "policy setting," but for the Group Policy Preferences.

It's my goal that after you work through this book, you'll be able to jump up on your desk one day and use all the vocabulary at once. Like this: "Hey! *Group Policy* isn't applying to our client machines! Perhaps a *policy setting* is misconfigured. Or, maybe one of our *Group Policy Objects* has gone belly-up! Heck, maybe one of the *preference items* is misconfigured. I'd better read about what's going on in Chapter 7, 'Troubleshooting Group Policy.'"

This terminology can be a little confusing—considering that each term includes the word *policy*. In this text, however, I've tried especially hard to use the correct nomenclature for what I'm describing. If you get confused, just come back here to refresh your brain about the definitions.

Note that there is never a time to use the phrase "Group Policies." Those two words together shouldn't exist. If you're talking about "multiple GPOs" or "multiple policy settings" or "policy settings vs. preference items," these are the preferred phrases to use, and never "Group Policies."

Where Group Policy Applies

Group Policy can be applied to many machines at once using Active Directory, or it can be applied when you walk up to a specific machine. For the most part, in this book, I'll focus on using Group Policy within an Active Directory environment, where it affects the most machines.

A percentage of the settings explored and discussed in this book are available to member or stand-alone Windows machines—which can either participate or not participate in an Active Directory environment.

However, the Folder Redirection settings (discussed in Chapter 10) and the Software Distribution settings (discussed in Chapter 11) are not available to stand-alone machines (that is, computers that are not participating in an Active Directory domain). In some cases, I will pay particular attention to non–Active Directory environments. However, most of the book deals with the more common case; that is, we'll explore the implications of deploying Group Policy in an Active Directory environment.

The "Too Many Operating Systems" Problem

If we line up all the operating systems that you (a savvy IT person) might have in your corporate world, we would likely find one or more of the following (presented here in date-release order):

- Windows 2000 (Workstation and Server), RTM through SP4
- Windows 2003 Server, RTM through SP2
- Windows XP, RTM through SP3
- Windows Vista, RTM through SP2
- Windows Server 2008, RTM (known as SP1, actually) through SP2
- Windows 7 RTM (no service packs yet, as of this writing)
- Windows Server 2008 R2 (no service packs yet, as of this writing)

For the love of Pete (whoever Pete is), that's a *lot* of potential operating systems. Okay, okay—perhaps you don't have *all* of them. You likely don't have any more Windows 2000 (or maybe you *do*, tucked in a back room somewhere, quietly processing something or other).

The point, however, is that Group Policy can apply to *all* of these systems. Under most circumstances, "old stuff" will work correctly on newer machines. That is, generally, something that can affect, say, an XP machine will also (generally) continue to affect a Windows 7 machine.

With that in mind, here's an example of what I'm *not* going to do. I'm *not* going to show you an example of something in the book, then say something like "… and this example is valid for Windows XP, Windows Vista, Windows Server 2008, Windows Server 2008 R2, and Windows 7."

My (and your) head will just explode if I do that and you need to read that each time.

So, here's what I *am* going to do. You'll read my discussion about something, then I'll say something like "… and this example is valid for Windows XP and later." That would mean that the concept, for example, policy setting, should work A-OK for XP and later machines (all the way to Windows 7 and also usually for servers, like Windows Server 2008, too). Similarly, if I say "… and this is valid for Windows Vista and later," that means you'll be golden if the target machine is Windows Vista and later (including Server 2008, Server 2008 R2, and Windows 7).

Of course, there are a handful of exceptions: things that only work on one particular operating system in a possibly peculiar way. For instance, there are a handful of Windows Vista–only settings that aren't valid for Windows 7 (or Windows Server 2008 R2) machines. And, on rare occasions, a particular service pack of a particular operating system is affected by a setting, where it wasn't previously available. Again, I'll strive for clarity regarding the exceptions—but the good news is, those are few and far between.

If you get lost, here's a quick cheat sheet to help you remember "which machines act alike":

- Windows 2000 Workstation and Windows Server
- Windows 2003 Server and Windows XP

- Windows Server 2008 and Windows Vista
- Windows 7 RTM and Windows Server 2008 R2

Most of the screen shots in the book are of Windows 7 and Windows XP. We'll also discuss Windows Server 2008 R2 when required, and also show a handful of Windows Vista shots. Where appropriate, I'll note the differences between the operating environments. Heck, I'll also express some concepts as originally found in Windows 2000. I like to talk about this "old school" way sometimes, because I find it helps explain why Windows does some things that seem, well, odd. But by explaining the original way with Windows 2000, then understanding modern Windows becomes much clearer.

A quick word about Windows Vista. Microsoft loves to tout bajillions of sales and oodles of "happy Vista customers." But ask a hundred IT shops, "Did you deploy Vista?" and you won't get much response. I honestly don't know what to believe other than what I see with my two eyes, and what people *tell* me. What I *see* and what people *tell* me is that they're basically "skipping Vista." They'll mostly be using Windows XP until they phase it out for Windows 7. So, of all the operating systems in this book, the one I'll be spending the least amount of time on is Vista itself.

But we also cannot deny the existence of Windows Vista.

Yes, friends. Vista happened.

It turns out that even though Microsoft "didn't quite get the taste right" with regard to Windows Vista, the individual ingredients continue to be the base of our Windows soup going forward. So, that means Windows 7 is, more or less, a minor upgrade from Vista. And pretty much everything that was once valid for Vista is *also* valid for Windows 7. Therefore, you'll see me write a lot about "… and this works for Windows Vista and later" or in some places, like table listings, you'll see "Valid for Vista+"—meaning that whatever I'm referencing will work on Vista (if you have it), but it will also work on Windows 7.

We can't deny that Windows Vista existed. It existed, and, well, now that it's reborn as Windows 7, the base that Windows Vista brought will be with us for a long time to come.

This Book and Beyond

Group Policy is a big concept with some big power. This book is intended to help you get a handle on this new power to gain control over your environment and to make your day-to-day administration easier. It's filled with practical, hands-on examples of Group Policy usage and troubleshooting. It is my hope that you enjoy this book and learn from my experiences, so you can successfully deploy Group Policy and manage your desktops to better control your network. I'm honored to have you aboard for the ride, and I hope you get as much out of Group Policy as I do from writing and speaking about it in my hands-on workshops.

As you read this book, it's natural to have questions about Group Policy or managing your desktops. To form a community around Group Policy, I have a popular community forum that can be found at www.GPanswers.com.

I encourage you to visit the website and post your questions to the community forum or peruse the other resources that will be constantly renewed and available for download. For instance, in addition to the forum at www.GPanswers.com, you'll find:

- Three extra downloadable chapters from this newest edition of the book
- Full downloadable PowerShell scripts from one of those downloadable chapters
- One older reference chapter (on ADM files) in case you need it
- Tips and tricks
- A third-party Group Policy Solutions Guide, and lots, lots more!

In case you're curious, here are the three downloadable chapters:

- Scripting Group Policy Operations with PowerShell (cowritten by PowerShell MVP Jeffrey Hicks)
- Advanced Group Policy Management (AGPM v4)
- Full Lockdown with Windows SteadyState

You'll love these extra chapters that we just couldn't fit in the book due to size constraints.

If you want to meet me in person, my website at www.GPanswers.com has a calendar of all my upcoming public training workshops, speaking engagements at conferences, and other events. I'd love to hear how this book met your needs or helped you out.

Group Policy Essentials

In this chapter, you'll get your feet wet with the concept that is Group Policy. You'll start to understand conceptually what Group Policy is and how it's created, applied, and modified, and you'll go through some practical examples to get at the basics.

The best news is that the essentials of Group Policy are the same in all versions of Windows 2000 onward. So as I stated in the introduction, if you've got Windows XP, Windows Server 2003, Windows Server 2008, Windows Vista, Windows 7—whatever—you're golden.

That's because Group Policy isn't a server-driven technology. As you'll learn in depth a little later, the magic of Group Policy happens (mostly) on the client (target) machine. And when we say "client," we mean anything that can "receive" Group Policy directives: Windows 7, Windows XP, or even Windows Server 2008 or Windows Server 2003; they're "clients" too.

So, if your Active Directory Domain Controllers are a mixture of Windows 2000 and/or Windows 2003 and/or Windows Server 2008, nothing much changes. And it doesn't matter if your domain is in Mixed, Native, or another mode—Group Policy works exactly the same in all of them.

There are occasional odds and ends you get with upgraded domain types. With the Windows 2003 or later schema, you'll get something neat called WMI filters (described in Chapter 4). Also note that in a Windows 2008 Functional mode domain level, the replication of the file-based part of a Group Policy Object (GPO) can be enhanced to use distributed file system (DFS) replication instead of system volume (SYSVOL) replication.

Regardless of what your server architecture is, I encourage you to work through the examples in this chapter.

So, let's get started and talk about the essentials.

Getting Ready to Use This Book

This book is full of examples. And to help you work through these examples, I'm going to suggest a sample test lab for you to create. It's pretty simple really, but in its simplicity we'll be able to work though dozens of real-world examples to see how things work. Here are the computers you need to set up and what I suggest you name them (if you want to work through the examples with me in the book):

DC01.corp.com   This is your Active Directory Domain Controller. It can be any type of Domain Controller, Windows 2000 and later. For this book, I'll assume you've loaded Windows Server 2008 and later on this computer and that you'll create a test domain called Corp.com.

In real life you would have multiple Domain Controllers in the domain. But here in the test lab, it'll be okay if you just have one.

I'll refer to this machine as DC01 in the book. We'll also use DC01 as a file server and software distribution server and for a lot of other roles we really shouldn't. That's so you can work through lots of examples without bringing up lots of servers.

XPPRO1.corp.com   This is some user's Windows XP machine, and it's joined to the domain Corp.com. I'll assume you've loaded Windows XP's SP3. Sometimes it'll be a Sales computer, other times a Marketing computer, and other times a Nursing computer. To use this machine as such, just move the computer account around in Active Directory when the time comes. You'll see what I mean. I'll refer to this machine as XPPRO1 in the book.

Win7.corp.com   This is some user's Windows 7 machine and it's joined to the domain Corp.com. I'll refer to this machine as WIN7 in the book. Like XPPRO1, this machine will move around a lot to help us "play pretend" when the times arise. Windows XP works a little differently than Windows 7, so having both a Windows 7 and a Windows XP machine in your environment will be good for testing if you are in charge of making both work under the same roof.

Win7management.corp.com   This machine is yours—the IT pro who runs the show. You could manage Active Directory from anywhere on your network, but you're going to do it from here. This is the machine you'll use to run the tools you need to manage both Active Directory and Group Policy. I'll refer to this machine as WIN7MANAGEMENT. As the name implies, you'll run Windows 7 from this machine. Note that you aren't "forced" or "required" to use a Windows 7 machine as your management machine—but you'll be able to "manage it all" if you do.

Figure 1.1 shows a diagram of what our test network should look like if you want to follow along.

 To save space in the book, we're going to assume you're using a Windows 7 machine as your management machine. If you're forced by some draconian corporate edict to use a Windows Vista or Windows XP (or earlier) machine as a management machine, you'll have to refer to previous editions of the book to get the skinny about using them.

For working through this book, you can build your test lab with real machines or with virtual hardware. Personally, I use VMware Workstation (a pay tool) and VMware Server (a free tool) for my testing. However, Microsoft's tools, like Virtual Server 2005

and Windows Virtual PC, or Sun VirtualBox (all free) are perfectly decent choices as well. Using virtual machines, if you don't have a bunch of extra physical servers and desktops around, you can follow along with all the examples anyway.

FIGURE 1.1   Here's the configuration you'll need for the test lab in this book. Note that the Domain Controller can be 2000 or above, but 2008 is preferred to allow you to work through all the examples in this book.

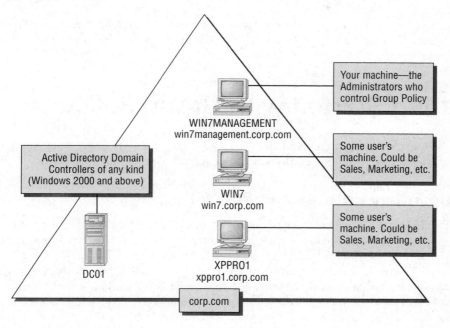

I suggest you build your test lab from scratch. Get the original media or download each operating system and spin up a new test lab.

You can find Windows Server 2008 trial download versions here:

www.microsoft.com/windowsserver2008/en/us/trial-software.aspx

And if you want to get Windows Server 2008 R2, you can find it here:

http://technet.microsoft.com/en-us/evalcenter/dd459137.aspx

If you want to get Windows 7 trial versions, here's the URL:

http://tinyurl.com/ktug5n

Microsoft usually also makes pre-built virtual hard disk (VHD) images for use with Virtual PC. It's your choice of course, but I prefer to fresh-build my lab instead of using the preconfigured VHD files.

And that's what I'll be doing for my examples in this book. If the URLs I've specified change, I'm sure a little Googling, er, Bing-ing will Bing it, er, bring it right up.

WARNING   Because Group Policy can be so all-encompassing, I highly recommend that you try the examples in a test lab environment first before making these changes for real in your production environment.

Note that from time to time I might refer to some machine that *isn't* here in the suggested test lab, just to illustrate a point. However, this is the minimum configuration you'll need to get the most out the book.

Getting Started with Group Policy

Group Policy is a big, big place. And you need a road map. Let's try to get a firm understanding of what we're about to be looking at for the next several hundred pages.

Group Policy Entities and Policy Settings

Every Group Policy Object contains two halves: a User half and a Computer half. These two halves are properly called *nodes*, though sometimes they're just referred to as either the *User half* and the *Computer half* or the *User branch* and the *Computer branch*.

A sample Group Policy Object with both the Computer Configuration and User Configuration nodes can be seen in Figure 1.2 (in the upcoming section "Local Group Policy on Pre-Vista Computers"). Don't worry; we'll show you how to get there in just a second.

NOTE   Just to make things a little more complicated, if you're deploying settings using Active Directory (the most usual case) as opposed to walking up and creating a "local GPO" as we do in Figure 1.2, the interface is a wee bit different and shows the Group Policy Preferences' node. Hang tight for more on that.

The first level under both the User and the Computer nodes contains Software Settings, Windows Settings, and Administrative Templates. If we dive down into the Administrative Templates of the Computer node, underneath we discover additional levels of Windows Components, System, Network, and Printers. Likewise, if we dive down into the Administrative Templates of the User node, we see some of the same folders plus some additional ones, such as Shared Folders, Desktop, and Start Menu and Taskbar.

In both the User and Computer halves, you'll see that policy settings are hierarchical, like a directory structure. Similar policy settings are grouped together for easy location. That's the idea anyway—though, admittedly, sometimes locating the specific policy or configuration you want can prove to be a challenge.

When manipulating policy settings, you can choose to set either computer policy settings or user policy settings (or both!). You'll see examples of this shortly. (See the section "Searching and Commenting Group Policy Objects and Policy Settings" in Chapter 2 for tricks on how to minimize the effort of finding the policy setting you want.)

Most policy settings are not found in both nodes. However, there are a few that overlap. In that case, if the computer policy setting is different from the user policy setting, the computer policy setting generally overrides the user policy setting. But, to be sure, check the Explain text associated with the policy setting.

Wait... I Don't Get It. What Do the User and Computer Nodes Do?

One of the key issues that new Group Policy administrators ask themselves is: "What the heck is the difference between the Computer and User nodes?"

Imagine that you had a combination store: Dog Treats (for dogs) and Candy Treats (for kids). That's right; it's a strange little store with seemingly two types of incompatible foods under the same roof. You wouldn't feed the kids dog treats (they'd spit them out and ignore the treat), and you wouldn't feed the kids' candy to a dog (because the dogs would spit out the sour candy and ignore the treat).

That's the same thing that happens here. Sure, it looks tempting. There are lots of treats on both sides of the store, but only one type of customer will accept each type of treat.

So, in practical terms, the Computer node (the first part of the policy) contains policy settings that are only relevant for computers. That is, if there's a GPO that contains Computer-side settings and it "hits" a computer, these settings will take effect. These Computer-side settings could be items like Startup Scripts, Shutdown Scripts, and how the local firewall should be configured. Think of this as every setting relevant to the *computer itself*—no matter who is logged on at that moment.

The User node (the second part of the policy) contains policy settings that are relevant only for users. Again, if there's a GPO that contains User-side settings and it "hits" a user, these settings will take effect for that user. These User-side items only make sense on a per-user basis, like logon scripts, logoff scripts, availability of the Control Panel, and lots more. Think of this as every setting relevant to the currently logged-on user—and these settings will follow the user to every machine they pop on to.

Feeding users dog treats, er, Computer settings doesn't work. Same thing with feeding computers User-side settings. When a GPO hits user objects with Computer policy settings or computer objects with User policy settings, it simply will *not* do anything. You'll just sit there and scratch your head and wonder why it doesn't work. But it's not that it's not working; this is how it's designed.

> Computer settings are for computer objects, and User settings are for user objects. If this is bad news for you, there are two ways to get out of the problem. One way is an in-the-box advanced technique called *loopback processing* that can help you out. Look for more information on loopback processing in Chapter 4. The other way is via a third-party tool called PolicyPak, which (among other things) can permit computers to embrace user-side settings. More on this in Chapter 6.

The 18 (Original) Categories of Group Policy

In this section, you'll learn how to gain access to the interface, which will let you start configuring these categories.

Now, as you're following along working through these examples (or you read Table 1.1 and want to get started right away), you might start to think to yourself, "Jeremy's screen shots don't look exactly like what I have on my screen." There's a simple answer for that.

There are, confusingly, various versions of the Group Policy Editor. If you're still using Windows XP as the place from which you manage Group Policy, your screens are going to look a little different from mine.

More modern clients (starting with Windows Vista/SP1 and onward to Windows 7) use a newer Group Policy Management Console (GPMC), which is found in a download called RSAT. RSAT stands for Remote Server Administration Toolkit and is akin to the old Adminpak download from the Server 2003 era. Inside the RSAT, you'll find tools like Active Directory Users and Computers as well as the GPMC, which we'll use right around the bend. Additionally, only RSAT's GPMC shows subnodes: Policies and Preferences, which will be important for Chapter 5. I'll show you how to get and install the RSAT tool with the updated GPMC in the section "Implementing the GPMC on Your Management Station" coming up a little later in this chapter, so don't worry about it for now.

Note that local policies are *not* split into two subnodes, though—that is because the Preferences node is only available within Active Directory GPOs. More on local policies vs. Active Directory–based policies, right around the corner.

 So, if in your real world you're missing the Policies and Preferences nodes within User Configuration and Computer Configuration right now, don't panic. You'll learn how to get those nodes introduced.

In this book, you'll learn about the major categories of Group Policy. Table 1.1 should be helpful if you're looking to get started working right away with a category. Again, your Group Policy Editor won't show the Policies or Preferences nodes unless you're using the RSAT tools with the updated GPMC and you're editing an Active Directory GPO.

TABLE 1.1 The Major Categories of Group Policy

Group Policy Category	Where in Group Policy Interface	Which Operating Systems Support It	Where to Find Information in the Book	Notes
Administrative Templates (also known as Registry Settings)	User or Computer ➤ Policies ➤ Administrative Templates	Windows 2000+	Many examples throughout the book	
Security Settings	Computer or User Configuration ➤ Policies ➤ Windows Settings ➤ Security Settings	Windows 2000+	Chapter 8	
Wired Network (802.3) Settings	Computer Configuration ➤ Policies ➤ Windows Settings ➤ Security Settings ➤ Wired Network (IEEE 802.3) Policies	Windows Vista+ only	Chapter 8	Be sure to read Chapter 8 before attempting to use these settings.
Wireless Network (802.11) Settings	Computer Configuration ➤ Policies ➤ Windows Settings ➤ Security Settings ➤ Wireless Network (IEEE 802.11) Policies	Windows XP and Windows Vista+ (set independently)	Chapter 8	Be sure to read Chapter 8 before attempting to use these settings for Windows Vista+.
Scripts	Computer Configuration ➤ Policies ➤ Windows Settings ➤ Scripts (Startup/Shutdown) and Policies ➤ Windows Settings ➤ Script (Logon/Logoff)		Chapter 12	
Group Policy Software Installation (also known as Application Management)	Computer or User Configuration ➤ Policies ➤ Software Settings	Windows 2000+	Chapter 11	

TABLE 1.1 The Major Categories of Group Policy *(continued)*

Group Policy Category	Where in Group Policy Interface	Which Operating Systems Support It	Where to Find Information in the Book	Notes
Folder Redirection	User Configuration ➤ Policies ➤ Windows Settings ➤ Folder Redirection	Windows 2000+; some additional options for Windows XP; many additional options for Windows Vista+	Chapter 11	
Disk Quotas	Computer Configuration ➤ Policies ➤ Administrative Templates ➤ System ➤ Disk Quotas	Windows 2000+	I don't cover this subject in this book. This content has been removed to make room for other material. Disk quotas have been covered in previous editions.	There is a brief article on disk quotas here: `http://support.microsoft.com/kb/183322`. You'll find another article here: `http://tinyurl.com/35mvny`.
Encrypted Data Recovery Agents (EFS Recovery Policy)	Computer Configuration ➤ Windows Policies ➤ Windows Settings ➤ Security Settings ➤ Public Key Policies ➤ Encrypting File System	Windows 2000+	Not covered	
Internet Explorer Maintenance	User Configuration ➤ Policies ➤ Windows Settings ➤ Internet Explorer Maintenance	Windows 2000+	Chapter 12	
Software Restriction Policies	Computer or User ➤ Policies ➤ Windows Settings ➤ Security Settings ➤ Software Restriction Policies	Windows XP+	Chapter 8	

TABLE 1.1   The Major Categories of Group Policy *(continued)*

Group Policy Category	Where in Group Policy Interface	Which Operating Systems Support It	Where to Find Information in the Book	Notes
Quality of Service (QoS) Packet Scheduler and Policy-Based QoS	Computer or User Configuration ≯ Policies ≯ Windows Settings ≯ Policy-based QoS	Windows XP+; Policy-based Enterprise QoS is Vista+ only.	Not covered	You can start your Windows Vista+ QoS journey here: http://tinyurl.com/yxglpp.
IPSec (IP Security) Policies	In XP: Computer Configuration ≯ Policies ≯ Windows Settings ≯ Security Settings ≯ IP Security Policies	Windows 2000+	Chapter 8	In Vista+, this is part of the Windows Firewall with Advanced Security section located under Computer Configuration ≯ Policies ≯ Windows Settings ≯ Security Settings.
Windows Search	Computer Configuration ≯ Policies ≯ Administrative Templates ≯ Windows Components ≯ Search	Windows Vista+	Not covered	See www.microsoft.com/windows/desktopsearch.
Deployed Printer Connections	Computer or User Configuration ≯ Policies ≯ Windows Settings ≯ Deployed Printers	Technically, Vista+ only; workaround available for Windows 2000+	Not covered	We'll leverage a better way to zap printers around. We'll learn about it first in Chapter 5, then deeply explore it in Chapter 12. If you want to learn more about the older "Deployed Printer Connections" see GPanswers.com's Newsletter #17.

TABLE 1.1 The Major Categories of Group Policy *(continued)*

Group Policy Category	Where in Group Policy Interface	Which Operating Systems Support It	Where to Find Information in the Book	Notes
Offline Files	Computer or User Configuration ➤ Policies ➤ Administrative Templates ➤ Network ➤ Offline Files	Different Group Policy "moving parts" to make this technology work in Vista+ and Windows Server 2008 than in previous operating systems; feature available in Windows 2000 and later.	Chapter 10	
Group Policy Preference Extensions	Computer or User Configuration ➤ Preferences (not available in local policies, only domain policies)	Group Policy Preference Extensions built in to Windows Server 2008 and Windows 7, but are an additional download and installation for Windows XP and Windows Vista; not supported on Windows 2000 machines.	Chapter 5	Adds 21 additional functions to the Group Policy universe.
Internet Explorer User Accelerators		Windows 7+	Not covered	
Internet Explorer Machine Accelerators		Windows 7+	Not covered	

Group Policy is a twofold idea. First, without an Active Directory, there's one and only one Group Policy available.

Officially, this policy directly on the workstation is called a *local policy*, but it still resides under the umbrella of the concept of Group Policy. Later, once Active Directory is available, the nonlocal (or, as they're sometimes called, *domain-based* or *Active Directory–based*) Group Policy Objects come into play, as you'll see later. Let's get started and explore both options.

> While you're plunking around inside the Group Policy Editor (also known as the Group Policy Management Editor, or Group Policy Object Editor), you'll see lots of policy settings that are geared toward a particular operating system. Some are only for specific operating systems, and others are more general. If you happen to apply a policy setting to a system that isn't listed, the policy setting is simply ignored. For instance, policy settings described as working "Only for Windows 7" machines will not typically work on Windows XP machines. Each policy setting has a "Supported on" field that should be consulted to know which operating systems can embrace which policy setting. Many of them will say something like "At least Windows XP" to let you know they're valid for, say, XP and onward.

Understanding Local Group Policy

Before we officially dive into what is specifically contained inside this magic of Group Policy or how Group Policy is applied when Active Directory is involved, you might be curious to see exactly what your interaction with Local Group Policy might look like.

Local Group Policy is best used when Active Directory isn't available, say either in a Novell NetWare environment or when you have a gaggle of machines that simply aren't connected to a domain.

Local Group Policy is different for Windows Vista and later versus the other Windows operating systems. Let's explore Local Group Policy on pre-Vista machines first and then move on to the features specific to Vista and Windows 7.

Local Group Policy on Pre-Vista Computers

The most expeditious way to edit the Local Group Policy on a machine is to click Start ➤ Run and type in **GPEDIT.MSC**. This pops up the Local Computer Policy Editor.

You are now exploring the Local Group Policy of this Windows XP workstation. Local Group Policy is unique to each specific machine. To see how a Local Group Policy applies, drill down through the User Configuration ➤ Administrative Templates ➤ System ➤ Ctrl+Alt+Del Options and select **Remove Lock Computer**, as shown in Figure 1.2. Once it's selected, choose the Enabled radio button and click OK.

FIGURE 1.2   You can edit the Local Group Policy using the Local Group Policy Editor (GPEDIT.MSC).

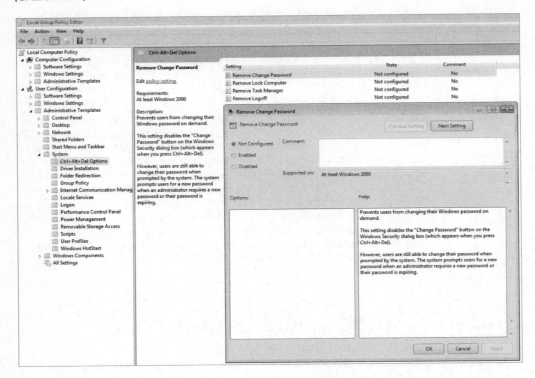

When you do, within a few seconds you should see that if you press Ctrl+Alt+Del, the Lock Computer option is unavailable.

To revert the change, simply reselect **Remove Lock Computer** and select Not Configured. This reverts the change back to the way the operating system works by default.

 You can think of Local Group Policy as a way to perform decentralized administration. A bit later, when we explore Group Policy with Active Directory, we'll saunter into centralized administration.

This Local Group Policy affects everyone who logs onto this machine—including normal users and administrators. Be careful when making settings here; you can temporarily lock yourself out of some useful functions. For instance, frequently administrators want to remove Run from the Start menu for Windows XP machines. Then, the first time they themselves want to go to a command prompt, they can't choose Start ➤ Run. It's just gone!

To get that Run command back, you'll have to click the MMC.exe icon in Explorer (or via command line/batch file) and manually load the Group Policy snap-in.

As I stated in the introduction, most of the settings we'll explore in this book are available to workstations or servers that aren't joined to an Active Directory domain. However, many functions, like Folder Redirection settings (discussed in Chapter 10), the Software Distribution settings (discussed in Chapter 11), and others are not available to stand-alone machines without Active Directory present.

You can point toward other computers' local policies by using the syntax gpedit.msc /gpcomputer:"*targetmachine*" or gpedit.msc /gpcomputer:"*targetmachine.domain.com*"; the machine name must be in quotes.

Local Group Policy on Vista and Later

It's true that you can also type **GPEDIT.MSC** at the Windows Vista or Windows 7 command prompt and get the same Local Computer Policy Editor you just saw in Windows XP.

However, Vista and later has a secret super-power that takes Local Group Policy to the next level.

Remember how, not more than three paragraphs ago, I stated this:

> "This Local Group Policy affects everyone who logs onto this machine—including normal users and administrators. Be careful when making settings here; you can temporarily lock yourself out of some useful functions."

True—for pre-Vista machines. On Vista and later, however, the superpower feature is that you can decide who gets what settings at a local level. This feature is called Multiple Local GPOs (MLGPOs).

MLGPOs are most often handy when you want your users to get one gaggle of settings (that is, desktop restrictions) but you want to ensure that your access is unfettered for day-to-day administration.

Now, in these examples we're going to use Windows 7, but this same feature is available on Vista and later (including Windows Server 2008 and of course Server 2008 R2). It's just not all that likely you'll end up using it on a Windows Server.

Understanding Multiple Local GPOs

The best way to understand MLGPOs is by thinking of the end product. That is, when we're done, we want our users to embrace some settings, and we (administrators) want to potentially embrace some settings. Or perhaps you want just one specific user to embrace a particular combination of settings.

When you type **GPEDIT.MSC** at a command prompt, it's just as if you did it on Windows XP: you're affecting all users—mere mortals *and* administrators.

But with Vista and later, there are actually three "layers" that can be leveraged to ensure that some settings affect regular users and other settings affect you (the administrator).

Let's be sure to understand all three layers before we get too gung-ho and try it out. When MLGPOs are processed, Windows Vista and later checks to see if the layer is being used and if that layer is supposed to apply to that user:

Layer 1 (lowest priority)   The Local Computer Policy. You create this by running GPEDIT.MSC.

- The settings you make on the Computer Configuration side are guaranteed to affect all users on this computer (including administrators).
- The settings you make on the User Configuration side may be trumped by Layer 2 or Layer 3.

Layer 2 (next highest priority)   Is the user a mere mortal *or* a local administrator? (One account cannot be both.) This layer cannot contain Computer Configuration settings.

Layer 3 (most specific)   Is this a specific user who is being dictated a specific policy? This layer cannot contain Computer Configuration settings.

You can see this graphically laid out in Figure 1.3.

If no conflicts exist among the levels, the effect is additive. For instance, let's imagine the following:

- Layer 1 (the Local Computer Policy level): The wish is to **Remove Lock Computer** from the Ctrl+Alt+Del area.
- Then, at Layer 2: We say "All local users" will have "Search" gone from the Start menu.
- Then, at Layer 3: We say Fred, a local user, will be denied access to the Control Panel.

The result for Fred will be the sum total of all edicts at all layers.

But what if there's a conflict between the levels? In that case, the layer that's "closest to the user" wins (also known as "Last writer wins"). So, if at the Local Computer Policy the wish is to **Remove Lock Computer** from the Ctrl+Alt+Del area, but that area is expressly granted to Sally, a local user on that machine, Sally will still be able to use the Lock command. That's because we're saying that she is expressly granted the right at Layer 3, which "wins" over Layers 1 and 2.

Trying Out Multiple Local GPOs on Windows Vista and Later

Just typing **GPEDIT.MSC** at the Windows Vista and later Start Search prompt doesn't give you the magical "layering" superpower. Indeed, just typing **GPEDIT.MSC** performs the exact same function as it did in Windows XP. That is, every edit you make while you run the Local Computer Policy affects all users logged onto the machine.

To tell Vista and later you want to edit one of the layers (as just described), you need to load the Group Policy Object Editor by hand. We'll do this on WIN7.

FIGURE 1.3   A block diagram of how MLGPOs are applied to a system

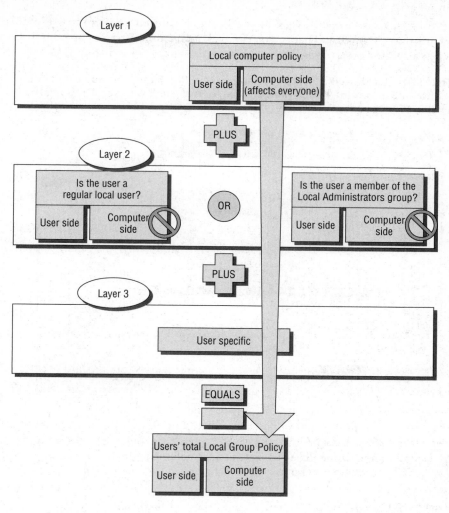

On WIN7, to load the Group Policy Object Editor by hand, follow these steps:

1. Click Start, and then in the Start Search box (which will run things), type **MMC**. A "naked" MMC appears. Note that you will have to approve the User Access Control (UAC) message (UAC is discussed in detail in Chapter 8).

2. From the File menu, choose Add/Remove Snap-in to open the Add/Remove Snap-in dialog box.

3. Locate and select the Group Policy Object Editor Snap-in and click Add (don't choose the Group Policy Management Snap-in, if present—that's the GPMC that we'll use a bit later).

4. At the "Select Group Policy Object" screen, note that the default Local Computer Policy is selected. Click Browse.

5. The "Browse for a Group Policy Object" dialog box appears. Select the Users tab and select the layer you want. That is, you can pick Non-Administrators or Administrators, or click a specific user, or the Administrator account as seen in Figure 1.4.

FIGURE 1.4 Edit specific layers of Windows MLGPOs by first adding the Group Policy Object Editor into a "naked" MMC. Then browse for the Windows Local Group Policy by firing up GPEDIT.MSC.

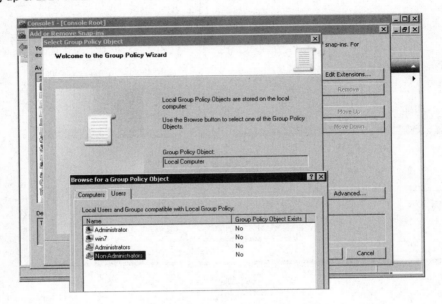

  In the Group Policy Object "Exists" column in the Users tab, you can also tell whether or not a local GPO layer is being used.

6. At the "Select a Group Policy Object" dialog box, click Finish.

7. At the "Add or Remove Snap-ins" dialog box, click OK.

You should now be able to edit that layer of the local GPO. For instance, Figure 1.5 shows that I've chosen to edit the Non-Administrators portion of the GPO (which is on level 2).
To edit additional or other layers of the local GPO, repeat the previous steps.

Here's an important point that bears repeating: Layers 2 and 3 of the MLGPO *cannot* contain overriding computer settings from Layer 1. That's why in Figure 1.5 you simply don't see them—they're not there. If you want to introduce a computer-side setting that affects everyone on the machine, just fire up GPEDIT.MSC and you'll be off and running. That's Layer 1, and it affects everyone.

FIGURE 1.5 Below the words Console Root, you can see which layer of the local GPO you're specifically editing.

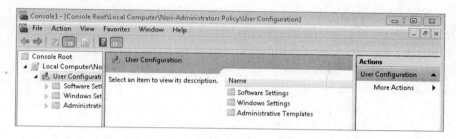

Local GPOs Final Thoughts

You can think of Local Group Policy as a way to perform desktop management in a decentralized way. That is, you're still running around, more or less, from machine to machine where you want to set the Local Group Policy.

The other strategy is a centralized approach. Centralized Group Policy administration works only in conjunction with Active Directory and is the main focus of this book.

 For more information, check out the article "Step-by-Step Guide to Managing Multiple Local Group Policy" from Microsoft. At last check, the URL was http://tinyurl.com/e4e9k. The specific guide is "Step-by-Step Guide to Managing Multiple Local Group Policy.doc" and is found toward the bottom. The guide is Vista specific, not Windows 7 specific, but all the steps should be the same.

In case you're curious, Local Group Policy is stored in the %windir%\system32\ grouppolicy directory (usually, C:\windows\system32\grouppolicy). The structure found here mirrors what you'll see later in Chapter 7 when we inspect the ins and outs of how Group Policy applies from Active Directory. Windows Vista and later store Local User Policies (level 3) inside %windir%\system32\grouppolicyusers.

You will notice one folder–per-user policy you have created, each named with the Security ID (SID) of the relevant user object.

Active Directory–Based Group Policy

To use Group Policy in a meaningful way, you need an Active Directory environment. An Active Directory environment needn't be anything particularly fancy; indeed, it could consist of a single Domain Controller (Windows 2000 and later) and perhaps just one Windows XP or Windows 7 workstation joined to the domain.

But Active Directory can also grow extensively from that original solitary server. You can think of an Active Directory network as having four constituent and distinct levels that relate to Group Policy:

- The local computer
- The site
- The domain
- The organizational unit (OU)

The rules of Active Directory state that every server and workstation must be a member of one (and only one) domain and be located in one (and only one) site.

In Windows NT, additional domains were often created to partition administrative responsibility or to rein in needless chatter between Domain Controllers. With Active Directory, administrative responsibility can be delegated using OUs.

Additionally, the problem with needless domain bandwidth chatter has been brought under control with the addition of Active Directory sites, which are concentrations of IP (Internet Protocol) subnets with fast connectivity. There is no longer any need to correlate domains with network bandwidth—that's what sites are for!

Group Policy and Active Directory

When Group Policy is created at the local level, everyone who uses that machine is affected by those wishes. But once you step up and use Active Directory, you can have nearly limitless Group Policy Objects (GPOs)—with the ability to selectively decide which users and which computers will get which wishes (try saying that five times quickly). The GPO is the vessel that stores these wishes for delivery.

 Actually, you can have only 999 GPOs applied and affecting a user or a computer before the system "gives up" and won't apply any more.

When we create a GPO that can be used in Active Directory, two things happen: we create some brand-new entries within Active Directory, and we automatically create some brand-new files within our Domain Controllers. Collectively, these items make one GPO.

You can think of Active Directory as having three major levels:

- Site
- Domain
- OU

Additionally, since OUs can be nested within each other, Active Directory has a nearly limitless capacity for where we can tuck stuff away.

In fact, it's best to think of this design as a three-tier hierarchy: site, domain, and each nested OU. When wishes, er, policy settings, are set at a higher level in Active Directory, they automatically flow down throughout the remaining levels.

So, to be precise:

- If a GPO is set at the site level, the policy settings contained within affect those accounts within the geography of the site. Sure, their user account could be in one domain and their computer account could be in another domain. And of course, it's likely that those accounts are in an OU. But the account is affected only by the policy settings here because the account is in a specific site. And logically, when a computer starts up in a new site, the User object will also get its site-based Group Policy from the same place. This is based on the IP subnet the user is a part of and is configured using Active Directory Sites and Services.

- If a GPO is set at the domain level, it affects those users and computers within the domain and all OUs and all other OUs beneath it.

- If a GPO is set at the OU level, it affects those users or computers within the OU and all other OUs beneath it (usually just called child or sub-OUs).

By default, when a policy is set at one level, the levels below *inherit* the settings from the levels above it. You can have "cumulative" wishes that keep piling on.

You might wonder what happens if two policy settings conflict. Perhaps one policy is set at the domain level and another policy is set at the OU level, which reverses the edict in the domain. The result is simple: policy settings further down the food chain take precedence. For instance, if a policy setting conflicts at the domain and OU levels, the OU level "wins." Likewise, domain-level settings override any policy settings that conflict with previously set site-specific policy settings. This might seem counterintuitive at first, so bear with me for a minute.

Take a look at the following illustration to get a view of the order of precedence.

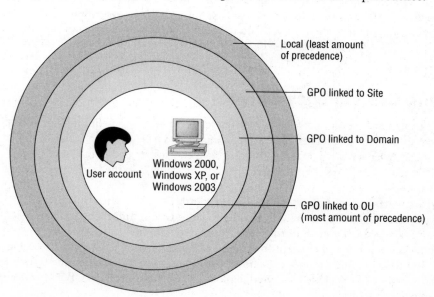

The golden rule with Group Policy is truly "Last writer wins." Another way to say it is "If any GPOs conflict, the settings contained in the last written GPO win."

However, don't forget about any Local Group Policy that might have been set on a specific workstation. Recall that for pre-Vista machines, everyone logging onto that workstation is affected by that policy setting. You just learned how Windows Vista's and Windows 7's MLGPOs add up to three layers of user settings (where Windows XP's Local GPOs have just one).

Regardless, once that local policy is determined, only *then* do policy settings within Active Directory (the site, domain, and OU) apply. So, sometimes people refer to the *four* levels of Group Policy: local workstation, site, domain, and OU. Nonetheless, GPOs set within Active Directory always trump the Local Group Policy should there be any conflict.

If this behavior is undesirable for lower Active Directory levels, all the settings from higher Active Directory levels can be blocked with the Block Inheritance attribute on a given OU. Additionally, if a higher-level administrator wants to guarantee that a setting is inherited down the food chain, they can apply the Enforced attribute via the GPMC interface. (Panic not! Chapter 2 explores both Block Inheritance and Enforced attributes in detail.)

Note that you cannot "Block Inheritance" between Local GPOs and Active Directory GPOs. But it is true that anything you set within Active Directory to inverse a Local GPO setting is always honored. Said another way, Active Directory edicts trump local edicts.

Don't sweat it if your head is spinning a little now from the Group Policy application theory. I'll go through specific hands-on examples to illustrate each of these behaviors so that you understand exactly how this works.

Linking Group Policy Objects

Another technical concept that needs a bit of description here is the "linking" of GPOs. When a GPO "appears" to be "created" at the site, domain, or OU level via the GUI (which we'll do in a moment), what's really happening is quite different. It's created in one, set "place," then merely "linked" there. (Yes, I know there are a lot of "quotes" in the last sentence, but sometimes that's how I "write.")

Anyway, when you tell the system, "I want to affect an OU with this new GPO," the system automatically creates the GPO in the fixed location, and then associates that GPO with the level at which you want to affect. That association is called *linking*.

Linking is an important concept for several reasons. First, it's generally a good idea to understand what's going on under the hood. However, more practically, the Group Policy Management Console (GPMC), as we'll explore in just a bit, displays GPOs from their linked perspective.

Let's extend the metaphor a little more.

You can think of all the GPOs you create in Active Directory as children in a big swimming pool. Each child has a tether attached around their waist, and an adult guardian is holding the other end of the rope. Indeed, there could be multiple tethers around a child's waist, with multiple adults tethered to one child. A sad state indeed would be a child who has no tether but is just swimming around in the pool unsecured. The swimming pool in this analogy is a specific Active Directory container named Policies (which we'll examine closely in Chapter 7). All GPOs are born and "live" in that specific domain. Indeed, they're replicated to all Domain Controllers. The adult guardian in this analogy represents a *level* in Active Directory—any site, domain, or OU.

In our swimming pool example, multiple adults can be tethered to a specific child. With Active Directory, multiple levels can be linked to a specific GPO. Thus, any level in Active Directory can leverage multiple GPOs, which are standing by in the domain ready to be used.

Remember, though, unless a GPO is specifically linked to a site, a domain, or an OU, it does not take effect. It's just floating around in the swimming pool of the domain waiting for someone to make use of it.

I'll keep reiterating and refining the concept of linking throughout these first four chapters. And, as necessary, I'll discuss why you might want to "unlink" a policy.

This concept of linking to GPOs created in Active Directory can be a bit confusing. It will become clearer later as we explore the processes of creating new GPOs and linking to existing ones. Stay tuned. It's right around the corner.

An Example of Group Policy Application

At this point, it's best not to jump directly into adding, deleting, or modifying our own GPOs. Right now, it's better to understand how Group Policy works "on paper." This is especially true if you're new to the concept of Group Policy, but perhaps also if Group Policy has been deployed by other administrators in your Active Directory.

By walking through a fictitious organization that has deployed GPOs at multiple levels, you'll be able to better understand how and why policy settings are applied by the deployment of GPOs.

Let's start by taking a look at Figure 1.6, the organization for our fictitious example company, Example.com.

This picture could easily tell 1,000 words. For the sake of brevity, I've kept it down to around 200. There are two domains: Example.com and Widgets.example.com. Let's talk about Example.com:

- The domain Example.com has two Domain Controllers. One DC, named EXAMPLEDC1, is physically located in the California site. Example.com's other Domain Controller, EXAMPLEDC2, is physically located in the Phoenix site.

- As for PCs, they need to physically reside somewhere. SallysPC is in the California site; BrettsPC and AdamsPC are in the Delaware site. JoesPC is in the Phoenix site.

- User accounts may or may not be in OUs. Dave's and Jane's account is in the **Human Resources** OU.

- Computer accounts may or may not be in OUs. FredsPC is in the **Human Resources** OU. AdamsPC is specifically placed within the **High Security** OU. JoesPC, SallysPC, and BrettsPC are hanging out in a container, and aren't in any OUs.

FIGURE 1.6 This fictitious Example.com is relatively simple. Your environment may be more complex.

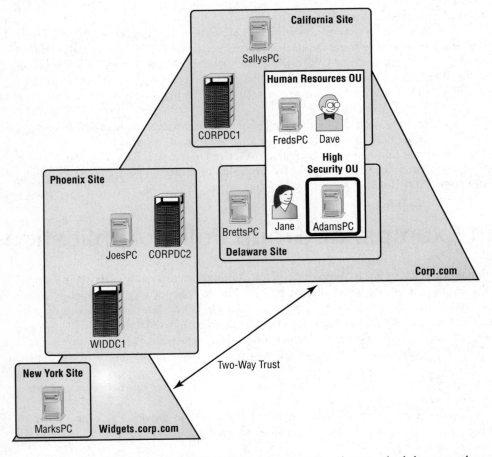

Using Active Directory Sites and Services, you can put in place a schedule to regulate communication between EXAMPLEDC1 located in California and EXAMPLEDC2 located in Phoenix. That way, the administrator controls the chatter between the two Example.com Domain Controllers, and it is not at the whim of the operating system.

Another domain, called Widgets.example.com, has an automatic transitive two-way trust to Example.com. There is only one Domain Controller in the Widgets.example.com domain, named WIDDC1, and it physically resides at the Phoenix site. Last, there is MarksPC, a member of the Widgets.example.com domain, and it physically resides in the New York site and isn't in any OU.

Understanding where your users and machines are is half the battle. The other half is understanding which policy settings are expected to appear when they start logging onto Active Directory.

Examining the Resultant Set of Policy

As stated earlier, the effect of Group Policy is cumulative as GPOs are successively applied—starting at the local computer, then the site, the domain, and each nested OU. The end result of what affects a specific user or computer—after all Group Policy at all levels has been applied—is called the *Resultant Set of Policy* (RSoP). This is sometimes referred to as the *RSoP calculation.*

Throughout your lifetime working with Group Policy, you will be asked to troubleshoot the RSoP of client machines.

Many of our dealings with Group Policy will consist of trying to understand and troubleshoot the RSoP of a particular configuration. Getting a good, early understanding of how to perform manual RSoP calculations on paper is important because it's a useful troubleshooting skill. In Chapters 3 and 7, we'll also explore additional RSoP skills—with tools and additional manual troubleshooting.

Before we jump in to try to discover what the RSoP might be for any specific machine, it's often helpful to break out each of the strata—local computer, site, domain, and OU—and examine, at each level, what happens to the entities contained in them. I'll then bring it all together to see how a specific computer or user reacts to the accumulation of GPOs. For these examples, assume that no local policy is set on any of the computers; the goal is to get a better feeling of how Group Policy flows, not necessarily what the specific end state will be.

At the Site Level

Based on what we know from Figure 1.6, the GPOs in effect at the site level are shown here:

Site	Computers Affected
California	SallysPC, EXAMPLEDC1, and FredsPC
Phoenix	EXAMPLEDC2, JoesPC, and WIDDC1
New York	MarksPC
Delaware	AdamsPC and BrettsPC

If we look at the graphic again, it looks like Dave, for instance, resides in California and Jane, for instance, resides in Delaware. But I don't like to think about it like that. I prefer to say that their accounts reside in OUs.

But users are affected by site GPOs *only* when they log onto computers that are at a specific site.

In Figure 1.6, we have Dave's and Jane's accounts in the Human Resources OU. And that's great. But they're only affected by California site-level GPOs if they travel to California. It doesn't matter where they usually reside; again, they're only affected by the site-level GPOs when they're physically present in that site.

So, don't think that user accounts *reside* at the site level. Rather, they reside in the OU level but are using computers in the site and, hence, get the properties assigned to all users at that site.

Sites are defined using the Active Directory Sites and Services tool. IP subnets that constitute a site are assigned using this tool. That way, if a new computer turns on in Delaware, Active Directory knows what site the computer is in.

At the Domain Level

Here's what we have working at the domain level:

Domain	Computers/Users Affected
Example.com Computers	SallysPC, FredsPC, AdamsPC, BrettsPC, JoesPC, EXAMPLEDC1, and EXAMPLEDC2
Example.com Users	Dave and Jane
Widgets.example.com Computers	WIDDC1 and MarksPC

At the OU Level

At the organizational unit level, we have the following:

Organizational Unit	Computers/Users Affected
Human Resources OU Computers	FredsPC is in the **Human Resources** OU; therefore, it is affected when the **Human Resources** OU gets GPOs applied. Additionally, the **High Security** OU is contained inside the **Human Resources** OU. Therefore, AdamsPC, which is in the **High Security** OU, is also affected whenever the **Human Resources** OU is affected.
Human Resources OU Users	The accounts of Dave and Jane are affected when the **Human Resources** OU has GPOs applied.

Bringing It All Together

Now that you've broken out all the levels and seen what is being applied to them, you can start to calculate what the devil is happening on any specific user and computer combination. Looking at Figure 1.6 and analyzing what's happening at each level makes adding things together between the local, site, domain, and organizational unit GPOs a lot easier.

Here are some examples of RSoP for specific users and computers in our fictitious environment:

FredsPC	FredsPC inherits the settings of the GPOs from the California site, then the Example.com domain, and last, the **Human Resources** OU.
MarksPC	MarksPC first accepts the GPOs from the New York site and then the Widgets.example.com domain. MarksPC is not in any OU; therefore, no organizational unit GPOs apply to his computer.
AdamsPC	AdamsPC is subject to the GPOs at the Delaware site, the Example.com domain, the **Human Resources** OU, and the **High Security** OU.
Dave using AdamsPC	AdamsPC is subject to the computer policies in the GPOs for the Delaware site, the Example.com domain, the **Human Resources** OU, and finally the **High Security** OU. When Dave travels from California to Delaware to use Adam's workstation, his user GPOs are dictated from the Delaware site, the Example.com domain, and the **Human Resources** OU.

At no time are any domain GPOs from the Example.com parent domain automatically inherited by the Widget.example.com child domain. Inheritance for GPOs only flows downward to OUs within a single domain—not between any two domains—parent to child or otherwise, unless you explicitly link one of those parent GPOs to a child Domain Container.

If you want one GPO to affect the users in more than one domain, you have four choices:

- Precisely re-create the GPOs in each domain with their own GPO.
- Copy the GPO from one domain to another domain (using the GPMC, as explained in the appendix).
- Use a third-party tool that can perform some magic and automatically perform the copying between domains for you.
- Do a generally recognized no-no called *cross-domain policy linking*. (I'll describe this no-no in detail in Chapter 7 in the section "Group Policy Objects from a Domain Perspective.")

Also, don't assume that linking a GPO at a site level necessarily guarantees the results to just one domain. In this example, as in real life, there is not necessarily a 1:1 correlation between sites and domains. Indeed, without getting too geeky here, sites technically belong to the forest, and not any particular domain.

At this point, we'll put our example Example.com behind us. That was really an on-paper exercise to allow you to get a feel for what's possible in Group Policy land. From this point forward, you'll be doing most items in your test lab and following along.

Group Policy, Active Directory, and the GPMC

The interface used to create, modify, and manipulate Group Policy in the original iteration of Active Directory when Windows 2000 was a pup had led to numerous missteps and head scratching when people try to figure out why something isn't going the way it should.

To make optimal use of Group Policy in an Active Directory environment, the Group Policy team at Microsoft introduced a free, downloadable tool for managing Group Policy in Active Directory in a meaningful way. It's called the Group Policy Management Console (GPMC), as mentioned earlier. The GPMC wasn't part of Windows 2000, or even Windows 2003. And it was "downloadable" for Windows XP operating systems.

It is, however, part of the shipping version of Windows Vista and Windows Server 2008, so no extra effort is required.

But wait!

Turns out, it's "gone again" with Windows Vista when SP1 is installed. Yep—the GPMC is "automatically removed" from Vista when its SP1 is applied. And to *reinstall* it, you have to fetch what's known as the *Remote Server Administration Tools (RSAT)*. Inside RSAT is the "updated GPMC."

And, it's not "in the box" for Windows 7 either.

I know, I know. This is all weird, right? I promise a detailed explanation of why in Chapter 2.

Kickin' It Old School

For the love of Pete, please don't tell me you're still using Windows 2000 or Windows 2003 "out of the box" to control your Active Directory.

Because if you are, that means you've never installed the GPMC; the tools built into Windows 2000 and Windows 2003 domains use the old-style interface. This old interface is built into Active Directory Users and Computer and Active Directory Sites and Services.

Hopefully, everyone is past this by now, but if you're not (or, you want a little nostalgia), here's a quick tour of the old-school interface. If you've never seen the old-style interface, you can do so right now before we leave it in the dust for the new GPMC in the next section.

If you don't yet have the GPMC installed on Windows Server 2003, and wish to see the old-style interface and create your first GPO at the domain level, follow these steps:

1. Log onto a Windows 2000 Server or Windows Server 2003 Domain Controller as the Administrator account (which is a Domain Administrator).

2. Choose Start ➢ All Programs ➢ Administrative Tools and select Active Directory Users and Computers. Alternatively, select Start ➢ Run and select dsa.msc to open Active Directory Users and Computers.

3. Right-click the domain name and choose Properties from the context menu.

4. Click the Group Policy tab.

5. Click the New button to spawn the creation of your first GPO.

6. For this first example, type **My First GPO**, as shown here.

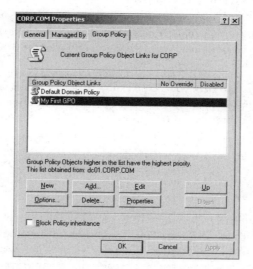

Highlight the policy and click Edit to open the Group Policy Management Editor.

At this point, things should look familiar, just like the Local Group Policy Management Editor, with the user and computer nodes. For example, if you drill down into the Administrative Templates folder in the User Configuration ➢ Policies folder, you can make a wish at the domain level and all your computers will obey.

For now, don't make any changes; just close the Group Policy Management Editor and read on. This was just a "fantasy walk down memory lane."

In our graphic earlier, we were able to create our first GPO (even though we didn't actually place any policy settings in there). The interface seems reasonable enough to take care of such simple tasks. And, heck, this interface is already part of the operating system, so why move away from it?

The old-school way of viewing and managing Group Policy just isn't scalable over the long haul. This interface doesn't show us any relationship between the GPO we just created and the domain it's in. As you'll see in this chapter, the new interface demonstrates a much clearer relationship between the GPOs you create, the links it takes to use them, and the domains where the GPOs actually "live."

The old-style interface also provides no easy way to figure out what's going on inside the GPOs you create. To determine what changes are made inside a GPO, you need to reopen each GPO and poke around. I've seen countless administrators open each and every GPO in their domain and manually document their settings on paper for backup and recovery purposes.

Indeed, backup and recovery is a really, really big deal, and the old-school mechanism (via NTBACKUP) provided no realistic way to back up and recover GPOs without copious amounts of surgery. The GPMC makes it a snap.

With that in mind, I encourage all of you—(and I know at least a few of you are still out there) if you're currently using the original Windows 2000 or Windows Server 2003 old-school way and haven't yet switched over to the GPMC, now is your time.

GPMC Overview

The Group Policy Management Console (GPMC) was created to help administrators work in a "one-stop-shop" place for all Group Policy management functions. Since 2003, it was freely downloadable as an add-on to either Windows XP or Windows Server 2003 systems. In Windows Vista, it was included in the box. Again, that is, until you load Windows Vista's SP1, when the GPMC is uninstalled until you fetch the RSAT tools. Again, the GPMC is built into Windows Server 2008 and Windows Server 2008 R2, and available for download and installtion for Windows 7 as part of the RSAT tools.

Even though I've said it before, it bears repeating: it doesn't matter if your Active Directory or domains or Domain Controllers are Windows 2000, Windows 2003, or Windows 2008 or whatever. You can use any flavor of the GPMC and create and use Group Policy, regardless of the domain type.

About the GPMC

The GPMC's name says it all. It's the Group Policy Management Console. Indeed, this will be the MMC snap-in that you use to manage the underlying Group Policy mechanism. The

GPMC just helps us tap into those features already built into Active Directory. I'll highlight the mechanism of how Group Policy works throughout the next three chapters.

One major design goal of the GPMC is to get a Group Policy–centric view of the lay of the land. Compared with the old interface (see the sidebar "Kickin' It Old School" earlier), the GPMC does a much better job of aligning the user interface of Group Policy with what's going on under the hood.

The GPMC also provides a programmatic way to manage your GPOs. In fact, the GPMC scripting interface allows just about any GPO operation. The older GPMC that works on XP and 2003 has a way to script using VBScript. The newer GPMC that works on Windows 7 and Windows Server 2008 R2 can use VBScript or PowerShell.

We'll explore scripting with the GPMC and PowerShell in a downloadable bonus chapter. So, if you're interested in scripting, you'll need to have the GPMC bits loaded on the Windows 7 system you want to script.

The GPMC scripts, which were previously part of the downloadable GPMC package, are not included in the newest GPMC. You have to specifically download them from the GPMC scripting center at http://tinyurl.com/23xfz3 or search for "Group Policy Management Console Sample Scripts" in your favorite search engine.

There are lots of ways you *could* manage your Group Policy universe. Some people walk up to their Domain Controllers, log onto the console, and manage their Group Policy infrastructure there. Others use a *management workstation* and manage their Group Policy infrastructure from their own Windows 7 (suggested) or Windows XP (if you must) management workstation.

I'll talk more about the use and best practices of a Windows 7 management workstation in Chapter 6.

Implementing the GPMC on Your Management Station

As I mentioned, the GPMC isn't built into Windows 7. But it is built into Windows Server 2008 and Windows Server 2008 R2. Remember earlier I stated that you could manage your Active Directory from anywhere. And this is true. You *could* walk up to a Domain Controller, you *could* install the GPMC on a Windows XP or Windows Server 2003 server, or you *could* use Terminal Services to remotely connect to a Domain Controller.

But in this book, you won't be. Your ideal management station is a Windows 7 machine (where we'll manually introduce the GPMC) or a Windows Server 2008 R2 machine (which is ready to go, no pesky downloads needed).

If you must use something else (Windows XP, Windows Server 2003, or Windows Vista RTM), you'll see me pepper in some advice for those. But you'll really want to use the recommended set to get the most out of this book.

Since I'd like to encourage you to utilize "the most modern GPMC" pos-sible, I'm going to specifically shun both Windows Vista and Windows XP from discussion here. Yes, it's true you could use Vista and you could use XP, but it's honestly not a great idea anymore. In Chapter 6, I will cover why this is the case, but for now, let's "get modern" and assume you'll be using a Windows 7 machine.

Using a Windows 7 or Windows Server 2008 R2 Management Station

For this book, and for real life, I recommend that you use what's known as a Windows 7 management station. And, to make use of it to implement Group Policy in your domain, you'll need to introduce the downloadable GPMC on it.

Note that you could *also* use a Windows Server 2008 R2 machine as your management station. Honestly, the Windows 7 GPMC that you'll download and the built-in GPMC for Windows Server 2008 R2 are equals. There's no difference. But it's simply not likely you're going to install Windows Server 2008 R2 on your laptop or desktop.

So, just to be clear, the following two ways to create and manage GPOs are equal:

- Windows 7 and the newly downloadable GPMC (contained within the RSAT tools)

- Windows Server 2008 R2 with built-in GPMC

I'll usually just refer to a Windows 7 management station, and when I say that, I mean what I have in that first bullet point. Just remember that you can use a Windows Server 2008 R2 machine as your management station too.

Now, to be supercrazy, ridiculously clear: you could also use any of the other GPMCs out there, and things will basically "work." I delve into this in serious detail in Chapter 6, but here's the Cliffs Notes, er, Jeremy's Notes version of "What GPMC should I use?":

- Always use Windows 7 (or Windows Server 2008 R2) as your management station and you'll always be able to control all operating systems' settings from all operating systems.

- The next best choice would be Windows Vista/SP1 (or SP2) and RSAT and/or Windows Server 2008. Those two GPMCs are equivalent.

- The next best GPMC would be the downloadable version for Windows Server 2003 and Windows XP.

But, if you have even one Windows 7 or Windows Vista client machine (say in Sales or Marketing), in order to manage all the settings, you're going to need to manage the machine using a "modern" GPMC. So I'm suggesting you just bite the bullet and get yourself a copy of Windows 7 and do your management from there.

Again, more details later, but here's the warning. If you create a GPO using a "newer GPMC" (say, using a Windows 7 or Windows Server 2008 R2 GPMC) but then edit it using an older operating system (say, a Windows XP GPMC), you might not be able to "see" all the configurable options. And what's worse, some settings might be set (but you wouldn't be able to see them!). Only the newest GPMC can see the "stuff" that the newest GPMC puts into the GPO.

What if you're not "allowed" to load Windows 7 on your own management station? Well, you've got another option. Perhaps you can create a Windows 7 or Windows Server 2008 R2 machine to act as your management station, say in the server room. Or, use VMware Workstation or Virtual PC to make an "almost real" management machine. Or, do create a real machine, but set up Terminal Services or Remote Desktop to utilize the GPMC remotely.

Again, in our examples we'll call our machine WIN7MANAGEMENT, but you can use either a Windows 7 or Windows Server 2008 R2 for your best management station experience.

Using a Windows Server 2008 R2 Machine as Your Management Station

The latest GPMC is available in Windows Server 2008 R2. However, it's not magically installed in most cases. The only time it is just "magically there" is when you make your Windows Server 2008 or Windows Server 2008 R2 machine a Domain Controller. In that case, the GPMC is automatically installed for you. You don't need to do the following procedure.

And, if you're following along in the labs, you've likely already made your Windows Server 2008 R2 machine a Domain Controller. But for practice, if you want to learn how to install it for when your Windows Server 2008 and Windows Server 2008 R2 computers are not acting like Domain Controllers, there are two ways to install the GPMC: using Server Manager and also by the command line.

To install the GPMC using Server Manager:

1. Click Start, then point to Administrative Tools and select Server Manager.

2. In the Server Manager's console tree, click Features and then select Add Features.

3. In the Add Feature wizard, select Group Policy Management Console from the list of features.

4. Click Install.

Close Server Manager once you're done.

You can also install the GPMC using the command line:

1. Open a command prompt as an Administrator.

2. In the command prompt, type **ServerManagerCmd -install gpmc**.

3. Close the command prompt when the installation has been completed.

For you PowerShell gurus, you could also use the "Add-WindowsFeature" cmdlet in Windows Server 2008 R2.

Using Windows 7 as Your Management Machine

The first step on your Windows 7 management-station-to-be is to install Windows 7. Next, you'll need to install RSAT. Find the RSAT for Windows 7 at http://tinyurl.com/qru5en.

RSAT installs like a hotfix, and you may or may not need to reboot after installation. Then, on Windows 7 go to Control Panel and select Programs. Select "Turn Windows features on or off." Locate the Feature Administration Tools and select Group Policy Management Tools. Also, since you're here anyway, locate the Role Administrator Tools, as seen in Figure 1.7, and select Active Directory Administrative Center.

FIGURE 1.7   The RSAT tools install like a hotfix but then must be individually selected using Control Panel ➢ Programs ➢ Turn Windows features on or off.

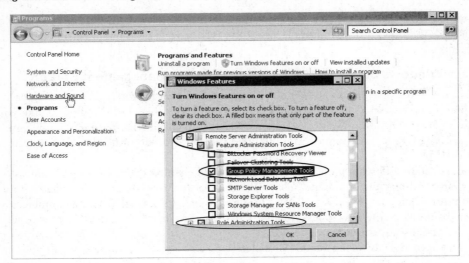

Once you're done, close the Windows Features window and, if prompted, reboot your Windows 7 machine. The next time you boot, you'll have Active Directory Users and Computers, the GPMC, and other tools available for use in the rest of the book.

If You Must Use a Windows Vista RTM, Windows Vista/SP1 (or SP2) and RSAT, Windows XP, or Windows Server 2003 Management Station

Again, I recommend against using any of the older GPMCs. If you positively cannot use a Windows Vista/SP1 and RSAT machine to be your management station, and you must limp along with a Windows Vista RTM, Windows XP, or Windows Server 2003 machine, you can.

But know that you won't get the full experience, and your screen might look different from my screen shots.

Read Chapter 6 for the full implications of being forced to use an older management machine.

If You Must Use a Windows Vista RTM Machine   On your Windows Vista machine, click Start, and in the Start Search prompt, type the **GPMC.MSC** command. With Windows Vista RTM, the GPMC will just fire right up.

If You Must Use a Windows Vista/SP1 (or SP2) and RSAT Machine   At last check, Vista's RSAT was found at `http://tinyurl.com/3cch2h`. This is preferred over the "in the box" GPMC that came with Windows Vista RTM.

If You Must Use a Windows XP or Windows Server 2003 Management Station   Now, what if you really, really cannot use a Windows 7 or, heck, even a Windows Vista or Windows Server 2008 management station? Well, then, sounds like you're stuck with Windows XP or Windows Server 2003. If you're being forced to use Windows XP or Windows Server 2003 as your management station, you can download the older GPMC for free from `http://tinyurl.com/566ru`.

To be honest, I don't know how much longer they'll maintain the original GPMC. I wouldn't be surprised if, some time soon, the only GPMC available will be inside the RSAT packages for Windows Vista and Windows 7. Again, you can install this older GPMC (downloaded as `GPMC.MSI`) on either Windows 2003 or Windows XP with at least SP1.

Creating a One-Stop-Shop MMC

As you'll see, the GPMC is a fairly comprehensive Group Policy management tool. But the problem is that right now the GPMC and the Active Directory Users and Computers snap-ins are, well, separate tools that each do a specific job. They're not integrated to allow you to work on both Users *and* Group Policy at the same time.

Often, you'll want to change a Group Policy linked to an OU and then move computers to that OU. Unfortunately, you can't do so from the GPMC; you must return to Active Directory Users and Computers to finish the task. This can get frustrating quickly. But that's the deal.

As a result, my preference is to create a custom MMC that shows both the Active Directory Users and Computers and GPMC in a one-stop-shop view. You can see what I mean in Figure 1.8.

You might be wondering at this point, "So, Jeremy, what are the steps I need in order to create this unified MMC console you've so neatly described and shown in Figure 1.8?"

Just click Start and type **MMC** at the Search prompt. Then add in both the Active Directory Users and Computers and Group Policy Management snap-ins, as shown in Figure 1.9.

You won't need the Group Policy Management Editor (which allows you to edit one Group Policy Object at a time), the Group Policy Object Editor (for Local Group Policy), or the Group Policy Starter GPO Editor (which we use in Chapter 2).

Once you have added both snap-ins to your console, you'll really have a near-unified view of most of what you need at your fingertips. Both Active Directory Users and Computers and the GPMC can create and delete OUs. Both tools also allow administrators to delegate permissions to others to manage Group Policy, but that's where the two tools' functionality overlap ends.

FIGURE 1.8   Use the MMC to create a unified console.

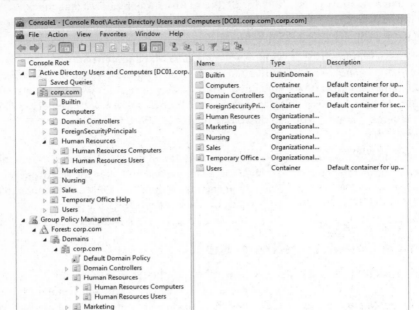

The GPMC won't show you the actual users and computer objects inside the OU, so deleting an OU from within the GPMC is dicey at best because you can't be sure of what's inside!

You can choose to add other snaps-ins too, of course, including Active Directory Sites and Services or anything else you think is useful. The illustrations in the rest of this book will show both snap-ins loaded in this configuration. I suggest you save your "one-stop shop" to the desktop and give it catchy name so you can quickly find it later when you need to.

Group Policy 101 and Active Directory

Let's start with some basics to ensure that things are running smoothly. For most of the examples in this book, you'll be able to get by with just the one Domain Controller and one or two workstations that participate in the domain, for verifying that your changes took place.

FIGURE 1.9   Add Active Directory Users and Computers and Group Policy Management to your custom view.

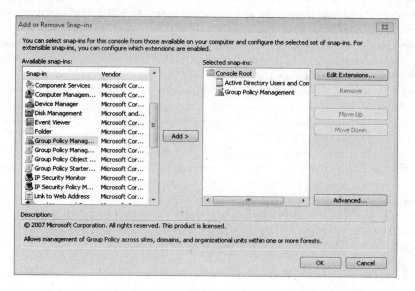

 For the examples in this book, I'll refer to our sample Domain Controller, DC01, which is part of my example Corp.com domain. For these examples, you can choose to rename the Default-First-Site-Name site or not—your choice.

Again, I encourage you to try these examples in your test lab and not to try them directly on your production network. This will help you avoid a CLM (career-limiting move).

For our examples, we'll assume you're using WIN7MANAGEMENT as your management station, which is a Windows 7 and RSAT machine.

Active Directory Users and Computers vs. GPMC

The main job of Active Directory Users and Computers is to give you an Active Directory object–centric view of your domain. Active Directory Users and Computers lets you deal with users, computers, groups, contacts, some of the Flexible Single Master Operations (FSMO) roles, and delegation of control over user accounts as well as change the domain mode and define advanced security and auditing inside Active Directory. You can also create OUs and move users and computers around inside those OUs. Other administrators can then drill down inside Active Directory Users and Computers into an OU and see the computers, groups, contacts, and so on that you've moved to those OUs.

But the GPMC has one main job: to provide you with a Group Policy–centric view of all you control. All the OUs that you see in Active Directory Users and Computers are visible in the GPMC. Think about it—it's the same Active Directory behind the scenes "storing" those details about the OU and its contents.

However, the GPMC just doesn't have a way to "view" the users, computers, contacts, and such. When you drill down into an OU inside the GPMC, you'll see but one thing: the GPOs that affect the objects inside the OU.

In Figure 1.8, you were able to see the Active Directory Users and Computers view as well as the GPMC view—rolled into one MMC that we created earlier. Even though it's not super-obvious from the screen shot, the Active Directory Users and Computers view of **Temporary Office Help** and the GPMC view of the same OU is radically different.

When focused at a site, a domain, or an OU within the GPMC, you see only the GPOs that affect that level in Active Directory. You don't see the same "stuff" that Active Directory Users and Computers sees, such as users, computers, groups, or contacts.

The basic overlap in the two tools is the ability to create and delete OUs. If you add or delete an OU in either tool, you need to refresh the other tool by pressing F5 to see the update. For instance, in Figure 1.8 you could see that my Active Directory has several OUs, including one named **Temporary Office Help.**

WARNING   Deleting an OU from inside the GPMC is generally a bad idea. Because you cannot see the Active Directory objects inside the OU (such as users and computers), you don't really know how many objects you're about to delete. So be careful!

If I delete the **Temporary Office Help** OU in Active Directory Users and Computers, the change is not reflected in the GPMC window until it's refreshed.

And vice versa.

So, let's summarize with three key points:

- Understanding that the two tools are "separate" and work on the same underlying database is key.

- Understanding that what you do in one tool (i.e., delete an OU) affects the other tool (because it's affecting the same underlying database) is also key.

- The final key is realizing that you will need to occasionally "refresh" the view of each tool. This is because other administrators might be "doing stuff" to the GPOs and/or Active Directory user accounts. You won't see their changes until you refresh *your* view.

Adjusting the View within the GPMC

The GPMC lets you view as much or as little of your Active Directory as you like. By default, you view only your own forest and domain. You can optionally add in the ability to see the sites in your forest as well as the ability to see other domains in your forest or domains in other forests, although these views might not be the best for seeing what you have control over.

Here's how to view the various other items you may need to within the GPMC.

Viewing sites in the GPMC   When you create GPOs, you won't often create GPOs that affect sites. The designers of the GPMC seem to agree; it's a bit of a chore to apply GPOs to sites. To do so, you need to link an *existing* GPO to a site. You'll see how to do this a bit later in this chapter.

However, you first need to expose the site objects in Active Directory. To do so, right-click the Sites object in GPMC, choose Show Sites from the context menu (see Figure 1.10), and then click the check box next to each site you want to expose.

FIGURE 1.10   You need to expose the Active Directory sites before you can link GPOs to them.

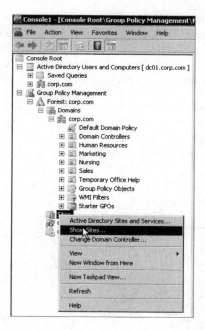

In our first example, we'll use the site level of Active Directory to deploy our first Group Policy Object. At this point, go ahead and enable the Default-First-Site so that you can have it ready for use in our own experiments.

Viewing other domains in the GPMC   To see other domains in your forest, drill down to the Forest folder in Group Policy Management, right-click Domains, choose Show Domains, and select the other available domains in your forest. Each domain will now appear at the same hierarchical level in the GPMC.

Viewing other forests in the GPMC   To see other forests, right-click the root (Group Policy Management) and choose Add Forest from the context menu. You'll need to type the name of the Active Directory forest you want to add. If you want to add or subtract domains within that new forest, follow the instructions in the preceding paragraph.

You can add forests with which you do not have a trust. However, GPMC defaults will not display these domains as a safety mechanism. To turn off the safety, choose View ➢ Options to open the Options dialog box. In the General tab, clear Enable Trust Detection and click OK.

Now that we've adjusted our view to see the domains and forests we want, let's examine how to manipulate our GPOs and GPO links.

The GPMC-centric View

As I stated earlier, one of the fundamental concepts of Group Policy is that the GPOs *themselves* live in the "swimming pool" inside the domain. Then, when you want to utilize a GPO from that swimming pool against a level in Active Directory, you simply link a GPO to that level.

Figure 1.11 shows what our swimming pool will eventually look like when we're done with the examples in this chapter.

FIGURE 1.11   Imagine your about-to-be-leveraged GPOs as just hanging out in the swimming pool of the domain.

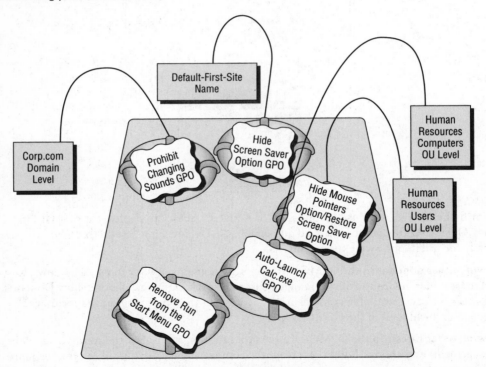

The Corp.com GPO Swimming Pool

Our swimming pool will be full of GPOs, with various levels in Active Directory "linked" to those GPOs. To that end, you can drill down, right now, to see the representation of the swimming pool. It's there, waiting for you. Click Group Policy Management ➢ Forest ➢ Domains ➢ Corp.com ➢ Group Policy Objects to see all the GPOs that exist in the domain (see Figure 1.12).

FIGURE 1.12 The Group Policy Objects folder highlighted here is the representation of the swimming pool of the domain that contains your actual GPOs.

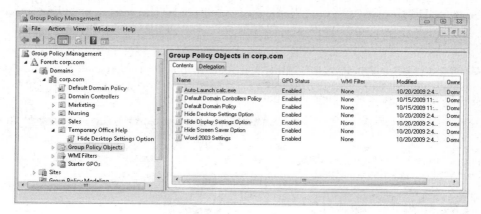

 If you're just getting started, it's not likely you'll have more than the "Default Domain Controllers Policy" GPO and "Default Domain Policy" GPO. That's OK. You'll start getting more GPOs soon enough. Oh, and for now, please don't modify the default GPOs. They're a bit special and are covered in great detail in Chapter 8.

All GPOs in the domain are represented in the Group Policy Objects folder. As you can see, when the **Temporary Office Help** OU is shown within the GPMC, a relationship exists between the OU and the "Hide Desktop Settings Option" GPO. That relationship is the tether to the GPO in the swimming pool—the GPO link back to "Hide Desktop Settings Option." You can see this linked relationship because the "Hide Desktop Settings Option" icon inside **Temporary Office Help** has a little arrow icon, signifying the link back to the actual GPO in the domain. The same is true for the "Default Domain Policy," which is linked at the domain level, but the actual GPO is placed below the Group Policy Objects folder.

Our Own Group Policy Examples

Now that you've got a grip on honing your view within the GPMC, let's take it for a quick spin around the block with some examples!

For this series of examples, we're going after the users who keep fiddling with their display doo-dads in Windows 7 and Windows XP.

If you want to see these examples in action using Windows XP, first start out on XPPRO1 by checking out the default Display Properties dialog box. Just right-click the Desktop and choose Properties from the context menu. You'll see several tabs, including Screen Saver, Appearance, and Settings, as shown in Figure 1.13 (left screen).

If you want to see these examples in action using Windows 7, first start out on WIN7 by looking at the "Personalize appearance and sounds" page, which is located by right-clicking the Desktop and choosing Personalize. You'll see several entries, including Screen Saver, Windows Color and Appearance, and Display Settings, as shown in Figure 1.13 (right screen).

FIGURE 1.13   In Windows XP, all the tabs in the Display Properties dialog box are available by default (left screen). In Windows 7, we can see lots of available areas in the Personalization screen, shown on the right.

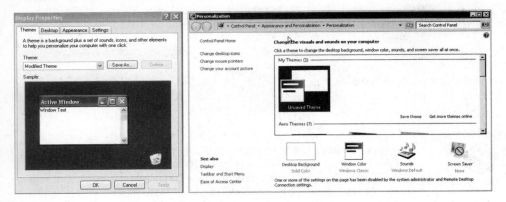

    Since they're called tabs in Windows XP and entries or options in Windows Vista and Windows 7, I'll just generally call them options from here on out.

For our first use of Group Policy, we're going to produce four "edicts" (for dramatic effect, you should stand on your desk and loudly proclaim these edicts with a thick British accent):

- At the site level, there will be no ability to change screen savers.

- At the domain level, there will be no ability to change Windows' sounds.

- At the **Human Resources Users** OU level, there will be no way to change the mouse pointers. And, while we're at it, let's bring back the ability to change screen savers!

- At the **Human Resources Computers** OU, we'll make it so whenever anyone uses a Human Resources computer, `calc.exe` automatically launches after login.

Following along with these concrete examples will reinforce the concepts presented earlier. Additionally, they are used throughout the remainder of this chapter and the book.

Understanding GPMC's Link Warning

As you work through the examples, you'll do a lot of clicking around. When you click a GPO link the first time, you'll get this message:

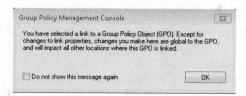

This message is trying to convey an important sentiment—that is, multiple levels in Active Directory may be linked back and use the exact same GPO. The idea is that multiple levels of Active Directory could use the exact same Group Policy Object contained inside the Group Policy Objects container—but just be linked back to it.

What if you modify the policy settings by right-clicking a policy link and choosing Edit from the context menu? All instances in Active Directory that link to that GPO embrace the new settings. If this is a fear, you might want to create another GPO and then link it to the level in Active Directory you want. More properties are affected by this warning, and we'll explore them in Chapter 5.

If you've squelched this message by selecting "Do not show this message again," you can get it back. In the GPMC in the menus, choose View ➢ Options and select the General tab, then select "Show confirmation dialog box to distinguish between GPOs and GPO links," and click OK.

More about Linking and the Group Policy Objects Container

The GPMC is a fairly flexible tool. Indeed, it permits the administrator to perform many tasks in different ways. One thing you'll do quite a lot in your travels with the GPMC is create your own Group Policy Objects. Again, GPOs live in a container within Active Directory and are represented within the Group Policy Objects container (the swimming pool) inside the domain (seen in Figure 1.11, earlier in this chapter). Any levels of Active Directory—site, domain, or OU—simply link back to the GPOs hanging out in the Group Policy Objects container.

To apply Group Policy to a level in Active Directory using the GPMC, you have two options:

- Create the GPOs in the Group Policy Objects container first. Then, while focused at the level you want to command in Active Directory (site, domain, or OU), manually add a link to the GPO that is in the Group Policy Objects container.

- While focused at the level you want to command in Active Directory (domain or OU), create the GPOs in the Group Policy Objects container and automatically create the link. This link is created at the level you're currently focused at *back* to the GPO in the Group Policy Objects container.

Which is the correct way to go? Both are perfectly acceptable because both are really doing the same thing.

In both cases the GPO itself does not "live" at the level in Active Directory at which you're focused. Rather, the GPO itself "lives" in the Group Policy Objects container. The link back to the GPO inside the Group Policy Objects container is what makes the relationship between the GPO inside the Group Policy Objects container swimming pool and the level in Active Directory you want to command.

To get the hang of this, let's work through some examples. First, let's create our first GPO in the Group Policy Objects folder. Follow these steps:

1. Launch the GPMC. Click Start, and then in the search box, type **GPMC.MSC**.

2. Traverse down by clicking Group Policy Management ➤ Forest ➤ Domains ➤ Corp.com ➤ Group Policy Objects.

3. Right-click the Group Policy Objects folder and choose New from the context menu, as shown in Figure 1.14, to open the New GPO dialog box.

4. Let's name our first edict, er, GPO, something descriptive, such as "Hide Screen Saver Option."

5. Once the name is entered, you'll see the new GPO listed in the swimming pool. Right-click the GPO, and choose Edit, as shown in Figure 1.15, to open the Group Policy Management Editor.

6. To hide the Screen Saver option, drill down by clicking User Configuration ➤ Policies ➤ Administrative Templates ➤ Control Panel ➤ Personalization. Double-click the **Prevent Changing Screen Saver** policy setting to open the policy setting. Select the Enabled setting, and click OK. You can see the new Windows 7 policy editor user interface in the sidebar "Old Policy Settings UI vs. New Policy Settings UI."

7. Close the Group Policy Management Editor.

Note that in earlier iterations of the GPMC, this setting was named differently and placed in another node. It used to be called **Hide Screen Saver Tab** and was located in the Display node within Control Panel. As you can see, as the operating system changes, so must the GPMC. Which is why it's pretty important to always use the "latest, greatest" GPMC, like we are using in this book.

FIGURE 1.14   You create your first GPO in the Group Policy Objects container by right-clicking and choosing New.

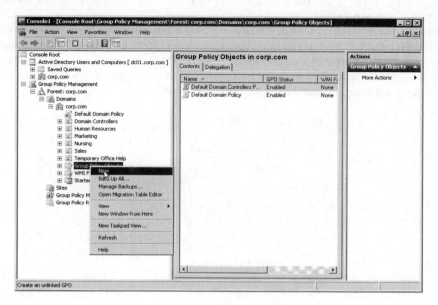

FIGURE 1.15   You can right-click the GPO in the Group Policy Objects container and choose Edit from the context menu to open the Group Policy Management Editor.

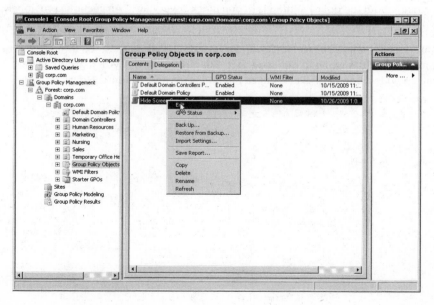

Old Policy Settings UI vs. New Policy Settings UI

If you've spent any amount of time in the Group Policy Editor over the years, this picture will be a familiar sight. Starting with Windows Vista, the Comment tab was added (and, don't worry; we'll examine it thoroughly in the next chapter.) But the problem with this UI is that it really wasn't "one-stop shop." It had two (now, more recently three) tabs to click through to see everything about the policy setting at once.

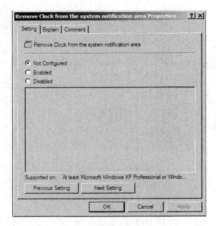

Now, starting with Windows 7 and Windows Server 2008 R2's GPMC, the UI has changed so that everything about the policy setting is in one quick "overview." All sections previously hidden behind the three tabs are all here.

This might freak out some seasoned Group Policy admins when they see it the first time. I know it took me a little while to get used to it. But in time, I think you'll grow to like it. Oh, and as an added bonus, you can resize the policy setting window. Neat.

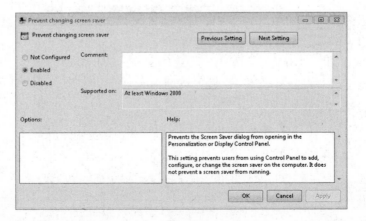

Understanding Our Actions

Now that we have this "Hide Screen Saver Option" edict, er, GPO floating around in the Group Policy Objects container—in the representation of the swimming pool of the domain—what have we done? Not a whole lot, actually, other than create some bits inside Active Directory and on the Domain Controllers. By creating new GPOs in the Group Policy Objects folder, we haven't inherently forced our desires on *any* level in Active Directory—site, domain, or OU.

To make a level in Active Directory accept our will, we need to *link* this new Group Policy Object to an existing level. Only then will our will be accepted and embraced. Let's do that now.

Applying a Group Policy Object to the Site Level

The least-often-used level of Group Policy application is at the site. This is because it's got the broadest stroke but the bluntest application. And more and more organizations use high-speed links everywhere, so it's not easy to separate computers into individual sites because (in some organizations) Active Directory is set up to see the network as just one big site!

Additionally, since Active Directory states that only members of the Enterprise Administrators (EAs) can modify sites and site links, it's equally true that only EAs (by default) can add and manipulate GPOs at the site level.

> When a tree or a forest contains more than one domain, only the EAs and the Domain Administrators (DAs) of the root domain can create and modify sites and site links. When multiple domains exist, DAs in domains other than the root domain cannot create sites or site links (or site-level GPOs).

However, site GPOs might come in handy on an occasion or two. For instance, you might want to set up site-level GPO definitions for network-specific settings, such as Internet Explorer proxy settings or an IP security policy for sensitive locations. Setting up site-based settings is useful if you have one building (set up explicitly as an Active Directory site) that has a particular or unique network configuration. You might choose to modify the Internet Explorer proxy settings if this building has a unique proxy server. Or, in the case of IP security, perhaps this facility has particularly sensitive information, such as confidential records or payroll information.

Therefore, if you're not an EA (or a DA of the root domain), it's likely you'll never get to practice this exercise outside the test lab. In upcoming chapters I'll show you how to delegate these rights to other administrators, like OU administrators around the bend.

For now, we'll work with a basic example to get the feel of the Group Policy Management Editor.

We already stood on our desks and loudly declared that there will be no Screen Saver options at our one default site. The good news is that we've already done two-thirds of what we need to do to make that site accept our will: we exposed the sites we want to manage, and we created the "Hide Screen Saver Option" GPO in the Group Policy Objects container.

Implementing GPOs linked to sites can have a substantial impact on your logon times and WAN (wide area network) traffic if not performed correctly. For more information, see Chapter 7 in the section "Group Policy Objects from a Site Perspective."

Now all we need do is to tether the GPO we created to the site with a GPO link.

To remove the Screen Saver option using the Group Policy Management Editor at the site level, follow these steps:

1. Inside the GPMC snap-in, drill down by clicking the Group Policy Management folder, the Forest folder, and the Sites folder.

2. Find the site to which you want to deliver the policy. If you have only one site, it is likely called Default-First-Site-Name.

3. Right-click the site and choose "Link an Existing GPO," as shown in Figure 1.16.

FIGURE 1.16   Once you have your first GPO designed, you can link it to your site.

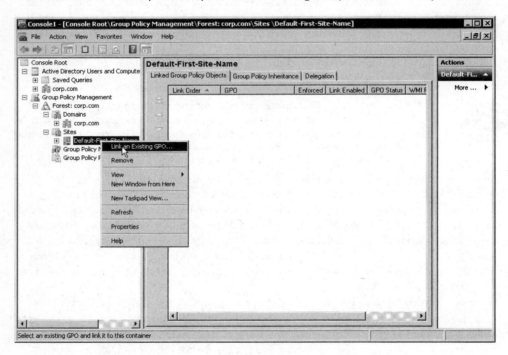

4. Now you can select the "Hide Screen Saver Option" GPO from the list of GPOs in the Group Policy Objects container within the domain.

Once you have chosen the GPO, it will be linked to the site.

Again, there is a good reason why GPOs for sites must be pre-created first. Since Sites does not belong to a specific domain, but rather the forest, you cannot assume which "domain swimming pool" they should be added to. By creating them this way, you know which domain you created them in first, and then to what site you want them linked.

> Did you notice that there was no "Are You Sure You Really Want To Do This?" warning or anything similar? The GPMC trusts that you set up the GPO correctly. If you create GPOs with incorrect settings and/or link them to the wrong level in Active Directory, you can make boo-boos on a grand scale. Again—this is why you want to try any setting you want to deploy in a test lab environment first.

Verifying Your Changes at the Site Level

Now, log onto any workstation or server that falls within the boundaries of the site to which you applied the sitewide GPO. If you didn't change any of the defaults, you should be able to log onto any computer in the domain (say, XPPRO1 or WIN7) as any user you have defined—even the administrator of the domain.

By right-clicking the Desktop and selecting Personalize (for Windows 7) or Properties (for Windows XP), you'll see that the Screen Saver option is, well, if not "gone" exactly, at least grayed out and cannot be selected, as shown in Figure 1.17.

FIGURE 1.17   The Screen Saver tab in Windows XP (shown on the left) is missing because the site policy is affecting the user. In Windows 7 (shown on the right), the Screen Saver entry on the Personalization page is disabled (grayed out).

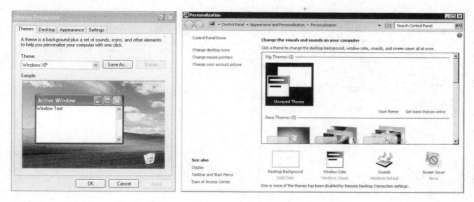

> Don't panic if you do not see the changes reflected the first time you log on. See Chapter 3, in the section "Background Refresh Policy Processing," to find out how to encourage changes to appear. To see the Screen Saver tab disappear right now, log off and log back on. The policy should take effect.

This demonstration should prove how powerful Group Policy is, not only because everyone at the site is affected, but more specifically because administrators are not immune to Group Policy effects. Administrators are not immune because they are automatically members in the Authenticated Users security group. (You can modify this behavior with the techniques explored in Chapter 3.)

Applying Group Policy Objects to the Domain Level

At the domain level, we want to deliver an edict that says that the Desktop Settings option in the Windows 7 Personalization page (or Desktop tab in the Display Properties dialog box for Windows XP) should be removed.

Active Directory domains allow only members of the Domain Administrators group the ability to create and link Group Policy directly on the domain level. Therefore, if you're not a DA (or a member of the EA group), or you don't get delegated the right, it's likely that you'll never get to practice this exercise outside the test lab. (We'll talk more about how to give others' rights to create and link GPOs besides Domain Admins a bit later.)

To apply the edict, follow these steps:

1. In the GPMC, drill down by clicking Group Policy Management ➤ Forest ➤ Corp.com.

2. Right-click the domain name to see the available options, as shown in Figure 1.18.

FIGURE 1.18 At the domain level, you can create the GPO in the Group Policy Objects container and then immediately link to the GPO from here.

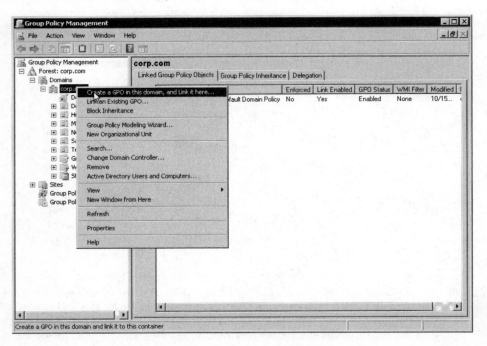

> ### "Create a GPO in this domain, and Link it here" vs. "Link an Existing GPO"
>
> In the previous example, we forced the site level to embrace our "Hide Screen Saver Option" edict. First, we created the GPO in the Group Policy Objects folder, and then in another step we linked the GPO to the site level. However, at the domain level (and, as you're about to see, the OU level), we can take care of both steps at once via the "Create a GPO in this domain, and Link it here" command. (Note, in previous versions of the GPMC, this was confusingly called "Create And Link A GPO Here." Being a grammar snob, this was a personal wish of mine to have clarified, and I'm happy to see Microsoft agreed and corrected it.)
>
> This command tells the GPMC to create a new GPO in the Group Policy Objects folder and then automatically link the new GPO back to this focused level of Active Directory. This is a time-saving step so we don't have to dive down into the Group Policy Objects folder first and then create the link back to the Active Directory level.
>
> So why is the "Create a GPO in this domain, and Link it here" option possible only at the domain and OU level and not the site level? Because Group Policy Objects linked to sites can often cause excessive bandwidth troubles when the old-school way of doing things is used. With that in mind, the GPMC interface makes sure that when you work with GPOs that affect sites, you're consciously choosing from *which* domain the GPO is being linked.

Don't panic when you see all the possible options. We'll hit them all in due time; right now we're interested in the first two: "Create a GPO in this domain, and Link it here" and "Link an Existing GPO."

Since you're focused at the domain level, you are prompted for the name of a new Group Policy Object when you right-click and choose "Create a GPO in this domain, and Link it here." For this one, type a descriptive name, such as **Prohibit Changing Sounds**. Your new "Prohibit Changing Sounds" GPO is created in the Group Policy Objects container and, automatically, a link is created at the domain level from the GPO to the domain.

 Take a moment to look in the Group Policy "swimming pool" for your new GPO. Simply drill down through Group Policy Management ➤ Forest ➤ Domains ➤ Corp.com and locate the Group Policy Objects note. Look for the new "Prohibit Changing Sounds" GPO.

Right-click the link "Prohibit Changing Sounds" (or the GPO itself) and choose Edit to open the Group Policy Management Editor. To make your wish come true and affect the Windows 7 Personalization page, drill down through User Configuration ➤ Policies ➤ Administrative Templates ➤ Control Panel ➤ Personalization, and double-click **Prevent Changing Sounds**. Change the setting from Not Configured to Enabled, and click OK. Close the Group Policy Management Editor to return to the GPMC.

Note that the policy setting will only affect Windows 7 or Windows Server 2008 R2 machines, so your Windows XP machines (if you have any) will ignore the policy setting.

Verifying Your Changes at the Domain Level

Now, log on as any user in the domain. You can log onto any computer in the domain (say, WIN7) as any user you have defined—even the administrator of the domain.

On WIN7, right-click the Desktop and click Personalize.

You'll see (in your tests) that the Sounds area is grayed out, as seen in Figure 1.19. Well, you might not be able to see it, exactly, in Figure 1.19, but, again, it's "locked out" for users.

FIGURE 1.19   The Sounds area is now grayed out because the user is affected by the domain-level policy.

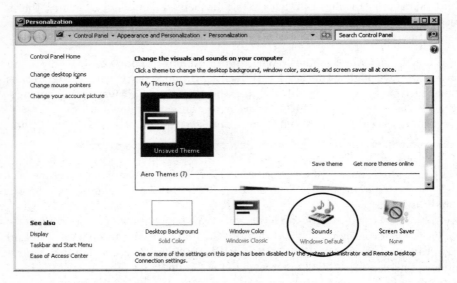

Once again, administrators are not immune to Group Policy effects. You can change this behavior, as you'll see in Chapter 2.

Applying Group Policy Objects to the OU Level

OUs are wonderful tools for delegating away unpleasant administrative duties, such as password resets or modifying group memberships. But that's only half their purpose. The other half is to be able to apply Group Policy.

You'll likely find yourself making most Group Policy additions and changes at the OU level, because that's where you have the most flexibility and the OU is the most refined instrument to affect users. Once OU administrators become comfortable in their surroundings, they want to harness the power of Group Policy.

Preparing to Delegate Control

To create a GPO at the OU level, you must first create the OU and a plan to delegate. For the examples in this book, we'll create three OUs that look like this:

- Human Resources
    - Human Resources Users
    - Human Resources Computers

Having separate OUs for your users and computers is a good idea—for both delegation of rights and also GPO design. Microsoft considers this a best practice. In the **Human Resources Users** OU in our Corp.com domain, we'll create and leverage an Active Directory security group to do our dirty work. We'll name this group HR-OU-Admins and put our first users inside the HR-OU-Admins security group. We'll then delegate the appropriate rights necessary for them to use the power of GPOs.

To create the **Human Resources Users** OU using your WIN7MANAGEMENT machine, follow these steps:

1. Earlier, you created a "unified console" where you housed both Active Directory Users and Computer and the GPMC. Simply use Active Directory Users and Computers, right-click the domain name, and choose New ➢ Organizational Unit, which will allow you to enter a new OU name. Enter **Human Resources** as the name. (Note that newer versions of Active Directory Users and Computers will ask you if you want to "Protect container from accidental deletion." It's your choice. I typically deselect the check box.)

2. Inside the **Human Resources** OU, create two more OUs—**Human Resources Computers** and **Human Resources Users**, as shown in Figure 1.20.

FIGURE 1.20   When you complete all these steps, your Human Resources OU should have a Human Resources Users OU and Human Resources Computers OU. In the users' side, put Frank Rizzo and the HR-OU-Admins.

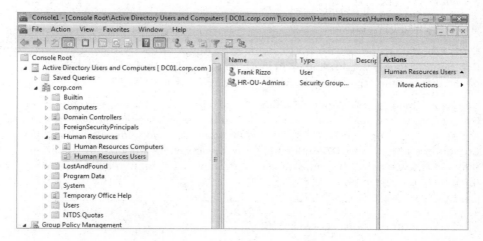

> Alternatively, you can create the OU in the GPMC. Just right-click the
> domain and choose New Organizational Unit from the context menu.

To create the HR-OU-Admins group, follow these steps:

1. In Active Directory Users and Computers, right-click the new **Human Resources Users**
   OU and choose New ➤ Group.

2. Create the new group HR-OU-Admins as a new Global Security group.

To create the first user to go inside HR-OU-Admins, follow these steps:

1. In Active Directory Users and Computers, right-click the **Human Resources Users** OU
   and choose New ➤ User.

2. Name the user **Frank Rizzo,** with an account name of **frizzo,** and click Next.

3. If you've established a Windows 2003 or later domain, you must now enter a complex
   password for a user. My suggested password in all my books is p@ssw0rd. That's a
   lowercase *p*, the at sign, an *s*, an *s*, a *w*, a zero, then *r*, and *d*.

4. Finish and close the wizard.

If you're following along, Frank Rizzo's login will be `frizzo@corp.com`.

Easily Manage New Users and Computers

The Computers folder and Users folder in Active Directory Users and Computers are *not*
OUs. They are generic *containers*. You'll notice that they are not present when using the
GPMC to view Active Directory. Because they are generic containers (and not OUs), you
cannot link Group Policy Objects to them. Of course, these objects will receive GPOs if
linked to the domain, because the containers are still *in* the domain. They just aren't OUs
in the domain.

These folders have two purposes:

- If you ever did an upgrade from NT 4 domains to Active Directory, these User and
  Computer accounts would wind up in these folders. (Administrators are then supposed to move the accounts into OUs.)

- The two folders are the default location where older tools drop new accounts
  when creating new users and computers. Additionally, command-line tools, such
  as net user and net group, will add accounts to these two folders. Similarly, the
  Computers folder is the default location for any new client workstation or server
  that joins the domain. The same goes when you create computer accounts using
  the net computer command.

So, these seem like decent "holding pens" for these kinds of objects. But ultimately, you don't want your users or computers to be in these folders—you want them to end up in OUs. That's where the action is because you can apply Group Policy to OUs, not to these folders! Yeah, sure, these users and computers are affected by site- and domain-level GPOs. But the action is at the OU level, and you want your computer and user objects to be placed in OUs as fast as possible—not sitting around in these generic Computers and Users folders.

To that end, domains that are at least at the "Windows 2003 functional level" have two tools to redirect the default location of new users and computers to the OUs of your choice. For example, suppose you want all new computers to go to a **NewComputers** OU and all new users to go to a **NewUsers** OU. And you want to link several GPOs to the **NewUsers** and **NewComputers** OUs to ensure that new accounts immediately have some baseline level of security, restriction, or protection. Without a little magic, new user accounts created using older tools won't automatically be placed there.

Starting with Windows 2003 Active Directory, Microsoft provided REDIRUSR and REDIRCMP commands that take a distinguished name, like this:

```
REDIRCMP ou=newcomputers,dc=corp,dc=com and/or
REDIRUSR ou=newusers,dc=corp,dc=com
```

Now if you link GPOs to these OUs, your new accounts will get the Group Policy Objects dictating settings to them at an OU level. This will come in handy when users and computers aren't specifically created in their final destination OUs.

To learn more about these tools, see the Microsoft Knowledge Base article 324949 at http://support.microsoft.com/kb/324949.

To add Frank Rizzo to the HR-OU-Admins group, follow these steps:

1. Double-click the HR-OU-Admins group.
2. Click the Members tab.
3. Add Frank Rizzo.

When it's all complete, your OU structure with your first user and group should look like Figure 1.20, shown previously.

Delegating Control for Group Policy Management

You've created the **Human Resources** OU, which contains the **Human Resources Users** OU and the **Human Resources Computers** OU and the HR-OU-Admins security group. Now, put Frank inside the HR-OU-Admins group, and you're ready to delegate control.

Performing Your First Delegation

You can delegate control to use Group Policy in two ways: using Active Directory Users and Computers and using the GPMC.

For this first example, we'll kick it old school and do it the Active Directory Users and Computers way. Then, in Chapter 2, I'll demonstrate how to delegate control using the GPMC.

To delegate control for Group Policy management, follow these steps:

1. In Active Directory Users and Computers, right-click the top-level **Human Resources** OU you created and choose Delegate Control from the context menu to start the "Delegation of Control Wizard."

2. Click Next to get past the wizard introduction screen.

3. You'll be asked to select users and/or groups. Click Add, add the HR-OU-Admins group, and click Next to open the "Tasks to Delegate" screen, as shown in Figure 1.21.

4. Click Manage Group Policy Links, and then click Next.

5. At the wizard review screen, click Finish.

FIGURE 1.21   Select the Manage Group Policy Links task.

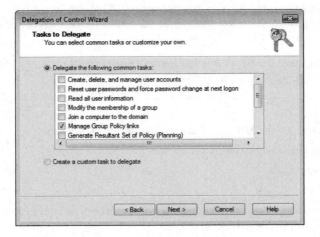

You might want to click some or all the other check boxes as well, but for this example, only "Manage Group Policy Links" is required. Avoid selecting "Generate Resultant Set of Policy (Planning)" and "Generate Resultant Set of Policy (Logging)" at this time. You'll see where these options come into play in Chapter 2.

The "Manage Group Policy Links" delegation assigns the user or group Read and Write access over the gPLink and gPOptions properties for that level. To see or modify these permissions by hand, open Active Directory Users and Computers and choose View ➤ Advanced Features. If later you want to remove a delegated permission, it's a little challenging. To locate the permission that you set, right-click the delegated object (such as OU), click the Properties tab, click the Security tab, choose Advanced, and dig around until you come across the permission you want to remove. Finally, delete the corresponding access control entry (ACE).

Adding a User to the Server Operators Group (Just for This Book)

Under normal conditions, nobody but Domain Administrators, Enterprise Administrators, or Server Operators can walk up to Domain Controllers and log on. For testing purposes only, though, we're going to add our user, Frank, to the Server Operators group so he can easily work on our DC01 Domain Controller when we want him to.

To add a user to the Server Operators group, follow these steps:

1. In Active Directory Users and Computers, double-click Frank Rizzo's account under the **Human Resources Users** OU.

2. Click the Member Of tab and click Add.

3. Select the Server Operators group and click OK.

4. Click OK to close the Properties dialog box for Frank Rizzo.

Normally, you wouldn't give your delegated OU administrators Server Operators access. You're doing it solely for the sake of this example to allow Frank to log on locally to your Domain Controllers.

Testing Your Delegation of Group Policy Management

At this point, on your WIN7MANAGEMENT machine, log off as Administrator and log in as Frank Rizzo (frizzo@corp.com). Heck, if you're using Windows 7 or Windows Server 2008 and later you can also use Switch User and stay logged in and just flip-flop back and forth as needed.

Now follow these steps to test your delegation:

1. Choose Start and type in **GPMC.MSC** at the Start Search prompt to open the GPMC.

2. Drill down through Group Policy Management, Domains, Corp.com, and Group Policy Objects. If you right-click Group Policy Objects in an attempt to create a new GPO, you'll see the context menu shown in Figure 1.22.

As you can see, Frank is unable to create new GPOs in the swimming pool of the domain. Since Frank has been delegated some control over the **Human Resources** OU (which also contains the other OUs), let's see what he *can* do. If you right-click the **Human Resources** OU in the GPMC, you'll see the context menu shown in Figure 1.23.

FIGURE 1.22   Frank cannot create new GPOs in the Group Policy Objects container.

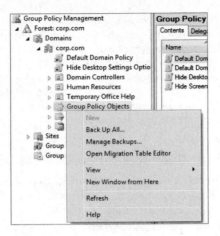

FIGURE 1.23   Frank's delegated rights allow him to link to existing GPOs but not to create new GPOs.

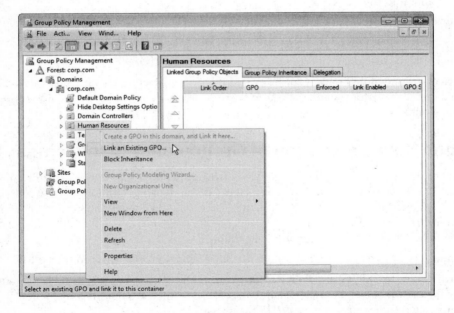

Because Frank is unable to create GPOs in the swimming pool of the domain (the Group Policy Objects container), he is also unable by definition to "Create a GPO in this domain, and Link it here." Although Frank (and more specifically, the HR-OU-Admins) has been delegated the ability to "Manage Group Policy Links," he cannot *create* new GPOs. Frank (and the other potential HR-OU-Admins) has only the ability to *link* an existing GPO.

Understanding Group Policy Object Linking Delegation

When we were logged on as the Domain Administrator, we could create GPOs in the Group Policy Objects container, and we could "Create a GPO in this domain, and Link it here" at the domain or OU levels. But Frank cannot.

Here's the idea about delegating the ability to link to GPOs: someone with a lot of brains in the organization does all the work in creating a well-thought-out and well-tested GPO. Maybe this GPO distributes software, maybe it sets up a secure workstation policy, or perhaps it runs a startup script. You get the idea.

Then, others in the organization, like Frank, are delegated just the ability to *link* to that GPO and use it at their level. This solves the problem of delegating perhaps too much control. Certainly some administrators are ready to create their own users and groups, but other administrators may not be quite ready to jump into the cold waters of Group Policy Object creation. Thus, you can design the GPOs for other administrators; they can just link to the ones you (or others) create.

When you (or someone with the right to link GPOs) selects "Link an Existing GPO," as seen in Figure 1.23, you can choose a GPO that's already been created—and hanging out in the domain swimming pool—the Group Policy Objects container.

In this example, the HR-OU-Admins members, such as Frank, can leverage any currently created GPO to affect the users and computers in their OU—even if they didn't create it themselves. In this example, Frank has linked to an existing GPO called "Word 2003 Settings." Turns out that some other administrator in the domain created this GPO, but Frank wants to use it. So, because Frank has Manage Group Policy Links rights on the **Human Resources** OU (and OUs underneath it), he is allowed to link to it.

But, as you can see in Figure 1.24, he cannot edit the GPOs. Under the hood, Active Directory doesn't permit Frank to edit GPOs he didn't create (and therefore doesn't own).

In Chapter 2, I'll show you how to grant specific rights to allow more than just the original creator (and now owner) of the object to edit specific GPOs.

Giving the ability to just link to existing GPOs is a good idea in theory, but often OU administrators are simply given full authority to create their own GPOs (as you'll see later). For this example, don't worry about linking to any GPOs. Simply cancel out of the Select GPO screen, close the GPMC, and log off from the server as Frank Rizzo.

Granting OU Admins Access to Create New Group Policy Objects

By using the "Delegation of Control Wizard" to delegate the Manage Group Policy Links attribute, you performed half of what is needed to grant the appropriate authority to Frank (and any additional future HR-OU-Admins) to create GPOs in the Group Policy Objects container and link them to the **Human Resources** OU, the **Human Resources Users** OU, or the **Human Resources Computers** OU. (Though we really don't want to link many GPOs directly to the **Human Resources** OU.)

FIGURE 1.24   The GPMC will not allow you to edit an existing GPO if you do not own it (or do not have explicit permission to edit it).

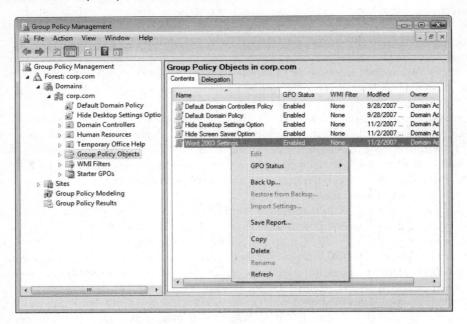

You can grant the HR-OU-Admins the ability to create GPOs in the Group Policy Objects container in two ways. For now, I'll show you the old-school way; in Chapter 2, I'll show you the GPMC way.

One of Active Directory's built-in security groups, Group Policy Creator Owners, holds the key to the other half of our puzzle. You'll need to add those users or groups whom you want to have the ability to create GPOs to a built-in group, cleverly named Group Policy Creator Owners. To do so, follow these steps:

1. Switch-User back to Domain Administrator.

2. Fire up Active Directory Users and Computers.

3. By default, the Group Policy Creator Owners group is located in the Users folder in the domain. Double-click the Group Policy Creator Owners group and add the HR-OU-Admins group and/or Frank Rizzo.

You will not be able to add the HR-OU-Admins group until the domain mode has been switched to at least Windows 2000 Native or Windows 2003 Functional level. Switch the domain by using Active Directory Domains and Trusts (or Active Directory Users and Computers). Switching the domain mode is a one-way operation, and disallows older operating systems as Domain Controllers. If you are not prepared to make the switch to Native mode, you'll only be able to add individual members—such as Frank Rizzo—and not a group.

In Chapter 2, you'll see an alternate way to allow users to create GPOs.

Creating and Linking Group Policy Objects at the OU Level

At the site level, we hid the Screen Saver option. At the domain level, we chose to get rid of the Sounds option in the Windows 7 Personalization page.

At the OU level, we have two jobs to do:

- Prevent users from changing the mouse pointers (a new Windows 7–only policy setting)
- Restore the Screen Saver option that was taken away at the site level

To create a GPO at the OU level, follow these steps:

1. Since you're on WIN7MANAGEMENT, log off as Administrator and log back on as Frank Rizzo (`frizzo@corp.com`).

2. Choose Start and type **GPMC.MSC** in the Start Search prompt.

3. Drill down until you reach the **Human Resources Users** OU, right-click it, and choose "Create a GPO in this domain, and Link it here" from the context menu to open the New GPO dialog box.

4. In the New GPO dialog box, type the name of your new GPO, say **Hide Mouse Pointers Option /Restore Screen Saver Option**. This will create a GPO in the Group Policy Objects container and link it to the **Human Resources Users** OU.

5. Right-click the Group Policy link and choose Edit from the context menu to open the Group Policy Management Editor.

6. To hide the Mouse Pointers Option in the Windows 7 Personalization page, drill down through User Configuration ➢ Policies ➢ Administrative Templates ➢ Control Panel ➢ Personalization and double-click the **Prevent Changing Mouse Pointers** policy setting. Change the setting from Not Configured to Enabled, and click OK.

7. To restore the Screen Saver setting for Windows 7 (or Screen Saver tab in Windows XP), double-click the **Prevent Changing Screen Saver** policy setting. Change the setting from Not Configured to Disabled, and click OK.

8. Close the Group Policy Management Editor to return to the GPMC.

By disabling the **Hide Screen Saver Tab** policy setting, you're reversing the Enable setting set at a higher level. See the sidebar "The Three Possible Settings: Not Configured, Enabled, and Disabled" later in this chapter.

Verifying Your Changes at the OU Level

On your test WIN7 machine, log back on as Frank. Because Frank's account is in the OU, Frank is destined to get the Site, Domain and now the new OU GPOs with the policy settings.

On WIN7, right-click the Desktop and choose Personalize from the context menu to open the Display Properties dialog box. In Figure 1.25, you can see the before (left) and after (right) when the policy is applied. Look closely, and note that the "Change mouse pointers" option is removed and that that the Screen Saver option is no longer grayed out and is now available.

In the book we've highlighted the areas that are affected. But because the book is printed in black and white it could be hard to see that the "Screen Saver" selection is, indeed, no longer grayed out, and, yes, quite clickable again, as seen in the right in Figure 1.25.

FIGURE 1.25   On the left, we have Frank's Personalization page before the policy applies. You can see the Screen Saver icon is unavailable, and the ability to change mouse pointers is still present. On the right, we have Frank's Personalization page after the policy applies. The ability to manipulate screen savers has returned, but he is now prevented from changing mouse settings.

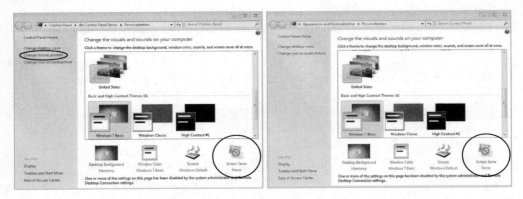

This test proves, once again, that even OU administrators are not automatically immune from policy settings. Chapter 2 explains how to change this behavior.

Group Policy Strategy: Should I Create More or Fewer GPOs?

At times, you'll want to lock down additional functions for a collection of users or computers. For example, you might want to specify that no users in the **Human Resources Users** OU can use the Control Panel.

At the **Human Resources Users** OU level, you've already set up a GPO that contained a policy setting to hide the mouse pointers option in the Windows 7 Personalization page. You can create a new GPO that affects the **Human Resources Users** OU, give it a descriptive name—say, **No One Can Use Control Panel**—and then drill down through User Configuration ➢ Policies ➢ Administrative Templates ➢ Windows Components ➢ Control Panel and enable the policy setting **Prohibit Access to Control Panel**.

Or you could simply modify your existing GPO, named Hide Mouse Pointers Option/ Restore Screen Saver Option, so that it contains additional policy settings. You can then rename your GPO to something that makes sense and encompasses the qualities of all the policy changes—say "Our Human Resources Users' Desktop Settings."

Here's the quandary: the former method (one policy setting per GPO) is certainly more descriptive and definitely easier to debug should things go awry. If you have only one policy set inside the GPO, you have a better handle on what each one is affecting. If something goes wrong, you can dive right into the GPO, track down the policy setting, and make the necessary changes, or you can disable the ornery GPO (as discussed in Chapter 2 in the section "Stopping Group Policy Objects from Applying.")

The second method (multiple policy settings per GPO) is a teeny-weeny bit faster for your computers and users at boot or logon time because each additional GPO takes some miniscule fraction of additional processing time. But if you stuff too many settings in an individual GPO, the time to debug should things go wrong goes up exponentially. Group Policy has so many nooks and crannies that it can be difficult to debug.

So, in a nutshell, if you have multiple GPOs at a particular level, you can do the following:

- Name each of them more descriptively.
- Debug them easily if things go wrong.
- Disable individually misbehaving GPOs.
- Associate that GPO more easily to a WMI filter (explored in Chapter 6).
- More easily delegate permissions to any specific GPO (explored in Chapter 2).

If you have fewer GPOs at a particular level, the following is the case:

- Logging on is slightly faster for the user (but really only slightly).
- Debugging is somewhat more difficult if things go wrong.
- You can disable individually misbehaving GPOs or links to misbehaving GPOs. (But if they contain many settings, you might be disabling more than you desire.)

So, how do you form a GPO strategy? There is no right or wrong answer; you need to decide what's best for you. Several options, however, can help you decide.

One middle-of-the-road strategy is to start with multiple GPOs and one lone policy setting in each. Once you are comfortable that they are individually working as expected, you can create another new GPO that contains the sum of the settings from, in this example, **Prevent Changing Mouse Pointers** and **Prohibit Access to Control Panel** and then delete (or disable) the old individual GPO.

Another middle-of-the-road strategy is to have a single GPO that contains only the policy settings required to perform a complete "wish." This way, if the wish goes sour, you can easily address it or disable it (or whack it) as needed.

Here's yet another strategy. Some Microsoft documentation recommends that you create GPOs so that they affect only the User half or the Computer half. You can then disable the unused portion of the GPO (either the Computer half or the User half). This allows you to group together policy settings affecting one node for ease of naming and debugging and allows for flexible troubleshooting. However, be careful here because after you disable half the GPO, there's no iconic notification (though there is a column labeled GPO Status that does show this). Troubleshooting can become harder if not performed perfectly and consistently. In all, I'm not a huge fan of disabling half the GPO.

Note that the policy changes we are making to the Windows 7 clients in the domain also take effect on Windows Server 2008 R2 machines.

Creating a New Group Policy Object Affecting Computers in an OU

For the sake of learning and working through the rest of the examples in this section, you'll create another GPO and link it to the **Human Resources Computers** OU. This GPO will autolaunch a very important application for anyone who uses these machines: calc.exe.

The setting we're about to play with also exists under the User node, but we'll experiment with the Computer node policy.

First, you'll need to create the new GPO and modify the settings. You'll then need to move some client machines into the **Human Resources Computers** OU in order to see your changes take effect.

To autolaunch calc.exe for anyone logging into a computer in the **Human Resources Computers** OU, follow these steps:

1. If you're not already logged in as Frank Rizzo, the **Human Resources** OU administrator, do so now on WIN7MANAGEMENT.

2. Choose Start and type **GPMC.MSC** in the Start Search prompt.

3. Drill down until you reach the **Human Resources Computers** OU, right-click it, and choose "Create a GPO in this domain, and Link it here" from the context menu.

4. Name the GPO something descriptive, such as **Auto-Launch calc.exe**.

5. Right-click the GPO, and choose Edit to open the Group Policy Management Editor.

6. We want to affect our client computers (not users), so we need to use the Computers node. To autolaunch **calc.exe**, drill down through Computer Configuration ➢ Policies ➢ Administrative Templates ➢ System ➢ Logon, and double-click **Run these programs at user logon**. Change the setting from Not Configured to Enabled.

7. Click the Show button, and the Show Contents dialog box appears. You'll see this policy setting has a little "table editor" associated with it. In the first "row," simply enter the full path to **calc.exe** as **c:\windows\system32\calc.exe** (or, if you want to be more general, **%Windir%\System32\calc.exe**) and click OK, as shown in Figure 1.26. Click OK to close the Show Contents dialog box, and click OK again to close the **Run these programs at user logon** policy setting.

FIGURE 1.26   When this policy setting is enabled and calc.exe is specified, all computers in this OU will launch calc.exe when a user logs in.

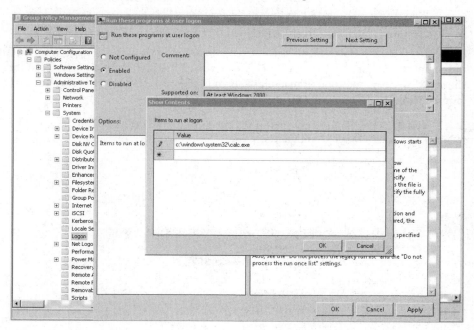

8. Close the Group Policy Management Editor to return the GPMC.

Be aware of occasional strange Microsoft verbiage when you need to enable a policy to *disable* a setting. Since Windows 2003, most policy settings have been renamed to "Prohibit *<whatever>*" to reflect the change from confusion to clarity.

Moving Computers into the Human Resources Computers OU

Since you just created a policy that will affect computers, you'll need to place a workstation or two inside the **Human Resources Computers** OU to see the results of your labor. You'll need to be logged on as Administrator on DC01 or WIN7MANAGEMENT to do this.

> Quite often computers and users are relegated to separate OUs. That way, certain GPOs can be applied to certain computers but not others. For instance, isolating laptops, desktops, and servers is a common practice.

In this example, we're going to use the Find command in Active Directory Users and Computers to find a workstation named XPPRO1 and the Windows Vista workstation named WIN7 and move it into the **Human Resources Computers** OU.

To find and move computers into a specific OU, follow these steps:

1. In Active Directory Users and Computers, right-click the domain, and choose Find from the context menu to open the Find Users, Contacts, and Groups dialog box.

2. From the Find drop-down menu, select Computers. In the Name field, type **WIN7** to find the computer account of the same name. Once you've found it, right-click the account and choose Move from the context menu, as shown in Figure 1.27. Move the account to the **Human Resources Computers** OU.

FIGURE 1.27   Use the Find command to find computers in the domain, then right-click on the entry and select Move to move them.

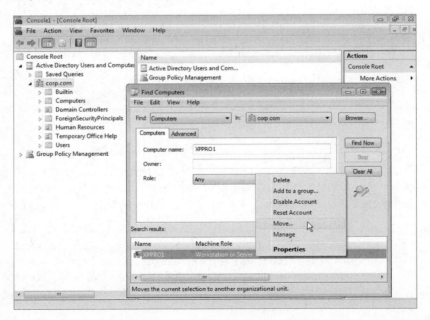

Repeat these steps for XPPRO1 and all other computers that you want to move to the **Human Resources Computers** OU.

3. Now that you've moved WIN7 (and maybe also XPPRO1) into the new OU, be sure to reboot those client computers.

After you move the computer accounts into the **Human Resources Computers** OU, it's very important to reboot your client machines. As you'll see in Chapter 3, the computer does not recognize the change right away when computer accounts are moved between OUs.

As you can see in this example (and in the real world), a best practice is to separate users and computers into their own OUs and then link GPOs to those OUs. Indeed, underneath a parent OU structure, such as the **Human Resources** OU, you might have more OUs (that is, **Human Resources Laptops** OU, **Human Resources Servers** OU, and so on). This will give you the most flexibility in design between delegating control where it's needed and the balance of GPO design within OUs. Just remember that for GPOs to affect either a user or computer, that user or computer must be within the scope of the GPO—site, domain, or OU.

Verifying Your Cumulative Changes

At this point, you've set up three levels of Group Policy that accomplish multiple actions:

- At the site level, the "Hide Screen Saver Option" GPO is in force for users.
- At the domain level, the "Prohibit Changing Sounds" GPO is in force for users.
- In the **Human Resources Users** OU, the "Hide Mouse Pointers Option/Restore Screen Saver Option" GPO is in force for users.
- In the **Human Resources Computers** OU, the "Auto-Launch calc.exe" GPO is in force for computers.

At this point, take a minute to flip back to Figure 1.11 (the swimming pool illustration) to see where we're going here. To see the accumulation of your policy settings inside your GPOs, you'll need to log on as a user who is affected by the **Human Resources Users** OU and at a computer that is affected by the **Human Resources Computers** OU. Therefore, log on as Frank Rizzo at WIN7.

If you're using Windows 7, right-click the Desktop and choose Personalize. Note that the "Change mouse pointers" option is still missing from the previous exercise (and the Screen Saver entry is restored). And, when you logged in, did the computer GPO autolaunch Windows Calculator?

These tests prove that even OU administrators are not automatically immune from GPOs and the policy settings within. Under the hood, they are in the Authenticated Users security group. See Chapter 2 for information on how to modify this behavior.

The Three Possible Settings: Not Configured, Enabled, and Disabled

As you saw in Figure 1.2 earlier in this chapter, nearly all administrative template policy settings can be set as Not Configured, Enabled, or Disabled. These three settings have very different consequences, so it's important to understand how each works.

Not Configured The best way to think about Not Configured is to imagine that it really says, "Don't do anything" or even "Pass through." Why is this? Because if a policy setting is set to Not Configured, then it honors any previously set setting (or the operating system default).

Enabled When a specific policy setting is enabled, the policy will take effect. In the case of the **Prohibit Changing Sounds** policy setting, the effect is obvious. However, lots of policy settings, once enabled, have myriad possibilities *inside* the specific policy setting! (For a gander at one such policy setting, use the Group Policy Management Editor and drill down to User Configuration ➢ Policies ➢ Administrative Templates ➢ Windows Components ➢ Internet Explorer ➢ Toolbars and select the policy setting named **Configure Toolbar Buttons**.) So, as we can see, Enabled really means "Turn this policy setting on." Either it will then do what it says or there will be more options inside the policy setting that can be configured.

Disabled This setting leads a threefold life:

- Disabled usually means that if the same policy setting is enabled at a higher level; reverse its operation. For example, we chose to enable the **Prevent Changing Screen Saver** policy setting at the site level. If at a lower level (say, the domain or OU level), we chose to *disable* this policy setting, the Screen Saver option will pop back at the level at which we *disabled* this policy. You can think of Disabled (usually) as "reverse a policy setting coming from a higher level."

- Additionally, Disabled often forces the user to accept the administrator's will. That is, if a policy setting is disabled, some default behavior of the policy setting is enforced and the user cannot change it. To see an example policy setting like this, use the Group Policy Management Editor and drill down through User Configuration ➢ Policies ➢ Administrative Templates ➢ Start Menu and Taskbar and select the policy setting named **Force classic Start Menu** (a setting meant for XP and Vista, but not Windows 7). Once this policy setting is set to Disabled, the policy forces Windows XP users to use Start Menu in the XP task-based style (as opposed to the old Windows 2000 style). The point here is that the Disabled setting is a bit tricky to work with. You'll want to be sure that when you disable a policy setting, you're doing precisely what you intend.

> - Disabled sometimes has a special and, typically, rare use. That is, something might already be hard-coded into the Registry to be "turned on" or work one way, and the only way to turn it off is to select Disabled. One such policy setting is the **Shutdown Event Tracker**. You disable the policy setting, which turns it off, because on servers since Windows 2003 it's already hard-coded on. In workstations Windows XP and later, it's already hard-coded off. Likewise, if you want to kill Windows XP or Windows 7's firewall, you need to set **Windows Firewall: Protect All Network Connections** to Disabled. (You can find that policy setting at Computer Configuration ➤ Policies ➤ Administrative Templates ➤ Network ➤ Network Connections ➤ Windows Firewall ➤ Domain Profile (and also Standard Profile) while editing GPOs on Windows XP/Service Pack 2 and above.) Again, that's because the firewall's defaults are hard-coded to on, and by disabling the policy setting, you're "reverting" the behavior back.
>
> So, think of Not Configured as having neither Allow nor Deny being set. Enabled will turn it on and possibly have more functions. Disabled has multiple uses, and be sure to first read the Help text for each policy setting. Most times it's simply directly spelled out what Enabled and Disabled does for that particular setting. Lastly, test, test, test to make sure that once you've manipulated a policy setting, it's doing precisely what you had in mind.

Final Thoughts

The concepts here are valid regardless of what your domain is running. It doesn't matter if you have a pure or mixed Active Directory domain with various and sundry Domain Controller types. The point is that to make the best use of Group Policy, you'll need an Active Directory.

You'll also need a Windows 7 or Windows Server 2008 R2 management station to do your Group Policy work. Again, we talk more about why you need a Windows 7 management station in Chapters 3, 6, and elsewhere.

Remember, the GPMC is built into Windows Server 2008 R2, but it's not installed unless the machine is also a Domain Controller. The GPMC isn't built into Windows 7 and is only available through the downloadable RSAT tools.

The more you use and implement GPOs in your environment, the better you'll become at their basic use while at the same time avoiding pitfalls when it comes to using them. The following tips are scattered throughout the chapter but are repeated and emphasized here for quick reference, to help you along your Group Policy journey:

GPOs don't "live" at the site, domain, or OU level. GPOs "live" in Active Directory and are represented in the swimming pool of the domain called the Group Policy Objects container. To use a GPO, you need to link a GPO to a level in Active Directory that you want to affect: a site, a domain, or an OU.

GPOs apply locally and also to Active Directory sites, domains, and OUs.   There is a local GPO that can be used with or without Active Directory. Everyone on that computer must embrace that local GPO. Then, Active Directory Group Policy Objects apply: site, domain, and then OU. Active Directory GPOs "trump" any local policy settings if set within the Local Group Policy. Active Directory is a hierarchy, and Group Policy takes advantage of that hierarchy.

Avoid using the site level to implement GPOs.   Users can roam from site to site by jumping on different computers (or plugging their laptop into another site). When they do, they can be confused by the settings changing around them. Use GPOs linked to the site only to set up special sitewide security settings, such as IPsec or the Internet Explorer Proxy. Use the domain or OU levels when creating GPOs whenever possible.

Implement common settings high in the hierarchy when possible.   The higher up in the hierarchy GPOs are implemented, the more users they affect. You want common settings to be set once, affecting everyone, instead of having to create additional GPOs performing the same functions at other lower levels, which will just clutter your view of Active Directory with the multiple copies of the same policy setting.

Implement unique settings low in the hierarchy.   If a specific collection of users is unique, try to round them up into an OU and then apply Group Policy to them. This is much better than applying the settings high in the hierarchy and using Group Policy filtering later.

Use more GPOs at any level to make things easier.   When creating a new wish, isolate it by creating a new GPO. This will enable easy revocation by unlinking it should something go awry.

Strike a balance between having too many and too few GPOs.   There is a middle ground between having one policy setting within a single GPO and having a bajillion policy settings contained within a single GPO. At the end of your design, the goal is to have meaningfully named GPOs that reflect the "wish" you want to accomplish. If you should choose to end that wish, you can easily disable or delete it.

As you go on your Group Policy journey...   Don't go at it alone. There are some nice third-party independent resources to help you on your way. I run www.GPanswers.com, which has oodles of resources, downloads, a community forum, downloadable eChapters, video tutorials, links to third-party software, and my in-person and online versions of my hands-on training seminars. Think of it as your secret Group Policy resource.

My pal (and technical editor for a previous edition) Darren Mar-Elia runs www.GPOguy.com.

My pal (and technical editor for a previous edition) Jakob Heidelberg has a lot of great articles (mostly on Group Policy topics) at http://www.windowsecurity.com/Jakob_H_Heidelberg, (http://tinyurl.com/ypar82).

2

Managing Group Policy with the GPMC

In Chapter 1, you got to know how and when Group Policy works. We used Active Directory Users and Computers to create and manage users and computers, but we used the Group Policy Management Console (GPMC) to manage Group Policy. We got a little workout with the GPMC when creating new GPOs and linking them to various levels in Active Directory.

And, for just a moment, we went back to the old-school way to delegate control to Frank and the HR-OU-Admins group to link existing GPOs to their **Human Resources** OU structure.

In this chapter, I'll cover the remainder of the daily tasks you can perform using the GPMC. As a reminder, the GPMC is for all implementations of Active Directory. That is, you can use the GPMC to manage your Active Directory—whatever the Domain Controllers are that constitute it.

You just need the GPMC loaded up on some machine. Now, in the previous chapter, I put a pretty fine point on it: you want this machine to be a Windows 7 or a Windows Server 2008 R2 machine. Here's the breakdown of the GPMC editions:

Windows XP/Windows Server 2003   Had (well, still has as of this writing) a download that you install on Windows XP or Windows Server 2003.

Vista RTM   Built into the shipping version of Windows Vista. Note that this GPMC is automatically removed when Windows Vista's SP1 is installed.

Windows Server 2008 or Windows Vista/SP1   Microsoft released the Remote Server Administration Toolkit (RSAT), an add-on for these machines. RSAT contained a newer GPMC. Note that RSAT is built into Windows Server 2008 and downloadable for Windows Vista (after SP1).

Windows Server 2008 R2/Windows 7   The "even newer" GPMC is contained within an "even newer" RSAT. Again, RSAT is built into Windows Server 2008 R2 and is downloadable for Windows 7.

So, ideally, your management station shouldn't just be any ol' Windows 7 machine, but rather one with the RSAT tools installed and the GPMC selected, as we already did in the previous chapter.

In short, if you don't use a Windows 7 machine (or Windows Server 2008 R2) as your management station, you won't have access to all the latest awesome powers in the Group Policy arsenal. In this chapter, you're going to be working again with your WIN7MANAGEMENT machine where you've already loaded the updated GPMC.

With that in mind, let's get to know the GPMC a bit better.

The unfortunate part of having multiple GPMCs out there is that, well, it's hard to describe, in language, *which* version we're talking about. Sometimes, in casual conversation I'll quip about doing something-or-other on "the updated GPMC." But the problem is, that's not its *official* name. And then, even if I do quip about "the updated GPMC," am I talking about the version that comes in the RSAT that's usable with Windows Vista or with the version that comes in the RSAT that's usable with Windows 7? Oy, confusing. The good news is that the advice always stands true: use the latest, greatest GPMC. And, since as of this writing, the "latest, greatest GPMC" can be found in Windows Server 2008 R2 and in the downloadable RSAT for Windows 7, that's what we'll call it: "the latest, greatest GPMC," or just the "updated GPMC."

I'm going to assume you've already installed the GPMC on either your Windows 7 management station (WIN7MANAGEMENT) or your Windows Server 2008 R2 Domain Controller (DC01). If you haven't already tackled those installation steps, go back to Chapter 1 and find the section "Implementing the GPMC on Your Management Station."

Once you're ready to get started, just click Start, and in the Start Search box, type **GPMC.MSC**.

Common Procedures with the GPMC

In Chapter 1, we created and linked some GPOs, which we can see in the Group Policy Objects container, to determine how, at each level, we were affecting our users. In this section, we'll continue by working with some advanced options for applying, manipulating, and using Group Policy.

Clicking a GPO (or a link) lets you get more information about what it does. For now, feel free to click around, but I suggest that you don't change anything until we get to the specific examples.

Various tabs are available to you once you click the GPO or a link. For instance, let's locate the GPO that's linked to the **Human Resources Users** OU. We'll do this by drilling down to Group Policy Management ➢ Forest ➢ Domains ➢ Corp.com ➢ Human Resources ➢ Human Resources Users and clicking the one GPO that's linked there: "Hide

Mouse Pointers Option/Restore Screen Saver Option." With that in mind, let's examine the various sections of a policy setting; you can flip through each of the tabs to get more information about the GPO you just found.

The Scope tab   Clicking a GPO or a GPO link opens the Scope tab. The Scope tab gives you an at-a-glance view of where and when the GPO will apply. We'll examine the Scope tab in the sections "Deleting and Unlinking Group Policy Objects" and "Filtering the Scope of Group Policy Objects with Security" later in this chapter, and in the WMI section of the next chapter. For now, you can see that the "Hide Mouse Pointers Option/Restore Screen Saver Option" GPO is linked to the Human Resources Users OU. But you already knew that.

The Details tab   The Details tab contains information describing who created the GPO (the owner) and the status (Enabled, Disabled, or Partially Disabled) as well as some nuts-and-bolts information about its underlying representation in Active Directory (the GUID). We'll examine the Details tab in the sections "Disabling 'Half' (or Both Halves) of the Group Policy Object" and "Understanding GPMC's Link Warning" in this chapter.

Should you change the GPO status here by, say, disabling the User Configuration of the policy, you'll be affecting all other levels in Active Directory that might be using this GPO by linking to it. See the section "Understanding GPMC's Link Warning" as well as the sidebar "On GPO Links and GPOs Themselves" a bit later in the chapter.

The Settings tab   The Settings tab gives you an at-a-glance view of what's been set inside the GPO. In our example, you can see the Enabled and Disabled status of the two policy settings we manipulated. You can click Hide (or Show) to contract and expand all the configured policy settings:

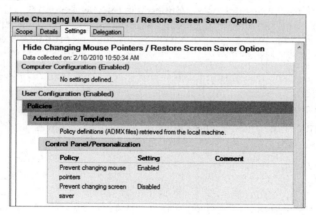

- Clicking Hide at any level tightens that level. You can expose more information by clicking Show.

- Clicking the policy setting name—for example, **Prevent Changing Mouse Pointers**—displays the help text for the policy setting (but note that this is only applicable to Administrative Template settings). This trick can be useful if someone set up a GPO with a kooky name and you want to know what's going on inside that GPO.

- If you want to change a setting, right-click the settings area and select Edit. The familiar Group Policy Management Editor will appear. Note, however, that the Group Policy Management Editor will not "snap to" the policy setting you want to edit. The editor always starts off at the root.

- Additionally, at any time you can right-click over this report and select Save Report, which does just that. It creates an HTML or XML report that you can then e-mail to fellow administrators or the boss, and so on. This is a super way of documenting your Group Policy environment instead of writing down everything by hand.

I've said it before, but it bears repeating: you can also edit the settings by clicking the GPO or any GPO link for that object and choosing Edit. However, you *always* affect all containers (sites, domains, or OUs) to which the GPO is linked. It's one and the same object, regardless of the way you edit it. See the sidebar "On GPO Links and GPOs Themselves" a bit later in the chapter to get the gist of this.

 If you chose to run the GPMC on a Windows Server, you may run into security pop-ups when clicking the Settings tab. Certain aspects of the GPMC, such as the Settings tab, utilize Internet Explorer to display their contents. Since Internet Explorer is hardened on Windows Server machines, you will have limited access to the whole picture. If you're presented with a warning box, simply add security_mmc.exe as a trusted website. This should make your problems go away. You can also turn off Internet Explorer Enhanced Security Configuration in Windows 2003 in Add/Remove Programs. In Windows Server 2008 or later, use Server Manager, and on the main screen, in the Security Configuration section, click Configure IE ESC, where you'll be able to enable or disable the annoying, I mean, informative pop-ups. This approach is recommended in test labs but not recommended on production servers.

The Delegation tab   The Delegation tab lets you specify who can do what with GPOs, their links, and their properties. You'll find the Delegation tab in a lot of places, such as when you do the following:

- Click a GPO link or click a GPO in the Group Policy Objects container
- Click a site
- Click a domain
- Click an OU
- Click the WMI Filters node
- Click a WMI (Windows Management Instrumentation) filter itself (covered in Chapter 4)
- Click on the Starter GPOs section

At each of these locations, the tab allows you to do something different. I'll discuss what each instance of this tab does a bit later in the section "Security Filtering and Delegation with the GPMC."

Raising or Lowering the Precedence of Multiple Group Policy Objects

You already know that the "flow" of Group Policy is inherited from the site level, the domain level, and then from each nested OU level. But, additionally, *within* each level, say at the **Temporary Office Help** OU, multiple GPOs are processed in a ranking precedence order. Lower-ranking GPOs are processed first, and then the higher GPOs are processed.

In Figure 2.1, you can see that an administrator has linked two GPOs to the **Temporary Office Help** OU. One GPO is named "Enforce 50MB Disk Quotas," and another is named "Enforce 40MB Disk Quotas."

FIGURE 2.1   You can link multiple GPOs at the same level.

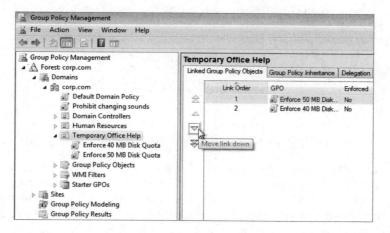

If the policy settings inside these GPOs both adjust the disk quota settings, which one will "win"? Client computers will process these two GPOs from lowest-link order to highest-link order. Therefore, the "Enforce 40MB Disk Quotas" GPO (with link order 2) is processed before "Enforce 50MB Disk Quotas" (link order 1). Hence, the GPO with the policy settings to dictate 50MB disk quotas will win.

So, if two (or more) GPOs within the same level contain values for the same policy setting (or policy settings), the GPOs will be processed from *lowest-link order* to *highest-link order.* Each consecutively processed GPO is then written. If there are any conflicts, the highest link order "wins." This could happen where one GPO has a specific policy setting enabled and another GPO at the same level has the same policy setting disabled.

Just to clear up a confusing little point: it turns out the highest-link order is not the highest numbered GPO listed at a level. Oh no—that would be too easy. Indeed, the highest-link order is shown as the lowest displayed number. Great. Just another fun fact to keep you on your toes.

Changing the order of the processing of multiple GPOs at a specific level is an easy task. For instance, suppose you want to change the order of the processing so that the "Enforce

40MB Disk Quotas" GPO is processed after the "Enforce 50MB Disk Quotas" GPO. Simply click the policy setting you want to process last and click the down arrow icon. Similarly, if you have additional GPOs that you want to process first, click the GPO and click the up arrow icon. The multiple arrow icons will put the highlighted GPO either first or last in the link order—depending on the icon you click.

Again—the "most last" applied GPO wins. So the GPO with a link order of 1 is always applied last and, hence, has the final say at that level. This is always true unless the Enforced flag is used (as discussed later).

Understanding GPMC's Link Warning

In the previous chapter, I pointed out that anytime you click a GPO link, you get the informational (or perhaps it's more of a warning) message shown in Figure 2.2.

FIGURE 2.2   You get this message anytime you click the icon for a link.

This message is trying to convey an important sentiment: no man is an island, and neither is a Group Policy Object. Just because you created a GPO and it is seen swimming in the Group Policy Objects container doesn't mean you're the only one who is possibly using it.

As we work through examples in this chapter, we'll manipulate various characteristics of GPOs and links to GPOs. If we manipulate any characteristics of a GPO we're about to play with, such as the following, then all other levels in Active Directory that also link to this GPO will be affected by our changes:

- The underlying policy settings themselves
- The security filtering (on the Scope tab)
- The WMI filtering (on the Scope tab)
- The GPO status (on the Details tab)
- The delegation (on the Delegation tab)

For instance, imagine you had a GPO linked to an OU called **Doctors** and the same GPO linked to an OU called **Nurses**. If you edit the GPO in the swimming pool, or click the link to the GPO in *either* **Doctors** *or* **Nurses** and click Edit, you're doing the same thing. Any changes made within the GPO affect *both* the **Doctors** OU and the **Nurses** OU.

This is sometimes a tough concept to remember, so it's good to see it here again. You can choose to squelch the tip if you like. Just don't forget its advice.

The difference between the GPO itself and the links you can create can be confusing. Be sure to check out the sidebar "On GPO Links and GPOs Themselves" a bit later in the chapter.

Another way to see this principle in action is by locating the "Auto-Launch calc.exe" GPO in either the link in the **Human Resources Computers** OU or the object itself within the Group Policy Objects container. Then, go to the Details tab and change the GPO status to some other setting. Then, go to the link or the actual GPO and see that your changes are reflected. You can even create a new OU, link the GPO, and *still* see that the change is there. This is because you're manipulating the *actual* GPO, not the link. If you choose to squelch the message, you can get it back by choosing View ➢ Options ➢ General and selecting "Show confirmation dialog to distinguish between GPOs and GPO links."

Stopping Group Policy Objects from Applying

After you create your hierarchy of Group Policy that applies to your users and computers, you might occasionally want to temporarily halt the processing of a GPO—usually because a user is complaining that something is wrong. You can prevent a specific GPO from processing at a level in Active Directory via several methods, as explained in the following sections.

Preventing Local GPOs from Applying

Before we get too far down the path with Active Directory–based GPOs, let's not forget that you might also want to stop a local GPO from applying. For instance, you might have walked up to 50 Sales computers and created a local GPO that prevents access to the Control Panel. However, now you want to reverse that edict. Instead of walking around to those 50 computers, you can just zap a Group Policy to those computers to inhibit the processing of local GPOs. Here's the trick, though: this technique only works for Windows Vista or later machines—not for earlier versions of the operating system.

To do this trick, you'll use the policy setting found at Computer Configuration ➢ Administrative Templates ➢ System ➢ Group Policy, and it's called **Turn off Local Group Policy objects processing**. Just remember to ensure that your computers are in the OU where this GPO is targeted to take effect.

Disabling the Link Enabled Status

Remember that all GPOs are contained in the Group Policy Objects container. To use them at a level in Active Directory (site, domain, or OU), you link back to the GPO. So, the quickest way to prevent a GPO's contents from applying is to remove its Link Enabled status. If you right-click a GPO link at a level, you can immediately see its Link Enabled status, as shown in Figure 2.3.

FIGURE 2.3   You can choose to enable or disable a GPO link.

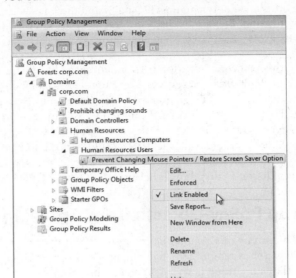

To prevent this GPO from applying to the **Human Resources Users** OU, simply click Link Enabled to remove the check mark. This will leave the link in the OU back to the GPO but disable the link, rendering it innocuous. The icon to the left of the name of the GPO will change to a scroll with the link arrow dimmed. You'll see a zoomed-in picture of this later in the section "GPMC At-a-Glance Icon View."

Disabling "Half" (or Both Halves) of the Group Policy Object

The second way to disable a specific GPO is by disabling just *one-half* of a Group Policy Object. You can disable either the User half or the Computer half. Or you can disable the entire GPO.

You might be wondering why you would want to disable only half of a GPO. On the one hand, disabling a GPO (or half of a GPO) makes startup and logon times a teeny-weeny bit faster for the computer or user, because each GPO you add to the system adds a smidgen of extra processing—either for the user or the computer. Once you disable the unused portion of the GPO, you've shaved that processing time off the startup or logon time. Microsoft calls this "modifying Group Policy for performance."

Don't go bananas disabling your unused half of GPO just to save a few cycles of processing time. Trust me, it's just not worth the headaches figuring out later where you did and did not disable a half of a policy.

Disabling half of the GPO makes troubleshooting and usage quite a bit harder, as you might just plumb forget you've disabled half the GPO. Then, down the road, when you modify the disabled half of the policy for some future setting, it won't take effect on your clients! You'll end up pulling your hair out wondering why once things *should* change, they just don't!

> **Why Totally Disable a Group Policy Object?**
>
> One good reason to disable a specific GPO is if you want to manually "join" several GPOs together into one larger GPO. Then, once you're comfortable with the reaction, you can re-create the policy settings from multiple GPOs into another new GPO and disable the old individual GPOs. If there are signs of trouble with the new policy, you can always just disable (or delete) the large GPO and re-enable the individual GPOs to get right back to where you started.
>
> You might also want to immediately disable a new GPO even before you start to edit it. Imagine that you've chosen "Create and link a new GPO here" for, say, an OU. Then, imagine you have lots of policy settings you want to place inside this new GPO. Remember that each setting is immediately written inside the Group Policy Management Editor. GPOs are replicated across all DCs (when it wants to, not when you want it to), and computers are continually requesting changes when their Background Refresh interval triggers.
>
> The affected users or computers might hit their Background Refresh cycle and start accepting the changes before you've finished writing all your changes to the GPO! Therefore, if you disable the GPO before you edit and re-enable the GPO after you edit, you can ensure that your users are getting all the newly changed settings at once.
>
> This tip works best only when creating new GPOs; if you disable the GPO *after* creation, there's an equally likely chance that critical settings will be removed while the GPO is disabled when clients request a Background Refresh. We'll discuss the ins and outs of Background Refresh in Chapter 3.

To disable an unused half of a GPO, follow these steps:

1. Select the GPO you want to modify. In this case, select "Auto-Launch calc.exe" and select the Details tab in the right pane of the GPMC.

2. Since the policy settings within the "Auto-Launch calc.exe" GPO modify only the Computer node, it is safe to disable the User node. Select the "User configuration settings disabled" drop-down box, as shown in Figure 2.4.

3. You will be prompted to confirm the status change. Choose to do so.

Here are some additional items to remember regarding disabling portions of a GPO:

- It is possible to disable the entire GPO (both halves) by selecting the GPO, clicking the Options button, and selecting the All Settings Disabled option. If you select All Settings Disabled, the scroll icon next to the name of the GPO "dims" to show that there is no way it can affect any targets. You'll see a zoomed-in picture of this later in the section "GPMC At-a-Glance Icon View."

- As I stated earlier in the section "Understanding GPMC's Link Warning," changing the GPO Status entry (found on the Details tab) will affect the GPO—everywhere it is linked—at any level, anywhere in the domain. You cannot just change the GPO status for the instance of this link—this setting affects all links to this GPO! The only good news here is that only the person who created the GPO itself (or anyone who has permissions to it) can manipulate this setting. To get the full thrust of this, be sure to read the sidebar "On GPO Links and GPOs Themselves" later in this chapter.

- In day-to-day use of this feature, the GPMC doesn't do a great job indicating (other than this "GPO status" area) that the link has been fully or half disabled. It's true that if you click the Group Policy Objects Container node (the swimming pool) and look at the GPOs in a list, you will see a column for GPO status. But I don't do that particular action much. Interestingly, in the old-school "Active Directory Users and Computers" interface in Windows 2003's old-and-crusty UI, you would at least see a yellow triangle warning icon next to the name of the GPO. But not in the modern GPMC. Weird (and potentially unsafe).

FIGURE 2.4 You can disable half the GPO to make Group Policy process a wee bit faster.

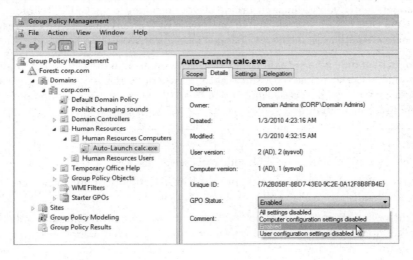

Deleting and Unlinking Group Policy Objects

As you just saw, you can prevent a GPO from processing at a level by merely removing its Link Enabled status. However, you can also choose to remove the link entirely. For instance, you might want to return the normal behavior of the computers so that calc.exe isn't launched whenever someone uses that machine. You have two options:

- Delete the link to the GPO
- Delete the GPO itself

Deleting the Link to the Group Policy Object

When you right-click the GPO link of "Auto-Launch calc.exe" in the **Human Resources Computers** OU, you can choose Delete. When you do, the GPMC will confirm your request and remind you of an important fact, as shown in Figure 2.5.

FIGURE 2.5   You can delete a link (as opposed to deleting the GPO itself).

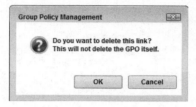

Recall that the GPO itself doesn't "live" at a level in Active Directory; it lives in a special container in Active Directory (and can be seen via the Group Policy Objects container in the GPMC). We're just working with a link to the real GPO. And, in Chapter 4, you'll see where this folder relates directly within Active Directory itself.

When you choose to delete a GPO link, you are simply choosing to stop using it at the level at which it was created but keeping the GPO alive in the representation of the swimming pool—the Group Policy Objects container. This lets other administrators at other levels continue to link to that GPO if they want.

Truly Deleting the Group Policy Object Itself

You can choose to delete the GPO altogether—lock, stock, and barrel. The only way to delete the GPO itself is to drill down through Group Policy Management ➢ Domains ➢ Corp.com, locate the Group Policy Objects container, and delete the GPO. It's like plucking a child directly from the swimming pool. Before you do, you'll get a warning message, as shown in Figure 2.6.

FIGURE 2.6   Here, you're deleting the GPO itself.

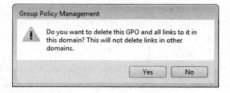

This action will remove the bits on the Domain Controller and obliterate it from the system. No other administrators can then link to this GPO.

Once it's gone, it's gone (unless you have a backup).

If you delete the GPO altogether, there's only one problem. There is no indication sent to the folks who are linking to this GPO that you've just deleted it. You might be done with the "Auto-Launch calc.exe" GPO and might not need it anymore to link to *your* locations in Active Directory, but what about other administrators? In this case, while I was out to lunch, Freddie, the administrator for the **Temporary Office Help** OU, has already chosen to link the "Auto-Launch calc.exe" GPO to his OU, as shown in Figure 2.7.

FIGURE 2.7   The "Auto-Launch calc.exe" GPO (lowest circle) is linked at both the Temporary Office Help OU (middle circle) and this Human Resources Computers OU (topmost circle).

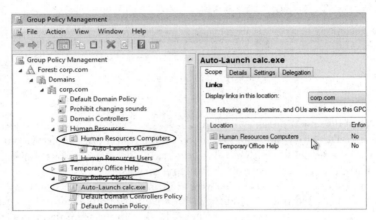

What if I had deleted the "Auto-Launch calc.exe" GPO? I'm pretty sure I would have received an angry phone call from Freddie. Or, maybe not—if Freddie didn't know who created (and owned) the GPO.

Since we only have a handful of OUs, this link back to the GPO was easy to find. However, once you start getting lots of OUs, locating additional links back to a GPO will become much harder. Thankfully, the GPMC shows you if anyone else is linked to a GPO you're about to delete. I call this ability, "look before you leap." You can just look on the Scope tab under the Links heading, as indicated in Figure 2.8. There you can see that both the **Temporary Office Help** OU and the **Human Resources Computers** OU are utilizing the GPO "Auto-Launch calc.exe."

If you're confident that you can still continue, you can delete the GPO contained within the Group Policy Objects container. However, for now, let's leave this GPO in place for use in future examples in the book.

The Scope tab shows you the links to the GPOs from your own domain. It is possible for *other* domains to leverage your GPOs and link to them. This is generally considered a "no-no" and is called Cross-Domain Linking. When you delete a GPO forever (and wipe it out of your swimming pool) you're deleting the ability for other domains to utilize that GPO as well. Note that there is a drop-down in the Scope tab labeled "Display links in this location." If you want, you can show Entire Forest. That way, if a GPO is being leveraged by doing a Cross-Domain Link, you can at least see if this GPO is linked to other areas you might not have intended it to be.

For now, don't delete the GPO. We'll use it again in later chapters. If you want to play with deleting a GPO, create a new one and delete it.

FIGURE 2.8 Use the Block Inheritance feature to prevent all GPOs (and the policy settings within them) from all higher levels from affecting your users and computers.

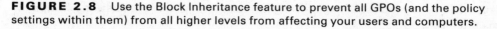
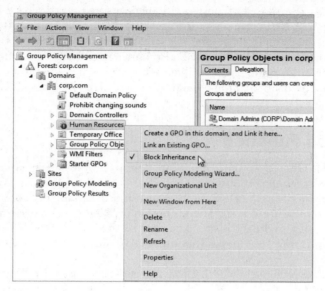

Block Inheritance

As you've already seen, the normal course of Group Policy inheritance applies all policy settings within GPOs in a cumulative fashion from the site to the domain and then to each nested OU. A setting at any level automatically affects all levels beneath it. But perhaps this is not always the behavior you want. For instance, we know that an edict from the Domain Administrator states there will be no Sounds option in the Windows 7 Personalization page.

This edict is fine for most of the OU administrators and their subjects who are affected. But Frank Rizzo, the administrator for the **Human Resources** OU structure, believes that the folks contained within his little fiefdom can handle the responsibility and gravitas of being able to change their own sounds. Remember a policy at the Domain level has performed this action. He also feels that they are grown-up enough to manage their own Screen Saver options (a policy at the Site level which has performed this action). Now, he wants to bring them back to his users. (But he's not ready to give back the ability to play around with the mouse pointers settings—a policy that is set at his level, the **Human Resources** OU level.

In this case, Frank can prevent GPOs (and the policy settings within them) defined at higher levels (domain and site) from affecting his users, as shown in Figure 2.8. If Frank chooses to select Block Inheritance, Frank is choosing to block the flow of *all* GPOs (with all their policy settings) from *all* higher levels.

When Frank does this, the **Human Resources** OU icon changes to include a blue exclamation point (!) as seen in Figure 2.8. Once the Block Inheritance upon the OU is performed and the GPOs are reprocessed on the client, only those settings that Frank dictates within his **Human Resources** OU structure will be applied.

If you want to see the effect of Block Inheritance, ensure that the check is seen as shown in Figure 2.8. Then, log on as any user affected by the **Human Resources** OU—say, Frank Rizzo. You'll notice that the screen saver options have returned as did the ability to manipulate sounds. But you'll also notice that the Mouse Pointers option in the Windows 7 Personalization page is still absent because that edict is contained within a GPO that's explicitly defined at the **Human Resources Users** OU level, which contains Frank's user account.

The Enforced Function

Frank Rizzo and his Human Resources folks are happy that the Screen Saver and Sounds options have made a triumphant return.

There's only one problem: the Domain Administrator has found out about this transgression and wants to ensure that the Sounds option in Windows 7 is permanently revoked.

The normal flow of inheritance is site, domain, and then OU. Super. If you've set a Block Inheritance on an OU (say, the **Human Resources** OU), then *all* settings to that OU are null and void.

But shouldn't there be some power to allow "bigger" administrators to get their wills enforced? Enforced! Heck, what a great term. I should trademark that. To trump a lower level's Block Inheritance, a higher-level administrator will use the *Enforced* function.

 Enforced was previously known as No Override in old-school parlance.

The idea behind the Enforced function is simple: it guarantees that policy settings within a specific GPO from a higher level are always inherited by lower levels. It doesn't matter if the lower administrator has blocked inheritance or has a GPO that tries to disable or modify the same policy setting or settings.

In this example, you'll log on as the Domain Administrator and set an edict to force the removal of the Sounds option in the Windows 7 Personalization page.

To use Enforced to force the settings within a specific Group Policy Object setting, right-click the "Prohibit Changing Sounds" GPO link and select Enforced, as shown in Figure 2.9.

Notice that the GPO link now has a little "lock" icon, demonstrating that it cannot be trumped. You can see this in the Prohibit Changing Sounds GPO link icon in Figure 2.9. You'll see a zoomed-in picture of this later in the "GPMC At-a-Glance Icon View" section.

To test your Enforced edict, log on as a user affected by the **Human Resources** OU—Frank Rizzo. In the Display Properties dialog box, the Sounds option in the Windows 7 Personalization page should be absent because it is being forced from the Enforced edict at the domain level even though Block Inheritance is used at the OU level.

FIGURE 2.9 Use the Enforced option to guarantee that settings contained within a specific GPO affect all users downward via inheritance.

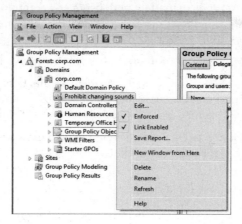

On GPO Links and GPOs Themselves

The GPMC is a cool tool, but shows you a bit *too* much. Sometimes, it can be confusing as to what can be performed on the GPO's link and what can be performed on the GPO itself. Remember that GPOs themselves are displayed in the GPMC via the Group Policy Objects container. The links back to them are shown at the site, domain, and OU levels. So here's a list of what you can "do" to a GPO link and what you can "do" to a GPO *itself*.

You can only do three things on a GPO link that applies to a site, a domain, or an OU:

- Link Enable (that is, enable or disable the settings to apply at this level).

- Enforce the link (and force the policy settings).

- Delete the link.

Everything else is always done on the *actual* GPO itself:

- Change the policy settings inside the GPO (found on the Settings tab).

- Apply security filters, rights (such as the "Apply Group Policy" privilege), and delegation (such as the "Edit this GPO" privilege), discussed in the section "Security Filtering and Delegation with the GPMC" later in this chapter.

- Enable/disable the Computer and/or User half of the GPO via the GPO status (found on the Details tab).

- Place a WMI filter on the GPO (discussed in Chapter 4).

If this seems clear as mud, consider this scenario:

- Fred and Ginger are the two Domain Administrators. By definition, they can create GPOs.

- Imagine that Fred designs the "Our Important Stuff" GPO (a poorly named GPO), which contains policy settings that affect both users and computers. Perhaps one user policy setting is **Remove Run off Start Menu**. Perhaps one computer policy setting is **Enforce disk quota limit**. And Fred sets the quota limit to 50MB.

- Fred links the Sounds GPO to the **Dancers** OU as well as the **Audition Halls** OU.

- Ginger gets a phone call from the folks in the **Audition Halls** OU. The users in the **Audition Halls** OU report that the 50MB disk quotas are too restrictive. "Can they just turn off the computer-side settings for us Audition Halls folks?" one of them cries.

- Ginger goes to the "Sounds" GPO link (which is linked to the **Audition Halls** OU), clicks the Details tab, and disables the computer settings using the GPO Status drop-down box.

- Fred then gets a phone call that the **Dancers** OU no longer has disk quotas being applied.

Why did this happen?

Because the Group Policy engine has certain controls on the GPO *itself* and has other controls on the Group Policy *link*. Because Fred and Ginger are both Domain Administrators, they jointly have ownership of the ability to change the GPO and the GPO link.

Whenever Ginger modifies any characteristic in the previous bulleted list, she's changing it "globally" for any place in Active Directory that might be using it. That's what the warning in Figure 2.2, earlier in this chapter, is all about.

If you'll allow me to get on my soap box for the next 10 seconds, the level of finite control over what Ginger can and cannot do to the GPO itself is fairly limited. In the future, I'd love to see the Group Policy engine extended so that we can delegate more aspects of control about the GPO link, not just about the GPO itself.

In any event, delegating what we can control over the GPO itself is precisely what the next section is about, specifically the "User Permissions upon Group Policy Objects" section.

Security Filtering and Delegation with the GPMC

You wouldn't want everyone in your domain to get every GPO applied to them. That would be crazy.

Likewise, you wouldn't want everyone in your domain to be able to modify every GPO. That would be "mega-crazy."

So this section will deal with both aspects of making sure users only get access (and application) to what they're supposed to. We'll talk about filtering a user (or computer) from getting specific GPOs. Then we'll move on to talking about ensuring that only the right users and admins have access to the underlying Group Policy system—by properly delegating who should have the ability to do what.

Turns out, to craft the solution to both of these problems, you leverage security pieces upon certain Active Directory aspects and also on specific GPOs.

It's not hard, but let's tackle these questions one at a time to locate all the places users and admins touch our Group Policy infrastructure, look at their access, and see where that access can be managed.

Filtering the Scope of Group Policy Objects with Security

The normal day-to-day Human Resources workers in the **Human Resources** OU structure are fine with the facts of life:

- The Enterprise Administrator says that no one at the site will have the Screen Saver option.

- The Domain Administrator says that no one will have the Sounds option in the Windows 7 Personalization page. He is forcing this edict with the Enforced option.

- Frank Rizzo, the **Human Resources** OU Manager, says that for the **Human Resources Users** OU, he will remove the Display Settings tab but restore the Screen Saver option. For the **Human Resources Computers** OU, he'll want to make sure that calc.exe launches whenever someone uses a Human Resources computer.

- Additionally, at the top-level **Human Resources** OU, he will enable the Block Inheritance setting to give back the Screen Saver option removed by the Enterprise Administrator at the site level. But Frank is forced to live with the fact that he won't be able to return the Sounds option in the Windows 7 Personalization page to his people. The Domain Administrator has taken this away and that's that.

But Frank and other members of the HR-OU-Admins security group are getting frustrated that they cannot access the Display Settings tab. And they're also getting a little annoyed that every time they use an Human Resources machine, calc.exe pops up to greet them.

Sure, it was Frank's own idea to make these two policy settings—one that affects the users he's in charge of and one that affects the computers he's in charge of. The problem is, however, it also affects Frank (and the other members of the HR-OU-Admins team) when they're working, and you can see where that can be annoying.

Frank needs a way to filter the *Scope of Management (SOM)* of the "Hide Mouse Pointers Option/Restore Screen Saver Option" GPO as well as the "Auto-Launch calc.exe" GPO. By scope or SOM, I mean how far and wide the GPOs we set up will be embraced.

Occasionally you will see references to SOM in your travels with Group Policy. An SOM is simply a quick-and-dirty way to express where and when a GPO might apply. An SOM can be nearly any combination of things: linking a GPO to the domain, linking a GPO to an OU, and linking a GPO to a site. However, if you start to filter GPOs within the domain, that's also an SOM. In essence, an SOM indicates *when* and *where* a GPO applies to a level in Active Directory.

In our case, the idea is twofold:

- Frank and his team are excluded from the "Hide Mouse Pointers Option/Restore Screen Saver Option GPO" edict.

- The specific computers that Frank and his team use are excluded from the "Auto-Launch calc.exe" GPO edict.

Recall from Chapter 1 that, despite the wording of the term *Group Policy*, Group Policy does not directly affect security groups. You cannot just wrap up a bunch of similar users or computers in an Active Directory security group and thrust a GPO upon them. There's nowhere to "link" to. You need to round up the individual user or computer accounts into an OU first and then link the desired GPO on that OU.

Here's the truly strange part: even though you can't round up users in security groups and apply GPOs to them, it's the security group that we'll leverage (in most cases) in order to enable us to filter Group Policy applications!

In order for users to get GPOs to apply to them, they need two under-the-hood access rights to the GPO itself:

- Read
- Apply Group Policy (known in shorthand as the AGP rights)

These permissions must be set on the GPO in question. By default, all Authenticated Users are granted the Read and AGP rights to all new GPOs. Therefore, anyone who has a GPO geared for them will process it.

The following two things might not be immediately obvious:

- Administrators are not magically exempt from embracing Group Policy; they, too, are members of Authenticated Users. You can change this behavior with the techniques described in the next section.

- Computers need love, too. And for computers to apply their side of the GPO, they need the same rights: Read and Apply Group Policy. Since computers are technically Authenticated Users, the computer has all it needs to process GPOs meant for it.

With these fundamental concepts in mind, let's look at several ways to filter who gets specific GPOs.

If you want to filter GPOs for either specific users or specific computers, you have three distinct approaches. For our three examples (which will all do the exact same thing), we want the "Hide Mouse Pointers Option/Restore Screen Saver Option GPO" to "pass over" our heroes in the HR-OU-Admins security group but to apply to everyone else who should get them. We also want the "Auto-Launch calc.exe" GPO to pass over the specific computers our heroes use at their desks.

How Is a Computer an Authenticated User?

I was shocked to learn that a computer falls under the category of an Authenticated User. It's true: the computer account has the Authenticated User's SID in its access token. I was skeptical, but über-guru Bill Boswell proved it to me. And you can prove it to yourself by following these steps on a Windows XP machine (they won't work on Windows Vista and later):

1. Use the at command and specify a time at least one minute ahead of the current time to open a system-level console:

   at *<one minute in the future>* /interactive cmd

2. Use WHOAMI to verify that the cmd has run as System. Now use WHOAMI /ALL to verify that you have the Authenticated Users group in the access token.

Note that System does not have domain credentials. When it touches another machine, it uses the Kerberos ticket issued to the local computer. You can take advantage of this for the following experiment:

1. Set the NTFS permissions on a folder in a shared volume on another machine to deny access to Authenticated Users but allow access by Everyone.

2. Map a drive from the system console to the share point and try to access the contents of the protected folder. You'll be denied access.

Because the Deny bit for Authenticated Users comes before the Allow bit for Everyone, you've proved that the computer account has the Authenticated Users group in its access token.

Group Policy Object Filtering Approach #1: Leverage the Security Filtering Section of the Scope Tab in GPMC

In the first approach, you'll round up only the users, computers, or security groups who should get the GPO applied to them. To make things easier, let's first create two Active Directory security groups—one for our users who will get the GPO and one for computers who will get the GPO. Good names might be:

　　People-Who-Get-the-HideDisplayMousePointersOption-and-RestoreSS

and

　　Computers-That-Get-the-Auto-Launch calc.exe-GPO

Remember, that first GPO does two things, so we've named it "Hide Changing Mouse Pointers / Restore Screen Saver Option." Making a group with something easy to remember but still only 64 characters can be tough. So, again, I'm recommending a group named People-Who-Get-the-HideDisplayMousePointersOption-and-RestoreSS.

The second group, for computers, is a little easier to make. The GPO we'll want to leverage with this group only does one thing: it automatically launches `calc.exe`. So, my suggested name is Computers-That-Get-the-Auto-Launch calc.exe-GPO.

Go ahead and do this in Active Directory Users and Computers, as seen in Figure 2.10.

FIGURE 2.10   Create a new Active Directory security group to which you want the GPO to apply. Create security groups for both users and computers based on the GPO you want to filter.

Next, add all user accounts that you want to embrace the GPO into the first security group.

You would then add all computer accounts that you want to get the GPO into the security group named Computers-That-Get-the-Auto-Launch calc.exe-GPO.

Because we don't want these GPOs to apply to Frank or Frank's computer (XPPRO1 or WIN7), don't add Frank to the first group (which contains users) and don't add XPPRO1 or WIN7 to the second group (which contains computers).

Next, click the link to the "Hide Mouse Pointers Option/Restore Screen Saver Option" GPO found in Group Policy Management ➢ Forest ➢ Domains ➢ Corp.com ➢ **Human Resources** OU ➢ **Human Resources Users** OU. In the Security Filtering section, you can see that Authenticated Users is listed. This means that any users inside the **Human Resources Users** OU will certainly get this GPO applied.

However, now we're about to turn the tables. We're going to click the Remove button to remove the Authenticated Users in the Security Filtering section; then we're going to add the People-Who-Get-the-HideDisplayMousePointersOption-and-RestoreSS security group, as shown in Figure 2.11.

Next, click the "Auto-Launch calc.exe" GPO link (which is under the **Human Resources Computers** OU). In the Security Filtering section of the Scope tab, you'll remove Authenticated Users and add the Computers-That-Get-the-Auto-Launch calc.exe-GPO security group.

FIGURE 2.11   When you remove Authenticated Users, no one will get the effects of the GPO. Add only the users or groups you want the GPO to affect.

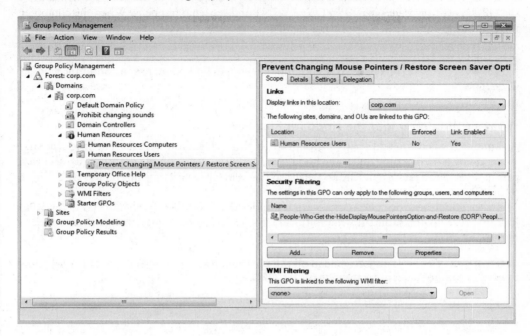

In both cases, what we're doing under the hood is giving these new security groups the ability to Read and Apply Group Policy. You'll see this under-the-hood stuff in a minute.

Testing Your First Filters

To see if this is working, log on XPPRO1 or WIN7 as Frank (frizzo). Even though the GPO applies to the **Human Resources Users** OU, the GPO will pass over him and anyone else not explicitly put into that security group since Frank is not a member of the People-Who-Get-the-HideDisplayMousePointersOption-and-RestoreSS-GPO security group.

For another test, add a new user account or two to the **Human Resources Users** OU (via Active Directory Users and Computers). Then, log on as one of these new users (in the OU) and verify that they, indeed, do not get the GPO. This is because the GPO is only set to apply to members of the security group. Then, add the user to the security group and log on again. The GPO will then apply to your test users (inside the security group) as well. In fact, you can add users to the security group by simply clicking the Properties button in the Security Filtering section. Doing so opens the Security Group Membership dialog box, in which you can add or delete users or computers.

Repeat your tests by adding XPPRO1 or WIN7 into the security group named Computers-That-Get-the-Auto-Launch calc.exe-GPO. When the computer is in the group, it will apply the GPO. Now, try removing XPPRO1 or WIN7 and see what happens. When the computer is out of the group, the GPO will pass over the computer.

You will have to reboot the machine to immediately see computer-side results.

What's Going on under the Hood for Filtering

As I implied, when you add security groups to get the GPOs in the Security Filtering section, you're doing a bit of magic under the hood. Again, that magic is simply granting two security permissions, Read and Apply Group Policy, to the users or security groups on the GPOs linked to the OU.

To see which security permissions are set under the hood for a particular GPO (or GPO link, because it's the same information), click the Delegation tab and click the Advanced button, as shown in Figure 2.12.

FIGURE 2.12 Clicking Advanced on the Delegation tab for the GPO (or GPO link) shows the under-the-hood security settings for the GPO.

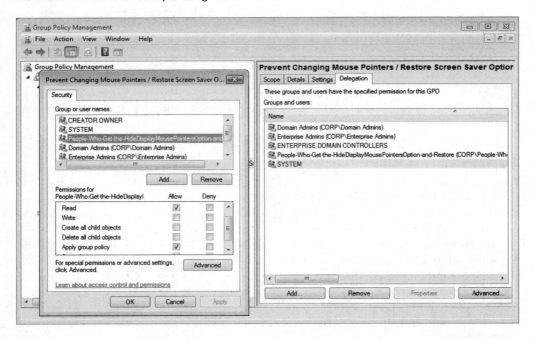

When you do, you can see the actual permission on the GPO itself. You can easily locate the security group named People-Who-Get-the-HideDisplayMousePointersOption-and-RestoreSS-GPO and see that they have both the Read and Apply Group Policy access rights set to Allow. This is why they will process this GPO.

Filtering Approach #2: Identify Those You Do Not Want to Get the Policy

The other approach is to leave the default definition in for the GPO such that the Authenticated Users group is granted the Read and Apply Group Policy attributes. Then, figure out who you *do not* want to have the policy applied to, and use the Deny attribute over the Apply Group Policy right.

When Windows security is evaluated, the designated users or computers will not be able to process the GPO due to the Deny attribute; hence, the GPO passes over them.

 See the sidebar "Positive or Negative?" later in this chapter before doing this in your real (production) environment.

For our examples, we want the "Hide Mouse Pointers Option/Restore Screen Saver Option" GPO to pass over our heroes in the HR-OU-Admins security group but to apply to everyone else by default. We also want the "Auto-Launch calc.exe" GPO to pass over the specific computers our heroes use at their desks.

To use this second technique, we'll use the Deny permission to ensure that the HR-OU-Admins security group cannot apply (and hence process) the "Hide Mouse Pointers Option/Restore Screen Saver Option" GPO. We'll also prevent Frank's computer, XPPRO1 or WIN7, from processing the "Auto-Launch calc.exe" GPO.

Again, you'll do this on the GPO (or the GPO link, because it's the same information); click the Delegation tab, and then click the Advanced button. Follow these steps:

1. Locate the People-Who-Get-the-HideDisplayMousePointersOption-and-RestoreSS-GPO security group and remove it.

2. Locate the Authenticated Users group, select the Read permission, select Allow, select Apply Group Policy permission, and select Allow.

3. If you used Frank's account to originally create this GPO, he is specifically listed in the security list. You want to remove Frank and add the HR-OU-Admins group. Click Frank, and then click Remove. Click Add, and add the HR-OU-Admins group.

4. Make sure the Apply Group Policy check box is set to Deny for the HR-OU-Admins group, as shown in Figure 2.13.

   Do not set the Deny check box for the Read and Write attributes from the HR-OU-Admins (the group you're currently a member of when logged in as Frank). If you do, you'll essentially lock yourself out, and you'll have to ask the Domain Administrator to grant you access again.

5. Click OK to close the Group Policy Settings dialog box. In the warning box that tells you to be careful about Deny permissions, click Yes.

6. Click OK to close the OU Properties dialog box.

FIGURE 2.13 Use the Deny attribute on the Apply Group Policy right to prevent Group Policy from applying.

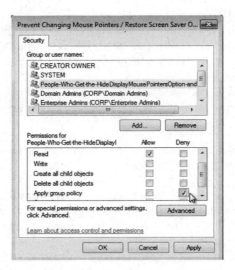

To test your first filter again, log onto XPPRO1 or WIN7 as Frank Rizzo. Note that the Settings tab has returned to him because he is part of the HR-OU-Admins group. The Hide Mouse Pointers Option/Restore Screen Saver Option GPO has passed over him because he is unable to process the GPO.

To bypass the "Auto-Launch calc.exe" GPO on XPPRO1 or WIN7, you'll perform a similar operation. That is, you'll modify the security on the GPO to pass over the computers our heroes use by denying those specific computer accounts the ability to Apply Group Policy. You can then test your second filter by logging on as anyone to XPPRO1 or WIN7. You should then see that calc.exe will not launch when a user uses that machine.

Turns out, however, there's a major problem in using the aforementioned method. That is, if you performed the previous exercise and used the Deny attribute to pass over the HR-OU-Admins group using the Security on the GPO, you've got a small problem. Sure, it worked! That's the good news. The bad news is that GPMC isn't smart enough to interpret quite what you did back on the Scope tab in the Security Filtering section shown in Figure 2.14.

Yes, it's technically true what the Security Filtering section says: Authenticated Users will apply this GPO. However, it doesn't tell us the other important fact: the HR-OU-Admins group *will not* process this GPO because they were denied the ability to Apply Group Policy.

The only way to get the full, true story of who will get the GPO applied to them is to look back within the GPO (or GPO link, because it's the same information), select the Delegation tab, and click the Advanced button to see who has Read and Apply Group Policy; then also see who is denied access to process the GPO via the Deny attributes.

FIGURE 2.14   The Security Filtering section on the Scope tab will not show you any use of Deny attributes under the hood.

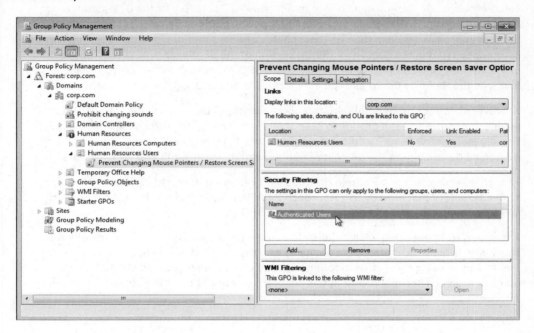

 With the updated GPMC (see the upcoming section "Searching and Commenting Group Policy Objects and Policy Settings"), you can leave a comment inside the GPO for others to read regarding who has been specifically denied AGP access. The only problem is someone might not read it.

The moral of the story? Always consult the Advanced tab to get the whole truth as to the security on the GPO.

Positive or Negative?

Now that you can see the two ways to filter users from processing GPOs, which should you use? Approach 1 (adding only those you want to get the GPO) or Approach 2 (denying only those you don't want to get the GPO)? The data reflected within the GPMC's Scope tab clearly wants you to take the first approach. However, many Active Directory implementations I know take the second approach (and, in fact, it was my advice to do so in the first several editions of this book).

Now, you and your team need to make a choice for your approach. As you saw, when you create new GPOs, you can choose to filter via the Scope tab or the Delegation tab's Advanced button. So which do you choose? If you're going to be religious about using the first approach, you can then be reasonably confident that only the users, groups, and computers listed in the Security Filtering section of the Scope tab will, in fact, be the only users, groups, and computers who will get the GPO. You can then reduce your need to dive into the Security Editor as seen in Figures 2.12 and 2.13, earlier in this chapter.

However, if you (or other administrators) occasionally choose to use the Deny attribute on users, computers, and groups to keep them from getting the GPO, you'll need to additionally inspect the Security Editor dialog box, which, again, you'll find by clicking the Advanced button within the Delegation tab as seen in Figures 2.12 and 2.13.

The GPMC encourages you to use Approach 1 for filtering. If you have older GPOs in your Active Directory that already use Approach 2 for filtering, consider changing it so that GPMC's Scope tab will reflect who will get the GPO.

There's no right or wrong answer here. The challenge is simply that the GPMC will not show who is expressly denied the ability to process the GPO. If you have an in-house system to compensate for that shortcoming (or you use the new updated GPMC Comment feature, which we'll explain later in this chapter), you might be able to make better use of Approach 2.

User Permissions upon Group Policy Objects

You already know the three criteria for someone to be able to edit or modify an existing GPO:

- They are a member of the Domain Admins group.
- They are a member of the Enterprise Admins group.
- They created the GPO themselves and hence are the owner. (We saw this in Figure 1.24 in Chapter 1 when Frank could edit his own GPOs, but couldn't edit the GPOs he didn't create.)

But sometimes, you also want to add rights on a GPO so other admins can modify it. As I previously suggested, the Delegation tab for a GPO (or GPO link, which reflects the same information) has a second purpose: to help you grant permissions to groups or users over the security properties of that GPO.

If you click Add on the Delegation tab, you can grant any mere mortal user, an admin, or group (even in other domains) the ability to manipulate a particular GPO, as seen in Figure 2.15.

FIGURE 2.15   You can set permissions of "who can do what" on a GPO.

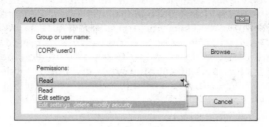

Once the permissions settings have been applied, the user has that level of rights over the GPO, as you can see in Table 2.1.

TABLE 2.1   GPMC vs. Genuine Active Directory Permissions

Permissions Option	Actual Under-the-Hood Permissions
Read	Sets the Allow permission for Read on the GPO.
"Edit settings"	Sets the Allow permission for Read, Write, Create Child Objects, and Delete Child Objects. See the note regarding "under-the-hood" attributes.
"Edit settings, delete, modify security"	Sets the Allow permission for Read, Write, Create Child Objects, Delete Child Objects, Delete, Modify Permissions, and Modify Owner. This is nearly equivalent to full control on the GPO, but note that Apply Group Policy access permission is not set. (This can be useful to set for administrators so they can manipulate the GPO but not have it apply to themselves.)
"Read (from Security Filtering)"	This isn't a permission located in the ACL Editor (see Figure 2.13); rather, this is only visible if the user has Read and AGP permissions on the GPO. This is a reflection of what is on the Scope tab.
Custom	Any other combinations of rights, including the use of the Deny permission. Custom rights are only added via the ACL Editor but can be removed here. They can be removed using the Remove button on the Delegation tab.

If you look really, really closely at the under-the-hood attributes specifically granted to the user when they are given "Edit settings" or "Edit setting, delete, modify security" rights, you'll note that Write isn't expressly listed. However, the ability to perform writes is granted because other subattributes that do permit writing are granted on the entry. To see those attributes for yourself, click the Advanced button while looking at the properties of the security on a GPO (like what we see in Figure 2.13).

Granting Group Policy Object Creation Rights in the Domain

As you learned in Chapter 1, a user cannot create new GPOs unless that user is a member of the Group Policy Creator Owners group. Dropping a user into this group is one of two ways you can grant this right.

However, the GPMC introduces another way to grant users the ability to have Group Policy Creator Owner–style access. Traverse to the Group Policy Objects container as seen in Figure 2.16, and click the Delegation tab. You can now click Add and select any user, including any user in your domain, say a user named Joe User, or users across forests, such as Sol Rosenberg, who is in a domain called bigu.edu. As you can see in Figure 2.16, both users have been added.

FIGURE 2.16 You can choose to delegate to users in your domain, in other domains, or in domains in other forests.

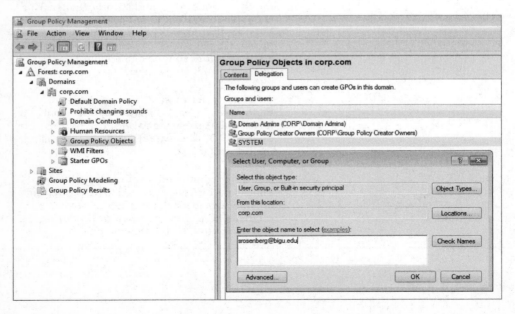

This can be handy if you have trusted administrators in other domains and you want to allow them to create GPOs in your domain. You might want to round them up into a group (instead of just listing them individually as Sol is listed here), but that's your option.

Special Group Policy Operation Delegations

You can delegate three special permissions at the domain and OU levels, and you can set one of those three special permissions at the site level. Clicking the level, such as an OU, and then clicking the Delegation tab for that level shows the available permissions, as seen in Figure 2.17.

FIGURE 2.17 These operations are equivalent to the Active Directory Users and Computers Delegation Wizard.

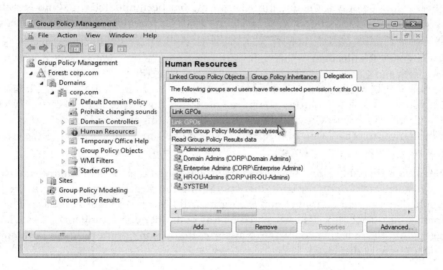

The interface is a bit confusing here. Specifically, you must first select the permission from the drop-down box. This lists the current users who currently have permissions. You can then click the Add, Remove, or Advanced button to make your changes.

You can select three permissions from the drop-down box, as seen in Figure 2.17:

Link GPOs   Of the three permissions here, this is the only permission that can be configured at all levels: site, domain, and OU. Recall in Chapter 1 that you ran Active Directory Users and Computers' "Delegation of Control Wizard" (see Figure 1.21). Instead of using Active Directory Users and Computers to perform that task, the GPMC can do the same job—right here.

Perform Group Policy Modeling analyses   This right performs the same function as if we had used Active Directory Users and Computers' "Delegation of Control Wizard" to grant the Generate Resultant Set of Policy (Planning) permissions, as you saw in Chapter 1,

Figure 1.21. The next section describes how to get more data about what's happening at the client. You'll see how to use this power in the section "What-If Calculations with Group Policy Modeling" later in this chapter. Group Policy Modeling lets you simulate what-if scenarios regarding users and computers.

By default, only Domain Admins have the right to perform this task. Domain Admins can grant other users or groups the ability to perform this function, such as the Help Desk, HR-OU-Admins, or your own desktop-administrator teams. You can choose to grant people the ability to perform Group Policy Modeling analyses on this specific container or this specific container and child containers. When you assign this right, the user performing the Group Policy Modeling analysis must have the delegated right on the container containing the what-if user and also the container containing the what-if computer. If you don't grant rights in both containers, only half the analysis is displayed.

This right is available only if the domain AD schema has been updated for Windows 2003 or later. Additionally, the Group Policy Modeling analyses function only when at least one Windows 2003 or later Domain Controller is available in the domain.

Read Group Policy Results data   This right performs the same function as if we used Active Directory Users and Computers' "Delegation of Control Wizard" to grant the "Generate Resultant Set of Policy (Logging)" permission (which isn't shown in Figure 1.21 but it would be there if you scrolled down a little). You'll see how to use this power in the section "What's-Going-On Calculations with Group Policy Results" later in this chapter. However, if you want to grant this power to others, you can. Again, a typical use is to grant this right to the Help Desk or other administrative authority.

When you assign this right, the user performing the Group Policy Results analysis must have the delegated right upon the container containing the target computer. Or this right can be applied at a parent container and the rights will flow down via inheritance. The user or group must also have this right delegated on any container containing any users who have logged onto the machine you want to analyze. If you don't grant rights in both containers, no analysis is displayed.

This right is available only if the domain AD schema has been updated for Windows 2003 and later.

Who Can Create and Use WMI Filters?

Okay, okay, okay. I know the subject of WMI filters has come up about 3,000 times already, and every time I refer you, the poor reader, to Chapter 4. Once you've read what they are and how to create them in Chapter 4, please come back here and read how to manage them.

Two types of people are involved in the management of WMI filters:

- Those who can create them
- Those who can use them

Delegating Who Can Create WMI Filters

By default, only the Domain Administrator can create WMI filters. However, you might have some WMI whiz kid in your company (and it's a good chance this isn't the same person as the Domain Administrator). With that in mind, the Domain Administrator can grant that special someone the ability to create WMI filters. To do this, drill down to the domain ➢ WMI Filters node, and then select Delegation in the pane on the right. You can now grant one of two rights, as shown in Figure 2.18.

FIGURE 2.18   These are controls over the creation of WMI filters.

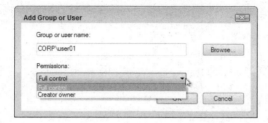

In Figure 2.18, we can see the two rights that appear in the drop-down box:

- Once a user has "Creator owner" rights here, they can create and modify their own WMI filters, but they cannot modify others' WMI filters. Note that members of the Group Policy Creator Owners security group have this right by default.

- A user with "Full control" rights here can create and modify their own WMI filters or anyone else's.

 These rights to create WMI filters are available only if the domain AD schema has been updated for at least Windows 2003.

Delegating Who Can Use WMI Filters

Once WMI filters are created (again, see Chapter 4), you'll likely want to assign who can apply them to specific GPOs. To do this, drill down to the specific WMI filter, as shown in Figure 2.19. Then click Add, and you'll see that two rights are available for the user you want.

In Figure 2.19, we can see the two rights that appear in the drop-down box:

- Once users have Edit rights here, they can edit and tailor the filter, as we do in Chapter 4.

- A user with "Full control" rights here can edit the filter as well as delete it and modify the security (that is, specify who else can get Edit or "Full control" rights here).

 The rights to use WMI filters are available only if the domain AD schema has been updated for at least Windows 2003.

FIGURE 2.19   These are controls over the WMI filters themselves.

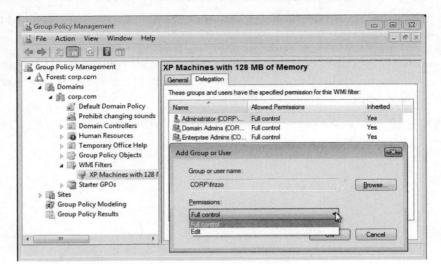

Performing RSoP Calculations with the GPMC

In Chapter 1, we charted out a fictitious organization's GPO structure on paper. We looked and saw when various GPOs were going to apply to various user and computers. Charting out the RSoP (Resultant Set of Policy) for users and computers on paper is a handy skill for a basic understanding of GPO organization and flow, but in the real world, you need a tool that can help you figure out what's going on at your client desktops.

The GPMC has a handy feature to show us all the GPOs that are going to apply for the users and computers at a specific level in Active Directory. In Figure 2.20, when you click the **Human Resources Users** OU and then click the Group Policy Inheritance tab, you can see a list of all the GPOs that should apply to the **Human Resources Users** OU.

The site level is not shown in this Group Policy Inheritance tab. Because computers, particularly laptops, can travel from site to site, it is impossible to know for sure what site to represent here.

As I said, this tab in Figure 2.20 should tell you what's going to happen. The operative word here is *should*. That's because a lot can go wrong between your wishes and what happens on the client systems. For instance, you already saw how to filter GPOs using security groups, which would certainly change the experience of one user versus another on the very same machine. And in Chapter 4, you'll learn about WMI filters, which limit when GPOs are applied even more.

FIGURE 2.20   The Group Policy Inheritance tab shows you which GPOs should apply.

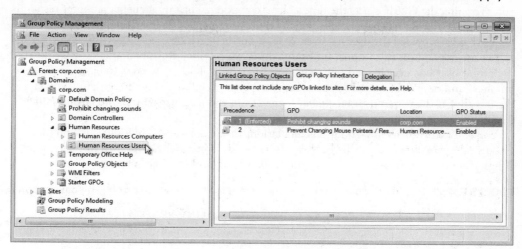

The point of all this RSoP stuff is to help us know the score about what's going on at machines that could be many hundreds of miles away. When users freak out about getting settings they don't expect or when they freak out about lacking settings they do expect, the point is to know which setting is causing the stir and which GPO is to blame for the errant setting.

We know one thing for sure: users do freak out a lot if anything changes, and it's our job to track down the problem (but not the user or computer). So the point of performing an RSoP calculation is to help you know what is going on and why it's going on that way. The GPMC can help with that.

What's-Going-On Calculations with Group Policy Results

If someone calls you to report that an unexpected GPO is applying, you can find out what's going on via the GPMC—as long as the machine in question is a Windows XP machine or higher. Sorry, Windows 2000 computers are left in the dust. (Windows 2000 computers are not left in the dust for the what-if calculations with Group Policy Modeling in the next section.)

Once the user with the problem has logged onto the machine in question, you can tap into the WMI provider built into all editions of Windows since Windows XP. Without going too propeller-head here, the upshot of this magic is that the GPMC (and the GPRESULT command, as you'll see in Chapter 7) can query any particular user that has ever logged on locally. It's then a simple matter to display the sexy results within the GPMC.

Once the results are displayed, you can right-click over the report and save them as an HTML or XML report.

The magic happens when the computer asking "What's going on?" (in this case, the computer running the GPMC) asks the target client computer. The target client computer responds with a result of what has happened—which GPOs were applied to the Computer side and to the User side (provided the user has ever, at least once, logged on).

Let me expand on this important point: this Group Policy Results magic only works if the target user has ever logged onto the target machine. They only need to have ever logged on once, and here's the amazing part: they don't even need to be logged on while you run the test. But if the target user has *never* logged onto the target machine, the Group Policy Results will not allow you to select that user.

You can run your what's-going-on calculations inside the GPMC by right-clicking the Group Policy Results node at the bottom of the GPMC's hierarchy, as shown in Figure 2.21. When you do, you can select the user and the computer and see their interaction.

FIGURE 2.21   The Group Policy Results Wizard performs what's-going-on calculations.

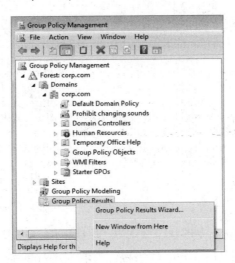

Keep in mind the following before trying to run the Group Policy Results Wizard to figure out what's going on:

- The target computer must be Windows XP or later.

- The target computer must be turned on and on the network. If this is not the case, you'll get an error to this effect. It will state that it cannot contact the WMI service via RPC.

- If the target machine has a firewall turned on, it must be disabled. Alternatively (in advance), you can open up ports 135 and 445 on the target machine. See the sidebar "Understanding Windows Firewall Settings (and Dealing with Group Policy Results)" for some ideas on how to mitigate this. If the machine is unreachable because the firewall is blocking access to port 135 or port 445, you'll get the same RPC Error as if the computer was off.

- The Windows Management Instrumentation service must be started.

- The user's local profile cannot be deleted. If the user has logged on but the administrator later whacks the local profile (or a Windows Vista or later–specific policy setting is enabled to auto-whack the local profile), WMI data will not be available.

Remember: the user you want to find out about must have logged onto the target computer *at least once* to be eligible to perform a Group Policy Results calculation.

Understanding Windows Firewall Settings (and Dealing with Group Policy Results)

Since Windows XP SP2 and Windows Server 2008, the Windows Firewall is automatically engaged—protecting your poor machines from the baddies out there.

Now, regular, everyday Group Policy stuff works just fine when the firewall is on. That's because the Group Policy client requests what he wants, then the results are returned through the requested ports.

But, as you just learned, the ability to get Group Policy Results is effectively disabled when the Windows Firewall is engaged. That's because firewalls reject unrequested stuff when engaged. So, it feels like the target computer is turned off.

There are some policy settings that will affect Windows XP or later found in two locations: Administrative Templates ➢ Network ➢ Network Connections ➢ Windows Firewall ➢ Domain Profile and Administrative Templates ➢ Network ➢ Network Connections ➢ Windows Firewall ➢ Standard Profile.

You can see that the exact same policy settings are listed for both the Standard Profile and Domain Profile nodes. The Domain Profile settings are what will take effect when users are inside your corporate network; that is, when they're actively logged in by a Domain Controller. The Standard Profile, on the other hand, is used for when users are out of the office (perhaps in a hotel or other public network where they cannot reach your company's Domain Controllers for authentication).

Once a machine receives the policy settings for both the Domain Profile and Standard Profile, that computer is ready to travel both in and out of the office. You can be sure that machine is embracing your company's firewall security policy both in the office and on the road.

If you're interested in learning more about how a computer makes a determination of whether it is supposed to use Domain Profile or Standard Profile policy settings, be sure to read Microsoft's "Network Determination Behavior for Network-Related Group Policy Settings" at:

    www.microsoft.com/technet/community/columns/cableguy/cg0504.mspx

(shortened to http://tinyurl.com/cao73).

Note that the details are different for Vista and later, but the net result is the same: you can use these Standard Profile settings or Domain Profile settings as you need to. You have three options if you want to restore the Group Policy Results functionality when you have Windows XP or later clients with the firewall on.

Approach 1: Kill the Windows XP/SP2 (or Later) firewall Now that you understand how to control Windows XP's (or later versions') firewall settings, one approach is to kill the firewall completely. If you do this, you understand that you're giving up any of the protection that Windows Firewall affords. However, by doing so, you will restore communication to the target computer. To kill the firewall, drill down to Administrative Templates ➢ Network ➢ Network Connections ➢ Windows Firewall ➢ Domain Profile and select **Windows Firewall: Protect all network Connections**. But here's the thing. You don't enable this policy to kill the firewall. You disable it. Yes, you read that right: you disable it. Read the help text in the policy for more information on specific usage examples.

Approach 2: Poke just the required holes in the firewall Instead of killing the firewall dead, you can simply open up the one port you need. Again, the idea is that if the target computer responds on port 135, you're golden. Windows has a policy setting you can enable named **Windows Firewall: Allow Inbound Remote Administration Exception**, which is located in Computer Configuration ➢ Administrative Templates ➢ Network ➢ Network Connections ➢ Windows Firewall ➢ Domain Profile. Again, when you do this, you're opening up the necessary port 135 (RPC). Note, however, that enabling this policy setting also opens up port 445 (SMB), which some security shops might object to.

Approach 3: Keep the firewall engaged, and don't use Group Policy Results You might opt for this third approach. That is, you really, really want to keep the firewall enabled and all ports closed on that target Windows machine. If so, how will you find out "what's going on" over there—on a target machine? There are two ways, both explored a bit later. One way is to trot out to the machine (or take remote control of it somehow) and run the GPRESULT command, which will tell you what's going on. Or, you can use a tool called GPMonitor (which we explore in the appendix). The idea is to have the target machines periodically push their Group Policy Results data to a location of your choosing. So, even if they're behind a firewall, you're still periodically able to see what's going on.

The output generated from the GPMC version when performing Group Policy Results RSoP calculations is quite powerful, as shown in Figure 2.22.

Similar to using the Settings tab, you can expand and contract the report by clicking Show and Hide. Inside, you can clearly see which GPOs have been applied and any major errors along the way. At a glance, you can see which GPOs have Applied and which were Denied (passed over) for whatever reason, such as filtering or that one-half of the GPO was empty.

The WMI filters category (shown in Figure 2.22) will not display data unless the target machine is running Windows XP with SP2 or later.

FIGURE 2.22   The Group Policy Results report shows lots of useful information.

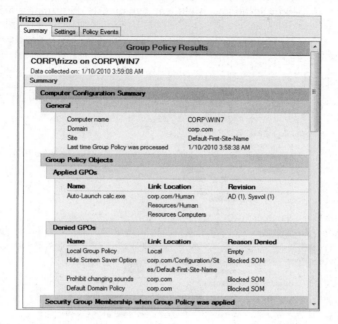

If you click the Settings tab here, you get an extra bonus: if conflicts exist along the scope of the GPO, you can see which other GPOs won in the contest for the ultimate Group Policy smackdown! Indeed, you can see this in Figure 2.23. Note, however, that the GPMC doesn't show you which GPOs lost when there was a conflict. This can sometimes mean more troubleshooting to determine other GPOs with conflicting settings.

There are one or two caveats about Group Policy Results data. Specifically, when you produce a Group Policy Results report, some data simply isn't reported! Depending on the circumstances, you might not see some of the following data in a report:

- IPsec policies
- Wireless policies
- Disk quotas policies
- Third-party client-side extension add-ins

Note, however, that after the report runs, you can right-click the entry for the report (located right under the Group Policy Results node, as seen in Figure 2.24) and select Advanced View. When you do this, you'll see an alternate view of the report. The report runs in an MMC snap-in, so it's not HTML. But the advantage of this Advanced report is that it can usually show extra attributes that are not always shown in the HTML report. But since the report is within an MMC, and isn't HTML, it's not really "portable," and you can't print it or send it in an e-mail. Also note that this tool hasn't been updated since Vista, so you might get some strange results when using it.

FIGURE 2.23   If specific settings conflict, you can quickly determine which GPO wins.

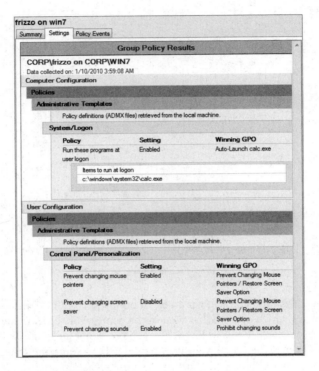

Additionally useful here is the Policy Events tab, which will dive into the target machine's Event Viewer and pull out the events related to GPOs, as shown in Figure 2.24. Just double-click the event to open it. Talk about handy!

The GPMC will also save the query so you can reuse it later if you want to retest your assumptions. For example, you might want to retry this after you've corrected your software installation failure, added a new GPO to the mix, or moved a machine from one OU to another.

If you move a computer from one OU to another, you might not get the correct results right away because the computer may not immediately recognize that it has been moved. If you move a computer from one OU to another, you might want to synchronize your Domain Controllers and then reboot the target machine to get accurate results right away. This is discussed in more detail in Chapter 3.

FIGURE 2.24 The Policy Events tab shows you events specific to this target computer.

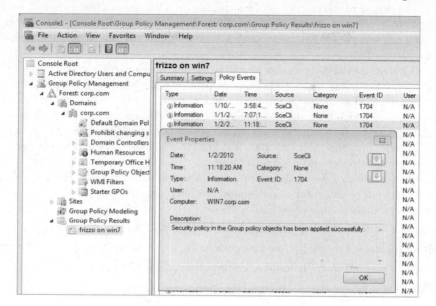

What-If Calculations with Group Policy Modeling

Finding out what's going on is useful if someone calls you in a panic. However, you might also want to plan for the future. For instance, would you be able to easily determine what would happen to the users in the **Human Resources Users** OU if a somewhat indiscriminately named GPO called "Desktop and User Stuff" was linked to it? Maybe or maybe not. (With a horribly named GPO like that, likely not.)

Or, what might happen if Frank Rizzo took a trip to another site? Which GPOs would apply to him then? Or which GPOs would apply if the HR-OU-Admins were granted different security rights (or had them revoked)? The Oracle, er, the Group Policy Modeling Wizard found in the GPMC can answer a million of these questions. Its job is to answer "What happens if?"

This function is available only if the domain schema has been updated for (at least) Windows 2003 and you have at least one Windows 2003 Domain Controller available. This is because a Windows 2003 or later Domain Controller runs a service that must be running for the calculation to occur.

The best news about what-if calculations is that Windows 2000 computers aren't left out of the picture. But the bad news is that the calculations shown for Windows 2000 machines are likely inaccurate. Modeling will happily tell you that your Windows 2000 machines will apply things only available for Windows XP and later machines, such as Wireless policy (when it's not possible for Windows 2000 machine to get these at all).

Again, the only catch to this magic is that when you want to run what-if modeling calculations, the processing of the calculations must occur on a Windows 2003 or later Domain Controller. Even if you have the GPMC loaded on a Windows 7 or Windows XP management station, you'll still have to make contact with a Windows 2003 or later Domain Controller to assist in the calculations.

You can kick off a modeling session by right-clicking the domain or any OU (as well as the Group Policy Modeling node) and selecting Group Policy Modeling Wizard. When you do, you'll be presented with the Group Policy Modeling Wizard Welcome screen.

You then choose which Domain Controller (2003 or 2008) will have the honor of performing the calculation for you. It doesn't matter which Domain Controller you choose—even those in other domains. Just pick one. Just note that it does need to be a Windows 2003 or 2008 Domain Controller and not anything less.

You'll then get to play Zeus and determine what would happen if you plucked a user and/or computer out of a current situation and modified the circumstances. In the wizard screens, you get to choose the following:

- Which user and/or computer (or container) you want to start to play with

- Whether to pretend to apply slow-link processing (if not already present on the target)

- Whether to pretend to apply loopback processing (if not already present on the target)

- The site in which you want to pretend the object is starting

- Where to move the user (if the user account moves at all)

- Where to move the computer (if it moves at all)

- Whether to pretend to change the user's security group membership

- Whether to pretend to change the computer's security group membership

- Whether to pretend to apply WMI filters for users or computers (if not already present on the target)

Now, to be clear: you don't have to tweak *all* these settings—maybe just one or two. Just whatever applies to your situation.

Also note that you will likely get inaccurate results if you try to do something that isn't possible. For instance, you can force the wizard into seeing what happens if Frank Rizzo's account is moved to another domain. But since there isn't a way to actually move Frank's account, the displayed results will be cockeyed. You'll learn more about some of the additional concepts, such as slow-link processing and loopback processing, in Chapter 4. You'll also learn more about WMI filters in Chapter 4.

The output in Figure 2.25 shows what would happen if Frank Rizzo were removed from the **Human Resources Users** OU (and plopped into the root of the domain).

When the calculations are complete, you'll get a results dialog box that looks quite similar to Figures 2.22 and 2.23. There, you can see how results will be displayed on both the Summary and Settings tabs. As a reminder, the Summary tab shows you which GPOs were applied; the Settings tab shows you which policies in the GPOs will win if there's a conflict. Present only in Group Policy Modeling output (not shown) is another item, called the Query tab, which can remind you of the choices you made when generating the query.

FIGURE 2.25   Here, the Group Policy Modeling summary screen shows you what you're about to simulate. For instance, you can simulate moving a computer and/or a user to other locations.

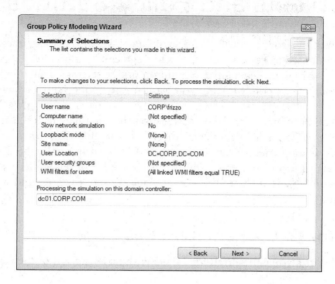

What to Expect from the Group Policy Modeling Wizard

When you first use the Group Policy Modeling Wizard, you may be surprised to see that it has Loopback, WMI Filters, and Slow Links options. At first, I was curious about why these were options in the wizard—if the wizard's whole job is to figure out what will be at the end of the simulation.

In a nutshell, the Group Policy Modeling Wizard allows you to simulate these additional items as if they all were *actually* going to be true. This way, you don't have to create an OU and/or a GPO with the specific policy settings (Loopback and so on) *just* to turn it on. This makes sense: if you enable these options on the real OU, you change the live environment.

The point of the Group Policy Modeling Wizard is to let you just simulate *what if* you did this on the target. When using the wizard and selecting Loopback, Slow Links, or WMI Filters, don't expect it to tell you that any of these things *are* true in the target. The simulation demonstrates what would happen *if* these properties came into the mix.

Note that the Group Policy Modeling Wizard is unable to take into account any Local Group Policy Object settings on the potential target workstation. That's because this wizard never queries a target computer. The calculations all happen on a Windows 2003 or Windows Server 2008 Domain Controller and are then output in the GPMC.

Searching and Commenting Group Policy Objects and Policy Settings

As your Active Directory grows, so will your use of GPOs. However, sometimes remembering the one GPO that you used to do some magic a while ago can be difficult.

And, moreover, with (what seems like) a bajillion policy settings available to choose from, finding the particular policy setting you want in the "policy setting haystack" is harder than ever.

To that end, the GPMC has some basic searching functionality for GPOs (the actual objects) and the Group Policy Management Editor has some filtering functionality for policy settings (the settings themselves, within the GPOs). Additionally, on each (the GPO itself or a policy setting) you can make "comments" to help you remember why you decided to do something—which can be helpful if you go back six months later and wonder why you did something.

Searching for GPO Characteristics

With the search feature, you can search for GPOs with any (and all) of the following characteristics:

- Display name (that is, friendly name)

- GUID

- Permissions on the GPO itself

- A link, if it exists (used in conjunction with the name, and so on)

- WMI filters used

- Specific client-side extensions if they were used for either the User or Computer side

To be clear, I'm talking about finding a specific GPO itself, not finding the settings *within* a GPO. To learn how to find specific settings contained within GPOs, well, that's coming right up.

To search for a GPO that matches the characteristics you're after, right-click the domain and choose Search, as seen in Figure 2.26. I show it here, specifically, because it can be a little hard to find.

Here's how it works:

- In the Search Item dialog box, pick the pre-canned search type, like GPO Name, or GUID.

- In the Condition drop down, select your condition, like "Contains," "Does not contain," etc.

- In the Value field, specifically enter criteria. Note: the Value field can change to a drop-down depending on what's utilized for the Search criteria, or it can be a free-form text box.

FIGURE 2.26 Right-click the domain name and select Search to start searching for GPO characteristics.

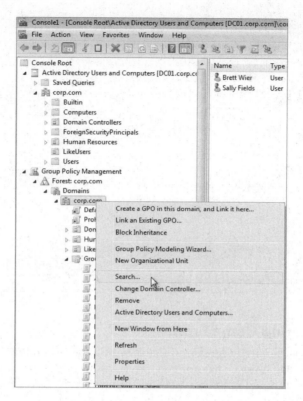

So, in Figure 2.27, I've selected "GPO Name" in the Search Item drop-down, and selected "Contains" in the Condition drop-down, and finally entered "hide" for Value. Lastly, I selected "Add" to add the whole criteria to the search engine, and clicked Search. The results in Figure 2.27 show all GPOs with *Hide* in the name.

Note that one thing *this* search engine *cannot* do is poke through each and every GPO to see where you configured some policy setting. That's done on a per-GPO basis while editing, which we'll cover, well, right here in the next section.

Filtering Inside a GPO for Policy Settings

How many individual Group Policy settings are there? Lots. There are now more than 2,800 with Windows 7 and Windows Server 2008 R2.

So, it's perfectly natural to feel like you're trying to find a needle in a haystack just locating a setting.

FIGURE 2.27   You can locate GPOs with lots of characteristics.

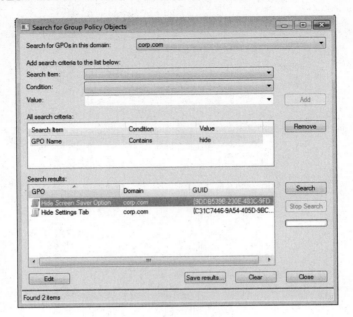

Where Did Filtering Come From?

The good news is that (finally!) Search is available within the Group Policy Management Editor (GPME). The bad news is that not every area within the GPME is searchable (boo!). Before we go into what is and is not available for the new search function, let's take a look at the historical archives for the Group Policy Filtering feature.

If you'll recall, the original Group Policy Editor (contained in the downloadable-for-XP version of the GPMC) *always* had a Filtering option. Really? You didn't know this? That's because it wasn't very well documented and kind of tucked away. If you still have an old XP machine with the GPMC kicking around, click on View ➢ Filtering option, seen in Figure 2.28.

This filtering option had simple abilities. You could check "Filter by Requirements information" and filter for policy settings that would, for example, only work on Windows XP or newer computers.

When you use the updated GPMC, you get a new ability to filter.

What's Available to Filter

The good news is that Filtering is available. The bad news is that only the Administrative Templates Group Policy settings are available to search. So, if you're looking to find that security policy setting that will set **Accounts: Rename guest account** or **Devices: Restrict CD-ROM access to locally logged in user only**, well, you're out of luck. These lie within Computer Configuration ➢ Windows Settings ➢ Security Settings ➢ Local Policies ➢ Security Options.

FIGURE 2.28   The pre–Windows Server 2003 GPMC Filtering option

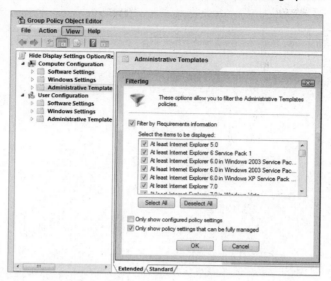

Anything that's not within the Administrative Template section is off-limits to the Filtering feature.

To get to the filter options, click anywhere within the User Configuration ➢ Policies ➢ Administrative Templates or Computer Configuration ➢ Policies ➢ Administrative Templates windows, then click View ➢ Filter Options, or right-click over the words "Administrative Templates" and select Filter Options, as seen in Figure 2.29. Once you do this, you'll get the Filter Options dialog box, shown in Figure 2.30. You could also right-click within Administrative Templates and select Filter Options.

FIGURE 2.29   The new updated GPMC Filter Options selection

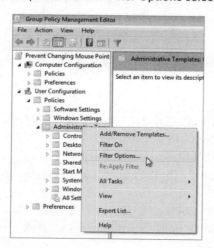

FIGURE 2.30   The new updated GPMC Filter Options dialog

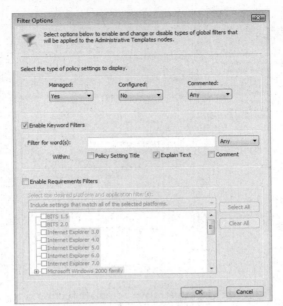

We'll discuss the dialog box in three parts: top (type of settings to display), middle (keyword filters), and bottom (requirements filters). We'll start in the middle with keyword filters, then move to the top, then finally the bottom.

There are lots and lots of reasons you might want to use the Filter Options dialog box. For instance, you might want to show only the policy settings that have been changed from their defaults. You can absolutely do that. But the most common reason for using the Filter Options dialog box is to hunt down settings you think (or hope) might be there. For instance, you already know there are some settings that do something to the Control Panel, but you may not know the exact setting names. You can use this dialog box to find the policy setting you seek.

We'll go through all the options in the Filter Options dialog box, but keep in mind that the most common use is to hunt down settings you want to muck with, er, *experiment* with inside your test lab.

Keyword Filters

Arguably the most useful part of the dialog box, the Keyword Filters option lets you type in something you know you want to do, then see which policy settings match that keyword. You can choose to search in the following three places:

Policy Setting Title   Searches text in the name of a policy setting, like Disable the Display Control Panel.

Help Text (also known as Explain Text)   Searches the help text within the Help section of each policy setting. Note that all policy settings that ship in the box have help text (though some policy settings from ADM or ADMX templates that you get on the Internet might not). It should also be noted that the help text keeps getting better and better with each new edition of Windows. Even the Security entries are mostly commented (but again, remember that we cannot filter based on Security entries).

Comment   We'll talk about comments a little later. But, in short, you can search for any text in comments within a particular GPO.

Let's say you wanted to find settings related to the Control Panel. Next to the "Filter for word(s)" line, you can see the default modifier Any, with All and Exact hiding underneath. Here's how the search for *Control Panel* would work with each modifier:

Any   Returns results where either the word *Control* or *Panel* or both are found. So, results like Turn Off Password Security in Input Panel would also appear along with Show Only Specified Control Panel Items.

All   Returns results where both *Control* and *Panel* are found, but would not display settings that contain only one or the other. Results would include Hide The Programs Control Panel and Hide Specified Control Panel Items. If there were a setting called Control a Panel of Experts to use Group Policy More, it would return that too, because both *Control* and *Panel* are in the name, even though they don't appear right next to each other. (Oh, if only there were a setting like that—but I digress.)

Exact   Returns results where the word *Control* is immediately followed by the word *Panel*. If those two words weren't in that exact order, that setting would not show up.

Note that all of these modifiers, including Exact, ignore case. So *Control Panel* is the same as *CoNTrol PANel*.

Type of Settings to Display

Part of this section of the dialog box can be seen in the following image. Here you'll be able to select three possible options:

Managed   You'll learn more about Managed (blue dot/list icon) versus Unmanaged (red dot/down arrow icon) policy settings in Chapter 6. The quick summary in 100 words or fewer is that *Managed* policies act like true Group Policy settings and *Unmanaged* policies will "tattoo" the Registry. For more information about tattooing, read Chapter 6.

I'm not quite sure why, but the default here is set to Yes. That would mean the results will be *only* Managed policy settings. Just to be on the safe side, selecting Any is likely a better bet because that way, you'll get back both managed and unmanaged policy settings. Again, I'll talk about this more in Chapter 6.

Configured   As you learned in Chapter 1, Administrative Templates policy settings can be set to Enabled, Disabled, or Not Configured. The default for Configured is No, which means the results will show only policy settings that haven't been configured. If you select Yes, the results will show only Enabled or Disabled policy settings. If you choose Any, the results will show Enabled, Disabled, or Not Configured. Selecting Any here seems to be your best bet for finding a policy setting you might want to experiment with.

Commented   You'll learn about comments later on in this chapter, so stay tuned. The default here is Any, which means it will look for commented or uncommented policy settings within this GPO. Selecting Yes will show only commented policy settings within this GPO. Choosing No will show only those policy settings without comments (which would typically be most of them).

Requirements Filters

If you click Enable Requirements Filters (seen in Figure 2.30 earlier), you can determine if you want to show policy settings that are meant for particular client types. Again, a Group Policy "client" can be anything that "receives" Group Policy. So, a Group Policy client can be Windows 2000 or later. The available platforms are listed for you to select, and the list includes various operating system parts that policy settings affect, such as Windows Media Player 10, Windows Installer 3.0, or NetMeeting 3.0. Just select the appropriate check boxes.

Note that there's a drop-down that changes the Filter results when you've checked multiple items. You can show All or Any of the selected platforms. To get your head around what these settings do, it's best to run through a "working example" on each.

Include settings that match any of the selected platforms   For argument's sake, let's say you select two categories using the Any drop-down. Let's say you select Windows XP SP2 and Windows 7. When you do this, you'll see policy settings results that are valid to be applied for lots of machine types: Windows 2000, Windows Vista, Windows 7, Windows Server 2008, and more. That makes sense. But, for example, what you *won't* see are policy settings that *only* apply to Windows 2000 machines. Again, some results (lots of them, actually) will be valid for, say, Windows 2000. And that's because lots of settings that *also* work for Windows XP SP2 and Windows 7 are perfectly happy and embraceable by Windows 2000 machines. But Windows 2000-only settings (that is, settings that Windows 2000 machines can use, but other machine types cannot use) are not listed in the results.

Include settings that match all of the selected platforms   For argument's sake, let's say you select the *same* two categories using the All drop-down. Let's say you select Windows XP SP2 and Windows 7. When you do this, you'll see lots of results. But surprisingly, none of the results show anything for, say, Windows XP SP2, nor do they show anything for Windows 7. You will see a lot of settings that say "At least Windows 2000" and "At least Windows XP Professional." Clear your mind for a second; here's why. The results you get back are correct. You're telling the system, "Show me the settings that are only valid for both Windows XP SP2 and also Windows 7." Well, older settings (Windows 2000–specific and original

Windows XP settings) fit that bill. Newer Windows XP settings, specifically Windows XP SP2 settings, might be perfectly valid on Windows 7. But those newest Windows 7 settings are *not* also valid on Windows XP. So the results you get are accurate. You're only seeing settings that will, indeed, *only* work on all the selected platforms—guaranteed. See Figure 2.31 (which shows Vista and Windows XP, but you get the idea).

FIGURE 2.31   You can select to filter by which platforms are supported.

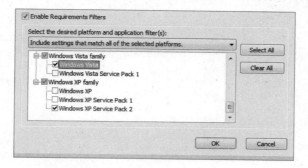

Note that the Windows Vista/Windows Server 2008 GPMC had problems with both the All and the Any filter feature. The Any function didn't always show the right results, and the All function was just broken with a capital B in the Windows Vista/Windows Server 2008 GPMC. It's been fixed in the most-modern Windows 7/Windows Server 2008 R2 GPMC.

Results of Your Filter

Once you've made your selections in the Filter Options dialog box, you're ready to click OK and watch the magic. Let's do a simple filter and look to find any unique Control Panel policy settings that we might want to check out. The filter selections can be seen in Figure 2.32. Here I've made sure to display all policy settings (managed or unmanaged), policy settings that are configured or not configured, and policy settings that are commented or uncommented (more on comments a little later). And for now, I'm just looking for the words *control panel* (in that exact order) to appear in any part of the setting title.

Browsing the Results

The results of applying your filter can be seen in multiple places. You can see the policy settings that affect the Control Panel in the User side by clicking User Configuration ➤ Policies ➤ Administrative Templates ➤ Control Panel (and also the folders within Control Panel named Display and Programs). An example is seen in Figure 2.33.

Note that the filter does not affect the Computer side. The filters are independently set. If you want to turn this on for the Computer side as well, you would need to manually find the Computer Configuration ➤ Policies ➤ Administrative Templates node and create a filter that filtered for the words *control* and *panel*.

FIGURE 2.32   Here I changed the Keyword Filter modifier to Exact to ensure that my results contained the exact phrase *control panel*.

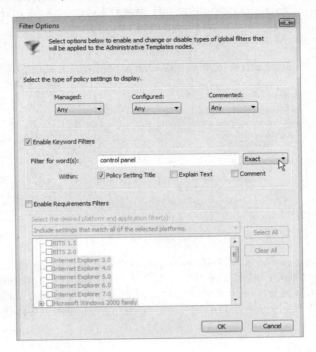

Filter Options On/Off

Once the filter is set to On, the icons around User Configuration ➢ Policies ➢ Administrative Templates and Computer Configuration ➢ Policies ➢ Administrative Templates change. Specifically, the icons take on a "funnel" image to demonstrate that you're looking through the filtered option. In Figure 2.34, I've "blown up" the User Configuration ➢ Policies ➢ Administrative Templates section to show you what I'm talking about.

FIGURE 2.34   The funnel icon shows you've got filtering enabled.

If you ever want to stop looking at only the filtered settings, it's easy. Just right-click anywhere within User Configuration ➢ Policies ➢ Administrative Templates or Computer Configuration ➢ Policies ➢ Administrative Templates and uncheck Filter On, as seen in Figure 2.35.

FIGURE 2.33 Browsing results of running the filter

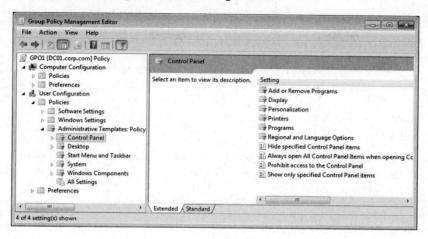

FIGURE 2.35 You can uncheck Filter On to disable the filter.

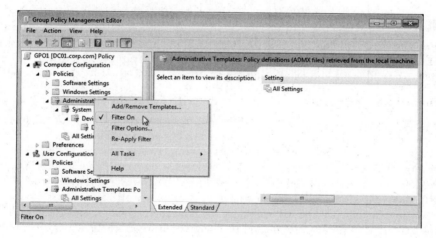

When you do, the filter immediately pops off, and you'll be looking at every possible policy setting again.

> The new updated GPMC filter settings "stick around," meaning that the last filter you use is remembered the next time you apply a filter. This is an advantage if you are searching for a specific setting through different GPOs. Sure, you still need to open each GPO one by one, but at least the last filter you created will be utilized.

Why "Reapply" a Filter?

In Figure 2.35, you can see the Re-Apply Filter option. Here's how that works.

Let's say you apply a filter to show only settings that contain the word *test* in the comment field. Your results show you the policy settings that currently match. However, what if you later add more comments to other policy settings that contain the word *test*? Your results won't show that new change immediately. That is, the change won't show until you reapply the filter!

You can see the same result if you choose to show only Not Configured policy settings but then later change one or a few of those to Enabled. Those changes will not be seen until you reapply the filter.

Reapplying the filter just sets filtering to Off and then turns it back on. Same result (but reapplying the filter is quicker).

The All Settings Node

Along with filters, the All Settings node is a feature in the updated GPMC. The idea is a little weird, so hang in here with me. There are two ways to leverage the All Settings node: when you're using filtering and when you're not.

Using the All Settings Node in Conjunction with Filtering

The idea is that you can see, at a glance, all the settings that tested "true" for the filter.

Since the results of filtering for *control panel* might exist in various nodes (User Configuration ➤ Policies ➤ Administrative Templates ➤ Control Panel, User Configuration ➤ Policies ➤ Administrative Templates ➤ Control Panel ➤ Display, and User Configuration ➤ Policies ➤ Administrative Templates ➤ Control Panel ➤ Programs), there are a lot of places you'd have to click to see all your results.

Instead, you can just click the All Settings node (and there's one for each side: User Configuration and Computer Configuration). There you'll see all the matches at a glance. Check it out in Figure 2.36.

In Figure 2.36, you'll also see some other interesting tidbits of information, like whether the policy has been configured (Enabled or Disabled) or if there's a comment within that policy setting (I promise you, we're getting to comments). Finally, it also shows the file path to the policy setting, in case you wanted to show others where to find this policy setting.

 The path is always relative to User Configuration ➤ Policies ➤ Administrative Templates or Computer Configuration ➤ Policies ➤ Administrative Templates, because that's the only place filtering is valid.

FIGURE 2.36 The All Settings node shows 100 percent of the returned filter results in one view.

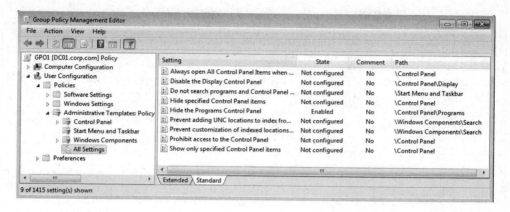

Using the All Settings Node without the Use of Filtering

There's another interesting way to use the All Settings node—when the filter is off. There are zillions of policy settings inside User Configuration and Computer Configuration.

What if you just wanted to quickly locate the policy settings with comments?

Or the policy settings that are configured?

Or quickly find a policy setting based on its name?

You could set up a filter (as previously discussed), but that takes *several whole seconds*! You don't have time for that! You're a busy IT professional!

If you had no filter configured, you could be a speed demon and just click the All Settings node, then click on the column you wish to sort. In Figure 2.37, I've turned off the Filter, then clicked User Configuration ➢ Policies ➢ Administrative Templates ➢ All Settings, and finally clicked the State column heading.

I can immediately see which policy settings have been configured in this particular GPO. No need to click, click, click my way through filters. This is life in the fast lane.

Comments for GPOs and Policy Settings

Imagine for a moment that you're in a large company—maybe you already are and it doesn't require much imagination. Perhaps there are 2, 5, or 50 other administrators. Wouldn't it be nice to be able to leave little messages inside the GPOs and particular GPO settings for other administrators who might happen to find a GPO you create?

That's what this section is all about: the Comment feature.

> Again, you'll only be able to leave comments and read others' comments if you use the updated GPMC. Admins using Windows XP (hence, the older GPMC) won't be able to read your comments. It only works with the updated GPMC.

FIGURE 2.37   Using the All Settings node with filtering turned off

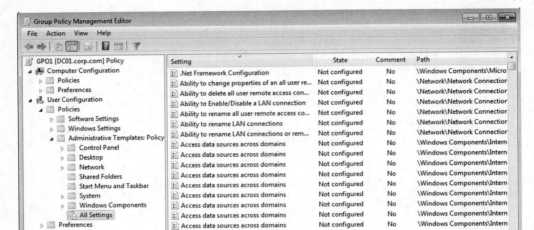

PolicySettings.XLS: Beyond the Filters Node

The Filters node is great. But it's missing one key, well, filtering ability.

It's missing the ability to show specifically what policy settings are available *only* for each operating system. That's right; there's no way of using the Filters to say "Show me only the new policy settings that only apply for Windows 7."

So, how do you do that?

You can download a spreadsheet from Microsoft from my website at www.GPanswers.com. Note, however, that Microsoft's spreadsheet doesn't go into much detail beyond the Explain Text setting for each policy setting. But they're all there and searchable, and you can sort by which operating systems will embrace which policy settings. It's quite good. Also, if you've got an older version, you should note that these settings are always updated whenever a service pack comes out. And, starting with Windows XP/SP2, Microsoft started to document some of the Security settings as well. And the most modern versions of the spreadsheet tries to express when a specific policy setting requires a logoff or a reboot.

Nice touch!

You can leave and read comments in exactly two places: in the GPO itself and inside a GPO's settings. We'll explore these two next.

Comments about a Specific GPO

In the real world, life moves fast. As a result, sometimes administrators don't always spend the time they would like when crafting the name of a GPO. For instance, you might see a poorly named GPO like Our Desktop Settings. It's poorly named because it doesn't explain what those settings are. Is that the Desktop background settings? Or the Control Panel settings? Both? Neither? You get the idea.

Fortunately, now you can choose to leave a comment inside a GPO. Here are some ideas as to what to include when you choose to leave a comment:

- Who's in charge of the GPO
- Who to call if there's a problem with this GPO
- Backup contact information
- Who is supposed to be affected by this GPO
- Detailed information about what the GPO is supposed to do
- Your favorite chocolate chip cookie recipe

Just kidding about that last one. But you get the idea.

Leaving a Comment inside a GPO

Leaving a comment is pretty easy to do, but the problem is that it's not super-duper obvious where to go to leave a comment. (And, as we'll see in the next section, not super-duper obvious where to pick them up, either.)

To leave a comment, you must first have rights to edit the GPO. Then, while you're editing the GPO, right-click the topmost node with the name of the GPO, then click Properties, as seen in Figure 2.38. Then you can type in your comment and click OK, as shown in Figure 2.39.

FIGURE 2.38   Leave comments while editing a GPO by going to its Properties dialog box.

FIGURE 2.39 Entering a comment inside a GPO

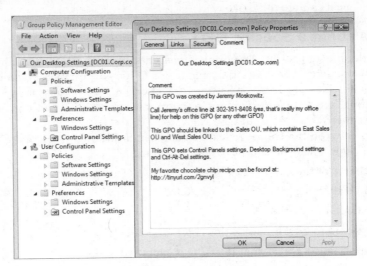

 The Comments feature includes some assistance for right-to-left languages like Arabic and Hebrew. You can find these while right-clicking inside the text field. Things like "Right to Left Reading Order," "Show Unicode Characters," and more are there for that kind of input.

Reading a Comment about a GPO

Reading comments sounds as if it should be easy, but for the uninitiated, they're not easy to find. If you're editing the GPO, you can right-click over the top node, select Properties, and click the Comment tab, as you saw in Figure 2.39. Then, instead of leaving a comment, you can just read the existing comment.

But a better option is found within the GPMC itself. Simply click on the GPO (or the link to the GPO), then click the Details tab, seen in Figure 2.40. You'll see the results in the Comment field below. The formatting is mostly kept the same as when the comment was typed into the Comment editor. And what's more, Unicode characters (like Japanese, Hebrew, etc.) are supported in the editor and the resulting display.

Comments about Specific GPO Settings

In the previous section you learned how to leave a comment about a particular GPO. Now let's explore the ability to leave comments about a particular Group Policy setting.

Like filters, comments about a specific GPO setting are available only to the Administrative Templates section. You cannot leave comments in other areas, like Security settings (which would be very useful) and the like. Note that Group Policy Preferences, which we talk about in Chapter 5, also have a Description field, which is nice.

FIGURE 2.40   The Details tab within the GPO shows the comments.

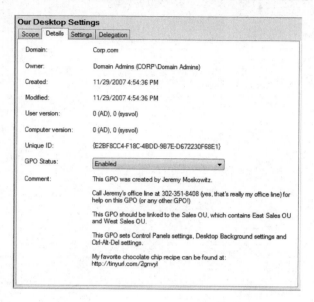

Leaving a Comment inside a Specific GPO Setting

For instance, let's say you wanted to explain why a particular policy setting was Enabled (or Disabled). Simply traverse to the policy setting, get to its properties, then select the Comment tab. Leave a comment like the one you see in Figure 2.41.

Reading a Comment inside a Specific GPO Setting

To quickly read any comments inside particular GPO settings, you have two techniques available. First, while you're editing the GPO, you can quickly check to see which policy settings (if any) contain comments. Second, you can see them while tooling around inside the GPMC.

Looking at Comments While Editing the GPO

Remember from my discussion of the All Settings node that if the filter is off, you can then just click either User Configuration ➢ Policies ➢ Administrative Templates ➢ All Settings or Computer Configuration ➢ Policies ➢ Administrative Templates ➢ All Settings and then click the Comment column to sort the ones with comments, which bubble to the top. You can see this in Figure 2.42. Then it's a simple matter of double-clicking the policy setting in question and clicking the Comment tab to read it.

FIGURE 2.41   Comments are available on a particular Group Policy setting.

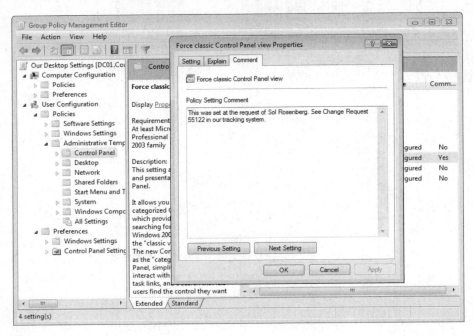

FIGURE 2.42   The All Settings node (and, actually, all nodes) within the GPME displays a Comment column that can be sorted.

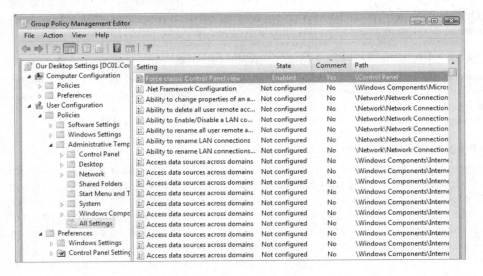

Looking at All Comments While inside the GPMC

The alternative way to see all comments about the policy settings inside the GPO is to view the settings report. Simply click on the GPO (or the link to a GPO) and click the Settings tab. When you do, any comments about any policy settings are displayed inline, as shown in Figure 2.43.

FIGURE 2.43   The comments can be seen inside your GPMC settings reports.

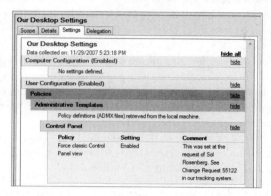

Where and What Are the Comments Anyway?

Behind the scenes, comments are really plain text or XML files placed in SYSVOL.

General GPO comments are placed in a plain-text file located here:

```
\\<domain>\SYSVOL\<domain>\Policies\<GPO GUID>\CPO.cmt
```

Individual comments for GPO settings are placed in two XML files for each GPO, one for Computer Configuration comments and another for User Configuration comments. The files are placed here:

```
\\<domain>\SYSVOL\<domain>\Policies\<GPO GUID>\Machine\Comment.cmtx
\\<domain>\SYSVOL\<domain>\Policies\<GPO GUID>\User\Comment.cmtx
```

Starter GPOs

The updated GPMC has another feature called Starter GPOs.

In big companies, there are often just a handful of people at the top who really "get" Group Policy. But there are a whole lot of people in the company who have to implement

it. Not everyone can take a master class on Group Policy (hint, hint: www.GPanswers.com/
training) or spend the time reading this book and working through all the examples.

With that in mind, Microsoft created Starter GPOs. The idea is that someone can create
a GPO with some baseline settings, including comments, and make them available for others
as a jumping-off point.

For instance, if you were the Domain Administrator and wanted to make sure that all
your OU administrators got a recommended group of settings for desktop configuration,
that would be easy. You would create a Starter GPO, then let them know they had a baseline of settings to leverage, or to edit as they so desired.

You could think of Starter GPOs as templates for making new policies. That way, you're
not back to nothing whenever you need to create a new GPO. The problem is, the word
template has a special meaning with Microsoft's pay Group Policy management tool—
AGPM, the Advanced Group Policy Management. That tool is discussed in downloadable
Bonus Chapter 3. Anyway, AGPM has a similar feature called templates, and that's likely
why this feature is called Starter GPOs and *not* Templates.

The updated GPMC has a new node called Starter GPOs. To get, er, started with
Starter GPOs, you need to have the Starter GPOs folder created in the domain. Click on
the Starter GPOs node and you'll see what's in Figure 2.44.

FIGURE 2.44   To create the Starter GPOs folder, just click on the big ol' button.

Starter GPOs in corp.com

Contents

The Starter GPOs folder does not currently exist in this domain.
Click on the button below to create this folder.

> Create Starter GPOs Folder

You might be asking yourself, "Where is this Starter GPOs folder being created?" Well,
we go into the "internals" of GPOs in the next chapter, but for the curious, its new directory
is created in the domain, inside the Domain Controller's SYSVOL container—specifically,
the <Domain>\SYSVOL\<Domain>\StarterGPOs folder.

During creation, something "extra special" happens.

If you're using the Windows 7 or Windows Server 2008 R2 GPMC, and you push the
"Create Starter GPOs Folder" button, Microsoft will auto-populate the Starter GPOs
folder with some preconfigured items for your use. You can see these in Figure 2.45.

FIGURE 2.45   The two types of Starter GPOs are Custom and System.

Starter GPOs in corp.com

Contents	Delegation	
Name		Type
Windows Vista EC Computer		System
Windows Vista EC User		System
Windows Vista SSLF Computer		System
Windows Vista SSLF User		System
Windows XP SP2 EC Computer		System
Windows XP SP2 EC User		System
Windows XP SP2 SSLF Computer		System
Windows XP SP2 SSLF User		System
My First Starter GPO		Custom

Note that you will not see these preconfigured Starter GPOs unless you're using the Windows 7/Windows Server 2008 R2 GPMC.

Also note that any new Starter GPOs you create will just appear alongside these existing Starter GPOs (also seen in Figure 2.45). The Type field for Starter GPOs that Microsoft provides are listed as System. The ones you create will be listed as Custom.

There are some differences in what Microsoft is able to put into their pre-created Starter GPOs vs. what you'll be able to do. We'll explore those differences here and in the sidebar "Microsoft's Pre-created Starter GPOs—Should You Use Them?"

Creating a Starter GPO

Simply right-click the Starter GPOs node and select New. When you do, you'll be prompted to give it a name and make some comments, as you see in Figure 2.46.

FIGURE 2.46 Add a useful comment when creating a new Starter GPO.

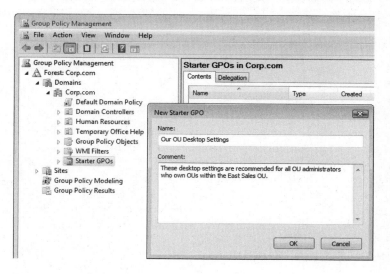

Editing a Starter GPO

Editing a Starter GPO is almost like editing a regular GPO. Just right-click the Starter GPO and select Edit. However, when you do, you'll notice it doesn't look exactly like what you're used to. In fact, only Computer Configuration ➢ Policies ➢ Administrative Templates and User Configuration ➢ Policies ➢ Administrative Templates are available as editable starter policy settings.

You can see this in Figure 2.47.

FIGURE 2.47 Starter GPOs allow for Administrative Templates settings along with comments inside any Administrative Templates settings.

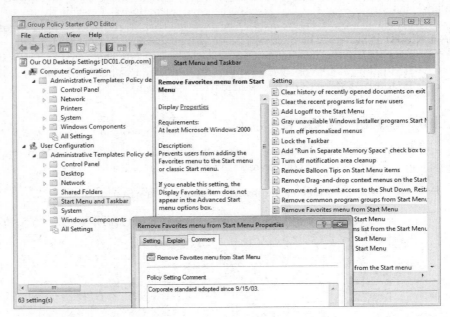

This is a real bummer; as most people (rightly so) think that Starter GPOs should encompass all the areas, not just Administrative Templates. The ability to use all areas, however, is possible, if you step up to Microsoft's pay Group Policy management tool—Advanced Group Policy Management (which we'll talk about in a downloadable Bonus Chapter 2). That feature is called Templates. It's like Starter GPOs, but all areas are available. Of course, AGPM costs money, and Starter GPOs are free. So, the free tool has at least something.

At this point, you can edit any settings you wish and even add comments about any particular policy settings.

Once you're finished, close the GPME.

 A keen eye will spot that the Group Policy Object Editor title bar name has changes to "Group Policy Starter GPO Editor" when you edit a Starter GPO.

Leveraging a Starter GPO

Now that you've created a Starter GPO, it's time for others to leverage your creation. To do that, an OU administrator (or Domain Admin, etc.) has two options: using the Starter GPOs node or just creating a new GPO as they normally would.

Using the Starter GPOs Node

Right-click the Starter GPO in the Starter GPOs node, and select New GPO From Starter GPO (as seen in Figure 2.48).

FIGURE 2.48   You can spawn a new GPO from the Starter GPOs node.

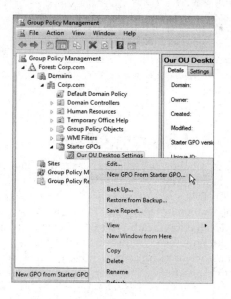

Next, the New GPO dialog box appears, and it auto-fills the Source Starter GPO field, as you can see in Figure 2.49.

FIGURE 2.49   The source Starter GPO is preset when you are modifying a Starter GPO.

Creating a New GPO and Selecting a Starter GPO

The other way to use a Starter GPO is to simply create a new GPO. This can be done either by right-clicking the Group Policy Objects node and selecting New or by clicking over the Domain or OU levels and selecting "Create a GPO in this domain, and link it here."

Regardless of which you do, you'll see the New GPO dialog box, shown in Figure 2.50. At this point, you can select Source Starter GPO and choose the Starter GPO you wish to use.

FIGURE 2.50   If you're creating a GPO normally, you can select a Source Starter GPO.

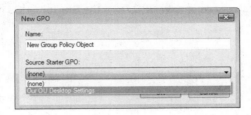

Delegating Control of Starter GPOs

The Starter GPOs section has a bug in its delegation section. That is, Starter GPOs cannot be delegated (beyond the Domain Administrators who already have access).

To access the Starter GPOs Delegation section, just click on the Starter GPOs node, then click the Delegation tab as seen in Figure 2.51. In Figure 2.51, we can see (oddly) that Authenticated Users is listed as having the ability to "...create Starter GPOs in this domain."

That's not true. And adding in a user you want to sanction, say, Frank Rizzo (also seen in Figure 2.51), also yields incorrect results. Also in Figure 2.51, we can see Frank trying to create a new Starter GPO even after he has been specifically delegated access. But creating Starter GPOs fails. Again, only (seemingly) Domain Admins have the ability to create Starter GPOs and not any kind of delegated users.

This bug has been around since the updated GPMC shipped in Windows Vista, and seems to affect all domain types under all circumstances.

If the status should change, you'll find out about it first with an update at www.GPanswers.com.

Wrapping Up and Sending Starter GPOs

One of the neat things about Starter GPOs is that you can give them to your friends—even if they belong to other domains. It's sort of like backing up a GPO, except all the guts are wrapped up into one file.

It's simple to do. Just click on the Starter GPOs node in the GPMC. Then find the Starter GPO you want to send to a friend. Then click "Save as Cabinet." This will save the file as a CAB file.

When your friend gets it, they simply click the "Load Cabinet" button to reverse the process. You can see the "Load Cabinet" and Save as Cabinet buttons in Figure 2.52.

Inside the CAB files are the guts, as seen in Figure 2.53.

FIGURE 2.51   Regular Authenticated users, thankfully, cannot manipulate Starter GPOs.

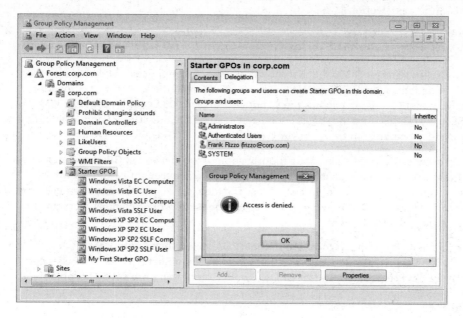

FIGURE 2.52   You can save and load Starter GPOs from CAB files.

FIGURE 2.53   The guts of the Starter GPO are in a CAB file.

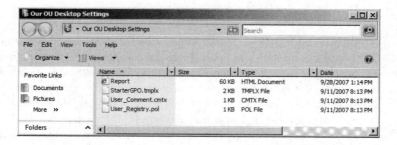

There doesn't seem to be a way to wrap up multiple Starter GPOs into a single CAB file. That would make transporting them enormously easier, but, alas. Additionally note that Starter GPOs are not backed up as part of the normal Group Policy backup (which we explore in the next section.)

Microsoft's Pre-Created Starter GPOs—Should You Use Them?

The Pre-Created Starter GPOs that Microsoft provides are supposed to be based on the recommendations in the Windows Vista Security Guide and the Windows XP Security Guide. Note that Microsoft also has the Windows Server 2008 Security Guide and Office 2007 Security guides. And they're all in one place: in the Security Compliance Management Toolkit pages, located at http://tinyurl.com/agkgzs.

And part of those downloads is a little (poorly named) tool called the GPOAccelerator tool. The GPOAccelerator tool's job is to help auto-create the same example GPOs from the prescriptive guidance in each of those guides. The idea is that, instead of you re-creating all the stuff inside a GPO, the GPOAccelerator tool does the work for you and creates the examples, so you don't have to.

So, the idea is that Microsoft took two of the GPOAccelerator's "outputs"—both from the Windows XP Security Guide GPOs and the Windows Vista Security Guide GPOs—and made those the Pre-Created Starter GPOs. Swell! Except there are several problems.

Problem #1:

You probably won't be using Vista. Most people are jumping right to Windows 7 from Windows XP. So the Pre-created Starter GPOs that are supposed to mirror the Windows XP Security Guide could be of limited value to you.

Problem #2:

You probably won't be using XP for much longer. So, same problem as above. Remember, the Pre-Created Starter GPOs come with only Windows Vista and Windows XP templates, not Windows Server 2008 and not Windows 7—the two most likely candidates for you to use them with.

Problem #3:

The Starter GPOs that Microsoft has created and supplied are incomplete. Remember: Starter GPOs have a big limitation. When we create our own Starter GPOs, we are only able to manipulate the Administrative Template settings. Turns out, underneath the hood, however, Starter GPOs can also allow for *some* security settings. (Note that we, as non-Microsoft insiders, cannot use Starter GPOs in this way—only the Microsoft templates are capable of leveraging this extra superpower.) But even then—they're still incomplete. If you do an apples-to-apples comparison between the Starter GPOs that are pre-created when you create the Starter GPOs folder against the GPOs from the GPOAccelerator tool, you'll find there's a lot more "stuff" inside the GPOAccelerator tool.

So, should you use the built-in Starter GPOs that are auto-created? My advice would be not to use them—for the three problems and reasons provided. I would leverage the ones that come from the security guide in its GPOAccelerator tool if I wanted to experiment. Besides, there's a higher likelihood that those security guides will be updated at some point, and you'll always be using the latest version and get the most "stuff" inside a GPO that corresponds to what's in the guidance.

On GPanswers.com, I interviewed a member of the Security Compliance team at Microsoft. You can listen to their take on the situation as an MP3 here: http://tinyurl.com/y9xrco3.

Back Up and Restore for Group Policy

Inadvertently deleting a single GPO can wreak havoc on your domain. Imagine what happens when a bunch of GPOs are inadvertently deleted. Let's just say that the users are suddenly happy because they can do stuff they couldn't normally do, and you're not happy because now *they're* happy. Ironic, isn't it?

It's not just the errant Group Policy deletion that could cause an issue. Another administrator could inadvertently delete a portion of the SYSVOL container on one Domain Controller, which will replicate to all Domain Controllers and quickly damage your GPOs.

In both of these example cases, you'll need a way to restore.

The Backup and Restore functions for GPOs are only meant to work within the same domain. However, you'll see in the appendix how the GPMC can be used to back up and import a GPO to get the same effect *between* domains.

In our case, if the policy settings inside the "Auto-Launch calc.exe" GPO were wiped out, the name of the GPO can surely help us put it back together. But the name alone might not be an accurate representation of what's going on inside the GPO.

Then, there are still other questions: Where was this GPO linked? What was the security on the GPO? Who owned it?

All said and done, you don't want to get stuck with a deleted or damaged GPO without a backup. Thankfully, the GPMC makes easy work of the once laborious task of backing up and restoring GPOs.

These techniques are valid for both all types and all configurations of Active Directory. So, back up those GPOs today with the GPMC regardless of your domain structure!

Backing Up Group Policy Objects

When you back up a GPO within the GPMC, you also back up a lot of important data:

- The settings inside the GPO.
- The permissions upon that GPO (that is, the stuff inside the Delegation tab).
- The link to the WMI filter—however, the actual filter itself is not preserved. (Again, I'll talk about WMI filters in Chapter 4.)

   However, it's also important to know what won't be backed up:

- Any WMI filters contained within Active Directory. You must back them up separately. You can see one way to do this in the section "Backing Up and Restoring WMI Filters" later in this chapter.
- IPsec settings themselves aren't backed up via the GPMC Backup and Restore function. They are backed up during a Domain Controller's System State backup. But discussing backing up and restoring them is a bit beyond the scope of this book. My best suggestion: manually document any GPOs with IPsec settings.
- GPO links aren't specifically backed up. Yes, you read that right. But before you panic, let me first explain how this is for your own protection. We'll examine this phenomenon in a bit and try to make you a believer in why this is a good thing.

   As you'll learn in Chapter 4, there are two parts of GPOs: the GPT (Group Policy Template) from Active Directory and the GPC (Group Policy Container) from within the SYSVOL. When a backup is performed, the GPT and GPC are wrapped up and placed as a set of files that can be stored or transported.

   What's additionally neat is that contained within the backup is a report of the settings inside that GPO you just backed up. So, if someone backs up a GPO named Sounds (again, a horrible name), you can at least see the report of just what is inside the GPO before you restore it to your domain.

   To back up a GPO, you need Read access to that GPO, as shown earlier in Figure 2.15. You can start by locating the GPO node in the GPMC and right-clicking it. Select either Back Up All or Manage Backups. For this first time, select Back Up All.

   You then select the location for the backup (hopefully some place secure) and click Backup. You'll then see each GPO being backed up to the target location, as shown in Figure 2.54. When you're finished, you can rest easy (or at least easier) that your GPOs are safe.

   You can inspect the directories that the backup produced if you like. You'll see a directory for each GPO, the XML file representing the GPT, and an XML report showing the settings. In the next section, you'll learn how to view the report (easily) by utilizing the View Settings button (as shown in Figure 2.55).

In Chapter 4, we'll learn more about the underlying nuts and bolts of GPOs. Specifically, you'll learn that the underlying name of a GPO relies on a unique GUID name being assigned to the GPO. What isn't immediately obvious here is that the directory names produced by the backup (which take the form of GUIDs) are *not* the same GUIDs that are used for the underlying identification of the GPO. These are additional, unique, random GUID directory names generated just for backup. This seemingly bizarre contradiction becomes useful when you read the next paragraph.

The backup is quick, painless, and rather reasonably sized. The best part about the backup facility is that it's flexible. When you choose to run your next backup, you can keep your backups in the same directory you just chose, and you'll keep a history of the GPOs, should anything change. It's the underlying random and unique GUID names for the directories that allow you to keep plowing more GPO backups right into the same backup directory—there's no fear of overlap. Or you can keep the backups in their own directory; it's your choice.

FIGURE 2.54   You can back up all your GPOs at once, if desired.

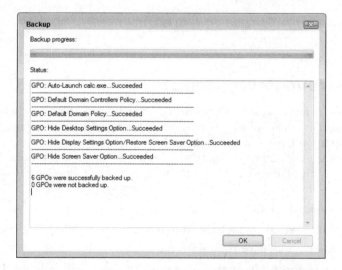

If you dare, go ahead and delete the "Hide Mouse Pointers Option/Restore Screen Saver Option" GPO. You'll restore it in the next section (I hope).

Now that you've backed up the whole caboodle, it should also be noted that you can back up just a solitary GPO. Right-click the *actual* GPO (which is located only in the Group Policy Objects container) and choose Backup. In the downloadable scripting chapter (Bonus Chapter 1), you'll find some scripts that enable you to automate your backups.

Be sure the place where you back up your GPOs is safe and that you can get to it in a pinch.

FIGURE 2.55   You can see all backups or just the latest versions.

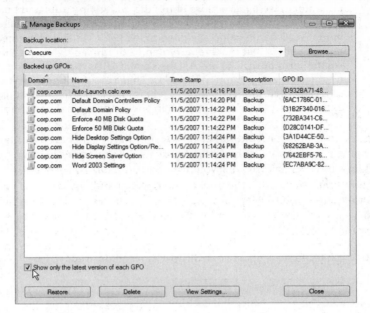

Restoring Group Policy Objects

The restore process is just as easy. It works for GPOs that were backed up in the same domain. Note that it's also possible to back up and restore between domains, but this is called a GPO Migration (see the appendix).

When you restore a GPO, the file object you created in the backup process is "unrolled" and placed within Active Directory. As you would expect, the following key elements are preserved:

- The settings inside the GPO

- The friendly name (which comes back from the dead)

- The GUID (which comes back from the dead)

- The security and permissions on that object (which come back from the dead)

- The link to WMI filters (which comes back from the dead)

 Whomping a GPO doesn't delete any WMI filters associated with a GPO itself. Any WMI filters are stored in a separate place in Active Directory. It's sort of like the Jacuzzi next to the swimming pool.

The GPO does not have to be deleted to do a restore. For instance, if someone changed the settings and you want to simply restore the GPO to get an older version of the policy settings, you can certainly restore over an existing GPO to put a previously known "good" version back in play.

Restoring GPOs requires the following security rights:

- If you want to restore on top of a GPO that already exists, you need Edit, Delete, and Modify rights, as seen back in Figure 2.15.

- If you want to restore a deleted GPO, you need to be a member of the Group Policy Creator Owners (or Domain Admins or Enterprise Admins) security group.

Warning: A Deleted GPO's Links Are Not Restored!

Assuming you went ahead in the last example and deleted the Hide Mouse Pointers Option/ Restore Screen Saver Option GPO and are now ready to restore it, there is something you need to know before proceeding. One critical item is missing: the Group Policy links to the GPO are *not* restored in this operation. The location of links is backed up, but during a restore, the links are *not* restored. You might be scratching your head wondering why this is.

Let's examine a theoretical timeline.

- On Day 0, a GPO named Sounds is linked to two OUs named **Doctors** and **Nurses**.

- On Day 1, the GPO is backed up.

- On Day 2, a fellow administrator unlinks the GPO from **Doctors**. Now, the GPO is linked only to **Nurses**.

- On Day 3, someone deletes the whole GPO (and hence its links).

- On Day 4, someone recognizes this deletion and restores the GPO.

Here's the $50,000 question: upon restore, where should the links be restored to?

Should the links be restored back to the last way it was *just before* the catastrophe on Day 3? Sure, that would be ideal, but how would the system know what happened between Day 2 and Day 4? As it is, on Day 4, the GPO is now linked *only* to **Nurses**, but how could the system know that now?

Should it link the GPO back to the *original* locations, as it was on Day 1? On Day 1, it was linked to **Doctors** and **Nurses**. But restoring those links to the same location could be a catastrophic mistake. Clearly, on Day 2 an administrator unlinked it from **Doctors** for some good reason! Restoring the link back on the **Doctors** could be detrimental to their health!

Instead of restoring the links, the GPMC does the smartest thing it can do during a restore: it doesn't restore the links. That's right—by not restoring the links, it ensures that you're not inadvertently relinking the GPO back to some location in Active Directory that shouldn't have it anymore.

However, as stated, the backup process does record where the links were at the time of backup. To that end, you can easily see where the links were at the time of backup, and if desired, you can manually relink the GPO back to the locations you want. To see where a GPO had links at backup time, here's what to do:

1. Right-click over the Group Policy Objects node and select Manage Backups.

2. In the Manage Backups dialog box, ensure that you're looking at the directory with the contents of the backup.

3. Locate, then select the GPO that was deleted.

4. Click the View Settings button (as seen earlier in Figure 2.55).

A report will be generated that, among other things, shows you where the GPO was linked. Then, once the GPO is restored, you can manually relink it where you need it to be linked.

You can start a restore by right-clicking the Group Policy Objects container and choosing Manage Backups. You'll be able to select a location that will house your GPO backups; you might have multiple locations.

If you've chosen to keep backing up the GPOs into the same backup directory, you can select the "Show only the latest version of each GPO" option, which shows you only the last backed-up version. If you've forgotten what is contained in a backup, simply click the backup name and choose View Settings. You can see these options in Figure 2.55.

When you're ready, click the GPO to restore, and then click Restore. It's really that easy.

You can also right-click the GPO itself (found only in the Group Policy Objects container) and choose "Restore from Backup," which in fact performs the same function. (See Bonus Chapter 1 for a script that will enable you to automate your restores.)

Backing Up and Restoring Starter GPOs

We just covered backing up and restoring GPOs. However, it should be noted that the backup that you normally do to protect yourself from GPO deletion, corruption, and plain ol' stupidity doesn't protect you here regarding Starter GPOs.

You'll have to occasionally right-click on the Starter GPOs node and select Backup. When you do, you'll be able to back up the Starter GPOs quite like backing up normal GPOs. You can see an example in Figure 2.56.

FIGURE 2.56   Backing up Starter GPOs is similar to backing up regular GPOs.

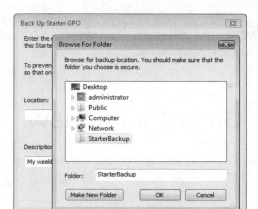

Other functions like Restore are completely analogous to what you just learned.

    Right now, there's no published scriptable interface for backing up and restoring Starter GPOs.

Backing Up and Restoring WMI Filters

As you read about WMI filters in Chapter 4 and learn what a pain in the tush they are to create, you'll be thankful that there's a mechanism that can back up and restore them. They are not backed up or restored in the process we just used. Rather, you must individually back up each WMI filter. Simply right-click the filter and choose Export. To restore, right-click the WMI Filters node and choose Import. Sometimes restoring a WMI filter adds excess and invalid characters to the query. Simply re-edit the query and clean up the characters and you're back in business.

In the previous section, you saw that GPO links are not restored when the GPO is restored. The same is true for WMI filters: the WMI filter links are not restored when the WMI filter is restored. Again, for information on how to automatically document this information, see Chapter 4.

Backing Up and Restoring IPsec Filters

As stated earlier, IPsec filters are not maintained as part of the normal Group Policy backup. I know—it's weird. We don't go much into IPsec policies in this book. But, in short, you create and configure IPsec policies using the Group Policy interface, but they're not stored inside the GPO itself.

With that in mind, to ensure your IPsec policies are backed up, use the IP Security Policy Management console, an MMC snap-in. Then use the All tasks ➤ Export Policies and All tasks ➤ Import Policies commands to, well, export and/or import.

It's still important to back up the GPOs that contain IPsec filters so you can "reconnect" a restored GPO to an IPsec filter—and also so you can "reconnect" a restored IPsec policy to a GPO.

GPMC At-a-Glance Icon View

Because the GPMC contains so many icon types, it can be difficult to know specifically what an icon represents. That's what Table 2.2 is all about.

TABLE 2.2 GPMC Icon List

Icon	Description	What the Icon Means
	Scroll.	A GPO itself. You'll only see this in the Group Policy Objects container.
	Scroll with arrow.	A link to an actual GPO.
	Scroll with arrow. Just the arrow is dimmed.	A GPO link that has Link Status disabled.
	Scroll with arrow. The whole icon is dimmed.	A link to a GPO whose status (on the Details tab) has been set to "All settings disabled."
	Scroll. The whole icon is dimmed.	The GPO whose status (on the Details tab) has been set to "All settings disabled."
	Scroll with arrow; additional lock icon.	Enforced link to this level.
	Blue exclamation point.	Block inheritance at this level.
	Folder with scroll.	Group Policy Objects container that actually holds the GPOs themselves.
	Folder with filter.	WMI Filters node.
	Filter.	A WMI filter.

The GPMC At-a-Glance Compatibility Table

You learned a lot in this chapter. Sometimes it can be confusing to know just when a feature is compatible with your setup in the office or the test lab. Hopefully, Table 2.3 will clear things up.

TABLE 2.3   Group Policy Functionality Compatibility Table

Function	Requirement	Where Discussed
Create and link GPOs and apply them to client systems.	Any Active Directory domain with Group Policy–capable clients Windows 2000 and later	Chapter 1
Back up and restore GPOs.	Any Active Directory domain plus the GPMC.	This chapter
Back up and restore Starter GPOs.	Any Active Directory with Windows 2008 schema plus the updated GPMC.	This chapter
Transfer (migrate) GPOs between same forest.	Any Active Directory domain plus the GPMC.	Appendix
Run Group Policy Results reports.	Any Active Directory domain plus the GPMC. Targets must be Windows XP or later. The target user must have logged on to the target machine at least once.	This chapter
Run Group Policy Modeling reports.	Any Active Directory domain plus the GPMC. Must have at least one Windows Server 2003 or 2008 Domain Controller available to run the calculations. Targets may be Windows 2000, but you might get inaccurate results with Windows 2000 clients.	This chapter
WMI filters.	Windows 2003 domain or Windows 2000 with an updated Windows 2003 schema via the ADPREP /Domainprep command. Additionally, XP clients or later required. Windows 2000 clients ignore WMI filters.	Chapter 4

TABLE 2.3   Group Policy Functionality Compatibility Table *(continued)*

Function	Requirement	Where Discussed
Delegate Group Policy Results ability.	At least Windows 2003 forest or Windows 2000 updated schema via ADPREP /forestprep. Use Active Directory Users and Computers or GPMC to delegate rights.	This chapter
Delegate Group Policy Modeling ability.	At least Windows 2003 forest or Windows 2000 updated schema via ADPREP /forestprep. Use Active Directory Users and Computers or the GPMC to delegate rights.	This chapter

Final Thoughts

While using the GPMC throughout this chapter, you ran queries and created several reports. What you possibly didn't know is that all that time you were creating HTML reports you can use to document your environment.

Back when you were first exploring a GPO's settings (see the screen shot in the section "Common Procedures with the GPMC" earlier in the chapter) and when you were creating RSoP reports (that is, Figures 2.23 and 2.24 and what would result after Figure 2.26), you were really generating HTML reports. Anytime you create those reports, you can right-click anywhere in the report and choose Save Report. Since these reports are standard HTML, you have an incredibly easy way to document just about every aspect of your Group Policy universe.

Backing up and restoring with the GPMC is simply awesome. But as you'll recall, when you restore a deleted GPO, you don't restore the links. You'll have to bring them back manually. Having good backups and good documentation about where each GPO is linked will always be your ace in the hole.

Something else not described here is that the GPMC provides a scriptable interface for many of our day-to-day GPO functions—including backups, creation, and management. You'll see that in the downloadable Bonus Chapter 1. Additionally, you can use the GPMC to migrate GPOs from one domain to another. I'll tackle that topic in the appendix.

Remember that the GPMC is now built into Windows Vista and Windows Server 2008, but the best version you can use is Windows Server 2008 R2 or Windows 7 when you download RSAT. Here are some parting tips for daily Group Policy Object management with the GPMC:

Use Block Inheritance and Enforced sparingly.   The less you use these features, the easier it will be to debug the application of settings. Figuring out at which level in the hierarchy one administrator has Blocked Inheritance and another has declared Enforced can eat up days of fun at the office. The GPMC makes it easier to see what's going on, but still, minimize your use of these two attributes.

Remember what can only be applied at the link.   Three and only three attributes are set on a GPO link: Link Enable (Enable or Disable the settings to apply at this level), Enforce the link (and force the policy settings), and Delete the link.

Remember what can be applied only on the actual GPO itself.   The following attributes must be set on the GPO itself: the policies and settings inside the GPO (found on the Settings tab), Security filters, permissions (as in the Apply Group Policy permission), delegation (as in the "Edit this GPO" permission), Enabling/Disabling half (or both halves) of the GPO via the GPO status (found on the Details tab), and WMI filtering (discussed in Chapter 4).

Remember that Group Policy is notoriously tough to debug.   Once you start linking GPOs at multiple levels, throwing in a Block Inheritance, an Enforced, and a filter or two, you're up to your eyeballs in troubleshooting. The best thing you can do is document the heck out of your GPOs. The GPMC helps you determine what a GPO does in the Settings tab, but your documentation will be your sanity check when trying to figure things out.

Use Microsoft's spreadsheet.   Microsoft has an Excel spreadsheet of all the administrative templates settings. (You'll learn more about why this is when you read Chapter 6.) My suggestion is to leverage this file every single time you create a new GPO and keep it in a common place for all administrators to reference to see what anyone else did inside a GPO. Be religious about it, and keep these files updated within your company. To locate the spreadsheet, go to www.GPanswers.com, in the "Microsoft Resources" section where I always have a link to it that's easy to find.

3

Group Policy Processing Behavior Essentials

After you create or modify a GPO in the domain, the policy's "wishes" are not immediately dropped on the target machines. In fact, they're not dropped on the target machines at all; they're requested by the client computer at various times throughout the day. GPOs are processed at specific times, based on various conditions. You could basically say that GPOs are created from your management machine, and plopped on the Domain Controllers for storage. Then those GPOs are simply "pulled" by the client.

It's likely that you have all sorts of client systems, including Windows 7, in your environment. And, again, when I say "client system" I mean "the client that receives Group Policy"—even if it's the server. Each operating system that receives Group Policy instructions processes Group Policy at different times in different ways. With different operating systems requesting different things at different times, the expected behaviors can get confusing quickly.

Additionally, other factors determine when and how a GPO applies. When users dial in over slow links, things can be—and usually are—different. And you can instruct the Group Policy engine (on a specific computer or all computers) to forgo its out-of-the-box processing behaviors for a customized (and often more secure) way to process.

Often, people throw up their hands when the Group Policy engine doesn't seem to process the dictated GPOs in an expected manner. Group Policy doesn't just process when it wants to; rather, it adheres to a strict set of processing rules. The goal of this chapter and the next is to answer this question: *When* does Group Policy apply?

Understanding the processing rules will help you better understand when Group Policy processes GPOs the way it does. Then, in Chapter 7 you'll get a grip on *why* and *how* Group Policy applies. Between these chapters, your goal is to discover how Group Policy can apply under different circumstances and how you can become a better Group Policy troubleshooter.

Group Policy Processing Principles

For you to best understand how Windows XP or Windows 7 processes GPOs, I'll first describe how Windows 2000 does its thing.

What? "That's lunacy!" I hear you cry. "Here it is, the year 2010" (or later, I suppose, depending on when you're reading this). "And you, Moskowitz, have the audacity to explain to me how a 10-year-old operating system works? Get modern, Mr. Caveman." Seriously. I can hear you—right now. It's like I'm right here.

Anyway, I know it's weird. But since Windows 2000 came out first, its behavior is critically important—especially because (and here's the punch line) I think you'll want to make your XP (or later) machines act like Windows 2000 by the time you're done reading this section.

You've read that right: I'm guessing you'll want to make your XP and later machines, like Windows 7, act like the 10-year-old Windows 2000 operating system.

Trust me. You'll want to learn how Windows 2000 does its thing first, before trying to understand the rest of the family.

Sure, Windows Server 2003 and Windows Server 2008 also process GPOs as a Group Policy client. We'll pepper in that information when necessary. But, as you're reading along, try to focus on the typical client computer.

To get a feel for how GPO processing works, we're going to walk through what happens to three users:

- Wally, who uses only a Windows 2000 Professional machine

- Xavier, who uses only a Windows XP machine

- Seven, who uses only a Windows 7 machine

 How can someone be named "Seven"? Check out this old Seinfeld episode, aptly named "The Seven": www.seinfeldscripts.com/TheSeven.html.

By using Wally, Xavier, and Seven as our three sample users (on our three sample computers), we can see precisely when Group Policy applies to them—when they're using Windows 2000 machines, Windows XP machines, and Windows 7 machines. Note that Windows Vista and Windows 7 act pretty much exactly alike. So, we'll "ignore" Windows Vista and just describe Windows 7 in these examples.

Before we go even one step further, let me debunk a popular myth about Group Policy processing: Group Policy is never *pushed* from the server and forced on the clients. Rather, the process is quite the opposite. Group Policy occurs when the Group Policy engine on a Windows client requests Group Policy. This happens at various times, but at no time can you magically declare from on high, "All clients! Go forth and accept my latest GPOs!" It doesn't work like that. Clients request GPOs according to the rules listed in this chapter.

In a nutshell, Group Policy is potentially triggered to apply at four times (and one special case we need to cover). Here's a rundown of those times; I'll discuss them in grueling detail in the next sections.

Initial policy processing   Initial policy processing is a fancy way of saying "the first cycle" of Group Policy. That first cycle happens for computers at startup time and for users at logon time.

At www.GPanswers.com, in the "Solutions Guide" I have pointers to two free downloads that can perform a "remote" Group Policy refresh. One is a command-line tool (rGPrefresh), and the other is a graphical snap-in to Active Directory Users and Computers (Specops GPUpdate). You can also check out Jakob Heidelberg's "How to Force Remote Group Policy Processing" solutions here:

www.windowsecurity.com/articles/How-Force-Remote-Group-Policy-Processing.html

(shortened to http://tinyurl.com/2opez6).

Background refresh policy processing (member computers)   Member machines (that is, non-Domain Controllers), check in with the Domain Controller to see if there are any new or changed Group Policy Objects. This occurs some time after the computer starts up and also for the user after the user logs on (usually at 90-minute intervals or so). A bit later, you'll see how Windows XP and Windows 7 leverage the background policy processing mechanism to a distinct advantage.

Background refresh policy processing (domain controllers)   Domain Controllers need love too, and to that end, all Domain Controllers perform a background refresh every 5 minutes (after replication has occurred).

Security policy processing   For all operating systems, only the security settings within all GPOs are reprocessed and applied every 16 hours regardless of whether they have changed. This safety mechanism prevents unscrupulous local workstation administrators from doing too much harm.

You can change the default behavior of certain nonsecurity policy settings so they are enforced in a manner similar to the way that security settings are automatically enforced. But you have to explicitly turn this feature on, and you have to do so correctly. In the section "Security Policy Processing," later in this chapter, I describe how to do this and give you several examples of why you would want to do so.

Special case: Moving a user or computer object   Although all the previous items demonstrate a trigger of when Group Policy applies, one case isn't trigger specific; however, it's important to understand a special case of Group Policy processing behavior. You might think that if you move a user or computer around in Active Directory (specifically, from one OU to another), then Group Policy is set to reapply—the system would "know" it's been moved around in Active Directory. But that doesn't happen. When you move a user or a computer from one OU to another, background processing may not immediately understand that something was moved. Some time later, the system should detect the change, and background processing should start normally again.

Don't Get Lost

There are definitely nuances in the processing mechanism among the various operating systems. The good news, if your head starts to swim a bit, is that you can dog-ear this page and highlight this little area for quick reference. If you remember one takeaway from this chapter, it should be that target computers fall into these three behavior types:

Behavior type 1   Windows 2000 Professional workstations, Windows 2000 member servers, Windows Server 2003 member servers, and Windows Server 2008 member servers

Behavior type 2   Domain Controllers of all sorts: Windows 2000 and Windows Server 2003 and Windows Server 2008

Behavior type 3   Windows XP, Windows Vista and Windows 7

It's important to understand the difference between these three behavior types. And once you understand the difference between them, you can decide if you want to take the machines that are in Behavior Type 3 (Windows XP and Windows 7) and make them act like machines that are in Behavior Type 1 (Windows 2000 and Windows Server 2003 and Windows Server 2008).

By now, you might have expunged Windows 2000 systems from your domain. However, I strongly encourage you to read about how all systems are processed.

I recommend this for three reasons:

- The behaviors described in the following sections are all based on the original "baseline" Windows 2000 behavior.

- It's easier to understand the Windows XP and Windows 7 behavior if you understand the original Windows 2000 behavior.

- Later in the chapter I'm going to encourage you to "Make your Windows XP and later machines act like Windows 2000." So, if you don't understand the Windows 2000 behavior, you won't know what I'm talking about.

Initial Policy Processing

Recall that each GPO has two halves: a Computer half and a User half. This is important to remember when trying to understand when GPOs are processed. All machines perform what is called *initial policy processing*. Again, that's just a way of saying "the first time policy is checked for after a computer is rebooted" and "the first time policy is checked for after a user logs on."

But Windows XP and later machines don't exactly perform the same steps as their Windows 2000 counterparts. Let's check it all out.

Windows 2000 (and Windows Server 2003 and Windows Server 2008) Initial Policy Processing

Our sample computer user Wally walks into his office and turns on his Windows 2000 Professional machine. The computer half of the policy is always processed at the target machines upon startup as his machine reboots. When a Windows 2000 or Windows 2003 machine starts up, it states that it is "Processing security policy" or "Applying Computer Settings." What this should say is "Processing Group Policy" (but it doesn't).

At that time, the workstation logs onto the network by contacting a Domain Controller. It finds the Domain Controller by looking up DNS records that say, "Hey, here's the name of a Domain Controller." The Domain Controller then tells the workstation which site it belongs to, which domain it belongs to, and which OU it is in. The system then downloads and processes the Computer half of Group Policy in that order. When the processing is finished, the "Press Ctrl+Alt+Delete to begin" prompt is revealed, and Wally can log on by pressing Ctrl+Alt+Delete and giving his username and password.

After Wally is validated to Active Directory, the User half of the GPO is downloaded and then processed in the same precise order: site, domain, and then each nested OU.

Wally's Windows 2000 Desktop is manipulated by the policy settings inside any GPOs targeting Wally's user or computer account. Wally's Desktop is displayed only when all the user-side GPOs are processed.

If you look at how all this goes, you'll see it's a lock-step mechanism. The computer starts up and then processes GPOs in the natural order: local, site, domain, and each nested OU. The user then logs on, and Group Policy is processed, again in the natural order: local, site, domain, and each nested OU. This style of GPO processing is called *synchronous processing*. That is, to proceed to the next step in either the startup or logon process, the previous step must be completed. For example, the GPOs at the OU level of the user are never downloaded and applied before the GPOs at the site level. Likewise, the GPOs at the domain level for Windows 2000 (and Windows Server 2003 and Windows Server 2008) are never downloaded before the site GPOs that affect a computer.

Therefore, the default for Windows 2000 (and Windows Server 2003 and Windows Server 2008) for both the computer startup and the user logon is that each GPO is processed synchronously. This same process occurs every time a user booting a Windows 2000 (or Windows Server 2003 or Windows Server 2008) machine turns on the machine and then logs on.

Windows XP and Later Initial Policy Processing

Xavier walks into his office and turns on his Windows XP machine. For a moment, let's assume this is the *first time* that this Windows XP machine has started up since joining the domain. Perhaps it just landed on Xavier's desk after a new desktop rollout of Windows XP. If this is the case, the Windows XP machine will act just like Windows 2000 (as described earlier). It will look to see which site, domain, and OUs the computer account is in and then apply GPOs synchronously. Likewise, let's assume this is the first time Xavier is logging into this Windows XP machine with his user account, which lives in Active Directory. Again, imagine that this machine just arrived after a desktop rollout. In this case, again, Windows XP will act like Windows 2000 (and synchronously process GPOs based on the site, domain, and OU Xavier is logging on from).

So far, so good. However, Windows XP performs this initial synchronous processing only in this special case described here. That is, either the computer has never started in the domain before or the user has never logged onto this particular Windows XP machine before.

Seven's experience on Windows 7 will be the same as Xavier's. That is, if Seven walks into her office and turns on her Windows 7 machine for the first time and logs into the machine for the first time, it will act like Windows 2000 and process GPOs synchronously for both the computer (during startup) and the user (during login). To understand Windows XP's normal default processing mode, take a deep breath and read on.

Background Refresh Policy Processing

Once Wally is logged onto Windows 2000 (or Windows 2003 or Windows Server 2008), and Xavier is logged onto Windows XP, and Seven is plugging along on Windows 7, things are great—for everyone. As the administrators, we're happy because Wally, Xavier, and Seven are all receiving our wishes. They're happy because, well, they're just happy, that's all.

But, now, we decide to add a new GPO or to modify a policy setting inside an existing GPO. What if something is modified in the Group Policy Management Editor that should affect a user or a computer? Aren't Wally, Xavier, and Seven already logged on—happy as clams? Well, a new setting is destined for an already-logged-in user or computer, and the new changes (and only the new changes) are indeed reflected on the user or computer that should receive them. But this delivery doesn't happen immediately; rather, the changes are delivered according to the *background refresh interval* (sometimes known as the *background processing interval*).

The background refresh interval dictates how often changed GPOs in Active Directory are pulled by the client computer. As I implied earlier, there are different background intervals for the different operating systems' roles (that is, member versus Domain Controller).

When the background refresh interval comes to pass, GPOs are processed *asynchronously*. That is, if a GPO that affects a user's OU (or other Active Directory level) is changed, the changes are pulled to the local computer when the clock strikes the processing time. It doesn't matter if the change happens at any level in Active Directory: OU, domain, or site. When changes are available to users or computers after the user or computer is already logged on, the changes are processed asynchronously. Whichever GPOs at any level have changed, those changes are reflected on the client.

 Standard precedence order is still applied: site, domain, OU. In other words, even though a new GPO linked to a site is ready, it isn't necessarily going to trump a GPO linked to the OU.

When does this happen? According to the background refresh interval for the operating system (discussed next).

Background Refresh Intervals for Windows 2000/2003/2008 Member Servers

It stands to reason that when we change an existing GPO (or create a new GPO), we want our users and computers to get the latest and greatest set of instructions and wishes. With that in mind, let's continue with our example. Remember that Wally is on his Windows 2000 machine, Xavier is on his Windows XP machine, and Seven is on her Windows 7 machine.

By default, the background refresh interval for Windows 2000 workstations and for Windows 2000 and Windows 2003 member servers is 90 minutes, with a 0–30 minute positive random differential added to the mix to ensure that no gaggle of PCs will refresh at any one time and clog your network asking for mass GPO downloads from Domain Controllers. Therefore, once a change has been made to a GPO, it could take as little as 90 minutes or as long as 120 minutes for each user or workstation that is already logged onto the network to see that change.

Microsoft's older documentation isn't consistent in this description. Some older Microsoft documentation will say the offset is 30 minutes (which could be interpreted as positive or negative 30 minutes). Indeed, in the first edition of this book, I incorrectly reported that "fact." However, since then, I have verified with Microsoft that the refresh interval is (and has always been) 90 minutes plus (not minus) 0–30 minutes.

Again, this is known as the background refresh interval. Additionally, the background refresh interval for the Computer half of Group Policy and the User half of Group Policy are on their own independent schedules. That is, the Computer half or the User half might be refreshed before the other half; they're not necessarily refreshed at the exact same moment because they're on their own individual timetables. This makes sense: the computer and user didn't each get Group Policy at the precise moment in time in the first place, did they?

You can change the background refresh interval for the Computer half and/or the User half using Group Policy, as described later in the section cleverly titled "Using Group Policy to Affect Group Policy."

You can set individual policy settings to prevent specific areas of Group Policy from being refreshed in the background, such as Internet Explorer Maintenance and Administrative Templates. See the section "Using Group Policy to Affect Group Policy" later in this chapter.

How Does the Group Policy Engine Know What's New or Changed?

The Group Policy engine on Windows 2000 and Windows XP can keep track of what's new or changed via a control mechanism called *version numbers*. Each GPO has a version number for each half of the GPO, and this is stored in Active Directory. If the version number in Active Directory doesn't change, nothing is downloaded. Since nothing has changed, the Group Policy engine thinks it has all the latest and greatest stuff—so why bother to redownload it (which takes time) and reprocess it (which takes more time)?

By default, when a background refresh interval arrives, a time-saving mechanism, "checking the GPO version numbers," is employed to minimize the time needed to get the latest and greatest GPOs. You'll learn more about GPO version numbers in Chapter 7.

To reiterate, when the background refresh interval arrives, only the new or changed GPOs are downloaded and processed.

Background Refresh Intervals for Windows 2000/2003/2008 Domain Controllers

Even though Wally, Xavier, and Seven are not logging onto Domain Controllers, other people might. And because Domain Controllers are a bit special, the processing for Domain Controllers is handled in a special way.

Because Group Policy contains sensitive security settings (for example, Password and Account Policy, Kerberos Policy, Audit Policy), any policy geared for a Domain Controller is refreshed within five minutes. This adds a tighter level of security to Domain Controllers. For more information on precisely how the default GPOs work, see Chapter 8.

You can change the background interval for Domain Controllers using Group Policy (as described later in the section "Using Group Policy to Affect Group Policy"). However, you shouldn't mess with the default values here—they work pretty well.

     You'll learn more about affecting Domain Controllers' security in Chapter 8.

Background Refresh Exemptions

Wally has been logged onto his Windows 2000 machine for four hours. Xavier has been logged onto his Windows XP machine, and Seven has been logged onto her Windows 7 machine for the same amount of time. Clearly, the background refresh interval has come and gone—somewhere between two and three times.

If any GPOs had been created or any existing GPOs had changed while Wally, Xavier, and Seven were logged on, both their user accounts and their computer accounts would have embraced the newest policy settings. However, four policy categories are exceptions and are never processed in the background while users are logged on:

Folder Redirection (explored in detail in Chapter 10)   Folder Redirection's goal is to anchor specific directories, such as the My Documents folder, to certain network shared folders. This policy is never refreshed during a background refresh. The logic behind this is that if an administrator changes this location while the user is using it (and the system responds), the user's data could be at risk for corruption. If the administrator changes Folder Redirection via Group Policy, this change affects only the user at the next logon.

Software Installation (explored in detail in Chapter 11)   Software Installation is also exempt from background refresh. You can use Group Policy to deploy software packages, large and small, to your users or to your computers. You can also use Group Policy to revoke already-distributed software packages. Software is neither installed nor revoked to users or computers when the background interval comes to pass. You wouldn't want users to lose applications right in the middle of use and, hence, lose or corrupt data. These functions occur only at startup for the computer or at logon for the user.

> Special Operations Software has a great third-party tool called Specops Deploy that will permit the deployment of software while the user is logged on. Check out www.GPanswers.com in the "Third-Party Solutions Guide" section for more information.

Disk quotas (explored in previous editions of the book)   Disk quotas are not run when the background processing interval comes around. They are run (changed, really) only at computer startup.

Logon, logoff, startup, and shutdown scripts (explored in detail in Chapter 12)   Technically, this entry shouldn't be here. Here's why: yes, it's true that these scripts are run only at the appointed time (at logon, logoff, startup, or shutdown). And, as expected, these scripts are not run again and again when the background processing interval comes around. But, technically, the Client-Side Extension (CSE) that implements scripts does run in the background. If it runs in the background, what is it doing? The Group Policy CSE will update the "values" like location and path changes. This can happen even after the user has already logged on. It's just that, of course, they won't run again until the appointed time. So, the important (and often misunderstood point) is that Group Policy itself doesn't run the scripts. That's handled by the logon process. The Group Policy part of the magic is always happening—just updating values (like location of the script) if they're changed within the GPO.

Windows XP and Later and Background Processing

As I stated in the introduction to this section, Windows XP and later do not process new Group Policy updates in the same way that Windows 2000, Windows Server 2003, and Windows Server 2008 do. Let's get a grip on how Windows XP and Windows 7 work.

Now that Xavier has logged onto his Windows XP machine for the first time and Seven has logged onto her Windows 7 machine for the first time, their sessions will continue to process GPOs in the background as I just described: every 90 minutes or so if any new GPOs appear or any existing GPOs have changed. Xavier now goes home for the night. He logs off the domain and shuts down his machine. When he comes in the next morning, he will not process GPOs the same way that Wally will on his Windows 2000 machine.

When Xavier (or Seven) logs on the second time (and all subsequent times) to a Windows XP or Windows 7 machine, initial policy processing will no longer be performed as described in the section "Initial Policy Processing" earlier in this chapter.

From this point forward, at startup or logon, Windows XP and Windows 7 will not process GPOs synchronously like Windows 2000; rather, GPOs will be processed only in the background.

If you're scratching your head at this point as to why Windows 2000 is different from Windows XP and Windows 7, here's the short answer. When Windows XP was in development, all the stops were pulled to make the "XPerience" as fast as possible. Both boot times and logon times were indeed faster than ever, but the trade-off came at a price.

By default, Windows XP and later won't wait for the network to be there in order to check for any updated GPOs. If the network is unavailable or slow, Windows XP and later will simply utilize the last-known downloaded GPOs as the baseline, even if GPOs have changed in Active Directory while the Windows XP or Windows 7 machine was turned off. Said another way, if Windows XP and later machines can't download anything new (quickly), they just maintain what they have, without any holdups.

While the network card is still warming up and finding the network and the first Domain Controller, the last-used computer GPOs are already just "there." Then, the "Press Ctrl+Alt+Delete to begin" prompt is presented to the user. While this prompt is presented, and once the network is ready, only then does Windows XP and later download and apply any new computer GPOs.

Assuming the user is now logged on, the Desktop and Start menu appear. Again, the system will not synchronously download the latest site, domain, and OU Group Policy Objects and apply them before displaying the Desktop. Instead, other activity is happening while the latest and greatest Group Policy is being downloaded, so the user might not see the effects right away.

Once the computer has started and the user is logged on, the Group Policy settings from "last time" are already there on the machine. Newly downloaded GPOs (and the policy settings inside) are then processed asynchronously in the background. This net result is a bit of a compromise. The user feels that there is a faster boot time (when the GPO contains computer policy settings) as well as faster logon time (when the GPO contains user policy settings). The most important policy settings, such as updated Security settings and Administrative Templates (Registry updates), are applied soon after logon—and no one is the wiser. Microsoft calls this Group Policy processing behavior *Fast Boot* (sometimes called *Logon Optimization*). Yes, it does speed things up a bit, but at a cost.

To keep things simple, we just walked through what would happen for Xavier on his Windows XP machine. However, the exact same behavior would occur for Seven on her Windows 7 machine. There is no difference between Windows 7, Windows XP, or Windows Vista in this respect.

Windows XP and Later Fast-Boot Results

Fast Boot affects two major components: Group Policy processing and user-account attribute processing. The (sometimes strange) results occur for both Xavier on his Windows XP machine and Seven on her Windows 7 machine when they have previously logged on. On his Windows 2000 machine, Wally is spared the Fast Boot behavior.

WINDOWS XP AND LATER FAST BOOT GROUP POLICY PROCESSING DETAILS

The immediate downside to the Windows XP and Windows 7 Fast Boot approach is that, potentially, a user could be totally logged on but not quite have all the GPOs processed. Then, once they are working for a little while—pop! A setting takes effect out of the blue. This is because not all GPOs were processed before the user was presented with the Desktop and Start menu. Your network would have to be pretty slow for this scenario to occur, but it's certainly possible.

The next major downside takes a bit more to wrap your head around. Some Group Policy (and Profile) features can potentially take Windows XP and later several additional logons or reboots to actually get the changes you want on them. This strange behavior becomes understandable when we take a step back and think about how certain policy categories are processed on Windows 2000. Specifically, we need to direct our attention to Software Distribution and Folder Redirection policy. I mentioned that on Windows 2000 these two types of policy categories (and some others) *must* be processed in the foreground (or synchronously) to prevent data corruption. That is, if there are Software Distribution or Folder Redirection edicts to embrace, they can happen *only* during startup or login.

But we have a paradox: if Windows XP and later only process GPOs asynchronously, how are the Software Distribution and Folder Redirection polices handled if they must be handled *synchronously*?

Windows XP and later fake it and tag the machine when a software package is targeted for the user or system. The *next time* the user logs on (or the computer is rebooted for computer-side policy), the Group Policy engine sees that the machine is tagged for Software Distribution and switches, just for this one time, back into synchronous mode. The net result: Windows XP and later machines typically require two logons (or reboots) for a user or computer to get a software distribution package.

Again, note that Windows 2000 Professional machines only require one logon (for user settings) or one reboot (for computer settings).

Folder Redirection is a wonderful tool. It has two modes: Basic Folder Redirection (which applies to everyone in the OU) and Advanced Folder Redirection (which checks which security groups the user is in). Windows XP and later machines won't get the effects of Basic Folder Redirection for two logons! And Windows XP and later machines won't get the effects of Advanced Folder Redirection for a whopping three logons. The first logon tags the system for a Folder Redirection change; the second logon figures out the user's security group membership; and the third logon actually performs the new Folder Redirection—synchronously for just that one logon.

We cover Folder Redirection in Chapter 10.

AUTOMATICALLY KILLING FAST BOOT WITH SPECIAL USER ACCOUNT ATTRIBUTES

Group Policy is only one of two areas affected by the Windows XP and later Fast Boot mechanism. If you change certain key user attributes, you could find that they are not updated until (you guessed it!) two logons. Those key attributes are:

- Roaming profile path (discussed in Chapter 9)
- The home directory
- Old-style logon scripts

Again, remember that Fast Boot is automatically disabled the first time any Windows XP or Windows 7 machine is started as a member of the domain. It is also disabled the first time any new user logs onto a Windows XP or Windows 7 client. In these situations, Windows XP and Windows 7 assume (correctly) that no GPO information is known and therefore must go out to Active Directory to get the latest GPOs. The net effect is that if settings for either (or both) Folder Redirection policy and Software Distribution policy already exist, the user will not require additional logons or reboots *the first time* they log onto a Windows XP or Windows 7 machine or when the computer is started for the first time after joining the domain.

This "Fast Boot" behavior can have another unintended side effect. That is, Group Policy-based logon scripts could possibly run *after* the user has already logged on. If that logon script was there to configure something important, the user's environment might not be ready for work until after this piece was complete!

But, once they are set (and detected), Fast Boot is officially, automatically killed by the system. From that point forward, since Fast Boot is turned off, changing those values again should only take one logon for you to see.

Read more about this topic here: http://support.microsoft.com/kb/305293.

MANUALLY TURNING OFF WINDOWS XP AND LATER FAST BOOT

If you want your Windows XP and later computers to start up a teeny-weeny bit faster (and have your users' Desktops pop up a teeny-weeny bit faster), by all means leave the default of Fast Boot on.

If you're doing some no-no's in Group Policy (namely setting up cross-domain Group Policy links or processing a lot of site-based GPOs), leaving Fast Boot on will, in fact, serve its purpose and likely make each and every startup and logon a wee bit faster.

My recommendation, however, is to get all your machines—Windows XP, Windows Vista, Windows 7, and Windows 2000 Professional—to act the same. That is, I suggest that you force your Windows XP and Windows 7 machines to act like Windows 2000 machines and perform synchronous policy processing during their startup and logon. To do this, you need to create a Group Policy that contains a setting to revert Windows XP and Windows 7 machines back to the old behavior. It might be a smidgen slower to log on, but no slower than your Windows 2000 machines already are.

This will make your Windows XP and Windows 7 machines perform initial policy processing at startup and logon—just like Windows 2000 machines. That is, the computer will start up, locate all GPOs, and then process them—before displaying the "Press

Ctrl+Alt+Delete to begin" prompt. Once the user is logged on, all GPOs are processed before the Desktop is displayed.

Troubleshooting Group Policy is now a heck of a lot more predictable because you're not trying to guess when Software Distribution, Folder Redirection, or even some settings from Administrative Templates are going to be processed. Since your Windows 2000 machines already act this way (and you can't make Windows 2000 Fast Boot like Windows XP), it probably would be a good enterprise supportability practice to have all machines in your environment act as similarly as possible—even if they are different operating systems.

To set Windows XP and later to the Windows 2000 synchronous behavior, for Initial Policy Processing, create and link a GPO (preferably at the domain level) to simply enable the policy setting named **Always wait for the network at computer startup and logon**. This policy can be found in the Computer Configuration ➢ Policies ➢ Administrative Templates ➢ System ➢ Logon. The name of this policy setting is a bit confusing. It would have been better, in my opinion, to name it **Make All Client Machines Process GPOs Like Windows 2000**. But they didn't.

Don't give the name of the policy setting **Always wait for the network at computer startup and logon** too much contemplation, even though it's confusing. It does not mean that the machine will just "hang" there until it sees the network during startup and logon. Its job is only to make Windows XP and Windows 7 machines act like Windows 2000.

Remember, to force Windows XP and Windows 7 machines to receive this computer policy (or any computer policy), the computer account must be within the site, domain, or OU where you set the policy. If you set this policy at the domain level (and enforce it to ensure that it cannot be blocked), you're guaranteed that all Windows XP and later machines in your domain will get the policy.

By performing this at the domain level and enforcing the link, all your machines—Windows XP, Windows 7, Windows 2000, and Windows 2003— will receive the message. But remember that policy settings meant for Windows XP or other operating systems won't affect Windows 2000 machines.

Forcing Background Policy Processing

You get a phone call from the person who handles the firewalls and proxy servers at your company. He tells you that he's added an additional proxy server for your users to use when going out to the Internet. Excitedly, you add a new GPO that affects Xavier's and Seven's user objects so they can use the new proxy server via Internet Explorer Maintenance Settings. But you're impatient.

You know that when you make this setting, it's going to take between 90 and 120 minutes to kick in. And you don't want to tell Seven or Xavier to log off and log back on to get the policy—they wouldn't like that much.

In cases like these, you might want to bypass the normal wait time before background policy processing kicks in. The good news is that you can run a simple command that tells the client to skip the normal background processing interval and request an update of new or changed GPOs from the server right now. Again, only new GPOs or GPOs that have changed on the server in some way will actually come down and be reflected on your client machines.

But, because you're impatient, you want to see Xavier on Windows XP and Seven on her Windows 7 machine start using that new proxy server setting that you plunked into that GPO right away. So you physically trot out to each of their machines, and enter the gpupdate command to manually refresh the GPOs.

Note that the gpupdate command can refresh either the User or the Computer half of a GPO, or both. The syntax is gpupdate /Target:Computer, /Target:User, or (again) just gpupdate by itself to trigger both.

Running gpupdate while Xavier is logged onto his Windows XP machine immediately gives him the new settings in the GPO you just set. This is, of course, provided the Domain Controller that Xavier and his Windows XP machine are using has the replicated GPO information. Ditto for Seven on her Windows 7 machine.

Additionally, gpupdate can figure out if newly changed items require a logoff or reboot to be active. Since Windows XP and later default behavior is to enable Fast Boot, Software Distribution and Folder Redirection settings are processed only at future logon times. Therefore, specifying gpupdate with a /Logoff switch will figure out if a policy has changed in Active Directory such that a logoff is required and then automatically log you off. If the updated GPO does not require a logoff, the GPO settings are applied and the currently logged-on user remains logged on.

Similarly, with Windows XP's and Windows 7's Fast Boot enabled, GPOs that have Software Distribution settings will require a reboot before the software will be available. Therefore, specifying gpupdate with a /boot switch will figure out if a policy has something that requires a reboot and automatically reboot the computer. If the updated GPO does not require a reboot, the GPO settings are applied, and the user remains logged on.

The /Logoff and /boot switches are optional.

> For information about how to turn off Windows XP's and Windows 7's Fast Boot and make it act like Windows 2000, refer to the section "Manually Turning Off Windows XP and Later Fast Boot" earlier in this chapter.

GPUpdate /force **Command for Windows XP vs. Windows 7 (and Windows Server 2008)**

There is one peculiarity about the gpupdate /force command when run in Windows XP. If there's a GPO that deploys software to your user or computer and you run the gpudpate /force command, sometimes it gets confused and thinks that the underlying GPOs have changed—even though they haven't. So, when it gets confused, gpupdate will express that a reboot (or logoff) is needed to get the full set of GPOs. However, this isn't strictly correct.

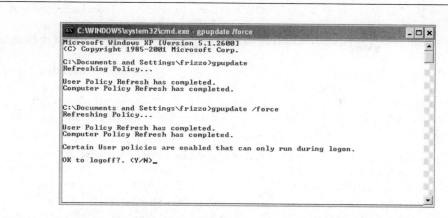

With Windows Vista and onward, Microsoft has cured this strange inconsistency. The newer gpupdate does something different: it informs you that during the next foreground refresh, it will occur synchronously to ensure that all policy is applied.

Security Background Refresh Processing

Even before Microsoft had the big, internal security hurrah, some modicum of security was built into the Group Policy engine. As I've stated, all Group Policy clients process GPOs when the background refresh interval comes to pass—but only those GPOs that were new or changed since the last time the client requested them.

Wally is on a Windows 2000 machine, and he's been logged on for four hours. Likewise, Xavier has been logged onto his Windows XP machine for four hours and Seven has been logged onto her Windows 7 machine for four hours.

Imagine for a second that there was a GPO in Active Directory named "Remove Run menu from Start Menu" and its function was to do just that. The client would certainly do so according to the initial policy processing rules and/or the background refresh processing rules.

Assuming that the underlying GPO doesn't get any policy settings modified or any new policy settings or that the GPO itself doesn't get removed, the client already knows to accept this edict. The client just accepts that things haven't changed and, hence, keeps on truckin'. Only a change inside the GPO will trigger the client to realize that new instructions are available, and the client will execute that new edict during its background policy processing.

Now, let's assume that we anoint Wally, Xavier, and Seven as local administrators of their Windows 2000, Windows XP, and Windows 7 machines, respectively. Since Wally, Xavier, and Seven are now local administrators, they have total control to go around the Group Policy engine processes and make their own changes. These changes could nullify a policy you've previously set with a GPO and allow them to access and change features on the system that shouldn't be changed. In this case, there are certainly going to be situations in which the GPOs on the Domain Controllers don't change, but certain parts of the workstation should remain locked down anyway.

Of course, the right answer is to only give people you absolutely trust access to local Administrator accounts. You should never give regular users Administrator accounts if you can possibly help it.

But, with that being said, let's examine two potential exploits of the Group Policy engine if a local administrator does choose to do so.

Group Policy exploit example #1: Going around an administrative template   Consider the calc.exe program we are forced to run every time someone uses a computer in Human Resources. We created a GPO named "Auto-Launch calc.exe" and enabled the policy setting named **Run these programs at user logon** within it. We linked the GPO to the Human Resources Computers OU. Our edict affected all users on our computers (including our administrators) so that calc.exe ran for everyone (because the GPO was linked to an OU containing the computer). Imagine, then, that someone with local administrative privileges (such as Wally) on the workstation changes the portion of the Registry that is affected, as shown in Figure 3.1.

FIGURE 3.1   A simple deletion of the Registry entry will nullify our policy setting.

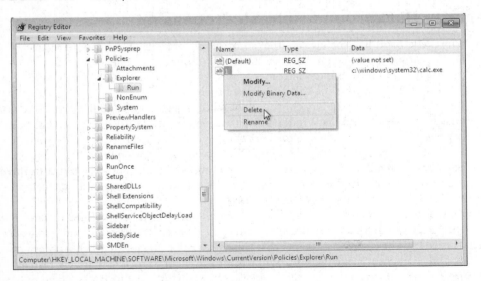

After the local administrator changes the setting, calc.exe simply won't run. (Again, only local administrators can make this change. Mere mortals do not have access to this portion of the Registry.) We're now at risk; a local administrator did the dirty work, and now all users on this workstation are officially going around our policy. Ninety minutes or so later, the background refresh interval strikes, and the client computer requests the background refresh from the GPOs in Active Directory. You might think that this should once again lock down the "Auto-Launch calc.exe" ability. But it doesn't. This ability won't get relocked down on reboot, either. Why? Because the Windows client thinks everything is status quo. Because nothing has changed in the underlying GPO in Active Directory that is telling the client its instruction set changed.

In this example, the Group Policy processing engine on the client thinks it has already asked for (and received) the latest version of the policy; the Group Policy processing engine doesn't know about the nefarious Registry change the local workstation administrator performed behind its back. Windows clients are not protected from this sort of attack by default. However, the protection can be made stronger. (See the section "Mandatory Reapplication for Nonsecurity Policy" later in this chapter.) Okay, this example exploit is fairly harmless, but it could be more or less damaging depending on precisely which policy settings we are forcing on our clients (as seen in this next example).

Group Policy exploit example #2: Going around a security policy setting   Via Group Policy, we use the material in the appendix to create a security template (and corresponding security policy) that locks down the \windows\repair directory with specific file ACLs (for Windows XP machines). For this example, imagine we set the \windows\repair directory so that only the Domain Administrators have access. Then, behind our backs, Xavier, now a local administrator, changes these file ACLs to allow everyone full control of these sensitive files. Uh-oh, now we could have a real problem on our hands.

Windows offers protection to handle cleanup for exploits of these two types. Let's see how that works.

In the first example, we went around the **Run these programs at user logon** policy setting by forcefully modifying the Registry. Running calc.exe for every user on a particular computer isn't considered a security setting. So, *by default* there is no protection for Exploit #1 (note the emphasis on "by default"). But, before you start panicking, let's examine Exploit #2, which attempts to go around a security policy we set.

Background Security Refresh Processing

The Group Policy engine tries to clean up after examples such as Exploit #2 by asking for a special background refresh—just for the security policy settings. This is called the *background security refresh* and is valid for every version of Windows.

Every 16 hours, a Group Policy client asks Active Directory for all the GPOs that contain "security stuff" (not just the ones that have changed). And, all that security stuff inside those GPOs are reapplied. This ensures that if a security setting has changed on the client (behind the Group Policy engine's back), it's automatically patched up within 16 hours.

To reiterate, background security refresh helps secure stuff on the client only every 16 hours and only if the setting is security related. So, within a maximum of 16 hours, the \windows\repair directory would have the intended permissions rethrust upon it. Okay, great. But in Exploit #1, our evil administrator went around the **Run these programs at user logon** policy setting. And the background security refresh would *not* have enforced our intended will upon the system. Running calc.exe is not considered a security policy setting. "How do we secure *those* exploits?" I hear you cry. "Read on," I reply. (Hey, that rhymed.)

You can manually change this security refresh interval in two ways. First, you can edit the local workstation's Registry at:

```
HKEY_LOCAL_MACHINE\SOFTWARE\Microsoft\
Windows NT\CurrentVersion\Winlogon\GPExtensions\
{827D319E-6EAC-11D2-A4EA-00C04F79F83A}\
MaxNoGPOListChangesInterval
```

and leverage a REG_DWORD signifying the number of minutes to pull down the entire security policy (by default, every 16 hours, so 960 minutes). You can also use the Security Policy Processing policy, which is described in the section "Using Group Policy to Affect Group Policy" later in this chapter. For more information, see Microsoft Knowledge Base article 277543 at http://support.microsoft.com/kb/277543.

Mandatory Reapplication for Nonsecurity Policy

Your network is humming along. You've established the GPOs in your organization, and you've let them sit unchanged for several months. Wally logs on. Wally logs off. So does Xavier. And Seven. They each reboot their machines a bunch. But imagine for a moment that the GPOs in Active Directory haven't changed in months.

When your users or computers perform initial Group Policy processing or background policy processing, a whole lot of nothing happens. If GPOs haven't changed in months, there's nothing for the clients to do. Since the engine has already processed the latest version of what's in Active Directory, what more could it possibly need?

True, every 16 hours the security-related policy settings are guaranteed to be refreshed by the background security refresh. But what about Exploit #1 in which Wally (who was anointed as a local workstation administrator) went around the **Run these programs at user logon** policy setting by hacking his local Registry?

Well, running calc.exe isn't a security policy. But it still could be thought of as a security hole you need to fill (if you were running something really important every time a user logged in). With a little magic, you can force the nonsecurity sections of Group Policy to automatically close their own security holes. You can make the nonsecurity sections of Group Policy enforce their settings, even if the GPOs on the servers haven't changed. This will fix exploits that aren't specifically security related. You'll learn how to do this a bit later in the section "Affecting the Computer Settings of Group Policy."

The general idea is that once the nonsecurity sections of Group Policy are told to mandatorily reapply, they will do so whenever an initial policy processing or background refresh processing happens.

You can choose to (optionally) mandatorily reapply the following areas of Group Policy, along with the initial processing and background refresh:

- Registry (Administrative Templates)
- Internet Explorer Maintenance

- IP Security

- EFS Recovery Policy

- Wireless Policy

- Disk Quota

- Scripts (by Scripts I mean the notification of changes to scripts, not the actual rerunning of scripts after the appointed time)

- Security

- Folder Redirection

- Software Installation

- Wired Policy

Note that most of the new CSEs for Windows 7 (like Printers and Windows Search) aren't in that list. But Wired (new for Windows 7) and Wireless Policy (updated for Windows 7) made it. Why some and not others? Beats me. I think someone just forgot to add them in during the rush-rush to get Vista out the door, and then, again for Windows 7. As it stands, you cannot change these defaults using any built-in policy settings.

As you'll see in the section "Affecting the Computer Settings of Group Policy," you can use the GUI to select other areas of Group Policy to enforce along with the background refresh.

To recap, if the GPO in Active Directory has *actually* changed, you don't have to worry about whether it will be automatically applied. Rather, mandatory reapplication is an extra safety measure that you can choose to place on your client systems so your will is always downloaded and re-embraced, not only if an existing GPO has changed or a new GPO has appeared. And, you can specify specific Group Policy sections that you wish to do this for.

 As you'll see in Chapter 7, a bit more is going on between the client and the server. Underneath the hood, the client keeps track of the GPO *version number*. If the version number changes in Active Directory, the GPO is flagged as being required for download; it is then redownloaded and applied. If the version number stays the same in Active Directory, the Group Policy isn't redownloaded or applied. Stay tuned for more on GPO version numbers in Chapter 7.

Manually Forcing Clients to Process GPOs (Revisited)

In "Forcing Background Policy Processing" earlier, I talked a bit about what happens if you set up a new GPO (or change an existing one) and get impatient. That is, you want to force your client systems to embrace your new settings.

As I've said, there's no way (with the tools in the box) from on high to shout to your client computers and proclaim, "Accept my latest GPOs, ye mere mortals and puny systems!"

If you want to kick off policy processing on a client, you need to trot on over to it to kick it in the shins.

You use gpupdate on Windows XP and later machines. But, again, note that the command-line tools have slightly different switches and behaviors.

The /force switch in GPupdate.exe will ensure that all policy-related settings are processed by the workstation—*regardless* of whether the underlying GPO has changed in Active Directory. Instead of waiting 16 hours, you can rush the hands of time and force the background policy refresh processing to strike.

The command is typically specified as:

gpupdate /force

Other options are available in conjunction with /force, such as the ability to log off the user or to reboot the machine should a foreground policy be required (in the case of, say, Software Distribution).

The Windows 7 (and Windows Server 2008) /force switch is a bit smarter than previous operating system versions. This is because in previous versions of the operating systems (like Windows XP), it might suggest a reboot or a logoff when one wasn't specifically needed. Here in Windows 7, it seems to know better than to make these suggestions when not needed.

Windows 2000 does not have the GPupdate.exe command; it uses Secedit.exe. With that in mind, you can perform the same "force" idea using the commands:

secedit /refreshpolicy machine_policy /enforce

and

secedit /refreshpolicy user_policy /enforce

Special Case: Moving a User or a Computer Object

When you move a user or a computer within Active Directory, Group Policy may not immediately apply as you think it should. For instance, if you move a computer from the **Human Resources Computers** OU to another OU, that computer may still pull GPOs from the **Human Resources Computers** OU for a while longer. This is because the computer may get confused about where the accounts it's supposed to work with are currently residing.

The userenv process syncs with Active Directory every so often to determine if a user or a computer has been moved.

This happens, at most, about every 30 minutes or so.

Once resynced, background processing continues as it normally would—only this time the user and computer GPOs are pulled from the new destination. If you move a user or a computer, remember that Group Policy processing continues to pull from the old location until it realizes the switch.

And don't forget that replication takes a while within your site and, also, potentially *between* Active Directory sites.

Altogether, the maximum wait time after a move to get GPOs pulled from a new location is as follows:

- 30 minutes (the maximum Active Directory synchronization time) *and*

- 90 minutes (the maximum Group Policy default background refresh rate) *and*

- 30 minutes (the maximum Group Policy default background refresh rate offset)

So that's the time it takes to replicate the change, plus a maximum of 150 minutes.

It could and usually does happen faster than that, but it can't take any longer. This behavior is important to understand if you move an entire OU (perhaps with many computers) underneath another OU!

Windows Vista and later machines are supposed to have a special trick up their sleeves. If you know the computer or user account has been moved (and, hence, would get different Group Policy settings), you can just run `gpupdate /force`, which double-checks where both the user and computer account live in Active Directory. Once the location is found, it applies GPOs specifically for that new location.

I say "supposed to" because in practice, I'm not sure it works perfectly 100 percent of the time. My suggestion is that if you move a user around, then log off and log back on. If you move a computer around, reboot the machine. Only then are you sure to get the latest settings.

An old KB article with an associated hotfix was supposed to shore up Windows XP and 2003, and you can find it here: `http://support.microsoft.com/kb/891630`. I tried it, and it just didn't work that great for me.

Policy Application via Remote Access, Slow Links, and after Hibernation

You will certainly have situations in which users take their Windows machines on the road and access your Active Directory and servers remotely via dial-up or VPN.

All versions of Windows, by default, will detect the speed of the connection and make a snap judgment about whether to process Group Policy. However, different operating systems determine the speed differently.

Windows 2000 and Windows XP Group Policy over Slow Network Connections

If the Windows 2000 or Windows XP machine uses TCP/IP to connect to the network and the connection is 500 kilobits/second (Kbps) or greater, it is considered fast enough to process Group Policy.

However, Windows 2000 and Windows XP sometimes have trouble figuring out what the speed actually is. Windows 2000 and Windows XP use ICMP (the same protocol that Ping utilizes) to figure out the speed. However, many router administrators have turned off ICMP at the routers. When this happens, and Windows 2000 and Windows XP can't ping their Domain Controllers, they just give up and don't process Group Policy.

And this is bad—because the whole point of figuring out the speed of the link is to help hone in on exactly which portions of Group Policy will apply over a slow link.

And what happens if your user's Windows 2000 or Windows XP laptop is off the network for three days? When they connect back, their Windows 2000 or Windows XP laptop will have tried and tried and tried to refresh policy. However, since a Domain Controller wasn't available, it just keeps on trying.

However, when the user finally does reconnect, Windows 2000 or Windows XP will finally find a Domain Controller. But this could take (you guessed it) up to 120 minutes (90 minutes, plus the 30 minute offset) for the refresh interval to finally come to pass. Vista and later improves on this (see the next section).

For the record, Windows Server 2003 acts the same way Windows XP does. But it's unlikely you're going to have Windows Server 2003 on a laptop that VPNs in from a hotel room.

Again, these machines use ICMP and Ping to figure out if they're on slow networks. For a very interesting sidebar, check out "Ping: Good, Evil, and Funny."

Ping: Good, Evil, and Funny

Ping, ping, ping.

Turns out that Ping (using the ICMP protocol) can carry a payload inside that ping packet. Turns out that ping payload can be used for good (i.e., the useful `ping` command), evil (look up "Ping of Death" on Wikipedia), or to make a funny.

Turns out that when Windows 2000 or Windows XP is pinging the server, it's got something in its payload. And guess what it is? It's a picture of the word "Microsoft." (Not really even the logo—just the word, as a graphic.)

If you read certain documentation regarding slow link detection, you will find Microsoft referring to the payload as a JPEG image—but they never tell or show you what it is.

Until now, this picture was a well-hidden secret. To dig it out, we—well, Thorbjörn, the book's technical editor—extracted it from the embedded resources in `userenv.dll`—where it is stored as a binary stream called "JPEG."

So, without further ado, the hidden message in Windows XP and Windows 2000's ping (presented in exact grainy quality and size) is:

Microsoft

Windows 7 Group Policy over Slow Network Connections

Windows Vista and later uses a different mechanism than Windows XP (or Windows 2000 or Windows Server 2003) to determine if the link is slow. Windows 7's Group Policy speed detection mechanism depends on an updated Windows component called *Network Location Awareness 2*, or *NLA 2*, for short.

NLA 2 is pretty simple (and there's nothing you need to configure). NLA 2 for Windows 7 has two jobs:

1. NLA 2 checks to see if the link is slow. This test doesn't use ICMP, so if router administrators have turned off ICMP, the calculation will still work. (See the next section, "What Is Processed over a Slow Network Connection?" for why you should care about what is processed over a slow network connection.)

2. NLA 2 calls out to the universe every so often and asks, "Is there a Domain Controller available NOW?" If the answer is "No!" then Group Policy cannot be updated. Pretty simple. However, if the answer is "Yes!" updated Group Policy could, theoretically, be processed, right?

This might be useful when a user has been working at the beach, disconnected for several days, then finally dials up or comes into the office. However, before doing anything, the Group Policy engine kicks in and asks one more question: "Did I miss the last background refresh interval?" (for instance, if the computer was hibernated, and therefore turned off, for three days).

If the answer is "Yes," then the Group Policy engine immediately performs (what amounts to) a `gpupdate` (no `/force`) to refresh Group Policy since the last time the user and computer made contact.

Why is the Group Policy engine so specific about finding out whether it missed the last background refresh interval? The Group Policy engine asks this question because NLA could have determined that the computer was ever-so-briefly off the network—and then back on again. And, if that's the case, there was nothing to miss, so nothing is updated. You wouldn't want it to trigger every time it went off and back on the network. That would be a veritable flurry of Group Policy updating! In other words, the Group Policy ensures that the Windows Vista and later machine was off the network for a goodly amount of time before asking for a refresh.

Again, Windows Server 2008 acts the same way Windows Vista and later do. But, it's unlikely you're going to have Windows Server 2008 on a laptop and VPN in from the beach.

What Is Processed over a Slow Network Connection?

So, if the connection is deemed fast enough, *portions* of Group Policy are applied.

Surprisingly, even if the connection is deemed "not fast enough," several sections of Group Policy are *still* applied. Security settings, Software Restriction Policy settings (Windows XP and later), and Administrative Templates are *guaranteed* to be downloaded during logon over a slow connection regardless of the speed. And there's nothing you can do to change that (not that you should want to). Additionally, included in security settings are EFS (Encrypting File System) Recovery Policy, and IPsec (IP Security) policy. They are also always downloaded over slow links.

WARNING   The Group Policy interface suggests that downloading of EFS Recovery Policy and IPsec policy can be switched on or off over slow links. This is not true. (See the note in the section "Using Group Policy to Affect Group Policy" later in this chapter.)

If the user connects using RAS before logging onto the workstation (using the "Log on using dial-up connection" check box as seen in Figure 3.2), the security and Administrative Templates policy settings of the Computer node of the GPO are downloaded and applied to the computer once the user is authenticated. Then, the security and Administrative Templates policy settings of the User node of the GPO are applied to the user.

FIGURE 3.2   If you select "Log on using dial-up connection," you first process GPOs in the foreground (when Fast Boot is disabled).

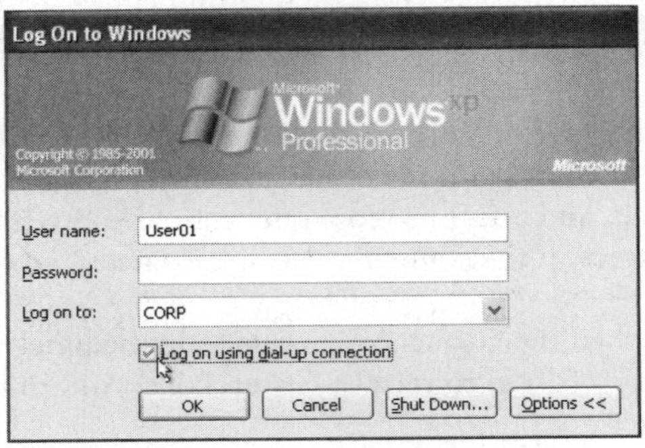

![Log On to Windows dialog box showing Windows XP Professional login with User name "User01", empty Password field, Log on to "CORP", and a checked "Log on using dial-up connection" checkbox, with OK, Cancel, Shut Down..., and Options buttons.]

If you've got a Windows 7 machine handy, you'll notice there is no "Log on using dial-up connection" available by default. To get this to show up, you'll need to create a VPN connection. And while creating it, select the option "Allow other people to use this connection." For more information, see an older Windows Vista posting here: http://tinyurl.com/ypgw8n.

Anyway, setting this up for Vista and Windows 7 machines is likely worth it; in doing so, you can enable users to achieve a foreground policy process. You can see the result of doing so in Figure 3.3.

If the user connects using RAS after logging onto the workstation (say, via VPN using the Network Connections icons), the security policy settings and the Administrative Templates policy settings for the user and computer are not applied right away; rather they are applied during the next normal background refresh cycle (every 90–120 minutes by default).

Other sections of Group Policy are handled as follows during a slow connection:

Internet Explorer maintenance settings   By default, these are not downloaded over slow links. (You can change this condition using the information in "Using Group Policy to Affect Group Policy" later in this chapter.)

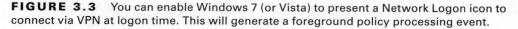

FIGURE 3.3   You can enable Windows 7 (or Vista) to present a Network Logon icon to connect via VPN at logon time. This will generate a foreground policy processing event.

Folder Redirection settings   By default, these are not downloaded over slow links. (Again, you can change this condition using the information in "Using Group Policy to Affect Group Policy.")

Scripts (logon, logoff, startup, and shutdown)   By default, script updates are not downloaded over slow links. (You can change this condition using the information in "Using Group Policy to Affect Group Policy." Also see the sidebar "Processing and Running Scripts over Slow Links" later in this chapter.)

Disk quota settings   By default, these are not downloaded over slow links. (You can change this condition using the information in "Using Group Policy to Affect Group Policy.") The currently cached disk quota settings are still enforced.

Software installation and maintenance   By default, these are not downloaded over slow links. More specifically, the offers of newly available software are not shown to users. Users do have the ability to choose whether to pull down the latest versions of applications at their whim. You can torture your dial-in users by changing the behavior of how offers are handled and by permitting the icons of new software to be displayed. They will hate you after you do this, but that is for you and them to work out. See the corresponding setting described later in this chapter in "Using Group Policy to Affect Group Policy." More information about Group Policy Software Installation can be found in Chapter 11.

Software Restriction policy (Windows XP and later)   These are guaranteed to download over slow links. You cannot turn off this ability. More information about Software Restriction Policy can be found in Chapter 8.

802.11 wireless policy (Windows XP and later)   By default, these are not downloaded over slow links. (You can change this condition using the information in "Using Group Policy to Affect Group Policy.") The currently cached 802.11 policy settings are still enforced.

802.3 wired policy (Windows Vista and later)   By default, these are not downloaded over slow links. (You can change this condition using the information in "Using Group Policy to Affect Group Policy.")

Administrative templates   These are guaranteed to download over slow links. You cannot turn off this ability.

EFS recovery policy   These are guaranteed to download over slow links. You cannot turn off this ability. The interface has an option that makes it appear as if you can turn off this ability, but you can't.

IPsec policy   These are guaranteed to download over slow links. You cannot turn off this ability. Again, the interface has an option that makes it appear as if you can turn off this ability, but you can't.

Group Policy Preference Extensions   The Group Policy Preference Extensions, which we'll explore in Chapter 5, are all guaranteed to download and process over slow links. You cannot turn off this ability.

You can change what is considered fast enough for all these policy categories from 500Kb to whatever speed you desire (independently for the Computer half and the User half). This is detailed in the section "Using Group Policy to Affect Group Policy."

Processing and Running Scripts over Slow Links

If your users try to run scripts while using slow links, they (and you) might notice some interesting behavior. First, computer startup scripts will not run over slow links. This just isn't supported by the Group Policy engine.

However, one enterprising friend of mine wrote his own service to explicitly do this *after* the user was logged on. Neato.

That being said, logon scripts are currently still fair game. However, many factors play into whether the scripts will run.

When a user is dialed in over a slow link, the scripts policy itself will not process. That is, it will not receive information about new or updated scripts. The actual *running* of the scripts is a different matter altogether and is irrespective of whether the user has a slow connection. Therefore, if you applied the script policy while on a high-speed connection (for example, a home office LAN) and then a user logs on over a dial-up connection, scripts will run; the script policy has already been downloaded and set for takeoff. Indeed, your script policy might tell the client to execute the script from the server, which may or may not be available.

But until your users come back to the headquarters, they won't get updates to that script policy if any have occurred. For instance, if the script policy states that the script should be run from an alternate server location, this information won't be downloaded until they come back into headquarters.

Windows 2000 and Windows XP (or later) have slightly different behaviors for the actual running of the scripts. Windows 2000 requires that the SYSVOL (NETLOGON share) be accessible for the scripts to even attempt to run. If the machine cannot see SYSVOL, no scripts will run.

Windows XP and later have addressed this problem, but it's thorny. If the machine is 100 percent offline (and, hence, SYSVOL isn't available), the scripts will indeed run. But if the system determines it's on a fast connection and SYSVOL is unavailable, scripts won't run.

Always Get Group Policy (Even on the Road) with DirectAccess and UAG (Maybe)

Microsoft is touting two technologies for "seamless network access"—DirectAccess (in Windows Server 2008 R2) and Unified Access Gateway (UAG).

Here's the idea of both (they're built on the same technologies).

In short, both technologies promise a way for laptops to simply "always be on the network"—if they're really at headquarters or in the coffee shop. Now if that sounds a little scary, there's supposed to be lots and lots of security involved getting these solutions up and going. And, personally, I haven't tried them out yet.

But the *promise* is quite interesting. The promise is that, once set up, your laptops are, well, "always on the network." And if they're always on the network, they just always get Group Policy, naturally.

Since I haven't tested these solutions, you'll have to stay tuned for an update on www.GPanswers.com. But for now, if you want to read about DirectAccess (part of Windows Server 2008), check out www.microsoft.com/directaccess.

If you want to read about UAG (part of Forefront), check out:

```
http://blogs.technet.com/edgeaccessblog/archive/2009/06/22/
introducing-uag-directaccess-solution.aspx
```

or

```
http://tinyurl.com/ykmgnkm.
```

Again, I think this is a great idea. Let's hope they deliver on the promise.

Using Group Policy to Affect Group Policy

At times, you might want to change the behavior of Group Policy. Amazingly, you actually use Group Policy settings to change the behavior of Group Policy! Several Group Policy settings appear under both the User and Computer nodes; however, you must set the policy settings in each section independently.

Affecting the User Settings of Group Policy

The Group Policy settings that affect the User node appear under User Configuration ➤ Policies ➤ Administrative Templates ➤ System ➤ Group Policy. Remember that user accounts must be subject to the site, domain, or OU where these GPOs are linked in order to be affected. Most of these policy settings are valid for any Windows machine, although some are explicitly designed and will operate only on Windows XP, Windows Vista, Windows 7, and so on.

The following sections list the policy settings that affect the user side of Group Policy.

Group Policy Refresh Interval for Users

This setting changes the default User node background refresh rate of 90 minutes with a 0–30 minute positive randomizer to almost any number of refresh and randomizer minutes you choose. Choose a smaller number for the background refresh to speed up Group Policy on your machines, or choose a larger number to quell the traffic that a Group Policy refresh takes across your network. There is a similar refresh interval for computers, which is on an alternate clock with its own settings. A setting of 0 is equal to 7 seconds. Set to 0 only in the test lab.

Group Policy Slow Link Detection

You can change the default definition of *fast connectivity for users* from 500Kbps to any speed you like. Recall that certain aspects of Group Policy are not applied to machines that are determined to be coming in over slow links. This setting specifies what constitutes a slow link for the User node. There is an identically named policy setting located under the Computer node (explored later in this chapter) that also needs to be set to define what is slow for the Computer node. Preferably set these to the same number. Note that you can set the **Group Policy Slow Link Detection** policy setting to zero to disable it.

Group Policy Domain Controller Selection

GPOs are written to the PDC emulator by default. When users (generally Domain Administrators or OU administrators) are affected by this setting, they are allowed to create new GPOs on Domain Controllers other than the PDC emulator. (See Chapter 7 for more information on this setting and how and why to use it.)

Create New Group Policy Object Links Disabled by Default

When users (generally Domain Administrators or OU administrators) are affected by this setting, the GPOs they create will be disabled by default. This ensures that users and computers are not hitting their refresh intervals and downloading half-finished GPOs that you are in the process of creating. Enable the GPOs when finished, and they will download during their next background refresh cycle.

Default Name for Group Policy Objects

If a user has been assigned the rights to create GPOs via membership in the Group Policy Creator Owners group and has also been assigned the rights to link GPOs to OUs within Active Directory, the default name created for GPOs is "New Group Policy Object." You might want all GPOs created at the domain level to have one name, perhaps AppliesToDomain-GPO, and all GPOs created at the **Human Resources** OU level (and all child levels) to have another name, maybe AppliestoHR-GPO. Again, in order for this policy to work, the user's account with the rights to create GPOs must be affected by the policy.

Enforce Show Policies Only

When users (generally Domain Administrators or OU administrators) are affected by this setting, the "Only show policy settings that can be fully managed" setting (explored in Chapter 6) is forced to be enabled. This prevents the importation of "bad" Administrative Templates (ADM files), which have the unfortunate side effect of tattooing the Registry until they are explicitly removed. (See Chapter 6 for more information on using all types of ADM templates.) Note, however, that the updated GPMC will always show "bad" ADM templates and, hence, this isn't needed when using the updated GPMC (the one with RSAT) on your management station.

Turn Off Automatic Update of ADM Files

You'll learn all about ADM files (and this particular policy setting) in Chapter 6. But, in essence, ADM template files are the underlying "definitions" of what's possible in Group Policy land (when you use pre-Vista management machine). When you use Vista (and later) management machines a new mechanism called ADMX files is used to define policy settings. Here's the 10-second "before Chapter 6" crash course. ADM templates start out in life on your local machine running the older GPMC. Then, they're "pushed up" into the GPO for future reference.

When it comes to ADM template behavior, the default behavior is to check the local machine's default location—that is, the \windows\inf folder—to see if the ADM template (locally) is newer than the one stored inside the GPO. If it's newer—bingo, the one in the GPO is overwritten.

By default, this check for an update occurs every time you double-click the Administrative Templates section of any GPO as if you were going to modify it. However, if you enable this setting, you're saying to ignore the normal update process and simply keep on using the ADM template you initially used. In other words, you're telling the system you'd prefer to keep the initial ADM template regardless of whether a newer one is available. (See Chapter 6 for critical information on updating ADM templates when service packs are available for Windows XP or Windows 2003.)

Disallow Interactive Users from Generating Resultant Set of Policy Data

Users affected by this setting cannot use gpresult.exe, the Group Policy Modeling, Group Policy Results tasks in the GPMC, or the old-and-crusty RSOP.MSC (which shouldn't be used anyway).

Enabling this setting locks down a possible entry point into the system. That is, it prevents unauthorized users from determining the current security settings on the box and developing attack strategies.

This policy setting is valid only when applied to Windows XP workstations and Windows 2003 servers (even though the policy specifies "At least XP and Server 2003").

In my testing, this setting did not affect Windows Vista and later machines.

Affecting the Computer Settings of Group Policy

The Group Policy settings that affect the Computer node appear under Computer Configuration ➢ Policies ➢ Administrative Templates ➢ System ➢ Group Policy. Once computers are affected by these policy settings, they change the processing behavior of Group Policy. Remember that the computer accounts must be subject to the site, domain, or OU where these GPOs are linked in order to be affected.

Turn Off Background Refresh of Group Policy

When this setting is enabled, the affected computer downloads the latest GPOs for both the user and the computer, according to the background refresh interval—but it doesn't apply them. The GPOs are applied when the user logs off but before the next user logs on. This is helpful in situations in which you want to guarantee that a user's experience stays the same throughout the session.

Group Policy Refresh Interval for Computers

This setting changes the default Computer node background refresh rate of 90 minutes with a 30-minute randomizer to almost any number of refresh and randomizer minutes you choose. Specify a smaller number for the background refresh to speed up Group Policy on your machines, or choose a larger number to quell the traffic a Group Policy refresh causes across your network. A similar refresh interval for the User node is on a completely separate and unrelated timing rate and randomizer. A setting of 0 equals 7 seconds. Set to 0 only in the test lab.

Group Policy Refresh Interval for Domain Controllers

Recall that Domain Controllers are updated regarding Group Policy changes within five minutes. You can close or widen that gap as you see fit. The closer the gap, the more network chatter. Widen the gap, and the security settings will be inconsistent until the interval is hit. A setting of 0 equals 7 seconds. Set to 0 only in the test lab.

User Group Policy Loopback Processing Mode

We'll explore this setting in detail in the next chapter.

Allow Cross-Forest User Policy and Roaming User Profiles

This policy is valid only in cross-forest trust scenarios. I'll describe how these work and how this policy works in Chapter 4 in the section "Group Policy with Cross-Forest Trusts."

This policy setting is valid only when applied to Windows XP/SP2 systems and later.

Group Policy Slow Link Detection

You can change the default definition of *fast connectivity* from 500Kbps to any speed you like. Recall that certain aspects of Group Policy are not applied to those machines that are deemed to be coming in over slow links. Independently, an identically named policy setting that exists under the User node (explored earlier) also needs to be set to define what is slow for the User node. Preferably, set these to the same number.

Turn Off Resultant Set of Policy Logging

As you'll see in Chapter 7, users on Windows XP can launch the Resultant Set of Policy (RSoP) snap-in by typing **RSOP.MSC** at the command prompt. Enabling this policy setting doesn't prevent its launch but, for all intents and purposes, disables its use. This policy setting disables the use for the currently logged-on user (known as the interactive user) as well as anyone trying to get the results using the remote features of the RSoP snap-in.

This policy setting is valid only when applied to Windows XP workstations and Windows 2003 servers (even though the policy specifies "At least XP and Server 2003").

In my testing, this setting did not affect Windows Vista and later machines. Your mileage may vary.

 On Windows Vista and later, regular users can only see the user half of the RSoP by default. They must be delegated the "Read Group Policy Results data" right over the computer they want to gather the information for. We talked about this in Chapter 2's "Special Group Policy Operation Delegations" section.

Remove Users' Ability to Invoke Machine Policy Refresh

By default, mere-mortal users can perform their own manual background refreshes using gpupdate. However, you might not want users to perform their own gpupdate. I can think of only one reason to disable this setting: to prevent users from sucking up bandwidth to Domain Controllers by continually running gpupdate. Other than that, I can't imagine why you would want to prevent them from being able to get the latest GPO settings if they were so inclined. Perhaps one user is performing a denial-of-service (DoS) attack on your Domain Controllers by continually requesting Group Policy—but even that's a stretch.

Even if this policy is enabled, local administrators can still force a gpupdate. But, again, gpupdate only works when run locally on the machine needing the update.

This policy setting is valid only when applied to Windows XP and newer and requires a reboot to kick in.

Disallow Interactive Users from Generating Resultant Set of Policy Data

This policy is similar to the **Turn off Resultant Set of Policy logging** setting but affects only the user on the console. Enabling this setting might be useful if you don't want the interactive user to have the ability to generate RSoP data but you still want to allow administrators to get the RSoP remotely. Again, RSoP and its related functions are explored in Chapter 3.

This policy setting is supposed to be valid only when applied to Windows XP and later. But I tried it on a Windows 7 machine and it had no effect. You may have a different experience.

Registry policy Processing (where *p* in policy is lowercase)

Yes, it's weird that I had to spell out the capitalization of the *P* in Policy here, because, depending on your circumstances, you might see two "Registry Policy Processing" entries: one with an uppercase *P* in Policy and with a lowercase *p* in Policy. Weird, right?

Totally weird. And I'll explain why you might have both "Registry Policy/policy Processing" nodes, or just one, a little later in this chapter in the sidebar "The Missing Group Policy Policy Settings."

This setting affects how your policy settings in the Administrative Templates subtrees react (and, generally, any other policy that affects the Registry). Once this policy setting is enabled, you have two other options:

Do Not Apply during Periodic Background Processing   Typically, Administrative Templates settings are refreshed every 90 minutes or so. However, if you enable this setting, you're telling the client not to ever refresh the Administrative Templates in the GPOs that are meant for it after the logon. You might choose to prevent background refresh for Administrative Templates for two reasons:

- When the background refresh occurs, the screen may flicker for a second as the system reapplies the changed GPOs (with their policy settings) and instructs Explorer.exe to refresh the Desktop. This could be a slight distraction for the user every 90 minutes or so.

- You might choose to disable background processing so that users' experiences with the Desktop and applications stay consistent for the entire length of their logon. Having settings suddenly change while the user is logged on could be confusing.

My advice is to leave this setting alone unless you're seriously impacted by the background processing affecting your users' experience.

Process Even If the Group Policy Objects Have Not Changed   If this setting is selected, the system will update and reapply the policy settings in this category even if the underlying GPO has not changed when the background refresh interval occurs. Recall that this type of processing is meant to clean up should an administrator have nefariously gone behind our backs and modified a local setting.

 You cannot turn off Registry policy processing over slow links. They are always downloaded and applied.

Internet Explorer Maintenance Policy Processing

Once enabled, this policy setting has three potential options:

Allow Processing across a Slow Network Connection   Select this check box to allow Internet Explorer Maintenance settings to download when logging on over slow links. Enabling this could cause your users to experience a longer logon time, but they will adhere to your latest Internet Explorer wishes.

Do Not Apply during Periodic Background Processing   If this option is selected, the latest Internet Explorer settings in Active Directory GPOs will not be downloaded or applied during the background refresh.

Process Even If the Group Policy Objects Have Not Changed   If this option is selected, it updates and reapplies the policy settings in this category even if the underlying GPO has not changed. Recall that this type of processing is meant to clean up should a user or an administrator have nefariously gone behind our backs and modified a local setting.

Software Installation Policy Processing

Once enabled, this policy setting has two potential options:

Allow Processing across a Slow Network Connection   As I stated, by default, software deployment offers are not displayed to users connecting over slow links. This is a good thing; allowing users to click the newly available icons to begin the download and installation of new software over a 56K dial-up line can be tortuous. Use this setting to change this behavior.

 If you have already distributed software via Group Policy and an offer has been accepted by a client computer (but perhaps not all pieces of the application have been loaded), setting this selection will likely not help, and your users may experience a long delay in running their application over a slow link. For more information on how to best distribute software to clients who use slow links, see Chapter 11.

Process Even If the Group Policy Objects Have Not Changed   For Software Installation, I cannot find any difference whether this option is selected or not, though Microsoft has implied it might correct some actions should the software become damaged. Since software deployment offers are only displayed upon logon or reboot (otherwise known as foreground policy processing), in my testing this setting seems not to have any effect.

Users can still get caught in a trap regarding Group Policy Software Installation and slow links. That is, if they accept a "partial offer" while connected over a fast link, then try to request more of the same application, the computer will attempt to download that part over a slow link. This happens regardless of how the "Allow Processing across a Slow Network Connection" policy setting is set. See the Software Installation settings described in Chapter 11 for more information.

Folder Redirection Policy Processing

Once enabled, this policy setting has two potential options:

Allow Processing across a Slow Network Connection   Recall that the Folder Redirection policy is changed only at logon time. Chances are you won't want dialed-in users to experience that new change. Rather, you'll want to wait until they are on your LAN. If you want to torture your users and allow them to accept the changed policy anyway, use this setting to change this behavior.

Process Even If the Group Policy Objects Have Not Changed   I cannot find any difference whether this setting is selected or not, though Microsoft has implied it might correct some folder-redirection woes should the username get renamed.

Folder Redirection settings are discussed in detail in Chapter 10.

Scripts Policy Processing

Once enabled, this policy setting has three potential options:

Allow Processing across a Slow Network Connection   Recall that, by default, new or changed startup, shutdown, logon, and logoff scripts are not downloaded over slow networks. Change this option to allow the download over slow links. The actual running of the scripts is a different process, as discussed earlier in the sidebar "Processing and Running Scripts over Slow Links."

Do Not Apply during Periodic Background Processing   This option will not allow the newest script instructions to be downloaded. See the sidebar "Processing and Running Scripts over Slow Links."

Process Even If the GPOs Have Not Changed   This option will allow the newest script instructions to be downloaded even if the GPOs have not changed. See the sidebar "Processing and Running Scripts over Slow Links."

Security Policy Processing

Once enabled, this policy setting has two potential options:

Do Not Apply during Periodic Background Processing   Recall that the security settings are refreshed on the machines every 16 hours, whether or not they need it. Checking this option will turn off that refresh. I recommend that you leave this as is. However, you might want to consider enabling this setting for servers with high numbers of transactions that require all the processing power they can muster.

Process Even If the GPOs Have Not Changed   Recall that after 16 hours, this policy category is always refreshed. With this option enabled, the security policies will be reprocessed during *every* refresh cycle.

IP Security Policy Processing

Once enabled, this policy setting has three potential options:

Allow Processing across a Slow Network Connection   When selected, this setting (shown in Figure 3.4) does nothing. IP Security settings are always downloaded, regardless of whether the computer is connected over a slow network. So, you might be asking yourself, what happens when you select this check box? Answer: nothing—it's a bug in the interface. To repeat: IP Security is always processed, regardless of the link speed.

 IPsec policies act slightly different from other policy setting categories. IPsec policy settings are not additive. For IP Security, the last applied policy wins.

Do Not Apply during Periodic Background Processing   If this option is selected, the latest IP Security settings in Active Directory GPOs will not be downloaded or applied during the background refresh.

Process Even If the Group Policy Objects Have Not Changed   If this option is selected, it updates and reapplies the policy settings in this category even if the underlying GPO has not changed. Recall that this type of processing is meant to clean up should a user or an administrator have nefariously gone behind our backs and modified a local setting.

EFS Recovery Policy Processing

Once enabled, this policy setting has three potential options:

Allow Processing across a Slow Network Connection   When this option is selected, it does nothing.

FIGURE 3.4 The "Allow processing across a slow network connection" setting is not used for IP Security or EFS settings (all versions of Windows).

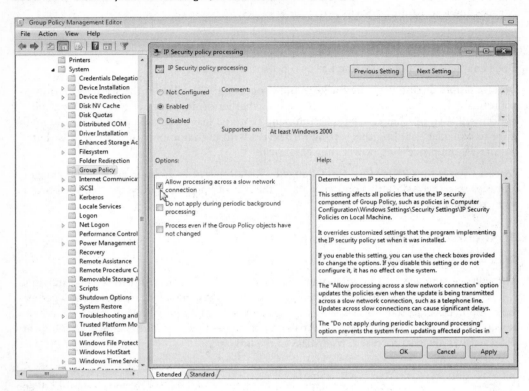

Like IP Security, the EFS recovery settings are always downloaded—even over slow networks. This is the same bug shown earlier in Figure 3.4. To repeat, EFS recovery policy is always processed, regardless of link speed.

 EFS recovery policies act slightly different from other policy setting categories. EFS recovery policies are not additive; the last applied policy wins.

Do Not Apply during Periodic Background Processing If this option is selected, the latest EFS recovery settings in Active Directory GPOs are not downloaded or applied during the background refresh.

Process Even If the Group Policy Objects Have Not Changed If this option is selected, it updates and reapplies the policy settings in this category even if the underlying GPO has not changed. Recall that this type of processing is meant to clean up should a user or an administrator have nefariously gone behind our backs and modified a local setting.

Wireless Policy Processing

If this policy setting is enabled, it has three potential options:

Allow Processing across a Slow Network Connection   Check this option to allow the latest wireless policy settings to download when the user is logging on over slow links. Enabling this could cause your users to experience a longer logon time.

Do Not Apply during Periodic Background Processing   If this option is selected, the latest wireless policy settings will not be downloaded or applied during the background refresh.

Process Even If the Group Policy Objects Have Not Changed   If this option is selected, it updates and reapplies the policy settings in this category even if the underlying GPO has not changed. Recall that this type of processing is meant to clean up should a user or an administrator have nefariously gone behind our backs and modified a local setting.

Wired Policy Processing

If this policy setting is enabled, it has three potential options:

Allow Processing across a Slow Network Connection   Check this option to allow the latest wired policy settings to download when the user is logging on over slow links. Enabling this could cause your users to experience a longer logon time.

Do Not Apply during Periodic Background Processing   If this option is selected, the latest wired policy settings will not be downloaded or applied during the background refresh.

Process Even If the Group Policy Objects Have Not Changed   If this option is selected, it updates and reapplies the policy settings in this category even if the underlying GPO has not changed. Recall that this type of processing is meant to clean up should a user or an administrator have nefariously gone behind our backs and modified a local setting.

This policy setting is valid only when applied to Windows Vista or later or Windows Server 2008.

Disk Quota Policy Processing

If this policy setting is enabled, it has three potential options:

Allow Processing across a Slow Network Connection   Check this option to allow the latest disk quota policy settings to download and apply when the user logs on over slow links. Enabling this could cause your users to experience a longer logon time.

Do Not Apply during Periodic Background Processing   If this option is selected, the latest disk quota policy settings will not be downloaded or applied during the background refresh.

Process Even If the Group Policy Objects Have Not Changed   If selected, this option updates and reapplies the policy settings in this category even if the underlying GPO has not changed. Recall that this type of processing is meant to clean up should a user or an administrator have nefariously gone behind our backs and modified a local setting.

Always Use Local ADM Files for Group Policy Object Editor

ADM files are the underlying language that creates policy settings in pre–Windows Vista versions. I'll talk more about ADM files and how to best use them in Chapter 6. However, for reference, if a computer is affected by this policy setting, the Group Policy Object Editor attempts to show the text within the ADM files from your local %windir%\inf directory (usually c:\windows\inf). If the ADM file is different inside the GPO than on your local c:\windows\inf directory, you could end up seeing different settings and Explain text than what's inside the GPO.

 This policy is valid only when applied to Windows 2003 servers but not **WARNING** (strangely) Windows XP management stations.

Indeed, if this policy is enabled, you might now see totally different policy settings than were originally placed in the GPO. However, you might want to enable this policy setting if you know that you will always be using one specific management station. Stay tuned for Chapter 6 to see how to use this function.

Turn Off Local Group Policy Objects Processing

If a Windows Vista or later computer is affected by this policy setting, then whatever is set within the local GPOs is ignored.

This can be useful if a machine is originally used in a workgroup (nondomain joined environment) and then it's joined to the domain. In that case, you might want to ensure that no user has any lingering policy settings that will specifically affect them. Hence, your desire would be to control everything from Active Directory and not anything from the local level.

Of course, this policy setting only works when being delivered from Active Directory (not when it's set locally).

This policy setting affects only Windows Vista and later machines (including Windows Server 2008 machines and later).

Startup Policy Processing Wait Time

This policy setting helps with timeouts when processing Group Policy. The policy setting only exists for Windows Vista and later; however, the facility to control these timeouts exists in other operating systems (like Windows XP/SP2 with a Registry hack).

Check out KB article 840669 (found here: http://tinyurl.com/88tbo) if you want to implement this setting for Windows XP/SP2 and earlier machines.

The Missing Group Policy Policy Settings

If you were just following along, book in your lap, Windows 7 management machine by your side, you likely didn't see anything strange or out of the ordinary.

But if you were following along with Windows Server 2008 (or 2008 R2) as your management machine, you might have seen a gaggle of "extra" policy settings that we didn't cover in the section "Using Group Policy to Affect Group Policy"

Seriously, this is weird, so stick with me. In Figure 3.5 you can see two screenshots. The left shows the Windows 7 management machine view of the Computer Configuration ➢ Policies ➢ Administrative Templates ➢ System ➢ Group Policy node. The right shows the same thing, except seen from a Windows Server 2008 management machine.

FIGURE 3.5 For Windows 7 (left) you'll see fewer policy settings in the Group Policy node as compared to Windows Server 2008 (right).

Setting	State	Comment
Allow Cross-Forest User Policy and Roaming User Profiles	Not configured	No
Software Installation policy processing	Not configured	No
Disk Quota policy processing	Not configured	No
EFS recovery policy processing	Not configured	No
Folder Redirection policy processing	Not configured	No
Internet Explorer Maintenance policy processing	Not configured	No
IP Security policy processing	Not configured	No
Registry policy processing	Not configured	No
Scripts policy processing	Not configured	No
Security policy processing	Not configured	No
Wired policy processing	Not configured	No
Wireless policy processing	Not configured	No
Disallow Interactive Users from generating Resultant Set of P...	Not configured	No
Turn off background refresh of Group Policy	Not configured	No
Turn off Local Group Policy objects processing	Not configured	No
Remove users ability to invoke machine policy refresh	Not configured	No
Group Policy slow link detection	Not configured	No
Group Policy refresh interval for computers	Not configured	No
Group Policy refresh interval for domain controllers	Not configured	No
Always use local ADM files for Group Policy Object Editor	Not configured	No
Turn off Resultant Set of Policy logging	Not configured	No
Startup policy processing wait time	Not configured	No
User Group Policy loopback processing mode	Not configured	No

Setting	State
Logging and tracing	
Allow asynchronous user Group Policy processing when logging o...	Not configured
Allow Cross-Forest User Policy and Roaming User Profiles	Not configured
Always use local ADM files for Group Policy Object Editor	Not configured
Applications Policy Processing	Not configured
Data Sources Policy Processing	Not configured
Devices Policy Processing	Not configured
Disallow Interactive Users from generating Resultant Set of Polic...	Not configured
Disk Quota policy processing	Not configured
Drive Maps Policy Processing	Not configured
EFS recovery policy processing	Not configured
Environment Policy Processing	Not configured
Files Policy Processing	Not configured
Folder Options Policy Processing	Not configured
Folder Redirection policy processing	Not configured
Folders Policy Processing	Not configured
Group Policy refresh interval for computers	Not configured
Group Policy refresh interval for domain controllers	Not configured
Group Policy slow link detection	Not configured
Ini Files Policy Processing	Not configured
Internet Explorer Maintenance policy processing	Not configured
Internet Settings Policy Processing	Not configured
IP Security policy processing	Not configured
Local Users and Groups Policy Processing	Not configured
Network Options Policy Processing	Not configured
Network Shares Policy Processing	Not configured
Power Options Policy Processing	Not configured
Printers Policy Processing	Not configured
Regional Options Policy Processing	Not configured
Registry policy processing	Not configured
Registry Policy Processing	Not configured
Remove users ability to invoke machine policy refresh	Not configured
Scheduled Tasks Policy Processing	Not configured
Scripts policy processing	Not configured
Security policy processing	Not configured
Services Policy Processing	Not configured
Shortcuts Policy Processing	Not configured
Software Installation policy processing	Not configured
Start Menu Policy Processing	Not configured
Startup policy processing wait time	Not configured
Turn off background refresh of Group Policy	Not configured
Turn off Local Group Policy objects processing	Not configured

So, what are these "missing" definitions? These are the settings used to control, manage, and monitor the Group Policy Preferences settings you'll learn about in Chapter 5. You'll see specific Group Policy Preferences items like **Printers Policy Processing, Shortcuts Policy Processing, Start Menu Policy Processing**, and all sorts of other Group Policy Preferences–specific settings.

And my favorite one is **Registry Policy Processing** (with an uppercase *P* in Policy) right next to its cousin **Registry policy processing** (with a lowercase *P* in policy.) The lower case *P* policy (**Registry policy processing**) is about how we handle the stuff inside the Administrative Templates node; you know—normal Group Policy settings like **Prevent Access to the Control Panel**. The uppercase *P* policy setting (**Registry Policy Processing**) is about the Registry node in the Group Policy Preferences (again, Chapter 5.)

Bizzaro, but now at least it's understandable.

Look closely, and you'll also see another whole node *within* the Group Policy node called "Logging and tracing."

Okay, so what gives?

We'll utilize and understand these settings in Chapter 5 and learn more about where they come from in Chapter 6. But since you can't wait that long, here's the abbreviated version. In short, the "definitions" of what's possible in Group Policy-land are stored in ADMX files (again, more detail—a lot more detail—in Chapter 6.) Turns out, though, that Windows 7's RSAT and Windows Server 2008 don't ship with the exact same definitions.

Kooky. The "missing" Group Policy settings are only available within Windows Server 2008 or Windows Server 2008 R2's "set" of definitions. And, yes, that set is downloadable if you don't want to rip it out of an existing Windows Server 2008 machine. This blog entry spells it all out: `http://tinyurl.com/kowj66` and the downloadable files are here: `http://tinyurl.com/mb6x5v` (though there are sure to be updates for Windows Server 2008 R2, so, I would try to track those down when available.)

In Chapter 6, we'll revisit this topic. I'll specifically show you how to make sure you always have the "latest set" of policy settings, so they're no mystery—you'll always have the latest set.

Final Thoughts

Group Policy doesn't just pick and choose when it wants to apply. Rather, a specific set of rules is followed when it comes time to process. Understanding these rules is paramount in helping you prevent potential Group Policy problems.

Many other things can affect the Group Policy engine, including loopback policy processing and how users connect over slow links. So be sure you really get these concepts before you run out and try them in real life.

Here are a few things to keep in mind:

Remember initial policy processing.   Windows 2000 (Workstation and Server), and all versions of Windows Server machines process all GPOs when the computer starts up or when the user logs on. And by default, XP and later perform initial policy processing only when a user has never logged in on the machine before (or if the computer has just joined the domain).

Remember background refresh policy processing (member servers).   For all machine types, regular member computers refresh some time after the user is logged on (usually 90 minutes or so).

Remember background refresh policy for Windows 7 and Windows XP.   By default, Windows XP and later workstations (like Windows 7) are unique and process GPOs *only* in the background (asynchronously). Some features, such as Software Distribution, Folder Redirection, and other functions, can take two reboots or logons to take effect.

Advanced Folder Redirection can take three logons to see an effect. This is because these special functions can be processed only in the foreground. You can turn off this feature as described earlier in this chapter.

Remember background refresh policy processing (Domain Controllers).   All Domain Controllers receive a background refresh every five minutes (after replication has occurred).

Security policy processing occurs every 16 hours.   For all operating systems, just the security settings within all GPOs are reprocessed and applied every 16 hours, regardless of whether security settings have changed. This ensures that all security functions in all GPOs are reprocessed if someone has manually gone around the security on the system.

Leverage "Process Even If the Group Policy Objects Have Not Changed."   You can force other Group Policy areas (such as Administrative Templates) to refresh during the background refresh interval. This will make those categories more secure and less susceptible to attack.

4

Advanced Group Policy Processing

In the previous chapter, we talked about basic Group Policy processing principles along with some special cases, including what happens over a slow link and how to manage the Group Policy engine itself—using Group Policy.

In this chapter, we'll explore some advanced scenarios. Here's the quick breakdown of what they are and why I think you'll be interested:

- If you've ever wanted to decide *when* and *where* a particular Group Policy should be applied, you're going to love WMI filters.

- If you've thought to yourself, "How do I get user-side settings to affect my computers?," you're going to love Loopback policy processing.

- And, if you've got multiple Active Directories tied together with cross-forest trusts, you'll want to understand how and when Group Policy applies.

So, let's get started with our advanced Group Policy processing.

 If you have any Windows NT machines kicking around out there, you might have old-school NTCONFIG.POL files, and you'll want to be sure to know how those fit together with modern Group Policy. Due to space constraints, we've taken that information out of this book. You can find it in any previous edition of this book.

WMI Filters: Fine-Tuning When and Where Group Policy Applies

In Chapter 2, I alluded to a power called WMI filters. I like to think of WMI filters as adding laser-sighting to the gun of Group Policy. With WMI filters, you can dive into and inspect the soul of your client machines, and if certain criteria are met, you can then apply the GPO to them.

While WMI filters can be used with any GPO, I find that people usually use them for targeting software via Group Policy Software Installation. I explore Group Policy Software Installation in Chapter 11.

Before we jump headlong into ferreting out the power of WMI filters, let's make sure we have the machinery necessary to wield this power:

- A domain with an updated schema (at least the Windows Server 2003 level)
- Your target clients are Windows XP or later

 Windows 2000 clients ignore WMI filters; for Windows 2000 clients, the GPO is always applied—regardless of the evaluation of the WMI filter.

WMI is a huge animal, and you can choose to filter on thousands of items. Hot items to filter on typically include the following:

- The amount of memory
- The available hard-drive space
- CPU speed
- A hotfix
- OS version or service pack level

But you don't have to stop there. You can get creative and filter GPOs on obscure items (if they exist and are supported by the hardware) such as the following:

- BIOS revision
- Manufacturer of the CD drive
- Whether a UPS is connected
- The rotational speed of the fan

The potential esoteric criteria you can query for, and then filter, goes on and on.

A silly example might be "Prevent Access to the Control when the machine has at least 128MB of memory."

Okay, perhaps that's a little too silly. You likely wouldn't care about showing or hiding desktop settings depending on the amount of RAM a computer has. But you can take the ideas here and use them in real examples. You can do things like this:

- "Only deploy Office 2007 when I have these hotfixes installed."
- "On Tuesdays at logon time, start up Excel."
- "Only install an operating system service pack when I have 256MB of RAM and 3GB of free hard drive space."

The idea is that either Group Policy will apply the GPO if the WMI filter evaluates to True or it will not apply the GPO if the WMI filter evaluates to False. Likewise, if "today" the GPO evaluates to True, but "tomorrow" it evaluates to False, the GPO will "fall out of scope" and then un-apply.

To give this a try, we'll first need some tools to help us figure out which pieces of WMI to query. We'll then take what we've learned and use the GPMC to create a WMI filter to specifically target the systems we want.

Unfortunately, I don't have room to dive into how or why WMI works on a molecular level. If you're unfamiliar with WMI, take a peek at:

```
http://msdn.microsoft.com/en-us/library/aa394582%28VS.85%29.aspx
```

shortened to `http://tinyurl.com/yjpojph`.

So, let's start off by creating a WMI filter and associating it with a GPO. Let's make an example that says "Turn off the ability to change Windows sounds when the RAM on the machine is over 128MB." Yes, yes, it's a positively silly example. But you'll be able to create your first WMI filter and associate it with a GPO, and see that it works.

Tools (and References) of the WMI Trade

To master WMI, you have to do a lot of work. You'll have to read up on and master four crucial pieces of WMI documentation, three of which are found at the following websites:

```
http://msdn2.microsoft.com/en-us/library/ms974579.aspx
```

(shortened to `http://tinyurl.com/yt4jlu`)

```
http://msdn2.microsoft.com/en-us/library/ms974592.aspx
```

(shortened to `http://tinyurl.com/2bjfkb`)

```
http://msdn2.microsoft.com/en-us/library/ms974547.aspx
```

(shortened to `http://tinyurl.com/2f464f`)

And you'll have to get the accompanying *Windows 2000 Scripting Guide* from Microsoft Press (2002)—the de facto (and very large-o) book on scripting—and work through all the hundreds of examples (at Amazon at `http://tinyurl.com/7yypc`). Yes, it's a Windows 2000 book, but it's awesome.

What? You don't have time for that? No problem! You can do the next best thing and "wing it." We'll use two tools to create WMI queries, and then we'll manually bend them into WMI filters.

- WMI CIM Studio is available on Microsoft's website. At last check, it was at `http://tinyurl.com/8zot`.

- And there's also the Scriptomatic version 2 tool (available at `http://tinyurl.com/5wdup`), which we'll be using for these examples.

The Scriptomatic tool was made by my pals, the "Microsoft Scripting Guys." The tool "enumerates" all the available WMI classes and then makes them available for an easy-breezy query. Note that you'll have to run the tool as an Administrator, or you'll get errors.

In Figure 4.1, the WMI class Win32_ComputerSystem is selected. Then, scriptomagically, all the WMI attributes in that class are exposed in a ready-to-run VBScript application. You can see them in Figure 4.1, including PartOfDomain, Status, WakeUpType, and the one we're after, TotalPhysicalMemory, which expresses the amount of RAM in this machine. Just click the Run button and you can see the output with the values on *this* machine.

FIGURE 4.1   The Scriptomatic version 2 tool from the "Microsoft Scripting Guys"

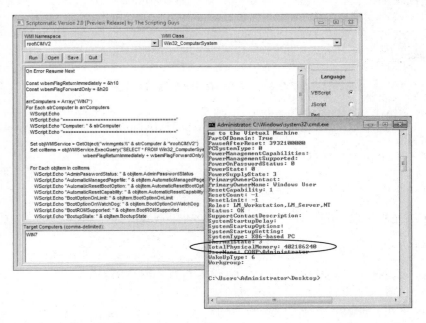

When you click Run, the script runs in a little prompt window. You can see that the TotalPhysicalMemory of this box is 402186240, which is 384MB. The point here, however, is that the unit measurement and expected output of this field is expressed in number of bytes. We'll leverage this information when we bend this WMI query into a WMI filter.

WMI Filter Syntax

You can start nearly all the WMI filters you'll create using Scriptomatic. All that's left is to wrap a little logic around the output. All the WMI filters we'll create have the following syntax:

```
SELECT * from Win32_{something}
WHERE {variable} [=,>,<,is, etc] {desired result}
```

Now, all we have to do is plug in the stuff we already know, and we're off and running. In this example, we're using `Win32_ComputerSystem`. We know the variable we want is *TotalPhysicalMemory*, and we know that we want it to be greater than 128MB, which we can represent as > 128000000. Yes, I know 128000000 isn't exactly 128MB of memory, but it's close enough. Anyway, when you put it all together, you get:

```
SELECT * from Win32_ComputerSystem WHERE TotalPhysicalMemory > 128000000
```

Easy as pie. However, not all WMI filters are this easy. Some WMI variable entries have text, and you must use quotes to specifically match what's inside the string to what's inside the WMI variable.

Creating and Using a WMI Filter

Once your WMI filter is in the correct syntax, you're ready to inject it into an existing GPO. Again, this can be any GPO you want.

Creating and using a WMI filter is a two-step process: creating and then using. (I guess that makes sense.)

WMI Filter Creation

Before you can filter a specific GPO, you need to define the filter in Active Directory. Follow these steps:

1. Fire up the GPMC, then drill down to the Forest ➤ Domains ➤ WMI Filters node.
2. Right-click the WMI Filters node and select New, as seen in Figure 4.2.

FIGURE 4.2 Right-click the WMI Filters node to create a WMI filter.

3. When you do, you'll be presented with the New WMI Filter dialog box, seen in Figure 4.3. You'll be able to type in a name and description of your new filter. Then, click the Add button, and in the Query field, just enter in the full SELECT statement from before.

FIGURE 4.3 This WMI query will evaluate to True when the machine has greater than 128MB of memory.

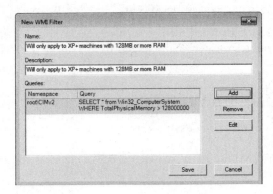

4. When you're done, click Save. Your query is now saved into Active Directory and can be leveraged for any GPO you want. We'll explore how to do that next.

WMI Filter Usage

Using the GPMC, it's easy to find the GPO you want and then leverage the WMI filter you just made. Follow these steps:

1. Locate the "Prohibit Changing Sounds" GPO you created (which should be linked to the domain level).

2. Click the Scope tab of the GPO.

3. In the WMI Filtering section, select the WMI filter you just created, as shown in Figure 4.4.

4. At the prompt, confirm your selection.

Now this GPO will only apply to Windows XP and later machines with 128MB of RAM or more. Note that Windows 2000 machines simply ignore WMI filters, so this GPO still (unfortunately) applies to them.

Final WMI Filter Thoughts

WMI filters can be a bit tough to create, but they're worth it. You can filter target machines that meet specific criteria for GPOs that leverage GPSI or any other Group Policy function. But keep two things in mind:

WMI performance impact WMI filters take some percentage of performance away each and every time Group Policy processing is evaluated. That is, at every logon, at startup, and every 90 minutes thereafter, you'll take a little performance hit because WMI filters are reevaluated. So, be careful and don't link a GPO to the domain level or every single Windows XP machine and later will work hard to evaluate that WMI query.

FIGURE 4.4   Choose the GPO (or GPO link) and select a WMI filter.

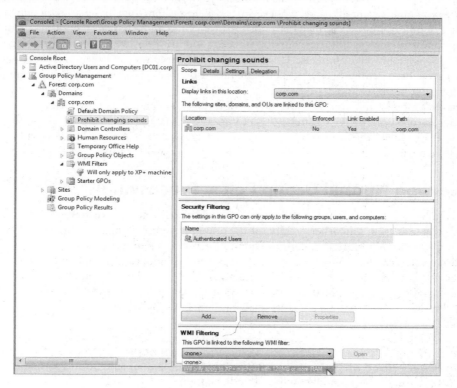

So, my example where I used the WMI filter on a GPO for the whole domain *isn't such a hot idea*. I did it only for the sake of the example, and you should try to avoid that kind of use in the real world.

The upshot: be careful where you link GPOs with WMI queries. You could seriously affect GPO processing performance. You'll definitely want to test your WMI filters first in the lab for performance metrics before you roll them out companywide.

WMI filters don't apply to Windows 2000   Windows 2000 machines are left out of the mix. They simply ignore the WMI filters placed on GPOs. When a Windows 2000 machine processes a GPO that leverages a WMI filter, it's as if the query always evaluates to True.

Return to Chapter 2 to review how to back up and restore WMI filters as well as how to delegate their creation and use.

Group Policy Loopback Processing

As you know, the normal course of Group Policy scope is local computer, site, domain, and then each nested OU. But sometimes it's necessary to deviate from the normal routine. For instance, you might want all users, whoever they are, to be able to walk up and log onto a specific machine and get the same User node settings. This can be handy in public computing environments such as libraries, nursing stations, and kiosks as well as manufacturing and production assembly environments. This is also critically necessary for Terminal Server environments, as discussed in the section "Group Policy Loopback—Replace Mode for Terminal Services" later in this chapter.

Wouldn't it be keen if you could round up all the special computers on which users need the same settings for an OU and force them to use these settings? Whoever logs onto those computers would get the same Internet Explorer settings (such as a special proxy) and logon scripts or certain Control Panel restrictions—just for those workstations.

Reviewing Normal Group Policy Processing

Recall that sometimes computers and users can each be relegated into different OUs. Indeed, any user from any other portion of the domain, say the Domain Administrator, could log onto WIN7 located under the **Human Resources Computers** OU.

When a user account contained in one OU logs onto a computer contained in another OU, the normal behavior is to process the computer GPOs based on the site, domain, and OU hierarchy and then process the user GPOs based on the site, domain, and OU hierarchy. This is true just by the rules of time: computers start up, their GPOs are processed, users log on, and their GPOs are processed.

Even when Windows XP/Windows 7's default of Fast Boot is turned off, that's generally the way things happen.

So, if the Domain Administrator were to sit down at the WIN7 machine in the **Human Resources Computers** OU, the normal course of events would apply the policy settings in the Computers node from the Default-First-Site, then the Corp.com domain, and then, finally, the **Human Resources Computers** OU. Next, the policy settings in GPOs linked to the user account would apply; first from the Default-First-Site and then only from the Corp.com domain (as the administrator account is not sitting under any OU in our examples).

With Group Policy Loopback processing, the rules change. There are two Group Policy Loopback modes: Merge and Replace. In both, the computer is tricked into forgetting that it's really a computer. It temporarily puts on a hat that says, "I'm a user," and processes the site, domain, and organizational unit GPOs as if it were a user. Kooky, huh? Let's take a look at the Merge and Replace modes.

For our examples, we'll pretend to have another machine called WIN7B. This is a new machine, just for this set of examples. It is not listed in Chapter 1 in the section "Getting Ready to Use This Book."

Group Policy Loopback—Merge Mode

When computers are subject to Group Policy Loopback—Merge mode, GPOs process in the normal way at startup (and at background refresh time): Computer node for site, for domain, and then for each nested OU. The user then logs on, and policy settings meant for that user are applied in the normal way: all GPOs are processed from the site, the domain, and then each nested OU.

But when computers are affected by Group Policy Loopback—Merge mode, the system determines where the computer account is and applies another round of User node settings—those contained in all GPOs that lead to that computer (yes, User node settings). This means that the logged-on user gets whacked with two different sets of User node policy settings. Here's the timeline:

- The computer starts up and gets the appropriate Computer node policy settings.

- The user logs on and gets the appropriate User node policy settings.

- The computer then puts on a hat that says, "I'm a user." Then all *User* node policy settings apply to the *computer*. Again, this happens because the computer is wearing the "I'm a user" hat.

The net result is that the user settings from the user's account and the user settings from the computer (which temporarily thinks it's a user) are equal to each other; neither is more important than the other, except when they overlap. In that case, the computer settings win, as usual.

The Group Policy Loopback—Merge mode is rarely used unless you need to modify a property in the user profile, but do it per computer.

Group Policy Loopback—Replace Mode

When computers are subject to Group Policy Loopback—Replace mode, Group Policy processes in the normal way at startup (and at background refresh time): Computer node for site, domain, and then each nested OU. The user then logs on, and GPOs meant for the user are totally ignored down the food chain for the logged-on user. Instead, the computer puts on an "I'm a user" hat, and the system determines where the computer account is but applies the User node settings contained in all GPOs that lead to that computer. Therefore, you change the balance of power so all users are forced to heed the User settings based on what is geared for the computer. Confused? Let's generate an example to "unconfuse" you.

By and large, Group Policy Loopback—Replace mode is more useful than Merge mode and works well in public computing environments such as labs, kiosks, classrooms, training machines, libraries, and so on. So let's work though an example to solidify our understanding of Replace mode. In this example, we'll perform a variety of steps:

1. Create a new OU called **Public Kiosk**.

2. Move a Windows 7 machine into the **Public Kiosk** OU. Again, use the WIN7B computer (a new computer for these examples.)

3. Create a new GPO for the **Public Kiosk** OU that performs two functions:

   - Disables the Control Panel so users cannot get to it.

   - Performs Group Policy Loopback—Replace mode processing so that *all* users are forced to embrace the setting. That is, no one logging onto the computers in the **Public Kiosk** OU will be unable to get into Control Panel—at all.

Setting All Who Log onto a Specific Computer to Use a Specific Printer

You might want to use the Group Policy Loopback—Merge mode to create a printer and apply it to anyone who uses a particular machine. For instance, you might want anyone who logs onto a machine on the fourth floor to automatically connect to the printer on the fourth floor. One way to do this is to run around to every machine on the fourth floor, log on as the user, and manually connect to the printer on the fourth floor.

If you've ever attempted this feat, you might have also tried to create a Group Policy startup script for a computer to attempt to connect everyone to a printer on the network—but it won't work. There is no user environment in which to house this newly created printer. So you have a paradox: how do you run a computer startup script for every user who sits down at a machine but run this startup script after the user is logged on? Group Policy Loopback—Merge mode comes to the rescue.

In both Loopback Processing modes, the computer doesn't think it's a computer. It temporarily puts on a user hat and processes the site, domain, and organizational unit GPOs as if it were a user.

With that in mind, you'll need to do several things:

1. Create a VB script that connects you to the printer you want. (Later in this sidebar, you'll see an example, ASSIGNHP4.VBS.)

2. Create an OU, say, **4th Floor Computers**, and move the computers on the fourth floor into it.

3. Create a new GPO on that OU and name it, say, "All computers get HPLJ4 Printer."

4. Drill down to the new GPO to Computer Configuration ➢ Policies ➢ Administrative Templates ➢ System ➢ Group Policy ➢ User Group Policy Loopback Processing mode, and specify that it be in Merge mode.

5. Drill down into User Configuration ➢ Windows ➢ Scripts ➢ Logon. Click Add to add a new file, click Browse to open the File Requester, copy the ASSIGNHP4.VBS script, and add it to the list to run.

Remember, in Loopback Processing mode, the computer thinks it's a user, so use User/Logon scripts, not Computer/Startup scripts.

Now, whenever you log on as any user to a computer in the **4th Floor Computers** OU, the GPOs meant for the user will be evaluated and run. The computer will then put on a user hat and run its own logon script, and you will get the printer assigned for every user on a computer.

Here is the ASSIGNHP4.VBS VB script you can use for the preceding example:

```
Set wshNetwork = CreateObject("WScript.Network")

    PrinterPath = "\\server1\HPLJ4"
    PrinterDriver = "HP LaserJet 4"
    WshNetwork.AddwindowsPrinterConnection PrinterPath, PrinterDriver
    WshNetwork.SetDefaultPrinter "\\server1\HPLJ4"
    Wscript.Echo "Default Printer Created"

Set wshNetwork = Nothing
```

Thanks to Richard Zimmerman of ABC Computers for the inspiration for this tip. Before you implement this tip, be sure to read Chapter 5 and Chapter 12, where I'll show you how to use ordinary Group Policy Preferences (GPPrefs) to get the same job accomplished. That is, I'll show you how to zap printers down to specific machines in a more efficient way. However, I'm leaving this example here because it's a firm demonstration, in general, of what Merge mode does.

Creating a New OU

To create a new OU called **Public Kiosk,** follow these steps:

1. Log onto the Domain Controller DC01 or Win7Management as Domain Administrator.

2. Choose Start ➢ All Programs ➢ Administrative Tools and select Active Directory Users and Computers.

3. Right-click the domain name, and choose New ➢ Organizational Unit. Enter **Public Kiosk** as the name in the New Object—New Organizational Unit dialog box.

WARNING
You are creating this new OU on the same level as **Human Resources.** Do not create this new OU underneath **Human Resources.**

Moving a Client into the Public Kiosk OU

In this case, we'll move a different computer, say WIN7B, into the **Public Kiosk** OU. Follow these steps:

1. In Active Directory Users and Computers, right-click the domain and choose Find to open the "Find Users, Contacts and Groups" dialog box.

2. In the Find drop-down, select Computers. In the Name field, type **WIN7B** (or the name of some other computer) to find the computer account of the same name. Once you've found it, right-click the account and choose Move. Move the account to the **Public Kiosk** OU.

Repeat these steps for all other computers you want to move to the **Public Kiosk** OU.

Creating a Group Policy Object with Group Policy Loopback—Replace Mode

We want the Display Properties dialog box disabled for all users who log onto WIN7B. To do this, we need to set two policy settings within a single GPO: **Prohibit Access to the Control Panel** and **User Group Policy Loopback Processing Mode**. Follow these steps using the GPMC:

1. Right-click the **Public Kiosk** OU, and choose "Create a GPO in this domain, and Link it here."

2. In the New GPO dialog box, name the GPO something descriptive, such as "No Control Panel—Loopback Replace."

3. Highlight the GPO and click Edit to open the Group Policy Management Editor.

4. To hide the Settings tab, drill down to User Configuration ➢ Policies ➢ Administrative Templates ➢ Control Panel ➢ and double-click the **Prohibit Access to the Control Panel** policy setting. Change the policy setting from Not Configured to Enabled, and click OK.

5. To enable Loopback processing, drill down to Computer Configuration ➢ Policies ➢ Administrative Templates ➢ System ➢ Group Policy and double-click the **User Group Policy Loopback Processing Mode** policy setting. Change the setting from Not Configured to Enabled, select Replace from the drop-down box, as shown in Figure 4.5, and click OK.

6. Close the Group Policy Management Editor.

Verifying That Group Policy Loopback—Replace Mode Is Working

You'll want to log onto WIN7B, but you'll need to restart it because Loopback processing doesn't seem to ever take effect until a reboot occurs. Since we're using Loopback Policy processing in Replace mode, you can choose any user you have defined—a mere mortal or even the administrator of the domain.

You should see that the link to Control Panel from the Start Menu is gone. But try this: right-click over the Desktop and select Personalize and note that no one can access the Display settings (which is part of Control Panel), as shown in Figure 4.6.

FIGURE 4.5   Choose the Loopback Processing mode desired, in this case, Replace.

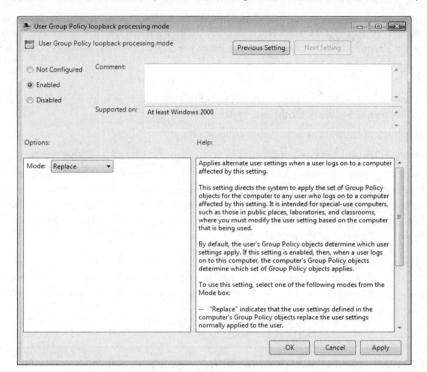

FIGURE 4.6   With Group Policy Loopback—Replace Mode processing enabled, all users are affected by a computer's setting.

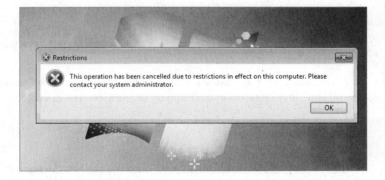

Group Policy Loopback—Replace Mode policy processing is powerful but is only useful for specialty machines. Additionally, you'll need to use it sparingly, because Loopback processing is a bit more CPU intensive for the client and servers and quite difficult to trouble-shoot should things go wrong.

Group Policy Loopback—Replace Mode for Terminal Services

Group Policy Loopback—Replace mode has one other major use: Terminal Services. If you have lots of servers and lots of users logging onto them, chances are you want everyone who logs onto your Terminal Services machines to have precisely the same settings, regardless of who they are.

The process of establishing these settings is straightforward:

1. Create an OU for your Terminal Services computers and give it an appropriate name, such as **Terminal Services Computers** OU.

2. Set Loopback Replace mode to apply to that OU.

3. Stuff your Terminal Services computer objects into the OU and reboot them.

Now any user policy settings within GPOs set on the **Terminal Services Computers** OU and everyone logging onto the Terminal Services computers will get the exact same settings.

All Windows Terminal Servers respond just fine to Loopback—Replace mode. Just be sure to stuff your Terminal Services computer objects into your designated OU, too, and then manually configure the policy settings on those computers as desired.

As an administrator, you might want to log onto Terminal Services machines, but you don't want the same settings as everyone else. To configure this, simply use the techniques found in Chapter 2 and filter the GPO containing the policy that performs the lockout for, say, Domain Administrators.

Yet Another Practical Use for Group Policy Loopback Mode

I don't know about you, but I just hate it when I walk up to a server and log on. Usually, I have no idea what the server's name, function, IP address, and so on could possibly be. In the NT 4 days, I used the following trick:

1. Fire up Windows Paint.

2. Create a BMP file that detailed the name, function, and IP address and save it as, say, c:\winnt\background.bmp.

3. Modify the .default user profile so that when no one was logged on at the console, the .bmp file was displayed. To do this, open the Registry of the local server and change:

   HKEY_USERS\.DEFAULT\Control Panel\Desktop\Wallpaper

to a path of c:\winnt\background.bmp.

But there was one major problem—as soon as I logged onto the server, the background went away (because my local profile took over), and 20 seconds later, I forgot what the machine's name, function, and IP address were. With Group Policy Loopback—Replace Mode policy, I discovered a cool trick; you can now force the same background BMP for every user who physically logs onto any given machine.

The idea is simple:

- Create the BMP file as explained earlier, and store it once again, locally, as c:\
windows\background.bmp.

- Create a new GPO on the Domain Controllers OU or on your own OU for your servers. Call the policy "Forced Background Wallpaper—Loopback Replace."

- Modify the User node of the policy as follows:

  1. Drill down through User Configuration ➤ Policies ➤ Administrative Templates ➤
  Desktop ➤ Active Desktop ➤ **Enable Active Desktop**, and set Enabled.

  2. Drill down through User Configuration ➤ Policies ➤ Administrative Templates ➤
  Desktop ➤ Active Desktop ➤ **Desktop Wallpaper**, and set Enabled. Set the wallpaper name to c:\windows\background.bmp.

  3. Drill down through User Node ➤ Administrative Templates ➤ Desktop ➤ Active
  Desktop ➤ **Allow Only Bitmapped Wallpaper**, and set Enabled.

  4. To modify the Computer node of the policy, drill down through Computer Configuration ➤ Policies ➤ Administrative Templates ➤ System ➤ Group Policy ➤
  and enable **User Group Policy Loopback Processing Mode**. Set to Loopback—Merge.

Now whenever anyone logs onto that server, they will get the exact same background
BMP! This is still true even if they usually get a background dictated via some other
Group Policy for their own personal account.

There is one more accompanying tip to seal the deal. If you've enabled Terminal Services Administration mode, by default you cannot see the wallpaper when coming in
over Terminal Services. Change the default behavior of Terminal Services by using the
Terminal Services Configuration application, right-clicking the RDP protocol, and selecting the Environment tab. Choose to view the wallpaper by deselecting the "Disable the
Wallpaper" check box.

A similar ability is available from the BGINFO tool, which you can download from
Microsoft's Sysinternals site at http://tinyurl.com/u6yy2. And it's dynamic, so if
something changes on the server, the background changes with it. However, this tip is
a useful example of how to use the Group Policy Loopback—Replace mode.

Additional Terminal Services Tips

As a side note, if your Terminal Services run at least Windows Server 2003, at your disposal
is an arsenal of policy settings designed to manage Windows 2003 Terminal Services. You'll

find two sets of Terminal Services policy settings for Windows 2003: one for users and one for computers:

- To manipulate Terminal Services computers, drill down to Computer Configuration ➢ Policies ➢ Administrative Templates ➢ Windows Components ➢ Terminal Services.

- To manipulate Terminal Services clients, drill down to User Configuration ➢ Policies ➢ Administrative Templates ➢ Windows Components ➢ Terminal Services.

Including information on how best to use the policy settings that configure Windows 2003 Terminal Services (and Windows Server 2008) is beyond the scope of this book. To that end, I recommend Christa Anderson's *Windows IT Pro Magazine* article "Using GPOs to Configure Terminal Services." You can find it at `http://tinyurl.com/2ojbyw`. Another interesting article from TechTarget can be found here: `http://tinyurl.com/lm7rek`.

Updates for Windows Server 2008 Terminal Server can be found at `http://tinyurl.com/m4muxd`.

One final parting tip regarding Terminal Services: Microsoft has a nice document that has a lot of tips and tricks for Terminal Services administrators vis-à-vis Group Policy. The document is named "Step-by-Step Guide for Configuring Group Policy for Terminal Services" and can be found here: `http://tinyurl.com/3dsydv`.

Group Policy with Cross-Forest Trusts

Windows 2003 domains brought a new trust type to the table: a forest trust (also known as a cross-forest trust). The idea is that if you have multiple, unrelated forests, you can join their root domains with one single trust; then, anytime new domains pop up in either forest, there is an automatically implied trust relationship.

Doing this requires a large commitment from all parties involved. All domains must be in at least Windows 2003 Functional mode, and all forests must be in Windows 2003 Functional mode. Only then is it possible to create cross-forest trusts via the Active Directory Domains and Trusts utility. For an example of an organization that might use this, see Figure 4.7.

In this example, all domains trust all other domains via the cross-forest trust. Indeed, a user with an account housed in bigu.edu, say, Sol Rosenberg, could sit down at a computer in either Corp.com or Widgets.corp.com and log onto his user account, which is maintained in bigu.edu.

When Sol (srosenberg) from bigu.edu logs onto any computer in domains below Corp.com (that is, Widgets.corp.com), the logon screen will not present BIGU as an option. To log on, Sol will need to type **srosenberg@ bigu.edu** as his logon ID along with his password. This is one of the limitations of cross-forest trusts.

FIGURE 4.7   Here's one example of how a cross-forest trust can be used.

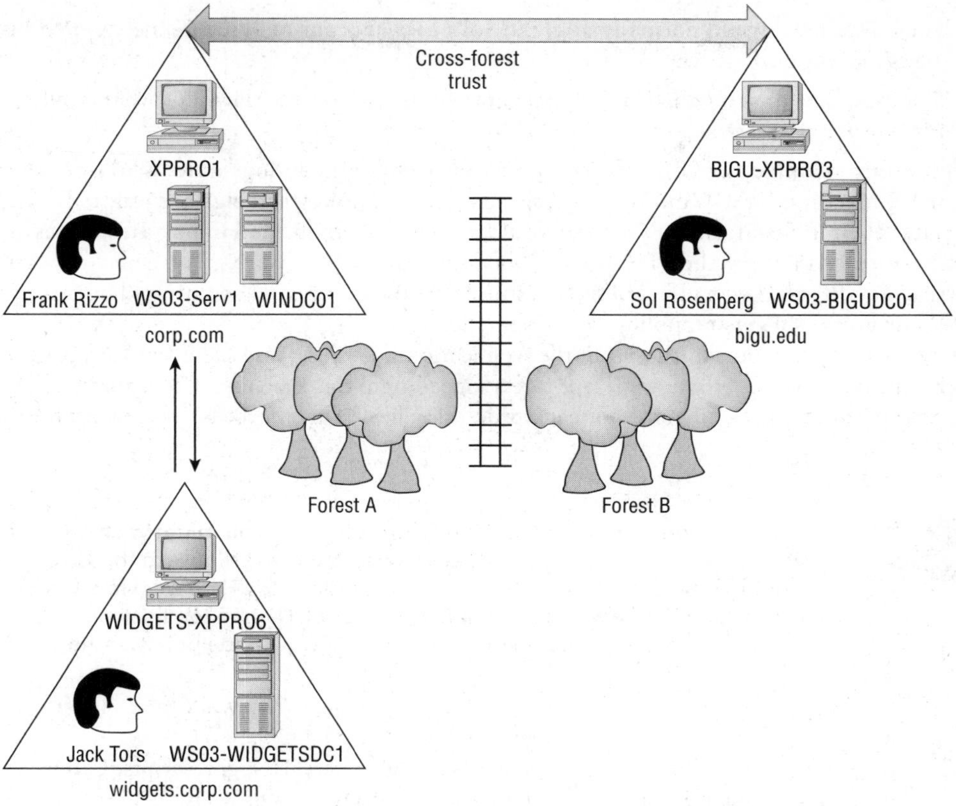

What Happens When Logging onto Different Clients across a Cross-Forest Trust?

So what happens when Sol from bigu.edu has access to various computer types in the Corp.com forest?

Here's where things get weird, so try to stay with me. Imagine that Sol Rosenberg in bigu.edu is also the SQL database administrator for a server named WS03-Serv1 over in Corp.com in the **Human Resources SQL-Servers** OU. From time to time, Sol gets in his car and travels from the BigU campus over to the WS03-Serv1 computer sitting at the Corp.com headquarters. He sits down, logs on locally to the console (where he's been granted access), and he *doesn't* get the GPOs meant for him (and therefore doesn't get his own policy settings).

Instead, the server processes GPOs as if it were using Group Policy Loopback Processing—Replace mode. What does this mean?

- The GPOs that would normally apply to Sol's user account in bigu.edu are ignored by the Windows 2003 server.

- The computer puts on an "I'm a user" hat and says, "Give me the GPOs that would apply to me if I were a user."

So, in our example, we can see that when Sol from bigu.edu logs onto WS03-Serv1 (or an XP machine, or a Windows 7 machine, etc.), his policy settings are ignored. The computer then looks at the GPOs that would apply to users in the **Human Resources SQL-Servers** OU (where the WS03-Serv1 account resides).

Since no GPOs linked to the **Human Resources SQL-Servers** OU contain policy settings geared for users, Sol gets no policy settings applied.

After logging on, you can check out the Application Event Log and see Event ID 1109, which states that Sol is "from a different forest logged onto this machine. Cross forest Group Policy processing is disabled and Loopback processing has been enforced in this forest for this user account."

 For your own testing and to solidify this concept, you might wish, just for now, to link an existing GPO (that has user policy settings) to the **Human Resources Computers** OU. For instance, link the "Hide Desktop Tab" GPO to the **Human Resources Computers** OU, then log back on as Sol. Sol's user account will be affected by the GPO with the policy setting.

At this point, you're likely scratching your head in disbelief. Why wouldn't Sol just get the "normal GPOs" that *should* affect him?

The answer is simple: if Sol were assigned software (Chapter 11), logon scripts, Group Policy Preferences (Chapter 5), or other potentially dangerous settings, *our* machine's stability could be affected.

By going into Loopback mode, our systems are protected from stuff that we might not want to happen to it. Since we're not administrating Sol, we don't know what potential harm Sol's settings might do.

Strange? Yes, but it works, and this becomes strangely more logical the more you think about it.

If you put your head around it for a while, you can design your Active Directory to account for this "phenomenon." That is, if you set up user-side policy settings for users and link them to OUs that contain computers, users from "foreign" domains across the cross-forest trust will get the user policy settings *you* intend for them to—not what *their* administrator wanted.

It's a mind-bender.

So, yes, this can be complicated, and thankfully, only a few administrators have to stay up nights thinking about it. But if you have cross-forest trusts—congrats—you're now one of us.

Turns out, something "extra" also occurs here that is out of the ordinary. That is, when users log onto your computers across a cross-forest trust, their user profiles are not allowed to be downloaded onto your machines either. That's right—user profiles from that foreign domain are apparently "potentially dangerous" too, like GPOs from that foreign domain.

So a user logging in from a foreign domain across a cross-forest trust might see something like what's in Figure 4.8.

FIGURE 4.8   When users log on across a cross-forest trust, their access to their own user profiles is restricted.

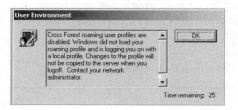

 Event ID 1109 will be generated on the client machine in the Application Event log stating that a user is "...from a different forest."

Disabling Loopback Processing When Using Cross-Forest Trusts

Let's recall the two things that happen across a cross-forest trust:

- Loopback Replace processing is turned on for users who use your computers across a cross-forest trust.

- Roaming user profiles are disabled for users who use your computers across a cross-forest trust.

Perhaps you want to restore the "normal" behavior. You can do that. Once you apply this setting, target users on these machines will get their "usual" set of policy settings (which, again, would come from their domain—not yours.)

To do this, you need to locate the **Allow Cross-Forest User Policy and Roaming User Profiles** policy setting. Drill down through Computer Configuration ➢ Policies ➢ Administrative Templates ➢ System ➢ Group Policy. Note that the policy setting says "At least Windows Server 2003" but it will affect Windows XP/SP2 machines and later as well.

Just create a GPO and link it to the computers you want to "make normal" again. But, again, the point is that this decreases the security on the system, because you won't know what "the other administrator" has dictated for the user. And then the user could be running evil nasty programs or scripts on your client machines.

Older Machine Types and Cross-Forest Trusts

Here's the weird—well, potentially weirdest—part. Until Windows 2000/SP4 and Windows XP/SP2, there wasn't any loopback behavior when coming over a cross-forest trust. That's because there was no Cross-Forest trust feature to care about.

Because of this, this is a "relatively new" feature in the "big-time line" of Windows. I'm sure you're all using Windows XP/SP2 and later at this point. But if you are using something older, you should know that those machines *don't go into loopback mode across a cross-forest trust.* That is, there's no protection from "the other administrators'" possibly bad software and scripts and Group Policy Preferences or other items.

In Table 4.1, I've spelled out which machines do what action when users log on across a cross-forest trust.

TABLE 4.1 Cross-Forest Trust Client Matrix

Client	What Happens When a User Logs on across the Cross-Forest Trust	Can Be Changed by the Allow Cross-Forest User Policy and Roaming User Profiles Policy Setting
Windows 2000 Server or Professional, with no service pack, SP1, SP2, or SP3	User gets user settings. Computer gets computer settings.	No
Windows 2000 Server or Professional, with SP4	User settings are ignored. Computer gets settings as if it were a user (that is, Group Policy Loopback—Replace mode).	Yes
Windows XP with no service pack or SP1	User gets user settings. Computer gets computer settings.	No
Windows XP with SP2+, Windows Server 2003, Windows Vista, Windows 7, Windows Server 2008	User settings are ignored. Computer gets settings as if it were a user (that is, Group Policy Loopback—Replace mode).	Yes

Understanding Cross-Forest Trust Permissions

If you're going to set up cross-forest trusts, here's a little extra takeaway to get you started.

Windows cross-forest trusts have two modes: Forest-wide Authentication and Selective Authentication, as shown in Figure 4.9. To view the screen shown here, open Active Directory Domains and Trusts, locate the properties of the trust, and click the Authentication tab.

FIGURE 4.9 You can set Forest-wide Authentication or Selective Authentication.

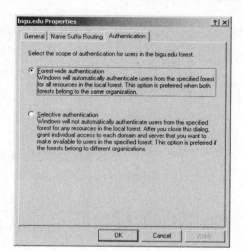

In a Windows 2003 (or later) Active Directory domain, Full Authentication mode permits Group Policy across forests to act as if it were one big forest. That is, GPOs are processed according to Table 4.1.

We already know that Sol is the SQL database administrator over at Corp.com, and we saw what happened when he logged onto the Windows 2003 member server WS03-Serv1. Twice a week, however, Sol works at Widgets.corp.com on the WIDGETS-XPPRO3 for some CAD work. Then, the unthinkable happens.

An attack originating at bigu.edu upon Corp.com's computers gets the two Domain Administrators in a heated battle. The Corp.com Domain Administrator decides he wants to prevent attacks from bigu.edu, so he enables Selective Authentication. Now no one from bigu.edu can log onto any of the machines in Corp.com or Widgets.corp.com. Ergo, Sol will not be able to log onto either his WS03-Serv1 Windows 2003 member server in Corp.com or his WIDGETS-XPPRO3 machine in Widgets.corp.com. Sol needs the "Allowed to Authenticate" right on the computer objects he will use. In this example, you can see what is done for WIDGETS-XPPRO3 in Figure 4.10.

Additional computers in Corp.com and Widgets.corp.com need these explicit rights if anyone else from bigu.edu is going to use them. Then, Group Policy will process as described earlier and summarized in Table 4.1.

Final Thoughts

In this chapter, you learned ways to utilize Group Policy in some interesting cases.

WMI filters are great; just be careful when you use them. They do take a little while to process on each machine, so be careful in the number of WMI filters you're asking your machines to process.

FIGURE 4.10 You need to specifically grant the "Allowed to Authenticate" right in order for Sol to use this machine.

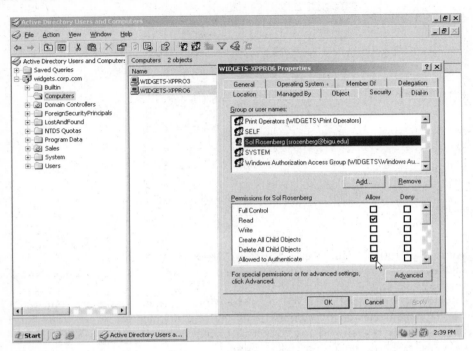

Loopback processing is great too; its job is to help you ensure that the same set of user settings affects a machine. It can be confusing to understand and use at first, so be sure to test this out in a test lab before running it in your production environment.

If you have cross-forest trusts, consider what happens over the trust. You can decide if you want to revert back to "standard" behavior (that is, you can retrain the system to allow Group Policy Objects to affect your user accounts) or stay with (Loopback) behavior. Group Policy processing with a cross-forest trust can be tricky because different operating systems and the roles they play in the domain dictate when Group Policy applies. And, sometimes, a service pack will change the behavior of some of the processing. But hopefully the text, examples, and Table 4.1 can help you with any problems.

As with all the advice in this book, test, test, test before you deploy.

5

Group Policy Preferences

Take a look at Figure 5.1. You'll see the Preferences node in the Group Policy editor.

You might be thinking to yourself, "Preferences? What's a preference? I thought this whole book was on Group Policy, so why is there a node called Preferences?"

And others might be thinking, "I've been using Group Policy for a long time, and never saw that Preferences node. Where did it come from and what do I download to start using it?"

Preferences are a relatively new part of the Group Policy world we've come to know, love, and inhabit.

Recall that a Client-Side Extension (CSE) is a way to "do more stuff" with Group Policy. Windows XP does more stuff than Windows 2000, and Windows Vista does more stuff than Windows XP, and Windows 7 does more stuff than Vista. That's because each operating system has more CSEs, which you learned about in Chapter 3. If you'll remember, they're just DLLs that process the directives contained in GPOs.

The Group Policy Preference Extensions are simply that: extension DLLs—really, one DLL that does a *lot* of stuff. Because Group Policy Preferences is kind of long to say, I'll abbreviate the Group Policy Preferences (the concept) as *GPPrefs*, and a specific Group Policy Preference extension as *a GPPrefs*, or just *an extension* or *node*—for instance, *the Registry preference extension* or *the Registry node*.

The first question you may have is, "What is all the awesome new power I'm gonna get?" Hang tight. That will be the first thing I show you.

But the next question you may have is, "Why the heck are they called *preferences* if they hook into Group Policy?" And, yes, I'll explain that in detail, too, I promise, but in short, they act like, well, preferences. That is, they don't "clean up" after themselves, like normal Group Policy settings do, and they don't "lock out" or restrict the user interface (under most circumstances). So, in short, they're not policies—they're preferences. They're settings administrators can deliver but users can work around. Indeed, it should be noted that Group Policy has always been able to deliver preferences; we'll see how to do it using ADM and ADMX files in the very next chapter.

Again, we're going to go into these details coming up, but it will take a lot of pages to answer both of these questions thoroughly. So I'll ask you to please hold your horses before running out and trying all these superpowers. You'll be really, really glad you waited and read this whole chapter to truly understand the powers you have rather than doing something you wish you hadn't done.

The technology is powerful and awesome; it extends Group Policy's reach and capabilities an astronomical amount. However, it must be fully understood and used with caution to get the most out of it, and so you don't shoot yourself in the foot as you're using it.

That's what this chapter is all about: the nuts, bolts, general use, and troubleshooting of the Group Policy Preferences. We won't be going over each and every new setting. That could be a whole book in and of itself. However, I will have more information about how to do some neat things using GPPrefs magic in Chapter 12.

FIGURE 5.1   Welcome to the new Preferences node in the Group Policy editor.

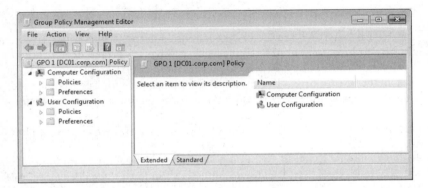

So, for this chapter, I'm going use the following roadmap to help you get a grip on what the GPPrefs are all about. Think about this chapter in four parts:

Powers of the Group Policy Preferences   You want to know what toys are in the toy box. I totally get it. Let's take a quick review of all the toys first, and then later, you can come back and use them (after you've learned how to do so safely).

Group Policy Preferences Architecture and Installation Instructions   In this section, you'll learn which operating systems have the Group Policy Preferences built in, and which need a boost in getting them installed.

Group Policy Preferences Concepts   In this meaty section, you'll learn more about policy versus preference, how the original Group Policy set and Group Policy Preferences can overlap but also work together. You'll also learn about the (sometimes confusing) red and green circles in the user interface. You'll learn about a concept called "CRUD modes" and learn about the Common tab.

Group Policy Preferences Tips, Tricks, and Troubleshooting   I think you can figure out what we'll learn in this section.

With that in mind, let's get going.

Note that the Group Policy Preferences are not available as Local Group Policy Objects. The Group Policy Preferences appear only when you use the GPMC and manage Active Directory GPOs.

> **G'bye Logon Scripts, Hello Group Policy Preferences**
>
> Here's one takeaway that you should start thinking about as you're reading this chapter: "Is there anything in my logon or startup process that I script today but could now start using Group Policy for?"
>
> Indeed, almost everyone sets Environment variables and maps drive letters using scripts. So, start thinking of pulling those things out of the logon scripts and making them more Group Policy-ish using the Group Policy Preferences.
>
> And, as you'll learn, since the GPPrefs can leverage variables, you'll have a lot more flexibility with GPOs and GPPrefs than you usually do with logon scripts.

Powers of the Group Policy Preferences

Before we dive into the power they behold, we need to first be super clear about how you can utilize them. First things first—once again—you don't need to have Windows Server 2008, Windows Server 2008 R2, or even Windows Server 2003. Group Policy (and Group Policy Preferences) does not concern itself with what domain controllers and type of DCs you have. All it cares about is if your clients are updated to receive the GPPrefs' goods from within a GPO.

Next, if you thought, "Why haven't I seen the Preferences node before?" there's an easy answer to that. You're not using the updated GPMC. Again, you'll need to be using (at least) a Windows Server 2008 or install the RSAT tools on a Windows Vista/SP1 (or SP2) machine. The best thing you can do is what you've (hopefully) been doing along in this whole book: use Windows 7+ RSAT (or Windows Server 2008 R2) as your management machine.

If you've been accustomed to the older GPMC (without the Preferences node), it doesn't have to be scary. The original "stuff" is now just tucked within the Policies node. Indeed, other than that, not much has changed there.

The new GPPrefs stuff is contained within its own new node called Preferences. Again, you won't see it until you use the updated GPMC.

The new Preferences node has lots of new categories on both the User and Computer side—and some even overlap! Indeed, not just overlap with itself (i.e., the same preference extension on both the Computer and User side), but also overlap with original Group Policy settings (which now live in the Policies nodes). Yikes! See the section "The Overlap of Group Policy vs. Group Policy Preferences and Associated Issues" a little later for more information on this particular issue.

In all, the Preferences node has 21 new categories of toys to play with. (Remember, I said I'd describe the powerful new abilities first, then we'll work on the understanding of that power second.)

You'll also see that these new Group Policy options are split between Windows Settings and Control Panel Settings.

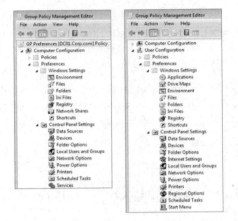

Computer Configuration ➤ Preferences

Again, this node is split in two: Windows Settings and Control Panel Settings. Let's check out each extension (in brief).

Computer Configuration ➤ Preferences ➤ Windows Settings

The Windows settings are settings you can make that, well, directly affect Windows. I know that's a little vague, but the other big category is Control Panel, which is also a little vague. In short, it doesn't matter why they're broken up this way; they just are.

Environment Extension

You can do two big things with the Environment preference extension:

- You can set user and system Environment variables.

- You can change or update the special Windows system Path variable.

You can best utilize this extension by using it to set specific Environment variables based on certain conditions. Then, in other GPPrefs, you can call these variables. For instance, you can define a variable like the one seen in the following image where we're defining NURSEFILES as C:\NURSEFILES. Then, later, you can recycle this variable when you want to use other GPPrefs to copy or utilize files based on this variable.

Files Extension

The Files preference extension lets you copy files from Point A to Point B. Point A can be a UNC path or the local machine, and so can Point B, though Point B usually is the local machine. The most common scenario is to copy a file (or three) from a share on a server to a user's My Documents folder, the desktop, or C:\ drive.

You can see a screen shot of the Files preference extension in the section "Environment Variables" a little later.

Folders Extension

This extension lets you create new folders and delete existing folders or wipe out their contents. In this example, I'm deleting the contents of the %NURSESFILES% folder, but only if the folder is empty.

.INI Files Extension

This extension allows you to perform a search and replace within existing .INI files. I have an example in the section "Environment Variables" a little later.

Registry Extension

This is a very powerful extension that can also be a little hard to handle. We'll use this extension later in some examples, but the idea is simple: punch in a particular Registry setting to your client machines.

You can see in the example here that I'm dictating a particular Registry setting to good ol' Notepad.

What's neat about the Registry extension is that you can send Registry punches normally designed for Users to both HKLM and HKCU. And you can send Registry punches normally designed for Computers to the HKLM.

> On the Computer side there's no way to get the HKCU except for the .Default profile. This is the account you see when no one is logged on, at the "Press CTL+ALT+DEL to Log On" prompt. Not sure why this is the only way you can get to the .Default profile and not normal users' settings by a computer using GPPrefs. Note, however, that PolicyPak (which you'll learn about in the next chapter) can overcome this limitation and deliver user-based Registry settings to anyone based on computers.

The Registry extension also allows you to set any type of Registry key, like REG_BINARY values, which has traditionally been impossible using ADM and ADMX files.

However, this extension needs to be handled with caution (as do others), especially when the "Remove this item when it is no longer applied" setting is chosen (which we'll discuss when we explore the Common tab a little later).

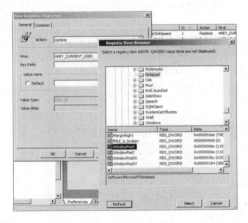

There are there several ways to utilize the Registry extension:

Registry item   This lets you specifically set an individual Registry setting. Again, all the major Registry types are supported (REG_SZ, REG_DWORD, REG_BINARY, REG_MULTI_SZ, and REG_EXPAND_SZ), and you can dictate to HKEY_LOCAL_MACHINE, HKEY_CURRENT_USER, HKEY_CLASSES_ROOT, HKEY_USERS, or HKEY_CURRENT_CONFIG.

Collection item　This is a fancy way of saying "a folder of stuff I want to lump together as a group." In short, by using this item, you can guarantee that groups of Registry settings will affect the machine at the same time. You'll use item-level targeting (ILT), which we'll discuss later, to ensure that your criteria are met *before* making the group of changes. For instance, you can check that the machine is manufactured by Dell before delivering all the Registry items in this group.

Registry wizard　This is a great way to take a sample machine's Registry, find a particular setting you want to manage, then manipulate and ultimately deliver the setting. You can select individual Registry settings or a whole Registry branch, change values if you want, then deliver all the changed values.

Network Shares Extension

This extension allows you to create new shares on workstations, or more commonly, servers. Or you can delete those shares.

You can also turn on Access-based Enumeration (ABE), available on Windows Server 2003 and Windows Server 2008, which will prevent someone who doesn't have proper rights from even seeing the shared directory.

Learn more about ABE at http://tinyurl.com/cwa8z, http://tinyurl .com/mmfhcf, and http://tinyurl.com/mgv5ch.

Note that this extension won't create the directory for the share; the directory must already exist. But, you can easily create the folders you need using the Folders extension, which we just explored.

Shortcuts Extension

This extension allows you to plunk both program and URL shortcuts on Desktops, in the Startup folder, in the Programs folders, and in a lot of other locations. In this example,

I'm plunking a link to www.GPanswers.com on the user's Desktop and selecting the little World icon.

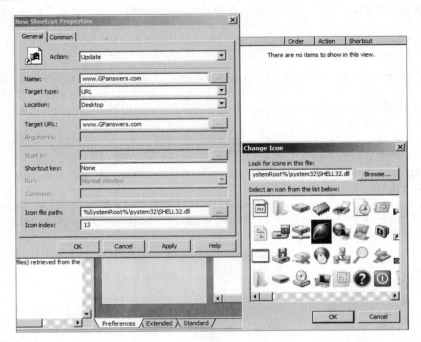

Note that you can also create shortcuts to shell objects. For instance, you can put a link to the Recycle Bin in the folders that users utilize most and even in the "Send to" flyout menu.

Note that the icon you select is "embedded" inside a DLL of your choosing. Indeed, you're really saying, "I want icon #6 inside Whatever.DLL." So, two things need to be true to get the same icon: that DLL needs to be on the target machine, and the icon needs to be in the same index within the DLL. I've seen people select one icon in the Group Policy editor, only to have another icon appear on the target machine. That's because either the DLL was not present on the target machine or the icon wasn't in the same place (the index) of the DLL.

Computer Configuration ➢ Preferences ➢ Control Panel Settings

Again, it's kind of unnecessary to have a division here and call out the specific "Control Panel" settings. But here are the ones listed within the Control Panel node.

Data Sources Extension

The Data Sources extension lets you set Open Database Connectivity (ODBC) data sources via Group Policy. Typically, this can be a 12-step process that you would normally have to run around and perform on every machine. Now it can be done via Group Policy in a snap.

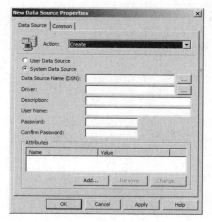

Devices Extension

This extension can disable a specific device or device class. There are similar original Group Policy settings that seemingly conflict with these.

Check out the section "Group Policy Device Installation Restrictions vs. GPPrefs Devices Preference Extension" for more information about which one does what and which ones are best to use.

Folder Options Extension

This extension exists in both the User and Computer sides. However, on the Computer side, it has only one possible function (whereas in the User side it has three functions). That is, you can associate a file extension with a particular class.

This part of this extension corresponds to Explorer's Tools ➢ Options ➢ File Types ➢ Advanced dialog box. Personally, in all my years working with Windows, I've never needed to modify anything in there, but clearly someone needed to or they wouldn't have put it in here.

Local Users and Groups Extension

In Chapter 8, we will explore a Group Policy concept called "Restricted Groups." I don't want to blow my whole story here, but that original tool is a toy compared with the Group Policy Preferences' Local Users and Groups. Here, you can jam users into groups, remove specific users from specific groups, change users' passwords, lock out accounts, and set password expirations.

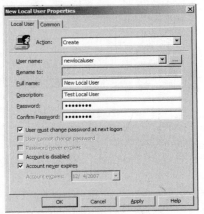

Network Options Extension

The Network Options extension allows you to configure the following connection types:

VPN connections   Previously, setting virtual private network (VPN) connections was tedious, arduous work. Now it's a snap.

DUN connections   Ditto for dial-up networking (DUN) connections.

Instead of running around to all your laptops and specifying these settings, you can be finished configuring an army of machines before breakfast. This is the "Cadillac" way to get the job done.

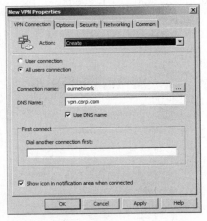

Power Options Extension

This preference item allows you to create new Power Schemes and Power Options for
Windows XP (and control existing ones) as well as manage Power Plans in Windows
Vista and later.

You can set things like the hard disk spin downtime, how long until the monitor
goes into stand-by mode, and what happens to laptops when you hit the power
button.

Again, because these settings are merely preferences, users can still change the
settings if they want to. So, be careful banking on the users maintaining the settings
you wanted.

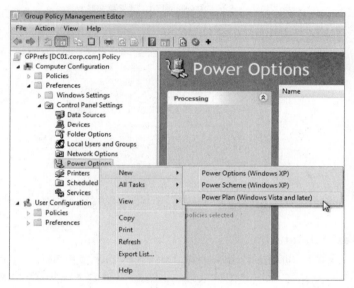

A little note regarding Vista. The Power Options extension is a bit tricky
because, as we'll learn in a minute, there is the "original" version of Windows Vista's Group Policy Preferences CSE and an "updated" version of
Windows Vista's Group Policy Preferences CSE available (well, *should*
be available by the time you read this, anyway). So, don't freak out if you
try to dictate Power Plan settings to your machines, and your Windows 7
machines cheerfully accept it but your Windows Vista machines don't do
what you want. Again, you'll need to apply the updated Windows Vista
Group Policy Preferences CSE, which, again, as of this writing, doesn't
exist yet.

Printers Extension

The Printers extension option might be one of those things you just fall in love with. But you have to contend with the fact that there's already a way to zap printers down via Group Policy, and we'll talk about it in the section "Group Policy Deployed Printers vs. GPPrefs Printers Extension."

In short, the Printers extension allows you to set TCP/IP and local and shared printers (though shared printers are available only on the User side).

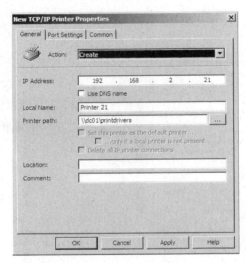

Scheduled Tasks Extension

You can set Version 1 scheduled tasks using this preference extension. Version 1 tasks are valid for Windows XP, Windows Server 2003, Windows Vista, Windows 7, and Windows 2008 machines.

However, Windows Vista, Windows 7, and Windows Server 2008 have more features available via Version 2 scheduled tasks, like interfacing with the Event log and such.

So, you can use the Scheduled Task preference extension to deliver tasks to all operating systems (Windows XP and later), but you cannot use this to take advantage of the Version 2–specific tasks that are available only on Windows Vista and later (including Windows 7, Windows Server 2008, and Windows Server 2008 R2).

You can set scheduled tasks and immediate tasks. *Immediate* is kind of a misnomer because in Group Policy, nothing is really "immediate." In reality, you'll have to wait until Group Policy refreshes on the client. When it does, the task is scheduled to run, and then poof, that's it.

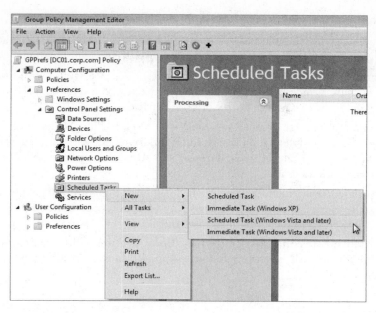

Poor Scheduled Tasks item. If only it worked the way we wanted it to. Here are the little, unfortunate "side notes" before you run out and try to use it:

Scheduled Tasks on XP Works as advertised. Have fun.

Scheduled Tasks on Windows 7 The CSE on Windows 7 (as it ships) appears to be "broken" with regard to "Version 2" immediate tasks. For now, those just seem to be broken. I would expect them to be fixed in a future hotfix or service pack.

Additionally, I found it hard to get Type 2 scheduled tasks working perfectly every time on my Windows 7 target machines. Sometimes I could see the tasks were getting into the target machines' scheduled tasks' queue, but I didn't always see the task fire off.

At least in my testing—your mileage may vary.

Scheduled Tasks on Windows Vista Like the Power Options, the Scheduled Tasks extension is also a bit tricky (and for the same reason). Again, there is the "original" version of Windows Vista's Group Policy Preferences CSE and an "updated" version of Windows Vista's Group Policy Preferences CSE available.

Again, it *may* be available by the time you read this. So, once again, don't freak out if you try to dictate Scheduled/Immediate tasks to your Windows Vista machines and they don't do your bidding.

Again, you'll need to apply the updated Windows Vista Group Policy Preferences CSE, which, again, as of this writing, doesn't exist yet.

So, let's recap:

- The Scheduled Task item works for Windows XP and later just fine. This creates "Type 1" tasks, and can successfully be embraced by Windows XP and later without issue.

- The "Immediate Task (Windows Vista and later)" doesn't work for Windows 7 out of the box because Windows 7 is just "broken" right now. No ETA on a solution, but it will likely be fixed in a future hotfix or service pack.

- Neither the "Immediate Task (Windows Vista and later)" or "Scheduled Task for Windows Vista and later" item works for Windows Vista with the "currently shipping" CSE. There should be an update out sometime that updates the Windows Vista CSEs and adds this feature.

- The "Scheduled Task" item for Type 2 scheduled tasks (Windows Vista and later) I found hard to get to work perfectly on Windows 7 and Windows Server 2008 R2; even though the tasks showed up in the target machines' queue.

So, it's entirely possible that the "Immediate Tasks" feature will work first on Windows Vista with an updated CSE even though it was supposed to work perfectly in Windows 7 out of the box.

Ironic.

Services Extension

You can manage just about every aspect of a client computer's services. This is especially useful if the target is a server machine and you have a pesky service that's running on multiple machines but you haven't gotten around to changing the service account in, well, years.

Simply change the password in Active Directory first, then deliver a Group Policy containing the Services item with your password change.

 The password is stored in encrypted form within the Group Policy's GPT. The password is 256bit AES encrypted. However, there is theoretically an embedded key available, so a determined hacker could crack it if necessary. See the sidebar "About Passwords inside Group Policy Preferences."

You can change the following items:

Startup   If you like, you can change the startup type to Automatic, Manual, or Disabled.

Service action   When the Group Policy runs, you can have it start, stop, or restart a service.

Log on as   You can configure the account that the service uses as well as change the password, as noted earlier.

Recovery   You can specify what will happen if the service fails on first, second, and subsequent failures. This equates to the Recovery options in the normal services dialog box.

Note that the original Group Policy has some ability to work with System Services. Be sure to check out the section "Group Policy System Services vs. GPPrefs Services Preference Extension" a little later for a breakdown on how each compares, head to head.

About Passwords inside Group Policy Preferences

There are numerous places to store a "password" field in the GPPrefs. You saw one in the Services extension. There's one in the Local Users and Groups, and another in the Scheduled Tasks extension.

And when you type the password, it looks like it's all nice and protected. You'll see "dots" replace what you type, and you get a warm, fuzzy feeling that you're all secure.

Except that you're not.

When you save the passwords inside the GPPrefs (which, of course, saves the password inside a GPO), you are actually creating a big-ish security hole.

Yes, the password is encrypted. However, let's break down the security problem in several steps to see how vulnerable that password is:

- The password is encrypted. It's encrypted in symmetric AES.

- The password is stored in the GPO.

- The GPO is readable by everyone (see the previous chapter; that's how anyone can process a GPO).

So, where's the problem? The problem is anyone with the source code to Windows can have the key. Yep—the same key I use in my GPPrefs is what you use. We both use the same key, because the key is stored in Windows itself, and not based on something only one of us has.

So, if you use any passwords in GPPrefs, you should consider them "well known" and, in my opinion "possibly pretty hackable."

This is even Microsoft's own opinion. Check out this blog article, which describes the situation:

> http://blogs.technet.com/grouppolicy/archive/2009/04/22/passwords-in-group-policy-preferences-updated.aspx

(shortened to http://tinyurl.com/ybsm884).

I suggest you be especially careful in using this to set local administrator passwords, service account passwords, or accounts dealing with scheduled tasks.

You might be okay, but in the end analysis, you could be vulnerable to attack. At least you know why.

User Configuration ➤ Preferences

On the User Configuration ➤ Preferences side of things, there are lots of preference extensions that overlap. In this section, we'll detail only ones that *don't* specifically overlap (or specific major features that don't overlap).

See Table 5.1 a little later for the bird's-eye view of where the overlaps are and to see what can specifically be accomplished on either the Computer or User side.

User Configuration ➤ Preferences ➤ Windows Settings

Let's explore the GPPrefs on the User ➤ Windows Settings side.

Applications Extension

This node is special because there are no configurable items available by default and no signs from Microsoft that it will be utilized. This was a special node when it was the pre-Microsoft product, but it doesn't appear Microsoft will be utilizing it. If something changes, I'll let you know on GPanswers.com.

Drive Maps Extension

Congratulations. You can finally get out of the "I have to map another network drive via logon scripts" business. It's *finally* come to Group Policy land.

The Drive Maps preference extension is like the Swiss Army knife of drive mappings, and you can create and delete drive mappings and assign letters with ease.

When this extension is combined with item-level targeting (which we talk about later), you'll be able to specifically dictate drive maps to users based on the specific circumstances they're in.

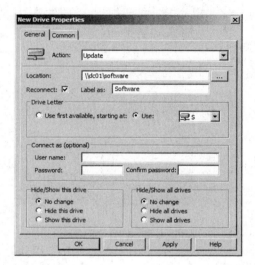

Note the Drive Maps Extension is a bit of an odd duck. All the rest of the Group Policy Preferences will apply in the background (that is, once a user is already logged on). However, if a user is already logged on and a drive maps directive is received, the user will not see the update. That's to prevent a user from having drive letter X: being mapped, say, to \\Server1\Share1 and then, oops, now he's magically remapped X: to \\Server2\Share2. That wouldn't be good.

User Configuration ➢ Preferences ➢ Control Panel

This is the final group of GPPrefs. Here we'll discuss the items that are available only on the User side of the house.

Folder Options Extension

While this exists on both the User and Computer side, they have different options. On the User side, you can right-click New ➢ Folder Options and see three options:

Folder Options (Windows XP)   This option is shown in the following screen shot. Although you could do a lot of these little tweaks by editing the Registry directly, there's a lot of "quick power" available in the Folder Options configuration item. These items mostly equate to Explorer's Tools ➢ Folder Options items that you would normally find inside every Explorer window. You can quickly turn on the ability to have Windows Explorer show hidden files, display the full path in the address bar, and show NTFS-compressed files with a different color.

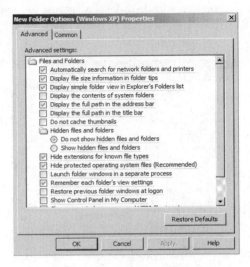

Folder Options (Windows Vista and Later) Very similar items to what's available for Windows XP, but specific to Windows Vista, Windows 7, Windows Server 2008, and Windows Server 2008 R2.

Open With This enables you to associate (or de-associate) applications from their extensions, so you can quickly configure a specific application on a machine to handle a particular document file.

 The only option on the Computer side for Folder Options is File Type.

Internet Settings Extension

You can set one of the following:

- Internet Explorer 5 and 6 settings (that's *one* kind of setting)
- Internet Explorer 7 settings
- Internet Explorer 8 settings

You can see Internet Explorer 8 settings here.

What's strange is that there are a lot of user interface elements that seemingly do, well, nothing. Several buttons are permanently grayed out and some tabs (like Privacy) are entirely grayed out.

Other than that, this is a stellar way to specify Internet settings. However, it should be noted that there are already two *other* ways to specify Internet Explorer settings via Group Policy. So, be sure to read the section "Group Policy Internet Explorer and Group Policy IE Maintenance Configuration vs. the GPPrefs Internet Settings Extension" a little later to figure out which one to use and when.

Printers Extension

Although this category exists on both the Computer and User sides, when settings are dictated to users, an additional option is available that allows for managing shared printers. Again, be sure to read the section "Group Policy Deployed Printers vs. GPPrefs Printers Extension" a little later for more information.

Regional Options Extension

This has always been something I wanted to set via Group Policy. It just seems obvious: depending on who the user is, you can immediately change their local settings. Now you can just do that, quickly and easily, using Group Policy.

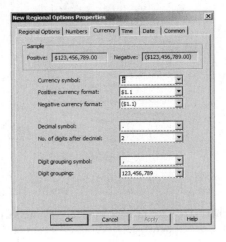

Start Menu Extension

While there are existing settings for controlling the Start menu, this extension provides a very easy way to make your changes. There are Start menu configurations for Windows XP and "Windows Vista and later." Note, the user interface could have been clearer here. The "XP" settings will mostly work just fine on Windows Server 2003, and the "Windows Vista and later" settings will mostly work just fine on Windows 7 and Windows Server 2008 and Windows Server 2008 R2.

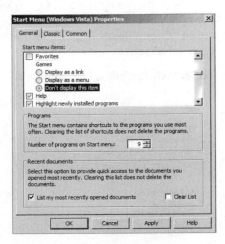

However, you might not want to try to change any of these settings until you read the section "Group Policy Start Menu Policy Settings vs. GPPrefs Start Menu."

Table 5.1 shows you where to find each Group Policy Preference Extension.

TABLE 5.1   Where to Find Group Policy Preferences

	Computer Configuration ➢ Preferences ➢ Control Panel	Computer Configuration ➢ Preferences ➢ Windows Settings	User Configuration ➢ Preferences ➢ Control Panel	User Configuration ➢ Preferences ➢ Windows Settings
Applications				X
Data Sources	X		X	
Devices	X		X	
Drive Maps				X
Environment		X		X
Files		X		X
Folder Options— Folder Options			X	
Folder Options— Open With			X	
Folder Options— File Type	X			
Folders		X		X
INI Files		X		X
Internet Settings			X	
Local Users and Groups— Local Group	X		X	
Local Users and Groups— Local User	X		X	

TABLE 5.1   Where to Find Group Policy Preferences *(continued)*

	Computer Configuration ➢ Preferences ➢ Control Panel	Computer Configuration ➢ Preferences ➢ Windows Settings	User Configuration ➢ Preferences ➢ Control Panel	User Configuration ➢ Preferences ➢ Windows Settings
Mail Profiles			X	
Network Options—VPN Connection	X		X	
Network Options—DUN Connection (Dial-up)	X		X	
Power Options—Power Options	X		X	
Power Options—Power Scheme	X		X	
Power Options—Power Plan (Vista+)	X		X	
Printers—Shared Printer			X	
Printers—TCP/IP Printer	X		X	
Printers—Local Printer	X		X	
Regional Options			X	
Registry		X		X
Scheduled Tasks	X		X	
Services	X			
Shortcuts		X		X
Start Menu			X	

Group Policy Preferences Architecture and Installation Instructions

As you'll recall from previous chapters, the magic of Group Policy happens in three steps:

1. You use a management station, which has the GPMC and Group Policy Management Editor, which has a snap-in editor for the item you want to use.

2. A GPO is created, lives, and is replicated to all Domain Controllers.

3. The directive you put into the GPO (from your management station) is processed by a particular CSE on the target system.

So, let's make a quick pit stop here to make sure you have all three ingredients necessary to make Group Policy Preferences magic happen.

First things first: your management station needs to have the updated capability of creating and managing new features. If you'll recall, you simply can't do these magic tricks from a Windows XP or Windows 2000 machine because that capability isn't contained within the power of that older Group Policy Object Editor. So, if you use Windows 7 as your management machine, you're good to go.

Second things second: the directive is stored within the GPO. That mechanism doesn't change.

Third things third: your target machine must have a CSE that implements the magic you created and stored within the GPO. That is, a moving part (a .DLL, actually) parses the GPO and performs the magic you want done. These could be settings like Disk Quotas, Folder Redirection, Internet Explorer settings, and so on. And now, the GPPrefs.

So, let's figure out what it's going to take to get both our management station and our target machines up to speed.

To get our management station up to speed (to create and manage the new settings):

- Your management station *must* be able to run the updated GPMC.

- Again, my pick is Windows 7 or Windows Server 2008 R2. Even though the updated GPMC is available for a Windows Vista or Windows Server 2008 machine, you won't be able to configure some items (like Internet Explorer 8, for instance).

To get our target systems up to speed (to embrace GPOs with the new changes):

- Your target system *may* be Windows XP with at least SP2, Windows Server 2003 with at least SP1, Windows Vista, or Windows Server 2008.

- Windows Server 2008 and later already has the GPPrefs CSEs built in. So, Windows Server 2008, Windows Server 2008 R2, and Windows 7 are all "ready to rock" with the Group Policy Preferences CSE preinstalled.

- Windows XP, Windows Server 2003, and Windows Vista need to have the GPPrefs CSEs installed on them to embrace the new functionality.

It's these two big items we're going to tackle in this section. That way, you're all set when you're ready to start using these new superpowers.

Installing the Client-Side Extensions on Your Client Machines

So, as you just learned, we'll need to get the GPPrefs CSEs on our target machines (except for Windows 7, Windows Server 2008, and Windows Server 2008 R2) to rock and roll with GPPrefs. Let's explore what we need to do on each machine to make sure they have the "set of instructions" required to embrace the GPOs we're about to create.

The CSEs for Windows 7, Windows Server 2008, Windows Server 2008 R2

Again, everything you need to take advantage of the Group Policy Preferences is already installed here.

So, if you wanted to get started using Group Policy Preferences, you can do so immediately.

Just fire up a Windows 7 management machine and get your own party started.

The CSEs for Windows Server 2003, Windows XP, and Windows Vista

Again, for Windows Server 2003, Windows XP, and Windows Vista you need to download pieces to make the magic happen. Let's examine each operating system, where to get the downloads, and how to install the pieces by hand.

The "main search" you'll want to look for is KB943729. Here, I've listed at last check, where you would find the Group Policy Preferences Extensions for various operating systems. These might change in the future.

- Windows XP/32-bit: http://tinyurl.com/mac4g7
- Windows XP/64-bit: http://tinyurl.com/nzafod
- Windows Vista/32-bit: http://tinyurl.com/ln8aw9
- Windows Vista/64-bit: http://tinyurl.com/n3va22
- Windows Server 2003/32-bit: http://tinyurl.com/cr3bwo
- Windows Server 2003/64-bit: http://tinyurl.com/kkavwm

Windows XP and Windows Server 2003 machines also need a prerequisite called XmlLite, and it can be found at http://support.microsoft.com/default.aspx/kb/914783.

Here's some key points about XmlLite:

- You may already "have all you need." That is, XmlLite is already built in to Windows XP/SP3 and part of IE 7. If you have already deployed either of those; skip ahead—you've got XmlLite already.
- Neither the XmlLite prerequisite nor the GPPrefs themselves are MSIs. Nope, they're *patches*. So, for Windows XP and Windows Server 2003, they're .EXE patches, and for Windows Vista they're a newfangled format called .MSU for Microsoft Update patch.

As we'll explore in Chapter 11, the Group Policy Software Installation engine cannot install MSP patches and it can't install newer MSU patches.

Bah.

You'll need a big tool like an SCCM 2007 or WSUS, which expressly handles patch management. Or, you'll need a script to install them for your systems.

Ugh, what a nightmare!

You'll always be able to install each piece by hand (which we'll explore first), but you'll also want a mass-deployment recipe to start really rolling this out. I'll provide a script that helps you roll this out to all your machines at once, so you're not running around from machine to machine doing all the dirty work.

Installing the Prerequisites and CSEs for Windows Server 2003 and Windows XP by Hand

So, we'll just want to make sure that our existing Windows Server 2003, Windows XP, and (in the next section) Windows Vista machines have the CSEs ready to accept our instructions from our management stations.

If you're installing the CSEs on Windows Server 2003, you'll likely do each one by hand. This makes sense, as mass deploying and mass rebooting live servers can be, well, not good for your users. However, if you wanted to do a mass rollout of the CSEs, check out the section "Installing the Prerequisites and CSEs for All Operating Systems Automatically."

Again, both Windows XP and Windows Server 2003 have the prerequisite of XmlLite. You can use the available command-line switches shown in Figure 5.2, if you want to be fancy, or you can just double-click the downloaded .EXE and kick off the installation.

FIGURE 5.2   The XmlLite command-line options

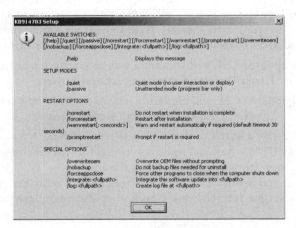

In my testing, the XmlLite components didn't require a reboot (but your mileage may vary). Knowing this fact will come in handy when we try to automate the whole thing using a script.

Next, I simply double-clicked the .EXE that contained the CSE.

Once again, it didn't even require a reboot and it appeared to be ready to go. You might want to reboot once just to be on the safe side.

You can verify the Group Policy Preferences installed on Windows Server 2003 or Windows XP by opening "Add or Remove Programs" and checking the "Show updates" check box. When you do, you'll see the hotfixes, like GPPrefs installation.

Installing the CSEs for Windows Vista by Hand

The Windows Vista CSE ships as an MSU, a Microsoft Update package, as seen in Figure 5.3. Just double-click it and then click OK to install—you're off to the races.

FIGURE 5.3   Installing the Windows Vista MSU file is like installing an MSI application.

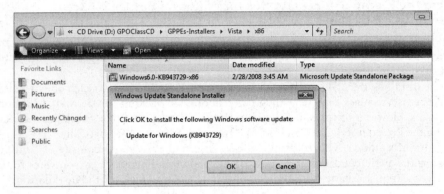

But here's the thing: there's (about to be) a newer version of the Windows Vista CSE. As of this writing, the current CSE is dated 6/23/2009 (and you can see what I'm talking about by going here: http://tinyurl.com/ln8aw9). Well, I know for a fact that the Windows Vista CSE is being updated to support two features we talked about earlier in this chapter:

- Windows Vista's updated CSE will contain a way to embrace new power settings directives (see the "Power Options Extension" section earlier).

- Windows Vista's updated CSE will contain a way to embrace new scheduled task directives (see the "Scheduled Tasks Extension" section earlier).

And, in January 7, 2010, a hotfix to that CSE was released here: http://support .microsoft.com/kb/KB977983. But, just to be confusing, this isn't the new update that is going to get you the new features. Just some bug fixes.

So, I still can't point you toward the new CSE, because, as I write this, it doesn't exist yet. It may be out by the time you read this. Check in at GPanswers.com in the blog section for updates.

When you get it, it should be an MSU file, like the one that's available as I write this. In my testing there was no need to reboot after installing the CSE, but it certainly couldn't hurt. You can verify that the Group Policy Preferences were properly installed by looking at Control Panel ➤ Programs ➤ Uninstall a program and then clicking "Turn Windows features on or off," as seen in Figure 5.4.

FIGURE 5.4　You can verify that the Group Policy Preferences were properly installed.

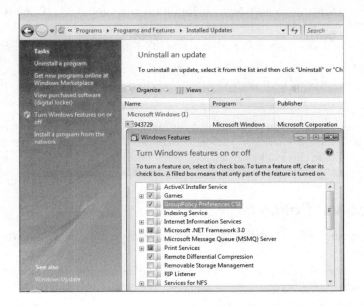

Note the Group Policy Preferences are on by default, and it's not such a hot idea to turn them off.

Installing the Prerequisites and CSEs for All Operating Systems Automatically

This gets a little trickier. And it takes a giant script to make it happen.

Fortunately, for you, we've put together that giant script and it's waiting for you at www.GPanswers.com in the Group Policy FAQs section. Right now it's Tip #18, but that could change.

Go grab it; then, if you don't want to use WSUS or a larger management tool like SCCM 2007, use the script to get the GPPrefs installed to all your clients.

Group Policy Preferences Concepts

The Group Policy Preferences look "different" than the rest of the Group Policy universe. That's because they *are* different. They were born at a company called DesktopStandard, and then integrated into existing Microsoft technology. It's kind of like the International Space Station. One minute, you're in the USA section and things are in English. Then you step into the Soyuz escape capsule, and all the markings are in Russian. It's not totally like that, but you can certainly see where things are significantly different.

And since there are a lot of holdovers from the originating technology, working with one, then the other, can be a little confusing.

Those confusing (but powerful) elements we'll cover here are as follows:

- The idea that they *aren't really policies* but rather are *preferences*. (Don't worry; we'll get to this bit of confusion right away.)
- The multicolored and dashed lines that are in some portions of the interface.
- The strange concept called the *CRUD method*.
- The Common tab, which allows you to do some high-power tricks.
- Using Group Policy Preferences "targeting" to further hone your wishes.

In all, it's a cool, cool brave new (or rather *additional*) world. But it does have tricks and pitfalls, and that's what we're going to explore here in this chapter. However, because we can't explore all 21 goodies in this book, <insert plug here> take my live or online Group Policy training class at www.GPanswers.com/training with hands-on labs for more information.

Preference vs. Policy

This is a quote from the Group Policy Preferences help file within the GPMC that pretty much sums it up:

> Unlike policy settings, by default preference items are not removed when the hosting GPO becomes out of scope for the user or computer.

Let's spend a little time breaking this apart, understanding the implications of getting our new superpowers before we proceed to do something we'll later regret.

Let me be really, really clear: please don't mass-deploy Group Policy Preferences settings to your clients until you understand the preference versus policy issues.

Why Group Policy Works—a Review

Let's recall a little more about what Group Policy does for you. Group Policy delivers settings. And the "target application"—say Windows Explorer, or Office 2003, or the WSUS client, or Windows Media Player, or Internet Explorer, or whatever—will pick up the settings and change their behavior based on what you want the application to do. For instance, if you use Group Policy and enable a setting like User Configuration ➤ Policies ➤ Administrative Templates ➤ Control Panel ➤ **Prohibit Access to the Control Panel**, your expectation is that Windows Explorer will do the dirty work for you and, well, prohibit access to the Control Panel.

Because that directive is written to a protected part of the Registry—in fact, to the "proper" Policies keys—the user cannot edit the Registry and "scoot" out of getting the setting. Again, we covered this in Chapter 3 and will cover it more in Chapter 6.

For now, I'll give you the crash course you need, but I won't go overboard.

Why ADM/ADMX Files Are and Aren't So Awesome

The whole idea that Group Policy is a massive "settings delivery machine" is great. And in the next chapter, you'll learn how the "underlying language" of Administrative Template policy settings is either ADM or ADMX. All ADM(X) files are is a simple language to describe what change you want made to the target computers' Registry, and where those changes should go.

You'll see that not all settings are exactly alike.

Some settings (indeed, all the ones that Microsoft ships) are "proper Policies." Their directives get put into special "Policies keys" in the Registry. When the GPO no longer applies, the setting is reverted.

We've already seen this in our travels. We create the policy, the action takes place. We remove the policy, the action is reverted. Neat, right?

But this "magic" is contingent upon the application knowing to look in these proper "Policies Keys" (again, more on this in the next chapter).

Many applications don't know to look in these specialized Policies Keys locations. So, you can implement your own ADM or ADMX file, only to push a setting like the startup sound to Windows XP. But then users can simply "walk around" your suggestion and make their own changes to the startup sound.

That's because Explorer doesn't know to protect that part of the world; it's not contained within the Policies keys.

And that's the same issue with the GPPrefs. The GPPrefs don't write their magical setting to these special Policies keys, like "proper" policy settings do.

And you might be asking yourself why. Again, the answer simple: the applications they control (Explorer, drive settings, ODBC settings, etc.) don't know to look in the Policies keys to pick up and revert settings. You're changing the values directly.

Group Policy Preferences Are Like ADM/ADMX Files (Mostly)

So, the GPPrefs specify where these applications should look for their settings. But the downsides in this scheme are the same downsides you would get when you create ADM and ADMX files:

- Settings you dictate with ADM/ADMX and GPPrefs can usually be changed, unset, or deleted by the end user (though there are some exceptions).

- If a user moves from one OU to another (or performs in some other way such that they fall out of scope of management), the setting will just stick there, tattooing the machine.

Hence, these new goodies are called Group Policy *Preferences*. And that's because they act more or less like the preferences we created when we created our own ADM and ADMX files.

Group Policy Preferences Advantages over ADM/ADMX Files

However, there is one additional distinction: ADM and ADMX files aren't usually "rewritten" after a user changes settings that are directed for them (though this can be changed via settings located within Computer Configuration ➢ Policies ➢ Administrative Templates ➢ System ➢ Group Policy, as we explored in Chapter 3 in the section "Affecting the Computer Settings of Group Policy").

GPPrefs are different. They hook into the "timing" of the Group Policy engine. So, even if a user changes the underlying settings (like, they delete a shortcut that is supposed to affect them using GPPrefs), the next time Group Policy refreshes, that shortcut will pop right back as if nothing had happened! Keen!

Now, as we'll see a little later, the GPPrefs have some extra superpowers available. These superpowers can all be found on the Common tab, and we'll cover these superpowers in detail a little later on.

Some options go above and beyond the original ADM/ADMX capabilities:

- "Remove this item when it is no longer applied" can help "peel off" settings when the user or computer falls out of scope of management. But this doesn't always work as you might expect, and we'll explore this a little later.

- "Apply once and do not reapply" changes the GPPref's default behavior. So instead of hooking into the timing of the Group Policy engine, settings are simply deployed once and never again—even if the user changes the settings the administrator wanted.

- "Item-level targeting" is sort of like WMI filters on steroids, and it's only available for GPPrefs settings, not original policy settings.

There are some more options where GPPrefs go above and beyond the original ADM/ADMX preferences, but these are the big ones.

The Overlap of Group Policy vs. Group Policy Preferences and Associated Issues

One of the strangest parts of the GPPrefs is that they bring totally new superpowers to the table yet overlap some existing areas. To some, this can be confusing to say the least, because how will you know which one to use?

Classic vs. Group Policy Preferences Overlap Areas

Some items cursorily overlap with other areas of Group Policy. For instance, drive mappings and Environment variables can also be set with login scripts, as could shortcuts and some other areas if you really put your mind to it. But in some instances, there is brand-new GPPrefs functionality that seems to "compete" with existing classic Group Policy functionality.

Microsoft doesn't like to think of the features as "competing." The idea is that you'll use some features for some reasons and other features for other reasons.

In practice, though, this is rarely 100 percent true.

In some cases, for some features, I'll make a judgment call. That is, there are "clear winners" in some GPPrefs features that you should simply use and stop using some of the original Group Policy features.

Yet, there are other times where one GPPrefs feature dovetails into an existing Group Policy feature. In those instances, I'll show you how to leverage the two features for a "better together" story.

Let's take a look and see the sights.

Group Policy Deployed Printers vs. GPPrefs Printers Extension

The Group Policy Deployed Printers feature debuted with Windows Server 2003 R2 and then made its way as a mainstream Windows Vista feature. You may be wondering why you've never heard of it and why I'm not covering it in other chapters. Well, in short, the feature is not wonderful. Check out www.GPanswers.com's Newsletter #17 for more information about deployed printers with Windows Server 2003 R2 and Windows Vista (and later, actually) if you like. But in short, the "policy-based" feature is difficult to implement, requires a schema update, and didn't work consistently.

For reference, this feature is found by traversing to Computer Configuration ➢ Policies ➢ Windows Settings ➢ Deployed Printers and User Configuration ➢ Windows Settings ➢ Deployed Printers.

In contrast, the new GPPrefs Printers extension feature is found in two places: in Computer Configuration ➢ Preferences ➢ Control Panel Settings ➢ Printers and User Configuration ➢ Preferences ➢ Control Panel Settings ➢ Printers.

The Group Policy feature only allows for shared printers, requires Windows Server 2003 R2 or greater, and only deploys "cleanly" to Windows Vista and Windows Server 2008. You can jury-rig it with the R2 executable PushPrinterConnections.exe (as detailed in www.GPanswers.com Newsletter #17).

This new Printers extension allows for TCP/IP, local printers, or shared printers (User side only), requires no schema changes, and, as long as the Group Policy Preferences are installed on the target machine, makes deploying printers a dream.

This one is a no-brainer: the Printers extension just clobbers the original Group Policy Printers capability. Start using it right away.

Group Policy Internet Explorer and Group Policy IE Maintenance Configuration vs. the GPPrefs Internet Settings Extension

There was already an overlapping message in Group Policy-land when configuring Internet Explorer (IE). The original policy settings can be found here:

- Computer Configuration ➢ Policies ➢ Administrative Templates ➢ Windows Components ➢ Internet Explorer.

- User Configuration ➢ Policies ➢ Administrative Templates ➢ Windows Components ➢ Internet Explorer. Inside, you'll see original policy settings for IE 5 and 6 and, more recently, IE 7 and now IE 8.

But then there are also the IE Maintenance settings, which are found at User Configuration ➢ Policies ➢ Windows Settings ➢ Internet Explorer Maintenance.

So, before we even add the GPPrefs, we have triple overlap.

Now, by adding the GPPrefs, there's a quadruple overlap. The new GPPrefs for the IE settings can be found at User Configuration ➢ Preferences ➢ Control Panel Settings ➢ Internet Settings, as seen in Figure 5.5.

With the overlap in IE, things get really confusing, really fast. What if you have IE settings contained within three or four areas? See the section "How Does the Group Policy Engine Deal with Overlaps?" where we discuss that problem.

FIGURE 5.5   This is the IE preference extension.

But my advice about which one to use and which one to dump is as follows:

- Abandon older IE 5 and 6 settings on the User side of things and use the Internet Explorer GPPrefs extension instead.

- However, the Internet Explorer extension for IE isn't available on the Computer side. So, in that case, see if you can use Computer Configuration ➤ Policies ➤ Administrative Templates ➤ Windows Components ➤ Internet Explorer and, only if you must, User Configuration ➤ Policies ➤ Windows Settings ➤ Internet Explorer Maintenance.

- As for IE 7 and 8, there are more and more items that can be done using policy. If you've got an IE 7 or 8 policy, I would use that. Then, whatever you cannot do using policy, use GPPrefs. But note again, users will be able to wiggle around your preferences.

Group Policy Power Management vs. GPPrefs Power Options Preference Extension

Original Power Management options were found in Computer Configuration ➤ Policies ➤ Administrative Templates ➤ System ➤ Power Management (and the various subnodes within). These settings deal with sleep options, what happens when you push various power buttons, spinning down the hard drive, and more.

There is also one lone User-side setting at User Configuration ➤ Policies ➤ System ➤ Power Management that deals with passwords when the laptop comes back from hibernation.

The new Power Options extension settings are found within Computer Configuration ➤ Preferences ➤ Control Panel Settings ➤ Power Options and User Configuration ➤ Preferences ➤ Control Panel Settings ➤ Power Options. In Figure 5.6 you can see the Power Plan settings available.

FIGURE 5.6   Power Plan settings for Windows Vista and Windows 7.

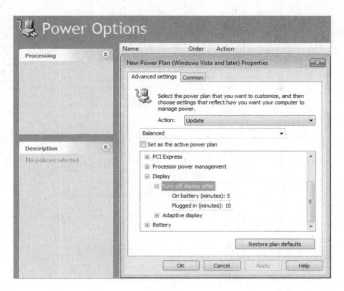

There is a degree of overlap here. In Figure 5.7, you can see what happens when I set the **Specify the System Sleep Timeout (Plugged In)** policy setting to "300 seconds" (not shown). You can see the result if the "Put the computer to sleep" option is set to five minutes, and users are locked out of that setting, plus they get a handy notification bar showing "Some settings are managed by your system administrator." Again, you'll only get the UI lockout and notification bar if you use true policy settings.

However, you are not able to create new Power Schemes (for XP) or Power Plans (Windows Vista or Windows 7) using policy settings. For that, you'll use GPPrefs.

And, what's also neat is that you can, say, create a new Power Plan using Group Policy Preferences, set it as the default, then start out to configure all the settings you want using preferences. Then, if there's a particular setting you want to lock down, you can do so, using policy (if it's available).

So, in short, more settings are available using preferences, but only policy performs a true UI lockout.

    Note that in my testing, creating a new Power Plan required a reboot for the target Windows 7 machine to see it.

Group Policy File Security vs. GPPrefs Files Preference Extension

Group Policy has a way to set security on files. But until the Files extension came along, there was no way to use Group Policy to get files on the Desktop or into folders (short of using a logon script to do it).

FIGURE 5.7   You can lock out various power settings using policy.

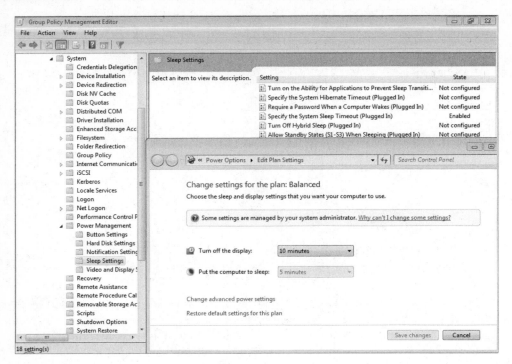

So, this situation is a little weird. It's like two halves that have always wanted to be together. So now with the Files extension (Computer Configuration ➢ Preferences ➢ Windows Settings ➢ Files), you can push a file to a client. And with Group Policy File Security (located within Computer Configuration ➢ Policies ➢ Windows Settings ➢ Security Settings ➢ File System), you can set the ACLs on those files.

What a magic combination!

Group Policy System Services vs. GPPrefs Services Preference Extension

The original way to control services is located in Computer Configuration ➢ Policies ➢ Security Settings ➢ System Services.

The GPPrefs way to control services is located in Computer Configuration ➢ Preferences ➢ Control Panel Settings ➢ Services.

Both have the ability to change the startup mode of a service to Automatic, Manual, or Disabled. However, here are the differences between the two tools:

- The original way can also set the security on the account (who can start, stop, and pause the service).

- The GPPrefs way can do the following things that cannot be done the original way:

- Change the service account password (see the earlier sidebar "About Passwords inside Group Policy Preferences" for the warning about using this).

- Start or stop the service once the Group Policy applies

- Change the recovery options if a service fails

- Change the program to run if a service fails and/or restart the computer if the service fails

So, while there is overlap here, you should ideally use the original way to change the security on the service if necessary but then use the Services extension to manage the rest of the properties, like local system account password and recovery options.

 Note that the management station needs to be running on a machine with the services you want to manage. This is the same behavior as the original Group Policy services node.

Group Policy Device Installation Restrictions vs. GPPrefs Devices Preference Extension

The original Device Installation Restrictions are found at Computer Configuration ➢ Policies ➢ System ➢ Device Installation ➢ Device Installation Restrictions, and we discuss them in detail in Chapter 8.

The new GPPrefs Devices extension node is found in Computer Configuration ➢ Preferences ➢ Control Panel Settings ➢ Devices and User Configuration ➢ Preferences ➢ Control Panel Settings ➢ Devices.

The original way works for only Windows Vista and later. The new way works for all operating systems.

However, the two technologies work fundamentally differently. The original technology's job is to prevent users from installing drivers for new hardware. So when you restrict a specific device from your Windows Vista machines, the driver is actually blocked from being installed. And this strategy works great if the device is unplugged and plugged back in a lot because during the next check, it will block the device. So, it works well for things like USB memory sticks and other things that are unplugged and plugged back in. However, the original technology didn't do such a hot job on devices that were already installed on the machine, such as CD-ROMs, SCSI cards, and scanners. Those device drivers are already installed, and you don't usually unplug them and put them back in. So the driver isn't ever rechecked.

The Devices Extension technology works differently. Its job is to disable the actual device or port, not prevent the driver from loading. So at first blush it would seem like the Devices Extension is the way to go. Except there are two flaws with GPPrefs Devices:

- With the GPPrefs Devices Extension, you cannot dictate a specific piece of hardware that you don't already have on your management station. So if you're looking to just ban 30GB color video iPods, you have to track one down and get it hooked into your management station so you can restrict that specific device type. If you can't find one, you can restrict an entire class that links to that, such as USB ports.

- Because it only disables the device (and doesn't prevent the device driver from installing), any user with appropriate rights can simply re-enable the device, as seen in Figure 5.8. However, regular users don't have access to this ability, so be sure to test this in your environment to see if it is a good fit.

FIGURE 5.8   If the Devices extension has disabled a device, users with Admin rights can re-enable it.

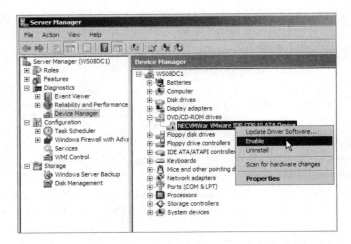

The original technology lets you specify GUIDs of specific hardware IDs. So all you need to do is locate the hardware ID of the device you're after and plunk it into the policy setting and you're golden. Moreover, the original Group Policy settings genuinely prevent the drivers from loading, so there's no way they can just re-enable a device if the drivers aren't even installed.

So, which one do you use where? Here's my advice:

- Use the Group Policy Device Installation settings when you have all Windows Vista or later machines. Preventing the driver is a better way to go overall. And, because you always use the Hardware ID when implementing the setting, you can be as specific or generic as you want.

- Use the Devices Extension settings when you have lots of Windows XP machines. Sure, it's not as industrial strength as preventing the driver from loading, but most users won't know to go around it anyway (and if they don't have rights to, this isn't a problem anyway).

- You might want to use Devices Extension with Windows Vista and Windows 7 machines *anyway*, because, don't forget, the Group Policy Device Installation only works when devices are removed and reintroduced. Devices Extension works great with devices when they're already used with the machine, such as CD-ROMs and SCSI cards, and so on. But again, it doesn't prevent users with rights from simply enabling these devices if they want to.

- Finally, in my testing, Devices Extension worked perfectly when I used Computer Configuration ➢ Preferences ➢ Control Panel Settings ➢ Devices. I restricted the hardware and did a gpupdate command, and my hardware was disabled. However, when I did the same thing using User Configuration ➢ Preferences ➢ Control Panel Settings ➢ Devices and restricted the same hardware, it didn't always take effect right away.

For more on the Devices preference extension versus Group Policy Device Installation settings, be sure to check out Chapter 12, where we have additional information on both solutions.

Group Policy Start Menu Policy Settings vs. GPPrefs Start Menu

The original Group Policy Start Menu policy settings are in User Configuration ➢ Administrative Templates ➢ Start Menu and Taskbar.

The GPPrefs Start Menu extension is located within User Configuration ➢ Preferences ➢ Control Panel Settings ➢ Start Menu.

Although there is a lot of overlap, we need to revisit the idea of policy versus preference. Since a policy is going to restrict the operating system (and force the user to accept the change), the policy settings can be heavy-handed. Heck, that may be just what you want.

On the other hand, the Start Menu extension settings are preferences, which means that they're more like suggestions for the user. So, if the user doesn't like your Start Menu preference settings, they can just reverse them if they so choose.

So, there's not one unified answer about which one you would always use.

Choose the Group Policy Start Menu policy settings when you want to guarantee your settings, and use the Start Menu extension settings when you want to set a baseline but permit the user to change them.

It should be noted that this GPPref (heck, all GPPrefs) will refresh every 90 minutes or so by default and wipe out their changed settings. But you can change this behavior later using information found in the sections about the Common tab, specifically in the section "Apply Once and Do Not Reapply."

Group Policy Restricted Groups vs. Local Users and Groups Preference Extension

The original Group Policy Restricted Groups is located within Computer Configuration ➢ Policies ➢ Security Settings ➢ Restricted Groups. We'll cover it in more detail in Chapter 8 if you're unfamiliar with it.

The GPPrefs Local Users and Groups is located within Computer Configuration ➢ Preferences ➢ Control Panel Settings ➢ Local Users and Groups and User Configuration ➢ Preferences ➢ Control Panel Settings ➢ Local Users and Groups.

Here's the "ever so brief" rundown. The original Group Policy Restricted Groups allows you to affect who is and who is not a member of either domain-based groups or local groups.

However, the Local Users and Groups GPPrefs extension is meant for, well, just local users and groups.

But Group Policy Restricted Groups does have some downsides. Its main goal is to strictly control the group membership, which might not be what you're looking to do. While it's possible to use Group Policy Restricted Groups to simply add a user to a group, it's not intuitive and it's a lot of work.

Moreover, the GPPrefs Local Users and Groups extension is available for both the User and Computer sides (which means it's more flexible), and you can also use it to add a new user account (complete with all account settings) to the computers of your choice. The Local Users and Groups extension can also delete local groups and cherry-pick specific users to delete from groups (super useful if you just want to pluck just one user out of, say, the local Administrators group).

So, the advice is simple:

- If you want to affect domain-based groups (like Backup Operators, Domain Admins, etc.), stick with Group Policy Restricted Groups.

- Use the Local Users and Groups extension for everything else. It's much easier to understand and implement and you'll likely be happier overall.

 This is kind of a "tip" with a "warning" edge. You can also use the Local Users and Groups extension to just mass-change the target machines' local Administrator password. Sounds great—except, again, you should check out the sidebar "About Passwords inside Group Policy Preferences" for a warning to decide if you still want to use this.

How Does the Group Policy Engine Deal with Overlaps?

Well, there's the short answer, the middle-length answer, and the long answer. Let's go over all of them. (We're old friends now—you knew I would anyway, right?)

The Short Answer: Policy Wins over Preferences

The short answer is that if there's a conflict between a policy setting and a preference setting, the policy setting will win. (So, for instance, items in Computer and User Configuration ➢ Policies should always win over Computer or User Configuration ➢ Preferences.)

Why?

Because only policies lock out the user interface of the application they manage (Explorer, Office 2003, etc.).

Preferences don't.

Remember, preferences are suggestions that you can give to the user's application, but the user can usually just wipe them out if they want (although GPPrefs will reapply again at policy refresh time by default).

Here's a quick example to prove the point. In the example in Figure 5.9, I'm clicking Help to ensure that the Help menu is on the Start Menu for all Windows 7 machines using GPPrefs. True, this is the default anyway, but by selecting it here, I'm laying down a preference that is always put on the machine.

FIGURE 5.9   By using GPPrefs, you're putting a preference on the client.

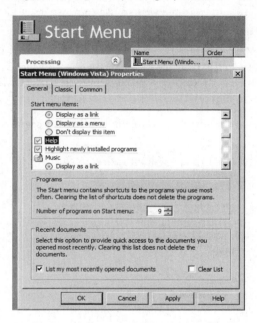

However, if I use the policy setting User Configuration ➢ Policies ➢ Administrative Templates ➢ Start Menu and Taskbar ➢ Remove Help menu from Start Menu, as seen in Figure 5.10, the Help option disappears in the Windows Vista/Windows 7 Start Menu.

FIGURE 5.10   This policy will positively remove Help from the Start Menu.

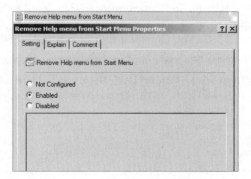

But the general case here is that policies always beat preferences. Rock always beats scissors. Or does it? Can the rock crumble when it's hit by the scissors? Let's continue to see at least one interesting case where it doesn't work that way.

The Middle-Length Answer: Sometimes Preferences Win over Policy

Microsoft's documentation expresses that policy *always* wins over preference. But in fact, that's not always true. Here's an example we can use to prove it:

1. Create a single GPO and link it to an OU containing users that you can test. In a minute, you'll have them log onto a Windows 7 machine.

2. Use the User ➤ Preferences ➤ Control Panel Settings ➤ Internet Settings preference extension to set the Internet Explorer 8 proxy server to 10.1.1.1 with port 8080. You can see a shot of this in Figure 5.11.

FIGURE 5.11   The Internet Settings extension lets you set preferences for users.

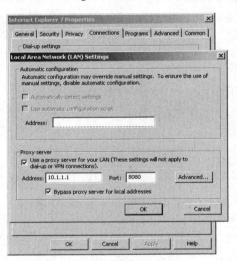

3. Then, in the same GPO locate User Configuration ➤ Policies ➤ Windows Settings Internet Explorer Maintenance ➤ Connection ➤ Proxy Settings to set the proxy to 10.2.2.2 with a port of 8282. You can see a shot of this in Figure 5.12.

4. Then, refresh your client via GPupdate and fire up Internet Explorer 8.

Which proxy server setting wins? Fire up IE 8, then use Tools ➤ Internet Options ➤ Connections ➤ LAN Settings and look at the Proxy page setting, where you'll see the delivered setting.

The preferences proxy server and port setting (10.1.1.1, port 8080) wins over the policy's 10.2.2.2 with port 8282!

Uh-oh. This seems to break the laws of nature! How can preferences win over policy? Because Internet Explorer Maintenance policy isn't really policy. Indeed, by setting the IE home page using Internet Explorer Maintenance, the value goes to:

`HKCU\Software\Microsoft\Windows\CurrentVersion\Internet Settings`

in a value called `ProxyServer`, as seen in Figure 5.13. And since this is not a place for a true policy, it must actually be a preference.

FIGURE 5.12   Setting the home page via IE Maintenance policy

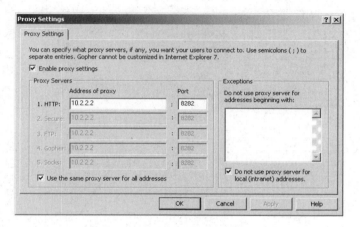

FIGURE 5.13   The value set by both Internet Explorer Maintenance and the IE Group Policy Preferences is the same. The Group Policy Preferences "wins" in this case.

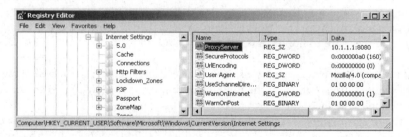

Indeed, the value that's being set is exactly the same for both the IE Group Policy Preference and Internet Explorer Maintenance.

Why does one win over the other? I'll show you the nuances of why in the next section.

But for now, it turns out there is a clever way to attain our goal: force an IE proxy server and lock it down so users cannot change it.

Check out an obscure Administrative Templates policy setting named **Disable changing proxy settings** (located in User Configuration ➢ Policies ➢ Administrative Templates ➢

Windows Components ➢ Internet Explorer). A-ha! That's true policy, so hopefully that will perform some kind of lockdown, as shown in Figure 5.14.

FIGURE 5.14   This policy performs a lockdown of IE.

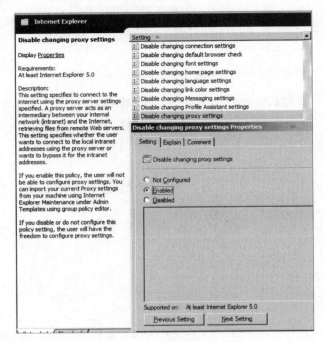

But why then does that Administrative Templates setting named **Disable changing proxy server settings** work in a way the other guys don't? Because IE 8.0 (and 7.0 and 6.0 and 5.0) are all coded to look in the proper policies keys. And if there's a value there that IE recognizes, then IE makes sure to honor that.

And it does.

The end result is that true policy wins. You can see this in Figure 5.15, where the proxy server entry's values are taken from the preferences but it's locked down via the policy.

For most people, the medium-length answer will be good enough.

But you're not most people. You're looking for the most detailed knowledge you can get. So if you're curious to know why the Internet Explorer GPPrefs won against the Internet Explorer Maintenance Group Policy settings, read on for the Longer Answer.

The Longer Answer: Understanding CSE Timing and Overlap

To get to the bottom of this mystery, we need to understand when Group Policy applies. Recall that the Group Policy system is a last-written-wins technology. So, if you have an overlap between, say, the domain level and the OU level, the default is that the OU level will win because it was written last.

FIGURE 5.15   True policy wins, and the user interface is locked out.

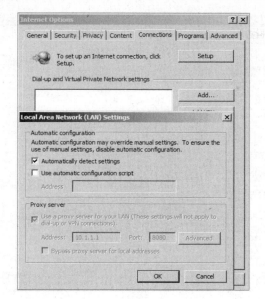

But now things become markedly more confusing. Not only is there overlap between Active Directory levels (site, domain, OU) for some of the features, there's overlap at the *feature* level, where two or three CSEs compete to write their data last.

Ow.

There is some order in this chaos. But to understand it you'll need an intimate understanding of what happens when the CSEs process (in the foreground and in the background). In short, the CSEs process in the order seen in Figure 5.16. This is a script you can download from http://tinyurl.com/23xfz3 called FindGPOsByPolicyExtension.wsf.

This exposes the same information as if you went to the following Registry key on a machine with the GPPrefs extensions loaded:

```
HKEY_LOCAL_MACHINE\SOFTWARE\Microsoft\
Windows NT\CurrentVersion\Winlogon\GPExtensions
```

There, you'll see the registrations for all CSEs. The GUID of each CSE dictates the order in which things will process. They'll process alphabetically, by GUID. So, Wireless Group Policy fires off first (that's a classic Group Policy setting), then Group Policy Environment (that's a new GPPrefs CSE), then Group Policy Local Users and Groups (another new GPPrefs CSE), then Folder Redirection (a classic Group Policy CSE), and so on.

So on the surface, it appears that if you had a conflict with both classic Group Policy settings and newer GPPrefs settings, you could just see which one ran last and bank on that setting always "winning."

But that's only true if the two CSEs end up writing to the *exact same places*.

FIGURE 5.16 All CSEs process in alphabetical order based upon GUID.

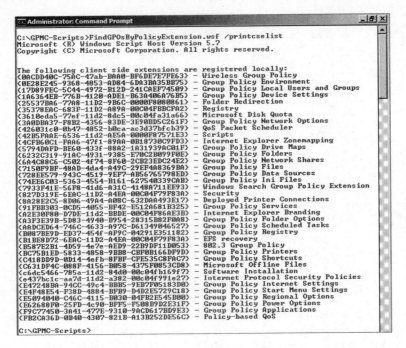

Although this is precisely what we encountered with the Internet Proxy server setting, the two technologies don't *usually* write to exactly the same place. The tie will be broken when an application is coded to look in the proper policies keys. And, if there's a policy setting in those keys, the target application will honor the policy, not the preference.

In our mystery, it's now easy to understand why the Internet Explorer GPPrefs (listed as Group Policy Internet Settings) in Figure 5.17 "won" over the IE Maintenance settings (listed as Internet Explorer Zonemapping and Internet Explorer Branding). The new Internet Explorer GPPrefs CSE (Group Policy Internet Settings) applies *after* the original Internet Explorer CSEs.

But in neither case are we applying actual "policy."

We're really just applying preferences—using two different kinds of technology.

We finally got it to work the way we wanted when a true policy was applied, and Internet Explorer saw the policy in the policies keys and acted accordingly.

Whew. All this stuff can give you a headache. This "who will win" stuff is really confusing, and I haven't tested every case. Be sure to test all interactions in a test lab before you roll out settings to production.

Other Items That Can Affect Group Policy and GPPrefs Processing

Recall that in Chapter 4 you learned about various policy settings found at Computer Configuration ➢ Policies ➢ Administrative Templates ➢ System ➢ Group Policy that have

the configuration option to "Process Even If the Group Policy Objects Have Not Changed."
(You can get a refresher back in Chapter 4 in the section "Using Group Policy to Affect
Group Policy.")

FIGURE 5.17   Many GPPrefs have action items, like this one.

If this option is turned on for a particular CSE, then that CSE will always try to rewrite
its configuration data—upon every single refresh. Again, that's not the default for classic
Group Policy, but it is an option on a CSE-by-CSE basis.

However, this same "always try to rewrite configuration data" mantra is held by the
GPPrefs CSEs *by default*, but it can also be set such that the data is laid down once and
never rewritten.

So knowing this information, you might have to do a little mental math to figure out
which one is going to win if you have conflicting policies *plus* the wildcard settings.

The Group Policy Results reports, as seen in Chapter 2, are going to be helpful in figuring
out *which* settings ultimately applied, but they're not going to be helpful in your understanding
of *why* the setting ultimately applied.

Hopefully, this section helps you out.

The Lines and Circles and the CRUD Action Modes

By this time, you might have spent a little time plunking around the new Group Policy
Preferences (but you haven't deployed them yet, because you haven't finished the chapter,
right?). And, indeed, you can see that they're really, really different than the original Group
Policy settings. Many of them (gasp!) kind of look like the thing they actually manage in
the Windows user interface! Mon Dieu!

If you haven't yet tried out GPPrefs and want to follow along with these examples, this would be a good time. That's because you'll learn about both the "lines and circles" and Action modes at the same time. I strongly suggest that you try these settings in a test lab and not in production until you've got a real grip on how everything works.

You'll note that many GPPrefs have an action item, and you can set it to Create, Replace, Update, or Delete. This is called the *CRUD method* for short. You'll also notice many GPPrefs have these thin solid green lines or thin dashed red lines underneath certain settings. These colorful lines express which settings could possibly affect your client.

We can use the Power Options preference extension in our examples because it has both CRUD ability *and* contains solid green lines for many options. To create a Windows XP power option for your users, dive down to User Configuration ➢ Preferences ➢ Control Panel Settings ➢ Power Options and select New Power Scheme (Windows XP). Alternatively, the same node exists on the Computer side if you wanted to play with that. When you do, you'll create a Power Options Preference item and see something similar to what I've got in Figure 5.17.

So both the lines and circles and CRUD action-item features can bite you in the butt—if you don't know what they mean and how they work. Let's explore those now. We'll tackle the colored lines first, then the CRUD. (That's it, I'm trademarking that phrase: www.GPanswers .com: *We Tackle the CRUD*.) Microsoft doesn't like to call it the CRUD method for obvious reasons. But I do. So that's what I'll be calling it.

The Lines and the Circles

Original Group Policy doesn't have any solid and dashed lines, but many of the new GPPrefs items do.

So, what's the deal with those solid and dashed lines? It's a way to craft which policy settings within a GPPrefs you want to affect a client machine.

Here's an example.

Let's say a user has gone in and made some settings they like to use. In our example, we'll assume users on laptops have created their own power schemes for when they're using the batteries on their laptops. And we trust that these laptop users have the scheme they need for their battery because they set it themselves.

However, we want to make sure they save power when they're plugged into the power outlets. No problem! We can use the Power Options extension to define what a Windows XP Portable/Laptop scheme is and how it uses power. You can see in Figure 5.17 that I've changed the scheme to Portable/Laptop and I'm ready to make changes.

But even though we're changing the "Plugged in" settings, we already said we don't want to disrupt any settings that might have already been made to the "Running on batteries" section of the scheme.

So, what are we going to do? By default *every* setting on this page has a thin green line beneath it. This means that if you update this power scheme, all green underlined settings will be delivered to the client machine. But, ouch! That's exactly what you *don't* want.

You want a way to update *some* of the settings, and not *all* of the settings. You need a way to prevent the processing of some of the settings on the page. To do this, highlight the setting (actually, pull down the pull-down) and then press the F7 key. This will change the thin green line to a thin dashed red line.

Now this setting (the one with the dashed red lines) is exempt from being applied within the edict.

So here's the thing that's misleading and potentially leads to misunderstanding: it doesn't matter what you configure the values to within the settings that now have the red dashed underline—because your client systems will never, ever pick those values up. This same behavior will hold true for check boxes, fill-in-the-blanks, and radio buttons. If there's a red dashed underline beneath the setting, your clients simply ignore the setting upon refresh.

Microsoft calls this "disabling the policy," but I don't love that term because I don't want to get mixed up in thinking somehow that I'm "disabling the functionality" the setting provides. By *disabling*, Microsoft means "disabling the processing of that particular setting."

So, in Figure 5.18 I've selected all the "Running on batteries" settings and disabled them by selecting each setting I wanted to skip the processing for, and then I pressed F7.

FIGURE 5.18   You can enable and disable individual settings using the function keys.

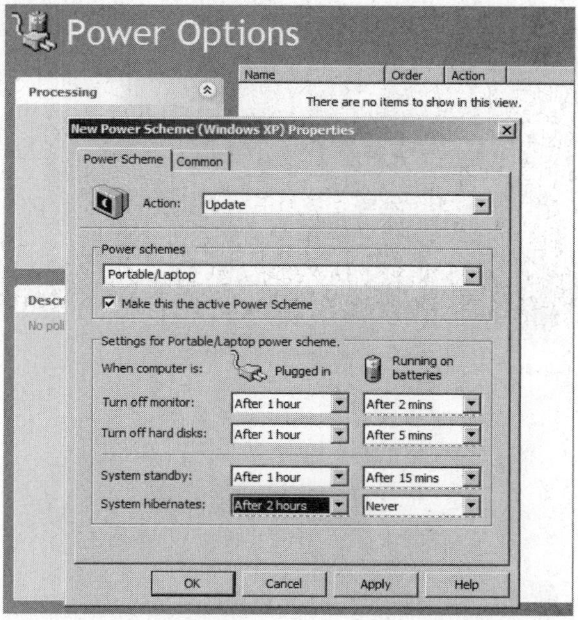

There are other function keys that have meaning in the interface as well. Here are all the function keys and what they do:

F5   Enables the processing of *all* settings on the page that need to be honored. Useful if you disabled some settings from being honored and want to reset the form.

F6   Enables the processing of one setting on the page that needs to be honored. Useful if you disabled one setting using F7 and want to change it back. Again, merely changing the value will not reset it to a green underline.

F7   Disables the processing of one setting on the page. Useful if you want to keep one setting from being updated or changed on the client.

F8   Disables the processing of all settings. Useful if you want to prevent all the settings on one tab from being honored on the client. Most useful when using the Internet Explorer settings because there are multiple tabs that hold a massive amount of settings. Perhaps you want to disable all settings (which means none will apply) but enable just one tab with two settings.

You'll also see that some settings in the extension have green circles (equivalent to the solid green underline) or red circles a la the "no" sign (which are the equivalent of the thin red dashed line). You can see an example in Figure 5.19, where I've explicitly disabled the processing of two settings within IE 7's Advanced tab. To disable the processing of those items, I simply selected the item and pressed F7. Again, it doesn't matter if the check box is actively checked or not: the value in the check box doesn't get processed if there's a little "no" sign next to it (or it has a red dashed underline).

FIGURE 5.19   The red and green circles in some areas of a preference extension are analogous to the red and green underlines.

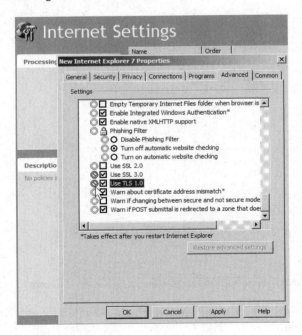

Warning: Visiting Multiple Tabs Can Be Hazardous to Your Network's Health

There are colored circles and lines for various Group Policy Preferences. Let's again take a look at Internet Explorer 8.

Internet Explorer 8, as an example, has lots of tabs. So the extension does a little helpful trick for you.

If you visit any tab, you'll see that many settings already have a green underline. You now know that any setting that has a green underline will have its value placed on the client (check box checked, radio button pushed, etc.).

But, again, most tabs have lots of stuff that *already* have green lines on most of the tabs. Does that mean that all those settings (even ones you likely don't care about) will be delivered to the client?

Well, *possibly*. There are the three cases to consider. We'll use Internet Explorer 8 properties as our example.

Case 1: Nothing actually created   Let's say you just want to poke around and see what's underneath the hood in the tabs. Of course you'll want to; you're naturally curious.

So you open up a Group Policy Object and create a new IE 8 Extension item and start poking around.

You can see it has a gaggle of tabs like General, Security, Privacy, Connections, Programs and so on. Some tabs have green underlines, and others have red underlines. Others have *both*. You know that green-underlined properties are going to be set on the target machine.

Except you haven't changed anything yet, have you? You're just exploring and poking around.

When you click Cancel, nothing's changed, because the preferences item isn't actually created.

Case 2: Quick visit to existing item, but no changes   Let's say you stumbled across someone else's IE 8 item, and you wanted to know what was set within the item.

So, you edit the item, and start exploring and poking around *but not changing anything*. You can click the Connections tab and see what's there or click the Advanced tab and see what's there. And you can see what changes were made.

But, again, this is just a quick visit, and you've changed nothing.

When you click Cancel, nothing's changed. That's because you didn't change anything.

Case 3: A visit with a change on any tab   Let's say you stumbled across someone else's IE 8 item, and you want to know what's set in some tabs (like Connections), *and* you want to change an item yourself in another tab (like Privacy).

So you edit the IE 8 item and check out the Connections tab, shown in the following image. As you can see, no check boxes or other values have been changed by the previous admin. You do see green lines underneath some values, however.

Now you visit the tab you really need to make changes on—the Privacy tab—and you click in one place, and, say, uncheck the "Turn on Pop-up Blocker," as seen in the second screen shot.

Here's the big warning: because you initially clicked on a tab (Connections) and that tab has green-line settings, then you visited a different tab (Privacy) to make a change, the green underlined settings as now specified on the Connections tab *will be set* (as well as all the green underlined settings in Privacy, because they're all green too!).

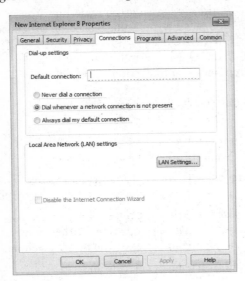 

This is very counterintuitive because, well, you didn't make any settings changes to Connections! You just visited one tab but made your changes in another tab.

But it doesn't matter. In this case, just looking at the tab (then making changes anywhere) does the damage.

The rule is simple: if you visit a tab (and the tab has green underlines) and you make any changes anywhere within the preference item, any tabs you visited will change the properties of their green underlined values.

The CRUD Method: Create, Replace, Update, or Delete

Let's continue with our power scheme for the XP example as we work through the next area: the CRUD method.

CRUD stands for Create, Replace, Update, or Delete. You'll notice these settings in the Action drop-down of many extensions, like the Power Scheme extension seen in Figure 5.20.

Here's what happens when an Action mode is chosen:

Create Create the setting, but only if it does not already exist. Check out Figure 5.20, where I'm creating a new power scheme for my whole company. Selecting Replace or Update (next options) wouldn't make sense because I'm not trying to modify an existing scheme. Only Create makes sense, because the whole scheme doesn't yet exist.

FIGURE 5.20   You use Create to dictate settings that you've never dictated before.

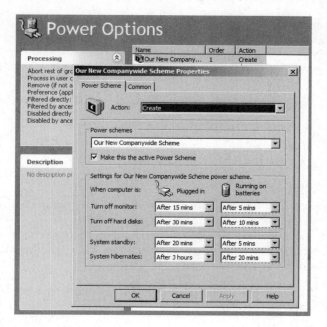

Replace   Delete the setting if it already exists. Then push down new settings. For this, the Power Options preference extension, the whole scheme "Our New Companywide Scheme" would be deleted. Then it would be re-created from scratch. A useful scenario might be after some company-wide power scheme was defined but perhaps defined incorrectly. In this case, choosing Replace would delete *any* settings if they exist. Then, you can reconfigure the GPO with exactly the settings you want to manage (and get it right this time).

Update (default)   This is the default action. This will create any new settings if they don't exist on the client. And if any settings do exist on the client, those with thin green underlines will also be updated with the values in the settings.

Delete   Delete the settings. In our example, Delete would delete the whole scheme. Poof.

Use this CRUD action item with caution. You can delete all sorts of things you wish you hadn't: power schemes, drive mappings, the local Administrators group, and more.

So really watch out, and especially test this action before you implement.

For many GPPrefs, you won't see the Action drop-down. In this case, that means there is only one way for these settings to work. It's usually Update.

Common Tab

If you notice back in some of the figures in this chapter, there's a tab that keeps showing up over and over again. It's called the Common tab, and it's full of many of the superpowers the GPPrefs provide.

If you click on any Common tab, you'll see that they all have exactly the same options, as follows:

- Stop processing items in this extension if an error occurs

- Run in logged-on user's security context (user policy option)

- Remove this item when it is no longer applied

- Apply once and do not reapply

- Item-level targeting

You can see the Common tab in Figure 5.21, with a little extra note when one of the items is selected. (We'll get to that note in this section as well.)

The idea is that each and every Group Policy preference item you create can also option- ally choose to leverage one or more of these extra options. Let's examine each of these items now in this section.

FIGURE 5.21 Be super, extra careful when you select the "Remove this item when it is no longer applied" option in the Common tab.

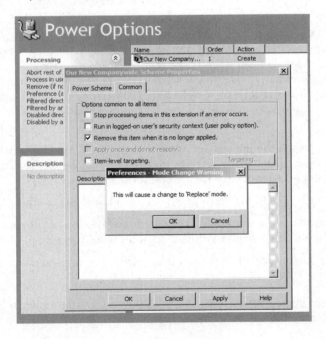

"Stop Processing Items in This Extension If an Error Occurs"

We'll start out with the least-used item of the bunch. The idea here is that if, when you're plunking down multiple preference items (within the same extension) there's a problem, then stop when the system encounters that problem. One situation where this might be helpful is when you use the Files extension. Perhaps you didn't want any files to be copied if, for some reason, the source file suddenly didn't exist. So, as soon as the GPPrefs engine realized one source file wasn't available, the whole Files preference extension CSE would stop. Other GPPrefs CSEs, like Drive Maps, Power Options, and Printers, would keep on chuggin'.

Again, this is the least-used option in the bunch.

"Run In Logged-on User's Security Context (User Policy Option)"

By default, the Group Policy engine runs all commands as SYSTEM, even though it's the user who's really logged in. This is awesome because it means you have some crazy superpowers, like the ability to zap any Registry key to anywhere in the Registry, restrict hardware regardless of who is logged on, and schedule tasks to run *right now*, even if no one is logged in.

There might be a time when you want to use this setting, but in my experience the times are few and far between. One example would be if you want to copy files in the user context and not the SYSTEM context.

There might be other times where GPPrefs just don't seem to take effect. One quick GPPrefs troubleshooting tip is to flip this setting on within the Common tab. There might be some occasion when trying to perform the action as the SYSTEM doesn't make the magic happen but performing the same action as the logged-in user does.

The other main use for this setting comes with the use of Environment variables, which we'll talk about in the next section, so hang tight.

Here are some quick notes about some behaviors of this policy:

- Note that this setting is grayed out when dealing with GPPrefs on the Computer side, and the behavior is then to *always* use the SYSTEM account.

- Drive mappings and printers (network printers and TCP/IP printers only) ignore this setting. They *always* use the user context, so checking this check box here shouldn't produce any discernable effect. Note that new drive mappings don't take effect until the next logon and aren't related to this discussion.

"Remove This Item When It Is No Longer Applied"

This is my favorite option because it's full of interesting opportunities, behaviors, and pitfalls. You can see in Figure 5.21, when you click on "Remove this item when it is no longer applied," you'll immediately get a pop-up saying, "This will cause a change to 'Replace' mode." If you click back over to, say, the Power Scheme tab (or whatever tab your GPPrefs uses that has a CRUD action item), you'll see that the action has automatically been set to Replace and is grayed out to stay that way.

Even though it sets it to Replace mode, you can think of this setting as Delete and not Replace. Heck, Delete isn't strong enough, really. Think of it as Nuke.

That's because it will nuke the settings if the preference goes out of the scope of management. If you'll recall from Chapter 3, a scope change can happen when any of the following are true:

- Group Policy security filters are used and the user/computer is filtered out (see Chapter 2).
- The Group Policy is deleted.
- The Group Policy is unlinked.
- The Group Policy's link is disabled.
- The preference is deleted.
- The WMI filter evaluates to false.
- And now, as we'll learn a little later, if "Item-level targeting" evaluates to false.

If any of these things happens, the target item is Nuked. Let's work through an example with one of my favorites, the Registry extension.

Finding a Value to Change with the Registry Extension

In this example, we're going to change the DoubleClickSpeed entry for all users in the **Human Resources** OU. That includes Sol Rosenberg and everyone else who's logged on. (Again, this is a working example to illustrate a point.)

In Figure 5.22, you can see the Mouse properties on the right and the underlying Registry entry HKEY_CURRENT_USER\Control Panel\Mouse\DoubleClickSpeed and its value of 500. If you move the Mouse properties slider to the right by two notches, the result is 340. Knowing this tidbit, if we use the Registry extension to dictate the DoubleClickSpeed value of 340, we'll be forcing our users to double-click slightly faster.

Using the Registry Preference Extension to Dictate the Setting to the Human Resources Users OU

Create and link a GPO over **Human Resources Users** OU. Then edit the GPO and dive into User Configuration ➢ Preferences ➢ Windows Settings ➢ Registry. Click New ➢ Registry Item.

- For Action, make sure Update is selected.
- For Hive, make sure you've chosen HKEY_CURRENT_USER.
- For Key Path, make sure you've selected (or typed in) Control Panel\Mouse.
- For Value name, make sure DoubleClickSpeed is entered (you can leave the Default check box unchecked).
- For Value type, make sure REG_SZ is selected.
- For Value data, enter **340** (the value we know we want to set).

You can see all of this in Figure 5.23.

FIGURE 5.22   We can figure out how the `DoubleClickSpeed` value works by playing with Explorer.

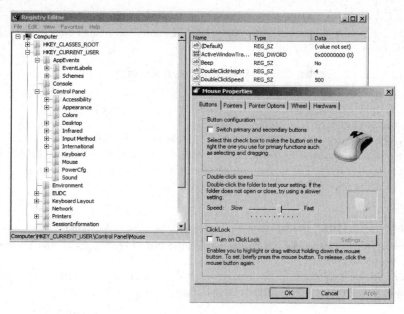

FIGURE 5.23   We can dictate specific settings using the Registry CSE.

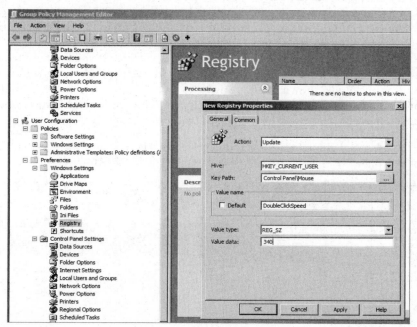

Testing the Delivery of Our Settings

At this point, log on as Sol Rosenberg to any machine, then check the double-click speed. You can check the slider in the Control Panel Mouse applet, but an even better check is running REGEDIT. Then dive down into HKEY_CURRENT_USER\Control Panel\Mouse and see if DoubleClickSpeed is set to 340.

Testing the Default Group Policy Preferences Behavior

At this point, move Sol Rosenberg's account from the **Human Resources Users** OU to the **Nurses** OU. (Don't worry, when we're done, we'll move him back.)

Log off, and log back on.

Then run the Registry editor (REGEDIT) and dive down into HKEY_CURRENT_USER\Control Panel\Mouse. What happened to the DoubleClickSpeed settings? Answer: nothing; they stay put because the Group Policy Preferences' default behavior is to maintain, or tattoo the Registry, even if the user falls out of the scope of management.

Log off as Sol.

Resetting for Our Next Test

At this point, move Sol Rosenberg's account from the **Nurses** OU back to the **Human Resources Users** OU.

Make sure you're logged off as Sol Rosenberg from the target computer.

Now, we're going to see what happens if we change the default behavior.

Turning on "Remove This Item When It Is No Longer Applied"

Now select the Common tab and select "Remove this item when it is no longer applied." You should get a pop-up box saying the mode has been changed to Nuke, er, Replace.

Back on the General tab, you should see that Replace is on and grayed out so it cannot be changed. Click OK to close the properties page. Now, before we continue, it should be noted that there is a signal of the (potential) devastation to come. If you look at the line item that's produced, you'll see a little red triangle next to the name showing you that the system is in Replace mode, shown in Figure 5.24.

Nothing "bad" will happen until something happens with the scope. Let's examine the normal course of action that could happen up to (and including) that point.

FIGURE 5.24   The red triangle next to the preference item shows we're in Replace mode (and also possibly in "Remove this item when it is no longer applied" mode).

Testing the Redelivery of Our Settings

Just for laughs, while logged on as Sol, reopen the Mouse applet in Control Panel and jam the double-click slider all the way to left. Now run GPupdate. Close and reopen the Mouse applet.

Did the slide jump back to the faster position we dictated?

Indeed, check the Registry on the machine just to be sure if you're not.

That's good: the default behavior of GPPrefs is working for you. That is, the default is that it will always reapply the settings, even if someone changes a setting by hand on the target computer.

Seeing the Result of "Remove This Item When It Is No Longer Applied"

At this point, move Sol Rosenberg's account from the **Human Resources** Users OU to the **Nurses** OU a second time.

Log off, and log back on. Then open rerun the Registry editor tool (REGEDIT) and dive down into HKEY_CURRENT_USER\Control Panel\Mouse.

And make a discovery.

That is, the whole DoubleClickSpeed *value has been deleted!*

You can see this in Figure 5.25. Or, rather, you *can't* see this in Figure 5.25, because it's GONE.

FIGURE 5.25   Once the "Remove this item when it is no longer applied" setting is checked, the DoubleClickSpeed Registry key is deleted. But, thankfully, the Mouse application doesn't seem to mind very much.

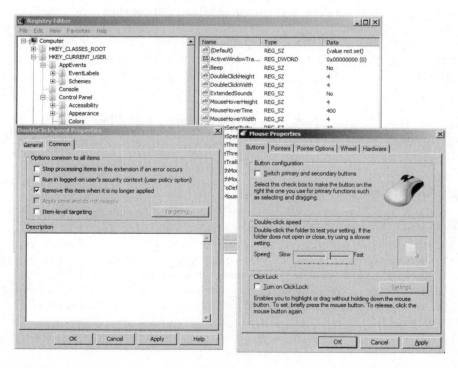

This isn't likely what you expected. You expected it to revert back to 500 or go to 0 or do something else predictable.

Right. Well, it doesn't.

By selecting "Remove this item when it is no longer applied," you Nuke the entry. It literally deletes the whole thing you're working on—in this case, a Registry setting; in other cases, power schemes, local users and groups, data sources, and other things you likely don't want to *delete*.

Putting the World Right Again for Sol

Put Sol's account back into the **Human Resources Users** OU.

Then log out and log back in. You should see the DoubleClickSpeed pop back in place with the value of 340.

Final Thoughts about "Remove This Item When It Is No Longer Applied"

Before we move on to the next topic, I do have some final thoughts about "Remove this item when it is no longer applied."

First, in our DoubleClickSpeed example, we didn't really do any "harm" to the system by deleting the DoubleClickSpeed key. In our examples, double-clicking will continue to work because the people who coded Explorer's mouse double-click feature must have said, "Well, if the DoubleClickSpeed key suddenly goes missing, we'll assume it's, oh, I dunno, how's 500?" And it keeps on working.

But that's because we're lucky!

If this was some Registry key to a custom application, you could have damaged the application, that's for sure.

Next, it isn't the Replace CRUD action that does this deed. It's positively the "Remove this item when it is no longer applied" check box. Again, think of this as Nuke. But the action item shows Replace, which is kind of misleading.

 If you're "freaking out" right now thinking "Nuke mode isn't what I want... I want a real way to revert settings back." Then don't panic. We'll learn about a tool called PolicyPak in the next chapter that does exactly that.

"Apply Once and Do Not Reapply"

This is the other setting in the Common tab that I like a lot. This setting does just what it says: it will plunk down the setting, then never reapply. This is good, and it's bad.

On the one hand, you're able to set a true preference for the user. That is, you're suggesting this setting for them, so it's laid down exactly one time. If they want to change it, they can, and your suggestion never "plows down" back on top of their selected setting.

On the other hand, you might have the occasion to want to perform a baseline push of certain values to the system again. And in that case, not even running gpupdate /force will reset the values.

Targeting Your Preference Items

The final superpower within the Common tab is item-level targeting (ILT). ILT provides a new way to indicate exactly when a specific preference item should apply. ILT is almost like WMI filters (which we explored in Chapter 4). But ILTs have some advantages over WMI filters:

- They're easier to set up and use immediately. You'll fall in love with the GUI interface of ILTs.

- You can do nested ANDs, ORs, and NOTs within ILTs, making them immediately more flexible than WMI filters.

- ILTs, in general, evaluate faster when run on the client. WMI filters really cut into the machine's heart to see what's going on to evaluate the query. ILTs use code within the GPPrefs CSE to perform the query, so they're usually much faster (in most cases). In most cases, overall there's hardly any processing penalty to using them.

The categories can be seen in Figure 5.26.

There are all sorts of queryable items, such as amount of RAM, CPU speed, available disk space, and more.

FIGURE 5.26   Item-level targeting lets you specify when specific preferences apply.

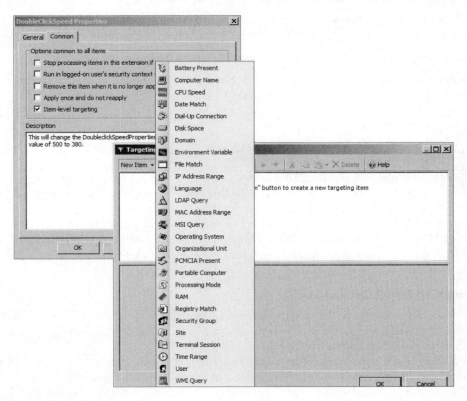

Note that one category within ILTs *is* WMI queries. So, you can leverage WMI queries within ILTs if you wanted to do something that wasn't part of the native ILT queries. The downside is that item-level targeting is only for GPPrefs and is simply not available for the other areas of original Group Policy.

How Are Item-Level Targeting Items Evaluated?

One question you might be asking yourself is, "In what context is the ILT evaluated?"

In some cases, the logged-in user might not have rights to determine if an item-level targeting item is true or not. Likewise, the computer (SYSTEM) might have too much power and inadvertently say that something is true when really it's not true for the user at all.

Thankfully, these scenarios have been thought out. In short, here's what happens:

- Most ILTs are checked in the SYSTEM context. Because the SYSTEM has more rights than the user, this is desirable.

- However, some items should only be determined from the viewpoint of the logged-on user. Here's the breakdown:

Security Group Targeting Item   Runs from the point of view of the logged-in user (except if you're checking to see if the computer is a member of a group)

Language Targeting Item   Runs from the point of view of the logged-in user

File Match Targeting Item   Runs from the point of view of the logged-in user; then, if that fails, runs in the SYSTEM context as a second try

---

The Targeting Editor

You'll craft your query in the Targeting Editor.

By default, all items are ANDed together. In this way, ILTs can be "banded together" to produce queries where multiple items need to be true for the action to take place.

In Figure 5.27, I've strung together a query to really and truly verify that DogFoodMaker 6.0 is installed on the machine—I'm checking that the MSI product code has been installed on the machine and also that the HKLM\Software\DogFoodMaker hive has a key called Ruff with a value of six.

Adding Additional Collections

Alternatively, if you want to do something fancier, you can select the Add Collection button and created nested groups of ILTs. For instance, you can have an ILT apply only when it hits User1 or the Administrator account.

To do that, you'd create two collections (be sure they're at the same level; you don't want to nest one within the other). Then, you'd highlight the second collection and click Item Options (next to Add Collection) and select OR. Now your second collection is OR.

Now, add your conditions in the first block and in the second block, and they'll be ORed together, as seen in Figure 5.28.

FIGURE 5.27   You can string together items in the Targeting Editor with AND.

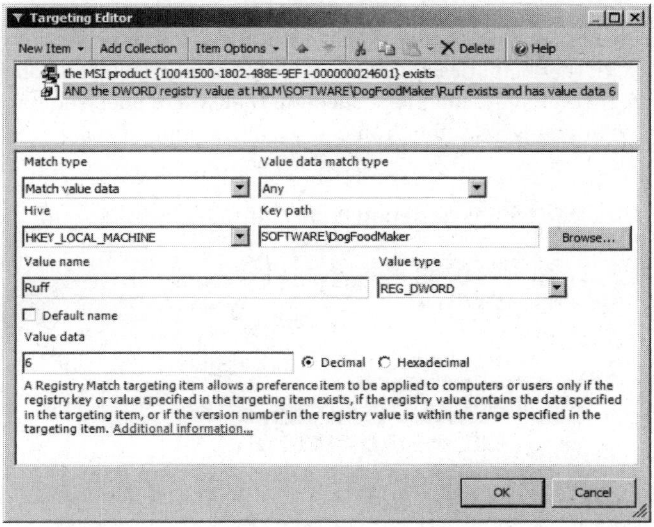

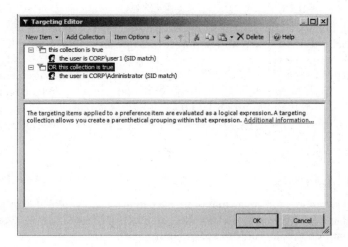

FIGURE 5.28   Using OR, you can ensure that your wishes take place when certain conditions are true.

Other Targeting Editor Tricks

You can usually drag and drop things around without thinking about it too much. The ILT editor was rewritten heavily (and heck, renamed!) since the acquisition of the product from DesktopStandard, and they really did a smashing job of cleaning it up and making it easier to use overall.

Be sure to experiment with the cut, paste, and copy items. You'll be able to rapid-fire-create ILTs once you play with these abilities a little more. Additionally, you can add a label to a collection. That way, if you have a complex collection that you're querying for, others can figure out precisely what you were doing. You can see an example of a collection query label in Figure 5.29.

FIGURE 5.29   You can label a targeting item.

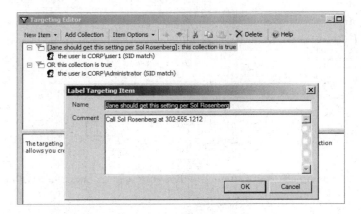

The one thing I really wanted in the ILT editor, I didn't get. I wanted a way to export the potentially rich target I created and import it into another GPPrefs. But I can't do that. There is no Export/Import feature.

However, a little later, in the section "Drag (or Paste) a Group Policy Preference Extension to a File," you'll learn how to see the underlying XML code for a GPPrefs. Inside that XML code is also the ILT information for that GPPrefs.

With that in mind, you could rip out the well-defined Filter section from one preference item and smash it into the preference item (of another type) you needed. Then, drag and drop the XML file back onto the GPPrefs Editor.

Description Field

This is the final Common entry regarding preference items. Here you're able to put in a simple description of what you're trying to do and notes about ILTs (if any.)

It's on the Common tab, as you can see in Figure 5.30.

FIGURE 5.30   Descriptions are GPPrefs item specific and appear in the Description field on the left only when you finally click OK (not Apply).

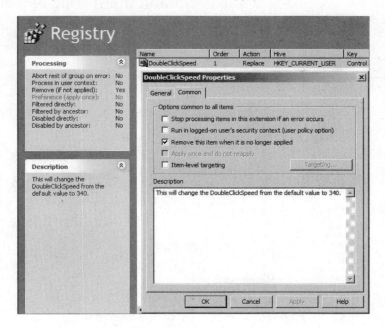

Group Policy Preferences Tips, Tricks, and Troubleshooting

Now that we're past the essentials, we're ready to move on to some useful tips and tricks to make us more productive with GPPrefs. And, of course, if something goes wrong, we'll need to troubleshoot our GPPrefs universe as well.

Quick Copy, Drag and Drop, Cut and Paste, and Sharing of Settings

I know this heading sounds like a lot of stuff, but it's really only one big thought. That is, the interface that allows you to create GPPrefs items lets you treat every setting like an object. I like to call this place the "GPPrefs editor" because it's the place within the Group Policy Management editor that you create GPPrefs items. So, you can do some neat tricks.

Quick Copy/Paste

In Figure 5.31, I'm about to make a copy of the DoubleClickSpeed Registry punch we dictated in a previous exercise.

FIGURE 5.31   You can right-click a preference item and select Copy (to paste it later).

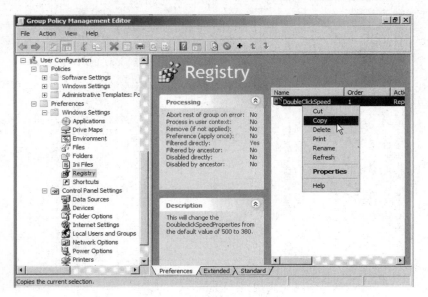

I can now do several things with this copy.

Right below the current entry, right-click and select Paste from the context menu. You'll see that a copy of the DoubleClickSpeed Registry punch is placed right next to it. We'll explore this in the next section, so hang tight.

Drag (or Paste) a Group Policy Preference Extension to a File

Go to your Windows Desktop and click Paste. (Yes, leave the Group Policy Management Editor, find the Windows Desktop, right-click, and select Paste.) A new document is automatically created with an XML extension. Alternatively, you can drag the line item from the GPPrefs editor right to the Desktop or a folder to create a file out of the contents.

You can see my document's icon and the contents of the document within Figure 5.32.

You can see that the file contains the Registry settings as well as the filters built in as one neat little package.

Sharing Your Wisdom with Others

At this point, you can e-mail this little gift of a file to a friend and they can drag and drop it into their own Registry Extension preference item list. In Figure 5.33, you can see what your other Administrator friend would do when he drags the corresponding file into his Registry preference extension item list.

FIGURE 5.32 Each preference item is exportable as an XML file.

FIGURE 5.33 You can share preference items with friends. Have your friend just drag and drop the XML right into the category as a preference item.

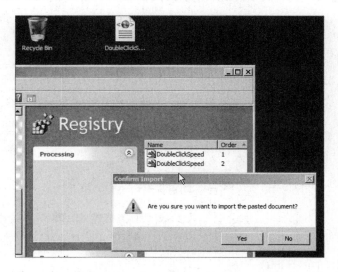

If you're going to share a GPPrefs XML file with other people outside your company, be careful to send only XML files that don't have any sensitive information contained within them, like SIDs, OUs, and other possibly sensitive information.

Multiple Preference Items at a Level

So an exercise or two ago, we copied our `DoubleClickSpeed` Registry entry. You can see this in Figure 5.22. But why would you want to do such a thing?

To be crafty, that's why!

Let's examine how to take advantage of this neat ability.

Filtering Each Preference Item at a Level

If you copy a preference item (which essentially makes two identical items at the same level), you can put a filter on one preference item and another filter on the other preference item. Of course, you'd change each item to act slightly differently, so that one item hits one set of users and the other item hits another set of users.

For instance, you could say Administrators get a DoubleClickSpeed of 300, but Users get a DoubleClickSpeed of 480. Just create two preference items (each changed slightly, and each with a different filter).

Again, a silly example, but you get the idea.

But, here's the kicker. GPPrefs process multiple preference items at a level by "counting up sequentially." So, if you had three preference items within the same extension, number 1 would be written first, number 2 would be written next, and number 3 would be written last.

If there was a conflict between any levels, the highest number would win.

Changing the Order of Preference Items at a Level

You change the order of the levels by clicking on the preference item you want and then using the menu bar's Up and Down arrows to change the order. So, for instance, in Figure 5.34 you can see that there are two preference items in the Start Menu extension. If you wanted to change the order, click on one of them, then select the menu bar's Up or Down arrow (seen in Figure 5.35). You can also see the full menu bar in Figure 5.35, which we'll refer to throughout the rest of this section.

FIGURE 5.34   You can have multiple, conflicting preference items inside a GPO.

FIGURE 5.35   The menu bar for Group Policy Preferences

This business of counting up sequentially within a GPPrefs extension is a little maddening to a Group Policy guy like me—especially because I usually have to explain how GPOs *themselves* are processed counting *down* sequentially. See the section "Raising or Lowering the Precedence of Multiple Group Policy Objects" in Chapter 2 for more information.

Renaming Preference Items at a Level

Since you copied DoubleClickSpeed, you now have what looks like two identical entries. But you don't. You have one filtered one way and another filtered another way. Why not right-click over each entry and rename it, being specific about what each entry now does, as shown in Figure 5.36?

FIGURE 5.36 If preference items within a GPO might potentially conflict, it's easiest to just rename them.

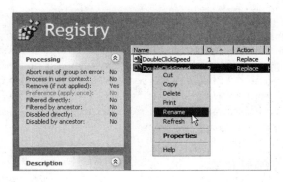

This will come in handy a little later when you learn about preference items and reporting.

Temporarily Disabling a Single Preference Item or Extension Root

Recall that Group Policy has the ability to remove the Link Enabled status from a GPO. When this happens, the GPO configuration stays in place, but it removes the GPO from processing (and usually reverts the setting back to an original setting).

GPPrefs have a similar ability, and it can be done at the preference item level or the GPPrefs extension root level *within* a GPO.

To do this, you can click on a preference item (like DoubleClickSpeed) and click the red No icon on the menu bar.

Or, if you want to do this on a GPPrefs extension root level, click on the Extension root, say the Registry extension, and click the No icon on the menu bar.

In Figure 5.37, I've disabled one preference item within the Registry extension, but I've also disabled the whole Registry extension—right at the root as well, just for show.

FIGURE 5.37   Both the first DoubleClickSpeed preference item and the Registry preference extension root are disabled.

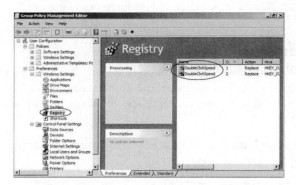

When you select the No icon, that icon will automatically change from red to green.

When either happens, the configuration is maintained within the extension, but it's taken out of processing. And, if the "Remove this item when it is no longer applied" setting is checked, the preference item falls out of the scope of management, so that value is usually deleted. So, again, be careful in using that setting.

To restore the preference extension or extension root itself for processing again, click the green No icon, which will put it back in play.

Environment Variables

One of the other superpowers the GPPrefs have is this idea of built-in, addressable variables in addition to the standard environment variables that Windows automatically sets, or ones that you set with logon scripts, or ones that you set using the Environment extension.

The idea is that GPPrefs bring these *additional* variables that allow you to specify the relative locations of many, many key items.

Here's a quick example (and there are about a zillion uses, so it was hard to just pick one). Imagine you had a file on a file share, named Everyone.txt, and you wanted to get it on everyone's machine. But you didn't just want to copy that file directly, no no! You wanted to rename it in the process to the name of the computer and *also* put it on everyone's Desktop folder. How could you possibly do that? Would you have to create a new GPO for everyone in the company!

Heck no!

With Environment variables, you can do this in one step. In Figure 5.38, I've used the Files Preference extension to specify the source file as \\dc01\share\everyone .txt. But for Destination File, before typing anything in, I hit the F3 key. When you do, the internal Environment variables pop up as a reference and you can select them to be automatically entered for you. For this example, I'll use one internal Environment variable (%CommonDesktopDir%) and one regular Windows Environment variable (%ComputerName%).

FIGURE 5.38   Hitting F3 when editing a preference item brings up the "Select a Variable" dialog box.

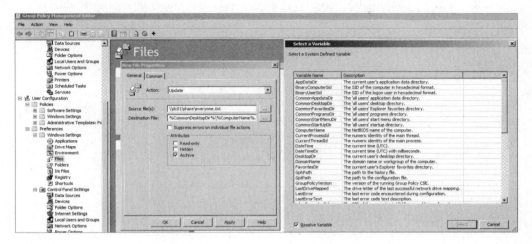

So, in Figure 5.38, I've specified %CommonDesktopDir%\%ComputerName%.txt as the destination filename.

Note the curious Resolve Variable check box when you hit the F3 key, as seen in Figure 5.39. The check box is on, which means variables like %ComputerName% resolve to WIN7. That's great; this makes sense and meets our goal.

However, strangely, there's also the ability to jam in the words that make up the variables—as variables! So, imagine you had an .INI file you wanted to change, but inside the .INI file, you wanted to jam in an actual variable. For instance, in DogFoodMaker 7.0, you needed to set the ruffcomputer property (located within the [ruffconfig] section) to have the word %ComputerName% (with percent marks included). You would uncheck the Resolve Variable check box, and what's put into the Property Value field is what's seen in Figure 5.39. That is, the variable name itself is contained within angle brackets (< and >) to signify that the variable %ComputerName% is jammed into the .INI file.

Managing Group Policy Preferences: Hiding Extensions from Use

There might be some times when you'll want to give someone rights to create GPOs but prevent them from utilizing some of the GPPrefs. For instance, maybe you didn't want them to be able to manipulate .INI settings or Registry settings. Well, you can take away that power if you want.

I wouldn't exactly call this a "security feature" because someone with enough know-how would be able to use another machine and jam in the underlying XML file into a GPO that they created and/or owned.

FIGURE 5.39   It's rare, but you may need to jam in the actual name of a variable, as seen here. Do this by putting angle brackets (< and >) around the variable name.

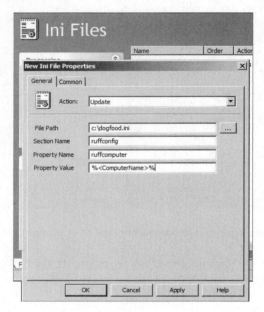

Regular Group Policy settings located at User Configuration ➢ Policies ➢ Administrative Templates ➢ Windows Components ➢ Microsoft Management Console ➢ Group Policy ➢ Preferences can help you perform the restrictions. You can see these policy settings in Figure 5.40.

The trick is, the Explain text is awful in these settings. For the ones I've tested, you need to disable the policy setting (yes, disable) to prevent the extension from showing.

In Figure 5.40, you can see I've disabled the .INI Files preference extension via its policy setting. In Figure 5.41, you can see the result; the extension to manipulate the .INI files is just—gone (in both the Computer and User sides)!

Now, this doesn't mean that GPOs that have any hidden extensions will stop working. It just means that some people (the people affected by these policy settings) cannot use the UI to manage that part of the world.

FIGURE 5.40 Use the settings seen here (and select Disable) to prevent the snap-ins from appearing within the MMC.

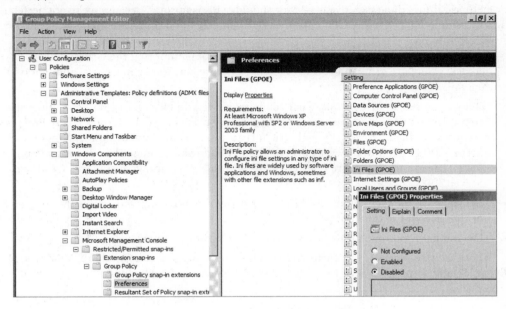

FIGURE 5.41 When admins affected by these policy settings try to create GPOs, the snap-ins are simply hidden.

Troubleshooting: Reporting, Logging, and Tracing

Sometimes, things don't exactly act as they should. This is normal, because we're not perfect, and the Group Policy Preferences make it easier than ever to do things we might not even really *want* to do.

To that end, we may need to spend some time on troubleshooting the Group Policy Preferences. Here are some quick things to check before you start going crazy and working with detailed logs:

- Before you pull your hair out when you're trying to troubleshoot your clients, the very first question you should ask yourself is, "Do my clients have the Group Policy Preferences installed?" Again, the only client that has it installed by default is Windows Server 2008, Windows Server 2008 R2, and Windows 7. You need to download and install the Group Policy Preferences for Windows XP, Windows Vista, and Windows Server 2003.

- Do you have the GPO linked to the correct place (site, domain, OU), and is the computer or user account in the right place?

- Do you have multiple preference items conflicting at the same level?

There are two places to get some dirt about what's going on: the Good Ol' Windows Event log and something new, the Group Policy Preferences Tracing logs.

Importing Group Policy Preferences

In the appendix, you'll learn how to use migration tables to migrate GPOs from one domain to another domain. However, it should be noted that migration tables do not support Group Policy Preferences. That is, as GPOs that contain preference items are imported, all settings are simply copied straight through, whether or not the value is valid in the target domain. AGPM 4.0 (the pay tool from Microsoft we talk about in a download-able bonus chapter) supports this function. However, you might also check out a free tool from my pal Mark Heitbrink, at http://tinyurl.com/lv8vbh, that can aid in this area. Don't be afraid of all the German on the page. The website may be in German, but the tool itself is in English.

Reporting: Settings Tab, GPMC Reporting, and GPresult

We have two usual ways of getting Group Policy results data: the Group Policy Results reports and the GPResult command. Let's see how each one responds to the Group Policy Preferences.

The Group Policy Results Reports from the GPMC

In a nutshell, the GPMC settings tab and GPMC HTML reports have all been modified to work with the new GPPrefs. The same Group Policy Results and Group Policy Modeling reports you know and love should work just the same with clients that have the Group Policy Preferences installed. There are some differences that need to be accounted for, though. For instance, if more than one preference item is at a level, you can see that within the Settings report of the GPO.

In Figure 5.42, you can see two Start Menu settings that conflicted. Of course, one has to eventually win.

However, when a Group Policy Results report is run, it has to figure not only which GPO wins, but also which preference item within a level wins. In Figure 5.43, we can see a Group Policy Results report, and the results are a little hard to read.

In Figure 5.43, we can see that Test GPP had some "Start Menu (Windows Vista and later)" settings win on the target machine. That's great. But there's like a billion settings within the Start Menu category. Which ones won? Well, even though the preference items are numbered inside the GPPrefs interface (remember Figure 5.34 when we talked about the GPPrefs order?), they're not labeled in the same order within the Group Policy Results reports.

FIGURE 5.42   Group Policy Preferences settings are reflected within the report.

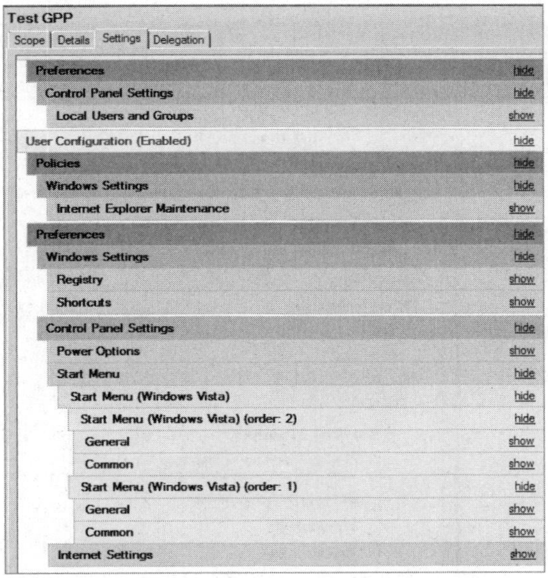

That's a bummer, because that's the kind of thing administrators want to know: which preference item (within the preference item order) won. But here's a tip. If we had used the rename function to rename a GPPrefs item, we can easily see which one won because the winning preference item bubbles up to the top by name.

Additionally, there seems to be no reporting of the ILTs. That's not exactly super helpful; I think I'd like to know why a specific preference item won over another one. So, again, if a specific ILT was found to be true, there doesn't seem to be any way to discover that from the Group Policy Results reports.

Gpresult.exe

I love the GPresult.exe tool. In XP and Vista there was no way to see the Group Policy Preferences "results" inside GPresult. However, with Windows 7 and later, you can run GPresult /H report.html (or any name) and out will pop an HTML file that shows the full RsOP that's occurred—including the Group Policy Preferences items. Again, that's only the HTML report.

If you try to run GPresult /R to get standard (text) output you'll see the GPOs themselves that affect the user or machine, but not the Group Policy Preferences inside those GPOs. Again, to see that data, use GPresult /H report.html.

Event Logs

The Windows Application log contains the really bad news about events that the Group Policy Preferences create. In Figure 5.44, we can see that something went wrong on the target machine (WS08DC1) when we attempted to apply Group Policy Shortcuts.

FIGURE 5.43   The winning preference item is the one that bubbles to the top.

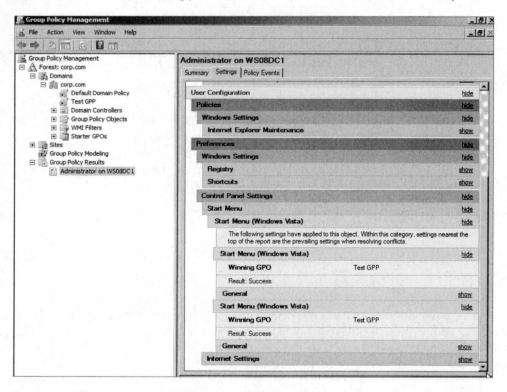

What's interesting is that each and every Group Policy Preference Extension category has its own source, so you can create custom views of the Application log, only showing the source you want (this applies to only Windows Vista and later clients, including Windows Server 2008 and Windows Server 2008 R2). In Figure 5.45, you can see that I'm creating a custom filter where you can select multiple sources (or just one) and show only the errors you want to expose in a single view.

Tracing

In Chapter 3, we talked about the Group Policy operational logs (for Windows Vista and Windows Server 2008) where you can get in-depth information about what's happening with regard to Group Policy. I haven't yet seen any Group Policy Preferences log information ever show up in the Group Policy Operational logs. That's because the Group Policy operational logs are for the processing of the GPOs themselves, not the specific settings *within* the GPO.

And because the Group Policy Preferences can be also be installed on Windows XP, as well as Windows Server 2003, it wouldn't be a great idea to put detailed Group Policy Preferences logs in a log file *only* for Windows Vista and later.

FIGURE 5.44 Group Policy Preferences' bad news can be found in the Application log.

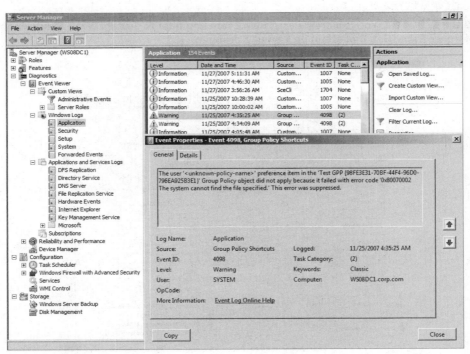

To that end, the Group Policy Preferences have their own detailed logs. The logs are called *trace logs*, and you turn them on them by enabling specific policy settings within Computer Configuration ➤ Policies ➤ System ➤ Group Policy ➤ Logging and tracing.

What? You've just gone to the "Group Policy" node on your Windows 7 management machine, and you don't see the "Logging and tracing" node? Don't panic!

As you learned in Chapter 3, the "missing" Group Policy settings are only built into Windows Server 2008's "set" of policy definitions. But those missing pieces are downloadable if you don't want to rip them out of an existing Windows Server 2008 machine. This blog entry spells it all out: `http://tinyurl.com/kowj66` and the downloadable files are `here http://tinyurl.com/mb6x5v` (though there could be updates for Windows Server 2008 R2, so, try to track those down when available). Once you've put the "missing" policy settings in place (again, see Chapter 6 for a how-to if needed) you can see the list of policy settings that control Group Policy Preferences in Figure 5.46.

Each Group Policy Preferences log, er, trace, can be set individually. By default they all push information to a shared log for each category.

The shared user log   The idea is that if the Group Policy Preference Extension is on the User side, it will write step-by-step data as to what it's doing within this log. The default location for the shared user log is:

```
%COMMONAPPDATA%\GroupPolicy\Preference\Trace\User.log
```

FIGURE 5.45   You can create your own Event Log filter to just show the Group Policy Preference Extension that might be having a problem.

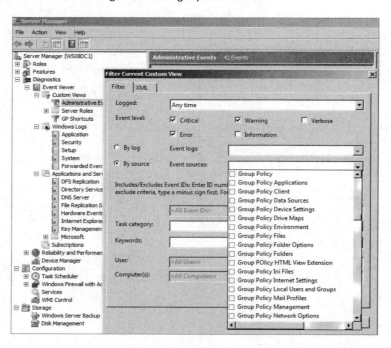

FIGURE 5.46   Tracing produces a lot of output. That's why there are two switches to enable it. First, enable the policy setting, and then select On from the Tracing drop-down or trace logs will not be produced.

The shared computer log   The idea is that if the Group Policy Preference Extension is on the Computer side, it will write step-by-step data as to what it's doing within this log. The default location for the shared user log is:

```
%COMMONAPPDATA%\GroupPolicy\Preference\Trace\Computer.log
```

The shared planning log   In ye olden days, when the product was younger (and owned by DesktopStandard), there was no GPMC reports integration. If you wanted to troubleshoot and learn what the RSoP was on the client, you needed to run the outmoded RSOP.MSC snap-in on the client system experiencing the problem. Well, those vestiges are still there. You can turn on the Planning log and run RSOP.MSC and see a log generated. There's little reason to do this because you can get reports, as we saw earlier, from GPMC's Group Policy Results reports. The default location for the shared Planning log is:

```
%COMMONAPPDATA%\GroupPolicy\Preference\Trace\Planning.log
```

The extra trick is that, after you enable the policy setting and ensure that the log files are in a place you can find, you still need to set the logging level, then finally (and here's the kicker) click the drop-down next to Tracing and select On. Yep, that's right. You enabled the policy setting, but that's not good enough. You also need to "double-enable" tracing.

When you do, your log file will appear in:

```
C:\ProgramData\GroupPolicy\Preference\Trace
```

as seen in Figure 5.47.

Finally, you might be asking why some settings, like Internet Settings, have both a Computer and a User log when the extension is applicable only on the User side. In short, it shouldn't be there, and it won't do anything.

FIGURE 5.47   Trace logs can be a bit hairy, but useful.

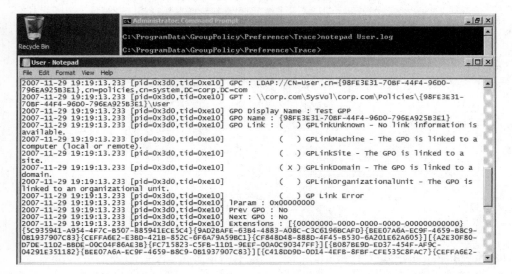

Final Thoughts

Let's do an ever-so-brief review of the top 10 things we've learned about Group Policy Preferences:

- Management station installation: You need a management station that has the Group Policy Preferences loaded.

- Client piece installation: There's a download for the Group Policy Preferences for Windows XP (at least) SP2, Windows Vista, and Windows Server 2003 (at least) SP1. It's built into Windows 7, Windows Server 2008, and Windows Server 2008 R2.

- Group Policy Preferences deliver preferences, whereas Group Policy (original) delivers policy settings. This usually means that users can undo settings that you deliver via Group Policy Preferences (but not always).

- There is some overlap between Group Policy (original) and Group Policy Preferences. But really, as we analyzed, there is more harmony between the two than overlap.

- Be sure you understand how the red and green lines and circles work in the interface.

- Know your CRUD Action modes and what each does. When in doubt, use Update. (When *really* in doubt, try it in a test lab first.)

- The Common tab is available for each preference item you create. Inside this tab are some superpowers, like ILT.

- Be super careful using the Common tab element "Remove this item when it is no longer applied." Remember, it's the equivalent of Nuke.

- Use the Windows Event logs and Group Policy Preferences tracing logs to help you determine whether or not your Group Policy Preferences wishes are being applied.

Again, on www.GPanswers.com in the forums you'll find lots of questions and answers about the Group Policy Preferences.

Also, if you were an original DesktopStandard PolicyMaker customer, check out http://tinyurl.com/l2gmn6 for a tool to help with the transition.

6

Managing Applications and Settings Using Group Policy

Let's take a step back, go to the 20-yard line, and remember why we're getting jazzed up about this Group Policy thing.

You're jazzed up because you're starting to realize the potential that Group Policy can bring: dictating settings for your operating system and making your world more "standardized."

As you poke around the Group Policy editor, you'll see there are lots of areas that you've already explored, and some we haven't yet explored. You've had a chance to handle the Administrative Templates section within policies. You've explored the Preferences area of the Group Policy Preferences. In the next chapter you'll explore the items in the Security section.

But let's take some time to focus on an important aspect of Group Policy: extending its use to wider areas of our desktop environment. Sure, Group Policy is neat because it can manage operating system settings—like how you prevented users from getting into the Control Panel, or how you launched calc.exe every time a user logged on.

But let's take it to the next level.

Let's start controlling our *applications*. True "control freaks" know that it's us, not the users, who should be in charge. And using the power of Group Policy we can manage our desktop applications like our operating system: let users change what we want, and also control and manage what we want.

To accomplish this, we need to understand the Administrative Templates section of the Group Policy editor. We need to know that those bazillions of Administrative Template settings come from somewhere—what they're made of and how they're built.

Even then, those built-in files might not be enough to perform true management under all circumstances. So in this chapter, we'll also explore a third-party add-on tool called PolicyPak that will help you manage your desktops beyond what's capable "in the box" and take your control-freak tendencies to the next level.

Here's the deal: I'm part owner of PolicyPak.

But before you throw your hands up in the air and cry, "Foul, Moskowitz; way to be a corporate sell-out!"—there's some good news. I built the tool with you, the cheapskate, er, "frugal master" in mind.

The tool has a 100 percent free "Community Edition" that gives all the functionality for limited use. It's my gift to all the readers of this book and the Group Policy community at large. I think you'll agree it's a nice (free) add-on to managing your desktop world. And when you're ready to unlock its full power to all your desktops and laptops—I'm here for you, too.

Administrative Templates: A History and Policy vs. Preferences

To understand how to better manage our world, we need to first understand a little history—where Administrative Templates came from, and where they are now.

Additionally, we'll need to clear up some vocabulary around policy versus preference. Yes, we've just learned about the Group Policy Preferences in the last chapter. But the idea of "what is a preference" can be further refined, as we're about to learn.

Administrative Templates: Then and Now

Take a look at Figure 6.1. First, you'll see the older XP version of the Group Policy editor. Then, you'll see the updated Group Policy editor, found within RSAT. If we ignore the fact that there's a Preferences node, we'll see that the Administrative Templates structure is pretty similar.

FIGURE 6.1   Here is the updated Group Policy editor. Then, in the next graphic is the older XP Group Policy editor. They both have Administrative Templates, which contain policy settings.

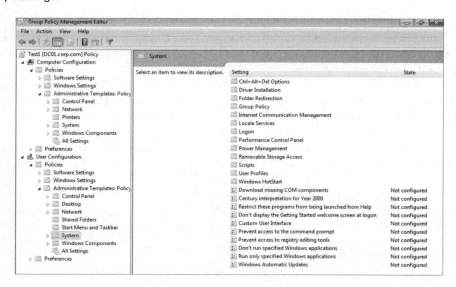

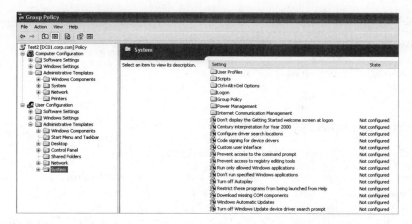

Sure, there are some little differences. Some of the policy settings have different names or have been moved around a bit. But the point is simple: both consoles contain Administrative Templates and both consoles contain policy settings. What's different is where each of these policy settings' definitions come from.

In Windows XP and earlier, the Administrative Templates section is born from what's known as ADM files. In the updated GPMC, that same section comes from new file types called ADMX and ADML files.

These files are what policy settings are born from.

The idea behind older ADM and newer ADMX files is pretty simple:

- Define a setting (i.e., give it a name)

- Describe what Registry punch it is to control

- Describe how administrators interface with the setting inside the Group Policy editor

Then, once wrapped up, we, as administrators, interact with these ADM and ADMX files inside the Group Policy editor interfaces (as seen in Figure 6.1). We just click a button, and "flick!" Our GPO contains Registry punch data to be delivered to the target machine. "Flick!" again, and that same Registry setting can be toggled off.

In this next section, "Policy vs. Preference," we'll explore the first "Flick": what happens when you dictate a Registry punch within a GPO. And, later on, we'll also answer the question about what happened with the next "Flick": what happens when that policy setting is to be removed.

Policy vs. Preference

Microsoft documentation states that four Registry areas are considered the approved places to create policies out of Registry punches:

- Computer settings, the preferred location:

```
HKLM\Software\Policies
```

- Computer settings, an alternative location:

  `HKLM\Software\Microsoft\Windows\CurrentVersion\Policies`

- User settings, the preferred location:

  `HKCU\Software\Policies`

- User settings, an alternative location:

  `HKCU\Software\Microsoft\Windows\CurrentVersion\Policies`

These locations are preferred because they have security permissions that do not allow a regular user to modify these keys. Again, the preferred locations are noted here, if any software developers are reading this book (and you know who you are).

When a policy setting is set to Enabled and the client embraces the Group Policy directives, a Registry entry is set in one of these keys. When the GPO that applied the keys is removed, the Registry values associated with it are also removed. However, it should be noted that the application (or operating system component) needs to look for changes to these keys in order for it to take effect. That is, the Group Policy engine doesn't "notify" the application—the application has to do its own checking. So, with this in mind, if an older operating system receives a policy setting for a newer operating system, nothing "bad" happens. It just gets ignored.

WARNING It should be noted that local administrators have security permissions to these keys and could maliciously modify delivered GPO settings because of rights within this portion of the Registry.

So "normal" Group Policy won't tattoo because it's being directed to go in a nonsticking place in the Registry. Turns out, every single "in the box" policy Microsoft has within its Administrative Templates section are all "normal" policy settings.

Flick! Hide the control panel.

Flick again! Bring it back.

Couldn't be simpler; and, again, it's because the operating system (really, `Explorer.exe` in this example) knows to look for proper Policies keys. And when they're not set any longer, poof! The directive is thrown away, and the setting reverts.

Let's take a different example, though.

Let's say you wanted to control a pet application, DogFoodMaker 6.1, that you have deployed in-house. Great—you've decided you want more control. Now, you need to determine which Registry values and data DogFoodMaker 6.1 understands. That could take some time; you might be able to ask the manufacturer for the valid Registry values, or you might have some manual labor in front of you to determine what can be controlled via the Registry. Consider using a tool like Process Monitor:

`http://technet.microsoft.com/en-us/sysinternals/bb896645.aspx`

or RegShot:

```
http://sourceforge.net/projects/regshot
```

You'll then be able to begin to create your own templates.

However, after you've determined how DogFoodMaker 6.1 can be controlled via the Registry, you'll find you have two categories of Registry tweaks:

- Values that fit neatly into the new Policies keys listed earlier
- Values that are anywhere else

You'll have some good news and some bad news. If DogFoodMaker 6.1 can accept control via the Registry, you can still create template files and control the application. The bad news is that if you try to utilize a Registry key that isn't part of the Policies keys, then you will *not* have proper policies. Rather, they become preferences.

Wait, wait, wait a second. Preferences? "Didn't I just read all about preferences in the last chapter?" Kind of. You read about Group Policy Preferences, or GPPrefs. GPPrefs is a collection of swell new stuff you can do—21 new functions you couldn't do earlier.

But the word "preference" has a second meaning (oh great). Let's examine the word preference, itself here for a second. Again, we're talking just about the word "preference," and not Group Policy Preferences or GPPrefs.

A preference is:

- A Registry punch that is not within the proper Policies keys (listed earlier).

- A setting which, once set, a user can work around. This is because there is no user interface "lockout" from Preferences (as explored in the last chapter). This is why Group Policy Preferences are called Group Policy *Preferences* and not Group Policy *MorePolicy* or something. Remember, as we learned in the last chapter, by and large, Group Policy Preferences can be worked around, even by regular users under most circumstances.

- A setting that, once set, stays set (or tattoos)—even when the setting should no longer apply. This is a weird one, because we're used to the "nice" behavior of policy settings. The idea that some settings stick around makes this idea of preferences kind of messy.

To reiterate, to be truly "Policy Enabled" a target application must be programmed to look for values in the Policies keys. Some applications, such as Word 2000, are coded to look at Policies keys, specifically:

```
HKEY_CURRENT_USER\Software\Policies\Microsoft\Office\9.0\Word\
```

Other applications, such as WordPad, do not "understand" the Policies keys. WordPad stores its settings in:

```
HKEY_CURRENT_USER\Software\Microsoft\Windows\CurrentVersion\Applets\Wordpad
```

Hence, WordPad wouldn't be a candidate to hand-create a template file for the purpose of coding for true policy settings. You could, however, still create your own *preferences* for

WordPad that modify and tattoo the Registry. Therefore, you will have to do the legwork to figure out if your applications are compatible with Policies keys.

Most aren't. Most applications are not still onboard the "True Policy" train. Most applications do not ship with any way to control them using Group Policy. And, again, even if you hand-created your own ADM or ADMX files, you still do not have the full control that you would likely desire. Again, remember, since most applications don't know to look in the Policies keys, they just store their information "wherever." There's no way to magically create an ADM or ADMX file and somehow make the application behave as if it's under control of true policy. In other words, there's no "in the box" way to policy-enable your apps with true lockdown—because they're not being controlled by true policy.

 There is some magical help on the way. In this chapter, we'll explore the third-party tool I alluded to earlier called PolicyPak. PolicyPak's job is to take non-policy applications and make them act as if they were truly policy enabled.

Because preferences and policies act so differently, you will need to quickly identify them within the Group Policy Object Editor interface. You will want to note whether you're pushing an actual new-style policy to them or a persistent old-style policy.

Take a peek back at Figure 6.1. Look at the "rows" of policy settings. When viewed with the updated GPMC, true policies are designated by little "paper" icons (the first screenshot). When viewed on Windows XP (the second screenshot), true policies are designated by little blue dots. (I know it's hard to tell they're blue because the book is printed in black and white. But trust me, they're blue.) Again, what you're looking at is "proper" or "true" policy settings because they modify the actual Policies registry keys listed earlier.

Policies that represent Registry punches in places *other* than the preferred Microsoft policies are designated another way. Take a look at Figure 6.2. In the updated GPMC editor (top graphic), they're represented by paper icons with a down arrow. In the older XP GPMC, they're designated by red dots. Again, trust me—it's red.

Don't panic; I'll show you a little later how I added these "extra" templates to my Group Policy editor. Well, honestly, I'm only going to show you how I did it for the updated GPMC. If you really need to still do it for Windows XP, refer to previous editions of this book.

Since the distinction of policies and preferences is an important one for the rest of this chapter, let's recap:

- Policies are temporary Registry changes that are downloaded at logon and startup (and periodically in the background). They don't tattoo the Registry (though they are maintained and stay persistent should the user log on while offline). These are set to modify the Registry in specific Microsoft-blessed Policies keys. Applications need to be coded to recognize the presence of the keys in order to take advantage of the magic of policies. In the updated GPMC's editor, true policies look like little paper icons.

- Preferences are persistent Registry changes delivered using the Group Policy infrastructure. Preferences typically tattoo the Registry until they're specifically changed or removed. In the updated GPMC editor interface, they look like paper icons with a little down arrow. Unlike policies, if you remove the GPO, you "tattoo" or "orphan" the settings on the target computer (no fun at all).

- A preference is just a fancy way of saying "a Registry punch that can live anywhere."

FIGURE 6.2   The updated GPMC shows preferences as seen in the first screenshot. The older GPMC (XP) shows preferences as seen in the second screenshot (with red dots).

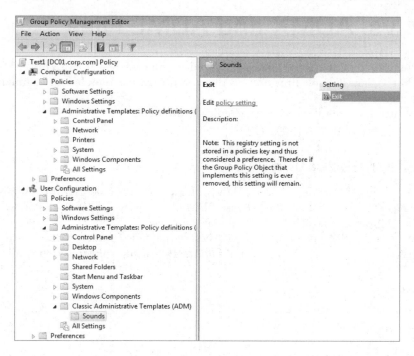

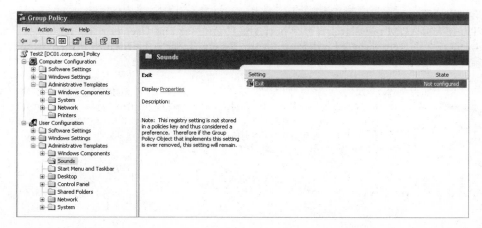

It should also be noted that policies don't "overwrite" user preferences if they exist. For instance, if a program like Microsoft Word is policy-enabled and a user specifies to enable "Correct two initial capitals," but later the administrator chooses to disable this setting with a GPO, the original user's desires will just magically "come back." So, when you remove a true policy setting from a GPO (that is, set to Not Configured), the original user preference will be "returned."

ADM vs. ADMX and ADML Files

So, the older (XP version) of the Group Policy editor and the newer (RSAT) version of the Group Policy editor present the Administrative Template in a similar fashion. Great.

But underneath the hood, honestly, it's radically different.

That's what we're going to explore in this section.

ADM File Introduction

If you use an older (XP) GPMC to create GPOs, you are using the older ADM (Administrative Templates) files stored on that machine. Those ADM files provide the definitions of "what's possible" in the Administrative Templates section.

Those default templates are stored in the %systemroot%\inf folder, which is usually c:\windows\inf. By way of example, you'll find the following templates are installed by default on Windows XP machines:

- Conf.adm
- Inetres.adm
- System.adm
- Wmplayer.adm
- Wuau.adm

These five ADM templates create both the Computer and User portion within Administrative Templates of a default Group Policy. Table 6.1 provides information about what each default template is and what lives inside it.

 NOTE inetcorp.adm and inetset.adm are two ADM templates that can alternatively be used to manipulate Internet Explorer settings. However, I don't advise that you use them, as they don't work well for newer versions of Internet Explorer.

TABLE 6.1   Default ADM Templates

ADM Template	Features	Where to Find in Interface
Conf.adm	NetMeeting settings.	Computer Configuration/User Configuration ➢ Administrative Templates ➢ Windows Components ➢ NetMeeting
Inetres.adm	Internet Explorer settings, including security, advanced options, and toolbar settings. It is equivalent to the options that are available when using the Internet Options menu inside Internet Explorer.	Computer Configuration/User Configuration ➢ Administrative Templates ➢ Windows Components ➢ Internet Explorer
Inetcorp.adm (not used in a GPO by default)	Used for Internet Explorer Maintenance Preference mode settings.	User Configuration ➢ Windows Settings ➢ Internet Explorer Maintenance. We won't be exploring this particular ADM template much. If you want more information on its ins and outs, read http://tinyurl.com/z3cae. I do not suggest you use Inetcorp.adm unless directed by a specific Microsoft document or PSS person.
Inetset.adm (not used in a GPO by default)	"Advanced Settings" for Internet Explorer 6.	User Configuration ➢ Windows Settings ➢ Internet Explorer Maintenance ➢ Advanced. Only visible in Internet Explorer Maintenance Preference mode (in Chapter 12, see the section "Internet Explorer Maintenance (IEM)"). I do not suggest you use Inetset.adm unless directed by a specific Microsoft document or PSS person.
System.adm	Operating system changes and settings. Most of the Computer and User Administrative Templates settings are in this ADM template.	Everything else under Computer Configuration/User Configuration ➢ Administrative Templates.
Wmplayer.adm	Windows Media Player 9 settings.	User Configuration ➢ Administrative Templates ➢ Windows Components ➢ Windows Media Player.
Wuau.adm	Controls client's access to Software Update Services servers.	Computer Configuration ➢ Administrative Templates ➢ Windows Components ➢ Windows Update.

Updated GPMC's ADMX and ADML Files

As we saw with the older GPMC, a mere handful of ADM files made up the bulk of our Administrative Template settings. When you use the updated GPMC, you no longer use built-in ADM files.

Instead, you use built-in *ADMX* and *ADML* files. And what was once a handful of files is now an entire growler-full.

 What's a growler? See http://en.wikipedia.org/wiki/Growler.

The updated GPMC's ADMX files are stored in the %systemroot%\PolicyDefinitions folder, which is usually c:\windows\PolicyDefinitions.

There are now about 132 ADMX files, which roughly cover the same settings found in Windows XP and all the new stuff in Windows Vista and Windows 7. They're generally component specific. For instance, you'll find things like WindowsMediaPlayer.admx and EventLog.admx, among others.

Here's something neat about ADMX files—they're language neutral. That is, the definitions for the Registry values that are controlled are inside the ADMX file. However, the text strings describing the policy and the Explain text are contained in a *separate* file called an ADML file—each ADMX file has a corresponding ADML file. These ADML files are located in specific subdirectories for each language within the c:\windows\PolicyDefinitions folder. For instance, U.S. English is contained within the en-US directory, which can be seen in Figure 6.3.

FIGURE 6.3 A quick list of some ADMX files. Note the language-specific directory here for English (en-US).

```
Administrator: Command Prompt                                         _ |□| x|

Directory of c:\Windows\PolicyDefinitions

11/08/2007  05:46 PM    <DIR>          .
11/08/2007  05:46 PM    <DIR>          ..
11/08/2007  05:41 PM             1,582 ActiveXInstallService.admx
11/08/2007  05:40 PM             4,714 AddRemovePrograms.admx
11/08/2007  05:41 PM             1,249 adfs.admx
11/08/2007  05:41 PM             3,796 AppCompat.admx
11/08/2007  05:41 PM             5,965 AttachmentManager.admx
11/08/2007  05:41 PM             2,883 AutoPlay.admx
11/08/2007  05:41 PM            17,197 Bits.admx
11/08/2007  05:41 PM             1,924 CaptureWizard.admx
11/08/2007  05:41 PM             1,767 CEIPEnable.admx
11/08/2007  05:40 PM             1,361 CipherSuiteOrder.admx
11/08/2007  05:41 PM             1,329 COM.admx
11/08/2007  05:41 PM            13,967 Conf.admx
11/08/2007  05:41 PM             2,600 ControlPanel.admx
11/08/2007  05:41 PM             6,959 ControlPanelDisplay.admx
11/08/2007  05:41 PM             1,293 Cpls.admx
11/08/2007  05:41 PM             1,933 CredentialProviders.admx
11/08/2007  05:41 PM            10,779 CredSsp.admx
11/08/2007  05:41 PM             1,746 CredUI.admx
11/08/2007  05:41 PM             2,141 CtrlAltDel.admx
11/08/2007  05:41 PM             2,437 DCOM.admx
11/08/2007  05:41 PM            12,707 Desktop.admx
11/08/2007  05:41 PM            14,686 DeviceInstallation.admx
11/08/2007  05:41 PM             1,093 DFS.admx
11/08/2007  05:41 PM             1,992 DigitalLocker.admx
11/08/2007  05:41 PM             3,034 DiskDiagnostic.admx
11/08/2007  05:41 PM             2,758 DiskNVCache.admx
11/08/2007  05:41 PM             6,123 DiskQuota.admx
11/08/2007  05:41 PM               989 DistributedLinkTracking.admx
11/08/2007  05:40 PM             9,671 DnsClient.admx
11/08/2007  05:41 PM             7,656 DWM.admx
11/08/2007  05:46 PM    <DIR>          en-US
11/08/2007  05:41 PM               962 EncryptFilesonMove.admx
11/08/2007  05:40 PM            21,738 ErrorReporting.admx
11/08/2007  05:40 PM             1,397 EventForwarding.admx
11/08/2007  05:41 PM            12,429 EventLog.admx
11/08/2007  05:41 PM             2,528 EventViewer.admx
11/08/2007  05:41 PM             2,840 Explorer.admx
11/08/2007  05:41 PM             2,141 FileRecovery.admx
```

The term *en-US* stands for U.S. English. For other locales, visit http://tinyurl.com/223ebg. For instance, HE is for Hebrew, RU is for Russian, DE is for German, and AR is for Arabic.

So, let me spell it out a different way:

- ADMX files store the same stuff as ADM files. Except now (whoopee...) they're XML based.

- ADML files are corresponding language files for ADMX files.

You may be wondering "what special superpowers do I get now that we use ADMX and ADML files?" Well, I dare say that you get "no new superpowers." Just because you're using ADMX/ADML files, you don't somehow magically get to "Group Policy enable" applications and their settings or have more Registry control.

But there has to be some benefit, right? Or else Microsoft wouldn't have done it, right? Yep. They're not superpowers, though. They're fixes to some thorny problems.

In the next section, let's explore the four problems that the construct of ADM files caused, and see how the newer construct of ADM and ADMX files fixes each of those problems.

ADM vs. ADMX Files—At a Glance

Our goal for the rest of the chapter is to give you an in-depth look at both ADM and ADMX files and for you to understand the differences between them. However, before we get going, here's a quick little reference table so you can see where we're going; you can also utilize this table as an ongoing reference.

ADM Files	ADMX Files
Lots and lots of definitions are packed into several large-ish files. The biggest one is SYSTEM.ADM.	Definitions are split logically into much smaller ADMX files, generally by Windows feature area.
Each ADM file contains settings in one specific language.	ADMX files are language neutral. Language-specific information is contained within a corresponding ADML file. Language-specific files live in hard-coded directories. For example, U.S. English language files live in %systemroot%\PolicyDefinitions\en-US.
Live on each Windows XP machine in %systemroot%\inf.	Live on each Windows Vista, Windows 7 and Windows Server 2008 machine in %systemroot%\PolicyDefinitions.

ADM Files

Every time a GPO is "born," it costs about 3MB on each Domain Controller because the ADM files are placed inside the GPO.

Use their own proprietary ADM syntax for describing Registry policy.

ADMX Files

GPOs created from ADMX files never have big space requirements. That's because the ADMX files are never pushed into the GPO themselves (whether or not the Central Store is used). We'll discuss the Central Store a bit later.

Use standard XML as the syntax for describing Registry policy.

ADMX and ADML Files: What They Do and the Problems They Solve

If ADM files were so wonderful, why did Microsoft have to (basically) dump this "tried and true" way for a newer construct of ADMX and ADML?

At first glance, it seems that ADMX and ADML files are more complex than ADMs. That's true, at least because now inside each file is gobbledy-gook XML code where, arguably, ADM files are easier to "read." Then, there's the complexity of having two (or more!) files, whereas before one ADM file seemed to be perfectly sufficient.

Problem is—it just wasn't. Let's examine the four problems that ADMs had and how ADMX and ADML files solve those problems.

Problem and Solution 1: Tackling SYSVOL Bloat

The older Group Policy editor pulls the ADM template files from the computer it is running on. And it copies these ADM template files from %systemroot%\inf—usually c:\windows\inf—directly into each GPO you edit. Each time you do this, you're burning about 3MB of disk space—on every Domain Controller. This is because all material inside the GPO is replicated to every Domain Controller.

Imagine you've created 100 GPOs using the older GPMC. In that case, you're using about 300MB to 500MB of disk space on every Domain Controller to store these ADM files! Ow! This problem is called SYSVOL bloat.

In Figure 6.4, you can see a sample SYSVOL with several GPOs. Recall that GPOs live on every Domain Controller in the sysvol\corp.com\Policies directory underneath their GUID. If you're using the older GPMC, each GPO will have an ADM directory each containing the same ADM templates at about 3MB each directory.

So, what does the updated GPMC do differently? Well, instead of copying stuff up from the local machine into the GPO, it just does "nothing." That's right—nothing. Figure 6.5 shows the difference between the older GPMC and the newer GPMC.

FIGURE 6.4 Every GPO created with an XP management station pushes about 3MB into SYSVOL.

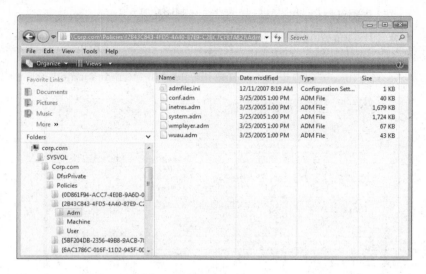

FIGURE 6.5 What's copied into the GPO when using the older and the newer GPMC

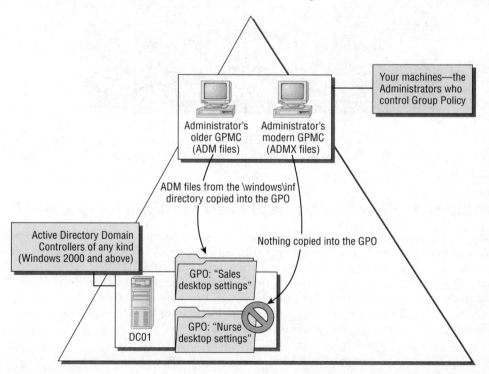

Don't believe it? Let's look at what's generated inside SYSVOL. In Figure 6.6, you can see that the top window was created using a modern GPMC, like what's available for Windows 7. You know this because there's no ADM directory.

FIGURE 6.6   The top window shows a GPO's contents when it's created using an updated GPMC management station. The middle window shows a GPO's contents when it's created using an older GPMC management station. The bottom window shows the contents of the ADM directory for the GPO created using the older GPMC management station.

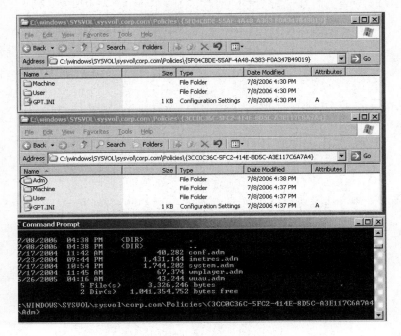

So, did we solve problem 1, SYSVOL bloat? You bet. Because there's no ADM directory (and no ADM files inside it), there's no wasted space (SYSVOL bloat) from ADM files.

Problem 2: How Do We Deal with Multiple Languages?

Let's imagine that you're a part of a big company (heck, maybe you are). And in this company you have multiple administrators speaking multiple languages. And these administrators need to modify GPOs. Worse, they sometimes have to modify each other's GPOs.

If you're using the older GPMC (which uses ADM files), this is a real problem. When Vlad in the Russian corporate office edits the GPOs, he wants to see those policy settings and help texts in Russian. When Sven in the Sweden corporate office edits GPOs, he wants to see those policy settings and help texts in Swedish.

The problem is, if Vlad creates and edits the GPO first using the older GPMC, Vlad's Russian ADM templates (which start out on Vlad's XP machine) go into the GPO. This is no big deal, until Sven wants to edit that same GPO. If Sven's ADM templates on his machine are *older* or have the same release date, then when Sven goes to edit the GPO that Vlad created, Sven will see the GPO's policy settings and help text in Russian, not Swedish.

Problem 3: How Do We Deal with "Write Overlaps"?

Let's extend problem 2 a little bit. Let's assume that in the previous example, Vlad's machine was an XP/SP2 machine. Let's also assume that in the previous example, Sven's machine was also an XP/SP2 machine.

Now, Sven is able to update his machine to XP/SP3, while Vlad still uses XP/SP2. Now when Sven goes to edit the GPO, Sven's ADM templates are *newer*. And because they're *newer*, they overwrite the ADM files *already inside* the GPO.

This is great news for Sven. Now when he edits the GPO, everything inside is Swedish! But this is bad news for Vlad, because now the GPOs he originally created, which had Russian policy settings and help text, will display in Swedish if Sven ever edits them.

Turns out the solution to solving problems 2 and 3 is exactly the same as solving problem 1. To solve the multiple languages problem (that's problem 2) and the "write overlaps" problem (problem 3), the updated GPMC once again simply "does nothing."

Since the updated GPMC doesn't use ADM files, it won't copy any definitions into the GPO at all. Not ADM, not ADMX/ADML. Nothing.

So why does this "do nothing" approach solve the problem? Because now when Vlad edits the GPO, Vlad uses his own local machine (say, a Windows 7 machine) for the Russian definitions. When Sven edits the same GPO, Sven uses his own local Windows 7 Swedish definitions.

See—I always thought world peace could be achieved if people just left each other alone; but alas, this isn't a political book.

This "do-nothing" approach really works, because there's never anything written into the GPO regarding definitions. Only the data, the "directives" are inside the GPO. And therefore each administrator simply uses his local `%systemroot%\PolicyDefinitions` folder to utilize his own ADMX and ADML definitions.

This "do nothing" approach seems great. It's now officially solved three of our four problems. Can we go four-for-four?

Problem 4: How Do We Distribute Updated Definitions to All Our Administrators?

Let's assume we have some software, and the manufacturer created, and then occasionally updates, some policy definition files. Microsoft, for instance, does this with the Office 2003 ADM files.

That's great. We get updates from the vendor; now assume we have 20 administrators at our company. Or even two—just Vlad and Sven.

How are we going to get those updated ADM files delivered to those administrators and make sure they're installed correctly? Are we going to e-mail these updates to each of them? Are we going to script these updates and hope the script correctly identifies our administrators and the machines they work upon?

In short, how the heck are we going to get our updated definitions to every administrator in a hurry?

Well, turns out that the updated GPMC has a trick up its sleeve, and it's called the "Central Store." We'll explore the Central Store in an upcoming section, but the idea is simple: rather than trying to get every administrator's machine up-to-date with ADMs, we'll use ADMX and ADML files, and just plunk them in a centralized place—a "Central Store" if you will.

Stay tuned—I'll show you exactly how that works in the next section.

Preventing SYSVOL Bloat If You're Still Using Pre-Vista Management Stations

There is a way to avoid copying the ADM files into the GPO and wasting about 3MB on each Domain Controller per GPO. The trick is to use a policy setting called **Always use local ADM files for Group Policy Object Editor** (located in Computer Configuration ➢ Administrative Templates ➢ System ➢ Group Policy) and have it affect your management station.

By enabling this policy, you're telling your management station, "I'm not going to push ADM files into the SYSVOL folder." Sounds great, right?

The downside, however, is that if you try to edit the GPO on a machine that doesn't have the same ADM templates as the GPO (or worse, the local machine is just plain missing an ADM template), you simply won't be able to edit the GPO the way you want. You'll have to track down the original machine that had the full complement of ADM templates to properly manage the GPO.

Because of the downsides, I suggest this workaround for only very large environments that have lots of GPOs that are taking a long time to replicate because of all the ADM template data being pushed into the GPO.

Here's the big ol' scary warning about the policy setting: it only works if the older GPMC application is installed on Windows Server 2003 (not Windows XP). Why? I have no idea. So, if you want to prevent SYSVOL bloat from ADM files, and you want to utilize this sneaky way to do it, you absolutely must make your older GPMC management station Windows Server 2003 (and not Windows XP).

Microsoft talks a bit more about this in Knowledge Base article 816662 found at http://support.microsoft.com/kb/816662.

The Central Store

As we discussed, in the ideal world you'd use only the updated GPMC for your management stations. Sure, that means you'd have to spin up one Windows 7 machine (and download and install the updated GPMC within RSAT or use a Windows Server 2008 machine).

But remember, if you have even one Windows Vista or Windows 7 client machine or one Windows Server 2008 machine out there in sales, marketing, human resources, and so on, you'll need to manage it *from* an updated GPMC machine. That's because the older GPMC (which runs on Windows XP and Windows Server 2003) won't have the definitions of the policy settings that the updated GPMC clients have.

So, we'll assume from here on that you'll be using only updated GPMC as your management station, eschewing older XP/2003 GPMC management stations.

As you're reading this right now, Microsoft has just shipped Windows 7. But let's fast-forward a bit and assume, oh, that we're up to Windows 7/SP3. Yep, Windows 7 Service Pack 3 has just been released and you need to control the new whiz-bang features that only come with Windows 7/SP3 client computers. (Again, I'm dreaming a little into the future here; new whiz-bang features might or might not come in service packs or other delivery vehicles, but stay with me through this example anyway.)

"No problem!" you say, "I'll just create a Windows 7/SP3 machine and put on the updated GPMC as my management station. That will always have the latest, greatest definitions in the local `PolicyDefinitions` folder." And you'd be right! Except that you already have an updated GPMC machine as your management station. So you wouldn't want to spin up a *whole new machine* just for this. You'd want to leverage the updated GPMC management station you already have, right?

Sure!

This is easy! You're a diligent administrator (you bought this book, subscribe to the `www.GPanswers.com` mailing list, and practice good Group Policy hygiene, after all), and you know you have three ways to update your current updated GPMC management station:

- If your updated GPMC management station is Windows 7, you would just apply Windows 7's SP3.That would update the ADMX files that live in `c:\windows\PolicyDefinitions`.

- Or, you could forgo applying SP3 to your Windows 7 management station and simply copy the ADMX (and associated ADML files) from another Windows 7/SP3 machine to your management station. Again, you'll plunk them in the `c:\windows\PolicyDefinitions` directory.

- Or, if your updated GPMC management station is Windows Server 2008, you could also just simply copy the ADMX (and associated ADML files) from another Windows 7 + SP3 machine to your Windows Server 2008 management station. Again, you'll plunk them in the `c:\windows\PolicyDefinitions` directory.

So, the message again sounds simple: whenever Microsoft has new ADMX/ADML files, get them into your updated GPMC management station.

Simple, yes—until you remember that you have 20 administrators in your company, each with their own Windows 7 management station. Or you remember those administrators who love to bounce from machine to machine because they have three sites to manage. Yikes! How are you going to guarantee that all of these administrators will use the updated ADMX files?

Let's assume you've successfully upgraded *your* Windows 7 management station to SP3, but only some of your 20 administrators successfully upgrade to Windows 7/SP3 (or have created custom ADMX files, or jam the ADMX files into their own local c:\windows\ PolicyDefinitions).

This becomes a big problem—fast. Here's why: if you create a new GPO, that GPO will have the definitions for all the whiz-bang stuff Windows 7/SP3 has to offer. However, when another administrator (who doesn't have the latest ADMX files) tries to edit or report on that GPO, they simply won't see the policy settings for Windows 7/SP3 available.

 GPMC reports about this newly created GPO would show the new whiz-bang features as "Extra Registry Settings," but actually trying to edit the GPO itself will not show them.

What you need is a way to ensure that all administrators who are using updated GPMC management stations have a one-stop-shop way to ensure that they're getting the latest ADMX files. That way, everyone will be on the same page, and there will be no challenges when one administrator creates a GPO and another tries to edit it.

The Windows ADMX/ADML Central Store

As described earlier, the updated GPMC has a trick up its sleeve.

That is, administrators using the updated GPMC can use a Central Store for ADMX and ADML files. Recall that the ADMX files are the definitions themselves, and the ADML files are the language-specific files for each ADMX file.

The idea is that the Central Store lives on every Domain Controller. So, after the Central Store is created, your updated GPMC management station simply looks for it—every time it tries to create or edit a GPO—and it will automatically use the definitions contained within the ADMX files inside the Central Store.

This means you don't have to worry about running around to each of your 20 management stations to update them whenever new ADMX files come out. You simply plop them in the Central Store and you're done. You don't even have to tell the updated GPMC management stations you did anything; they'll just automatically look and use the latest definitions!

Here's the best part: it doesn't matter what kind of Domain Controllers you have. Doesn't matter if you have Windows 2000, Windows Server 2003, Windows Server 2008, or a mix of all three. It's the updated GPMC that is doing the work to look for the Central Store in the place on the Domain Controller.

Wait, I'm going to stop here, and take a big deep breath and say it one more time. Because I know you're reading fast and want to get to the good stuff. So, say it out loud if you have to. It doesn't matter if you have Windows 2000, Windows Server 2003, Windows Server 2008, or a mix of all three. It doesn't matter what domain mode you're in. It's the updated GPMC that is doing the work to look for the Central Store in the prescribed place on the Domain Controller.

Got it? You don't have to "sell" your boss on upgrading the whole Domain Controller back end just to get this cool Central Store stuff. With one updated GPMC management station, you've basically got the magic you need.

So, let's read on and make it happen.

Creating the Central Store

Creating the Central Store must be done by a Domain Administrator because only a Domain Administrator has the ability to write to the location we need in SYSVOL. You can do this operation on any Domain Controller, because all Domain Controllers will automatically replicate the changes we do here to all other Domain Controllers via normal Active Directory/ SYSVOL replication. However, it's likely best to perform this on the PDC emulator because that's the default location the GPMC and Group Policy Object Editor use by default.

To create the Central Store:

1. On the PDC emulator, use Explorer or the command line to create a directory in:

```
%systemroot%\windows\sysvol\sysvol\<domain name>\policies
```

(That's the usual location; yours could be different.) You want to create a directory called `PolicyDefinitions` as seen in Figure 6.7.

FIGURE 6.7 Create a new directory called `PolicyDefinitions` in the `Policies` folder of SYSVOL.

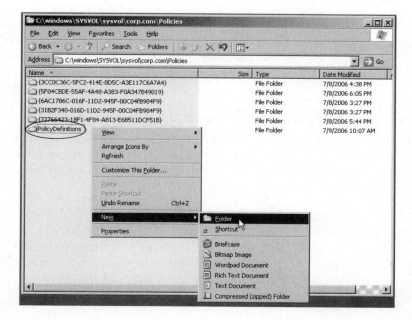

2.   We need a location to store our language-specific ADML files. Within
     PolicyDefinitions you'll create a directory for each locale. Again, U.S. English
     is en-US. For other locales, visit http://tinyurl.com/qpomo.

Note that the directory name must be the same as specified in the locale
reference page. If it's not, the ADMX file will not find its corresponding
ADML file for that language.

Populating the Central Store

Now, you simply have to get the latest, greatest ADMX and ADML files from your updated
GPMC machine into the Central Store.

There are a zillion possible ways to copy the files there. But the steps are most easily
done with two xcopy commands. This will work if your Windows 7 management station
has access to the Domain Controller and if you have write rights.

To copy the ADMX files into the Central Store from your Windows 7 management station:

```
xcopy %systemroot%\PolicyDefinitions\*
   %logonserver%\sysvol\%userdnsdomain%\
               policies\PolicyDefinitions
```

To copy in the ADML files into, say, the U.S. English directory we created earlier:

```
xcopy %systemroot%\PolicyDefinitions\EN-US\*
   %logonserver%\sysvol\%userdnsdomain%\
               policies\PolicyDefinitions\EN-US\
```

You can also get a free graphical utility for creating and populating the
Central Store automatically at www.gpoguy.com/Free-GPOGuy-Tools.aspx.

Verifying That You're Using the Central Store

Once you've created the Central Store directories in SYSVOL and copied the ADMX and
ADML files to their proper location, you're ready to try it out. Start by closing the updated
GPMC if it's already open, then reopen it. You can fire up the GPMC by clicking Start and
in the Run box typing **gpmc.msc**.

And then just create and edit a GPO.

However, can you be sure you're really using the Central Store?

The updated GPMC's Group Policy Management Editor will tell you if you're using
local policy definitions or using the Central Store. In Figure 6.8, you can see a GPO where
the Administrative Templates are retrieved from the local machine. However, as soon as the
Central Store is available, that same notice changes to what's seen in Figure 6.9.

FIGURE 6.8   Policy definitions are originally pulled from the local machine.

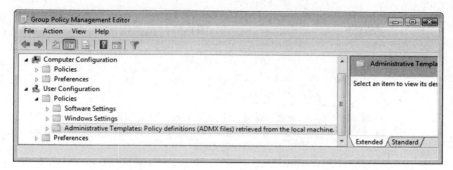

FIGURE 6.9   Policy definitions can be pulled from the Central Store.

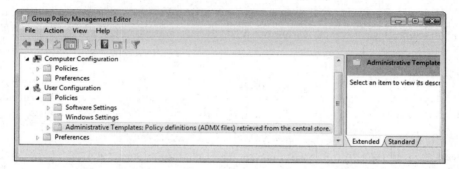

There is a secondary test as well to help you verify that you're using the Central Store. That is, when you create and edit a GPO, then click the Settings tab in the GPMC, you'll see a line under either Computer Configuration or User Configuration that says "Policy definitions (ADMX files) retrieved from the Central Store." You can see this in Figure 6.10.

Updating the Central Store

ADMX and ADML files will be updated at some point. If your management machine is already Windows Vista, well then, as expected the ADMX and ADML files from Windows 7 are newer.

Likewise, when Windows 7's SP2, SP3, and so on comes out, those will be newer still, and so on.

When this happens, you'll need to update the Central Store, which couldn't be easier. Simply copy the latest and greatest ADMX files to the `PolicyDefinitions` directory you created in SYSVOL, and copy the latest and greatest ADML files to the language-specific directory within `PolicyDefinitions`.

Then you're done.

FIGURE 6.10   Anytime you click the Settings tab, the impromptu report will demonstrate if you are using the Central Store for your ADMX files.

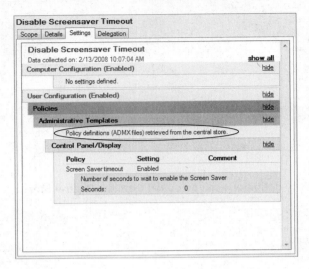

Additionally, other products, like Office 2007, will have ADMX and ADML files. If you wish to make those available to all administrators, just do the same thing. Drop them into the Central Store and you're done. (More about Office 2007 ADMX files a bit later.)

Office 2007 has, confusingly, both ADM templates and ADMX templates. You can find the ADM and ADMX/ADML templates at http://tinyurl .com/2rr8c2, but don't bother putting ADM files in the Central Store because ADM templates and the Central Store don't mix.

Creating and Editing GPOs in a Mixed Environment

I know I've suggested about 8 million times now that you use the "updated" GPMC. And that updated GPMC is found within RSAT for Windows Vista, Windows 7, Windows Server 2008, and Windows Server 2008 R2. That's a lot of opportunity to do things *right*.

The problem is, for many of you, you're ready to upgrade your own management machine to, say, Windows 7 but your friend Billy in the branch office is still using a Windows XP/SP2 machine from 2004.

Ow.

So, here's where things get complicated. That is, you could have the four following situations:

Scenario 1   Start out by creating and editing a GPO on an older GPMC management station (like Windows 2000, Windows XP, Windows Server 2003, and so on). Edit using another older GPMC management station. In this scenario, no modern Windows is involved.

Scenario 2   Start out by creating and editing a GPO on an older GPMC management station. Edit using a modern management machine station.

Scenario 3   Start out by creating and editing a GPO on a newer management station. Edit using another newer management machine station.

Scenario 4   Start out by creating and editing a GPO on a newer management machine. Edit using an older GPMC (i.e., Windows XP) management station.

Scenario 1: Start Out by Creating and Editing a GPO Using the Older GPMC. Edit Using Another Older GPMC Management Station.

Again, here, the new updated GPMC isn't involved. In this scenario, it's all about using the older GPMC with old-school ADM templates and ADM template behavior. And, of course, note that by creating a GPO using an older GPMC machine, you won't be able to get to any of the Windows 7 or Windows Server 2008 goodies—that's because all the Windows 7 and Windows Server 2008 goodies are available only when you use an updated GPMC management station.

So, let's imagine that you've created 86 GPOs using an old and crusty Windows XP machine with the older GPMC loaded. Of course, all 86 GPOs have the original Windows XP versions of those ADM templates (yes, old and crusty).

Now, you learn about a policy setting in Windows XP/SP2 that requires the corresponding Windows XP/SP2 templates. What are you going to do?

Easy! Jump on a Windows XP/SP2 machine and edit the GPO using the GPMC!

This is because, as we already understand, the ADM template files used to modify and update a GPO are always copied from your management station. Older ADM templates inside GPOs are automatically updated when you re-edit a GPO on a machine that has new ADM templates.

When you edit the GPO on your older GPMC management station and merely look at the policy settings in the Administrative Templates section, the editor will say, "Ah-ha! I've got Windows XP/SP2 templates available to me! This specific GPO's ADM templates are only the original old and crusty Windows XP templates. I can tell because the date is so old. I'll update the underlying ADM templates automatically from c:\windows\inf in Windows XP—without even saying a word. That's because I have newer ones!"

And it then proceeds. And it proceeds because the time/date stamp for Windows XP ADM templates your editor has access to is more recent than the time/date stamp for Windows 2000 ADM templates. It's doing you a favor behind your back. You must repeat for every old GPO you want to update. If you want to update all your GPOs with Windows XP/SP2 ADMs, you simply have to open each old GPO and look at the policy settings in the Administrative Templates section. But again, you need to do this from a Windows XP/SP2 management station. Then they'll be updated.

Again, there's no universal master update location where you can just "drop in" your latest ADM templates and be done.

Scenario 2: Start Out by Creating and Editing a GPO with the Older GPMC. Edit Using the Updated GPMC.

This will be the common "upgrade" scenario. That is, you've already got your gaggle of GPOs created. You created them using Windows XP's GPMC. Now, you've got the updated GPMC installed on, say, a Windows 7 machine, and you're ready to use it. What happens?

Not much! If you start to use a Windows 7 management station and edit an existing GPO created by XP, nothing happens in SYSVOL. No updated GPMC ADMX files are copied anywhere, and very little happens overall.

However, while you're editing the GPO, you'll have access to all the latest and greatest policy settings, one of which is shown in Figure 6.11.

For argument's sake, let's say you decided to enable **Turn off Windows HotStart**—a Windows Vista and later–only feature.

FIGURE 6.11 Editing an existing GPO with an updated GPMC gives you the ability to see updated settings.

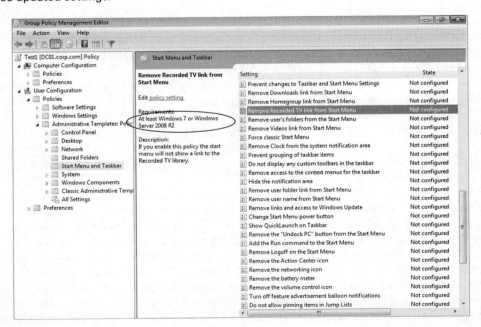

Now, what happens if you try to edit and/or report on those settings using the older GPMC using Windows XP? Short answer: it's not good. That's because the older GPMC doesn't know how to interpret the Vista (and later) specific settings you've set within the GPO. If you try to edit the GPO on an older GPMC machine, you simply won't see the newly available policy setting.

And if you try to look at it using the older GPMC's Settings Report feature, the Vista (and later) specific settings show up as "Extra Registry Settings," as seen in Figure 6.12.

FIGURE 6.12 Windows XP doesn't know how to interpret Vista and later settings within a GPO. These settings show up as "Extra Registry Settings."

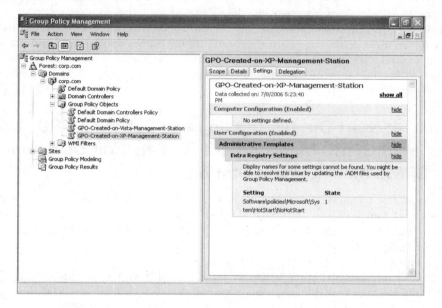

In Figure 6.12 you can see the Settings tab from GPMC running on an older GPMC machine running Windows XP, which is a report of what's going on inside the GPO.

Again, if you were to continue to use your older GPMC management station to *edit* the GPO, you simply wouldn't be able to find the **Remove Recorded TV link from Start Menu** policy setting—or any other Windows 7–specific policy setting for that matter.

Although it's clearly not a good idea, there is nothing that technically prevents you from using Windows XP to make a change to a GPO that was created using an older GPMC management station. In short, you simply can't see the updated settings.

If a custom ADM file has been added to the GPO (yes, ADM), then your updated GPMC will display it.

Scenario 3: Start Out by Creating and Editing a GPO Using the Updated GPMC. Edit Using Another Updated GPMC Management Station.

This is the scenario you want to strive for. That is, always use the updated GPMC to create and edit your GPOs.

Without the Central Store in place, everyone will use their local ADMX and ADML policy definitions. At least the new "do nothing" behavior of the GPMC will cheerfully keep the GPOs "bloat free" and you don't have to worry about multilanguage issues or overwriting each others' definitions inside the GPO.

If you've got the Central Store in place, even better. That way, all your administrators are utilizing the same definitions. Even if various administrators update their own management machines with service packs, everyone is still using the same centralized policy definitions. Then, once those are updated by a domain administrator, again, everyone is immediately updated.

Scenario 4: Start Out by Creating and Editing a GPO Using an Updated GPMC Management Station. Edit Using an Older GPMC Management Station.

Avoid this scenario whenever possible. This is the worst of all worlds because when you originally created the GPO on your updated GPMC management station, you did so without copying the 3MB of ADM files (remember, the updated GPMC doesn't natively use ADM files to define Group Policy settings).

So, you did good here!

However, by merely *viewing* the GPO using the older GPMC, you end up pushing up the 3MB of ADM files into the GPO. So, every time you do this, you'll see an ADM directory inside the GPO because they were pushed up from your older GPMC machine.

And it's done "invisibly."

So, don't do this. Create a corporate-wide edict to ditch the older GPMC and try to engage all administrators to use the updated GPMC whenever possible to avoid this problem.

ADM and ADMX Templates from Other Sources

The templates Microsoft provides with Windows are just the beginning of possibilities when it comes to Administrative Templates. The idea behind additional templates is that you or third-party software vendors can create them to restrict or enhance features of either the operating system or applications.

If you know what to control, you're in business. Just code it up in an ADM or ADMX file and utilize it. Again, however, be mindful that your application itself needs to be coded to be "policy aware" or else you're just zapping Registry edicts around as "preferences."

If you're starting from scratch and have a choice, you'll want to use ADMX files instead of ADM files. That's because you can leverage the Central Store for ADMX files instead of remembering to copy ADM files to every management station.

However, it should be noted that you might already be using an ADM file or three. If you are, how do you get them to the ADMX "promised land"? A free tool, of course. Before we get into that, I will say that's the best option: get those custom and additional ADM files into ADMX format and leverage the Central Store. However, for completeness, I do want to explain what happens if you try to introduce an ADM file directly into a newer GPMC management station.

Recall that ADM templates are the older way to make definitions of what we can control. And recall that there are both true *policies* and *preferences* that can be defined within an ADM file (or, ADMX file too).

Policies write to the "correct" place in the target computer's Registry. And when the user or computer falls out of the "scope of management" of the GPO (that is, it doesn't apply to them anymore), the setting should revert back to the default.

Preferences write anywhere in the Registry that the application might be looking for it. Preferences tattoo the Registry. So, when the user or computer falls out of the scope of management of the GPO, the setting just sticks around.

You have the ability to get some ADM files from various sources. These ADM files sometimes have definitions for true policies. Other ADM files have definitions for preferences. How do you know which are which? The good news is, the Group Policy Management Editor interface shows you a difference between the two.

The editor for the older GPMC shows blue for policies and red for preferences. In the updated GPMC, it shows a little paper icon for policies and a paper icon with a down arrow for preferences. That way, you can make an informed decision on whether or not you want to implement a preference.

Indeed, on GPanswers.com in the Tips and Tricks section we have a gaggle of downloadable ADM templates that people have created to control various aspects of applications and of their systems.

Leveraging ADM Templates from Your Windows Management Station

If you want to leverage and load one of these ADM templates into an existing GPO, simply edit it by using the GPMC and bringing up the Group Policy Object Editor, as shown in Figure 6.13. Then, choose either User Configuration ➤ Policies ➤ Administrative Templates or Computer Configuration ➤ Policies ➤ Administrative Templates, right-click over either instance of Administrative Templates, and choose Add/Remove Templates to open the Add/Remove Templates dialog box.

FIGURE 6.13 You can still Add/Remove Templates from a GPO you create with a modern GPMC.

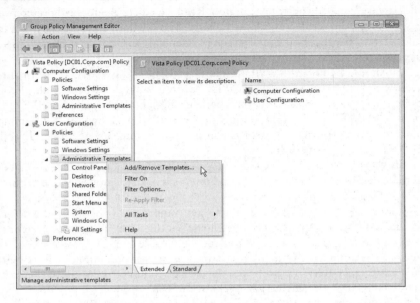

Click the Add button to open the file requester, and select to load the ADM template you want. I'll show you in the next section or two where to track down more ADM files, but I wanted to show you this first so you'd know how to use them.

The original default location to start looking for ADM files is `\windows\inf`; however, in practice you could store your ADM files anywhere. Just remember that every time you use an ADM template, you're copying that file directly into the GPO within SYSVOL.

> When you're adding an Administrative Template, the interface suggests that you can choose to add it from either the Computer Configuration or the User Configuration node. In actuality, you can add the ADM template from either section and the appropriate policy settings appear under whichever node the ADM template was designed for.

Once ADM templates are added using an updated GPMC management station, they show up within the Group Policy Object Editor under a special node called Classic Administrative Templates (ADM), as seen in Figure 6.14. In Figure 6.14, I've loaded an ADM template for Word 2003 (again, I'll show you where to get these templates in a minute so you can experiment, too).

Again, ADM files can have definitions for true policies or for old-style preferences. If you load additional ADM templates into the Group Policy Management Editor that contain old-style preferences, you will also see them. If you go back to Figure 6.2, you'll see it right there.

Once you're editing a preference, you'll notice that old-style preferences have a paper icon with a down arrow on them. This is to indicate that this is a preference and not a true policy, and these values will stick around even after the policy no longer applies to the user or computer. You can see the little down arrow icon for any tattooing preference.

FIGURE 6.14   ADM templates are permitted in GPOs created from newer management stations.

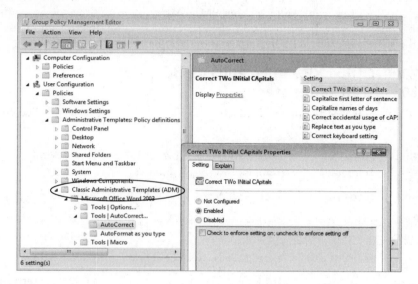

Indeed, the Group Policy Editor is nice enough to even tell you this fact, as you can see in Figure 6.2.

Microsoft Office ADM Templates

If you are also interested in deploying Office 2000, Office XP, Office 2003, or Office 2007, you'll be happy to know that they each come with a slew of customized ADM templates for you to import and use to your advantage.

- For Office 2000, download the Office 2000 Resource Kit tools at:

  `http://office.microsoft.com/en-us/ork2000/HA101693191033.aspx`

- For Office XP, download the Office XP Resource Kit tools at:

  `http://office.microsoft.com/en-gb/help/HA011362921033.aspx`

- Office 2003 templates are located in the Office 2003 Resource Kit. Visit `www.microsoft` `.com/office`. At last check, some even newer templates are available in the Office 2003/ SP2 Resource Kit at `http://tinyurl.com/4wxxn`.

- Office 2007 ADM and ADMX templates are located at `http://tinyurl.com/2w9qs7`. However, Office 2007 is the first to utilize ADMX templates.

> For information on how to automatically deploy Office 2000, XP, or 2003 (with patches and personalized customizations) to your users, see Chapter 11.

The file you're looking for (with either Office 2000 or XP) is called `Orktools.exe` (for Office 2003, it's `Ork.exe`), and it's about 9MB. After you install the corresponding Resource Kit on your management station, the files in the next section are automatically placed in the `\windows\inf` folder for importation like the other ADM files.

Office 2000, Office XP, Office 2003, and Office 2007 ADM Templates

Here is a list of the ADM templates available for Office 2000, Office XP, Office 2003, and Office 2007:

Office 2000 Templates	Office XP Templates	Office 2003 Templates	Office 2007 Templates	Description
access9.adm	access10.adm	access11.adm	access12.adm	Access settings
clipgal5.adm	gal10.adm	gaal11.adm	N/A	Restrict access to media clips
excel9.adm	excel10.adm	excel11.adm	excel12.adm	Excel settings
frontpg4.adm	fp10.adm	fp11.adm	N/A	FrontPage settings
instlr1.adm	instalr11.adm	instalr11.adm	N/A	Windows Installer settings
office9.adm	office10.adm	office11.adm	office12.adm	Common Office settings
outlk9.adm	outlk10.adm	outlk11.adm	outlk12.adm	Outlook 2000 settings
ppoint9.adm	ppt10.adm	ppt11.adm	ppt12.adm	PowerPoint settings
pub9.adm	pub10.adm	pub11.adm	pub12.adm	Publisher settings
word9.adm	word10.adm	word11.adm	word12.adm	Word settings
N/A	N/A	N/A	visio12.adm	Visio Settings
N/A	N/A	aer.adm	N/A	Corporate Windows Error Reporting (See the section "Microsoft Corporate Error Reporting" later in this chapter.)

Office 2000 Templates	Office XP Templates	Office 2003 Templates	Office 2007 Templates	Description
N/A	N/A	rm11.adm	N/A	Microsoft Relationship Manager File location
N/A	N/A	scrib11.adm	onent12.adm	Microsoft OneNote 2003 settings
N/A	N/A	N/A	cpao12.adm	Calendar Printing Assistant for Outlook 2007
N/A	N/A	N/A	groove12.adm	Groove 2007
N/A	N/A	N/A	ic12.adm	Office InterConnect 2007
N/A	N/A	N/A	inf12.adm	InfoPath 2007
N/A	N/A	N/A	proj12.adm	Project 2007
N/A	N/A	N/A	spd12.adm	SharePoint Designer 2007

Implementing a Customized Office Policy

After the Office templates are on the server, you can simply load them alongside the currently loaded templates. You can load all, some, or none—it's up to you.

In this example, we'll make believe we need to set up a custom Word 2003 policy for a collection of users. Normally, as in this example, Office template settings are meant for users, not computers. However, Office does include Computer-side settings that you can use to override User-side settings if you want.

 If you don't want to use the Office 2003 ADM templates in this example, you can substitute Office XP or Office 2000 templates. Just make sure you also have the corresponding Office suite installed on the target machine.

Here, you'll see how to use an additional template. We'll load the word11.adm template alongside our current default templates. Then we'll change the default behavior of our Human Resources users for Word 2003 as follows:

- The grammar checker is turned off while we type in Word.
- The spell checker is turned off while we type in Word.
- Word will ignore words in uppercase during spell check.
- Word will ignore words with numbers during spell check.

To change Word's default behavior for the **Human Resources Users** OU, follow these steps:

1. Log onto your management machine as the Domain Administrator.

2. Download the Office 2003 Resource Kit tools and make sure the ADM templates are properly installed in the \windows\inf folder.

3. Fire up the GPMC.

4. Right-click the **Human Resources Users** OU and select "Create and link a GPO here."

5. Create a new GPO called "Word 2003 Settings."

6. Edit the "Word 2003 Settings" GPO.

7. Choose either User Configuration ➢ Policies ➢ Administrative Templates or Computer Configuration ➢ Policies ➢ Administrative Templates, right-click over either instance of Administrative Templates, and choose Add/Remove Templates to open the Add/ Remove Templates dialog box.

8. Click the Add button to open the file requester, and select to load the Word11.adm template from the \windows\inf folder. Click Close to close the Add/Remove Templates dialog box to return to the Group Policy Object Editor.

9. To turn off the "Check grammar as you type" feature, drill down to User Configuration ➢ Policies ➢ Administrative Templates ➢ Classic Administrative Templates (ADM) ➢ Microsoft Office Word 2003 ➢ Tools ➢ Options ➢ Spelling & Grammar ➢ Check grammar as you type. Then, enable the setting, but do *not* select the check box. This forces the policy on the user, but clearing the check box forces it off.

10. Repeat step 9 for "Check spelling as you type," "Ignore words in UPPERCASE," and "Ignore words with numbers."

You can try this exercise with the other Office 2003–supplied templates listed earlier. These will affect Excel, PowerPoint, Access, and the like.

To test your new policy on the **Human Resources Users** OU, simply log onto any machine loaded with Word 2003 as a user who would be affected by the new policy. For instance, log on to XPPRO1 as Frank Rizzo, our old HR pal from Chapter 1 (assuming you have Word 2003 loaded).

Then in Word, choose Tools ➢ Options to open the Options dialog box, and make sure the settings reflect the policy settings you dictated.

Now, in this example we just explored, we were using the raw ADM files. Again, you can (as you'll discover a little later) take these ADM files and covert them—lock, stock, and barrel—into ADMX files to be used in the Central Store.

Also note that Office 2007 now has downloadable ADMX files—no need to convert or do anything fancy. Just plop 'em in your Central Store and start using them. We'll talk more about the Office 2007 ADMX files a little later. Check it out in the upcoming section "Using ADMX Templates from Other Sources."

Other Microsoft ADM Templates

Microsoft has two additional applications outside the Office family of products that leverage the Group Policy infrastructure by using ADM templates.

Microsoft Software Update Services (SUS) and Windows Server Update Services (WSUS)

The job of Windows Server Update Services (WSUS) is to ensure that patches are deployed to your Windows 2000, Windows XP, and Windows 2003 client systems. After a server is set up to deploy the patches, the client system learns about the server by way of a custom ADM template.

The template is built into Windows 2003 and Windows 2000/SP4 as `Wuau.adm`. However, the template is not built into Windows 2000/SP3.

You can learn more about WSUS, how to deploy it, and how to use the ADM templates from several places, here's two.

Microsoft has an excellent guide to the policy settings with regard to WSUS available at `http://tinyurl.com/ytwg39`. Here's an older article I wrote on the subject `http://tinyurl.com/yad8q7t`.

Microsoft Corporate Error Reporting

Microsoft has a service that lets corporate IT administrators "trap" error messages to a central server, instead of allowing them to be sent directly to Microsoft; it's called Corporate Error Reporting (CER). CER can help track systems that frequently crash and can provide an easier way to connect with Microsoft if a system does fail often. It can trap information for many of Microsoft's most popular applications, including Office XP, Windows XP, Windows 2003, Project 2002, and SharePoint Portal Server.

Microsoft CER uses the ADM file `Cer2.adm`. You can get more information on CER at `http://tinyurl.com/2n233o`. You'll find the ADM file in the "toolbox" section of the web page.

Corporate Error Reporting is built into Office 2003, and more information can be found here: `http://tinyurl.com/3bnvlw`.

The MDOP tools (available for Microsoft Software Assurance customers for an extra fee) also comes with a package named Microsoft System Center Desktop Error Monitoring for industrial-strength reporting.

Using ADMX Templates from Other Sources

You'll get ADMX files the same way you got ADM files: companies like Microsoft will make them available to control the products they support, and enterprising geeks will produce ADMX files that control other parts of the operating system and third-party applications.

The same basic note and warning applies, though: ADMX files can contain both (or either) true policies or old-school preferences.

ADMX Templates for Office 2007

The most current version of Office, right now, is Office 2007. About nine months after Office 2007 was released, so was its corresponding ADMX files. You can download the ADM and ADMX (and a lot of language-specific ADML files) here: `http://tinyurl.com/2w9qs7`.

And when you download them, you already know what to do. Just chuck 'em in the Central Store (both ADMX and ADML files in the appropriate places) and you'll be golden. Then all the new GPOs that you create will be able to control Office 2007 when you use an updated GPMC management station.

ADMX Templates from Other Sources

Will other Microsoft products have ADMX files? We hope so. So, while I have nothing specific to report now, check in every so often on www.GPanswers.com (especially the newsletters, where I'll try to let you know about any new ones that pop up).

Darren Mar-Elia, who runs www.GPOguy.com, has an ADMX version of his troubleshooting tool, GPOLOG.adm, at www.gpoguy.com/Free-GPOGuy-Tools.aspx.

Deciding How to Use ADMX Templates

Once you have the ADMX templates, you need to decide how to use them. If you've already created the Central Store, terrific. Just plop them into the Central Store and you're done. However, note that this means that all administrators who have access to create GPOs using management stations will be able to leverage all ADMX files.

You might not want to enable all administrators to leverage all ADMX templates.

If that's the case, you have only one option: put the specific ADMX files you only want some administrators to get only on the management station you want them to use. The downside, however, is that if another Group Policy administrator (on his management station) tries to edit the GPO or report on it, he won't get the same view of all the settings that you do. That's because his management station doesn't contain the ADMX file you're using.

So, best practice is to use the ADMX file Central Store whenever possible.

ADMX Migrator and ADMX Editor Tools

Yes, it's true. We've just seen that it's possible to import older-school ADM files into GPOs on our updated management machine.

But that gets complex.

Wouldn't it be a better idea to just utilize ADMX files everywhere? That way, you can just plop 'em all in the Central Store and be done. If you already have custom ADM files and need to get them to ADMX land, there's a utility that was written by FullArmor Corporation and licensed by Microsoft to give to you for free.

It's got a silly name: the ADMX Migrator tool. Doesn't it sound like it migrates ADMX files? Well, it doesn't. Maybe it should have been called ADM2ADMX or something, but regardless of the name, that's its job. You can download the tool from Microsoft here: http://tinyurl.com/ydb6ub. Note that it requires the .NET Framework 2.0 to be currently installed.

Additionally, inside the ADMX Migrator tool package is a basic (very, very basic) ADMX editor to help you handcraft your own ADMX files from scratch. The idea is that you don't have to "learn" a new language and hand-code it using, say, Notepad. Just use the tool to create your own ADMX files and you're in business.

Problem is, though, that the ADMX Migrator tool is not super intuitive. You might also want to check out an alternative ADM and ADMX creation and migration tool from SysPro at `www.sysprosoft.com/adm_summary.shtml`.

For these examples, I'm running the tools on my Windows Win7 management station, but they'll work just fine on a Windows XP that has the .NET Framework 2.0 loaded as well.

ADMX Migrator

There are lots of places you can get premade ADM files. You might try leveraging some right now—some are at `www.GPanswers.com`; others are found online at various other websites. Here's an example of a simple ADM file if you want to follow along. Just take this text and copy it into Notepad and save it as `Sounds.ADM`.

```
CLASS USER

CATEGORY "Sounds"
    POLICY "Sound to hear when starting Windows XP"
        KEYNAME "Appevents\Schemes\Apps\.Default\SystemStart\.Current"
        PART "What sound do you want?" EDITTEXT REQUIRED
        VALUENAME ".default"
        END PART
    END POLICY

END CATEGORY
```

Then run the tool `faAdmxConv.exe` against the ADM file you have. It can be as simple as just pointing to the file, but there are more switches if you have specific requirements.

Once run, it will create an ADMX and ADML file for the ADM. The documentation swears that it will put them in a temporary directory on the running user's profile, but in my tests, the resulting files seem to go to the root of the `c:\` drive. Be sure to look for your new ADMX file in `c:\` and the ADML file in `c:\en-US`.

To prevent this behavior, you can also just specify an output directory like this:

```
faAdmxConv.exe admname.adm c:\outputdirectory
```

Once you're in the directory of your choice, the resulting files are ready to be put in the Central Store (or, if you're not using the Central Store, then with individual updated GPMC management stations). You can see the program run and its output in Figure 6.15.

The ADMX Migrator tool sometimes can't handle the SUPPORTED keyword. In this example, I've removed the SUPPORTED keyword to ensure that conversion occurs properly. However, in the conversion you'll see the warning, as seen in Figure 6.15.

FIGURE 6.15   The faAdmxConv.exe tool will take your ADM and convert it into an ADMX and ADML file.

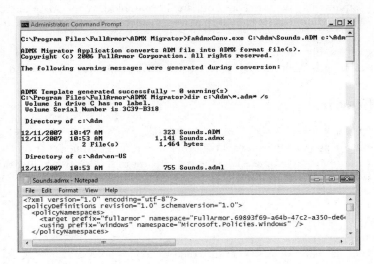

Then, if you want to leverage ADMX and ADML files in the Central Store, put the ADMX file in the \PolicyDefinitions directory within the SYSVOL and the ADML file in the language directory (en-US for English).

The ADMX Migrator tool sometimes appears to be hit or miss during conversion. The latest version (1.3 as of this writing) seems to clear up many of the bugs that I recorded and sent in. Some remain, though, and it's unclear whether FullArmor has intentions of updating the tool in the future.

ADMX Editor

In the previous example, we leveraged an existing ADM file that modified Windows XP's startup sound. What if you wanted to create the ADMX file from scratch?

Creating an ADMX template can sometimes be difficult. The hardest part can be figuring out which Registry setting you need to modify on the client system. Again, tools like Process Monitor or RegShot (URLs located earlier in chapter) can help point out what's changing on the client.

Then, armed with that information, you can triumphantly create your own custom ADM or ADMX template and try it. That's where the ADMX editor, also in the ADMX Migrator download, comes in.

Start the ADMX Editor by clicking Start ➢ All Programs ➢ FullArmor ➢ FullArmor ADMX Migrator ➢ ADMX Editor.

Once you fire it up, you'll be able to create a new ADMX file and add categories like "Misc XP Sounds" as seen in Figure 6.16. Note that it's not easy (at all) to realize you need to click to the right of Display Name to get that field to turn on. Once you do, you can enter the name.

FIGURE 6.16   Once you create a new ADMX file, you can create your first category, such as "Misc XP Sounds."

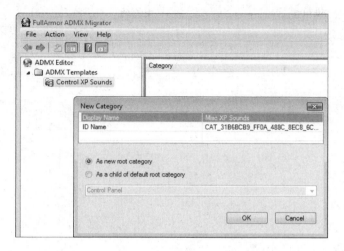

Then, right-click over your new category and enter your first policy setting. Here, we're only entering one: **Sound to hear when starting Windows XP.** We then give it the Registry key (seen in the previous ADM listing) and the Registry value name (also seen in the previous ADM listing) and finally specify that it's a User-side setting with the pull-down menu next to Class. You can see these all entered in Figure 6.17.

Then, you can add different elements such as a DropdownList, ComboBox, and more, as shown in Figure 6.18. You can also enter your own Explain text and Supported On text.

FIGURE 6.17   You can create your own policy settings within the categories you previously created.

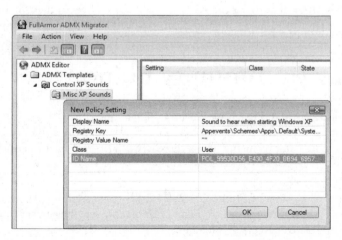

FIGURE 6.18 You can add various elements like TextBox requesters, DropdownLists, and more.

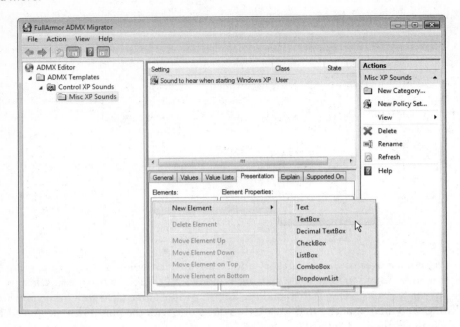

When ready, you can right-click over the ADMX file (in my example the node labeled "Control XP Sounds") and click Save As. This will create an ADMX and ADML file. Be sure to (again) move the ADMX into the Central Store and the ADML file into the language directory (en-US) for English.

I really wish there was some kind of "preview mode" to see if you got it right before you went through the motion of copying the ADMX and ADML files to their final location—because there's potentially a lot of trial and error involved before you get it just right.

PolicyPak Community Edition

So, I've been working with and teaching Group Policy a long time.

And one day, it hit me. Like Sir Isaac Newton sitting under the apple tree. Bonk. "There's something missing from the 'in the box' stuff. Stuff we need. I should invent something."

What was my epiphany?

Let's review the "current state of affairs" of the stuff in the box:

- Using ADM or ADMX templates, you can craft a very, very basic user interface. You can describe and deliver Registry punches.

- Those "preference" Registry punches just "stay there" after the GPO delivering the setting is removed. There's no way to "revert" to a known setting.

- Some applications, like Office, support true lockout. That's because those applications are coded to look in the proper policies keys. Because of this, those applications get an advantage—their UI gets to be truly "locked out" when policies are applied, because, again, they're true policy and not preferences.

- The Group Policy Preferences Registry extension is neat; it lets you quickly deploy a Registry setting just about anywhere. But when that policy is deleted, if the "Remove this value when it no longer applies" check box is set, the value is not reverted back—it's obliterated. Poof. Gone. Uh-oh.

Policy can get you so far. Preferences can get you so far.

To me, what was missing was clear: a way to deliver Registry settings wherever I needed (like preferences), but also a way to lock out application's user interfaces (like true policy). I also wanted a way to ensure that settings "went away" when I was done using them (also like policy).

Basically, I wanted the best of both worlds.

So I founded a software company and invented PolicyPak.

PolicyPak is both a free and commercial product that fills the gap. PolicyPak enables you to do the following:

- Quickly create a rich user interface inside the Group Policy editor that mirrors the user interface of your application

- Deploy Registry punches and other application changes anywhere your applications need them

- Lock down most applications' user interfaces as if the application was truly policy-enabled

- Automatically stop applying and revert these lockdown settings when the GPO no longer applies

Now, don't just throw your hands in the air and say, "This is too good to be true, at least for a free product." Yes, there is a catch, plain and simple, and here it is: PolicyPak Community Edition allows you to do all of this whiz-bang stuff for *one* application with up to 25 "controls" or "elements" like check boxes and drop-downs.

So, if you have a pet application, like DogFoodMaker 8.6, or WinZip, or Acrobat Reader, or anything, and you want to control it using Group Policy and truly policy-enable it, you can do so, right now, for no cost at all. When you're ready, PolicyPak Software will be happy to sell you a license that unlocks the software for unlimited use on each target machine.

Everything we'll explore in this section is 100 percent free. We don't have enough space to run through everything that PolicyPak can do. But as part of the download at www.PolicyPak.com there's a PDF manual that also has some walkthroughs and extended use cases.

For purposes of this section, I'll assume you went to PolicyPak.com and downloaded the latest version of PolicyPak. Note that the features are always increasing, so what you see here might not exactly match what the interface looks like in your download.

PolicyPak Concepts and Installation

PolicyPak's job is to help you re-create an existing application's user interface and help you describe the Registry punches each user interface element performs. Then, you'll control the application using a regular GPO.

You'll do this in four steps:

1. Import the UI of existing applications using an included (free) PolicyPak tool (PPAutoUI).

2. Describe the Registry behavior for check boxes and drop-downs and the link using the PolicyPak Design Studio tool.

3. Compile your work into something you can use inside the Group Policy editor.

4. Deploy your new PolicyPak like any other Group Policy setting and watch the magic happen.

Before we get started, though, you'll have to do a little installation. In the download, you'll see some key files. Here are the files, what they do, and where to install them:

PolicyPak CSE.msi (client-side extension)   Hand-install or use Group Policy Software Installation (Chapter 11) and get it on your client machines. Client machines can be XP and later, including Windows 7, 64-bit machines, and Terminal Services/Citrix. So, in this book, you'll likely want to install PolicyPak CSE.msi on XPPRO1 and/or WIN7. Be sure to install the 32-bit CSE on 32-bit clients and 64-bit CSE on 64-bit clients.

PolicyPak Admin Console.msi   Hand-install or use Group Policy Software Installation (Chapter 11) and get this file installed where you have the GPMC installed. When you do, you'll see a new PolicyPak node. For this book, I suggest you install it on WIN7MANAGEMENT.

PolicyPak Design Studio.msi   This is the PolicyPak "Toolkit," which will enable you to create your own PolicyPaks. You can install them on the same machine as your management machine or on another machine. For our examples, I again suggest you install it on WIN7MANAGEMENT.

There is one more prerequisite that needs to be on your PolicyPak creation station. That's the (free) Microsoft Visual C++ Express Edition. To be clear—this doesn't have to be on every machine. This only needs to be on the machine where you create PolicyPaks from. It's a whopper of a download, and can be found here:

www.microsoft.com/express/download/#webinstallUT

Be sure to pick the right one (the orange one) or you'll be kicking yourself wondering why step 3 doesn't work.

That's it. There are no server components to load, nothing installed on Domain Controllers, and no schema updates.

For more details on installation, see the PolicyPak manual accompanying the download.

For this super-fast tutorial, we won't go into every feature. In this chapter, I just want you to get a taste for what it can do and show you the end results. For more details, you can read the PolicyPak manual.

Creating Your First PolicyPak

In this example, we'll assume you want to control and manage an application like WinZip. For this section, you'll be running all steps on your PolicyPak Creation Station. For these examples, WinZip should already be installed on your PolicyPak Creation Station machine (for now) and also on your target systems for later control. WinZip can be found here: www.winzip.com/downwz.htm.

The PolicyPak AutoUI Wizard

On your PolicyPak Creation Station, open WinZip's Options ➢ Configuration page, and click Passwords, as shown in Figure 6.19.

FIGURE 6.19   Applications like WinZip can (and should) be controlled using Group Policy.

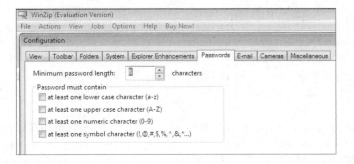

Leave this configuration page open as you proceed and run the PolicyPak AutoUI Wizard tool. The PolicyPak AutoUI Wizard tool's job is to take the interfaces from your existing applications, like WinZip, and bring them into the PolicyPak format for later use.

Now, run the PolicyPak AutoUI Wizard by clicking Start ➢ PolicyPak ➢ PolicyPak AutoUI Wizard. When you do, the PolicyPak AutoUI Wizard will run. Select "Start a new project."

When you do, you'll see a list of all the processes that are running that might have a user interface (UI) for PolicyPak to capture. In the top pane (Processes), select WinZip. In the bottom pane (Windows), select Configuration. You'll need to have WinZip's Configuration window open in order to see it listed in the Windows pane.

Once WinZip is selected, as shown in Figure 6.19, click Next. You'll then be prompted to name your project. I suggest you change the default from "WinZip (Evaluation Version)" to "WinZip."

At this point, the PolicyPak AutoUI Wizard will bring the Passwords tab into the Configuration window, as Figure 6.20 shows.

FIGURE 6.20 The PolicyPak AutoUI capture wizard can immediately make your applications' UI ready for Group Policy.

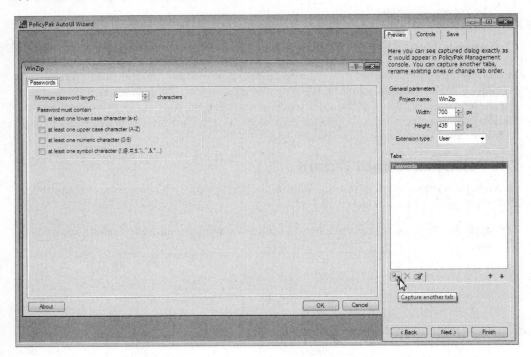

In Figure 6.20, you can see the mouse is highlighting a button that will let you capture additional tabs. Click the button and select the Cameras tab. After you do, switch back to the PolicyPak AutoUI capture tool, and you'll see the Cameras tab auto-captured.

For our examples, don't select any more tabs for now.

Once the Passwords and Cameras tabs are captured, click Finish. You'll be prompted to save your PolicyPak file. This file is called a "pXML" file. Save it in a location you can easily find and remember, like the Desktop or My Documents. Note that in practice you'll likely want to store the file in a more specific location for future reference. You may name the file anything you like.

For now, close the PolicyPak AutoUI Wizard (leaving WinZip running) and continue.

The PolicyPak Design Studio

Now that you've saved your project, you can open the PolicyPak Design Studio. To do so, select Start ➢ Programs ➢ PolicyPak ➢ PolicyPak Design Studio.

The PolicyPak Design Studio enables you to load PolicyPak pXML-based files that you've created using the PolicyPak AutoUI Wizard, or preconfigured pXML "paks" that you downloaded from the PolicyPak "Trading Post" part of the website.

Choose File ➢ Open and select the `WinZip.xml` file you created earlier using the PolicyPak AutoUI Wizard. When you do, you'll be prompted with a warning explaining the PolicyPak Community Edition limitations. That is, PolicyPak will only process the first 25 elements (check boxes, radio buttons, etc.) when in Community Edition.

The PolicyPak Design Studio allows you to modify what you've already got from a PolicyPak AutoUI capture, or create a new user interface from scratch. (No need to hand-create anything; the PolicyPak tools do all the work.)

Setting Registry Punches Using PolicyPak Design Studio

For now, click the Passwords tab, then click the "at least one symbol character (!,@,#,$,%,^,&,*…)" element, as seen in Figure 6.21.

FIGURE 6.21   Use the PolicyPak Design Studio to manage UI, Registry, and other settings.

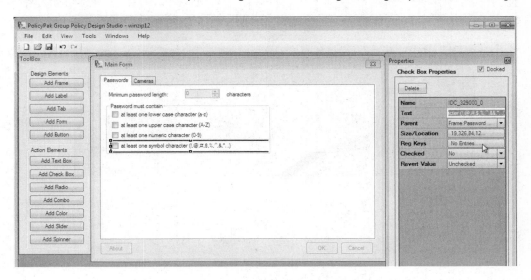

Click the "RegKeys ➢ No Entries…" check box property, also seen highlighted in Figure 6.21. When you do, you'll be prompted for the Checkbox Wizard.

There are two ways to use the Wizard:

- If you know the exact Registry entry associated with the check box, you can click Browse and get started.

- If you don't know the exact Registry entry, you can find it quickly with the Capture Wizard tool.

It's a bit too many steps to show the (really neat) Capture Wizard tool. You're welcome to check it out and have it automatically determine the Registry entry associated with the check box.

So, for now, just click Browse, and locate HKEY Current User ➢ Software ➢ Nico Mak Computing ➢ WinZip Policies. Select "passwordreqsymbol" (if present) or type it in as the Key Value Name.

When this value is "unchecked," you want the value to be set to 0.
When this value is "checked," you want the value to be set to 1.
You can see the result you're looking for in Figure 6.22.

FIGURE 6.22 Set what happens in the Registry when you click check boxes in the applications' UI.

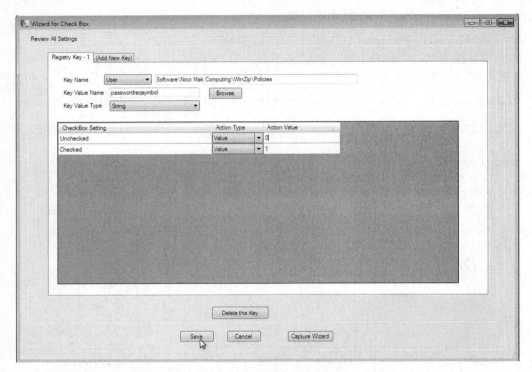

Click Save to save the value to the check box.

In real life you use the PolicyPak Design Studio and figure out (automatically if you liked) which check boxes, radio buttons, and drop-downs performed what actions on your client machines. Again, you can check out how to do that in the PolicyPak manual. For now, to save time, we'll ensure that just this one entry for "at least one symbol character (!,@,#,$,%,^,&,*...)" is entered correctly, and move on directly to testing.

Compiling Your PolicyPak in Group Policy

Now you're ready to make your "working" PolicyPak by compiling it. Choosing Tools ➢ Compile and PolicyPak Design Studio will use the Microsoft C++ 2008 Express Edition compiler you loaded on your PolicyPak Creation Station. Again, this is a massive download, but it's a required component in order to compile your PolicyPak into something we can use.

You may get a warning message because you didn't "complete" the project and define all areas. But for the purposes of a quick demonstration, that's okay. Click to continue.

You should get a message saying that your compile was successful and the creation of your PolicyPak is now complete. Click OK to exit and then close the PolicyPak Design Studio if you like.

Deploying Your First Compiled PolicyPak Extension

At this point, you've successfully compiled your first PolicyPak project into an extension. Now you're ready to create a GPO and affect your target users who are already using this application.

For this quick example, we're assuming that the machine you used as your PolicyPak Creation Station is *also* acting as your Group Policy management station. Therefore, we'll assume you already loaded the GPMC and the PolicyPak MMC snap-in (PolicyPak Admin Console.msi).

Now, let's create a GPO to affect our users. Fire up the GPMC by choosing Start ➢ Run and typing **GPMC.MSC** in the Run box.

We can now create a GPO and link it to the **Human Resources Users** OU and give the GPO a name, like WinZip Settings Test.

You should now be in the Group Policy Editor. Drill down to User Configuration ➢ PolicyPak ➢ Applications. Then, right-click Applications and select New ➢ Application and select your PolicyPak as seen in Figure 6.23.

FIGURE 6.23   Use the PolicyPak node inside the Group Policy editor to manage your applications.

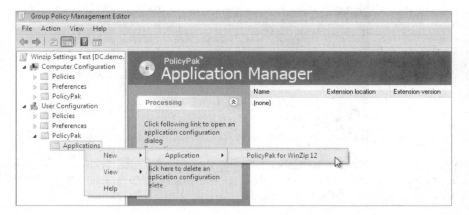

If you don't see the PolicyPak node, you likely did not install the PolicyPak Admin Console.MSI file from the download on the machine running the GPMC. You need to do this to see the PolicyPak node.

You will see a PolicyPak item fill in under Name, Extension Location, and Extension Version. Double-click the entry to open it. When you do, it should look exactly like the WinZip application we captured earlier and then modified with PolicyPak Design Studio. Again, in our quick example, we captured just two tabs. In real life you'll likely want to capture all tabs.

To test our PolicyPak, click the "at least one symbol character (!,@,#,$,%,^,&,*...)" entry on the Passwords tab. When you do, it will underline the value, showing enforcement.

Additionally, for this test, right-click over the setting and select "Revert this policy setting to the default value when it is no longer applied," as seen in Figure 6.24. Additionally, select "Disable corresponding control in target application," also shown in Figure 6.24.

FIGURE 6.24 PolicyPak lets you set enforcement modes (first block), Reversion modes (second block), and PolicyPak AppLock™ modes (third block).

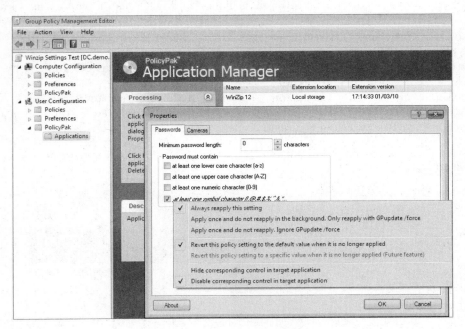

Finally, click the Cameras tab. Right-click over some blank space on the Passwords tab and select "Hide all controls in target application (for this tab)," as seen in Figure 6.25.

Click OK to apply your PolicyPak settings.

Testing Your PolicyPak

Now we need to log onto a client machine for testing. PolicyPak is ready to work when the following is true:

- The PolicyPak CSE is installed on a client computer that the user is logging onto. In our examples, I'm hoping you installed it on XPPRO1 or WIN7.

- The target computer (XPPRO1 or WIN7) already has the test application (WinZip) loaded.

- The user account is contained within the affected OU (in our testbed, that would be any account in the **Human Resources Users** OU, like Frank Rizzo).

FIGURE 6.25   Use PolicyPak to hide unused settings.

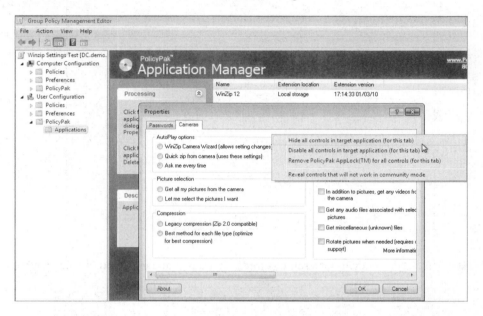

If you're sure these items are true, then log onto your test computer as an affected user. After logging on as a user in the **Human Resources Users** OU, run WinZip 12. Then, click Options ➢ Configuration and select the Passwords tab.

You should see that your setting to enforce "at least one symbol character (!,@,#,$,%,^,&,*…)" is set, as seen in Figure 6.26. Also note that the setting is grayed out so that users cannot mess with it.

Additionally, in Figure 6.26, you selected to hide all the options on the Cameras tab. Click the Cameras tab to see what has occurred. In Figure 6.27, you can see that none of the values on the Cameras tab are available for the user to change.

Now, let's simulate what would happen if the user changes job roles or the GPO should no longer be applied. Find Frank Rizzo's account using Active Directory Users and Computers to move the account to another OU, or the Users folder if need be.

Next, as Frank, on the target computer log off and then back on. Since the GPO no longer affects Frank, the GPO's settings should revert when applicable.

In Figure 6.24, you right-clicked over the "at least one symbol character (!,@,#,$,%,^,&,*…)" setting and selected "Revert this policy setting to the default value when it is no longer applied."

FIGURE 6.26 PolicyPak can deliver the settings, then gray out (disable) items your users shouldn't have access to.

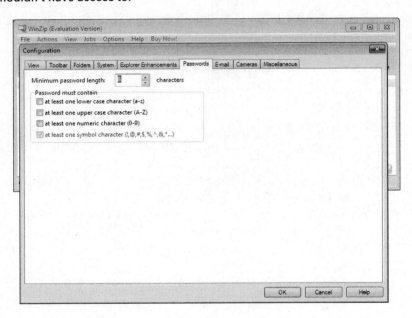

FIGURE 6.27 PolicyPak can remove (hide) settings that users shouldn't have access to.

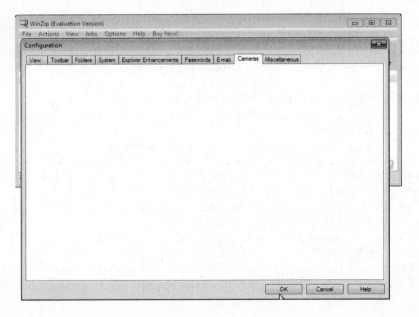

As Frank, run WinZip, select Options ➢ Configuration, and look at the Passwords tab. The check box in the "at least one symbol character (!,@,#,$,%,^,&,*...)" setting should be removed, because it is no longer applied. And, inspecting the Passwords tab, all the elements should unhide and allow the user to manipulate them.

Easy, right?

Let's wrap up by moving Frank's account back into the **HR-OU-Admins** OU and deleting or unlinking the GPO that contains the PolicyPak affecting him with WinZip.

Final Thoughts

Managing your applications requires that you extend Group Policy a bit. You can do so with ADM, ADMX, or PolicyPak.

Remember—if you use ADM or ADMX files, only applications smart enough to read Registry settings from the Policies keys will be true policies. They will be applied and removed when different users log on or off. They will not tattoo. They will appear with a paper icon (in the updated GPMC) or a blue dot (in the older GPMC) in the Group Policy Object Editor.

Most applications are not yet Policies key–aware, which means if you want to create your own modifications, you'll likely need to make them preferences. Preferences do not modify the Policies keys. They tattoo the Registry. They're left behind when the policy no longer applies. They will appear with a down arrow (in Windows 7) or a red dot (in pre–Windows Vista versions) in the Group Policy Object Editor.

If you have an ADM file you want to use in the Central Store, you'll have to convert it to ADMX first. Use the downloadable ADMX Migrator tool to perform that magic. On GPanswers.com, we will also maintain the previous edition's "ADM Template Syntax" section as a downloadable PDF should you need that, as well. Arguably, it's easier to first create an ADM file by hand, then convert it using the ADMX migration tool. Last, check out Microsoft's document Step-by-Step Guide to Managing Group Policy ADMX Files at

`http://go.microsoft.com/fwlink/?LinkId=55414`

And for the truly geeky, you can check out the ADMX schema, located at `http://tinyurl.com/28k56v` if you have wild dreams of hand-coding your own ADMX files.

PolicyPak's goal is to truly policy-enable your applications—even if the underlying Registry punches are really just preferences. PolicyPak can deliver the settings anywhere in the Registry, then lock down the user interface so users cannot change things.

PolicyPak Community Edition works for up to 25 elements in one PolicyPak. So get started today to control one pesky application (for free). Download it at `www.PolicyPak.com`.

7

Troubleshooting Group Policy

Working with Group Policy isn't always a bed of roses. Sure, it's delightful when you can set up GPOs with their policy settings from upon high and have them reflected on your users' desktops. However, when you make a Group Policy wish, a specific process occurs before that wish comes true. Indeed, the previous chapter discussed *when* Group Policy applies. Now you understand the general rules of the game and when they occur.

But what if the unexpected happens? More specifically, it's difficult to determine *where* a policy setting comes from and *how* it's applied. Or if Group Policy isn't working, *why* not, and *what's* going on? Additionally, you're usually after *whom* to blame, but that's actually something that auditing (discussed in Chapter 8) can help with. Additionally, check out our information on third-party tools in the appendix.

A user might call the help desk and loudly declare, "Things have just changed on my Desktop! I want them back the way they were!" Okay, sure, you want things better too. But a lot of variables are involved. First, there are the four levels: Local Group Policy (and potentially multiple local GPOs in Windows Vista and later) site, domain, and each nested OU (so perhaps even more levels). Then, to make matters worse, what if multiple administrators are making multiple and simultaneous Group Policy changes across your environment? Who knows who has enabled what Group Policy settings and how some user is getting Group Policy applied?

Additional factors are involved as well. For instance, you could have an Active Directory with cross-forest trusts to another forest, and users are logging in all over the place—not to mention a whole litany of things that could possibly go wrong between the time you make your wish and the time the client is expected to honor that wish.

Here's a taste of what to expect while troubleshooting GPOs:

Disabled GPOs   If the GPO is disabled or half the GPO is disabled, you need to hunt it down. Maybe someone decided to disable a GPO link and didn't tell you?

Inheritance troubles and trouble with WMI filtering   Between local, site, domain, and multiple nested OUs, it can be a challenge to locate the GPO you need to fix. Also, introducing WMI filters can make troubleshooting even harder.

GPO precedence at a given level   With multiple GPOs linked to a specific level in Active Directory, you might have some extra hunting to do.

Permissions problems   Ensuring that users and computers are in the correct site, domain, and OU is one battle; however, ensuring that they have the correct permissions to access GPOs is quite another.

Windows XP and later processing   Windows XP and later change the way GPOs are processed. And cross-forest trusts can be somewhat confusing as well.

Replication problems   The health of the GPO itself on Domain Controllers is important when hunting down policy settings that aren't applying.

Infrastructure problems   Group Policy processing requires that all pieces of your infrastructure are healthy, including such seemingly unrelated pieces as DNS, the services running on the client, and the ability to pass network protocols between clients and domain controllers. Good Active Directory design equals good (consistent) Group Policy processing. The first place to look when Active Directory (or replication) behaves strangely is DNS. As my good friend Mark Minasi likes to say, "The second place to look for replication problems is DNS, too." That's because problems with Active Directory almost always result from the DNS misconfiguration.

Loopback policy processing   Sometimes, by mistake, an administrator has enabled loopback policy processing for a computer (or multiple computers). When this happens, the user sees unexpected behavior because the GPOs that would normally apply to him are suddenly out of the ordinary. Just understanding how loopback policy processing works can be a tricky matter. Not only do we have two different modes (Replace or Merge), on top of that you can have complex permission settings on the GPOs themselves, making it hard to calculate which settings a given user will take on.

Slow links   You've rolled out your RAS (Remote Access Service) or new Windows Server 2008 R2 DirectAccess. Now how and when are your clients going to process GPOs?

These are just a few places where you might encounter trouble. Between various client types with different processing behavior, these problems and the occasional solar flare make things crazy. Troubleshooting can get complicated. Fast.

In this chapter, we'll first dive into *where* Group Policy "lives" to give you a better sense of what's going on. We'll then explore some techniques and tools that will enable you to get an even better view of *why* specific policies are being applied.

Now you might be running any number of operating systems at this point: Windows XP, Windows Vista, Windows 7, Windows Server 2003, Windows Server 2003 R2, Windows Server 2008, and Windows Server 2008 R2. Ow.

We'll be focusing on troubleshooting Windows XP and Windows 7 in this chapter. Sorry, Vista. You had your shot.

That said, here's the "chart" in case you need to understand and troubleshoot others:

- Windows XP and Windows Server 2003 share the same "guts" so they're generally troubleshot the same. Look for references to Windows XP.

- Windows 7, Windows Vista, Windows Server 2008, and Windows Server 2008 R2 all troubleshot the same. Look for references to Window 7 or "Windows Vista and later."

There may be a case where one operating system doesn't "fit the mold." In that case, I'll expressly call it out for you.

Under the Hood of Group Policy

As stated in Chapter 1, Group Policy scope has four levels: Local Group Policy (including Multiple Local Group Policy Objects) and then the three levels of Active Directory–based Group Policy—site, domain, and OU. When troubleshooting Group Policy, one approach is to first get a firm understanding of what's going on under the hood. As a kid, I took things apart all the time. My parents went mental when they came home and the dishwasher was in pieces all over the kitchen floor. It wasn't broken; I just wanted to know how it worked. If you're like me, this section is for you.

Inside Local Group Policy

Remember that a GPO is manipulated when someone walks up to the machine, runs the Local Group Policy Object Editor (GPEDIT.MSC), and makes a wish or three. Remember that in Windows XP, there is only one local GPO on a machine and local GPOs affected everyone who logged on to that machine. In Windows 7, there are Multiple Local GPOs (MLGPOs.)

Enterprise Admins, by default, do not have local administrator rights on individual client machines. Domain Admins, but not Enterprise Admins, have rights to Local Group Policy Objects (LGPOs).

Where Local Group Policy Lives

Once wishes are made with GPEDIT.MSC and a Local Group Policy is modified, the Local Group Policy lives in two places. The first part is file based, and the second part is Registry based:

The file-based part of local Group Policy (all versions of Windows)   The file-based part of the default local GPO can be found in %windir%\system32\grouppolicy.

The file-based part of local Group Policy for MLGPOs   Remember that in Windows Vista and later there are now Multiple Local GPOs (MLGPOs). Because of this, the storage of those user-specific and group-specific GPOs is in a different location than the default local GPOs. Namely, they are stored in a new subfolder of \Windows\SYSTEM32 called GroupPolicyUsers, as shown in Figure 7.1.

As you can see in the figure, there are three SID-named folders that contain the user-specific portion of the local GPO. (Remember that the computer portion applies to everyone, and, hence, there is no computer portion represented here.) You might have more than three folders here. In my example, the first SID you see in the list (with a SID of S-1-5-21-2410154586-1371493383-3297913877-1000) is the SID of a user account for whom I created a user-specific local GPO.

FIGURE 7.1   Viewing the directories of Windows 7 local GPOs

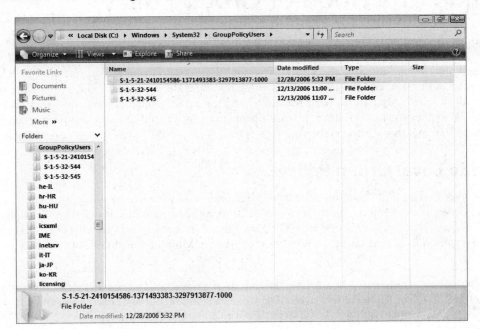

And, again, as you know from Chapter 1, I could have any number of user-specific local GPOs defined. And for each of those user-specific GPOs, each one would have its own SID-based folder.

In addition, the two other folders that you see in Figure 7.1 are ones you will find on your Windows Vista and later systems if you decide to define local GPOs specific for the Administrators group and still another folder that holds LGPO information for non-administrators. The folder called S-1-5-32-544 defines the Administrators GPO (and not coincidentally, that is the SID of the built-in Administrators group). Likewise, the folder named S-1-5-32-545 is the SID of the built-in Users group, which represents the non-administrators local GPO.

Again, you should notice one major difference between the default local GPO and these user-specific local GPOs: the default local GPO includes a computer-specific Machine folder in addition to the default User folder. However, any user-specific local GPO only contains a User folder (since it only contains user-specific policy settings).

The files and folders found in the local GPO mirrors, for the most part, the way the file-based portion of an Active Directory–based GPO stores its stuff. This is good news, as it makes understanding the two types of GPOs (local versus domain-based GPOs) nearly equal.

> Feel free to inspect the %windir%\system32\grouppolicy folder, and then jump to the section "Group Policy Templates" later in this chapter to get the gist of the file structure. Note, however, that not all the structure may be present until the local GPO is edited. For Windows XP and later operating systems, one major difference between local and Active Directory–based GPOs is that, when you make a policy change to the security attributes within the local GPO, that change is made directly to the workstation you're editing instead of being stored in the file system. So, if you change, for example, the password policy on the local GPO, you won't find evidence of it stored anywhere but in the local computer's Security Accounts Manager (SAM) database.

Three Use-at-Your-Own-Risk Local Group Policy Tips

Here are three tips that you are welcome to try—but use at your own risk. I cannot vouch for their validity or soundness, so you're on your own.

Tip 1 (for Windows XP): Ensure that admins (and other users) avoid Local Group Policy.   Perhaps you've set it up so that your users do not have access to the Start ➤ Run command. However, when you're logged in as the local administrator, you want the Run command. Then, check out support.microsoft.com/kb/293655. This tip shows you how admins (and other users) can override Local Group Policy for XP (and 2000 and Server 2003). Note that in Windows Vista and later, with the Multiple Local GPO feature, this tip is no longer required to segregate administrative policy from nonadministrative policy. However, this tip is valid only when the workstation isn't a domain member.

Tip 2: Reset Local Group Policy to the defaults.   If you've set up a Local Group Policy and want to restore it to its default configuration, there's no easy way. However, my good pal Mark Minasi has a newsletter (#32) on the subject. Track it down at www.minasi.com/ archive.htm. Even Mark admits that this solution might not be totally complete.

Tip 3: Copy a local GPO from one computer to another.   This tip works in all versions of Windows, including Windows 7. If you have the need to replicate a local GPO from one machine to another, it's possible (but not advisable). In fact this tip is expressly untested, unverified, and unsupported by the Group Policy team. Anyway, if you choose to proceed, you could simply copy the files contained within %systemroot%\system32\GroupPolicy from the source machine to the target machine. But note that not everything will come over. Scripts and Administrative Templates will come over, but other stuff like security will not, because as I mentioned earlier, security policy settings on the Local GPO are not stored within the file system. In short, if you try this trick, be sure to test the results to make sure all the stuff you want to come across does come across.

As you're performing this tip, be sure that you also hand-modify the gpt.ini found in the root of this directory. In short, make sure the number present here is greater than the number found in the gpt.ini of your target machines. As you'll learn later, the gpt.ini houses the *version number* of a GPO. If you don't set the version number higher than what is already present on the target computer, the local GPO engine doesn't know anything has changed, and hence you won't see the updated settings. And it's not just a matter of setting the version number to the same number plus one. Version numbers are a bit more complicated than that. So, before you run off and try this tip, you'll also need to learn more about how version numbers work. See the sidebar "Understanding Group Policy Version Numbers" later in the chapter, which should give you the data you need.

With Windows Vista and later, you can copy the user-specific MLGPOs from the %systemroot%\system32\GroupPolicyUsers directory on the source system to the same location on the target system. But, you will need to rename the directory to the correct SID of a user on the target system, and you will need to change the security permissions on the copied folder too.

Likewise, you can copy the administrators' and the nonadministrators' specific MLGPOs by copying the appropriate folders (S-1-5-32-544 and S-1-5-32-545). However, this is not supported in any way, and I recommend that you test this thoroughly if you need it in a production environment.

Inside Active Directory Group Policy Objects

Here's the strange part about Group Policy (as if it weren't already strange enough). Chapter 1 discussed how creating a GPO involves two steps. First, the GPO is written in the Group Policy Objects container, and then it is *linked* to a level—site, domain, or OU. So, we know that GPOs don't really "live" at the level where they're linked. Specifically, all GPOs live inside the Group Policy Objects container in the domain. That is, they're always kept nestled inside this container yet are logically linked to (but not stored in) the other levels to which they point. I referred to the GPOs we created as swimming around in a virtual pool within the domain.

So far in our journey, we created four new GPOs that affect our storyline:

- "Hide Changing Screen Saver," which we applied to the Default-First-Site Name site

- "Prohibit Changing Sounds," which we applied to the Corp.com domain

- "Hide Mouse Pointers Option / Restore Screen Saver Option," which we applied to the **Human Resources Users** OU

- "Auto-Launch Calc.exe," which we applied to the **Human Resources Computers** OU

We can check in with our concept of these GPOs as floating in a swimming pool within the Group Policy Objects container as shown here.

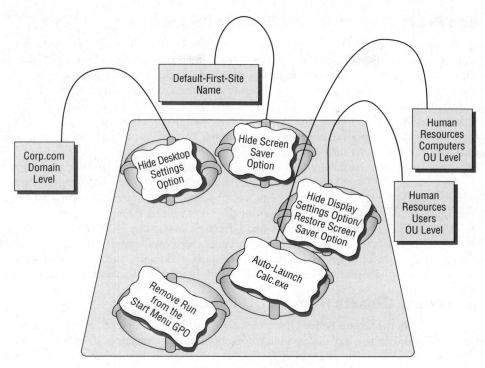

The Corp.com GPO Swimming Pool

As you can see, the GPOs never "live" at any level in Active Directory. They aren't stored at any particular level, although it might appear (using the old-school interface) that they are.

To reiterate, if you leverage a GPO that is supposed to affect a site, an OU, or even a domain, the GPO itself is not stored directly at that level. Rather, the GPO is simply linked to the level in Active Directory. When a GPO is called to be used, it has to request a Domain Controller to fetch it from the Group Policy Objects container (and from its parts in SYSVOL) and pull the information out.

Each time you create a new GPO, it's born and placed into the swimming pool within the domain—ready for action if linked to a level in Active Directory. You can reuse a GPO at multiple levels in Active Directory simply by linking it to another level of Active Directory.

So, when GPOs are created for use at the site, domain, or OU level, they're always created within the domain swimming pool, the Group Policy Objects container, where we just link to the GPOs we need when we need them.

We're going to continue this discussion a little out of order here. We'll be talking about domain-linked GPOs, OU-linked GPOs, and then round out with site-linked GPOs. Yes, yes, we all know the "right" order is site, domain, OU—so bear with me here (I think you'll understand why we're going out of order by the time this section is complete).

Group Policy Objects from a Domain Perspective

Since we know that all GPOs are just hanging out in the Group Policy Objects container waiting to be used, we can take this one step further. That is, even those GPOs linked to the domain level aren't exempt from having to be "fetched." When clients use domain-linked GPOs, they have to make the same requests and "ask" the Domain Controller for the GPOs that apply to them.

This is usually not a problem; the Domain Controller doesn't have far to go to get the GPO in the swimming pool to apply it to the domain. But this is precisely why doing *cross-domain* GPO linking is so slow and painful.

For instance, in an environment with multiple domains, it might appear to be easier to recycle an existing GPO that lives in another domain. But when it comes time to grab the information inside the GPO, it needs to be brought back all the way from Domain Controllers in the originating domain. Again, this cross-domain GPO linking is very, very painful and should be avoided at all costs. In the appendix, I describe how to copy GPOs from one domain to another. This avoids the problem altogether because there's no "penalty" for creating a copy from a source domain and then having the copy live in your domain. Sure, it takes up a wee bit of storage in the new domain's swimming pool. But it's better than Cross-Domain Linking.

Group Policy Objects from an OU Perspective

Since GPOs live in the Group Policy Objects container at the domain level, a distinct advantage is associated with the way Group Policy does its thing: it's tremendously easy to move, link, and unlink GPOs to the domain and/or its OUs. You could, if you desired, simply unlink a GPO in the domain or OU and link it back to some other OU. Or you could link one GPO to the domain and/or multiple OUs.

It's typical and usual that you'll use OUs to apply most of your GPOs. If GPOs live in the Group Policy Objects container swimming pool, it's easy for multiple, unrelated OUs to reuse the same GPOs and just create new links to existing GPOs.

Group Policy Objects from a Site Perspective

Site-level GPOs are a bit unique. If you used (or continue to use) the old-school interface via Active Directory Sites and Services to dictate a site-based GPO, you might be in for a world of pain. By default, all site-level GPOs created using the old-school interface will live in the Group Policy Objects container of the Domain Controllers of the *root* domain—and only the root domain, that is, the first Active Directory domain brought online. Then, every time a GPO meant for a site is called for use by a client system, a Domain Controller from the root domain must fetch that information. If the closest Domain Controller from the root domain is in Singapore, so be it. You can see where the pain could get severe.

The GPMC basically forces us to create site-based GPOs in a thoughtful way. Specifically, you need to create the GPO in the domain swimming pool of your choice. Then, you need to link the GPO from the domain to the site you want. As you saw in Chapter 1, we first create the GPO in the Group Policy Objects container.

The idea is to create the GPO in the domain that makes sense and is closest to where the site-linked GPO will be used. Then, once we expose the site, we just add a link to our existing

GPO, which is already in the domain swimming pool. In short, we get the site GPO to leverage the closest domain's swimming pool. Sure, it takes a little extra planning to think about which swimming pool is closest to the users and computers in the site—but it's worth it. That way, we're not asking some Domain Controller in Singapore to serve our New York users.

> **WARNING**   Remember, by default, only members of the Enterprise Administrators group (or members of the Domain Admins group in the root domain) can create new site-level GPOs or link to existing GPOs from the site level. Optionally, this right can be delegated.

The Birth, Life, and Death of a GPO

Now that you understand where GPOs live, we can take the next step: understanding the "journey" of a GPO. Specifically, a GPO is born and must stay healthy if it's going to stay alive. If its usefulness becomes depleted, you can call in the Soprano boys to whack it—never to be seen again.

How Group Policy Objects Are "Born"

Before you can give birth to GPOs, you need rights to do so, and you can get these rights in two ways. First, you can be a member of the Group Policy Creator Owners or Domain Admins security group.

> **NOTE**   If you're a member of the Group Policy Creator Owners group, you have rights to create but not link GPOs. Domain Administrators can create GPOs and link them to where they want.

You can also be granted explicit rights via the Delegation tab in the Group Policy Objects container via the GPMC (as you saw in Chapter 2).

A new Group Policy Object is born when you right-click the Group Policy Objects container and choose New. Now you're setting into motion a specific chain of events.

First, by default, the PDC emulator is contacted to see if it's available for writing. If not, the user is prompted about how to proceed, as shown in Figure 7.2.

GPOs are initially born when you use the GPMC to create a new GPO. They are created on the PDC emulator, and then, a bit later, they are replicated to the other Domain Controllers within the site and then between sites. Assuming the PDC emulator is available, you can give your GPO a friendly name, say "Hide Mouse Pointers Option / Restore Screen Saver Option," as we did in Chapter 1.

FIGURE 7.2   If the PDC emulator is not available for writing, the user is prompted for an alternate location.

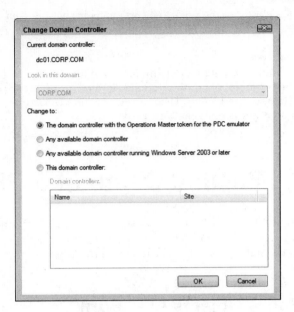

Once that happens, your GPO is officially "born." The PDC emulator has already performed certain functions on your behalf:

- The GPO was given a unique ID that takes its form as a globally unique identifier (GUID).

- It created a *Group Policy Container (GPC)* object in the Policies folder of the system container in the Active Directory domain partition. Think of this as a reference in Active Directory for your new GPO.

- It created a *Group Policy Template (GPT)* folder in the SYSVOL Policies directory of the PDC emulator. This is where the real files that make up your GPO live. They're replicated to every Domain Controller for quicker retrieval.

- Additionally, if "Create a GPO in this domain, and Link it here" is used when focused on the domain or OU level (or the old-school interface is used), the new GPO you just created is automatically *linked* to the current level you were focused at—domain or OU.

When you inspect the properties of any new GPO, you'll see the unique ID it is automatically given, as shown in Figure 7.3.

So, every GPO is made up of two components (the GPC and GPT), and those components are split between two places on that Domain Controller. The good news, though, is that it all ties back to the GPO's GUID. We'll explore each of these components in the next two sections.

FIGURE 7.3   Every GPO gets a unique name.

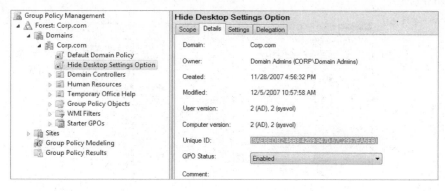

How a GPO "Lives"

A GPO in Active Directory is made up of two constituent parts. One part isn't enough, and the GPO cannot live without both parts. Both parts are required in order to communicate the GPO message.

As you'll see in a bit, the GPO derives its life from these two parts.

Group Policy Containers (GPCs)

The Active Directory database contains the first half of a GPO. Not to get too geeky, but these are just objects (of class groupPolicyContainer), which we refer to as the Group Policy Containers (GPCs). Each GPO defined in a domain has exactly one GPC object defined for it. Then, it's this GPC object that can hold multiple properties related to the Group Policy Object—for instance, version and display information and some policy settings. A GPC has a unique name that takes the format of a globally unique identifier (GUID)—see the sidebar "GPC Attributes." The GUID is *not* the friendly name we use when administering the GPO. The friendly name is stored as an attribute—called displayName—on that GPC object in Active Directory.

You can see the GPCs for every Group Policy you create by diving into the Active Directory Users and Computers console.

To view the GPCs and their GUIDs, follow these steps:

1. Log onto the server DC01 as Administrator of the domain.

2. Choose Start ➢ All Programs ➢ Administrative Tools ➢ Active Directory Users and Computers.

3. Choose View ➢ Advanced Features, as shown in Figure 7.4, to display the Policies folder.

4. Expand the System folder to display the Policies folder along with the GPCs, as shown in Figure 7.5.

FIGURE 7.4 Turn on the Advanced Features setting to see the Policies folder (and a whole lot more).

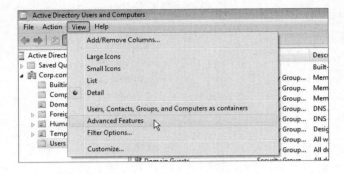

FIGURE 7.5 Expand the Policies folder to expose the underlying GPC objects.

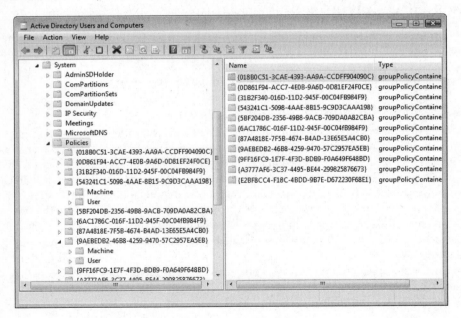

Up to this point, we've been using the GPMC interface to create GPOs. When we use the GPMC to create GPOs, we've made reference to the Group Policy Objects container within the GPMC as a representation of the swimming pool. But the GPMC isn't showing you the real swimming pool—it's showing you a *representation* of the swimming pool. What it's showing you is the GPC part of the swimming pool. The other "half" of the swimming pool is the GPT (which we'll talk about next), the files that live in the replicated SYSVOL folder that exists on every domain controller in an Active Directory domain. The path to the GPT is `\\<domain name>\sysvol\<domain name>\policies`.

GPC Attributes

When a GPC object is created, it is given several attributes:

Common Name (CN)   In Active Directory, you'll see that this attribute is called `cn`. An LDAP (Lightweight Directory Access Protocol) designation for the name is assigned to an object. GPC names use the GUID format to ensure uniqueness throughout a forest—for example, `CN={2C53BFD6-A2DB-44AF-9476-130492934271}`.

Distinguished Name (DN)   In Active Directory, you'll see an attribute called `distinguishedName`. This is the object's common name plus the path to the object from the root of the LDAP tree—for example, `CN={2C53BFD6-A2DB-44AF-9476-130492934271}`, `CN=Policies, CN=System, DC=corp, DC=com`.

Display Name   In Active Directory, you'll see an attribute called `displayName`. This is the friendly name assigned to the Group Policy in the user interface—for example, the Hide Screen Saver Tab GPO.

Version   In Active Directory, you'll see an attribute called `versionNumber`. This is a counter that keeps track of updates to a GPC object (more on this topic a little later).

GUID   In Active Directory, you'll see an attribute called `objectGUID`. This is the GUID assigned to the object itself.

You might find it a little confusing for the GPC object to have a GUID that refers to the object itself and a name that uses a GUID format. For an important reason, Microsoft needed a way to make the underlying, real name of GPOs unique, independent of their friendly names. Suppose two administrators create two (or more) GPOs with the same friendly name on their own Domain Controllers. When these GPC objects replicate, one of them has to be discarded, overwritten, or renamed, depending on the exact circumstances of the replication collision. That could be a bad thing. Therefore, Microsoft solves this problem by using underlying unique names formatted with the GUID format. There is a negligible chance of identical GUIDs being created, not only within one Active Directory but also across the entire world, should the need arise to coexist with GPOs in other forests (such as with cross-forest trusts).

When you drill into a GPC container in Active Directory, you should see one GUID-named folder for every GPO you have created, plus two more for the two default GPOs—the Default Domain Policy and the Default Domain Controllers Policy (which we'll explore in Chapter 8).

In Figure 7.5, I have lots of GPOs already created; therefore, I have lots of containers. You might have fewer.

Those two default GPOs, in fact, have what are referred to as "well-known GUIDs." That is, the GUID for each of those two GPOs will be the same no matter what AD domain you look at. They are the same in your AD domain as mine. That makes it easy to find them. When you're used to seeing those two GUIDs time and again, you will know right away which GPOs they represent.

When you try to drill down into the subcontainers, some will and some will not expand past the *{GUID}\Machine* and *{GUID}\User levels*. Those that do expand do so because you have set up policy settings in that specific GPO that Active Directory needs to maintain information on, such as when you Publish or Assign applications. We'll look at where each policy area stores its settings after the section on the GPT.

We explore how to Publish and Assign applications in Chapter 11.

Don't be surprised if, at this stage in working through the book, you do not have any fully expandable subfolders as shown in Figure 7.5. The subfolders that don't expand simply don't have any Group Policy settings stored within them. Almost everything else the GPO needs in order to be useful is stored in the GPT, which is explored in the next section.

Who Really Has Permissions to Do What?

In Chapter 2, we applied various permissions on the GPO, including who had "Read" and "Apply Group Policy" permissions, as well as who could see the settings or edit the stuff inside the GPO. The locking mechanism for "Who really has what permissions" on a specific GPO is found right here, at the Policies folder:

- On the one hand, the locking mechanism on the Policies folder itself dictates who can and cannot create GPOs. However, it should be noted that these permissions are not inherited to the GUID-named GPT folder itself.

- See the note following Figure 7.8 for specific information on how to change the default permissions.

- On the other hand, the locking mechanism on the GUID-named GPT folders underneath the Policies folder dictates which users have access to "Read" and "Apply Group Policy," or can change the GPO itself.

In reality, the permissions that you see in GPMC for a given GPO reflect the permissions of *both* the GPC and GPT. Although the permissions that you can grant to an Active Directory object do not map one-to-one to the permissions that you can grant to a file system folder like those found in SYSVOL, they roughly translate into the same permissions. For this reason, it's very important that you *not* try to directly modify the permissions on a GPO by simply modifying the permissions on either the GPC or the GPT independently. The best tool for this task is the GPMC's security filtering and delegation features.

However, in my GPanswers.com newsletter #13 (found at www.GPanswers .com/newsletter), you will find a tip that does walk through how to expressly change the underlying permissions in an emergency. Note that in that article, it's a special case and, again, should only be performed as described in that particular emergency.

Who Can Create New Group Policy Objects?

Right-click the Policies container, select Properties, then click the Security tab to display several names, some of which should be familiar, including the Group Policy Creator Owners and Domain Administrators groups. Additionally present will be anyone you explicitly added via the Delegation tab upon the Group Policy Objects container in GPMC. You saw how to do this in Chapter 2. At that time, we added a user named Joe User from our domain.

If you examine the properties of the Policies container (as shown in Figure 7.6), you'll see the Group Policy Creator Owners group. Joe is also listed (because he was expressly granted permission via the GPMC). Note also that the Domain Admins and Enterprise Admins groups are also present, but those names are at the top of the list, so you can't see them in Figure 7.6.

You can click the Advanced button to display Joe's precise "Special Permissions." Indeed, Joe has only one permission, and it's called "Create `groupPolicyContainer` Objects." Once he has this right, the system permits him to create GPC folders and populate them with Group Policy information when he creates a new GPO.

FIGURE 7.6   Expand the Policies folder to expose the underlying GPC objects.

Active Directory Users and Computers			
File Action View Help			

Domain Controllers
ForeignSecurityPrincipals
Human Resources
LostAndFound
Program Data
System
  AdminSDHolder
  ComPartitions
  ComPartitionSets
  DomainUpdates
  IP Security
  Meetings
  MicrosoftDNS
  Policies
    {018B0C51-3CAE-4393-AA9A-CCDFF904090C
    {0D861F94-ACC7-4E0B-9A6D-0D81EF24F0CE}
    {31B2F340-016D-11D2-945F-00C04FB984F9}
    {543241C1-5098-4AAE-8B15-9C9D3CAAA198}
    {5BF204DB-2356-49B8-9ACB-709DA0A82CBA}
    {6AC1786C-016F-11D2-945F-00C04FB984F9}
    {87A4818E-7F5B-4674-B4AD-13E65E5A4CB0}
    {9AEBEDB2-46B8-4259-9470-57C2957EA5EB}

Policies Properties

General | Object | Security | Attribute Editor

Group or user names:

SYSTEM
Joe User (user@Corp.com)
Domain Admins (CORP\Domain Admins)
Enterprise Admins (CORP\Enterprise Admins)
Group Policy Creator Owners (CORP\Group Policy Creator Own...
Administrators (CORP\Administrators)

Add...   Remove

Permissions for Joe User   Allow   Deny

Read
Write
Create all child objects
Delete all child objects
Special permissions

For special permissions or advanced settings, click Advanced.   Advanced

Learn about access control and permissions

OK   Cancel   Apply   Help

The Group Policy Creator Owners group has many, many more unnecessary permissions on the Policies folder, including "Create all child objects," "Create User Objects," and a whole lot of stuff that, really, doesn't have anything to do with Group Policy. Indeed, if you log on as someone in the Group Policy Creator Owners group and right-click the Policies folder, you can do some things you really shouldn't do, as you can see in Figure 7.7.

FIGURE 7.7   For the love of Pete, please don't do this.

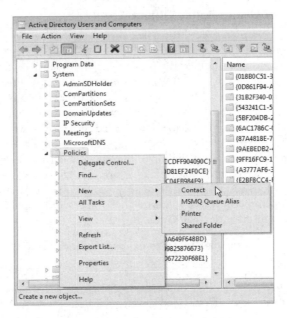

 The system (thankfully) won't let you do *all* the functions listed here, but it does let you do *some* of them. And, again, you really shouldn't be poking around like this. Of course, the "right" thing to do is to set permissions only via the GPMC. However, I show you these things for demonstration purposes so you can get a better feeling for what is different between someone in the Group Policy Creator Owners Group versus someone who has been explicitly delegated rights via the Delegation tab upon the Group Policy Objects container in GPMC.

The Domain Administrators group and the Enterprise Administrators group also have explicit permissions here. When they create new GPOs, they do so because of their explicit permissions, not because they are members of the Group Policy Creator Owners group.

Who Can Manipulate and Edit Existing Group Policy Objects?

Right-click a GPO folder (with the name of a GUID) under the Policies folder and choose Properties to display the Security tab (see Figure 7.8), which will show the same information as when, in Chapter 2, you used the Deny attribute to pass over certain security groups. That is, the same information is shown here as when we clicked the Advanced button in the Delegation tab when focused on the GPO (or GPO link, because it's using the same information taken from the actual GPO).

FIGURE 7.8   Each GPC can display the underlying permissions of the GPO.

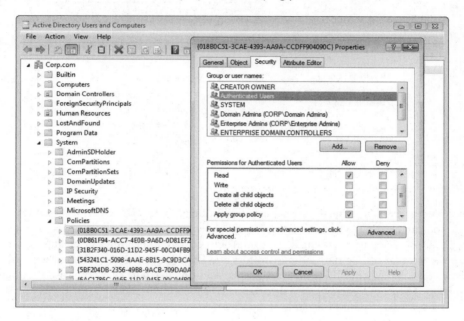

 The permissions that a new GPO gets when it's created are controlled by the DefaultSecurityDescriptor attribute on the groupPolicyContainer class within the Active Directory schema. If you want your GPOs to get different default permissions when they're created, you can modify the schema instance of this attribute. The Microsoft Knowledge Base article at http://support.microsoft.com/kb/321476/en-us describes how to do that.

Unless otherwise delegated, the person or group who created the GPO is the only one other than Domain Admins and Enterprise Admins who can modify or delete the GPO. However, this may be a particularly sensitive issue if you have many Domain Administrators—as they all have "joint ownership" of the GPOs they create. There is a serious potential risk in one administrator taking the reins and modifying another administrator's GPOs.

However, as you saw in Chapter 2, you can also grant someone explicit rights via the Delegation tab upon the GPOs container via the GPMC. In this example, I have done this for Joe. Figure 7.9 shows the properties of a GPO that Joe has created.

FIGURE 7.9   If Joe creates a GPO, he owns the GPO. No one else (other than Domain Admins or Enterprise Admins) can edit it.

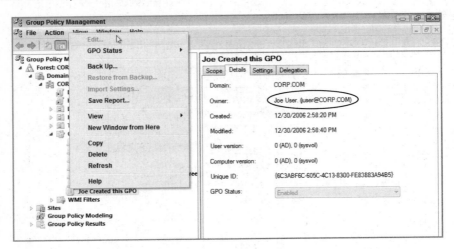

Since Joe has explicit permissions to create GPOs, he becomes the owner of the GPOs he creates. You can clearly see that Joe created it, and now he owns it. Hence, Joe doesn't have to worry about other explicitly anointed users or groups changing the GPOs he creates and owns. Note, however, that the Domain Administrators and Enterprise Administrators group will, in fact, be able to change any GPOs that Joe creates. Additionally, note that other users within Group Policy Creator Owners cannot dive in and edit Joe's GPOs. Again—Joe owns it; it's his.

Using LDP to See the Guts of a GPC

The GPC object itself holds even more critical attributes for GPOs:

gPCFileSysPath   The physical path to the associated Policies folder, or GPT, stored in SYSVOL. The Policies folder has the same name as the GPC, which is another reason that uniqueness is so important. The GPT is discussed in the next section.

gPCMachineExtensionNames   This is a list of GUIDs of the computer-related CSEs (*Client-Side Extensions*)—and the MMC snap-in that manages them—that will be called for this particular GPO. For instance, if a GPO has policy set on the Administrative Templates node under the Computer Configuration node in the Group Policy Object Editor, the gPCMachineExtensionNames list includes the GUID of the Registry CSE and the GUID of the MMC snap-in for the Administrative Templates node. CSEs are discussed later in this chapter in the section "How Client Systems Get Group Policy Objects."

gPCUserExtensionNames   This is a list of the GUIDs of the CSEs and their MMC snap-ins, called by a user-related Group Policy. Again, I'll discuss CSEs a bit later in this chapter.

There are several ways you can see this entry. You could use the updated RSAT's Active Directory Users and Computers to see them (on the Attribute Editor tab). Or you could use the ADSI Edit MMC snap-in or the LDP tool, which is an LDAP browser tool. Both tools are found by loading the support tools from the SUPPORT\TOOLS folder on the Windows Server 2003 CD (Windows Server 2008 has the tools built in).

I'm suggesting LDP for these examples. LDP lets you perform LDAP queries right into the actual guts of Active Directory. Using LDP, you can see these attributes. Normally, you wouldn't want or need to go poking around in here, but taking the time to learn just where attributes are can help you understand what constitutes a GPO.

To query a specific GPO to see its underlying attributes, follow these steps:

1. After loading the Support tools on the Domain Controller, choose Start ➢ Run to open the Run dialog box, and in the Open field, type **LDP** and press Enter to select the domain of your choice.

2. Choose Connection ➢ Bind, and in the dialog box type the administrative credentials to the domain. In the Domain field, you'll need to type the DNS name of the domain, for example, **Corp.com**. If you successfully connect, you'll see your first query results in the right pane of the LDP window.

3. Choose View ➢ Tree to open a dialog box that lets you specify the distinguished name of the domain. If your domain is Corp.com, enter **dc=corp, dc=com**. If you do that correctly, your left pane will show the domain name with a plus (+) sign. You should be able to double-click the plus sign and expand the contents within the domain.

4. Find the System container and double-click it to expand it.

5. Find the Policies container and double-click it to expand it.

6. Find the unique name of the GPO you want to inspect and double-click it to expand it. (For information about how to find a specific unique name of a GPO, see the earlier section "How Group Policy Objects Are 'Born.'") In the following illustration, the attributes are highlighted.

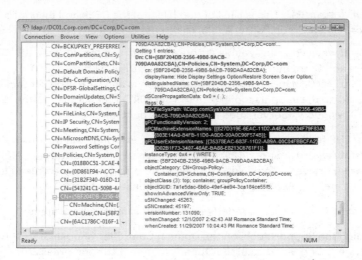

Once you find the unique name, the resultant LDP query will show you the properties on that GPO.

There is one more important attribute to inspect by using LDP: gPLink. Recall that a GPO can be linked by one level, multiple levels, or no levels. If a GPO is to be linked to a site, a domain, or an OU, that level needs to have a *pointer* or *link* to the GPO. When clients log on (computer and user), they use LDAP to query to each level they are a part of (site, domain, OUs) to find out if the level has the gPLink attribute set. If so, the client makes an LDAP query to find out what GPOs are meant for it. With the information in hand, it determines what files to download from the SYSVOL share on its logon server. (You can see these queries happening for yourself, when you inspect Userenv.log, explored later in the section "Turning On Verbose Logging.")

> To see the gPLink attribute, you can simply click the level you want to inspect. In this case, click the **Human Resources Users** OU you created in Chapter 1.
>
> In the right pane, find LDP's query results. The gPLink attribute has LDAP pointers to the unique names of the GPOs. In this case, the **Human Resources Users** OU has links to the "Hide Mouse Pointers Option / Restore Screen Saver Option" GPO, in my case, 5BF204DB-2356-49B8-9ACB-709DA0A82CBA.

Group Policy Templates

As we just learned, GPCs are stored in the Active Directory database and replicated via normal Active Directory replication. A Group Policy Template (GPT), on the other hand, is stored as a set of files in the SYSVOL share of each Domain Controller. Each GPT is replicated to each Domain Controller through FRS (File Replication Service).

When we used the Properties tab of the GPO, we were able to find its unique name (as we did earlier in Figure 7.3). We can use the unique name to locate the GPC in Active Directory, and it's the same unique name we can use to locate the GPT in the SYSVOL.

To see the GPTs in SYSVOL, follow these steps:

1. On a Domain Controller in the domain, open Windows Explorer.
2. Change the directory to the SYSVOL container. Its usual location is `C:\Windows\SYSVOL\SYSVOL\<domain name>` (in this case, `C:\Windows\SYSVOL\SYSVOL\corp.com`).
3. Change into the Policies folder. You'll see a list of folders. The folder names match the GPC GUID names stored in Active Directory (seen in the previous exercise). Figure 7.10 shows a Policies folder containing many GPOs.

Double-clicking a Policies folder inside SYSVOL displays the contents of the GPT. Inside, you'll see several subfolders and a file. The first entry on this list is the file (`gpt.ini`); the rest are subfolders.

`gpt.ini`   The one file you will always find under the GUID folder. It holds the version number of the GPT as well as the equivalent information to the `gpcMachineExtensionName` and `gpcUserExtensionName` attributes found on the GPC object in Active Directory. Namely, these two keys within the `gpt.ini` list the GUIDs of the CSEs and their associated MMC snap-in extensions that have been implemented within the GPO. This lets the client know which CSEs need to be called when GPOs are processed. (You'll read about version numbers in the next section.) For very old GPOs, you might also see a little text snippet in the `gpt.ini` that says "displayName=New Group Policy Object." This snippet of text is the same when using very old Group Policy creation tool. This entry is vestigial and has never been used.

`\Adm`   If you create your GPOs using a Windows 7 management station (as we discussed in Chapter 1 and explored in depth in Chapter 6), you won't see an ADM directory in any of your newly created GPOs. However, if you create GPOs from XP machines, this directory is created to house policy settings called Administrative Template files. In short, when you create or edit a GPO from an XP machine, the Administrative Templates (.adm files) are copied from the \Windows\INF folder. Again, this happens from the machine where you're editing that GPO, into the GPT's \Adm folder.

FIGURE 7.10 The unique names of the GPOs are found as folder names in SYSVOL. This is the unique name for the "Hide Mouse Pointers Option / Restore Screen Saver Option" you saw in the last graphic in the sidebar "Using LDP to See the Guts of a GPC."

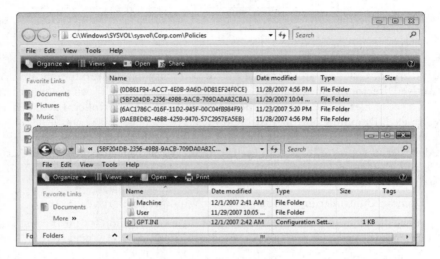

By default, those .ADM files are Conf.adm, Inetres.adm, System.adm, wmplayer.adm, and wuau.adm.

Double-clicking the \Adm folder displays the templates. Note that the \Adm folder will not exist until the GPO is opened for the first time from an XP machine and you click either the Computer or the User Administrative Template node. Again, feel free to review the material in Chapter 6 for more on this topic.

 Note that the presence of the \Adm folder in the GPT is an artifact of pre–Windows Vista operating systems. When you create and edit a new GPO using Windows 7, no \Adm folder is created because Windows 7 no longer copies the ADM files up to the GPT—they are held locally in C:\windows\policydefinitions or in the "Central Store." However, if you edit a GPO that was first created on a modern GPMC, then later edit it using an older GPMC (for example, XP, 2003, and so on), the \Adm folder will get created and populated in the GPT. Note that this behavior—editing a GPO from a down-level version of Windows—is generally not a good idea. Once you've gone Windows 7 from a Group Policy creation and editing perspective, it's best to continue to edit those GPOs using a modern client from then on. You can check out Chapter 6, which describes the Central Store and ADMX files in great detail and explores this particular problem more.

\Machine   This folder contains the settings for the Computer side of the GPO, including startup and shutdown scripts (though there's nothing requiring them to live here; they could be located in other places as well), pointers to applications that are assigned, and Registry settings (among other settings). The actual contents of the \Machine folder depend on the computer options specified in the GPO. The potential contents include the following:

> **The Registry.pol file**   Holds the Registry settings set in Computer Configuration ➢ Policies ➢ Administrative Templates as well as settings for Software Restriction Policy under Computer Configuration ➢ Policies ➢ Windows Settings ➢ Security Settings ➢ Software Restriction Policies.

> **The \Applications folder**   Stores pointer files called Application Advertisement Scripts, or AAS files. These files are used in conjunction with Group Policy Software Deployment. These are the instructions that the client computers use to process Software Installation. Software Installation is further discussed in its own chapter, Chapter 11, but AAS files are described further in the sidebar entitled "Inside .AAS Files."

Inside .AAS Files

The .AAS file serves a specific role in the context of Software Installation Policy. This file is created when you first deploy an MSI package. It contains information related to the advertisement of the package.

Advertisement is an MSI feature that allows you to deploy part of an application (you can think of it like a shortcut or file extension association) to a computer or user. The whole application is not installed right away; instead, when the user first clicks the shortcut or activates a file extension associated with the advertised package, the installation proceeds at that time. This feature is known as *Install-On-First-Use*.

The .AAS file holds that advertisement information specific to the package you've deployed. It also contains the hard-coded path to the package you've specified. This is why you cannot easily change the path to a package once you've deployed it via Software Installation Policy. This .AAS file must be regenerated and the path to the package that is referenced in the GPC portion of the GPO must also be updated.

The \Microsoft\Windows NT\Secedit folder   Stores a file called GptTmpl.inf. This file holds various computer security settings, defined under the Computer Configuration ➢ Policies ➢ Windows Settings ➢ Security Settings portion of the GPO. You can also set up these settings in advance and deploy them *en masse* using the techniques described in Chapter 8.

The \Scripts\Shutdown folder   Contains the instructions for which shutdown scripts to run and, optionally, the actual files used for computer shutdown scripts. The instructions as to which scripts will run and where the scripts are stored are held in a file called scripts.ini, within this folder. It can be of any scripting file type (that the ShellExecute process can run), including .BAT, .CMD, .VBS, .JS, and others. You'll see how to use this in Chapter 8.

The \Scripts\Startup folder   Contains the instructions for which startup scripts to run and, optionally, the actual files used for computer startup scripts. The instructions as to which scripts will run and where the scripts are stored are held in a file called scripts.ini, within this folder. Can be of any scripting file types (that the ShellExecute process can run), including .BAT, .CMD, .VBS, .JS, and others. You'll see how to use this in Chapter 8.

\User   This folder contains the settings for the User side of the Group Policy coin, including logon and logoff scripts, pointers to applications that are published or assigned, and Registry settings. Depending on the options used on each GPO, it represents what is in the \User folder under the computer side of the GPT.

> **The Registry.pol file**   Holds the Registry settings set in User Configuration ➢ Policies ➢ Administrative Templates, as well as settings for Software Restriction Policy under User Configuration ➢ Policies ➢ Windows Settings ➢ Security Settings ➢ Software Restriction Policies.

> **The \Applications folder**   Stores pointer files called .AAS files for applications deployed with Group Policy Software Installation.

> **The \Documents and Settings folder**   Contains a file called Fdeploy.ini, which stores applicable Folder Redirection settings. You can learn more about Folder Redirection in Chapter 10.

> **The \Microsoft\IEAK folder**   Stores files to represent the changes made in User Configuration ➢ Policies ➢ Windows Settings ➢ Internet Explorer Maintenance.

> **The \Microsoft\RemoteInstall folder**   Stores Oscfilter.ini, which specifies Group Policy Remote Installation Services settings. Remote Installation Services isn't used anymore. Its successor, Windows Deployment Services, has taken its place.

> **The \Scripts\Logon folder**   Contains the instructions for which logon scripts to run and, optionally, the actual files used for user logon scripts. The instructions as to which scripts will run and where the scripts are stored are held in a file called scripts.ini, within this folder. Can be of any acceptable file type, including .BAT, .VBS, .JS, and others—and, now with Windows 7, PowerShell scripts. You'll see how to use this folder in Chapter 12.

> **The \Scripts\Logoff folder**   Contains the instructions for which logoff scripts to run and, optionally, the actual files used for user logoff scripts. The instructions as to which scripts will run and where the scripts are stored are held in a file called scripts.ini, within this folder. Can be of any acceptable file type, including .BAT, .VBS, .JS, and others. You'll see how to use this folder in Chapter 12.

Group Policy Settings Storage

As I've indicated, Group Policy settings, the things that you set when you're editing a GPO, are stored within one half of the GPO—either the GPC or the GPT. The decision as to which is used to store a given setting varies with the size of the data being stored. Typically, because

Active Directory is not designed for storing large blocks of data, those settings that require big chunks of stuff are stored in the GPT instead of the GPC.

But it really does vary by each CSE. Table 7.1 indicates where each CSE stores its settings.

TABLE 7.1   Client-Side Extensions and Their Storage Locations

Client-Side Extension	Storage Location	Comments
Wireless	Stored in AD, under the GPC container for a given GPO, within the path `CN=wireless,CN=Windows,CN=Microsoft,CN=Machine`.	Wireless policies are stored in AD as objects of the class `msieee80211-Policy`. This class is supported only in AD domains of Windows Server 2003 and newer AD domains. So, even though this CSE is on Windows XP, the policy must still be defined in domains that have that minimum schema level. Note that there is also a required schema update to support the enhanced Wireless policy that's only supported on Windows Vista and later clients. This is further explained in Chapter 8.
Folder Redirection	Stored in SYSVOL, under the GPT container for a given GPO. Folder Redirection policy is stored in a file called `fdeploy.ini` in the subfolder `User\Documents and Settings` within the GPT.	
Administrative Template Policy	Stored in SYSVOL, under the GPT container for a given GPO. Administrative Templates policy is stored in a file called `registry.pol`, which can be defined per user and per computer. Within a given GPT, if you've defined both user and computer Administrative Templates policy, you will see a `registry.pol` file under both the user and machine subfolders.	If the GPO was created with an older GPMC, then you'll see ADM files for any given GPO that are stored with the GPO in the GPT. Note ADMs can also be added with the updated GPMC, but not usually. In both cases, you'll find ADMs in a folder called ADM, off the root of the GPT for a given GPO. Thus, each GPO that sets Administrative Templates policy will store its own copy of the ADM files used to edit it, even if they are the same as another GPO. Note that GPOs do not store ADMX files within the GPO, as they are with ADMX files. See the previous chapter for all the gory details.

TABLE 7.1 Client-Side Extensions and Their Storage Locations *(continued)*

Client-Side Extension	Storage Location	Comments
Disk Quota	Stored in SYSVOL, under the GPT container for a given GPO. Disk quota policy is also stored in registry.pol; however, you'll only find it in the copy of registry.pol stored under the machine folder, as this is a per-machine policy only.	
QoS Packet Scheduler	Stored in SYSVOL, under the GPT container for a given GPO. QoS policy is also stored in registry .pol; however, you'll only find it in the copy of registry.pol stored under the machine folder, as this is a per-machine policy only.	
Startup/Shutdown and Logon/Logoff Scripts	Stored in SYSVOL under the GPT container for a given GPO. Machine-specific scripts are stored in the machine\scripts\ startup and machine\ scripts\shutdown folders. User-specific scripts are stored in the user\logon and user\logoff folders.	Note that script files themselves do not have to be stored in SYSVOL. You can reference scripts located anywhere on your network, as long as they are accessible to the computer or user. The scripts.ini file found in the computer\scripts folder and user\scripts folder in SYSVOL contains the actual references to any scripts that you've defined.
Internet Explorer Maintenance and Zonemapping	Stored in SYSVOL under the GPT container for a given GPO. Specifically, IE Maintenance settings are stored in the GPT under the \User\ Microsoft\IEAK folder.	Basic "branding" settings are stored in a file under this folder called install.ins. Security zone settings are stored in a subfolder called Branding and are stored as .inf files.
Security Settings	Stored in SYSVOL under the GPT container for a given GPO. Security settings are stored in the Machine\ Microsoft\Windows NT\ SecEdit folder in a file called GptTmpl.inf.	The format of this file is identical to those created when you use the MMC Security Templates editor to create a Security Template. The exception to this is Software Restriction Policy, which is stored in the registry.pol file.

TABLE 7.1 Client-Side Extensions and Their Storage Locations *(continued)*

Client-Side Extension	Storage Location	Comments
Software Installation	Stored in both the GPC and the GPT. Within the GPT, deployed package information is stored under the container machine (or user)\Applications, within an Application Advertisement File, or AAS file. Within the GPC, a special object of class packageRegistration is created for each application deployed. This object can be found in the GPC for a GPO under machine (or user)\Class Store\Packages.	packageRegistration objects found in the GPC contain information such as the path to the MSI file, any transforms (modifications) that have been selected, and whether the application is published or assigned. (See Chapter 11 for more details.)
IP Security	IPsec policy is a special case. Settings are stored as special objects strictly in Active Directory but *not* within the GPC. Namely, IPsec policy settings are stored under the CN=IP Security, CN=System container within a domain. Therefore, IP Security settings are stored domain wide and can be referenced by any GPO in the domain. When you *assign* a particular IPsec policy to a GPO, an additional object is created within the GPC of the GPO—specifically, an *ipsecPolicy* object is created under the Machine\Microsoft\Windows container under the GPO. This object stores the association between the available IPsec policies in the domain and that GPO.	

TABLE 7.1 Client-Side Extensions and Their Storage Locations *(continued)*

Client-Side Extension	Storage Location	Comments
Windows Search (Vista+ only)	Stored in SYSVOL, under the GPT container for a given GPO. Windows Search policy is also stored in `registry.pol`; however, you'll find it only in the copy of `registry.pol` stored under the machine folder, as this is a per-machine policy only.	
Offline Files (Vista+ only)	Stored in SYSVOL, under the GPT container for a given GPO. Offline Files policy is also stored in `registry.pol`, within both the machine and user folders, depending on which side is being set.	
Deployed Printer Connections (Vista+ only)	Stored in AD, under the GPC container for a given GPO, within the path `CN=PushedPrinterConnections,CN=Machine` (or `CN=User`).	Deployed Printer Connection policies are stored in Active Directory as objects of class `msPrintConnectionPolicy`. This class is only supported in Windows Server 2003 R2 (and later) domains. Therefore, this feature, Deployed Printer Connection policy, can be defined only in domains that have that minimum schema level.
Enterprise QoS Policy (Vista+ only)	Stored in SYSVOL, under the GPT container for a given GPO. Enterprise QoS policy is also stored in `registry.pol`, within both the machine and user folders, depending on which side is being set.	
802.3 and Wireless Policy (Vista+ only)	Both of these policy areas are stored in AD in the GPC but require a schema update.	See Chapter 8 for the required schema update to support both Wired and Wireless schema policy.

Understanding Group Policy Version Numbers

If you take a peek at any GPO's gpt.ini, you'll see its version number. You can see the same number if you dive into the GPC using the directions found in the sidebar "Using LDP to See the Guts of a GPC," later in this chapter.

So, how is that version number constructed? The idea is that it's a 32-bit value where the most significant 16 bits are the user value, and the least 16 significant bits are the computer value.

In decimal, here's the formula:

Version = (Number of user section changes × 65536) + (Number of computer section changes)

So, when you create a new GPO, the version number is 0. Click Edit over a GPO and begin editing, and then the numbers start going up. Enable a policy on the Computer side and click OK. Then set it back to Not Configured. That'll add 2 to the version number. Edit a policy on the User side and click OK. That'll add 65536. Change it back to Not Configured and it'll add another 65536. The version number's largess isn't super important here. That is, it doesn't matter how huge the number gets.

So, how do we, in our daily lives, see the version number? In the Details tab of any Group Policy, as shown here:

In this example, we can see that the User side has been modified twice (2 * 65536) and the computer version has been modified three times (add 3 to that). So, if we peek in the gpt.ini of this GPO, the version number should be 131075.

Again, both the GPC and the GPT store the version number for the GPO. But, as we've described, there could be situations where replication hasn't finished and the GPC and GPT version numbers don't agree. In that case, the GPMC (which shows the version numbers via the Details tab of a GPO) will *always* use the GPC version number as the final reference but will give you a message if these are not in sync.

The Group Policy team at Microsoft has an interesting blog entry on the subject. Check it out at http://tinyurl.com/2gfmmg.

Verifying That GPCs and GPTs Are in Sync

The two pieces of information that make up a GPO are GPCs and GPTs:

- GPCs are stored in the Active Directory database and are replicated via normal Active Directory replication.

- GPTs are stored in the SYSVOL folders of every Domain Controller and are replicated using FRS replication.

Here's the trick: for Windows 2000, for Group Policy to be applied, both the GPC and the corresponding GPT need to be synchronized. *Synchronization* simply means that the versionNumber attribute on the GPC object for a given GPO needs to be the same as the versionNumber key found in the GPT's gpt.ini file for that same GPO.

For all versions of Windows after Windows 2000, the GPC and GPT no longer need to have the same version for Group Policy processing of that GPO to proceed.

Recall that both the GPC and GPT are originally written to the PDC emulator by default. Once they're written, the goal is to replicate the GPC and GPT to other Domain Controllers. With just one Domain Controller in a domain, there are no replication issues because there are no other Domain Controllers to replicate to; it's all happening on one system. But when multiple Domain Controllers in a domain enter the picture, things get a little hairier. This is because normal Active Directory replication and FRS replication are on completely independent schedules (though under normal circumstances, they take the same path).

An administrator can create or modify a GPO, and the GPC might not replicate in lock-step with the files in the GPT. This isn't normally a problem because, over time, all Domain Controllers end up with exactly the same information in their replicas of the Active Directory database and in their SYSVOL folders. But during a given replication cycle, there may be intervals when the GPC and GPT *don't* match on a particular Domain Controller.

Additionally, the GPC and GPT share a *version number* for each half of the GPO— Computer and User. The version numbers are incremented each time the GPO is modified and are included in the list of attributes that are replicated to other Domain Controllers. Remember in Chapter 1 I stated that if a specific GPO doesn't change, the default for the client is to not process the GPO. After all, if nothing's changed, why should the client bother? The client uses these version numbers to figure out if something has changed. The client keeps a cache of the GPOs it last applied along with the version number within the Registry. Then, if the GPO has been touched, say, by the modification of a particular policy setting or the addition of a policy setting, the version number of the GPO in Active Directory changes. The next time the client tries to process GPOs, it will see the change, and the client will download the entire GPO again and embrace the revised instruction set! So, version numbers are important for clients to recognize that new instructions are waiting for them.

So far, so good. Now, there's a bit more to fully understanding version numbers. According to Microsoft, here's the secret to figuring out whether a GPO is going to process on a workstation:

- Both the GPC and GPT parts of the GPO must be present on the Domain Controller the workstation uses to log on.

- If the client processing Group Policy is Windows 2000, then the GPC and GPT must have the same version number.

- If it's XP or later, the GPC and GPT can have different version numbers and Group Policy processing will still occur.

- In all cases, if the version number held in the GPC or GPT is different than the version number held in the Registry from the last time that GPO was processed, Windows considers that a change has occurred and goes ahead and processes policy.

The main point here is that for early versions of Windows (Windows 2000), Group Policy processing would fail if the version numbers didn't match up. It's still important for the two pieces to synchronize at some point. If they aren't synchronized at some point, this implies that one piece doesn't have the latest information for settings. At some point, the replication should complete and all Domain Controllers will have the same Group Policy data; then, machines and users will get the latest version of Group Policy settings. If this *never* happens, you have a problem with your domain and should follow up with the tools and techniques in this section.

 Version numbers aren't the only thing that would constitute a "change." A change could also be a removed GPO (or added GPO), a change in security group membership, and a new or removed WMI filter. Also, it's important to point out that if one GPO changes, the CSEs that process that GPO must reprocess *all* GPOs in the list, not just the one that changes.

Changing the Default Domain Controller for the Initial Write of Group Policy Objects

GPOs are, by default, created and edited using the Domain Controller that houses the PDC emulator. Of course, over time, those new and modified GPOs make it to all other Domain Controllers using replication. However, sometimes in large Active Directories, you may not want to leverage the PDC emulator as the "go to" place when creating and editing Group Policy.

Imagine this scenario: there is one domain but two sites—the United States and China. The U.S. site holds the Domain Controller designated as the PDC emulator. Therefore, whenever an administrator in China writes a GPO, they must connect across the WAN to write the GPO and then wait for the entire GPO (both the GPC half and the GPT half) to replicate to their local Domain Controllers.

You can, however, specify which Domain Controller to write the GPO to, which is a two-step process:

1. Select a Domain Controller to be *active*. Open the GPMC, right-click the domain name, select Change Domain Controller, and select the Domain Controller to which you want the Group Policy to apply.

2. Create your GPO and edit it. At the root node of the Group Policy snap-in, choose View ➢ DC Options. Now you have the following three choices:

    ▪   "The one with the Operations Master token for the PDC Emulator." The default behavior, this option finds the PDC emulator in the domain and writes the GPO there. Replication then occurs, starting from the PDC emulator.

    ▪   "The one used by the Active Directory snap-ins." Since you just selected the *active* Domain Controller, this is your best bet because you know exactly which Domain Controller you selected in the first step.

    ▪   "Any available Domain Controller." The odds are good that you will get a local Domain Controller to write to (based on Active Directory site information), but not always.

Therefore, the best course of action is to select the Domain Controller you want to initially write to and then select "The one used by the Active Directory snap-ins" to guarantee it.

Sound like too much work for each GPO? Alternatively, you can create a GPO that affects those accounts that can create GPOs. Use the policy setting located at User Configuration ➢ Policies ➢ Administrative Templates ➢ System ➢ Group Policy setting named **Group Policy Domain Controller Selection**. You'll get the same three choices listed earlier. Set it, and forget it.

Here's a parting tip for this sidebar. Often, GPOs are created with the additional intent to use security groups to filter them. After creating a GPO with the GPMC, an administrator will also create some security groups using Active Directory Users and Computers to filter them. However, after creating the GPO and the security groups, many admins are surprised that the security groups they want to add "now" are not immediately available. This is because the GPMC is using one Domain Controller and the Active Directory Users and Computers tool is using another Domain Controller. Therefore, replication of the group has not yet reached the Domain Controller the GPMC is using! So the tip is to manually focus both the Active Directory Users and Computers and/or GPMCs explicitly on the same Domain Controller (or just the PDC emulator) before creating GPOs where you'll also want to filter using groups.

Using *Gpotool.exe*

If you suspect you're having problems with keeping your GPTs and GPCs in sync, you can use `Gpotool.exe`, a tool included with the Windows 2000 and Windows 2003 Resource Kits. You can run `Gpotool.exe` on any Domain Controller to verify that both the GPCs and GPTs are in sync and have consistent data among all Domain Controllers in the domain. At last check, the `Gpotool.exe` (and other Group Policy–related tools) can be downloaded from `http://tinyurl.com/ydjmm3`.

As of this writing, there isn't an updated `Gpotool.exe` for Windows Server 2008, and there may not ever be one. The current version seems to work just fine with GPOs that live on domains of all types.

Running the `Gpotool` command without any parameters verifies that all GPCs and GPTs are synchronized across all Domain Controllers in the domain. If you are having trouble with only one GPO, however, you might not want to go through the intense process required to check every GPO's GPC and GPT on every Domain Controller. Instead, you can use the `/gpo:` switch, which allows you to specify a friendly name or GUID of a GPO you are having problems with. For instance, if you suspect that you are having problems with "Hide Mouse Pointers Option / Restore Screen Saver Option" GPO we created in Chapter 1, you can run `Gpotool /gpo:Hide` to search for all GPOs starting with the word *Hide*, as shown in Figure 7.11.

FIGURE 7.11   Use Gpotool to see if your GPCs and GPTs are synchronized across your Domain Controllers.

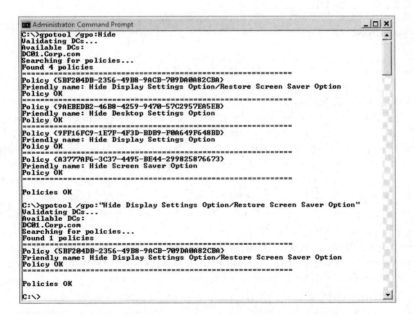

> To specifically verify the "Hide Mouse Pointers Option / Restore Screen Saver Option" setting, you can also run Gpotool /gpo:"Hide Settings Tab / Restore Screen Saver Tab" as seen in Figure 7.11. Note that the /gpo: switch is case sensitive. For instance, running Gpotool /gpo:Hide is different from running GPOTOOL /gpo:hide.

This example shows when things are going right. This next example (see Figure 7.12) shows when things might be wrong.

FIGURE 7.12   Gpotool has found trouble in paradise.

In this example, we are verifying the synchronization of the GPO named "Broken2." In this case, the versions between the GPC and GPT do not match. You can see this when comparing what the tool calls the DS version with the SYSVOL version. The DS version represents the GPC, and the SYSVOL version represents the GPT.

Before panicking, recall that this "problem" might not actually be a problem. Remember, the GPC and the GPT replicate independently. The DC our clients are currently using might have simply received the SYSVOL (GPT) changes before the Active Directory changes (GPC), or vice versa. Wait a little while, and the two versions might converge. If they do not converge, this problem could indicate either Active Directory or FRS replication issues.

Here are some additional tips about using Gpotool:

- Running Gpotool on a large domain with lots of GPOs can take a long time and bog down your Domain Controller performance. If possible, run Gpotool only after hours, when the fewest number of people will be affected.

- If you must run it during working hours, you might want to specify the /dc: option and specify to check only the GPOs on the PDC emulator (the place where GPOs are initially born and initially modified). If you're going to have a problem, it's quite likely to be initially pinpointed on this key Domain Controller.

- Gpotool has one extra super-power: it can also verify the underlying ACLs of the GPT part of a GPO. Recall that the GPT is the part of the GPO that lives in SYSVOL. To perform this extra check, you need to specifically specify it on Gpotool's command line as `Gpotool /checkacl`. By default, this test is not run because it is additionally time and resource intensive. There is one key point about the `/checkacl` switch: it checks only the ACL inheritance flag on the SYSVOL `Policies` folder itself, not the ACLs on the individual folders that contain the guts of the GPO. So, if you have a specific permissions problem on the folder containing a GPO, the `/checkacl` switch won't help you ferret that out.

- One caveat about Gpotool—it only checks to see if the version numbers are the same between the GPC and GPT. It does not check to see, say, if all the files that are supposed to be in the GPT are there. If you're having FRS replication problems, for example, only some of the GPT files may have replicated to a given DC, and Gpotool won't tell you that if it finds that the `gpt.ini` file has the information it needs.

Using *Replmon* to See the Version Numbers

The Replmon (Replication Monitor) tool is available as part of the support tools on the Windows 2003 (or Windows 2000) Server CD. Replmon is one of the most useful free tools Microsoft has ever created. As of this writing, Replmon isn't available for Windows Server 2008. That's okay. You can just run it from a Windows Server 2003 machine on your domain.

For our purposes, we'll use it in a fashion similar to how we used Gpotool; that is, Replmon can tell us if a GPO's GPC and GPT are in agreement with the version numbers.

First, load the support tools in the \SUPPORT\TOOLS folder on a Windows Server 2003. Then, choose Start ➢ Run to open the Run dialog box, and type **Replmon** in the Open box. Right-click the Monitored Servers icon and choose Add Monitored Server. For now, just add the PDC emulator. In my case, I'll add DC01. Once the server is being monitored, right-click it and choose Show Group Policy Object Status to display a screen like that shown in Figure 7.13.

FIGURE 7.13   Replmon can show you the version numbers of all your GPOs.

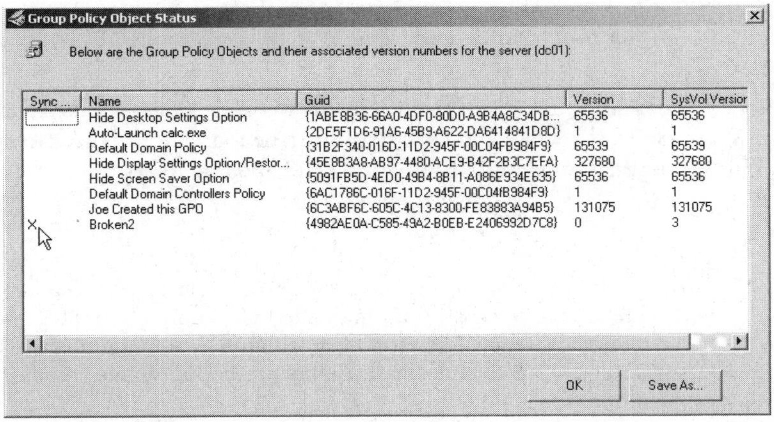

In Figure 7.13, you can see that the GPO named "Broken2" has an X in the Sync Status column. The version numbers are dissimilar in the GPC and GPT. Again, this might not be a real "problem" because the GPC and GPT are being independently replicated. Perhaps this Domain Controller did not yet get the latest updates.

Isolating Replication Problems

You can try to see if Active Directory replication is working (and, hence, if GPC replication is working) by performing several "litmus tests." Here are some examples:

- Create a new GPO in the Group Policy Objects container. Just create it with no policy settings, and don't link it anywhere.
- Create a new OU in Active Directory Users and Computers or the GPMC.
- Add a new user in Active Directory.

In each case, you want to see if these objects are replicated to other DCs. After creating your objects on one Domain Controller, use the Active Directory Users and Computers and/or GPMC to check other Domain Controllers. Simply right-click the domain and choose another Domain Controller.

If these litmus tests fail, you can try to force replication using Active Directory Sites and Services. If you need extra-strength replication, Replmon can help force replication in multiple ways.

You can try to see if SYSVOL replication is working via FRS (and, hence, if GPT replication is working) by simply throwing any file—say, a Readme.txt file—into the SYSVOL share of any Domain Controller and seeing if it is replicated to the other Domain Controllers' SYSVOL shares. If it is not automatically copied to the other Domain Controllers, test each machine's connectivity using the ping command.

Here are some additional tips for troubleshooting FRS replication:

- Microsoft TechNet has an excellent feature-length article, "Troubleshooting FRS," at the TechNet home page at http://tinyurl.com/yobuf4. Microsoft has a tool, Sonar (part of the Windows 2003 Resource Kit), that can dramatically help with FRS troubleshooting.
- Microsoft has another tool, Ultrasound, which surpasses Sonar's ability to help troubleshoot FRS.

Ultrasound and Sonar are available on the Microsoft website. At last check, Sonar can be found at http://tinyurl.com/5ouk9 and Ultrasound can be found at http://tinyurl.com/odgu. General FRS troubleshooting and information can be found at www.microsoft.com/frs as of this writing.

The Microsoft Knowledge Base articles Q221112, Q221111, Q272279, and Q229928 are good starting points to learn more about FRS and how to troubleshoot SYSVOL replication problems by debugging FRS. See Q229896 and Q249256 for details on how to debug Active Directory replication.

21st Century Replication Using DFSR Instead of FRS

Most Active Directory implementations don't have any issues with the in-the-box replication that has been there since Windows 2000 days: File Replication Service (FRS). FRS is what makes the stuff in SYSVOL "magically" go from Domain Controller to Domain Controller.

However, there is some percentage of customers who have major issues with FRS. FRS kind of "freaks out" when tasked with replicating large files or lots and lots of files. And, GPOs (GPTs, really), are just files that FRS moves around. And, if FRS freaks out, you could find yourself knee deep in the ghastly world of morphed files, journal wraps, and a whole lot of other scary errors and conditions.

To that end, it's possible to migrate the SYSVOL replication from FRS to DFSR, the more modern "DFS Replication." You can only opt to do this if all your DCs in a domain are Windows Server 2008 or higher, and once performed, there's no going back.

On this page:

```
http://blogs.technet.com/askds/archive/2009/05/01/sysvol-migration-from-
frs-to-dfsr-whitepaper-released.aspx
```

(`http://tinyurl.com/yc634nr`) you can find a variety of useful documents to help make that transition.

- SYSVOL Replication Migration Guide: FRS to DFS Replication (TechNet Version)

- SYSVOL Replication Migration Guide: FRS to DFS Replication (Word Doc Version)

You can also find the following "possibly useful" (their words, not mine) documents:

- Verifying File Replication during the Windows Server 2008 DFSR SYSVOL Migration—Down and Dirty Style

- DFSR SYSVOL Migration FAQ: Useful Trivia That May Save Your Follicles

- KB968733 (Hotfix for Migration under Certain RODC Scenarios)

- KB967326 (Hotfix for Migration under Disjoint Name Space Scenarios)

In short, that web page is your "go to" home for FRS to DFSR conversion.

Death of a GPO

As you saw in Chapter 2, there are three ways to stop using a GPO at a level in Active Directory. One way is to "Delete the link" to the GPO at the level being used in Active Directory. In the swimming pool analogy, we're simply removing the tether to our child in the pool, but we're leaving the object swimming in the pool should other levels want to use it.

The other is "Disabling the link." This leaves the tether in place but basically prevents the level from receiving the power within the OU.

The final way to stop using a GPO is to delete it. With the GMPC, you can delete a GPO only by traversing to the Group Policy Objects node, right-clicking it, and choosing Delete, as you saw back in Figure 2.6. But, again, be careful; other levels of Active Directory (including those in other domains and forests) might be using this GPO you're about to whack.

 As we've discussed in previous chapters, Cross-Domain Linking of GPOs is a no-no. And, if you whack the GPO in the source domain, it won't clean up links to *other* (target) domains.

How Client Systems Get Group Policy Objects

The items stored on the server make up only half the story. The real magic happens when the GPO is applied at the client, usually a workstation, although certainly servers behave in the same way. Half of Group Policy's usefulness is that it can apply equally to servers and desktops and laptops. Indeed, with the advent of Windows 2003, Windows Server 2008 and, of course, Windows Vista and Windows 7, the new policy settings they bring to the table mean you can control and configure more stuff than ever. So the details in this section are for all clients—servers and workstations.

When Group Policy is deployed from on high to client systems, the clients always do the requesting. This is why, when the chips are down and things aren't going right, you'll need to trot out to the system and crack open the Event Log (among other troubleshooting areas) to help uncover why the client isn't picking up your desires.

Microsoft doesn't provide a way to instantaneously "push" the policy settings inside GPOs to clients, even if you think they should get a new change right now. Out of the box, there's no "push the big red button and force the latest Group Policy to all my clients" command to make sure every client gets your will. This can be a little disappointing, especially if you need a security setting, such as a Software Restriction Policy, propagated to all your clients right now. There are several ways, however, to make this a reality:

- In the Third-Party Group Policy Solutions Guide on www.GPanswers.com is a link to a free tool called RGPrefresh, which also performs this function. Alternatively, you can download that tool right from my fellow MVP Darren Mar-Elia's website at http://tinyurl.com/ycsnfqt.

- Also in the Third-Party Group Policy Solutions Guide on www.GPanswers.com is a link to another free tool called SpecOps GPupdate, which also performs this function. This tool is graphical, hooks into Active Directory Users and Computers, and allows you to perform four functions on your client machines: Group Policy Refresh, reboot, shutdown, and startup (if the client machine has a wake-on-LAN card).

- These and additional examples are explained in Jakob H. Heidelberg's article "How to Force Remote Group Policy Processing" at `http://tinyurl.com/2opez6`.

But, without these "tricks," unfortunately, Group Policy is processed only when the computer starts up, when the user logs on, and at periodic intervals in the background, as discussed in Chapter 4. In that chapter, you learned "when" Group Policy is processed; in this section, you'll learn both "how" and "why" Group Policy is processed.

The Steps to Group Policy Processing

Group Policy processing on the client is broken down into roughly two parts. The first part is called "core" or "infrastructure" processing. We'll break it down for Windows XP and Windows 7, the two types of computers you're likely to have.

Core Processing for XP Machines

During the core processing stage of Group Policy processing, Windows tries to accomplish a number of tasks. Chief among them:

- To determine if the connection to the Domain Controller is over a slow link
- To discover all of the GPOs that apply to the computer or user
- To discover which Client-Side Extensions have to be called
- To discover whether anything has changed (GPOs, security group memberships, WMI filters) since the last processing cycle
- To create the final list of GPOs that need to be applied

In order to perform these tasks, Windows requires a number of network protocols be successfully passed between the client and the DC that it's paired with. These protocols, and their usages, are listed here:

- ICMP for slow link detection
- RPC (TCP port 135 and some random port that's greater than port 1024) for authentication to AD
- LDAP (TCP port 389) for querying AD to determine the list of GPOs, group membership, WMI filters, and so on
- SMB (TCP port 445) for querying the GPT in SYSVOL

If the client tries to get to the server and any of the protocols listed here are blocked (usually by a firewall), then all Group Policy processing will fail. Thus it's important that Windows clients have unimpeded access to all potential domain controllers that will respond to authentication and Group Policy requests for these protocols. Again, it's not super-common in the Windows world (yet) to turn the firewalls on for Domain Controllers and servers.

Another point to note is that Group Policy processing in Windows XP runs within the privileged Winlogon process. Winlogon is a system service and thus has the highest level of privilege within Windows. For that reason, poorly behaved CSEs could potentially crash Windows. This didn't happen often (or ever, to my knowledge, but it was certainly possible).

As we'll see in the next section, the inner workings of Group Policy has changed in Windows Vista and later, as we'll see with the *Group Policy Client Service*.

Once the core steps are complete, each CSE DLL is called by the Winlogon process, in the order that they are registered in the Registry under:

```
HKLM\Software\Microsoft\Windows NT\CurrentVersion\Winlogon\GPExtensions
```

(with the exception of Administrative Templates Policy, which always runs first), and each CSE processes the GPOs that have been discovered during the core processing cycle.

Core Processing for Windows 7

So, Microsoft made a significant change to the Group Policy processing engine in Windows Vista. And that work was maintained in Windows 7 and Windows Server 2008 and Windows Server 2008 R2.

It has moved the engine from Winlogon into a separate service, called the *Group Policy Client* **Service**. This service is "hardened" so that even an administrator cannot easily stop it dead.

This is probably a good thing because there are not too many situations where you'd want to disable Group Policy processing completely. As I mentioned, a normal administrator cannot easily stop the Group Policy Client Service. If you go into the Services MMC snap-in and highlight the service, you'll notice that the options to stop and start the service are grayed out. It takes a bit of work to stop the service, and when you do, it will automatically restart itself after a short period of time. However, if you want to see this in motion, here is the general process.

If you want to try this out (just for fun), you'll need to start the Windows Task Manager and select the Services tab. Locate the service called gpsvc, and note the process ID listed next to it, as shown in Figure 7.14. Next, move to the Processes tab in Task Manager and locate the svchost process with the same process ID as the gpsvc entry. Highlight that svchost process and click the End Process button to end the service.

FIGURE 7.14   Viewing the Group Policy Client Service process

That's all there is to it!

Except in a few minutes, you'll see the gpsvc spring back to life in a bit. Which is good.

Now, the main difference between core processing for Windows Vista and Windows 7 versus the older operating systems is the ICMP slow link detection process. Even though, underneath the hood, there's lots of new stuff for Vista and later, it *acts* pretty much like XP. Except in one big respect I mentioned, and that's the slow link detection process. This is described next.

Windows 7's Slow Link Detection

Windows Vista and later use a completely different mechanism to detect a slow link. Instead of using ICMP pings, Windows Vista and later rely on the Network Location Awareness (NLA) service that is part of the operating system. The NLA service uses a series of higher-level communications with Domain Controllers to determine when a Domain Controller is available and at what link speed it is available. The NLA process is more dynamic and thus is able to inform the Group Policy engine when a Domain Controller becomes available (where the previous mechanism was not). Because of this, it's important to understand under what scenarios GP processing occurs when NLA detects that a DC is available. We'll discuss this later in the chapter in the section "Troubleshooting NLA in Windows 7."

If you were to use Windows Server 2008 as your Group Policy client over a slow link, it would detect slow links the same way. But how often are you using Windows Server 2008 to dial up from a hotel room?

Client-Side Extensions

When a Group Policy "clock" strikes, the client's Group Policy engine springs into action to start processing your wishes. The GPOs that are meant for the client are downloaded from Active Directory, and then the client pretty much does the rest.

When GPOs are set from on high, usually not all policy setting categories are used. For instance, you might set up an Administrative Template policy but not an Internet Explorer Maintenance policy. The client is smart enough to know which policy setting groups affect it.

The client knows which policy setting groups affects it specifically because it asks each GPO which extensions have been set within it through the gpcMachineExtensionName and gpcUserExtensionName attributes in the GPC that we introduced earlier.

This happens during the "core" processing part of Group Policy. During this core processing cycle, the client queries Active Directory to get its list of GPOs, figures out which ones actually apply to it, and makes a list of the CSEs that will need to run for the GPOs found. Once all that core work is done, each CSE is called in turn to do its thing.

CSEs are really DLLs (Dynamic Link Libraries) that perform the Group Policy processing. These DLLs are called by the system Winlogon process (or the Group Policy Client Service in Windows Vista and later). These CSEs are automatically registered in the operating system and are identified in the Registry by their GUIDs.

Additional CSEs can be created by third-party programmers who want to control their own aspects of the operating system or their own software. See the sidebar "Group Policy Software Vendors with Their Own CSEs" for a sampling.

Group Policy Software Vendors with Their Own CSEs

The whole idea of CSEs is that if you have a great idea, and you want to make that idea happen via Group Policy, you can do it. Several vendors have stepped up and created their own CSEs that implement their ideas. Come to www.GPanswers.com for the latest look at products that have their own CSEs. As of this writing, the following companies have products with their own CSEs:

Specops Software   Specops Software has products that feature CSEs.

> **Specops Deploy**   This CSE enables you to perform several Group Policy Software Installation tasks (discussed in Chapter 11) that you can't natively perform. For instance, you can distribute software to users and computers that are already logged on as well as get a detailed log of which computers received software. Found here:
>
> www.specopssoft.com/products/specopsdeploy
>
> **Specops Inventory**   This product performs hardware and software inventory via the Group Policy engine and provides detailed reports of what software and hardware your enterprise is using. Found here:
>
> www.specopssoft.com/products/specopsinventory

BeyondTrust Software   BeyondTrust has a bunch of Windows and Linux products. However, their Privilege Manager is a true CSE. Its job is to allow your applications to run as administrators, while keeping your users with user rights. Check it out at:

> http://pm.beyondtrust.com/products/PrivilegeManager.aspx

PolicyPak Software   The PolicyPak family of tools can be found at www.PolicyPak.com. You learned all about PolicyPak in Chapter 6, but in short PolicyPak enables you to configure and lock down both applications and operating system settings beyond what ADM and ADMX files are capable of. So, if you wanted to manage Adobe Acrobat Reader or WinZip or your own home-grown application via Group Policy, you could create your own PolicyPak and manage them centrally.

In Windows 2000, the OS shipped with 9 CSEs. In Windows XP and 2003, Microsoft added 2 more, for a total of 11 CSEs. With Windows XP SP2 another CSE was added. Vista adds an additional 5 for a total of 17.

Once the Group Policy Preference Extensions are added to Windows XP or Windows Vista, another 21 are added. Or, since they're in the box for Windows Server 2008, the in-the-box number jumps to a total of 38.

Windows 7 contains the 38 CSEs just mentioned plus another 5, specific to Windows 7.

 The three Windows XP SP2 and Windows 2003 SP1 CSEs are Internet Explorer Zonemapping, 802.11x Wireless policies, and Quality of Service Packet Scheduler policies. Vista added the Enterprise QoS, 802.3, Offline Files, Deployed Printer Connections, and Windows Search CSEs. Some additional policy functionality, such as Software Restriction Policies, was added in XP and Windows 2003 but was implemented within an existing CSE. Windows 7 adds two "Accelerators" for Internet Explorer, a CSE for DirectAccess (called "Connectivity Platform"), and two for TCP/IP control.

To take a look at the CSEs on a workstation or server, follow these steps:

1. On Windows XPPRO1 or WIN7, log on as Administrator.

2. For Windows XP, choose Start ➢ Run (for Windows 7, just type **regedit** in the Search dialog box) to open the Run dialog box; then in the Open box type **Run Regedit** and press Enter to open the Registry Editor, as shown in Figure 7.15.

FIGURE 7.15 The Client-Side Extension DLLs actually perform the GPO processing.

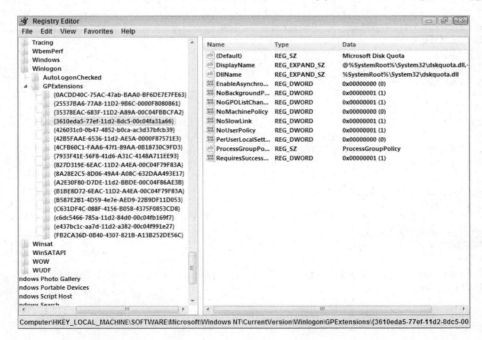

3. Drill down into HKLM ➤ Software ➤ Microsoft ➤ Windows NT ➤ Current Version ➤ Winlogon ➤ GPExtensions. Here you will find a list of GUIDs, each representing a CSE.

Let's take a look at the next sections to understand precisely what we're seeing.

CSEs for XP Machines

Figure 7.15 shows a sample CSE and the settings for disk quotas. See Table 7.2 for the CSEs listed by GUID, the functions they perform, and the associated DLLs. Note that a particular DLL can be responsible for more than one function.

TABLE 7.2 GUIDs, Their Functions, and Their Corresponding DLLs for Pre–Windows Vista Machines

Class ID	Function	DLL
{C6DC5466-785A-11D2-84D0-00C04FB169F7}	Software deployment	appmgmts.dll
{3610EDA5-77EF-11D2-8DC5-00C04FA31A66}	Disk quotas	dskquota.dll
{B1BE8D72-6EAC-11D2-A4EA-00C04F79F83A}	EFS recovery	scecli.dll
{25537BA6-77A8-11D2-9B6C-0000F8080861}	Folder redirection	fdeploy.dll
{A2E30F80-D7DE-11d2-BBDE-00C04F86AE3B}	Internet Explorer settings	iedkcs32.dll
{e437bc1c-aa7d-11d2-a382-00c04f991e27}	IP security	gptext.dll
{35378EAC-683F-11D2-A89A-00C04FBBCFA2}	Registry settings (Administrative Templates)	userenv.dll
{42B5FAAE-6536-11D2-AE5A-0000F87571E3}	Scripts	gptext.dll
{827D319E-6EAC-11D2-A4EA-00C04F79F83A}	Security	scecli.dll
{0ACDD40C-75AC-47ab-BAA0-BF6DE7E7FE63}	Wireless (802.11x) (Windows XP+ only)	gptext.dll
{4CFB60C1-FAA6-47f1-89AA-0B18730C9FD3}	Internet Zone Mapping (Windows XP+)	iedkcs32.dll

TABLE 7.2 GUIDs, Their Functions, and Their Corresponding DLLs for Pre–Windows Vista Machines *(continued)*

Class ID	Function	DLL
{426031c0-0b47-4852-b0ca-ac3d37bfcb39}	Quality of Service Packet Scheduler (Windows XP+ only)	gptext.dll
None	Software Restriction (Windows XP+ only)	None
None	Remote Installation Services (RIS) (Windows Server 2003 and earlier)	None

> Why don't all CSEs have DLLs? Neither Remote Installation Services (RIS) nor Software Restriction polices require CSEs to be associated with DLLs. RIS is active *before* the operating system is. Software Restriction policies don't require CSEs because they "tag along" on the functionality of another CSE.

CSEs for Windows Vista and Windows Server 2008 Machines

See Table 7.3 for the Windows Vista–specific CSEs listed by GUID, the functions they perform, and the associated DLLs. Again, all the pre-Vista CSEs are also on Windows Vista, so they're not repeated in this table since they're already listed in Table 7.2. Note that a particular DLL can be responsible for more than one function.

TABLE 7.3 CSE GUIDs, Their Functions, and Their Corresponding DLLs That Exist Only on Windows Vista and Server 2008 Machines

Class ID	Function	DLL
{7933F41E-56F8-41d6-A31C-4148A711EE93}	Windows Search	srchadmin.dll
{7B983727-8072-47ea-83A4-39C6CE25BAE6}	Offline Files (see note)	cscobj.dll
{8A28E2C5-8D06-49A4-A08C-632DAA493E17}	Deployed Printer Connections	gpprnext.dll
{B587E2B1-4D59-4e7e-AED9-22B9DF11D053}	802.3 Policy	dot3gpclnt.dll
{FB2CA36D-0B40-4307-821B-A13B252DE56C}	Enterprise QoS	gptext.dll

Offline Files existed before Windows Vista (in Windows 2000 and Windows XP), but in Vista it became its own CSE.

CSEs for Windows 7 and Windows Server 2008 R2 Machines

It's true that Windows 7 and Windows Server 2008 R2 (and Windows Server 2008 for that matter) all have the Group Policy Preferences CSEs. In Table 7.4 I list the specific CSEs that only they have.

TABLE 7.4 Windows 7 and Windows Server 2008 R2 CSE GUIDs, Their Functions, and Their Corresponding DLLs That Exist Only on Windows 7 and Windows Server 2008 R2 Machines

GUID	Function	DLL
{7B849a69-220F-451E-B3FE-2CB811AF94AE}	Internet Explorer 8 User Accelerators	iedkcs32.dll
CF7639F3-ABA2-41DB-97F2-81E2C5DBFC5D}	Internet Explorer 8 Machine Accelerators	iedkcs32.dll
{CDEAFC3D-948D-49DD-AB12-E578BA4AF7AA}	TCP/IP v6 handlers	gptext.dll
{e437bc1c-aa7d-11d2-a382-00c04f991e27}	IPSEC Security Policies	polstore.dll
{fbf687e6-f063-4d9f-9f4f-fd9a26acdd5f}	Connectivity Platform / DirectAccess	gptext.dll

Additional CSEs for the Group Policy Preferences

These are the Group Policy Preference Extensions, which we explored in Chapter 5.

Again, to be super clear: they're already in the box for Windows 7, Windows Server 2008, and Windows Server 2008 R2, and they're downloadable for Windows XP, Windows 2003, and Windows Vista. They won't install on Windows 2000.

In Table 7.5, you can see the list of Group Policy Preferences CSEs, their GUIDs, and the corresponding functions.

 There's no mistake in Table 7.5. All the new Group Policy Preference Extensions use the *same* DLL, but if you look at the actual Registry entry, you'll see that each one's Displayname key notes the DLL name (gppprefcl.dll) with an entry point ID.

TABLE 7.5 CSE GUIDs, Their Functions, and Their Corresponding DLLs That Exist Only When You Add the Group Policy Preference Extensions

CSE GUIDs	Function	DLL
{0E28E245-9368-4853-AD84-6DA3BA35BB75}	Group Policy Environment	gpprefcl.dll
{17D89FEC-5C44-4972-B12D-241CAEF74509}	Group Policy Local Users and Groups	gpprefcl.dll
{1A6364EB-776B-4120-ADE1-B63A406A76B5}	Group Policy Device Settings	gpprefcl.dll
{3A0DBA37-F8B2-4356-83DE-3E90BD5C261F}	Group Policy Network Options	gpprefcl.dll
{5794DAFD-BE60-433f-88A2-1A31939AC01F}	Group Policy Drive Maps	gpprefcl.dll
{6232C319-91AC-4931-9385-E70C2B099F0E}	Group Policy Folders	gpprefcl.dll
{6A4C88C6-C502-4f74-8F60-2CB23EDC24E2}	Group Policy Network Shares	gpprefcl.dll
{7150F9BF-48AD-4da4-A49C-29EF4A8369BA}	Group Policy Files	gpprefcl.dll
{728EE579-943C-4519-9EF7-AB56765798ED}	Group Policy Data Sources	gpprefcl.dll
{74EE6C03-5363-4554-B161-627540339CAB}	Group Policy INI Files	gpprefcl.dll
{91FBB303-0CD5-4055-BF42-E512A681B325}	Group Policy Services	gpprefcl.dll
{A3F3E39B-5D83-4940-B954-28315B82F0A8}	Group Policy Folder Options	gpprefcl.dll
{AADCED64-746C-4633-A97C-D61349046527}	Group Policy Scheduled Tasks	gpprefcl.dll
{B087BE9D-ED37-454f-AF9C-04291E351182}	Group Policy Registry	gpprefcl.dll
{BC75B1ED-5833-4858-9BB8-CBF0B166DF9D}	Group Policy Printers	gpprefcl.dll

TABLE 7.5 CSE GUIDs, Their Functions, and Their Corresponding DLLs That Exist Only When You Add the Group Policy Preference Extensions *(continued)*

CSE GUIDs	Function	DLL
{C418DD9D-0D14-4efb-8FBF-CFE535C8FAC7}	Group Policy Shortcuts	gpprefcl.dll
{E47248BA-94CC-49c4-BBB5-9EB7F05183D0}	Group Policy Internet Settings	gpprefcl.dll
{E4F48E54-F38D-4884-BFB9-D4D2E5729C18}	Group Policy Start Menu Settings	gpprefcl.dll
{E5094040-C46C-4115-B030-04FB2E545B00}	Group Policy Regional Options	gpprefcl.dll
{E62688F0-25FD-4c90-BFF5-F508B9D2E31F}	Group Policy Power Options	gpprefcl.dll
{F9C77450-3A41-477E-9310-9ACD617BD9E3}	Group Policy Applications	gpprefcl.dll

Inside CSE Values

For each CSE, several values can be set (or not). Not all CSEs use these values. Indeed, Microsoft does not support modifying them in any way.

You can see a list of the values listed here:

http://msdn.microsoft.com/en-us/library/aa373494%28VS.85%29.aspx

(shortened to http://tinyurl.com/y9ydmcx).

They are presented at that URL for your own edification, but in most circumstances, you should not be modifying them unless explicitly directed to do so by Microsoft Product Support Services (PSS).

 WARNING Remember, the CSE sets these values—you don't, unless you're directed by Microsoft PSS to help make sure the CSE is working the way it's supposed to.

Note that many of the options listed at that URL 6 (for example, NoSlowLink, NoBackgroundPolicy, and NoGPOListChanges) can be set within the Computer Configuration ➤ Policies ➤ Administrative Templates ➤ System ➤ Group Policy section of a GPO. When they are set through policy, the values shown in the Registry value column listed in the table are ignored.

I hope you won't have to spend too much time in here. But I present this information so that if you need to debug a certain CSE, you can go right to the source and see how a setting might not be what you want.

Remember that most of these settings are either established by the system default or can be changed. You can modify the settings yourself—such as the ability to process over slow links, the ability to be disabled, or the ability to be processed in the background—using the techniques described near the end of Chapter 3.

Where Are Administrative Templates Registry Settings Stored?

This section is the mini-review of everything you already learned in Chapter 6. But because Administrative Templates is one of the most commonly applied policy settings, let's take a minute to learn specifically how the client processes Administrative Templates.

Here, we're just talking about proper "policies" and not "preferences" (which are discussed in Chapter 5).

Remember: Group Policy's strength is that the "in the box" policy settings do not tattoo the Registry. That is, once a setting is applied, it applies only for that computer or user. When the user or computer leaves the scope of the GPO (for example, when you move the user from the **Human Resources Users** OU to the **Accounting Users** OU), the Registry settings that applied to the user are removed and the new Registry settings then apply. Similarly, if a computer was in, say, the **Human Resources Computers** OU and moved to the **Accounting Computers** OU, the settings linked to within the **Human Resources Computers** OU settings would peel off.

Administrative Templates Group Policy settings are usually stored in the following locations:

User settings   `HKEY_CURRENT_USER\Software\Policies`

Computer settings   `HKEY_LOCAL_MACHINE\Software\Policies`

Alternatively, some applications may choose the following locations:

User settings   `HKEY_CURRENT_USER\Software\Microsoft\Windows\CurrentVersion\Policies`

Computer settings   `HKEY_LOCAL_MACHINE\Software\Microsoft\Windows\Currentversion\Policies`

Microsoft is encouraging third-party developers to write their applications so that they utilize `HKEY_CURRENT_USER\Software\Policies` or `HKEY_LOCAL_MACHINE\Software\Policies` to become Group Policy enabled.

Knowing how this works helps us understand why each version of Windows increases the number of Administrative Templates policy settings that can apply to it. It's quite simple: the specific program that's targeted for the policy setting looks for settings at these two Registry locations. Sometimes that application is one we overlook a lot—Explorer.exe! For Windows XP, Explorer.exe has been "smartened up." Same with Windows 7. It's Explorer.exe even smarter still, being able to control many dozens of new items. Same with Internet Explorer, or the Windows Firewall; as they grow up, so do the number of items that be managed.

This also answers the question of why Windows XP machines seem to "overlook" policy settings that are designed only for, say, Windows 7 computers.

In short, "older" operating systems (which are really applications) simply don't know to "look" for new policy settings (even though those settings are written into the target machine's Registry). So, all operating systems (which, again, are really applications) that can download the policy settings *do*. But who cares? If an older system applies a policy setting, the Registry is modified and then it's generally ignored by the applications running on it. "Old" Windows just doesn't know to look for the new Registry changes. Occasionally, with the release of a service pack, the application in question might get a new lease on life and understand some new policy settings—because the application has now been updated to look for them in the Registry. This has already happened for Explorer, Software Update Services, Windows Media Player, and Office, to name a few.

 If you have a mixture of Windows servers and clients, you might need to keep track of policy settings that affect only XP, for example. It's likely a good idea to create GPOs with names specific to which operating system they apply to: Windows XP, Windows Vista, Windows 7, etc.

Because the settings inside Administrative Templates are written to only these four locations, we are free from the bonds of having our Registries tattooed. The Administrative Templates CSE (Userenv.dll) applies the settings placed in any of these four locations to the current mix of user and system.

As you move users in and out of OUs, or change group membership, the settings that apply to them change as well. Under the covers, this process is a bit more subtle. The way the nontattooing behavior works is that when Registry settings are first applied, they are merged into files that are stored on the computer in per-computer and per-user areas— each file is called ntuser.pol. The next time the Administrative Templates CSE runs, it looks into these stored files and makes a list of all the policy settings that exist in the four "special" keys I mentioned previously (at the beginning of this section). It then deletes all those settings, as specified by that file. Then, the CSE re-creates that file with all the new Administrative Template settings that currently apply to the computer or user. Finally, it applies those values to the computer or user portions of the Registry.

Any settings that are outside the four "special" locations are *not* covered by this removal process, and thus you have the tattooing behavior.

Why Isn't Group Policy Applying?

At times, you set up Group Policy from on high and your users or workstations do not receive the changes. Why might that be the case?

First, remember how Group Policy is processed:

- The GPO "lives" in the swimming pool in the domain.

- The client requests Group Policy at various times throughout the day.

- The client connects to a Domain Controller to get the latest batch of GPOs. (Group Policy isn't somehow "pushed" from on high.)

- If it's status quo, meaning that:

  - Nothing has changed inside the GPO (based on changed version number)

  - The location of the user or computer hasn't changed in Active Directory

  - The user or computer hasn't changed group memberships

  - Any WMI filters set on the GPO haven't changed

  the default behavior is to not reprocess the GPOs (though this can be changed, as explored in Chapter 3).

- If there is a change (with respect to any of these previous bullet points), then all applicable CSEs reprocess all applicable GPOs.

That's the long and the short of it.

Now, if you think all this is happening properly, try to answer the questions in the following sections to find out what could be damming the proper flow of your Group Policy process.

Reviewing the Basics

Sometimes, it's the small, day-to-day things that prevent a GPO from applying. By testing a simple application that has normal features, you can often find problems and eliminate them, which allows Group Policy to behave the way you expect.

Is the Group Policy Object or Link Disabled?

Recall from Chapter 1 that there are two halves of the Group Policy coin: a Computer half and a User half. Also recall that either portion or both can be disabled. Indeed, a GPO itself can be fully disabled (see Figure 7.16).

Check the GPO itself or any related GPO links. Click the Details tab and check the GPO Status setting. If it is anything other than Enabled, you might be in trouble.

 If you change the status of the GPO, that status changes on all links that use this GPO.

FIGURE 7.16   You can disable the entire GPO if desired.

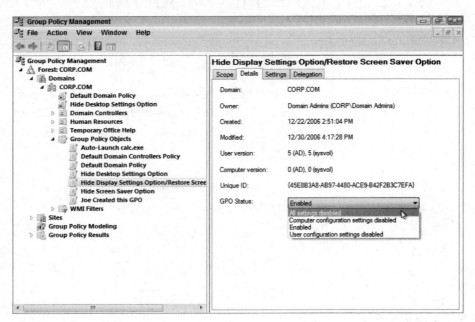

Are You Sure about the Inheritance?

Recall that Group Policy flows downward from each level—site, domain, and each nested OU—and is cumulative. Also recall that in XP, there is only one Local Group Policy for a computer, which is applied first.

And, in Windows Vista and later there are three levels of MLGPOs. See Chapter 1 for the full rundown. Remember, in MLGPOs it's a "last written wins" policy.

Are You Trying to Apply Policy to a Group Inside an OU?

This bears repeating: you can't just plunk an NT-style/Active Directory group that contains users into an OU and expect them to get Group Policy. Group Policy doesn't work that way; you can only apply Group Policy directly to users or computers in an OU. Not a group.

Multiple Group Policy Objects at a Level

Also recall that there can be many GPOs at any level, which are applied in the reverse order—that is, from bottom to top, as described in Chapter 2. Since any two (or more) GPOs can contain the same or even conflicting settings, the last-applied GPO wins. If you mean for one GPO to have higher precedence, use the Up and Down buttons to manipulate the order. Remember, the GPO with the *lowest* number gets the *highest* priority. Confusing, I know, but that's the deal.

Examining Your Block Inheritance Usage

The GPMC gives you a quick view of all instances of Block Inheritance with the Blue Exclamation Point (!). Remember: once you select to block inheritance, *all GPOs* from higher levels are considered null and void—not just the one policy setting or GPO you had in mind to block. It's as if you were starting from a totally blank slate. Therefore, whenever you block inheritance, you must start from scratch—either creating and linking new GPOs or simply linking to existing GPOs already swimming in the GPOs container.

Examining Your "Enforced" Usage

Conversely, be aware of all your "Enforce" directives. The Enforce icon is a little lock next to the GPO link. Enforce specifies that the policy settings selected and contained within in a *specific* GPO cannot be avoided at any inherited level from this point forward. Note that Block Inheritance applies to a container in Active Directory (for example, a domain or an OU), while Enforced applies to a GPO link. So if you have a GPO linked to four containers in Active Directory, you could have only one of those links "Enforced," two of them or all of them (or none!). When Block Policy Inheritance and Enforce are seemingly in conflict, Enforce always wins. Recall that Enforce was previously known as No Override in the old-school parlance.

Are Your Permissions Set Correctly?

Recall from Chapter 2 that two permissions—"Read" and "Apply Group Policy"—must be set so that the affected user processes a specific GPO. By default, Authenticated Users have these two rights, but you can remove this group and set your own filtering via the Security Filtering section on the Scope tab of a GPO link.

In Chapter 2, I showed you two ways to filter:

- Round up only the users, computers, or security groups who *should* get the GPO applied to them.

- Figure out who you *do not* want to get the GPO applied to them, and use the "Deny" attribute over the "Apply Group Policy" right.

When all is said and done, users will need both "Read" and "Apply Group Policy" permissions on the GPO itself to apply GPOs. And, you can prevent a GPO from applying by simply setting "Deny" access on one or the other of these two rights. However, if you're going to use this technique, best practices dictate to always try to deny access on "Apply Group Policy" and not "Read."

Try to always deny "Apply Group Policy" (and not "Read") because later, that user might need to be able to modify the GPO. And, without read access, they cannot modify it.

Having only one of those permissions means that Group Policy will not apply when processing is supposed to occur. Additionally, make sure to remember that the "Deny" attribute always trumps all other permissions. If an explicit "Deny" attribute is encountered, it is as if it were the only bit in the world that matters. Therefore, if a specific GPO is not being applied to a user or a group, make sure that "Deny" isn't somehow getting into the picture along the way.

 Any use of the "Deny" attribute is not displayed in the Security Filtering section of the Scope tab, so you have no notification if it's being used. This is a common reason for Group Policy not applying; the old-school way to perform Group Policy filtering involved heavy use of the "Deny" attribute, and now the GPMC will not easily display this fact unless you use the Group Policy Results Wizard (or gpresult.exe).

Advanced Inspection

If you've gone through the basics and nothing is overtly wrong, perhaps a more subtle inter-action is occurring. See if any of the following questions and solutions fit the bill.

Is Windows XP (and Later) Fast Boot On?

The default behavior of Windows XP and later is different from that of Windows 2000. The default behavior of Windows 2000 is to process GPOs in the foreground (at computer startup or user logon) synchronously. That is, for the policy settings that affect a Windows 2000 computer (which will take effect at startup), every GPO is applied—local, site, domain, and each nested OU—even before the user has the ability to press Ctrl+Alt+Del to log on. Once the user logs on, the policy settings that affect the User side are applied—local, site, domain, and each nested OU—before the user's Desktop is finally displayed and they can start working.

This usually isn't too much of a problem for the policy settings within GPOs that affect computers, but it can seriously affect your user's experience if enabled for user policy pro-cessing. Even *after* a user is logged on, GPOs can suddenly be downloaded and policy set-tings start popping up and changing the user's environment.

Moreover, as I stated in Chapter 3, by default several key items in Windows XP and later take between two and three reboots to become effective. To that end, I suggest you modify the default behavior. The strongest advice I can give you is to create and link a new GPO at the domain level. Name your new GPO something like "Force XP and later machines to act like Windows 2000," and enable the **Always wait for the network at computer startup and logon** policy setting. Then, select Enforced so it cannot be blocked.

To find this policy setting, drill down through the Computer Configuration ➤ Policies ➤ Administrative Templates ➤ System ➤ Logon branch of Group Policy. (For more information, see Chapter 3.)

Therefore, if you have erratic Group Policy application (especially for Software Installation, Folder Redirection, or Profile settings), see if the Windows XP and later default of Fast Boot is still active.

Is Asynchronous Processing Turned On in Windows 2000?

Not that you have Windows 2000 machines around anymore, but for completeness, we'll mention this tidbit. Windows 2000 was born with a way to try to act like Windows XP and later and process GPOs asynchronously. However, doing so is not recommended, as amazingly unpredictable results can occur. Windows XP was built from the ground up to do asynchronous processing; Windows 2000 really wasn't. So, in a nutshell, don't turn on asynchronous processing for Windows 2000 machines. It's a bad idea.

Asynchronous processing is independent for both the Computer and the User sides.

Are Both the GPC and GPT Replicated Correctly?

As stated in the first part of this chapter, Group Policy is made up of two halves:

- The GPC, which is found in Active Directory and replicated via normal Active Directory replication
- The GPT, which is found in the SYSVOL share of one Domain Controller and replicated via FRS to other Domain Controllers

Both the GPC and GPT are replicated independently and can be on different schedules before converging.

Use the techniques described earlier in conjunction with Gpotool and Replmon to diagnose issues with replicating the GPC and GPT.

Did You Check the DNS Configuration of the Server and Client?

In order for the GPC and GPT to replicate correctly, the DNS structure must be 100 percent kosher at all times—both on the server and at the client. If you suspect that the GPC and GPT are not being replicated correctly, you might try to see if the DNS structure is the way you intend. If it is, I don't recommend you rip it all up and reconfigure it if everything else is working. The Microsoft Knowledge Base article at:

    http://support.microsoft.com/kb/291382/en-us

provides a good foundation for understanding how to create a healthy DNS infrastructure.

In some cases, one Domain Controller might not be providing Group Policy to your clients. In the next section, I'll show you how to find out if your clients are really logged on and, if so, what Domain Controller the computer and user are using for logon.

Are You Really Logged On?

Windows 2000 doesn't perform the logon process precisely the same way that later operating systems do. Specifically, when a user logs on to a Windows XP or later machine, that machine might or might not have made contact with a Domain Controller to validate that user and give them a Kerberos ticket to the network. Kerberos is the newer authentication mechanism that has supplanted NTLM. Windows XP and later will try its darnedest to speed things up (again) and log on with cached credentials. Windows XP and later will then try to contact a Domain Controller and get the Kerberos ticket for the user.

In Windows 2000, it is easy to identify the Domain Controller where the local Desktop authenticated. You issue a set command at a command prompt and look for the contents of the *LOGONSERVER* variable, as shown in Figure 7.17.

FIGURE 7.17 The LOGONSERVER variable shows the Domain Controller where this Windows 2000 client is picking up its Group Policy settings.

```
C:\WINNT\system32\cmd.exe                                          _|□|x|
C:\>set
ALLUSERSPROFILE=C:\Documents and Settings\All Users
APPDATA=C:\Documents and Settings\User01\Application Data
CommonProgramFiles=C:\Program Files\Common Files
COMPUTERNAME=W2KPRO
ComSpec=C:\WINNT\system32\cmd.exe
HOMEDRIVE=C:
HOMEPATH=\
LOGONSERVER=\\DC01
NUMBER_OF_PROCESSORS=1
OS=Windows_NT
Os2LibPath=C:\WINNT\system32\os2\dll;
Path=C:\WINNT\system32;C:\WINNT;C:\WINNT\System32\Wbem
PATHEXT=.COM;.EXE;.BAT;.CMD;.UBS;.UBE;.JS;.JSE;.WSF;.WSH
PROCESSOR_ARCHITECTURE=x86
PROCESSOR_IDENTIFIER=x86 Family 6 Model 14 Stepping 8, GenuineIntel
PROCESSOR_LEVEL=6
PROCESSOR_REVISION=0e08
ProgramFiles=C:\Program Files
PROMPT=$P$G
SystemDrive=C:
SystemRoot=C:\WINNT
TEMP=C:\DOCUME~1\User01\LOCALS~1\Temp
TMP=C:\DOCUME~1\User01\LOCALS~1\Temp
USERDNSDOMAIN=CORP.COM
USERDOMAIN=CORP
USERNAME=User01
USERPROFILE=C:\Documents and Settings\User01
windir=C:\WINNT
```

In Windows 2000, if you aren't logged on to a Domain Controller, you see the variable set to the local computer name.

In Windows XP and later, you simply cannot trust this *LOGONSERVER* variable to tell you the truth. Additionally, you cannot trust the Windows XP or later SYSTEMINFO utility either, which claims to provide this data.

Just based on the way Windows XP and later do their logon thing, you cannot use these aforementioned methods. XP will simply tell a bald-faced lie and say that you are logged on (via the *LOGONSERVER* variable, with the information from the last Domain Controller it contacted).

With Windows XP and later, to ensure that your user and computer are really logged on the network, you can count on just one tool—Kerbtray (or the command-line equivalent, klist.exe). Kerbtray and klist are found in the Windows 2003 Resource Kit and are small enough to be put on a USB stick and run on a suspect machine. When you run Kerbtray, it puts a little icon in the notification area. If the computer and user have Kerberos tickets, the icon turns green and you know you're really logged on. However, if the Kerbtray returns a graphic of a bunch of loose keys (that, in my opinion, look like question marks), as shown in Figure 7.18, you know you're not actually logged on and, hence, not downloading the most recent GPOs. Again, if you were really logged on, the graphic would be a green ticket.

FIGURE 7.18 The Windows XP and later LOGONSERVER variable cannot be trusted. Use Kerbtray instead, which is shown running in the notification area.

In Figure 7.18, you can see several things:

- The computer's network card is disabled (as shown in the Network Connections window).

- The *LOGONSERVER* variable is set to a Domain Controller (as shown in the CMD prompt window). Feel free to simply say out loud, "If the network card is off, this is bloody impossible."

- Kerbtray, thankfully, returns that icon of a bunch of loose keys verifying that we're not really logged on.

So, to find out if you're really logged on when using a Windows XP or later computer, it's "Kerbtray or the highway." Once you've validated with Kerbtray that the computer has really logged on, you can *then* use the *LOGONSERVER* variable to make sure which Domain Controller the Windows XP or later machine has used. Because, you'll know the truth: whether or not you're really logged on.

Did Something Recently Move?

If a computer account or a user account is moved from one OU to another, Windows (all versions) can wait as long as 30 minutes to realize this fact. Once it does, it might or might not apply background Group Policy processing for another 90 minutes or more! Running GPUpdate (or SECEDIT for Windows 2000 machines) will not help.

However, if you're expecting a specific setting to take effect on a user or computer that has moved more than 150 minutes ago, you'll then need to figure out if the move has been embraced by the Domain Controller the workstation used to authenticate. (See the previous section for information about how to determine the Domain Controller via the *LOGONSERVER* variable, but make sure you're really logged on!)

You can then fire up Active Directory Users and Computers and connect to the Domain Controller in question, as shown in Figure 7.19.

FIGURE 7.19 You can always manually connect to a Domain Controller to see if Active Directory has performed replication.

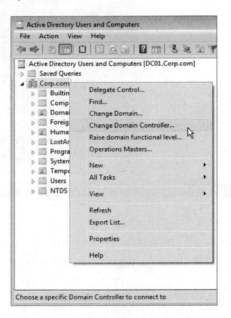

If the target computer's local Domain Controller does not know about the move, you might want to manually kick off replication using Active Directory Sites and Services. If the target computer's local Domain Controller *does* know about the move, you might want to try logging the user off and back on or restarting the computer. Although using SECEDIT (for Windows 2000 machines) or GPUpdate (for Windows XP and later) to refresh the GPO is a good option, it's best to log off and/or reboot the machine to guarantee that the computer will perform the initial policy processing as described in Chapter 3.

I've seen Microsoft documentation that states that running GPUpdate /force on a Windows XP/SP2 machine will "jump-start" the machine and/or user account into recognizing that it has moved around in Active Directory. I've done extensive testing but get inconsistent results. Sometimes it seems to work; other times it doesn't. In short, when a user or computer is moved around in Active Directory, I always re-log on as the user, or reboot the computer. It's slightly better with Windows Vista, and even better still with Windows 7—but even then, I've seen it work and also fail to work.

Is the Machine Properly Joined to the Domain?

This is weird, so stay with me. In short, sometimes you can find yourself in a situation where the computer has de-joined from the domain. This can happen in virtual environments, especially in testing, when a client computer (say, Windows 7 or XP) was joined at one time, but the VMs were "rolled back" to an earlier date and time.

There are other circumstances, too, which could cause computer de-joining, but that one happens to me all the time. And here's the weird part: if you try to log on, sometimes it just inexplicably *works*—even though it shouldn't.

But then, like Stephen King's *Pet Sematary*, suddenly things feel "not quite right." You get User-side policy, and maybe even Computer-side policy—for a while. Then you might lose Computer-side policy. GPresult /R starts to fail with strange error messages.

In short, you're not joined anymore, *and you don't even know it*.

What's happened is that the *computer trust*, also known as a *secure channel*, is broken. To see if the computer trust (secure channel) to the domain is damaged, you can use NLTEST, which is available here: http://tinyurl.com/4uhnu. The verification syntax is nltest /sc_query:domain_name. If the test passes, then you're kosher. If not, the fix is simple: just disjoin and rejoin the device to the domain.

Is Loopback Policy Enabled?

Enabling Loopback policy will turn Group Policy on its ear: Loopback forces the same user policy settings for everyone who logs on to a specific computer. If you're seeing user policy settings apply but not computer policies, or if things are applying without rhyme or reason, chances are Loopback policy is enabled. Review Chapter 4 to see in depth how it works, when you should use it, and how to turn it off.

In Windows XP, determining you are in Loopback mode is difficult.

In Windows Vista and later, it's a little easier. Look for Event ID 5311 in the Windows Group Policy Event Logs. In the guts of the event, you'll see if Loopback policy processing mode is set to Replace, Merge, or not enabled. We show this a little later in Figure 7.29.

How Are Slow Links Being Defined, and How Are Slow Links Handled?

If you notice that Group Policy is not applied to users coming in over a slow link, remember the rules for slow links:

- Registry and security settings are always applied over slow (and fast) links.

- EFS (Encrypting File System) and IPsec (IP Security) policies are *always* applied over slow links. You cannot turn off this behavior, even though settings found under the Computer Configuration ➢ Policies ➢ Administrative Templates ➢ System ➢ Group Policy branch imply that you can. This is a bug in the interface, as described in Chapter 3.

- By default, Disk Quotas, Folder Redirection, Internet Explorer settings, and Software Deployment are not applied over slow links. Updated and new logon scripts are also not downloaded over slow links. You can change this default behavior under Computer Configuration ➢ Policies ➢ Administrative Templates ➢ System ➢ Group Policy, as described in Chapter 3. Note that there is a difference between processing scripts policy and running scripts. The scripts themselves run only during logon and boot (computer startup or user logon), but the *updating* of the list of scripts that needs to run can be done in the background. That updating is what I'm referring to here.

Additionally, you can change the definition of what equals a slow link. By default, a slow link is 500Kb or less. You can change the definition for the user settings in User Configuration ➢ Policies ➢ Administrative Templates ➢ System ➢ Group Policy ➢ **Group Policy Slow Link Detection** and for the computer settings in Computer Configuration ➢ Policies ➢ Administrative Templates ➢ System ➢ Group Policy ➢ Group Policy Slow Link Detection. Figure 7.20 shows the user settings. If Group Policy is not being applied to your slow-linked clients, be sure to inspect the slow link definition to make sure they fit.

FIGURE 7.20   Make sure you haven't raised the bar too high for your slower-connected users to receive Group Policy.

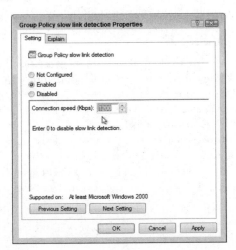

Last, don't forget about your broadband users on DSL or cable modem. Those speeds are sometimes faster than 500Kb and sometimes slower than 500Kb. This could mean that your broadband users might get GPOs on weekends but not when logged on during peak usage times. Therefore, if this happens, set the definition of slow link up or down as necessary.

Finally, it should be noted that if you set the slow link threshold to 0, the client will always assume it's on a fast link.

Troubleshooting NLA in Windows 7

If you're working on a Windows 7 (or Windows Vista) client, you may need to determine if an NLA (Network Location Awareness) refresh has occurred. As I mentioned earlier, NLA is the service that replaces ICMP slow link detection when determining link speed and Domain Controller availability when your client is Windows Vista and later.

If the Domain Controller is not available to the client, either because the client is remote and not connected to the company network or because the Domain Controller is simply not available, Group Policy processing will fail.

When the Domain Controller becomes available again, NLA will detect its presence and trigger an immediate request to perform a background refresh of Group Policy. But here's the trick: NLA will perform this refresh *only* if the previous refresh of Group Policy has failed. If the previous Group Policy refresh succeeded, and *then* the Domain Controller becomes unavailable and *then* available again (before the next Group Policy processing cycle), NLA will not trigger a background refresh. You will be able to see NLA-based Group Policy refresh by looking at the Group Policy Operational Log, described later in the section "Verbose Logging in Windows 7." The event will look identical to that shown in Figure 7.21.

Note that it took as long as 10 minutes for NLA to complete its detection of the Domain Controller and trigger a background Group Policy processing cycle in my testing. So, don't expect an NLA-based Group Policy refresh to happen immediately after your DC becomes available. Depending on your system and network, your mileage may vary.

FIGURE 7.21   Viewing an event indicating an NLA-based Group Policy refresh

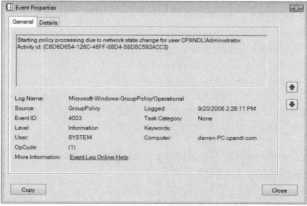

Are the Date and Time Correct on the Client System?

Time differences greater than five minutes between the client system and the validating Domain Controller will cause Kerberos to simply not permit the logon. If you don't have Kerberos, you've got a logon problem, and that's going to yield a Group Policy problem.

Are Your Active Directory Sites Configured Correctly?

Sometimes Group Policy won't apply if your client isn't in a properly defined Active Directory site (that has IP information associated with it). With that in mind, check the subnet the client is on, and verify that it is correctly associated to an Active Directory site and that the site has Domain Controller coverage.

Did You Check the DNS Configuration of the Client?

One of the most frequently encountered problems with Active Directory networks is that things just "stop working" when DNS gets out of whack. Specifically, if you're not seeing Group Policy apply to your client machines, make sure their DNS client is pointing to a Domain Controller or other authoritative source for the domain. If it's pointing to the wrong place or not pointing anywhere, Group Policy will simply not be downloaded. As a colleague of mine likes to say, "Healthy DNS equals a healthy Active Directory."

Moreover, since Windows 2003 and its multiple forests with cross-forest trusts, Group Policy could be applying from just about anywhere and everywhere. It's more important than ever to verify that all DNS server pointers are designed properly and working as they should. For instance, if clients cannot access their "home" Domain Controllers while leveraging a cross-forest trust, they won't get Group Policy.

Finally, to put a fine point on it, Group Policy leverages *only* the fully qualified name. It's not enough to verify that you can resolve a computer named XPPRO1 as opposed to XPPRO1 .corp.com. The first is the NetBIOS name and *not* the fully qualified domain name. The second is the fully qualified domain name. If you find yourself in a DNS resolution situation where resolving the NetBIOS name will work but the fully qualified name will not work, you have a DNS problem that needs to be addressed.

Are You Trying to Set Password or Account Policy on an OU?

As you'll see in Chapter 8, certain Group Policy items, namely password and account policy, cannot be set at the OU level. Rather, these policy settings are only domain wide. The GUI lets you set these policy settings at the OU level, but they don't affect users or machines. Well, that's not true, as you'll see in Chapter 8, but for the purpose of troubleshooting, just remember that you can't have, say, 6-character passwords in the **Sales** OU and 12-character passwords in the **Engineering** OU. It won't work. (You will see in Chapter 8 where password policy affects local accounts in an OU. Stay tuned for that later.)

Did Someone Muck with Security behind the Group Policy Engine's Back?

As you saw in Chapter 3, there are a number of ways to "go around" the back of the Group Policy engine. Remember, though, that these exploits require local administrative access.

However, this implies that users with local administrative access can manually hack the Registry and return their systems to just about however they want. Then, as I've described, Group Policy will not reapply upon background refresh, logon, or reboot. It reapplies changes only when something related to Group Policy has changed, as previously mentioned.

Windows 2000 uses the SECEDIT command to refresh Group Policy, but, as I've stated, it still won't forcefully reapply all the settings—even if the /enforce switch is used (which just forcefully reapplies security settings). Windows XP and later's GPUpdate command will refresh changed Group Policy as well, but its /force switch is quite powerful and will reapply all settings—even those that have not changed.

Is the Target Computer in the Correct OU? Is the Target User in the Correct OU?

This is my personal sore point. This is the one I usually check last, and it's usually what's at fault. That is, I've simply forgotten to place the user object or the computer object into the OU to which I want the GPO to apply. Therefore, the object isn't in the "scope" of where Group Policy will apply.

You can configure all the user or computer policy settings on an OU that you like, but, quite obviously, unless that user or computer object is actually *in* the OU, the target computer will simply not receive the message you're sending. And, no, you cannot just move a security group that contains the user or computer objects and plunk it in the desired OU. Group Policy doesn't work that way. That actual user or computer object needs to be in the site, domain, or OU that the GPO applies! And since no two objects can be in any two OUs at the same time, this can be a challenge.

Security groups are irrelevant—except for filtering.

Is There a Firewall on (or between) Your Domain Controllers?

Windows XP/SP2 and later get a lot of press because they ship with the firewall turned on. And now Windows Server 2008 has the firewall turned on by default, too.

But Windows 2003 (with and without SP1) *also* has a firewall. It's just that, by default, Windows 2003's firewall isn't turned *on*.

So, whatever your Domain Controllers types are, if someone has misconfigured the built-in firewall, your clients will not be able to make contact to then download the Group Policy Objects.

Note that on Windows Server 2008 and later (like Windows Server 2008 R2), your Domain Controllers should automatically open up the correct ports when they're upgraded from a mere server to a Domain Controller. However, I have seen times when they haven't. In such a case, you might need to remove the Active Directory "role" and reinstall it to get the ports to open properly.

Likewise, if someone has put up a hardware firewall or some other software firewall barrier between your client and your Domain Controllers and it's blocking some of the core protocols required by the client to communicate with a Domain Controller, you simply won't be able to get the Domain Controller's attention, and hence you can't download Group Policy.

Did You Disable ICMP (Ping) from Your Clients to Your Domain Controllers? (For XP Machines)

Once a client system makes contact with a Domain Controller to download its Group Policy Objects, it then immediately does a quick "speed test" to see whether it's on a fast network or a slow network. It does this by using the ICMP protocol, more commonly described as Ping.

Before we get into what happens when clients cannot ping Domain Controllers, let's first examine why they might not be able to ping Domain Controllers:

- There's a firewall between the client and Domain Controller that prevents ICMP.

- There's a firewall on the Domain Controller itself (such as Windows 2003's firewall) that prevents ICMP.

- You have a router between the client and the Domain Controller that doesn't like the size of the ICMP test packets the client is using (2048 bytes is the default ICMP packet size used by slow link detection). Therefore, the ICMP test packets are being discarded, and it's as if they're never reaching the Domain Controller at all. Microsoft has a Knowledge Base article about this specific problem and its resolution at `http://tinyurl.com/df9bx`.

Let's examine the first two issues (which are really the same thing). That is, what if ICMP simply cannot be passed along to the Domain Controller? Perhaps a corporate decision to squash ICMP packets has been passed down, and now you just have to "handle it."

If ICMP is disabled, and slow link detection has not been disabled on the client, then no Group Policy processing will occur. It simply fails. Either you have to disable slow link detection or you need to allow ICMP to pass unrestricted between the client and the Domain Controller. Note that when slow link detection is disabled, a "fast link" is *always* assumed. With that in mind, be sure to consider the impact when Software Installation and Folder Redirection come into play.

 You can disable slow link detection by following the instructions in the Microsoft Knowledge Base article at `http://support.microsoft.com/kb/227260/en-us`.

Did Someone Muck with the ACLs of the GPT Part of the GPO in SYSVOL?

There is very, very little reason to manually dig into the guts of the GPO within SYSVOL (that's the GPT part) and manually manipulate the file ACLs. However, uninitiated

administrators will sometimes play—with nasty consequences. And, as stated earlier, Gpotool
/checkacl won't validate the file ACLs on the GPO's GPT parts. In other words, if the ACLs on the GPT are damaged, your best bet is to whack the GPO and restore from backup. The restore process should create the GPO with the correct ACLs upon its re-creation. You can also try using the GPMC to simply make a modification to a damaged GPO's ACLs. Any change will do. By doing so, this can sometimes "re-synchronize" the ACLs on the GPC and GPT, though it depends on how badly the GPT's ACLs have been modified as to whether this method will work.

Client-Side Troubleshooting

One of the most important skills to master is the ability to determine what's going on at the client. By and large, the Group Policy Results tool, which you run from the GPMC, should give you what you need. However, occasionally, only trotting out to the client can truly determine what is happening on your client systems.

You could be roaming the halls, just trying to get the last Krispy Kreme glazed doughnut from the break room, when someone snags you and plops you in their seat for a little impromptu troubleshooting session. They want you to figure out why Group Policy isn't the same today as it was yesterday or why they're suddenly getting new or different settings.

This section will describe the various means for determining the RSoP (Resultant Set of Policy) while sitting at a client or using some remote-control mechanism such as Microsoft SCCM (Systems Center Configuration Manager), VNC (Virtual Networking Client), or even, in the case of Windows XP or Windows 7, Remote Desktop (or Remote Assistance).

As you saw in Chapter 2, the GPMC has two tools to help you tap into this data: Group Policy Results and Group Policy Modeling. However, you have other client-side tools at your disposal. Additionally, I'll describe how to leverage a function in Windows XP, Windows 2003, and Windows 7 to determine a target user's and computer's RSoP remotely.

Let me add a word about Group Policy troubleshooting technique before you run off and try to troubleshoot things. There is a good progression to things that is worth following:

- The first step you should take is to use the RSoP capabilities I describe in the next sections to make sure you know what's happening—which GPOs are applying, which aren't, and why.

- Once you've got that under your belt and still can't find the problem, the next step is to dive into the logs—starting with the Application Event Log on the problem client.

- Then proceed to the userenv.log file for Windows XP (described later in the section "Advanced Group Policy Troubleshooting with Log Files") or the Group Policy Event Logs for Windows 7 (also described later in the section "Leveraging Windows 7 Admin Logs for Troubleshooting").

- If userenv.log doesn't yield results, and you still can't find the problem, progress to CSE-specific logs.

This approach will minimize the time you spend solving a problem and leaves the most complex troubleshooting tasks as a last resort.

RSoP for Windows Clients

Windows Vista and later greatly expand our capacity to determine the RSoP of client machines and users on those machines. In this section, we'll explore several options. The first stop is a grown-up GPResult to help us get to the bottom of what's happening on our client machines. It should be noted that GPResult provides the same information as the GPMC's Group Policy Results Wizard, which can be used to generate the same data if a graphical tool is desired over the GPResult command-line variety.

GPResult for Windows 2003, Windows Vista RTM, and Windows XP

GPResult for Windows Vista, Windows 2003, and Windows XP is more advanced than its Windows 2000 counterpart because it relies on the WMI-based RSoP infrastructure that was added in these newer operating systems. Indeed, you can run GPResult when you're sitting at a user's desktop or at your own desktop, or you can run it remotely and pretend to be that user. If you're running it while sitting at someone's desktop, you'll likely use the following options:

- /v is for verbose mode. It presents the most meaningful information.

- /z is for zuper, er, super-verbose mode. Based on the types of policy settings that affect the user or computer, it displays way more information than you'll likely ever want to see.

- /scope user limits the output to the User-side policy settings, and /scope computer limits the output to the Computer-side policy settings.

> **WARNING**   There was a change in GPResult.exe for Windows Vista and later. Namely, as a regular, nonelevated user running GPResult.exe in Vista and later, you will get only User-side results from the tool. If you attempt to report on Computer-side settings, you will get an Access Denied error until you run the command in an elevated context. Note that you could delegate specific users or groups the right to read this data using the GPMC.

You can mix and match the options. For instance, to display verbose output for the user section, you can run GPResult /v /scope user.

GPResult for Windows 7, Windows Vista/SP1, and Windows Server 2008 and R2

GPResult for Windows 7, Windows Vista/SP1, and Windows Server 2008 and R2 acts a little differently. You can't just type a single gpresult.exe at a command prompt to get data. That's right. One minute you're running plain ol' GPResult on your Windows machine, and now you must run gpresult.exe /R to return the same data.

That's our pals at Microsoft. Just keeping us on our toes.

But the good news is that there are also two new output options:

- `GPResult /H:File.html` will output the results as HTML to a file named `File.html`.
- `GPResult /X:File.xml` will output the results as XML to a filename.

Windows Vista and Windows Server 2008's `GPresult /H` won't show the contents of the Group Policy Preferences in the report. But the Windows 7 and Windows Server 2008 R2 versions, thoughtfully, will.

GPResult in a Modern World

There is one special note about running GPResult for Windows Vista and later: if you try to run it as a regular user to get your RSoP data, you'll only be able to see the User-side settings. Why? Because that's all you have access to in this more secure Windows world. To address this, you have two choices:

Choice 1 Run GPResult twice: once as the user in question, and again as an admin. (You run GPResult as an admin by running a command prompt as an administrative user.) This way, you take the User-side RSoP (that you just ran as the user) and the Computer-side RSoP (that you just ran as an administrative user). Then, both of those halves make up the genuine RSoP. Frustrating, but necessary with the way the security within Windows Vista and later prevents regular users from seeing this. What makes this more frustrating is that if you (the Administrator) have never logged in to a particular client machine, you get an error from GPResult that expresses that there is no RSoP data for that admin account. So, in the following screen shot, we're logged in as Joe User trying to get his RSoP data (top window). As stated, the Computer side is inaccessible to him by default. So, we perform the runas command to get our own command-line window as the Administrator (bottom window). To counter, we then run GPResult /scope:computer. We still get an error about the *User* side not having data (bottom window), even though we simply want the *Computer* side of the equation. Frustrating to the max.

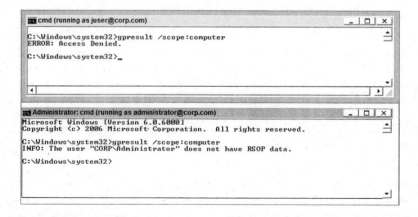

Choice 2   Use the GPMC to delegate users the ability to see their own Computer-side RSoP data. Again, this isn't permitted by default in a Windows Vista or Windows 7 world. This works just fine for XP machines. So, in my opinion, there's very little reason not to just permit the user to see it.

Assuming you wanted to permit everyone in the domain to see their own RSoP data, we need to review how to perform delegation (discussed in Chapter 2). If we wanted to perform this delegation, we would use the GPMC, click the domain level, and click the Delegation tab. In the Permission drop-down, we would select "Read Group Policy Results data," then add in Authenticated Users (or modify the rights over the Domain Users group, which is always already listed) and select to apply to "This container and all child containers."

You can see a screen shot of this process here.

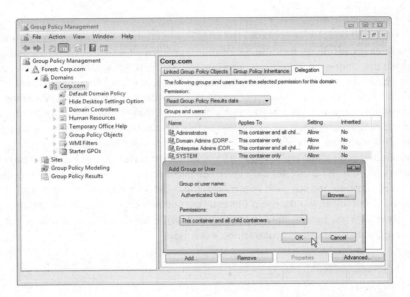

In this sidebar we talked about what it takes to get the RSoP of a machine if we're physically sitting down at it. It's a totally different story if you're looking to get this data remotely, from another machine. And the equation gets even more intense if you're looking to delegate rights to a nonadministrative user (like someone on the help desk). A little later in this chapter, we review how to successfully retrieve Group Policy Results and Group Policy Modeling data as a nonadmin user. Be sure to read those sections to get the full picture, or you'll be left out in the cold wondering why you're getting Access Denied messages.

Those sections are "Remotely Calculating a Client's RSoP (When You've Delegated Permissions to Someone Who's Not a Local Administrator of the Target Machine)" and "Remotely Calculating a Client's Group Policy Modeling Analysis Data (When You've Delegated Permissions to Someone Who's Not a Local Administrator of the Target Machine)."

Here's the result of running GPResult with no arguments while logged on to the XPPRO1 workstation (which is in the **Human Resources Computers** OU) as Frank Rizzo (who is in the **Human Resources Users** OU). I have slightly modified the output for formatting purposes. Note that some of the display might be somewhat different from yours.

```
Microsoft (R) Windows (R) XP Operating System Group Policy Result tool v2.0
Copyright (C) Microsoft Corp. 1981-2001


Created On 12/30/2010 at 10:00:40 PM



RSOP results for CORP\frizzo on XPPRO1 : Logging Mode
----------------------------

OS Type:                    Microsoft Windows XP Professional
OS Configuration:           Member Workstation
OS Version:                 5.1.2600
Domain Name:                CORP
Domain Type:                Windows 2000
Site Name:                  Default-First-Site-Name
Roaming Profile:
Local Profile:              C:\Documents and Settings\frizzo
Connected over a slow link?: No


COMPUTER SETTINGS
---------
    CN=XPPRO1,OU=Human Resources Computers,OU=Human Resources,DC=CORP,DC=COM
    Last time Group Policy was applied: 12/30/2010 at 9:58:06 PM
    Group Policy was applied from:    dc01.CORP.COM
    Group Policy slow link threshold:  500 kbps

    Applied Group Policy Objects
    ----------------
        Auto-Launch calc.exe
        Default Domain Policy

    The following GPOs were not applied because they were filtered out
    ----------------------------------
        Prohibit Changing Sounds
            Filtering:  Not Applied (Empty)
```

    Prevent Changing Screen Saver
       Filtering: Not Applied (Empty)

    Local Group Policy
       Filtering: Not Applied (Empty)

The computer is a part of the following security groups:

    BUILTIN\Administrators
    Everyone
    BUILTIN\Users
    XPPRO1$
    Computers-That-Get-the-Auto-Launch Calc.exe-GPO
    Domain Computers
    NT AUTHORITY\NETWORK
    NT AUTHORITY\Authenticated Users

USER SETTINGS

    CN=Frank Rizzo,OU=Human Resources Users,OU=Human Resources,DC=CORP,DC=COM
    Last time Group Policy was applied: 12/30/2010 at 9:59:44 PM
    Group Policy was applied from: dc01.CORP.COM
    Group Policy slow link threshold: 500 kbps

    Applied Group Policy Objects

       Hide Mouse Pointers Option / Restore Screen Saver Option
       Default Domain Policy
       Prohibit Changing Sounds
       Prevent Changing Screen Saver
       Local Group Policy

    The user is a part of the following security groups:

       Domain Users
       Everyone
       BUILTIN\Users
       LOCAL
       NT AUTHORITY\INTERACTIVE
       NT AUTHORITY\Authenticated Users

You can redirect the output to a text file with GPResult > filename.txt.

You can glean all sorts of juicy tidbits from GPResult. Here are the key areas to inspect when troubleshooting client RSoP:

- Find the "Applied Group Policy Objects" entries for both the user and computer. Remember that Group Policy is applied from the local computer first, then the site level, then the domain level, and then each nested OU. If a setting is unexpected on the client, simply use the provided information along with the Group Policy Object Editor to start tracking the errant GPO.

- Use the "Last time Group Policy was applied" entry to see the last time the GPO was applied—via either initial or background refresh processing. Use GPUpdate to refresh this, and then ensure that the value is updated when you rerun GPResult.

- Use the spelled-out distinguished name of the computer and user objects (for example, CN=Frank Rizzo, OU=Human Resources Users, DC=corp, and DC=com) to verify that the user and computer objects are located where you think they should be in Active Directory. If they are not, verify the location of the user and computer accounts using Active Directory Users and Computers. You might need to reboot this client machine if the location in Active Directory doesn't check out.

- Use "The user is a part of the following security groups" and "The computer is a part of the following security groups" sections to verify that the user or computer is in the groups you expect. Perhaps your user or computer object is inside a group that is denied access to either the "Read" or "Apply Group Policy" permissions on the GPO you were expecting. Note that if you make a change to a computer's security group membership, Group Policy will not pick up that change unless you reboot the computer. There is no way around this, unfortunately. The same holds true for user group changes—the user will need to re–log on before the security group changes take.

- Find the "Connected over a slow link?" entry for the log and the "Group Policy slow link threshold" entries for both the user and computer. Remember that the various areas of Group Policy are processed differently when coming over slow links. (See Chapters 3.)

- Find the section "The following GPOs were not applied because they were filtered out" for both the user and the computer halves. If you have GPOs listed here, the user or computer was, in fact, in the site, domain, or OU that the GPO was supposed to apply to. However, the GPOs listed here have not applied this user or computer for a variety of reasons. GPResult can tell you why this has happened. Here are some of the common reasons:

Denied (Security) The user or computer has been explicitly denied "Read" and "Apply Group Policy" rights to process the GPO. For instance, in the previous example, the "Auto-Launch Calc.exe" doesn't apply to XPPRO1 because in Chapter 2, we explicitly denied the XPPRO1 computer object the ability to process the "Apply Group Policy" attribute.

Not Applied (Empty)   This GPO doesn't have any policy settings set in the user or computer half. For instance, in the previous example, the "Prohibit Changing Sounds" GPO doesn't have any Computer-side policy settings. Hence, this GPO doesn't apply to Frank's computer object. Specifically, here the Group Policy engine is seeing that the number of revisions for either the User or Computer half is 0. This is tied to the version number of the GPO, so if the version number is not updated correctly when a GPO change is made, the GPO could be mistakenly viewed as empty.

Not Applied (Unknown Reason)   Usually Block Inheritance has been used, or the user doesn't have rights to read the GPO (though other, truly "unknown reasons" could also be valid). In the previous example, the "Prevent Changing Screen Saver" GPO, which is set at the site level, won't apply to Frank because we've blocked inheritance at the Human Resources OU.

Three Different GPResults—Three Different Outputs!

If you want to take GPResult to the next level, use it with the /v switch. You can then see which Registry settings are specifically being altered by the GPOs. This could be useful if you want to manually dive into the Registry and perform the same punch the policy setting is doing on a machine that isn't connected to Active Directory and see if you get the same results.

However, running GPResult /v on various machine types (Windows 2000, Windows XP, Windows 2003, Windows Server 2008, Windows Vista, or Windows 7) can return different outputs. For the sake of brevity, here are three comparison snippets to illustrate some additional information possible with GPResult /v. This output has been taken out to show you some specific details and also formatted slightly for readability.

GPResult /v for Windows XP is the least useful. When you run it, you'll get output similar to the following:

```
Administrative Templates
GPO: Prohibit Changing Sounds
Setting: Software\Microsoft\Windows\CurrentVersion\Policies\System
State:   Enabled
```

This output merely tells you that the GPO "Prohibit Changing Sounds" manipulates a Registry key somewhere in the path specified in the Setting field. Whoopee.

When you run the command on a Windows Server 2008, Windows 2003, Windows Vista, or Windows 7 computer, you get the following:

```
Administrative Templates
-------------
GPO: Prohibit Changing Sounds
```

```
KeyName: Software\Microsoft\Windows\CurrentVersion\Policies\
System\NoDispBackgroundPage
Value: 1, 0, 0, 0
State: Enabled
```

This output is more useful, because it shows you that it's the NoDispBackgroundPage Registry entry with the value of 1 in the Registry that is performing the function. I'm guessing the difference in output between Windows XP and Windows 2003 and Windows Vista is just a GPResult bug. But the point is that with GPResult on Windows XP, the output displayed is, in fact, not as useful as the output from the other operating systems.

However, the most useful GPResult /v output comes from the GPResult in the Windows 2000 Resource Kit! (Yes! Windows 2000!)

```
The user received "Registry" settings from these GPOs:
    Prohibit Changing Sounds
        Revision Number:   3
        Unique Name:    {1ABE8B36-66A0-4DF0-80D0-A9B4A8C34DB1}
        Domain Name:    corp.com
        Linked to:      Domain (DC=corp,DC=com)
    The following settings were applied from: Prohibit Changing Sounds
        KeyName:     Software\Microsoft\Windows\CurrentVersion\Policies\System
        ValueName:   NoChangingSoundScheme
        ValueType:   REG_DWORD
        Value:    0x00000001
```

The Windows 2000 GPResult /v shows you the ValueName (like the Windows 2003 version), but it also shows you the ValueType (REG_DWORD). Additionally, it can easily show you the association between the GPO friendly name (say, "Prohibit Changing Sounds") and the GUID (in my case, {1ABE8B36-66A0-4DF0-80D0-A9B4A8C34DB1}). You might need this information later with other tools such as the Event Viewer, which may or may not use the friendly name.

So my advice? The GPResult built into Windows XP and later is much better for basic troubleshooting. Its output describing *why* specific GPOs are not being processed is excellent. However, keep a copy of the Windows 2000 version of GPResult handy. It runs just fine on all versions of Windows, and because of its additional functions in displaying both the Registry and the GPO GUID, you can get a lot closer to knowing *what* has been changed.

Remotely Calculating a Client's RSoP (Using the GPResult from Windows XP and Later)

The Windows 2000 version of GPResult doesn't work the way that the Windows XP and later version does. The more modern version of GPResult has a secret weapon tucked up its sleeve. You can almost hear it say, "Are you talkin' to me?"

Its weapon is that it can tap into the WMI provider built into those operating systems. GPResult is like the GPMC's Group Policy Results Wizard. That is, it can be run from any Windows XP and later machine, and, provided the target machine is turned on, the system can collect information about any particular user who has ever logged on locally. It's then a simple matter of displaying the results. You run GPResult, point it to a system, and provide the name of the user whose RSoP data you wish to collect.

This magic only works on Windows XP and later machines, as both source computers and target computers. Windows 2000 computers don't have a tap into this WMI magic, so they can't play.

There are two more important cautions here (which I talked about in the section "GPResult in a Modern World." That is, this magic works only if the target user has ever logged on to the target machine. They only need to have logged on just once, and they don't even need to be logged on while you run the test. But if the target user has *never* logged on to the target machine, remotely calculating GPResult for that user will fail. Additionally, remotely trying to get a Windows XP/Service Pack 2 and later's RSoP via GPResult will fail if the Windows Firewall is enabled.

As described in Chapter 2, either turn off the Windows Firewall or enable the Windows XP/Service Pack 2 policy setting **Windows Firewall: Allow Inbound Remote Administration Exception**, which can be located in Computer Configuration ➢ Policies ➢ Administrative Templates ➢ Network ➢ Network Connections ➢ Windows Firewall ➢ Domain (or Standard) Profile. This setting does affect Windows XP/SP2 and later machines.

Or, for your Windows 7 clients, you can really be gung ho and use the new Windows Firewall with Advanced Security (which you'll learn about in Chapter 8), which of course has an alternate method only valid for Windows Vista and Windows 7.

This would be found under Computer Configuration ➢ Policies ➢ Windows Settings ➢ Security Settings ➢ Windows Firewall with Advanced Security ➢Inbound Rules.

With that in mind, here are your additional Windows XP and later `GPResult` options:

- `/s <target system name or IP address>` points to the target system.
- `/user <optional domain\username>` collects RSoP data for the target user.

You can combine any of the aforementioned GPResult switches as well. If you log onto DC01 and want to see only the User-side policy settings when Frank Rizzo logs onto XPPRO1, type the following:

```
gpresult /user frizzo /s xppro1 /scope:user
```

Again, this command succeeds only if Frank has ever logged on to XPPRO1 (which he has).

GPResult is much better at telling you *why* a GPO is applying rather than *what* specific policy settings are contained within a GPO. For instance, notice that at no time did GPResult tell us what policy settings were contained in the local GPO. And, even when we performed a `GPResult /v`, we only found out the Registry keys that were modified—not the proper name of the specific policy setting that is doing the work. For these tasks, we'll need to use the GPMC (as seen in Chapter 2).

Remotely Calculating a Client's RSoP (When You've Delegated Permissions to Someone Who's Not a Local Administrator of the Target Machine)

In Chapter 2 (and to a lesser extent in this chapter), we talked about the idea of opening up the Windows XP or Windows 7 firewall to **Windows Firewall: Allow Inbound Remote Administration Exception**. Again, this policy setting is located in Computer Configuration ➢ Policies ➢ Windows Firewall ➢ Domain Profile.

The idea is that you can't remotely grab an RSoP using either `GPResult.exe` or the GPMC's Group Policy Results Wizard without being able to communicate to the WMI provider on the target machine. To do this, at a minimum you need to open up ports 135 and 445, which is precisely what this particular policy setting will do on a computer.

But there's a little twist (which we've already discussed): you need rights to view the RSoP data. Now, if you're a local administrator on the target machine, you already have all the rights you need. You just have to open up that firewall enough to get that data.

But if you want to delegate rights to, say, the help desk (or another nonadministrative group), you do, in fact, need an extra boost to ensure that they can read the RSoP data. (If you need a refresher on how to delegate the permission in the first place, be sure to read the section "Special Group Policy Operation Delegations" in Chapter 2.) Again, this area is located in the Delegation tab on the OU (or domain or site) you want to delegate rights to.

Once you've performed the delegation of the "Read Group Policy Results data" right on the user and/or computer you want, you also need to perform these very important additional delegation steps. (Again, these steps are required only if you've delegated this ability to a non-administrator of the target machine.)

For instance, let's assume that Tom User (from the help desk) needs access to read Group Policy Results data from a computer that Brett Wier is using (Win7.corp.com). First, you delegate rights upon the OU that contains Win7.corp.com and ensure that Tom can "Read Group Policy Results data." But even if you do that, as soon as Tom tries to run the Group Policy Results Wizard, he gets an "Access is denied" message as seen in Figure 7.22.

To open it up a little (and decrease your security a little, too), you'll need to create and link a GPO that affects the target computer's OU. Then, make sure the following policy settings are enabled within that GPO:

1. We already covered this one, but just to be sure you have it in place: Computer Configuration ➢ Policies ➢ Administrative Templates ➢ Network Connections ➢ Windows Firewall ➢ Domain Profile ➢ **Windows Firewall: Allow Inbound Remote Administration Exception**. Choose which subnets to allow inbound requests from (or specify * to allow all subnets).

2. Computer Configuration ➤ Policies ➤ Windows Settings ➤ Security Settings ➤ Local Policies ➤ Security Options ➤ **DCOM: Machine Access Restrictions in SDDL syntax.** When you edit the policy setting, you'll first select "Define this policy setting," then click Edit Security, add in Tom User, and specify to allow Remote Access. When you do this, a security descriptor is (thankfully) automatically built, like O:BAG:BAD:(A;;CDCLC;;;) and is usually quite long. You can see a screen shot of this in Figure 7.23 (though the security descriptor isn't in the screen shot, because I haven't hit OK yet).

FIGURE 7.22 Tom doesn't have access to run Group Policy Results against machines for which he isn't also a local administrator.

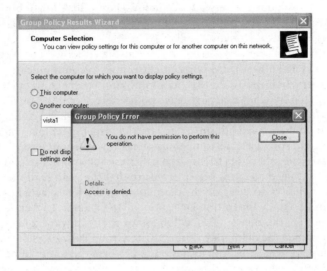

3. Computer Configuration ➤ Policies ➤ Windows Settings ➤ Security Settings ➤ Local Policies ➤ Security Options ➤ **DCOM: Machine Launch Restrictions in SDDL syntax.** Again, be sure to click "Define this policy setting." Then, add in the same person (Tom User) and grant the "Remote Launch: Allow" and "Remote Activation: Allow" rights.

Since you've changed the Computer-side settings, be sure to run gpupdate /force on the target machine (or just reboot it).

When you do, you'll give nonadministrative users the ability to read another computer's RSoP data using the GPMC's Group Policy Results Wizard.

After these steps are performed, you've delegated a user (or group, like the Help Desk) and have now enabled the ability to "reach out" and see what's going on at other machines—even if they're not a local admin. Don't forget about the golden rule here, though: if the target machine's firewall is blocking your incoming request, even though you've now delegated the permission, it still ain't gonna work.

FIGURE 7.23   For each DCOM permission, add in the delegated user and specify they have Remote Access: Allow permissions.

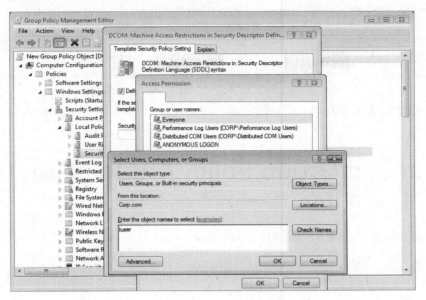

Remotely Calculating a Client's Group Policy Modeling Analysis Data (When You've Delegated Permissions to Someone Who's Not a Local Administrator of the Target Machine)

This is a similar situation to what we encountered earlier. Imagine you've given Tom User from the help desk the rights to "Perform Group Policy Modeling analyses." If you need a refresher on how to delegate the permission in the first place, read Chapter 2's "Special Group Policy Operation Delegations" section. Be sure to delegate the permission on both the OUs that contain the user and computer accounts or you'll be stuck with seeing only half the results data. However, just performing the delegation steps isn't enough—you'll still get an Access Denied message from the Group Policy Modeling Wizard as soon as you try to pick the Domain Controller on which to perform the calculations.

So, since Windows Server 2003/SP1, the default security for DCOM permissions has changed, requiring changes akin to what you saw in the previous section. But here's the trick: you're not modifying the target computer's DCOM settings; you're modifying the Windows Server 2003/SP1's Domain Controller settings. To do this, create and link a GPO on the **Domain Controllers** OU. I suggest you *don't* modify the default Domain Controller for this purpose, though it would work just fine. Then, modify the GPO as follows:

1. Computer Configuration ➢ Policies ➢ Windows Settings ➢ Security Settings ➢ Local Policies ➢ Security Options ➢ **DCOM: Machine Access Restrictions in SDDL syntax.**

When you edit the policy setting, you'll first select "Define this policy setting," then click Edit Security, add in Tom User, and specify to allow Remote Access. When you do this, a security descriptor is (thankfully) automatically built, like O:BAG:BAD:(A;;CDCLC;;;) and is usually quite long. You can see a screen shot of this in Figure 7.23.

2. Computer Configuration ➢ Policies ➢ Windows Settings ➢ Security Settings ➢ Local Policies ➢ Security Options ➢ **DCOM: Machine Launch Restrictions in SDDL syntax**. Again, be sure to click "Define this policy setting." Then, add in the same person (Tom User) and grant the "Remote Launch: Allow" and "Remote Activation: Allow" rights.

Now, Tom User from the help desk can see Brett Wier (and Brett's computer) Group Policy Analysis data using the Group Policy Modeling Wizard.

Advanced Group Policy Troubleshooting with Log Files

We've already explored some of the techniques used to troubleshoot Group Policy applications. You can enable some underlying operating system troubleshooting tools to help diagnose just what the heck is going on when the unexpected occurs.

Using the Event Viewer

Quite possibly, the most overlooked and underutilized tool in Windows is the Event Viewer. The client's Event Viewer logs both the successful and unsuccessful application of Group Policy (see Figure 7.24).

FIGURE 7.24   The Event Viewer is a terrific place to start your troubleshooting journey.

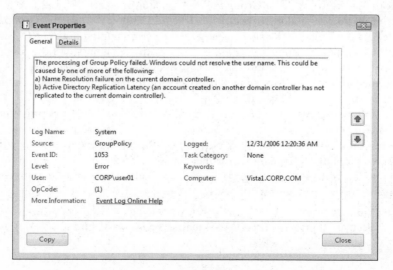

Before beating your head against the wall, check the client's Event Log for relevant Group Policy records. The Event Log in Windows XP and Windows 2003 spits out much more information and many more warnings than did the Event Log in Windows 2000—so take advantage of it.

In Windows 7, the Event Log takes on a whole new importance with respect to Group Policy troubleshooting. In fact, as we talk in this section about logs that are useful in troubleshooting, we'll talk about how this all changes in a Windows Vista/Windows 7 world.

In Figure 7.24, the Event Log returned an error code of 1053. Doing a quick search in Microsoft TechNet, you can find a related article, 261007 (http://support.microsoft.com/kb/261007), which shows that the client is pointing to an incorrect DNS server. Again, search the Microsoft Knowledge Base when you find an event that might be at fault. You might find a hidden gem there—perfectly ready to solve your problem.

Diagnostic Event Logging (for XP)

If you want to go bananas, you can enable *diagnostic logging* to supercharge your Event Log in Windows 2000, Windows XP, and Windows 2003. To do so, you must create a Registry key to the client machine. Traverse to

```
HKEY_Local_Machine\Software\Microsoft\Windows NT\CurrentVersion
```

Create a Diagnostics key, but leave the Class entry empty. You can specify logging types by creating one of two REG_DWORD keys:

RunDiagnosticLoggingGroupPolicy   Create this REG_DWORD to log only Group Policy events. To enable logging, set the data value to 1. Log entries appear in the Application Log.

AppMgmtDebugLevel   Create this REG_DWORD, but do so with a data value of 4b in hexadecimal. At the next targeted software deployment, you'll find a log in the local \windows\debug\usermode folder named appmgmt.log, which can also aid in troubleshooting why applications fail to load.

> Some older Microsoft documentation also shows RunDiagnosticLogging-IntelliMirror and RunDiagnosticLoggingAppDeploy keys as viable options for the Diagnostics key. These entries are apparently documentation bugs and do absolutely nothing in Windows.

When you've finished debugging, delete the Diagnostic keys so your Event Logs don't fill up.

Diagnostic Event Logging (Windows 7)

In Windows Vista and later (like Windows 7 and Windows Server 2008), Event Log entries related to Group Policy have changed significantly. First of all, Group Policy–related events have moved from the Application to the System Log. The system generates Group Policy events with an event source of (who woulda guessed?) GroupPolicy, as shown in Figure 7.25.

FIGURE 7.25   Viewing the Windows 7 system log and Group Policy events

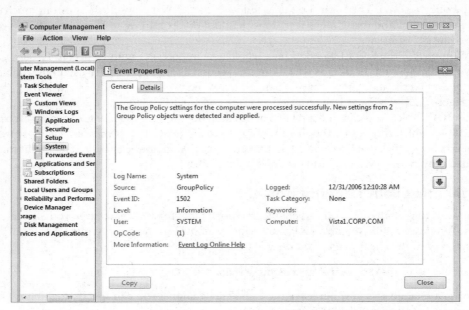

The logging of Group Policy events in Windows 7 is on by default, so you don't need to enable anything specifically. You can simply filter events in this log with a source of GroupPolicy and get a snapshot of GP Processing. The events recorded in this log related to Group Policy are a summary of each processing event—they tell you things like whether Group Policy processing proceeded successfully, which Domain Controller was used to process policy, and how many GPOs were processed. They do not provide deep levels of detail. In the next section, we'll talk about how you can get that detail out of the Event Log in Windows 7.

Turning On Verbose Logging

Sometimes, all the server pieces are working perfectly, but the end result on the client is cockeyed. You can examine Group Policy step by step by turning on *verbose logging*, which goes beyond the diagnostic Event Log Registry hacks.

Verbose Logging (for XP)

When you enable verbose logging by editing the Registry at the client, you are telling the system to generate extra events in a file called USERENV.LOG in the \windows\debug\usermode folder for XP (or \winnt\debug\usermode for Windows 2000). By default, this file is enabled in Windows XP and Server 2003 but is not set to verbose mode. You can then examine the file to see what the client thinks is really happening.

To enable verbose logging, follow these steps:

1. Log on locally to the client system as the Administrator.

2. Run REGEDIT.

3. In the Registry Editor, traverse to HKEY_Local_Machine\Software\Microsoft\Windows NT\CurrentVersion\Winlogon.

4. In the Edit DWORD Value dialog box, add a REG_DWORD value by entering **UserEnvDebug-Level** in the Value Name box, and in the Value Data box, enter the hex value of **10002**, as shown in Figure 7.26. Click OK.

FIGURE 7.26   Verbose logging requires a hack to the Registry.

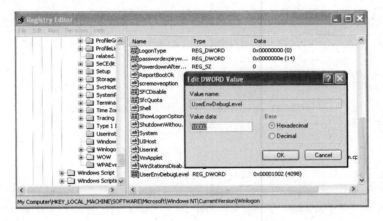

5. Close the Registry Editor.

The hex value 10002 signifies verbose logging. The hex value 10001 signifies to log only errors and warnings. The hex value 10000 doesn't log anything.

Note that after you make this entry in Windows XP or Windows 2003, verbose logging is enabled right away, but Windows 2000 often requires a reboot for the logging change to take effect. After you modify the entry, log off as the local Administrator, and log on as someone with many GPOs that would affect their user object—say, Frank Rizzo in the **Human Resources Users** OU. After logging on as Frank, you can immediately log off and back on as the Administrator for the workstation and then read the log file.

You can also hack the Registry at a command prompt. You can use the RUNAS command to run the command prompt as the Administrator. For this system, type **runas /user:XPPro1\administrator cmd**, and type the password to log on as the Administrator.

In the Userenv.log file in the \windows\debug\usermode folder, you should come across the following snippet. The output here has been truncated and formatted for better reading and for the sake of example. Additionally, line headers such as ProcessGPOs, AddGPO, and SearchDSObject have all been removed.

```
Starting user Group Policy (Background) processing...
Starting computer Group Policy (Background) processing...
User name is:  CN=Frank Rizzo,OU=Human Resources Users,
OU=Human Resources,DC=corp,DC=com,
Domain name is:  CORP
Domain controller is:  \\DC01.corp.com  Domain DN is corp.com
network name is 192.168.2.0


User name is:  CN=XPPRO1,OU=Human Resources Computers,
OU=Human Resources,DC=corp,DC=com,
Domain name is:  CORP


Domain controller is:  \\DC01.corp.com  Domain DN is corp.com
Calling GetGPOInfo for normal policy mode



No site name defined.  Skipping site policy.

Searching <OU=Human Resources Users,OU=Human Resources,DC=corp,DC=com>
Found GPO(s):
<[LDAP://cn={45E8B3A8-AB97-4480-ACE9-B42F2B3C7EFA},
cn=policies,cn=system,DC=corp,DC=com;0]>

Searching <OU=Human Resources,DC=corp,DC=com>
Found GPO(s):  < >
<OU=Human Resources,DC=corp,DC=com> has the Block From Above attribute set
Searching <DC=corp,DC=com>

Found GPO(s):
<[LDAP://cn={45E8B3A8-AB97-4480-ACE9-B42F2B3C7EFA},
cn=policies,cn=system,DC=corp,DC=com;0][LDAP://CN=
{31B2F340-016D-11D2-945F-00C04FB984F9},CN=Policies,CN=System,DC=corp,DC=com;0]>

GPO will not be added to the list since the
Block flag is set and this GPO is not in enforce mode.
```

```
Searching
<CN={45E8B3A8-AB97-4480-ACE9-B42F2B3C7EFA},CN=Policies,CN=System,DC=corp,DC=com>
User does not have access to the GPO and so will not be applied.
Found functionality version of:  2
Found file system path of:
<\\corp.com\SysVol\corp.com\Policies{45E8B3A8-AB97-4480-ACE9-B42F2B3C7EFA} >
Sysvol access skipped because GPO is not getting applied.
Found common name of:  < {45E8B3A8-AB97-4480-ACE9-B42F2B3C7EFA} >
Found display name of:
<Hide Display Settings Option / Restore Screen Saver Option >
Found user version of:  GPC is 2, GPT is 65535
Found flags of:  0
Found extensions:  [{35378EAC-683F-11D2-A89A-00C04FBBCFA2}
{0F6B957E-509E-11D1-A7CC-0000F87571E3}]
```

You can learn a lot quickly by doing a little sleuthing inside the results. First, the computer is processing in Normal mode (as opposed to Loopback mode). And, while you're here, you can sniff out three back-to-back "errors" that I've detailed next.

The first error occurred due to some Active Directory site misconfiguration error. The text is clear: "No site name defined. Skipping site policy."

The second error occurred when the GPO represented by GUID {45E8B3A8-AB97-4480-ACE9-B42F2B3C7EFA} wasn't applied. This is the "Prohibit Changing Sounds" GPO we created and linked to the domain. The report states that the "GPO will not be added to the list since the Block flag is set and this GPO is not in enforce mode." This indicates that the GPO isn't being enforced while the OU level (**Human Resources**) is blocking inheritance.

The last error occurred when the GPO with the {45E8B3A8-AB97-4480-ACE9-B42F2B3C7EFA} was not applied due to "User does not have access to the GPO." In my case, the GUID matched with the "Hide Mouse Pointers Option / Restore Screen Saver Option" GPO. Back in Chapter 2, one example denied the HR-OU-Admins security group the access to read that GPO, so it would not apply to them. Frank Rizzo is a member of the HR-OU-Admins group and, hence, does not get the GPO.

You might also want to check out a free tool that can make the job of parsing this log a bit easier. The guys at SysPro have a free tool that does the hard work. Check it out at www.sysprosoft.com/policyreporter.shtml. It's also listed on www.GPanswers.com in the "Third-Party Solutions" guide.

Some other information you can glean from this file includes the timestamp when the event occurred. Each line of the userenv.log file includes some text that looks like the following:

```
USERENV(2b8.2bc) 09:09:57:250
```

The meaning of this text is relatively straightforward. Userenv is the process under which these events are occurring. (2b8.2bc) indicates, in hexadecimal form, the process and thread ID of this particular event, and then the time shown indicates the time that this event is occurring. The time is broken down as hour:minute:second:hundreths-of-a-second. The process and thread ID tag is useful if, for example, you are troubleshooting Group Policy processing after issuing a gpupdate command. Because GPUpdate runs both computer and user processing at roughly the same time, each of these will have unique thread IDs but events will be intertwined with each other. So, you can use the thread ID to distinguish a user processing event from a computer processing one.

Additionally, the one piece of information that userenv.log will tell you (that you can't get very easily elsewhere) is the time interval until the *next* background processing update. This usually comes at the end of a given processing cycle and looks something like this:

```
USERENV(2b8.908) 09:15:41:062 GPOThread:
Next refresh will happen in 105 minutes
```

The downside to userenv.log is that it also logs user profile activity, which can muddy up your Group Policy troubleshooting. Because of this, I usually just delete or rename the existing userenv.log file in the C:\windows\debug\usermode folder. Then, I'll run GPUpdate. When it's finished, my userenv.log file contains *only* the data from that last Group Policy processing cycle. In short, this process makes it much easier to troubleshoot.

Other Types of Verbose Logging

In addition to userenv.log, some of the individual CSEs provide their own verbose log files that you can enable with Registry tweaks. When you can't get the information you need from the Event Log or userenv.log, your next step is to try to track down the problem with one of these CSE-specific logs. While not every CSE creates its own log file, most of the important ones do, and you can use these logs to get more detailed information about a particular Group Policy area that has gone awry. The following table lists all available CSE-specific logs and Registry values needed to enable them.

Component	Location of Log	Location in Registry	Value
Security CSE	%windir%\Security\Logs\WinLogon.log	HKLM\Software\Microsoft\Windows NT\CurrentVersion\Winlogon\GPExtensions\{827d319e-6eac-11d2-a4ea-00c04f79f83a}	ExtensionDebugLevel DWORD 2

Component	Location of Log	Location in Registry	Value
Folder Redirection CSE	%windir%\Debug\ UserMode\FDeploy .log (Windows XP and 2003 only) Windows 7 / Vista / 2008 in Application Log.	HKLM\Software\ Microsoft\Windows NT\CurrentVersion\ Diagnostics	FDeployDebugLevel DWORD 0x0B
Software Installation CSE	%windir%\ Debug\UserMode\ AppMgmt.log	HKLM\Software\ Microsoft\Windows NT\CurrentVersion\ Diagnostics	AppMgmtDebugLevel DWORD 0x9b

See Darren Mar-Elia's website www.GPOguy.com, for a great ADM template that helps automate these Registry punches, if needed, on your client machines.

Verbose Logging in Windows 7

Windows Vista introduced major changes to the information that the Group Policy engine provides for you to troubleshoot problems. And that same information is also now available for Windows 7 and Windows Server 2008 and R2.

This is great news! But in order to best leverage that new data, you're going to need to know where and how to find it. This section is devoted to that task.

The newer operating systems no longer keep verbose Group Policy logging information in userenv.log. Instead, this type of detailed logging has moved to the System Event Log—which in the context of Group Policy is referred to as the *Admin Log*—and into a new place called the *Group Policy Operational Log*.

Both of these logs leverage the new features in the code-named "Crimson" Event Log system. This is a good thing because the events logged here are now clearer and more easily collected than they were in the userenv.log file. Crimson also has some neat features, such as subscription, that I'll introduce here and that can further help with your Group Policy troubleshooting tasks. The Group Policy logs are also enabled as verbose by default, so you don't need to bother with turning on and off Event Logs with Registry hacks.

To find the Group Policy Operational Log, simply open the Event Viewer and drill into Applications and Services Logs ➢ Microsoft ➢ Windows ➢ Group Policy ➢ Operational. What you'll get is a set of events similar to those found in Figure 7.27.

FIGURE 7.27   Viewing the Group Policy Operational Log in Windows 7

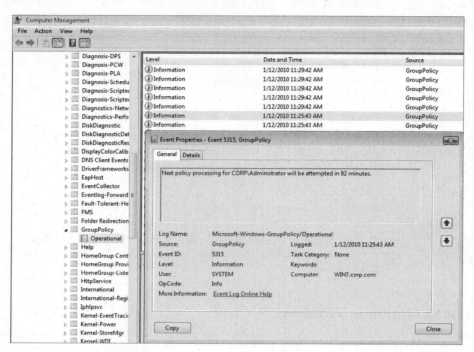

As you can see from the figure, the Group Policy Operational Log has more detailed and useful information than the userenv.log, such as the amount of time it took to process Group Policy for a user. If you're using Windows Vista or later, the Operational Log is going to be your best Group Policy friend and will provide almost all the information you need to track down Group Policy problems. I say "almost" because while Windows Vista and later has made great strides in consolidating the userenv.log file into the Event Logs, the CSE-specific logs that I mentioned earlier for previous versions of Windows still exist in the modern operating system and are still stored in separate text files that must be explicitly enabled.

Leveraging Windows 7 Admin Logs for Troubleshooting

Let's look at how you might use the Windows Vista and later Admin Log for troubleshooting a Group Policy problem.

The System Log is designed to give you high-level information about the state of the Group Policy engine. So it will tell you things such as if computer Group Policy processing succeeded or failed, but it won't necessarily tell you what happened or why (see Figure 7.28).

One other useful piece of information the Admin Log will give you is the time it took for Group Policy processing to occur. You can see this in the event in Figure 7.28 by clicking the Details tab in the lower preview pane of the Event Viewer, as shown in Figure 7.29.

FIGURE 7.28   Viewing a Group Policy Admin Log event

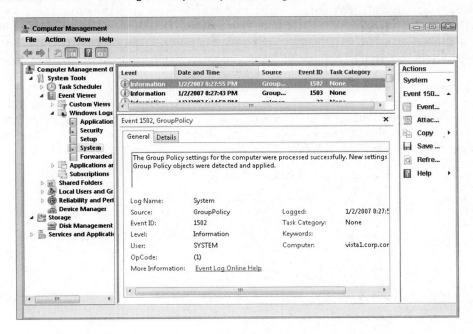

FIGURE 7.29   Viewing the Group Policy processing time

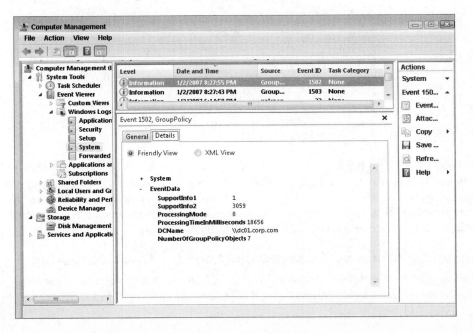

Note that in Figure 7.29, the ProcessingTimeInMilliseconds field shows 18656 milliseconds, or 18.656 seconds. That is how long it took for computer processing to occur. Also note that the ProcessingMode is listed as 0. That indicates that the computer is working in normal processing mode, as opposed to loopback processing. If the value were 1 or 2, that would indicate that loopback in Merge mode or Replace mode, respectively, was enabled. And, of course, the DCName field indicates which Domain Controller serviced the Group Policy engine's request for Group Policy processing during the last cycle.

In addition to telling you when things are good with Group Policy, the System Log will tell you when things aren't so good. And, new to Windows Vista and Windows Server 2008, the failure logs will also try to give you some hints as to why things aren't working. For example, check out the event in Figure 7.30.

FIGURE 7.30   Viewing a Group Policy failure event

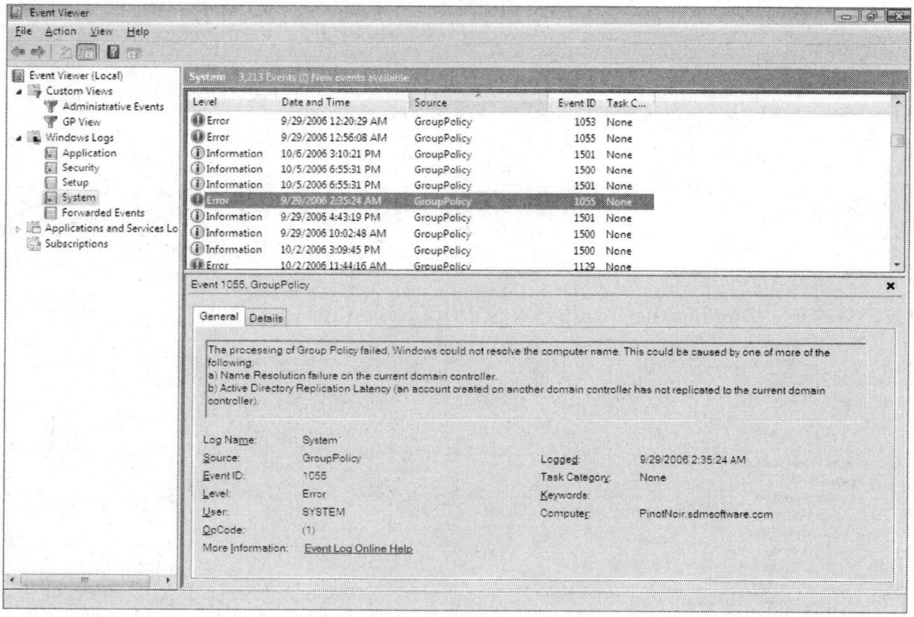

As you can see from Figure 7.30, not only does the event tell you that Group Policy processing has failed because it couldn't resolve the computer name, but it also gives you several possible reasons why that failure occurred. Additionally, if you were to click the "Event Log Online Help" link at the bottom of the page, you would be taken to a Microsoft website that contains more detailed information about this event ID.

Leveraging Windows 7 Operational Logs for Troubleshooting

Assuming that the Windows Vista and later Admin Logs don't help you track down the problem, the next step would be the Group Policy Operational Logs. As I mentioned, these logs provide the same level of detail that the userenv.log file provided in prior Windows versions, but in a nice Event Log format.

This is great, but how can you use this data to troubleshoot a problem when there are so many events generated in a given processing cycle? For example, a given Group Policy processing cycle could generate 20 to 30 Operational Log events, and the Operational Log itself could contain hundreds of these events. The goal is to narrow in on *one* Group Policy processing cycle and walk through the steps that it took to either succeed or fail. You can accomplish this task using a custom view, a feature of the Crimson Event Log system.

Each instance of a Group Policy processing cycle is uniquely identified by a field in the event called a *Correlation Activity ID*. This is akin to the thread ID I mentioned earlier when discussing the userenv.log file. By creating a custom view that filters events by this ActivityID, you can get a listing of only those Group Policy Operational events related to a given processing cycle. Let's walk through how to do that.

To filter the Operational Event Logs by a specific Group Policy Activity ID:

1. Start the Event Viewer utility.

2. The first thing you need to do is find the activity ID for the Group Policy processing cycle you're interested in. You can do that by going into the Operational Log, finding an event that is part of the cycle in question, clicking the Details tab in the lower preview pane, as shown in Figure 7.31. Copy this activity ID someplace safe—we'll need it in a second.

FIGURE 7.31 Locating the Correlation ActivityID in a Group Policy Event

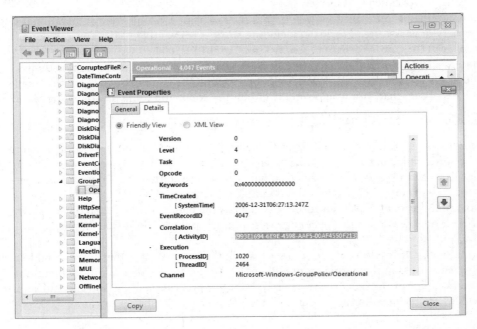

3. On the left-hand pane of the Event Viewer, right-click the Custom Views node and choose Create Custom View.

4. The Create Custom View dialog box appears on the Filter pane, but for this exercise, we're going to enter the XML filter directly rather than using the check boxes. So, click the XML tab and check the box that says "Edit query manually."

5. Paste the following XML query string into the filter query box:

```
<QueryList><Query Id="0"
 Path="Application">
<Select Path="Microsoft-Windows-GroupPolicy/Operational">*
[System/Correlation/@ActivityID='{INSERT ACTIVITY ID HERE}']
</Select></Query></QueryList>
```

6. Place the ActivityID you found in step 2 in the spot that says, "INSERT ACTIVITY ID HERE." Once you do that, click OK twice and the upper-right results pane of the Event Viewer will show only a filtered view of your Group Policy events.

GPLogView

Now that we've filtered the events down to a single Group Policy cycle, you might be saying to yourself, "Gee, that's pretty hard to see what's going on given that I have to scroll through each event without getting to see them all in a single view." Well, for that reason, Microsoft has created a tool called GPLogView.

This command-line utility lets you output the events of a Group Policy Operational Log to a variety of easy-to-read formats, including straight text and HTML. You can download the tool at http://go.microsoft.com/fwlink/?LinkId=75004.

Here is a taste of what GPLogView can do. You can use it to do the exact same thing we did in the previous custom view description—output the events associated with a single ActivityID. To do that, you would run the gplogview command using the following syntax:

```
Gplogview -a 9A867233-04FF-4625-B7D1-6DEB763E2DCA -o ouput.txt
```

This generates a step-by-step listing of all events with the ActivityID we've supplied to an output file called output.txt. If we open output.txt in Notepad, we see a nice listing, similar to what we've got in userenv.log but without the clutter and unintelligible references to APIs. Figure 7.32 shows a small sample of the output.

Note that it provides useful information such as the bandwidth detected during slow link detection, the time until the next processing cycle, which GPOs were applied and denied, and why.

Additionally, if you look at the actual events in the Event Viewer that correspond to each of the events listed in the output from GPLogView, you can get some additionally useful information. For example, at the start of every policy processing cycle, some useful summary flags are included in each event under the Details tab, as shown in Figure 7.33.

FIGURE 7.32 Viewing the output from GPLogView

FIGURE 7.33 Viewing summary flags for a Group Policy Operational event

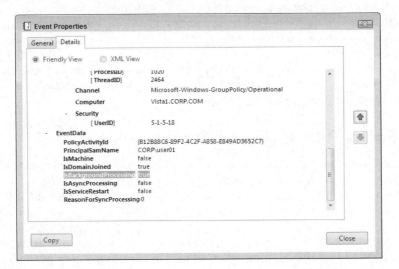

The flags you see in this figure can provide a glimpse into the kind of processing that is occurring. For example, the isBackgroundProcessing = true flag indicates that this is a background processing cycle rather than a foreground one. This is important because certain CSEs, such as Software Installation and Folder Redirection, don't run during background processing. This summary view also provides useful information such as whether processing occurred asynchronously (IsAsyncProcessing) and whether machine or user processing is being logged (IsMachine).

Overall, the Group Policy Operational Log is the place to be when it comes to troubleshooting Group Policy problems in Windows Vista and later.

> Microsoft has an indispensable document on Group Policy troubleshooting and the Event Logs for Windows Vista and later (including Windows 7). It's called (cleverly enough) "Troubleshooting Group Policy with Event Logs." You should be able to find it on www.GPanswers.com in the Microsoft Resources section. Or, just Google for the name of the white paper. Note that the information is "all about Windows Vista"; but since Windows Vista and Windows 7 are basically identical in this respect, don't panic too much.

Enabling Tracing for the Group Policy Preference Extensions

The Group Policy Preference Extensions don't produce any direct log files by default. The assumption is that "they're working fine" unless you want to get more information out of them.

To do that, there are a slew of policy settings that enable tracking logs. We explored tracing for the Group Policy Preferences in Chapter 5, but for completeness, I'm putting a reference to their existence here, in this troubleshooting chapter, as well.

You can find the Group Policy Preference Extensions tracing policy settings at Computer Configuration ➢ Policies ➢ Administrative Templates ➢ Group Policy ➢ Logging and Tracing.

You can see the Group Policy Preference Extensions tracing options in Figure 7.34.

For more information on Group Policy Preferences troubleshooting, check out "Troubleshooting: Reporting, Logging, and Tracing" in Chapter 5.

Group Policy Processing Performance

I often hear the question, "Is it better to have fewer, bigger GPOs or more GPOs with fewer settings?" The answer to that question is the basis for this section.

The bottom line to Group Policy processing performance is that the time it takes to process Group Policy is highly dependent on what you're doing within a given set of GPOs and the state of your environment. If you think about all the things we've discussed in this chapter about how Group Policy is stored and processed, then you have probably discovered that there is a lot of variability in the process. For example, setting Administrative Templates policy is a lot less time consuming than re-permissioning a large file tree using File Security policy. Likewise, installing Microsoft Office using Software Installation Policy is going to take more time than setting users' rights on a given system.

FIGURE 7.34 You use these policy settings to troubleshoot the Group Policy
Preference Extensions.

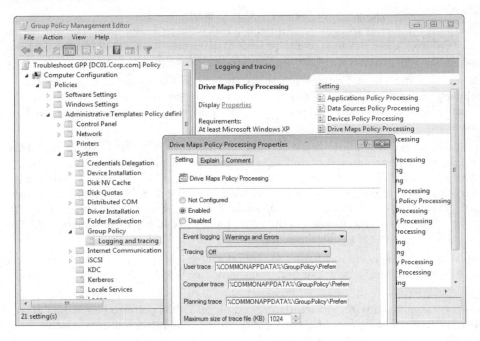

Additionally, the time that Group Policy processing spends during the core processing phase, where the client communicates with AD to determine which GPOs to apply, is typically a small percentage of the overall processing time as compared to the CSE processing part of the cycle. Thus, having to enumerate more GPOs or less GPOs will have a negligible effect on the overall processing time as compared to having to perform the more time-intensive CSE processing. And, it's also important to remember that Group Policy processing only occurs if something changes in the Group Policy infrastructure for a given computer or user. So, in most environments, days may go by before changes to GPOs are made or a new GPO is created. Given that, the question of performance gets down to what's acceptable in your environment.

The best thing you can do to optimize processing performance is measure and understand where time is being spent during a given processing cycle. You can do this using any number of the tools we've mentioned in this chapter. For example, the `userenv.log` file in pre–Windows Vista versions of the OS will timestamp each step of the processing cycle, letting you see where time is being spent. Similarly, the Group Policy Operational Log will do the same thing in Windows Vista and later. In addition, you can download a free command-line utility called `gptime.exe` at `www.gpoguy.com/Free-GPOguy-Tools.aspx` that outputs the time spent processing Group Policy for either a local or remote computer.

A number of factors can affect Group Policy processing performance more than just the number of GPOs you have applied to a given user or computer. Some of these are highlighted here:

- Keep the number of security groups applied to a GPO to a minimum. The more security groups a client has to read and process to determine if a GPO applies or does not apply, the more time is spent during the core processing phase.

- Make sure that you are not forcing policy application for a given CSE (by enabling the relevant policy under `Computer Configuration\Policies\Administrative Templates\System\Group Policy`) during every refresh cycle unless you absolutely have to.

- Make sure that you minimize the amount of "expensive" operations that your GPOs do. Expensive operations include Folder Redirection of large amounts of user data, Software Installation of large applications over the network, and re-permissioning of large file or Registry trees. Additionally, Scripts policy can be problematic if the scripts are performing complex tasks that can hang. The default script timeout in Group Policy is 10 minutes. That means a script could hang there for up to 10 minutes, with your users waiting, until it finally times out.

- WMI Filters (discussed in Chapter 5) also take a big chunk of processing time to figure out if the condition is "true" or not. You should use WMI filters if you need them, but not to excess.

So, in the end, the question of whether fewer, bigger GPOs perform better than more, smaller GPOs is probably not the right question to ask. The better question is which configuration is easier to manage. Once you answer that question, you can optimize for performance using the tips I've described in this section.

Final Thoughts

You want to be a better troubleshooter for Group Policy issues? You're well on the way.

In the previous chapter, you learned when Group Policy is supposed to apply. It doesn't just happen when it wants to; it happens according to a set of precise timings. In this chapter, you learned two more key items to help on your troubleshooting journey. First, you learned the real story about what's going on under the hood. Then, you learned how to take that knowledge and troubleshoot Group Policy. Hopefully, every page in this chapter will help you further troubleshoot Group Policy should something go awry. However, here are some parting tips when troubleshooting Group Policy:

Check the basics.   When troubleshooting, first check the basics. Make sure you're not using Block Inheritance or Enforced where you shouldn't.

Check permissions.   Users need both "Read" and "Apply Group Policy" permissions to the GPOs. Computers do too. If a user (or group the user is in) is "Denied" access to either of these permissions, then the GPO will not apply.

Leverage the built-in tools.   Use the built-in debugging tools, such as the Event Viewer, supercharged with the Diagnostics key to help troubleshoot even tougher problems.

Leverage additional tools.   You have lots of additional troubleshooting tools at your disposal. Be sure to check out the appendix, in which I introduce WinPolicies, GPMonitor, GPInventory, and more.

Remember which operating systems act alike.   In this chapter we basically focused on XP and Windows 7. But many people have Windows Vista out there too, and of course, there's Windows Server 2003 and Windows Server 2008 and their R2 cousins! When it comes to troubleshooting, remember that Windows Vista, Windows Server 2008, and Windows Server 2008 R2 are all just like Windows 7 and that Windows Server 2003 is just like XP.

Verify that replication is working.   If a client isn't getting the GPOs you think they should, it just may be that normal replication hasn't finished yet. GPCs replicate via Active Directory replication. GPTs replicate via FRS replication. They are supposed to take the same path, but sometimes they don't. Use Gpotool and Replmon to troubleshoot.

Check out Microsoft's troubleshooting documentation.   There are two official white papers on Group Policy troubleshooting from Microsoft. One can be found at `http://go.microsoft.com/fwlink/?LinkId=14949`.

There's also another, more modern version at `http://tinyurl.com/3ceraj`. I was one of the reviewers who provided input into this later document.

Remember all the log files at your disposal.   In this chapter, we've discussed a few log files. However, there are many more available. As we'll see in other chapters along our journey, there are log files for many processes related to Group Policy. We've just seen `UserEnv.log`, but additionally, there is `FDeploy.log` (examined in Chapter 10), `Appmgmt.log` (examined in Chapter 11), and others. Reference the two aforementioned Microsoft documents on Group Policy troubleshooting for the additional logs, in areas such as troubleshooting "internal" GPMC or Group Policy Object Editor workings via `Gpmgmt.log` and `GPedit.log`, respectively.

8

Implementing Security with Group Policy

There is a little aphorism that's grown on me over time. It's a simple mantra, which hopefully you can agree with:

> *If you don't know Group Policy, you don't know security.*

That's because Group Policy and security are so intrinsically linked. Not only are you setting configuration items (which will make you more secure), and not only are you setting security items (which will also make you more secure), but you also need to know the ins and outs of where Group Policy applies, who it applies to, and when that magic is going to happen.

But Group Policy is a big, big place, and we simply don't have room to go over *all* the stuff you can do with Group Policy or even all the *security* stuff you can do with Group Policy. So I'm picking the most important things to show you in this chapter with the amount of room I have.

In this security chapter we've got an enormous amount to cover. Here's the list:

Default GPOs We'll first look at the two default GPOs—the "Default Domain Policy" GPO and the "Default Domain Controllers Policy" GPO—and how they help tighten security.

Password policy Ah, passwords. They're so easy to manage, right? Ahem. Well, don't shoot the messenger as you read this update for Windows Server 2008 domains. It's even more fun now!

Auditing servers and Group Policy usage Who is using our clients and servers? You'll find out how to find out. You'll also find out what's changed for Windows Server 2008, Windows Server 2008 R2, and Windows 7.

Restricted groups You'll learn how to force group membership and nested group membership.

Software restriction policies and AppLocker Put the smack down and allow/disallow specific applications to run.

Controlling user account control "Are you sure you want to do that?" That question pops up time and time again in Windows Vista and Windows 7. Want to control it? This is your section.

Wireless and wired network policies   Windows Vista and later have some new controls around wireless and wired network policies. Set up both wired and wireless security using these techniques.

Windows firewall with advanced security   Windows XP has a built-in firewall. Windows Vista and Windows 7 have a lot more going on. Find out what the hubbub is all about in this section.

Obviously, there's a lot more to an overall security strategy. And, in other chapters, and the Appendix, we'll cover some other items you may want to check out if you're crafting a security policy for your environment. The topics I think you should check out are

- Internet Explorer Settings (Chapter 12)
- Security Templates (Appendix)
- Security Configuration Wizard (Appendix)
- ADM/ADMX/PolicyPak for controlling your applications (Chapter 6)

The Two Default Group Policy Objects

Whenever you create a new domain, three things automatically happen:

- The initial (and only) OU, named **Domain Controllers**, is created automatically by the DCPROMO process.
- A default GPO is created and linked to the domain level, called "Default Domain Policy."
- A default GPO is created for the **Domain Controllers** OU, called "Default Domain Controllers Policy."

This section helps answer the question, why are these GPOs different from all other GPOs?

These two GPOs are special. First, you cannot easily delete them (though you can rename them). Next, it's a best practice to modify these GPOs only for the security settings that we'll describe in this section. Too often, people will modify the "Default Domain Controller Policy" GPO or "Default Domain Policy" GPO only to mess it up beyond recognition. So, these special default GPOs shouldn't be modified with the "normal stuff" you do day to day. In general, stay clear of them, and modify them only when a setting prescribed for them is required.

Instead of modifying the "Default Domain Controller Policy" GPO or "Default Domain Policy" GPO for normal stuff, you should create a new GPO and link it at the level you want, then implement your policy settings inside that new GPO. And it's a best practice to always be sure that the defaults are highest in the link order (that means they're the most powerful if anything should conflict in another GPO at the same level).

It's not that the GPOs themselves are all that different, but rather that their location is special, as you'll see later in this chapter. The locations in question are the domain level and the **Domain Controllers** OU.

The "Default Domain Policy" GPO and "Default Domain Controllers Policy" GPO can be deleted, but I strongly recommend that you *don't ever delete these*. If you truly want to delete either of the default policies, you'll need to add back in the "Delete" access control entry to a group you belong to—Domain Administrators, for instance. Even then, I can't see why you would want to delete them. If you want to disable their link for some reason (again, I can't imagine why), do that, but leave the actual GPOs in place. If you do run into a situation where these are deleted, use the command dcgpofix.exe (described in detail in the section entitled "Repairing the Defaults for Windows 2003 / 2008 Domains") to get them back.

GPOs Linked at the Domain Level

If you take a look inside the domain level, you'll see one GPO that was created by default: the "Default Domain Policy." The purpose of this GPO is to set the default configurations for the Account Policies branch in the Group Policy Object Editor. These Account Policies encompass three important domain-wide security settings:

- Password policy
- Account Lockout policy
- Kerberos policy

You can see these settings in Figure 8.1.

FIGURE 8.1 The "Default Domain Policy" GPO (linked to the domain level) sets the domain's default Account Policies, Kerberos policy, and Password policy. If you link GPOs containing these policy settings anywhere else, they are ignored when Active Directory is being used.

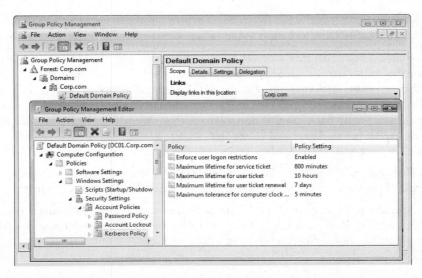

Again, the default policy settings are set inside the "Default Domain Policy" GPO and linked to the domain level. However, you can change the defaults of the Account Policies in one of two ways:

- By modifying the "Default Domain Policy" GPO directly
- By creating your own GPO linked to the domain level and changing the precedence order within the domain level

You'll see how shortly.

Again, the special part about the domain level of Group Policy is that this is the only place these three Group Policy settings can be set for the domain, and the default settings for the domain are prespecified in the "Default Domain Policy" GPO.

If you try to set Password policy, Account Lockout policy, or Kerberos policy anywhere else in the domain (say, at any OU or on any site), the settings are ignored when users log onto the domain; they don't matter, and only those linked to the domain level take effect.

Microsoft has taken a lot of heat for the fact that Account policies must agree for all the accounts in the domain. Up until recently, that meant if two administrators of two OUs couldn't agree on equal Account policies (usually things like password length), they would have needed to split those users between two domains—a major administrative overhead nightmare.

So they changed it in Windows Server 2008. It's not a light-year improvement, but it does do the job. We'll explore that here as well.

Special Policy Settings for the Domain Level

In addition to Password policy, Account Lockout policy, and Kerberos policy, five additional policy settings take effect only when a GPO is linked to the domain level. They are located under Computer Configuration ➤ Policies ➤ Windows Settings ➤ Security Settings ➤ Local Policies ➤ Security Options:

Network Security: Force logoff when logon hours expire   You can set up accounts so that users logged onto Active Directory must log off when they exceed the hours available to them.

Accounts: Rename administrator account   You can use this policy setting to forcibly rename the Administrator account. This works only for the Domain Administrator account when set at the domain level. This is useful as a level of "extra protection" so that no matter what the Administrator account is renamed to in Active Directory Users and Computers, it will "snap back" to this name after Group Policy refreshes. The "display name" in Active Directory Users and Computers won't change, but the underlying "real" name of the account will be changed.

Accounts: Rename guest Account   You can rename the domain Guest account using this policy setting. This works only for the Guest account when set at the domain level.

Accounts: Administrator account status   This setting is valid only for Windows 2003 domains (and higher). You can forcibly disable the Administrator account using this setting. See this tech note for more information: http://tinyurl.com/y36ths.

Accounts: Guest account status   This setting is valid only for Windows 2003 domains (and higher). You can forcibly disable the Guest account using this setting. See this tech note for more information: http://tinyurl.com/y39kqp.

Setting these five special security settings at any other level has no effect on domain accounts contained within Active Directory. However, if you linked a GPO containing these settings to an OU, the local computer would certainly respond accordingly.

> Again, these policies cannot affect domain accounts when a GPO containing these settings is linked to, say, the **Sales** OU or **Marketing** OU. This is because these policies must specifically affect the Domain Controllers computer objects.

Modifying the "Default Domain Policy" GPO Directly

You can dive into the "Default Domain Policy" GPO in two ways. Use the Group Policy Management Console (GPMC) and click the domain name. You'll see the "Default Domain Policy" GPO linked to the domain level. If you try to edit the GPO at this level, you'll see the standard set of policy settings you've come to know and love while inside the Group Policy Object Editor (though again, as I've stated, you won't want to add "normal stuff" to this GPO).

Here, for instance, you can specify (among other settings) that the password length is 10 characters, the user is locked out after the third password attempt, and Kerberos ticket expiration time is 600 minutes. But these values are only valid for the entire domain.

> Again, if you want to add more policy settings at the domain level (which would affect all users or computers in the domain)—great! But try to leave the "Default Domain Policy" GPO alone, except when you need to change the "special" policy settings as described in this section.

Creating Your Own Group Policy Object Linked to the Domain Level and Changing the Precedence

Recall that at any level (site, domain, or OU), all the policy settings within all the GPOs linked to a level are merged unless there is a conflict. Then, the GPO with the highest precedence "wins" at a level. I talked about this in Chapter 2. The same is true regarding the settings special to the domain level: Password policy, Account Lockout policy, and Kerberos policy.

The defaults for these three policies are set within the "Default Domain Policy" GPO, but you could certainly create and link more GPOs to the domain level that would override the defaults. That doesn't necessarily mean that you should. Take a look at the example in Figure 8.2.

Here, a GPO is higher in priority than the "Default Domain Policy." If you do this, you better know precisely what you are doing. Again, this is because any policy setting within any GPO with a higher priority than the "Default Domain Policy" GPO will "win."

Which Approach Do You Take?

As you've seen, you can either modify the "Default Domain Policy" GPO or create your own GPO and ensure that the precedence is higher than the "Default Domain Policy" GPO. If you need to modify a special domain-wide account policy setting, which approach do you take? Here are the two schools of thought:

School of thought 1   Modify only the Account policies settings in the "Default Domain Policy" GPO. Then, ensure that it has the highest precedence at the domain level. This guarantees that if anyone does link other GPOs to the domain level, this one always wins.

School of thought 2   Leave the defaults in the "Default Domain Policy" GPO. Never modify the "Default Domain Policy" GPO—ever. Create a new GPO for any special settings you want to override in the "Default Domain Policy" GPO. Then, link the GPO to the domain level, and ensure that it has higher precedence than the "Default Domain Policy" GPO (as seen in Figure 8.2).

FIGURE 8.2   If you have a GPO with a higher precedence than the "Default Domain Policy" GPO, it will "win" if there's a conflict.

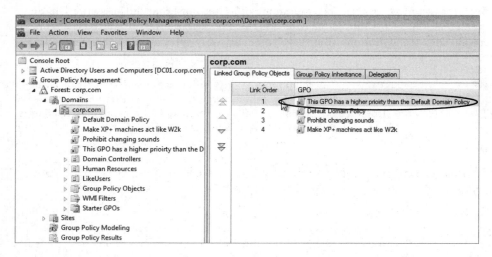

Various Microsoft insiders have given me different (sometimes conflicting) advice about which to use. So what do I think?

If you want to modify any special domain-wide security settings, use School of Thought 1. This is the simplest and cleanest way. If you do it this way, you'll always treat the "Default Domain Policy" GPO with kid gloves and know it has a special use. And you can check in on it from time to time to make sure no one has lowered the precedence on it. Additionally, some applications, such as Microsoft SMS, will specifically modify the "Default Domain Policy" GPO. Hence, if you want that application to run smoothly, it's best to let it do what it wants to do.

School of Thought 2 has its merits. Leave the "Default Domain Policy" GPO clean as a whistle, and then create your own GPOs with higher precedence settings. However, I don't think this is a great idea, because you might forget that you set something important inside this new GPO.

Either way works, but my preference is for School of Thought 1.

Group Policy Objects Linked to the Domain Controllers OU

How is the **Domain Controllers** OU different? You can see there is also a default GPO linked, named the "Default Domain Controllers Policy" GPO. But before we dive into it, let's take a step back. First, it's important to think of all the Domain Controllers as essentially equal. If one Domain Controller gets a policy setting (Security setting or otherwise), they should all be getting the same policy settings. On logon, users choose a Domain Controller for validation at random; however, you want the experience they receive to be consistent, not random. Moreover, when you, as the Domain Administrator, log onto a Domain Controller at the console, you also want your experience to be consistent.

Oh, and did I mention that when servers are finished being promoted into Domain Controllers via DCPROMO, they automatically end up in the **Domain Controllers** OU? So, that's where the "Default Domain Controllers Policy" GPO comes into play. Again, it's easy to find the "Default Domain Controllers Policy" GPO. It's linked to the **Domain Controllers** OU.

Again, since all Domain Controllers are, by default, nestled within the **Domain Controllers** OU, all Domain Controllers are affected by all the aspects inside the "Default Domain Controllers Policy" GPO. Of specific note are the Security Settings, as shown in Figure 8.3.

For instance, you'll want the same Event Log settings for all Domain Controllers. You'll want to set it once, inside a GPO linked to the **Domain Controllers** OU, and have it affect all Domain Controllers. By default, the "Default Domain Controllers Policy" GPO has the following set to specific defaults, which should remain consistent among all Domain Controllers.

Right-click any node and choose Export List from the context menu to export to a text file for an easy way to document complex settings, such as User Rights Assignments.

Audit Policies   Located in Computer Configuration ➢ Policies ➢ Windows Settings ➢ Security Settings ➢ Local Policies ➢ Audit Policy. Here you can change the default auditing policies of Windows 2000, Windows 2003, or Windows 2008. We talk about auditing later in this chapter in the section "Inside Auditing with and without Group Policy."

FIGURE 8.3   The "Default Domain Controllers Policy" GPO affects every Domain Controller in the Domain Controllers OU.

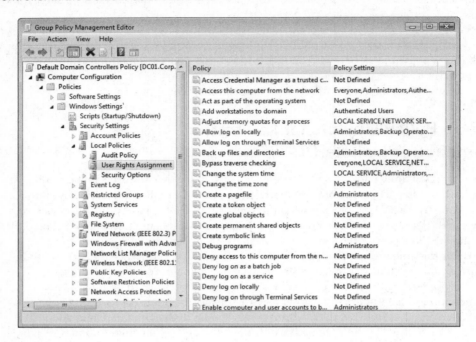

User Rights Assignment   Located in Computer Configuration ➢ Policies ➢ Windows Settings ➢ Security Settings ➢ Local Policies ➢ User Rights Assignment. Here you can configure which accounts you will "Allow log on locally" or "Log on as a service" among other specific rights.

Domain Controller Event Log Settings   Located in Computer Configuration ➢ Policies ➢ Windows Settings ➢ Security Settings ➢ Event Log. Set them here, and all Domain Controllers in the Domain Controllers OU will obey. Settings such as the maximum size of logs are contained here. Note, however, that decreasing the size of an Event log will not take effect on the DCs; you can enforce a log size increase, but not a decrease.

Various Security Options   Located in Computer Configuration ➢ Policies ➢ Windows Settings ➢ Security Settings ➢ Local Policies ➢ Security Options. Here you'll find settings such as "Domain controller: LDAP server signing requirements" and other items that might be specifically relevant to Domain Controllers. Note that GPOs created on Windows 7 machines will have more Windows Vista and Windows 7–specific security options available. The Group Policy spreadsheet (found at www.GPanswers.com in the Microsoft Resources section) has a list of all the security options and what target machines can be affected.

The same rules apply to the **Domain Controllers** OU as they do for the domain level. That is, you can put a GPO in at a higher precedence than the "Default Domain Controllers Policy"

GPO. However, my recommendation is to use the "Default Domain Controllers Policy" GPO for the "special" things that you set at this level, and ensure that it's got the highest precedence when being processed within the OU.

Oops, the "Default Domain Policy" GPO and/or "Default Domain Controllers Policy" GPO Got Screwed Up!

If you modify the "Default Domain Policy" GPO or "Default Domain Controllers Policy" GPO such that you want to return it back to the defaults, you might just have a shot. The procedure is different for Windows 2000 domains or those with Windows 2003/Windows Server 2008 Domain Controllers. First, you'll need to determine which default GPO got screwed up; then you need to take the appropriate steps. These procedures are among the most popular requests for Microsoft Product Support Services. However, these tools should be performed only as an absolute last resort because it will restore your defaults as if the installation were done "out of the box." So, be careful. If you have a backup of your defaults, you should try to perform a restore first—before using these "emergency-only" tools.

Repairing the Defaults for Windows 2003/2008 Domains

As long as you have even one Windows 2003 Domain Controller, you have it made in the shade. Well, not too made, as you might already be in the doghouse if the default GPOs are screwed up. However, Windows 2003 domains with their Windows 2003 Domain Controllers come with a command-line tool, DCGPOFIX, to make it easy to restore back to the defaults. You can tell DCGPOFIX to restore the "Default Domain Policy" GPO (with the /Target:Domain switch) or the "Default Domain Controllers Policy" GPO (with the /Target:DC switch). Or you can restore both with the /Target:BOTH switch, as shown in Figure 8.4. The command-line tool did not change functionality in Windows Server 2008.

FIGURE 8.4 Use DCGPOFIX with Windows 2003 Domain Controllers to restore the defaults if necessary.

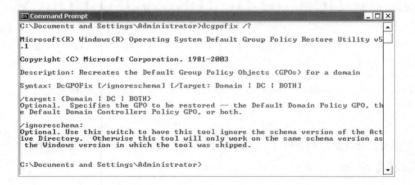

Optionally, you can simply reset the User Rights Assignment for Windows 2003/Windows Server 2008 instead of plowing back the entire "Default Domain Controllers" GPO. To do so, see the Microsoft Knowledge Base article "How to Reset User Rights in the Default Domain Group Policy in Windows Server 2003" (KB 324800) at `http://support.microsoft.com/kb/324800`.

However, you might also encounter a strange situation if you're trying to bring back one of the default GPOs but you've updated the schema to some later version. If that happens, `DCGPOFIX` won't proceed unless you add the `/ignoreschema` switch in front.

The idea is that it will bring back the default GPO you choose based on the schema it knows (originally), not the one you might have upgraded to. There's a Microsoft Knowledge Base article here on it: `http://support.microsoft.com/kb/932445`. In short, you might have to run `DCGPOFIX` with the `/ignoreschema` switch, even though it appears there's no reason you might need it.

This article states that nothing was modified in the schema that would affect Group Policy from Windows Server 2003 to Windows Server 2003 R2, but I don't know what that means in terms of Windows Server 2008 or, even the latest Windows Server 2008 R2.

If you have to restore the default GPOs for some reason, you might be in heap of trouble anyway and might want to call Microsoft Product Support Services for extra guidance.

Repairing the Defaults for Windows 2000 Domains

If the "Default Domain Policy" GPO or "Default Domain Controller Policy" GPO for a Windows 2000 domain get irreparably damaged, you can download and run a tool that was previously available only to customers when they called Microsoft Product Support Services. That is, Windows 2000 also has an equivalent to Windows 2003/Windows Server 2008's `DCGPOFIX`. Its name is `RecreateDefPol`, and you have to download it. Here's a shortened link to the tool: `www.tinyurl.com/3yyr3`.

The Strange Life of Password Policy

If you create a new GPO, link it to any OU, and then edit your new GPO, it certainly appears as if you *could* set the Password policy and Account Lockout policy using a GPO

But does it do anything? Let's find out.

Additionally, we'll talk about a new function in Windows Server 2008 called Fine-Grained Password Policy.

What Happens When You Set Password Settings at an OU Level

For example, I have a **Sales** OU in which I recently placed WIN7. As you can see in **Figure 8.5**, I created and linked a GPO, called "Sales Password Policy," to the **Sales** OU. I am setting the Password policy so that the minimum password length is 10 characters.

At first glance this would seem to be counterproductive, because, as already stated, these policy settings only take hold of the accounts in the domain via the "Default Domain Policy" GPO. But administrators might actually want to perform this seemingly contradictory action. That is, when the user logs on locally to the Windows workstation, the account policy settings contained in the GPO linked to the OU will have been magically planted on their machine to take effect for *local* accounts. In Figure 8.6, I have logged in as the local administrator account on the workstation.

Again, this won't affect users' accounts when users are logging onto the domain; rather, it affects only the local accounts on the targeted computers. This could be helpful if you grant local administrator rights to users on their workstations or laptops and want to set a baseline.

FIGURE 8.5   It might seem counterproductive to set the Password policy at any level but the domain.

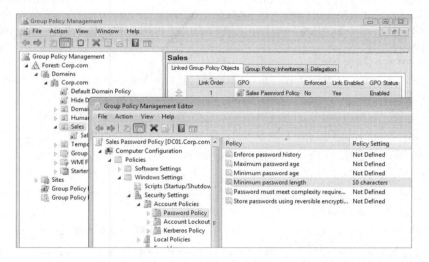

FIGURE 8.6   Setting a Password policy in the domain (other than at the domain level) will affect passwords used for local accounts on member machines.

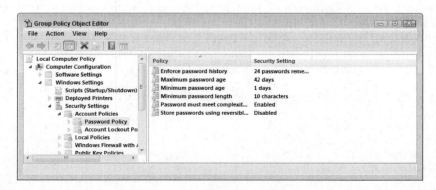

If you are still using Windows 2000 machines, Figure 8.6 would show both "Local" and "Effective" settings for Windows 2000 Professional machines. However, because of the behavior described here, the effective settings might not be accurate. Again, this is noted in the old Microsoft Knowledge Base 257922 article "Local Security Policy May Not Accurately Reflect Actual System Settings."

Fine-Grained Password Policy with Windows Server 2008

So if setting Password policy at an OU level doesn't affect your domain users, is there a way to set password policies on specific users in the domain such that they have different password requirements?

Short answer: yes. It's called Fine-Grained Password Policy (FGPP) and it's built into Windows Server 2008.

Longer answer (here goes):

You can do this with Windows Server 2008 if all Domain Controllers are Windows Server 2008, and...

The domain functional level has been raised to Windows Server 2008, and...

You can accept that you can't set Fine-Grained Password Policy on OUs, and...

You accept that you can't use Group Policy to do it.

Oh wait, there's more:

Setting it up is a real bear. We'll be going through that in a second, but I just wanted to give you a heads-up now.

And, finally, did I mention that you can't use Group Policy and affect an entire OU?

Wouldn't that be nice? You bet, and it's quite simply not part of the deal here.

Now, this is a Group Policy book, but I'm going to give you the ever-so-brief run-through anyway, because you might want to get a feel for how this works. I'll have some links a little later for you to get super-deep with FGPP if you'd like to.

Let me jump to the end of the story, though, and say, quite simply, if you want to have a Fine-Grained Password Policy, where you can specify those policies toward specific OUs (or specific people) *and* you want to use Group Policy to manage it all—well, then, you can do so using a third-party add-on option via a company called Specops Software. Their product is called Specops Password Policy. And you can check it out at

`www.specopssoft.com/products/specopspasswordpolicy/`

(shortened to `http://tinyurl.com/yw8rr9`).

A little later, after I've described all the gyrations required to get native Windows Server 2008 FGPP working, I'm also going to talk about a free Specops tool (with a darn similar name) called Specops Password Policy Basic. Stay tuned. We'll be working with that tool to help us with FGPP a little later.

So, with all those caveats behind us, what does FGPP bring to the table? It brings us the ability to dictate a specific password policy for a user account or an Active Directory global security group the user is a member of. The key takeaway here is the word *group* and not *OU*.

Let's check it out to see how it works. You'll want to perform these steps directly on your Windows Server 2008 Domain Controller.

Getting Ready for Fine-Grained Password Policy

Most domains will default to Windows Server 2003 functional level. However, if you're going to make use of this new feature, the domain functional level must be Windows Server 2008. You can check and/or raise the functional level by using Active Directory Users and Computers, right-clicking over the domain name, and selecting "Raise domain functional level," as seen in Figure 8.7.

FIGURE 8.7   Use Active Directory Users and Computers to raise the domain functional level (if needed).

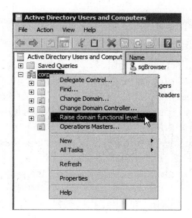

When you do, you can see the current domain functional level and/or change to Windows Server 2008 functional level if necessary, as shown in Figure 8.8. You'll need to do this if you want to proceed.

Creating a Password Setting Object (PSO)

Now, most people will run screaming when I mention the tool we'll be using for FGPP. It's (wait for it) ADSI Edit (which is now part of the Windows Server 2008 operating system and not an add-on tool).

FIGURE 8.8 You must be in Windows Server 2008 Functional Level (which you raise here if necessary) to get Fine-Grained Password Policy.

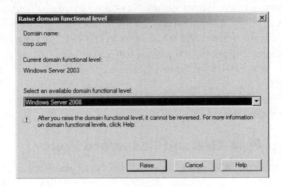

ADSI Edit will help us create the unit we need, called a Password Setting Object (PSO). Here's the breakdown of what we need to do to make the magic happen:

1. Create a PSO in the Password Settings Container (PSC) using ADSI Edit.

2. Configure the PSO options by completing the ADSI wizard.

3. Link the PSO to a user account or a global security group.

It's a long road, so let's get started.

Creating a Password Settings Object

Again, the tool we use is (shudder) ADSI Edit. So, start out by clicking Start ➢ Run and typing **adsiedit.msc** in the Run box. When you do, ADSI Edit will appear.

Right-click over the only node available (ADSI Edit) and select "Connect to." At the Connections Settings screen, accept all the defaults and click OK. You should be able to drill down into your Active Directory.

At this point, find Default naming context ➢ <domain FQDN> ➢ CN = System ➢ CN = Password Settings Container. Then right-click and select New ➢ Object, as seen in Figure 8.9.

Next you'll be presented with a crappy little wizard that walks you through the process, as seen in Figure 8.10.

With his permission, I'm borrowing my pal Jakob Heidelberg's excellent write-up of this subject from his blog, but also including some additional items. You'll see this write-up in Table 8.1. (I'll give you a link a little later to his write-up on the subject.) Each item in the table represents a step in the wizard, so be sure to read my notes carefully if you try to tackle this.

Note that some of the numbers are calculated as negative numbers. Yikes. So, how do you calculate these numbers? With this web page, which has a calculator script, of course:

`http://msdn2.microsoft.com/en-us/library/ms974598.aspx`

(shortened to `http://tinyurl.com/yuekhs`).

FIGURE 8.9   You start setting Fine-Grained Password Policy using ADSI Edit.

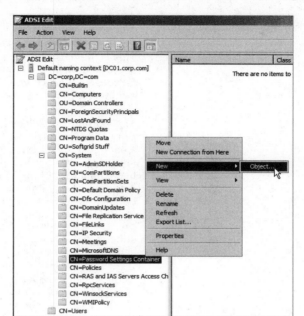

FIGURE 8.10   One screen of the Fine-Grained Password Policy Wizard (if you can call it that)

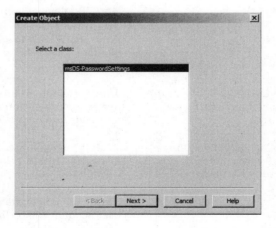

In our example here, we've suggested some values and provide their corresponding meaning as a baseline.

TABLE 8.1 Required Attributes to Set in Fine-Grained Password Policy

Attribute	Value	Meaning
Cn	SalesPasswords	This is the name of the policy. Try to come up with a naming convention for these policies if you will have lots of them.
msDS-PasswordSettingsPrecedence	10	This number is used as a "cost" for priority between different policies in case a user is hit by multiple PSOs. Be sure to leave space below and above for future use. The stronger the PSO password settings are, the lower the "cost" should be. In other words, use low numbers for PSOs you want to "win" if there's a precedence collision. (See more on this subject in the "Resulting Set of PSOs" section a little later.)
msDS-PasswordReversibleEncryptionEnabled	False	Boolean value to select if passwords should be stored with reversible encryption (usually not a good idea).
msDS-PasswordHistoryLength	32	How many previously used passwords should the system remember?
msDS-PasswordComplexityEnabled	True	Should the users use a complex password (Boolean value)?
msDS-MinimumPasswordLength	16	What should be the minimum number of characters in the user accounts password?
msDS-MinimumPasswordAge	−864000000000 (9 zeros; enter as negative value)	What is the minimum password age? (In this case, 1 day.) Note the minus sign to enter this as a negative value.
msDS-MaximumPasswordAge	−36288000000000 (9 zeros; enter as negative value)	What is the maximum password age? (In this case, 42 days.) Note the minus sign to enter this as a negative value.
msDS-LockoutThreshold	5	How many failed attempts before the user account will be locked?
msDS-LockoutObservationWindow	−18000000000 (9 zeros; enter as negative value.)	After how long should the counter for failed attempts be reset? (In this case, 6 minutes.) Note the minus sign to enter this as a negative value.

TABLE 8.1   Required Attributes to Set in Fine-Grained Password Policy *(continued)*

Attribute	Value	Meaning
msDS-LockoutDuration	−18000000000 (9 zeros; enter as negative value)	For how long should the user account object be locked in case of too many bad passwords entered? (In this case, 6 minutes.) Note the minus sign to enter this as a negative value.

When you've finished entering the values in Table 8.1 into the wizard, you can (get this) continue to optionally enter even *more* values. But for now, just click Finish at the end of the wizard. At this point, you should see your PSO in the Password Settings Container object.

Double-click it to get its properties. We need to set a filter on it. In the lower-right corner of the PSO's properties, you'll see a Filter button (not shown in Figure 8.11). When you click it, the Filtering options appear (as in Figure 8.11). You can see the various default filter options.

FIGURE 8.11   You need to change the filter options.

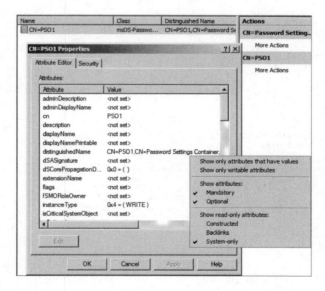

Change the filter so the following options are selected:

- Show attributes: Mandatory, Optional
- Show read-only attributes: Constructed, Backlinks, and System-only

Leave the following two unchecked:

- Show only attributes that have values
- Show only writable attributes

You can see the desired filter state in Figure 8.12.

Now, inside the PSO, you should be able to see the msDS-PSOAppliesTo attribute as shown in Figure 8.13. Click Edit, then select Add Windows Account and pick the users and/or groups you want to get this particular password policy. In this case, I'm assigning the PSO to EastSalesUser1 and EastSalesUser2.

You'll see the msDS-PSOAppliesTo variable changes to reflect the SIDs of the users and groups you just added.

When you're done losing your mind inside ADSI Edit, close the tool.

FIGURE 8.12 The changed filter options

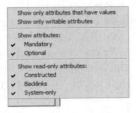

FIGURE 8.13 You can assign specific PSOs to user accounts.

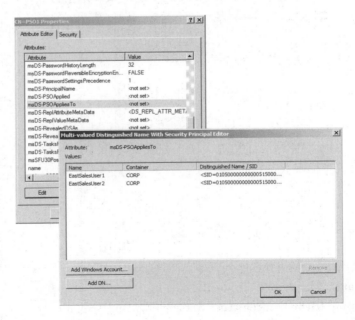

Resulting Set of PSOs

In our previous example, we created one PSO and linked it to some user accounts. But how can we see the results of our labor?

The Active Directory Users and Computer Attribute Editor

You can validate your efforts by firing up Active Directory Users and Computers. But Active Directory Users and Computers needs to be running in a special mode called Advanced Features to see the results of what we just performed. So, after running Active Directory Users and Computers, select View ➢ Advanced Features, as seen in Figure 8.14.

FIGURE 8.14   Use Active Directory Users and Computers Advanced Features to see if your users are receiving Fine-Grained Password Policies.

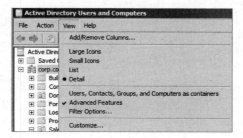

Then, find and open the user account. Click the new Windows Server 2008 Attribute Editor tab, seen in Figure 8.15. Now, the defaults won't show what we need, which means we have to click Filter and reselect the filter options we selected earlier in Figure 8.12. Once you do that, you should see an attribute called `msDS-ResultantPSO`, shown in Figure 8.16. This is the PSO that is ultimately applied to the user.

FIGURE 8.15   The attribute we need, `msDS-PSOApplied`, isn't shown by default.

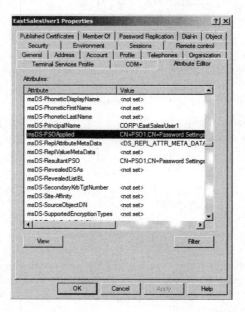

PSO Precedence

Now in all this hubbub of creating a PSO for your users and groups, you might have forgotten all about the Default Domain Policy. Turns out, it's still working for you, behind the scenes in case you never touch PSOs.

FIGURE 8.16 The attribute we need, `msDS-ResultantPSO`, is shown only when properly filtered.

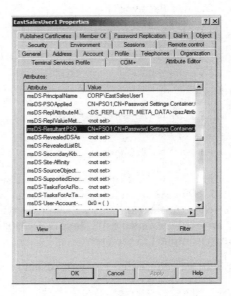

Here's the breakdown of what happens now that you have PSOs set up:

1. If a user has a PSO linked directly to him, that PSO automatically wins. If there are multiple PSOs linked to the user, you'll see a warning in the Event log on the Domain Controller, and the one with the *lowest* precedence value is the resultant PSO. If the user doesn't have a PSO linked directly to him, see step 2.

2. If the user is a member of a global security group, he gets a PSO linked to that security group. If the user is a member of multiple groups with PSOs linked to them, see step 3.

3. All the global groups of which the user is a member (and has PSOs linked) are compared. The one with the lowest precedence dictates his resultant PSO.

4. If none of these applies (no PSOs on his account or any group he's a member of), the Default Domain Policy is applied.

So one good strategy is to ensure that your Default Domain Policy password settings are really tough by default. That way, if you make some mistake with FGPP, and someone "defaults" to the Default Domain Policy, you've still got nice, tough security on those passwords. Basically, you'll be "secure by default."

Using Specops Password Policy Basic (Free Edition)

So, let me get this straight: you didn't like entering all that data using the crappy wizard, running scripts to calculate negative values, and then linking it over to the user or group accounts?

Right.

If there were only a free GUI tool to help you through that minefield. Well, there is, and it's called Specops Password Policy Basic and is available at www.specopssoft.com (specific link http://tinyurl.com/33s7bt). Note that you'll need to have PowerShell installed on the management station on which you install this tool.

In Figure 8.17, you can see how easy it is to configure a new PSO, provide parameters, and then address which members should get the policy.

FIGURE 8.17　Specops Password Policy Basic makes quick work of complicated Fine-Grained Password Policy.

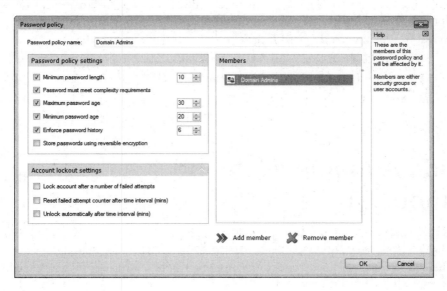

Easy!

Specops Password Policy Basic also allows you to see which PSOs "win" if multiple PSOs address a user, a group, or both.

It's free, so positively check it out.

Again, their pay tool, Specops Password Policy (not basic or free) enables you to perform Fine-Grained Password Policy directly to users or OUs, using Group Policy. Ah, joy.

Command-Line PSO Management

If you're a command-line freak and don't want to deal with the hassle of the ADSI Edit GUI we saw, Joe from www.Joeware.net has a great tool called PSOmgr that will do just the trick. Just head over to

www.joeware.net/freetools/tools/psomgr/index.htm

I also found a set of tools by Christoffer Andersson that you might find useful. It's called the "Fine Grain Password Policy Tool 1.0" and it found here: `http://tinyurl.com/ygwux9w`.

More Information on Fine-Grained Password Policy

Before we leave this section, it should be noted that there are three attributes that, on a per-user basis, can always override the PSO:

- Reversible password encryption required

- Password not required

- Password does not expire

If any of these attributes are set directly on a user using Active Directory Users and Computers, they will be honored, and the PSO policy for those attributes will be ignored.

If you'd like to spend more quality time with FGPP, here are some great links for you to explore.

- Microsoft's documentation on this topic: `http://tinyurl.com/2xubeo`

- Step-by-step guide from Microsoft: `http://tinyurl.com/287260`

- Jakob Heidelberg's take on FGPP: `http://tinyurl.com/2x1d67`

- And his Part 2: `http://tinyurl.com/2241yj`

- And Ulf B. Simon-Weidner's blog at `http://tinyurl.com/22h4sf`

Inside Auditing With and Without Group Policy

Auditing is a powerful tool. It can help you determine when people are doing things they shouldn't as well as help you determine when people are doing things they should.

But here's the trick: turning on and using auditing can be confusing. So, here's the little cheat-sheet we'll use for this section:

- Some auditing is turned on using Group Policy. This is the easy case. We'll explore this first.

- Some advanced auditing is turned on using a command-line tool. This tool is called `Auditpol.exe`, and is only needed if you have Windows Vista or Windows Server 2008 machines upon which you wish to perform the advanced auditing.

- Because `Auditpol.exe` is such a pain to work with, `Auditpol.exe`'s necessity goes away if the target is Windows Server 2008 R2 or Windows 7.

So, again, we'll first examine the auditing possibilities with Group Policy; that is, the stuff you can actually audit when you use Group Policy to enable the auditing. Then, we'll talk about auditing Group Policy itself.

Finally, we'll review the new advanced features that are available from Windows Vista and Windows Server 2008 and later.

We'll cleanly use Group Policy to manage auditing for our Windows Server 2008 R2 and Windows 7 machines, but be forced to use the command-line tool `Auditpol.exe` for our Windows Vista and Windows Server 2008 machines.

Auditable Events using Group Policy

So, Group Policy can be used to turn on many auditable events.

Certain aspects of auditing you'll turn on at the **Domain Controller** OU level, inside the "Default Domain Controllers Policy" GPO. Other aspects of auditing you'll typically turn on at other OU levels (via a GPO linked to the OU containing the systems you want to audit).

In Figure 8.18, you can see the default auditing settings contained within the "Default Domain Controllers Policy" GPO. The left screenshot shows a new Windows Server 2003 domain. The right screenshot shows a new Windows Server 2008 domain.

The list of possibilities for auditing are numerous and confusing. Table 8.2 shows what can be audited, along with where you should perform the audit.

FIGURE 8.18   Windows 2003 Default Domain Controller policy (left) and Windows Server 2008 Default Domain Controller Policy (right)

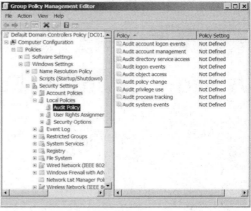

No matter how much you audit, it does you no good unless you're actually reviewing the logs. There is no way out of the box to centralize the collection of logs from your Domain Controllers, servers, or workstations. Consider a third-party tool, such as Microsoft SCOM or Event Log Sentry II from www.engagent.com.

TABLE 8.2 Auditable Events

Auditing Right	What It Does	Where You Should Set It	Is It On by Default in Windows 2003 Active Directory?	Is It On by Default in Windows 2008 Active Directory?	Notes
Audit account logon events	Enters events when someone attempts to log onto Active Directory.	In the "Default Domain Controllers Policy" GPO to monitor when anyone tries to log onto Active Directory.	Yes.	Yes. Hard-coded on, even though the GPO doesn't show it enabled.	By default, only successes generate events. Settings can be changed to record logon failures as well.
Audit account management	Enters events when someone creates, deletes, renames, enables, or disables users, computers, groups, and so on.	In the "Default Domain Controllers Policy" GPO to generate events for when users, computers, and so on are created in Active Directory. Set at the OU level to generate events on file servers or workstations for when users and groups are created on member machines.	Yes. Enabled on Domain Controllers, which log Active Directory events only. Not enabled on member servers.	Yes. Hard-coded on, even though the GPO doesn't show it enabled.	By default, only successful object manipulations generate events. Settings can be changed to record failures as well.

TABLE 8.2   Auditable Events *(continued)*

Auditing Right	What It Does	Where You Should Set It	Is It On by Default in Windows 2003 Active Directory?	Is It On by Default in Windows 2008 Active Directory?	Notes
Audit directory service access	Enters events when Active Directory objects are specified to be audited.	In the "Default Domain Controllers Policy" GPO.	Yes. In the "Default Domain Controllers Policy" GPO, which will log Active Directory access and GPO creation, deletion, and modification. See the section "Auditing Group Policy Object Changes." Not enabled on member servers.	Yes. Hard-coded on, even though the GPO doesn't show it enabled.	Works in con-junction with the actual attribute in Active Direc-tory that has auditing for users or computers enabled. Can be used to audit other aspects of Active Direc-tory. See the section "Audit-ing Group Policy Object Changes."
Audit logon events	Enters events for interactive logon (Local logon) and network logon (Kerberos).	Set at OU level to generate logon events on servers you want to track access for.	Yes. In "Default Domain Con-troller Policy" GPO, which affects only Active Direc-tory logons.		Set this set-ting to deter-mine if UserA touches a shared folder on ServerA. This will constitute an auditable event for "Audit logon events."

TABLE 8.2 Auditable Events *(continued)*

Auditing Right	What It Does	Where You Should Set It	Is It On by Default in Windows 2003 Active Directory?	Is It On by Default in Windows 2008 Active Directory?	Notes
Audit object access	Enters events when file objects are specified to be audited.	If you store files on your Domain Controllers, you can set this at the "Default Domain Controllers Policy" GPO. Otherwise, set it at the OU level to monitor specific files within member machines.	No.	No.	Works in conjunction with the actual file on the file server having auditing enabled. See the section "Auditing File Access."
Audit policy change	Enters events when changes are made to user rights, auditing policies, or trust relationships.	In the "Default Domain Controllers" GPO to monitor when changes are made within Active Directory. Set at OU level to monitor when changes are made on member machines.	Yes. In "Default Domain Controllers Policy" GPO, which affects only Active Directory events.	Yes. Hard-coded on, even though the GPO doesn't show it enabled.	See discussion in the next section.

TABLE 8.2 Auditable Events *(continued)*

Auditing Right	What It Does	Where You Should Set It	Is It On by Default in Windows 2003 Active Directory?	Is It On by Default in Windows 2008 Active Directory?	Notes
Audit privilege use	Enters events when any user right is used, such as backup and restore.	In the "Default Domain Controllers Policy" GPO to generate events for when accounts in Active Directory are used. Set at the OU level to generate events on file servers when accounts on member machines are used.	No.	No.	
Audit process tracking	Enters events when specific programs or processes are running.	In the "Default Domain Controllers Policy" GPO to affect Domain Controllers. Set at the OU level to monitor processes on specific servers within the OU.	No.	No.	This is an advanced auditing feature that can generate a lot of events once turned on. Only turn this on at the behest of Microsoft PSS or another troubleshooting authority.

TABLE 8.2 Auditable Events *(continued)*

Auditing Right	What It Does	Where You Should Set It	Is It On by Default in Windows 2003 Active Directory?	Is It On by Default in Windows 2008 Active Directory?	Notes
Audit system events	Enters events when the system starts up or shuts down, or any time the security or system logs have been modified.	In the "Default Domain Controllers Policy" GPO to determine when Domain Controllers are rebooted or logs have been modified. Set at an OU level to monitor when member machines are rebooted or logs have been modified.	Yes. In "Default Domain Controllers Policy" GPO, which affects only Domain Controllers.	Yes. Hard-coded on, even though the GPO doesn't show it enabled.	

Auditing File Access

Let's start with something simple.

Let's assume you want to enable auditing when users attempt to access files on file servers. You could run around to each server and turn on file auditing. Or (insert fanfare music here), you could use Group Policy to do it in one fell swoop.

So, to leverage file auditing on a wide scale, you need to do the following within Active Directory:

- Create an OU.

- Move the accounts of those file servers in the OU.

- Create a GPO linked to the OU.

- Enable the **Audit object access** policy setting inside the GPO linked to the OU.

Once you do this, you then specify which files or folders on the target file server you wish to audit. To do so, follow these steps:

1. At the target file server itself, use Explorer to drill down into the drive letter and directory that you want to audit. Right-click the folder (or just one specific file), and choose Properties from the context menu to open the Properties dialog box.

2. Click the Security tab, and then click the Advanced button to open the Advanced Security Settings for the share.

3. Click the Auditing tab.

4. Click Add to open the Auditing Entry dialog box, seen in Figure 8.19. This dialog box will allow you to add users to the auditing entries.

The simplest and most effective entry you can add is the Everyone group, as shown in Figure 8.19. When anyone tries to touch the file, you can audit for certain triggers, such as the "Read" permission.

FIGURE 8.19   Set auditing for files on the file or folder on the target system.

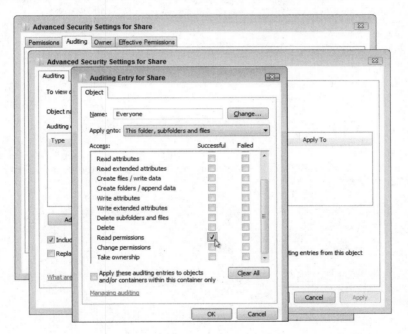

Auditing Group Policy Object Changes

You might be asked to determine who created a specific Group Policy and when it was created. To that end, you can leverage Active Directory's auditing capability and use Group Policy to audit Group Policy. Whenever a new Group Policy is born, deleted, or modified, various events such as the 566 Event in Figure 8.20 (for Windows Server 2003) and the 4662 Event in Figure 8.21 (for Windows Server 2008) are generated.

FIGURE 8.20   Event 566s are generated when GPOs are created or modified (Windows Server 2003).

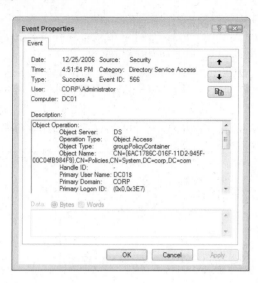

FIGURE 8.21   Event 4662s are generated when GPOs are created or modified (Windows Server 2008).

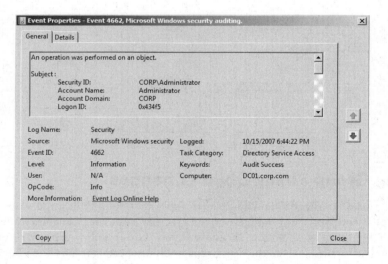

These events are generated on the Domain Controllers because two things are automatically set up by default in Active Directory (since Windows Server 2003):

- **Audit directory service access** is enabled in the "Default Domain Controllers Policy" GPO. You can see this in Figure 8.18, earlier in this chapter. In 100 percent new Windows Server 2008 domains, this isn't set "on" in the GPO; it is just hard-coded "on" by default regardless of the value in the GUI. This setting likely comes from the security database that is applied during the Domain Controller promotion process.

- Auditing is turned on for the "Policies" object container within Active Directory. The Policies folder is where the GPC (Group Policy Container) for a given GPO is stored in Active Directory. Auditing is turned on so that events are generated when anyone creates, destroys, or modifies any objects inside the folder.

To view the Policies container, follow these steps:

1. Launch Active Directory Users and Computers.

2. Choose View ➢ Advanced Features. This enables you to see some normally hidden folders and security rights within Active Directory Users and Computers.

3. Drill down into Domain ➢ System ➢ Policies.

4. Right-click the Policies folder, and choose Properties from the context menu to open the Properties dialog box.

5. Click the Security tab.

6. Click the Advanced button to open the Advanced Security Settings for Policies window.

7. Click the Auditing tab, which is shown in Figure 8.22.

If you drill down even deeper, you'll discover that the Everyone group will trigger events when new GPOs are modified or created. It is this interaction that generates events, such as those shown in Figure 8.20 and Figure 8.21.

If you wanted to hone in on who triggered events (as opposed to the Everyone group), you could remove the Everyone group from being audited (shown in Figure 8.22) and plunk in just the users or groups you wanted to monitor.

Group Policy Auditing Event IDs for Windows Server 2003

As you saw in Figure 8.19, the Event ID for GPO Auditing on Windows Server 2003 is Event ID number 566. However, there are numerous instances of Event 566, each with information that depends on precisely what you do to the GPO. The bad news is that the audit doesn't show you the GPO's "friendly name"; rather, it shows only the GUID, which is a little disappointing and makes things difficult to track down.

Table 8.3 shows what to expect when looking within Event 566.

FIGURE 8.22 Auditing for GPO changes is set on the Policies folder within Active Directory Users and Computers.

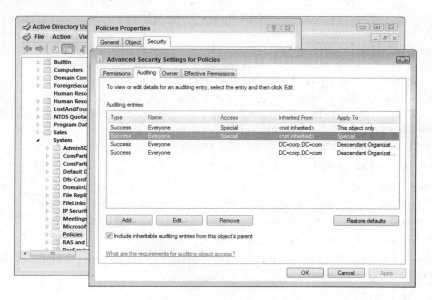

TABLE 8.3 The Contents of Event 566

Action That Occurred	Field to Look For	What It Shows in the Field
Create a new GPO	Accesses	Create Child groupPolicyContainer
Modify a GPO	Properties	Write Property—Default property set versionNumber gPCMachineExtension-Names groupPolicyContainer
Remove a GPO	Access	WRITE_DAC
Remove a GPO	Properties	WRITE_DAC groupPolicyContainer
Change GPO status	Properties	Write Property—Default property set flags groupPolicyContainer
Remove the Link Enabled status or remove the link from an OU	Properties	Write Property—Default property set gPLink organizationalUnit
Enforce/unenforce a GPO link	Properties	Write Property—Default property set gPLink organizationalUnit (or domain-DNS if done at the domain level)

TABLE 8.3   The Contents of Event 566 *(continued)*

Action That Occurred	Field to Look For	What It Shows in the Field
Block/unblock inheritance on an OU	Object Type	OrganizationalUnit
Block/unblock inheritance on an OU	Properties	Default property set gPOptions organizationalUnit
Change permissions	Properties	WRITE_DAC groupPolicyContainer

Windows 2000 shows these as Event 565, whereas Windows 2003 shows them as Event 566. The "Field to Look For" column and the "What It Shows" column may not be precisely the same for Windows 2000 domains.

Windows 2000 will also pop up Event 643 whenever the "Default Domain Policy" GPO is processed (whether changed or unchanged). You might see a lot of these, and you can safely ignore them.

Group Policy Auditing Event IDs for Windows Server 2008

The Event ID number changes from 566 in Windows Server 2003 to 4662 in Windows Server 2008. You can see an example in Figure 8.23, which shows that a specific GPO is being changed.

FIGURE 8.23   The GUID of the GPO is listed in the auditing trail.

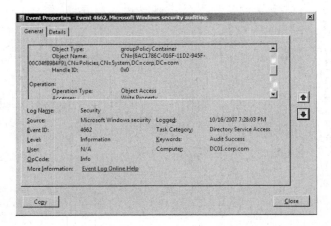

Whoopee.

I'm more than a little disappointed that Windows Server 2008 (as well as Windows Server 2008 R2) brings basically zero improvements in figuring out what's changed within a GPO. And what's more, reading the Event log details of a changed GPO is harder than trying to figure out what's going on in the movie *Pulp Fiction* the first time you watch it.

Advanced Audit Policy Configuration

Windows Server 2008 and Windows Vista introduced some potentially useful new auditing capabilities. You have the same general updated abilities when using Windows Server 2008 R2 and Windows 7, but the way you turn them on is a little different.

I'm not going to be able to go into all the various new capabilities. There's just too many of them. We'll focus on one of them—an important one, in just a bit.

First I'll show you where to find these settings if you want to examine and, optionally, set them. From your Windows 7 management machine, open a new GPO and traverse to Computer Configuration ➢ Policies ➢ Windows Settings ➢ Security Settings ➢ Advanced Audit Policy Configuration, as shown in Figure 8.24.

FIGURE 8.24   We'll explore the "Audit Directory Service Changes" policy.

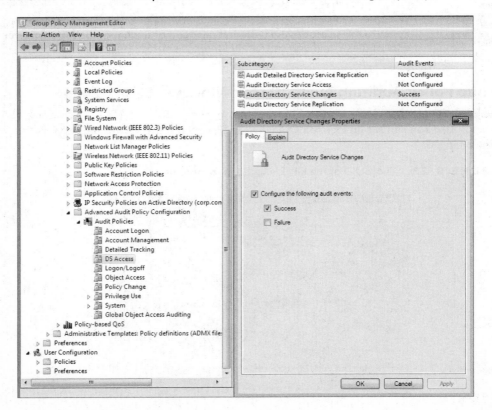

Now, you might look at this list of 10 categories and 50+ subcategories and think, "Whoa. What does each one do?" Well, the good news is, I'm not going to bore you to death with all that. I am, however, going to point you toward all that boring material for when the time comes. The link to find this is `http://tinyurl.com/yfj412a`. In case the article moves, just Google, or Bing, for "Advanced Security Audit Policy Settings."

As you can see in Figure 8.25, I'm using that link and drilling down to learn more about the DS Access category and the Audit Detailed Directory Service Replication subcategory. You can see the events it generates and other helpful information. Note that some of that same information is in an Explain tab right inside the policy itself—but I suggest reading both to get super clarity.

So, again, there are lots of Advanced Audit Policy Configuration settings that are perfectly valid on Windows Server 2008, Windows Server 2008 R2, Windows Vista, and Windows 7.

FIGURE 8.25   The Microsoft TechNet articles on advanced auditing

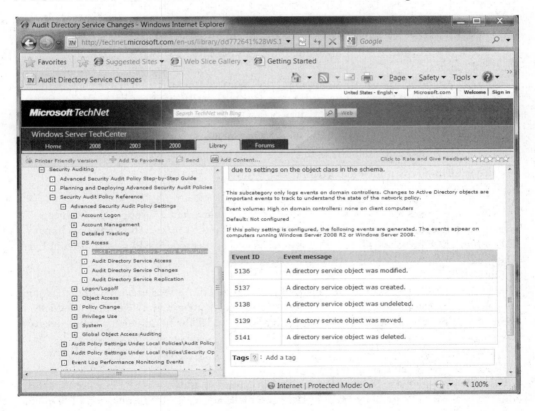

But, let's be super-duper "couldn't be clearer" clear:

- If you turn on these advanced auditing settings using Group Policy, your Windows XP and Windows Server 2003 machines will ignore them.

- If you turn on these advanced auditing settings using Group Policy, your Windows Server 2008 and Windows Vista machines will ignore them.

- If you turn on these advanced auditing settings using Group Policy, your Windows Server 2008 R2 and Windows 7 machines embrace them.

However, the caveat to bullet 2 is that you can make your Windows Server 2008 and Windows Vista machines do the advanced auditing. The trick is that they use an annoying tool called `Auditpol.exe`, whereas Windows Server 2008 R2 and Windows 7 are happy-as-clams to use Group Policy.

Let's work through one example that might be useful—we'll do it on both Windows Server 2008 (which requires `Auditpol.exe`) and Windows Server 2008 R2, which is happy to use the built-in Group Policy way to do things.

Advanced Auditing Example: Auditing Directory Service Changes

Let's check out Advanced Auditing using one example category: Auditing Directory Service Changes.

Looking up in the Microsoft documentation I pointed to earlier, I learned that I can turn on the ability to show four new Event ID types for when stuff happens in Active Directory. Here are the Event IDs and what they show:

- Event 5136: Show modified attributes

- Event 5137: Show created attributes

- Event 5138: Show undeleted attributes

- Event 5139: Show moved attributes

I was initially excited about these events, thinking that when a Group Policy Object was created or changed it would show me Event 5137 and 5136 and show me the changes *within the GPO*. It doesn't. It tells you a new GPO was created (but I knew that from Event IDs 4662).

Oh well.

However, these events *do* show you what has changed in Active Directory after the magic happens. So if EastSalesUser9 was renamed to Sally. In that case, you'll get multiple 5136 events because there are a gaggle of things that go on under the hood when a simple user rename occurs.

Make sense?

So how do you enable these new gifts?

Now, before I give you the secret sauce here, you need to ask yourself, "How useful is this going to be for me?" Already you could audit if something changed. The question is, "Do you want to see before and after results of the auditing?" The second question you need to ask yourself is, "Am I prepared to perform multiple steps along anywhere in Active Directory I want to actually audit for these special events?" If the answer is "Yes," then go for it.

Again, I'm picking an example category that makes sense mostly for Domain Controllers: Windows Server 2008 and Windows Server 2008 R2. So, that's what I'll show you here.

Enabling Advanced Auditing for Windows Server 2008 R2 and Windows 7

Again, enabling Advanced Auditing for Windows Server 2008 R2 (in my example) is easy as pie. Just drill down to the Computer Configuration ➢ Policies ➢ Windows Settings ➢ Security Settings ➢ Advanced Audit Policy ➢ DS Access and enable **Auditing Directory Service Changes**, as seen in Figure 8.24 earlier.

The trick, again, however, is to ensure that a Windows Server 2008 R2 machine receives the GPO. If a Windows Server 2008 machine (or Windows Server 2003 machine) embraces the GPO, it will do nothing.

Enabling Advanced Auditing for Windows Server 2008 and Windows Vista

If you wanted to turn on the same level of auditing (Auditing Directory Service Changes) on Windows Server 2008 DCs, you're going to have to do some manual labor.

You'll need to perform a command-line execution, by hand, on every Windows Server 2008 Domain Controller. And you do this on every Windows Server 2008 DC because you don't want some Windows Server 2008 DCs to log these new items and others missing out. Remember: your Windows Server 2008 DCs will ignore the Group Policy we created that will only work with Windows Server 2008 R2, so you'll have to run around to your remaining Windows Server 2008 DCs.

To turn them on you'll use the `auditpol.exe` command on your Windows Server 2008 Domain Controller.

The command you need to type is this (as seen in Figure 8.26):

```
auditpol /set /subcategory:"directory service changes" /success:enable
```

FIGURE 8.26   Turn on the new Event IDs.

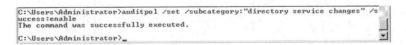

Okay. Maybe that wasn't too terrible. But I hate having to ask you to either create a startup script, or, worse, run around to each Windows Server 2008 machine—when our newer Windows Server 2008 R2 machines can just accept the edicts using Group Policy controls.

Auditing the Specific OU

So you've enabled the configuration using Group Policy (if your target is Windows Server 2008 R2) or using `Auditpol.exe` (if your target is Windows Server 2008).

But wait! There's more you have to do. Specifically, you have to turn on auditing at the OU level. At least, it's an OU in my example; you can audit other areas of Active Directory as well. Here's what to do next:

1. Using Active Directory Users and Computers, right-click the OU (or any object) for which you want to enable auditing, and then click Properties.

2. Click the Security tab, then click Advanced, and finally click the Auditing tab.

3. Click Add, and under "Enter the object name to select," type **Everyone** (or anyone you want to specifically audit for), then click OK.

4. In "Apply onto," click "Descendant User objects" (which is really far down the list). Note that you could also audit other objects if the container you're auditing contains other objects.

5. Under Access, select the Successful check box for "Write all properties."

6. Click OK in all open windows.

The Results

To see your results, just rename a user within that OU you just adjusted for auditing. In Figure 8.27, you can see that I've renamed EastSalesUser9 to Sally.

FIGURE 8.27   Here you can see that the AttributeValue of Sally is placed on the ObjectDN of EastSalesUser9.

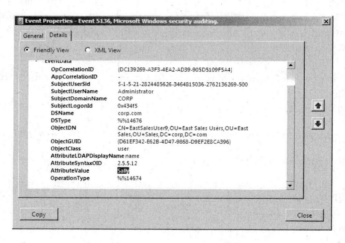

Is this useful? Possibly.

Well, here's the thing: you'd still get 4662 events that express that something's happened to the account anyway.

There's got to be someone out there who requested these advanced auditing features. Maybe you'll find them useful as well.

If you want more information from the source, here's a little guide:

- Lots of Auditpol advice can be found here: http://tinyurl.com/2qwu9e.

- A decent step-by-step guide on advanced auditing can be found here: http://tinyurl .com/ykju5q3.

- A very lengthy article describing how to "mass roll out" Auditpol.exe settings is here: http://support.microsoft.com/kb/921469. This document also describes a specific technique to ensure that "normal" auditing events don't overwrite the advanced auditing events. Look for it. It's a special policy setting called **Audit: Force audit policy subcategory settings (Windows Vista or later) to override audit policy category settings.**

Reading and testing is a must before rolling out into production.

Restricted Groups

In the last section, we conquered auditing. In this section, we'll move on to a new topic. The idea is simple—ensure the right people are always in the right groups. Sounds easy, right? Well, with a special security-related Group Policy function, you can use Restricted Groups to strictly control the following tasks:

- The membership of security groups that you create in Active Directory
- The security group membership on groups created on member machines (workstations or servers)
- The security groups that are nested within each other

You might want to strictly control these security groups or nestings to make sure that users in other areas of Active Directory, say, other domain administrators, don't inadvertently add someone to a group that shouldn't be there. Here are some practical uses of this technology:

- Ensure that the domain's Backup Operators group contains only Sally and Joe.
- Ensure that the local Administrators group on all desktops contains the user accounts of the help desk and desktop support personnel.
- Ensure that the domain's Sales global group contains the domain's East Sales, West Sales, North Sales, and South Sales local groups.

You set up these Restricted Groups' wishes via a GPO. You might be thinking to yourself that if the domain administrator creates the GPO, can't any domain administrator just delete the GPO and work around the point of the Restricted Groups settings? Yes, but the point of Restricted Groups is additional protection, not ultimate protection.

An analogy might be "museum putty." The idea behind museum putty is that you attach it to your precious objects as extra protection in case an object gets bumped from the shelf. You can see museum putty here: http://tinyurl.com/ycxc78. The idea is that if someone tries to "bump" users in or out of the group, this will keep just the users you want in place.

Here's the trick about the Restricted Groups function: it's younger, more capable brother just came back from college with the football trophy. I'm talking about the "Local Users and Groups" Group Policy Preferences function. Here's my honest opinion: I'd rather see you use Local Users and Groups Group Policy Preferences than the Group Policy Restricted Groups function—when it comes to manipulating local computers' groups, like the local Administrators group.

Here's why:

It just works.

The interface is obvious about what you want to do, and what's going to happen.

You can easily "laser beam" add or remove a particular user from a group.

And you can do more (like setting passwords on user accounts).

With that in mind, if you have a need to manipulate local users and groups—great. Use the Group Policy Preferences and be done. You'll be happier all around.

However, there is one use for Group Policy Restricted Groups that should not be overlooked—and we'll cover it right now. That's when you want to ensure who is a member of an Active Directory group.

Ah-ha! So the younger, more capable brother has a little Achilles heel. But this is his only one. So, if you'd like to learn how to utilize Group Policy Restricted groups to control Active Directory groups, then read on.

To save space, in this edition of the book I've cut the material about how to use Group Policy Restricted Groups for any use on local groups. Again, in those cases, I couldn't recommend the Group Policy Preferences Local Users and Groups (Chapter 5) highly enough.

Strictly Controlling Active Directory Groups

The ideal way to strictly control Active Directory groups with specific Active Directory users is to create a new GPO and link it to the **Domain Controllers** OU.

You *could* modify the "Default Domain Controllers Policy" GPO directly, but as stated earlier, it's better to create a new GPO when dealing with "normal" settings such as this one. This keeps the "Default Domain Controllers Policy" GPO as clean as possible. Likewise, you *could* modify the "Default Domain Policy" GPO. But, again, keeping away from the defaults for other than their special uses (as previously discussed) is preferred.

If you set up Restricted Groups policies at multiple levels in Active Directory, there is no "merging" between Restricted Groups policy settings. The "last applied" policy wins. For example, if you set up a Restricted Groups policy, link it to the domain level, create another Restricted Groups policy, and link it to the **Domain Controllers** OU, the one linked to the **Domain Controllers** OU "wins."

To get started with restricted groups:

1. Open the GPO and traverse to Computer Configuration ➢ Policies ➢ Windows Settings ➢ Security Settings ➢ **Restricted Groups**.

2. Right-click Restricted Groups, and choose Add Group from the context menu, which opens the Add Group dialog box.

3. Click Browse to open the Browse dialog box, and browse for a group, say, the domain's Backup Operators; then click OK.

4. When you do, the Backup Operator Properties dialog box, shown in Figure 8.28, appears.

FIGURE 8.28   You can specify which users you want to ensure are in specific groups.

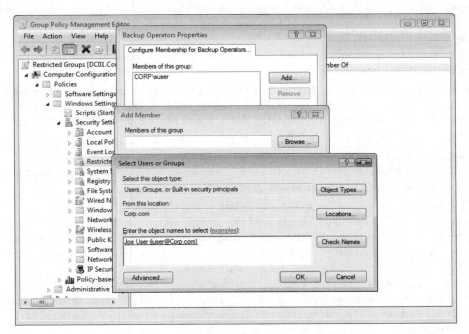

You can now choose domain members to place in the "Members of this group" list. In Figure 8.28, I have already added Sally User's account, which is in the domain, and I'm about to add Joe User's domain account.

WARNING   Be careful about just typing in the user account names without either browsing the domain or manually entering the domain with the DOMAIN\ user syntax. Restricted Groups in Active Directory will not apply correctly unless you do this.

When Restricted Groups Settings Take Effect

After you enter the users in the "Members of this group" list and click OK, you can sit back and wait for all Domain Controllers to get the change and process Group Policy. However, if you have only one Domain Controller in your test lab, this change should occur quickly. You can run GPUpdate to make it occur even faster in this case. This happens because any new GPO you create and link to the **Domain Controllers** OU should get picked up and applied right away—about 5 minutes after replication occurs.

Now, take a look inside the Backup Operators group using Active Directory Users and Computers. Sally and Joe's accounts should be forced inside Backup Operators.

When Restricted Groups Settings Get Refreshed

If someone were to *remove* Sally and Joe from Backup Operators in Active Directory Users and Computers, their accounts would be repopulated during the background security refresh, which is every 16 hours.

As described in Chapter 3, you have two choices if you don't want to wait 16 hours for the background security refresh:

- Link a GPO to the **Domain Controllers** OU level, with the **Security policy processing** policy setting with the "Process even if the Group Policy objects have not changed" flag set. Then, the Background Security Refresh will process with the normal background refresh (every 5 minutes for DCs).

- Force a manual refresh by running GPUpdate /FORCE on your Domain Controller. Recall that GPUpdate /FORCE may be used when the underlying GPO hasn't changed and you want your changes reflected immediately.

The users removed from Backup Operators will pop right back in!

There is one caveat with the "Members of this group" section of Restricted Groups: this is an explicit list. If you later add more users using Active Directory Users and Computers, they will also be removed when the Restricted Groups policy is refreshed. Only the users listed in the "Members of this group" section will return.

Note that there is a way to work around this, but it's an unsupported "trick." I had the exact how-to in the last edition of the book, but I've since taken it out. Why? Because Group Policy Preferences' Local Users and Groups function can do it in a "non-tricky" way, and that's more supportable in the long run.

Strictly Applying Group Nesting

Another trick Restricted Groups can perform is that it can ensure that one domain group is nested inside another. Like the "Strictly Controlling Active Directory Groups" trick, you need a GPO linked to the **Domain Controllers** OU.

The interface is a bit counterintuitive; the idea is that you name a group (say, HR-OU-Admins) and then specify the group of which it will be a member.

To nest one group within another:

1. Open the GPO and traverse to Computer Configuration ➢ Policies ➢ Windows Settings ➢ Security Settings ➢ **Restricted Groups**.

2. Right-click Restricted Groups, and choose Add Group from the context menu, which opens the Add Group dialog box.

3. Click Browse to open the Browse dialog box, and locate the first group. Click OK in the Add Group dialog box to select your group.

4. When you do, the Properties dialog box appears, as shown earlier in Figure 8.28 earlier.

5. Then, you'll click the Add button in the "This group is a member of" section of the Properties dialog box (not shown in Figure 8.28). You'll then be able to specify the second group name.

When you're finished, and the Group Policy applies, the result will be that the first group will be forcefully nested within the second group. In order for this to work well, it helps to remember that different domain modes allow for different levels of group nesting. Here's the super-speedy version:

- Windows 2000 Mixed mode domains and Windows 2003 Interim mode domains can nest global groups only into domain local groups.

- Windows 2000 and higher Native mode domains can nest global groups into domain local groups. Additionally, global groups can be nested into global groups.

WARNING While you are creating a Restricted Groups policy, take care. Results can be unpredictable when you mix the "This group is a member of" and "Members of this group" sections. If you have ensured a group's membership using the "Members of this group" setting, don't attempt to further modify that group's membership by feeding the "This group is a member of" users (by lying to the Restricted Groups function) to extend the original group's membership! On occasion, the "This group is a member of" and "Members of this group" will conflict if you try to add users to both headings.

Which Groups Can Go into Which Other Groups via Restricted Groups?

The processing of Restricted Groups can sometimes be picky depending on the scenario. (This is officially documented in the Microsoft Knowledge Base article 810076 at http:// support.microsoft.com/kb/810076.) And the out-of-the-box processing changes a bit and becomes more standardized for the most up-to-date clients: Windows 2003, Windows 2000/SP4, and Windows XP/SP2.

Microsoft Knowledge Base article 810076 now has several tables to help you during your testing of this feature. Again, to ensure that the tables work for you, you need Windows 2003, Windows 2000/SP4, or Windows XP/SP2, or you need the hotfix in the Microsoft Knowledge Base article 810076 applied to machines that will receive the forced users or groups.

No operating systems past Windows XP are represented in this table yet. While I haven't tested every combination, I'm told iterations of the operating system from Windows XP/SP2 and later are supposed to also act like Windows XP/SP2.

Restrict Software: Software Restriction Policy and AppLocker

Windows, as a product, is successful. And the reason for that is pretty simple: it runs a lot of software. Running a lot of software sounds good, until you're on the other end of the equation and, as an IT professional, you want to start *preventing* some of that software from running.

Many viruses show up in your users' inboxes as either executables or .VBS scripting files. Just one launch within your confines, and you're cleaning up for a week. Additionally, users will bring in unknown software from home or download junk off the Internet, and then, when the computer blows up, they turn around and blame you. What an injustice!

To that end, there are two separate mechanisms to squelch which software will run: Software Restriction Policies (SRP) and AppLocker:

- Software Restriction Policies is available when the target machine is Windows XP or later.

- AppLocker is available when the target is Windows 7 and Windows Server 2008 R2.

Let me jump to the end of the story. If you're using mostly Windows XP, then, yes, go ahead and learn about Software Restriction Policies in this next section. However, if you're using mostly Windows 7, then still read the Software Restriction Policies section for concepts. We'll build on those concepts and ideas, but then utilize AppLocker for Windows 7.

But wait. There is one major caveat around AppLocker, which I want to just "get out there" right now before you get all hot under the collar about it. That is, it's not available on every version of Windows 7.

In this document (`http://tinyurl.com/yjvh34d`), Microsoft is very clear: AppLocker is only available for the Enterprise (and Ultimate) versions of Windows 7. It is not available in the Professional version of Windows 7.

Ouch. That potentially puts this real neat security feature out of reach for a lot of people.

Inside Software Restriction Policies

Software Restriction Policies enable you, the administrator, to precisely dictate what software will and will not run on your Windows XP desktops.

To that end, Microsoft developed Software Restriction Policies, which can put the kibosh on software that shouldn't be there in the first place. You can restrict software for specific users or for all users on a specific machine. You'll find Software Restriction Policies in Computer Configuration ➢ Policies ➢ Windows Settings ➢ Security Settings ➢ **Software Restriction Policies**. Just right-click over the Software Restriction Policies node, and select New Software Restriction Policies, as shown in Figure 8.29, to get started.

Software Restriction Policies is also available as a node under User Configuration ➤ Policies ➤ Windows Settings ➤ Security Settings ➤ **Software Restriction Policies**, which can also be seen in Figure 8.29.

FIGURE 8.29   Software Restriction Policies are available in both the Computer and User nodes.

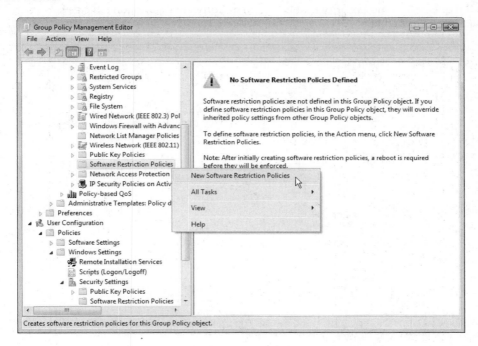

Like other policies that affect users or computers, you'll need an OU containing the user or computer accounts you want to restrict, and you'll need a GPO linked to that OU. Or you can set a GPO linked to the domain level, which affects all machines (or, alternatively, users). Typically, you'll use the Computer side branch of Software Restriction Policies. That way, all users on a specific machine are restricted from using specific "known bad" applications.

Software Restriction Policies are also valid when set on a local computer within a local policy (via GPEdit.msc). This can be particularly useful for a Windows 2003 or Windows Server 2008 acting as a Terminal Server. Software Restriction Policies are meant to replace the APPSec.exe tool.

GPOs containing Software Restriction Policies might be common in environments that include any variety of Windows machines. However, Windows 2000 machines that are affected by GPOs containing Software Restriction Policies will simply ignore the settings and restrictions contained within.

Software Restriction Policies' "Philosophies"

Using Software Restriction Policies with your Windows users involves three primary philosophies. You can choose your philosophy by selecting the Security Levels branch of Software Restriction Policies, as shown in Figure 8.30.

FIGURE 8.30   The Security Levels branch of Software Restriction Policies sets your default level of protection.

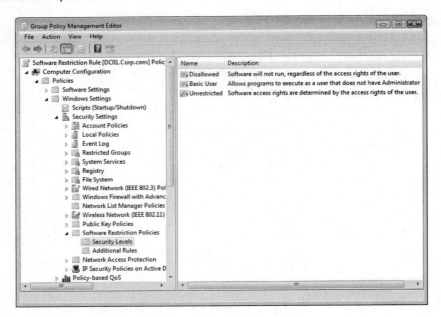

Philosophy 1 (aka "The Black List") *Allow everything to run except specifically named items.* Here, we've chosen the default that the Unrestricted option is selected. Windows will allow all programs to run, like normal. However, if the administrator names certain applications, such as a virus or a game, it will be prevented from running. It's as if you're putting the things you don't want on the "black list" but allowing everything else to run.

Philosophy 2 (aka "The Doggie Door") *Don't allow programs of a certain type to run.* Allow only specifically named items of that type to pass. I nickname this one "The Doggie Door." The Unrestricted option is selected. You can choose to squelch all files of a certain type, say, all .VBS files. However, you can instruct Windows to allow .VBS files that are digitally signed from your IT department to run.

Philosophy 3 (aka "The White List") *Nothing is allowed to run but the operating system and explicitly named items.* This is the "Full Lockdown" approach. The Disallowed option is selected. This is the most heavy-handed approach but the safest. Only operating system components will run, unless you specifically open up ways for programs to be run. Be careful when using this method; it can get you into a lot of trouble quickly.

Within these philosophies, you have one extra super-power if you use Windows Vista or Windows 7 as your target machine: you can specify that specific software can only be run with Basic User credentials. That is, if you decide that you want to run a specific application but are concerned that in doing so it might run with too many rights, you can specify it to run as a "Basic User."

 You cannot select the Basic User security level for a Certificate Rule (described next).

Software Restriction Policies' Rules

Once you've chosen your philosophy, you can choose how wide the door is for other stuff. There are four rules to either allow or deny specific software:

- Hash
- Path
- Certificate
- Network zone (or Internet zone on pre-Vista management stations)

To create a new rule, select the Additional Rules folder, and right-click in the right pane to see your choices, as shown in Figure 8.31.

FIGURE 8.31   The Rules of Software Restriction Policy

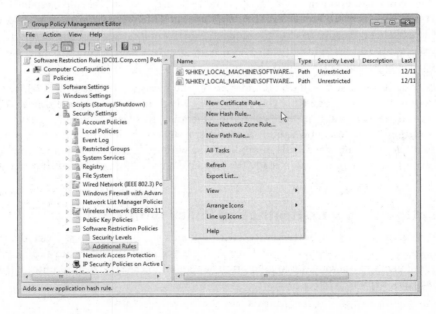

By default, some path rules are set that enable access to critical portions of the Registry. These are enabled so that the operating system can write to the Registry even if the Disallowed option is set in the Security Levels branch.

Hash Rule   In computer science terms, a hash value is a numeric representation, or fingerprint, that can uniquely identify a file should it be renamed. It's sort of like a "checksum" value. For instance, if I rename Doom.exe to Gloom.exe, the actual bits, the 1s and 0s, contained within the .EXE file are the same. Therefore, the hash value is the same. However, if any changes are made to the file (even if one bit is changed), the hash value is different. Hash rules are quite useful in containing any application that's an .EXE or a .DLL.

Sure, it's true that a user could use a hex editor (such as FRHED from http://frhed .sourceforge.net/) and change just one bit in an .EXE or .DLL file to get a new hash value, but it's bloody unlikely. And, the .EXE could be damaged and unusable in the process! And that's reasonably good protection for most of us.

Path Rule   You can specify to open (or restrict) certain applications based on where they reside on the hard drive. You can set up a path rule to specify a specific folder or full path to a program. Most environment variables are valid, such as %HOMEDRIVE%, %HOMEPATH%, %USERPROFILE%, %WINDIR%, %APPDATA%, %PROGRAMFILES%, and %TEMP%. Additionally, path rules can stomp out the running of any file type you desire, say, VBScript files. For example, if you set up a path rule to disallow files named *.vb*, all VBScript file variants will be unable to execute.

Certificate Rule   Certificate rules use digitally signed certificates. You can use certificate rules to sign your own applications or scripts and then use a certificate rule to specify your IT department as a Trusted Publisher. Users, admins, or Enterprise Admins can be specified as trusted publishers. Be sure to read the sidebar "Software Restriction Policies and Digital Signatures" before rolling out certificate rules. Note that this rule is unable to specify the Basic User security level as previously described.

Network Zone Rule   Users will download crap off the Internet. This is a fact of life. However, with Network Zone Rule you can specify which Internet Explorer zones are allowed for download. You can specify Internet, Intranet, Restricted Sites, Trusted Sites, and My Computer. The bad news about zone rules, however, is that they simply aren't all that useful. They prevent downloads of applications with the MSI format but nothing else. So, in my opinion, they're not quite ready for primetime use. (Note that we talk more about MSI files in Chapter 11.)

Setting Up a Software Restriction Policy with a Rule

As stated, you can craft your Software Restriction Policies in myriad ways. Space doesn't permit explaining all of them, so I'll just give you one example. We'll test our Software Restriction Policies by locking down a nefarious application that has caused untold distress to innumerable, hapless people: Solitaire!

To restrict Solitaire from your environment, follow these steps:

1. Create a new hash rule as seen in Figure 8.31 earlier in this chapter.
2. Click Browse and locate sol.exe.

You might have to type **\\XPPR01\c$\windows\system32\sol.exe** to point to a copy of Solitaire on one of your Windows XP machines if you're logged on at a Domain Controller (because Solitaire isn't present on Windows 2003 servers). If you have Windows XP/SP2 loaded on your client system, you can't do this until the SP2 firewall is turned off.

In Windows XP, the "File hash" entry is filled in with the file hash value of Sol.exe from the machine, as shown in Figure 8.32.

In the updated GPMC, there isn't a file hash that's shown, but it's still doing the work.

Under the hood, the Software Restriction Policies editor actually created *two* file hashes. One hash is an MD5 hash (for older Windows XP and Windows Server 2003 clients) and another is an SHA-256 hash for newer XP, Windows Server 2003, and Windows Vista and later clients. Windows Vista and later still reads MD5 hashes created using older Windows XP management stations.

Now let's be super-clear: the hash value for sol.exe on Windows XP won't equal the hash value for sol.exe on Windows Vista. Heck, the hash value for sol.exe on Windows XP/SP2 might not equal the hash value for sol.exe on Windows XP/SP3! With that in mind, if you want to restrict sol.exe everywhere, you'll need to get ahold of each and every sol.exe variant and add it as a hash value.

FIGURE 8.32 Once you specify the file, the hash value is filled in.

Testing Your Software Restriction Policies

In the previous example, you could create a Software Restriction Policy that affects users or computers. If your policy is for users, for this very first test, log off. If your policy is for computers, reboot the machine. Follow these steps to immediately demonstrate the desired behavior of Software Restriction Policies:

1. Log on the machine that should get the Software Restriction Policies.

2. Choose Start ➢ Run to open the Run dialog box.

3. In the Open box, type **so1.exe**. You'll see the message shown in Figure 8.33.

   If you were to open a command prompt and then type **so1.exe**, you would also be restricted. You'd see the message "The system cannot execute the specified program," which is what you might expect.

FIGURE 8.33   On Windows XP machines, Solitaire is prevented from running.

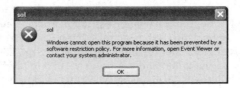

Software Restriction Policies and Digital Signatures

Note that there is a security policy setting named **System settings: Use Certificate Rules on Windows Executables for Software Restriction Policies** located in Computer Configuration ➢ Policies ➢ Windows Settings ➢ Security Settings ➢ Local Policies ➢ Security Options.

You'll need to enable this policy setting if you create a certificate rule on a *digitally signed* .EXE. You can tell if a file is digitally signed by checking out its properties and looking for a Digital Signatures tab, as seen here in the file's properties. WINWORD.EXE has a Digital Signatures tab, while So1.exe has none.

If you were to restrict a digitally signed .EXE, such as WINWORD.EXE, this policy setting would be necessary for the certificate rule to be embraced by your client systems.

As stated, this policy setting is only necessary for digitally signed .EXEs. However, if you only deal with digitally signed .VBS or .MSI files, you don't have to worry about this setting at all.

Understanding When Software Restriction Policies Apply

When you log onto a machine, you're running a shell program that launches other programs. This is sometimes called a "launching process." That shell program (or launching process) is familiar—`Explorer.exe`. Whenever `Explorer.exe` (or other launching processes) launches restricted software, it checks a portion of the Registry for any restrictions. How does this help determine when Software Restriction Policies apply?

 Software Restriction Policies are housed in `HKEY_LOCAL_MACHINE\ SOFTWARE\Policies\Microsoft\Windows\Safer\CodeIdentifiers`.

A Software Restriction Policy affects a machine as soon as it's downloaded via the Group Policy engine. After that, no new instances of that application are possible. It doesn't matter if the launching program (i.e., Explorer) has already been started; it doesn't need a refresh. It just restricts the software as specified in the Software Restriction Policies as soon as the Group Policy containing the Software Restriction Policies is applied. Note, however, that programs *already* running don't magically stop running. This will only prevent future instances of the specified application from running. So, if `Sol.exe` is already running, then a Software Restriction Policy comes down to disable it—as long as `Sol.exe` is running, it stays running. When you close it, however, it cannot be reopened again because Explorer has checked in with the Registry and prevents it.

Troubleshooting Software Restriction Policies

You can troubleshoot Software Restriction Policies in two primary ways:

- Inspect the Registry to see if the Software Restriction Policies are embraced.
- Enable advanced logging.

Inspecting the Software Restriction Policies Location in the Registry

If Software Restriction Policies aren't being applied, and you logged off and back on, log on again as the administrator at the target machine and check `KEY_LOCAL_MACHINE` or

`HKEY_CURRENT_USER\SOFTWARE\Policies\Microsoft\Windows\Safer\CodeIdentifiers`

Inside, you'll see numbered branches containing the rules. In Figure 8.34, you can see `Sol.exe` being restricted by a hash rule.

Note that operating system files change with service packs—sometimes even innocuous things like `Sol.exe`! If, after a service pack, your client isn't restricting applications as you expect (because the hash value changes even after a tiny change), make sure the version number of the restricted application matches the version located on the client. More specifically, make sure the hash values match.

FIGURE 8.34 The Registry lays out what will be restricted.

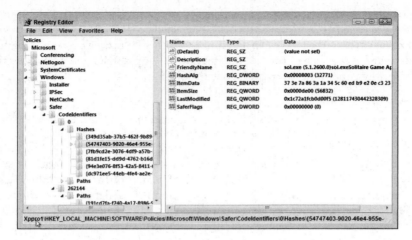

Software Restriction Policies Advanced Logging

You can troubleshoot Software Restriction Policies via a log file. To do so, follow these steps:

1. In the Registry, traverse to

   KEY_LOCAL_MACHINE\SOFTWARE\Policies\Microsoft\Windows\Safer\CodeIdentifiers

2. Create a new string value named LogFileName.

3. In the Data field of the new Registry key, enter the full path and name of a log file—for example, **c:\srplog.txt**.

Now whenever an application runs, a line is written to the log file explaining why it can or cannot run. Here are two lines from that log file: the first when I run Notepad (which is free to run) and the second when I run the Sol.exe (which is restricted):

```
cmd.exe (PID = 1576) identified C:\WINDOWS\system32\notepad.exe as Unrestricted
    using path rule, Guid = {191cd7fa-f240-4a17-8986-94d480a6c8ca}

cmd.exe (PID = 1576) identified C:\WINDOWS\system32\sol.exe as Disallowed using
    hash rule, Guid = {e669efa3-96d8-4c16-b506-2fec88fbee33}
```

You'll find a great article on Software Restriction Policies in TechNet at http://technet.microsoft.com/en-us/library/bb457006.aspx. If it's not there, then just search for an article named "Using Software Restriction Policies to Protect Against Unauthorized Software." Also check out this small article series on the subject by my pal Jakob H. Heidelberg called "Default Deny All Applications" (part 1 at http://tinyurl.com/ysb6wu and part 2 at http://tinyurl.com/2hdz7s).

Oops, I Locked Myself Out of My Machine with Software Restriction Policies

If you make a Software Restriction Policy too tight, you can lock yourself right out of the system! Don't panic. If the policy is a GPO in Active Directory, remove the policy setting or disable the GPO. After Group Policy processes on the client, log on again as the user and you should be cleared up.

However, if you make a Software Restriction Policy using the local policy editor (GPEDIT.MSC) and you lock yourself out, you have a slightly longer road to recovery. Follow these steps:

1. Reboot the machine, and press F8 upon startup to open the Advanced Options menu at boot time.

2. Select SAFE MODE and allow the computer to continue to finish booting.

3. Log on as the machine's local administrator.

4. Dive in to

   `HKLM\Software\Policies\Microsoft\Windows\Safer\CodeIdentifiers`

   Delete everything below the `CodeIdentifiers` key.

5. Reboot the machine.

You should be out of the woods now.

However, if the policies were set on a given user, the steps are a bit different. Just drill down to that user's HKCU hive file and nuke them there.

More Software Restriction Policies resources can be found at

`www.microsoft.com/technet/security/prodtech/windowsxp/secwinxp/xpsgch06.mspx`

(shortened to `http://tinyurl.com/mx96v`).

Restricting Software Using AppLocker

I'm going to let you in on a little secret: Microsoft loves to market things. Really. It's true. So this newfangled "AppLocker" thing we're about to talk about is really (under the hood) called Software Restriction Policy v2. Really! So, while some may tell you that AppLocker is revolutionary, it's more evolutionary. But that doesn't mean it isn't useful.

Anyway, so AppLocker is the "more modern" way that Microsoft has provided to restrict software. You'll find the AppLocker controls only if your GPMC is the Windows 7 with RSAT or Windows Server 2008 R2 version.

And, again, you can only set AppLocker policies for Windows 7 and Windows Server 2008 R2 machines. Not that I think that you'll use it very much, if ever, on a Windows Server 2008 R2 machine. The only foreseeable time would be if you're using Windows Server 2008 R2 as a Terminal Server where real users log on.

AppLocker is an important evolution compared to Software Restriction Policies. AppLocker's has three "Laws" to determine whether files should execute on the system. "Laws" is my word, not Microsoft's, but I think it explains AppLocker's "brain" pretty well.

Here are the AppLocker Laws:

- Law 1: Explicit deny: A specific rule that denies an action.

- Law 2: Explicit allow: A specific rule that allows an action.

- Law 3: Implicit deny: All files that are not specifically named by an Allow rule are automatically blocked.

So, Software Restriction Policies did a reasonable job at controlling applications on Windows XP. But, on the other hand, it was missing (in my opinion) two key ingredients to make it a blockbuster:

- One problem is that there was no easy way to state: "Allow software to run from Manufacturer X, Product ABC, if Product ABC is above a certain revision." So, in our examples, we'll make an AppLocker policy that says: "Allow software from Adobe, specifically Acrobat Reader, when it's version is greater than 9.0."

- The other problem was that while Software Restriction Policies had the concept of "Allow" and "Deny" there was no great way of quickly telling Software Restriction Policies about all the "good" software you had. It was tedious, if not impossible, to make the list so that it worked well. With AppLocker, we can quickly spawn a list of "good stuff" we want to allow to run based on a "template machine."

So, we'll try and put both of these Software Restriction Policies problems behind us, and bury them using AppLocker in these examples.

To prepare for these examples, we'll need both Acrobat Reader 8.1.2 and 9.0. Note that Acrobat Reader 8.1.2 is, well, a little old. And that's the idea. We'll start out with Acrobat Reader 8.1.2 (the previous version) and create some rules. Then we'll upgrade to Acrobat Reader 9.0 and see how AppLocker handles it. I was able to find both the new and older versions of Acrobat on this page at Adobe: http://tinyurl.com/yowttp. Use the downloads in the "Full Download" section.

We'll need to install them on WIN7MANAGEMENT and also on our WIN7 client. You'll see why in a bit. So, again, install Acrobat Reader 8.1.2 on both WIN7MANAGEMENT and WIN7 if you want to walk through these examples with me.

AppLocker has three required pieces we need to configure in order to make it work:

- The AppLocker policy itself, which describes the applications and circumstances to be on the lookout for

- An "overall" policy describing if you want to really lock out, or just perform an "audit" (more later)

- A service that must be actively running on the Windows 7 or Windows Server 2008 R2 client

We'll break down each piece, and additionally walk through where AppLocker has a leg up on its predecessor, Software Restriction Policies.

AppLocker: Rules and Rule Conditions

Let's start out by creating and linking a GPO to our Human Resources Computers OU and call it AppLocker Tests. You'll find AppLocker abilities tucked under Computer Configuration ➢ Policies ➢ Windows Settings ➢ Security Settings ➢ Application Control Policies ➢ AppLocker. (Why they chose to use a separate subnode called AppLocker underneath Application Control Policies, I will never know.) Inside, you'll see there are three types of *rules*: Executable Rules, Windows Installer Rules, and Script Rules. Let's review each before we dive into them for testing:

- Executable Rules: Allow or Prevent specific `.EXE`s, `.COM`s, `.DLL`s, or `.OCX`s to run
- Windows Installer Rules: Allow or Prevent specific `.MSI` (Windows Installer) and `.MSP` (Windows Patching) setup files to run
- Script Rules: Allow or Prevent scripts to run. Limited to `.PS1`, `.BAT`, `.CMD`, `.VBS`, and `.JS` files only.

Now, in a second, we'll create a rule. And for each of the rules, there are three types of *rule conditions*:

- Path Rule Condition: Similar to what we've learned about in Software Restriction Policies, you can Allow or Deny based on where the file resides.
- File Hash Rule Condition: Again, similar to what we've learned about in Software Restriction Policies, you can Allow or Deny based on the hash of a file.
- Publisher Rule Condition: This is unique to AppLocker, and allows you to specify a Publisher you want to Allow or Deny. This assumes the files you want to run are digitally signed by the publisher.

Using the GPO we have open, let's right-click Executable Rules and immediately select "Create Default Rules," as seen in Figure 8.35.

The Default Rules won't come into play right now, but they're a good habit to get started with. The Default Rules ensure that (at least) Windows system files will always be able to run, when you start to put the smack down on your applications.

But, since we're looking at them now, anyway, let's examine the default rules and understand what they allow us to do:

- Allow anything to run that's already installed in Program Files
- Allow anything to run if it's in the Windows folder
- Allow local administrators to run any file

Remember AppLocker's Law 3: everything is denied unless we've specifically set up a rule to allow it. So, setting up the default rules is a good idea, so that anything and everything running inside Program Files will just work.

FIGURE 8.35   "Create Default Rules" to ensure safe passage using AppLocker.

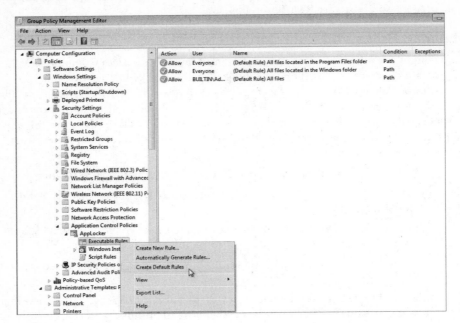

Leveraging Law 1: Blacklisting Specific Applications with an Explicit Deny

You've already installed Acrobat Reader 8 on your WIN7 machine. It's already inside the Program Files directory, running along. And, you've got a default rule in place that enables you to run it. (Remember, one of those rules allows anything inside Program Files to run.)

But since it's out there and installed already, how can we control it using AppLocker?

To do this, we'll create an Explicit deny to put the kibosh on Acrobat Reader.

Let's right-click over Executable Rules and select "Create New Rule." When you do, you'll be prompted with a wizard and "Before You Begin" page (not shown). Click Next to get started. You'll then see a "Permissions" page where you can select to Allow or Deny applications. Let's select Deny (not shown), leave the "User or Group" selection set to Everyone (default), and select Next.

When you do, you'll see the Conditions page shown in Figure 8.36.

In our examples, we'll want to restrict Acrobat Reader based on who published it—Adobe. So select Publisher and click Next. When you do, you'll see the Publisher screen shown in Figure 8.37.

FIGURE 8.36 Select Publisher to restrict based on digitally signed applications.

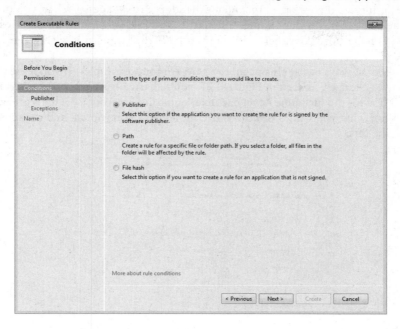

FIGURE 8.37 You can select a file which contains a digital signature, then dictate which values you want to restrict against.

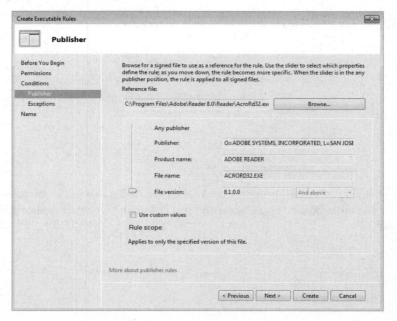

For our examples, click the Browse button, and then find `AcroRd32.exe` (which usually lives under `C:\Program Files\Adobe\Reader 8.0\Reader`). When you do, you'll see the Publisher, Product name, File name, and File version all automatically populate. This is because AppLocker is reading the digital signature within the Acrobat Reader file.

There are lots of ways to use this page, but here are some examples. If you leave the slider as is, making no changes, as seen in Figure 8.37, you're basically saying "Deny Acrobat Reader 8.1.0.0, with the file name `AcroRd32.exe`, published by Adobe." That's great, but maybe that's not what you want. You can move the slider up one notch, and the screen should look like this:

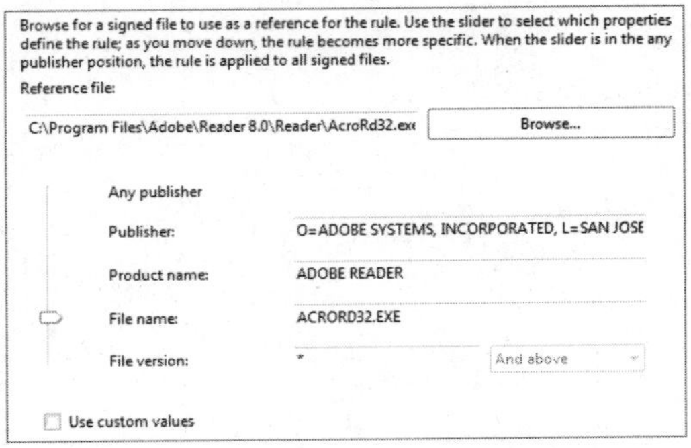

The File Version selection goes to "*" which means "all versions." So, now you're saying "Deny All Versions of Acrobat Reader, with the file name `AcroRd32.exe` published by Adobe." What happens if you move the slider up *another* notch, as seen here?

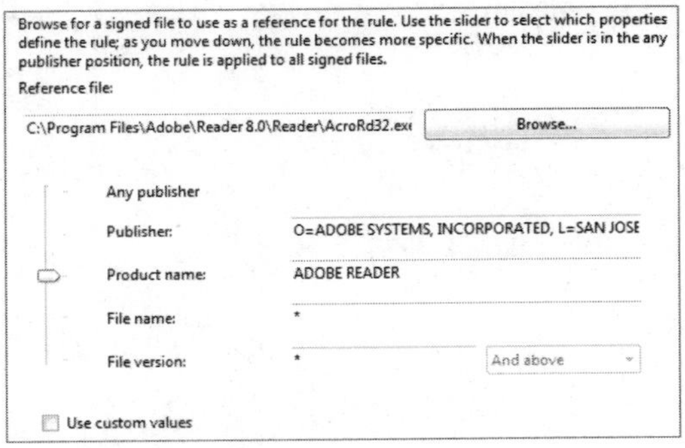

Now you're saying "Deny all products by Adobe that are known as Adobe Reader."

Move it up one more notch as seen here, and you're saying "Deny all applications by the publisher Adobe."

And, you can put it one *more* notch up, and deny All Publishers as seen here! (Don't really do this; I don't advise doing so right now.)

Wow! That's some serious power!

Turns out, though, none of these configurations is what I want us to work through for the real example. So, click the "Use custom values" check box. Then change the File Version from 8.1.0.0 to 8.2.0.0 and select "And below," as seen here:

Now our rule says "Deny Acrobat Reader from Adobe when the File Version is below 8.2.0.0."

Click Next to visit the Exceptions page (not shown). Here you can make an exception to your rule. We're not going to do this for now, but it's good to know there are ways we can permit specific applications from publishers if we really crank down, say, denying all applications based on Publisher. So on the Exceptions page, click Next.

The final page is called "Name and Description." The system guesses at a good name for your AppLocker rule. Feel free to change if you like and/or add a description. This page is not shown here. Click Create to finish up and present the rule. When you do, you'll see the rule created, as seen in Figure 8.38.

FIGURE 8.38   Your Deny rule is set to restrict Acrobat Reader 8.2 and below.

Action	User	Name	Condition	Exceptions
✅ Allow	Everyone	(Default Rule) All files located in the Program Files folder	Path	
✅ Allow	Everyone	(Default Rule) All files located in the Windows folder	Path	
✅ Allow	BUILTIN\Ad...	(Default Rule) All files	Path	
🚫 Deny	Everyone	ACRORD32.EXE, version 8.2.0.0 and below, in ADOBE READ...	Publisher	

You might think that you're ready to go. Oh, no. There are two more big steps you must do before testing can commence.

AppLocker Actions: Enforcement or Auditing

AppLocker does nothing at all once you've created your rules.

It can be kind of a letdown if you're not prepared for it.

You have to determine what actions you want to take when your AppLocker rule comes to pass. So, to get the party started (or, more accurately, be the wet blanket *on* the party) you need to turn on Enforcement rules.

You find this by again, locating Computer Configuration ➢ Policies ➢ Windows Settings ➢ Security Settings ➢ Application Control Policies ➢ AppLocker, right-clicking it, and selecting Properties.

When you do, you'll see what's in Figure 8.39.

For our example, we've only configured an Executable rule (with a Publisher Rule Condition). So, we have to decide what action we want: Enforcement or Auditing.

Auditing will simply log results to the target machine's event log. Specifically, the results will go into the AppLocker log (which can be found in Event Viewer.) If you want to see them, then drill down into "Application and Services Logs," select Microsoft ➢ Windows ➢ AppLocker. Inside there, you'll find the logs for "EXE and DLL." There's another log as well for "MSI and Script."

If you'd like to try AppLocker in Auditing mode, you're on your own; I don't have enough space to cover it. You can also read this document from Microsoft about AppLocker and auditing to see the event IDs generated: http://tinyurl.com/yjdm8j6.

FIGURE 8.39 You can decide to start enforcement, or simply audit for who is actually running your application.

For our example, we'll select "Enforce rules" for executable rules. Do that now and click OK.

Note that you can optionally enable DLL and OCX blocking if you choose to peek at the Advanced tab. There's a warning about some potential slowdowns when engaged, but I feel it's worth it in the name of security. Additionally, you'll have to be diligent. If you select to enable the stomping of DLLs, you'll need to ensure that every DLL that is used by your approved applications is in there. That could get difficult, fast. An application can just stop working if you forget to add a DLL.

Anyway, you would think that now you're done and ready for testing, right? Nope. One more big hurdle to overcome.

AppLocker: The AppID Service

It's almost as if Microsoft doesn't want you to use the AppLocker service. They've made it so you have to first create a rule, turn on the rule action (Auditing or Enforcement), and now, one last hurdle. And that hurdle must be performed on each and every Windows 7 and/or Windows Server 2008 R2 machine on which you wish AppLocker to work.

You need to turn on and change the startup mode for the AppLocker service. Really, it's called the "Application Identity," or AppID service.

There are two ways I will suggest for you to accomplish this task: manually or using the Group Policy Preferences.

Turning On the AppID Service Manually

If you want to turn on the AppID service manually, on your target machine (WIN7) right-click Computer from the Start menu. Then select Manage.

Drill down to Computer Management ➤ Services and Applications ➤ Services and select "Application Identity," as seen in Figure 8.40.

FIGURE 8.40   The Application Identity service must be started (and configured to start at Startup) in order to process AppLocker edicts.

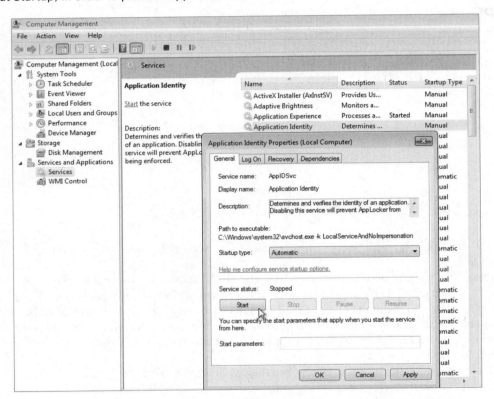

Change the service Startup Type to Automatic and click Start and then OK. When you do, you should see the service start right up and be set to Automatic startup going forward.

This technique is great if you want to test one or two machines. But it falls down if you have 10, 100, or 10,000 machines you want to utilize with AppLocker.

Turning On the AppID Service "En Masse" Using Group Policy Preferences

Instead of running around from machine to machine, you can optionally use the Group Policy Preferences' Services extension to mass-change and enable the AppIDSvc (Application Identity Service).

As you can see in Figure 8.41, I'm using the Group Policy Preferences to select the AppIDSvc, change Startup to Automatic, and set "Service Action" to "Start service."

Use the same GPO you've already used for this AppLocker exercise, or create a new GPO. Just make sure your edict is linked to where your Windows 7 and/or Windows Server 2008 machines are, and you're golden. The next time Group Policy refreshes on those machines, the AppID service will start up and be ready to start on every reboot thereafter.

AppLocker: Testing It Out

Whew. Now that your rule is set up, your actions are set, and your service is started, you're finally ready to test your AppLocker work.

Log on as Frank Rizzo to WIN7. Now, remember that AppLocker policies are Computer side, not User side. And it could take up to 120 minutes before this policy becomes active on the computer.

Or, you could run GPUpdate after you log on as Frank and get the latest policies for both Frank (who just logged on anyway) and the computer (which might have just been sitting around a while). Or you can reboot the computer. Your choice.

FIGURE 8.41   Use the Group Policy Preferences to mass-enable the AppIDSvr (Application Identity) service on your Windows 7 and/or Windows Server 2008 R2 machines.

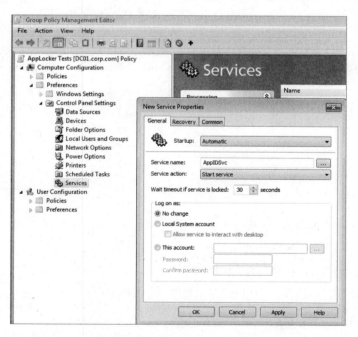

When you try to launch Acrobat Reader 8.1 as Frank, you should encounter a road-block, as seen in Figure 8.42.

This is expected because the rule matched, and you have enforcement enabled. Success!

FIGURE 8.42   The default message when AppLocker kicks in

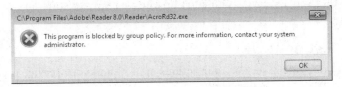

AppLocker: Modifying What the Client Sees

Users see the default message when an AppLocker rule kicks in, as you saw in Figure 8.42. However, there is an alternate message you can display for users if you like.

You can set the policy found at Computer ➤ Policies ➤ Administrative Templates ➤ Windows Components ➤ Windows Explorer ➤ **Set a Support Web Page Link**.

The goal is to point users to click on a custom URL, which, for instance, has your corporate rules listed in clear language, or a phone number for the help desk, or some other explanation as to why they were denied the ability to run the application.

Now, when users encounter a rule that blocks them, they'll get a different message, as seen in Figure 8.43.

FIGURE 8.43   Alternative AppLock message with "More information" link

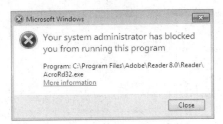

The user now can be redirected to your URL by clicking the "More information" link as you've defined it.

AppLocker: Wrapping Up Our Tests

So, we've created a rule that blocks the execution of Acrobat Reader 8.2 and earlier. So our Acrobat Reader 8.1 is stopped dead in its tracks. To complete the test, on WIN7 upgrade Acrobat Reader to a version greater than 8.2, say, version 9.

You should see it run, because the rule was only set to restrict Acrobat Reader 8.2 and earlier.

Leveraging Laws 2 and 3: Whitelisting Only Known Good Applications

In the previous example, we denied one publisher and its one application: Adobe. That Explicit deny rule would be helpful in two circumstances:

- If Acrobat Reader 8.2 was already installed in Program Files
- If Acrobat Reader 8.2 was already installed anywhere else

I know that seems like a weird way to describe what we did, but logically, that's the way we must express it. That's because we already had the default rule that would allow it to run inside Program Files. And our new Explicit deny rule stomps it out both in Program Files, and anywhere else it's ever discovered (say, in some alternate directory).

Okay, great. We've now stamped out *one* little fire. Yippee.

What about the zillions of other applications we might want to protect ourselves against? And then, how can we specifically okay the apps we know are good?

Well then, you might want to consider AppLocker's "whitelist" approach. Let's recall our three AppLocker laws from earlier:

- Law 1: Explicit deny: A specific rule that denies an action.
- Law 2: Explicit allow: A specific rule that allows an action.
- Law 3: Implicit deny: All files that are not specifically named by an Allow rule are automatically blocked.

So, if we look at the laws carefully, we can see that if we turn AppLocker on, and, well, "do nothing," then all files that are not specifically named are going to be automatically blocked.

Wow, can that really be true? Let's try it out.

Testing AppLocker's Law #3: Default Deny

Let's start out by editing the one AppLocker GPO you created and removing the one Deny rule you had. At this point you should have nothing but the default rules again, as seen in Figure 8.35.

On WIN7, make sure you're logged in as Frank Rizzo. Run GPUpdate to get the changed AppLocker rules from the GPO. Now, you should be able to run Acrobat Reader 8 or 9 (if you upgraded as I suggested for testing). Again—this runs because the default rules are saying "Go ahead and let anything in Program Files run A-OK." And since Acrobat Reader is already installed there, it runs, A-OK.

Now, as Frank, download the latest WinZip setup program. I found it here: http://www.winzip.com/downwz.htm. Now, as Frank, try to run the setup .EXE. You should get what's shown in Figure 8.44.

See? AppLocker specifically denies WinZip's setup program. It's not already installed and living in Program Files, so the default rule doesn't apply. It's immediately blocked.

Automatically Generating Rules for AppLocker Whitelisting

So, we can see that AppLocker will just auto-smack-down anything that isn't expressly listed by an Allow. You've likely come to the conclusion, however, that you'll have to generate some lengthy "Allow" list that contains all your applications.

FIGURE 8.44 AppLocker's Law 3 ensures that anything that isn't specifically listed is automatically denied.

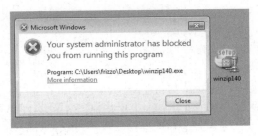

And you're right. That's the hard part. You will have to figure out what the Sales team is using, and the Marketing team, and Human Resources, and so forth. It's not easy or fun. But there is good news: AppLocker can automatically generate rules and then add them to a whitelist, as shown in Figure 8.45.

FIGURE 8.45 Automatically generate rules to add them to the whitelist.

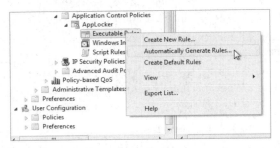

What you'll do is this:

- Find a representative machine from the department you want to control—say, Human Resources. We'll call this your AppLocker "template machine."
- On this machine, you'll need to have the GPMC running.
- You'll utilize the "Automatically Generate Rules" wizard.

When the wizard is over, you'll have (a start at least) of the applications you know are good and should pass through and allow to run. Sure, you'll have to trim a bit, use your brains for a little while, as well as use a little elbow grease to make sure nothing bad slipped through.

But it's a quick way to get started. Right-click over Executable Rules and select "Automatically Generate Rules" to open the wizard to the "Folder and Permissions" screen shown in Figure 8.46.

The default is c:\Program Files, but you're welcome to create rule sets for anyplace you wish. Indeed, for x64 machines, you should run the wizard again, and be sure to include, say, c:\program files (x86) because otherwise all 32-bit apps on the 64-bit system will be missed. Additionally, be sure to add in any custom applications in c:\DogFoodMaker or the like.

The next screen is Rule Preferences, as seen in Figure 8.47. I recommend taking the defaults, as it does a pretty decent job, but you're welcome to try other options.

FIGURE 8.46 Specify where you want to start your analysis.

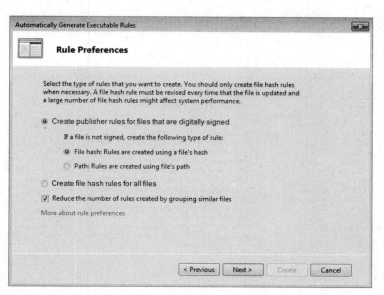

FIGURE 8.47 Utilize the defaults to create rules based on signed files with file hashes as a backup.

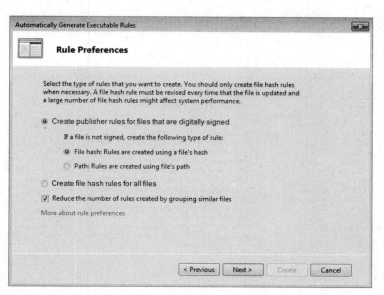

You'll then come to the Review Rules screen, shown in Figure 8.48. At this point the rules aren't yet created. You can select "Review files that were analyzed" if you want to explicitly remove a file from consideration. You can also preview the rules before they get codified.

When ready, click Create. When you do, the rules for your particular machine will be populated into the GPO, as seen in Figure 8.49.

FIGURE 8.48   You can explicitly remove a file from consideration using the "Review files that were analyzed" selection.

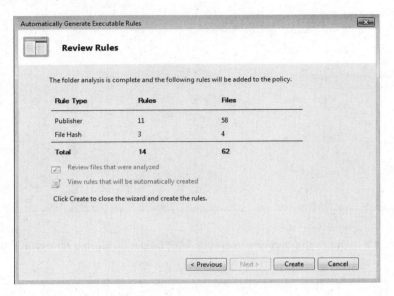

FIGURE 8.49   AppLocker allows you to autogenerate rules for whitelisting.

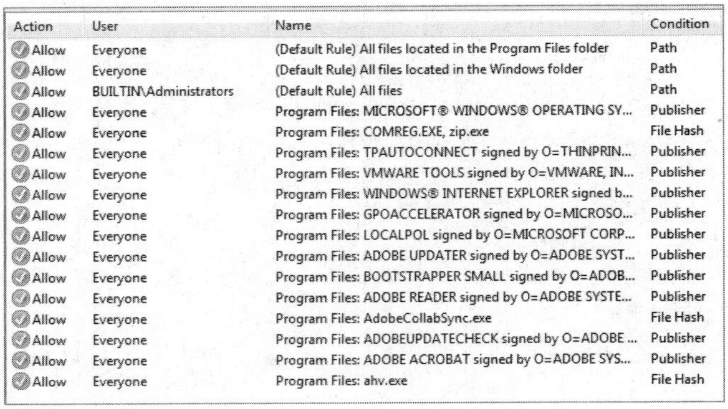

Action	User	Name	Condition
Allow	Everyone	(Default Rule) All files located in the Program Files folder	Path
Allow	Everyone	(Default Rule) All files located in the Windows folder	Path
Allow	BUILTIN\Administrators	(Default Rule) All files	Path
Allow	Everyone	Program Files: MICROSOFT® WINDOWS® OPERATING SY...	Publisher
Allow	Everyone	Program Files: COMREG.EXE, zip.exe	File Hash
Allow	Everyone	Program Files: TPAUTOCONNECT signed by O=THINPRIN...	Publisher
Allow	Everyone	Program Files: VMWARE TOOLS signed by O=VMWARE, IN...	Publisher
Allow	Everyone	Program Files: WINDOWS® INTERNET EXPLORER signed b...	Publisher
Allow	Everyone	Program Files: GPOACCELERATOR signed by O=MICROSO...	Publisher
Allow	Everyone	Program Files: LOCALPOL signed by O=MICROSOFT CORP...	Publisher
Allow	Everyone	Program Files: ADOBE UPDATER signed by O=ADOBE SYST...	Publisher
Allow	Everyone	Program Files: BOOTSTRAPPER SMALL signed by O=ADOB...	Publisher
Allow	Everyone	Program Files: ADOBE READER signed by O=ADOBE SYSTE...	Publisher
Allow	Everyone	Program Files: AdobeCollabSync.exe	File Hash
Allow	Everyone	Program Files: ADOBEUPDATECHECK signed by O=ADOBE ...	Publisher
Allow	Everyone	Program Files: ADOBE ACROBAT signed by O=ADOBE SYS...	Publisher
Allow	Everyone	Program Files: ahv.exe	File Hash

AppLocker: Importing and Exporting Rules

Since you're doing all of these wonderful tests in the test lab, you might be wondering how you're going to take your (potentially complex) rule set and export those rules—then, in the real world, how you're going to import them. It's easy. Look at Figure 8.50.

FIGURE 8.50   Use AppLocker's Export and Import Policy to move rules from your test lab to the real world.

You can also utilize Export and Import to take one GPO's rules in the real world, export them, and import them into another one for transfer or clean up.

AppLocker Final Thoughts and Resources

We used AppLocker in two ways: we explicitly denied an application (blacklisting), and we also implicitly denied everything and specified the good applications (whitelisting).

My final parting thought here is to use AppLocker with as many "Allow" rules as you can. That's because denying specific things (Law 1) is going to be less secure than relying on Law 3 to auto-smack-down stuff that shouldn't be running.

If a really smart user wanted to subvert your AppLocker policies, here's how they could do it:

Path Rules   They could figure out where an application *isn't* allowed to run, and move it to a place that *is* allowed to run. This could take some trial and error, but is certainly in the realm of possibility.

File Hash Rules   A user could use a hex editor (explained earlier) to modify the file hash. This does increase the risk of the application breaking, however.

Publisher Rules   A user could inject the executable with a signed (Allowed) certificate. They would need the private key of the certificate, which would not be possible under almost all circumstances. This is a pretty low probability problem.

True, most places won't have to worry about these kinds of attacks. But if you use whitelisting (Law 3), you won't have to worry about them at all. I've provided a thorough workout of AppLocker here, but if you're still hungry for more, here are some pointers:

- TechNet Article by Greg Shields: http://tinyurl.com/ylkrs5z or

http://technet.microsoft.com/en-us/magazine/2009.10.geekofalltrades.aspx

- A four-part series by Brien Posey:

  www.windowsnetworking.com/articles_tutorials/Introduction-AppLocker-Part1.html

- Microsoft Technical Documentation on AppLocker: http://tinyurl.com/yhcw83f
- PowerShell and AppLocker: http://tinyurl.com/otdo8a and
  http://tinyurl.com/yj2cfv8

Controlling User Account Control (UAC) with Group Policy

UAC is the User Account Control feature for Windows Vista and later. You might see it as the "annoying extra pop-up box I need to click in order to do anything useful!" Well, sometimes it might seem that way. But that's not exactly accurate. What's really happening is that you're seeing a prompt for anything that requires administrator rights (that is, that affects the entire computer and all users on that computer).

Since UAC is available for Windows Vista and later, instead of saying "Windows Vista and later" each time it comes up, I'll just say "for Windows" in the general case, and if there's something specific about a particular version of Windows, I'll let you know.

For instance, on Windows Server 2008, you might not see the prompts as much because if you log on with the local Administrator account, UAC prompts are largely not presented. However, if you log on as just about anyone else, like a Server Operator, you will see the UAC prompts that we'll discuss here using Windows 7 examples.

In reality, it's not that bad; UAC is designed to put a (small) roadblock in front of administrative tasks and applications so that only administrators can do anything with these items.

An example of a UAC dialog box that can pop up based on the types of actions and programs you want to run is shown in Figure 8.51, where a mere mortal is trying to "Allow a program through Windows Firewall" and is prompted for local administrator credentials.

In UAC parlance, a mere mortal, or regular user, is officially called a *Standard User*. There are three types of prompts you might get when UAC is active:

- Teal bar plus a shield: This program is a part of Windows.

- Gray plus a shield with an exclamation mark: This is signed and trusted by Windows. Trusted means that the certificate used to sign the application "chains" to a certificate in the computer's Trusted Root Certificate Store. Note: The Trusted Root Certificate Store can also be managed via Group Policy.

- Orange plus a shield with an exclamation mark: This program isn't part of Windows and is either unsigned or signed but not yet trusted.

And, at first blush, you might be right. It might be annoying to provide that one extra click or provide alternate credentials. But the underlying idea of UAC is a really good one: regular users need permissions to do the more privileged operations on a Windows machine.

FIGURE 8.51 Anytime a user clicks on an action with a shield icon, they are prompted for credentials.

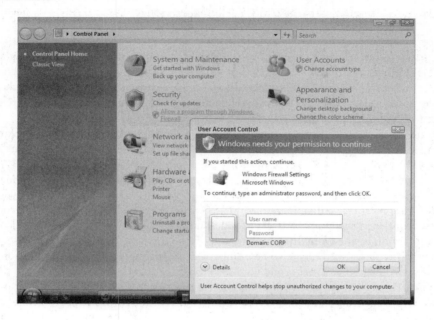

 In the short term, you might see the UAC prompts a lot. That's because when you're first configuring Windows, there will be a lot of systemwide changes you'll want to make. But over time, how often are you really making those kinds of changes? Once the computer is configured for your specific environment and the bulk of the software is installed, you will rarely ever see a UAC dialog box again.

Additionally, when you log on as an Administrator (local or Domain Administrator), you get "stripped" of your admin rights until you click to say you want to leverage them. UAC's goal is to implement the "Principle of Least Privilege": only use privileged user rights when needed.

The UAC prompts leverage of a technology called UIPI (UI Process Isolation) and another called MIC (Mandatory Integrity Control). The idea is that the operating system is protected from nonprivileged processes. Only certain types of Windows messages and input are permitted to interact with this dialog box. Therefore, previous attacks where the malware would simply click the security dialog box before the user ever saw the prompt are thwarted—only privileged processes can interact with the UAC dialog boxes. This helps prevent what is known as process injection and shatter attacks.

NOTE Learn more about process injection and shatter attacks at http://en.wikipedia.org/wiki/Code_injection and http://en.wikipedia.org/wiki/Shatter_attack.

What's the upshot? Sure, it's one extra click (as an admin) or the fuss of providing admin credentials (for users who aren't admins). But what's the benefit? In short, even admins get the benefit of not doing something potentially harmful because there's one extra click in the way. (How many times have you wished you could have taken an extra "beat" before doing something potentially harmful?)

The other big goodness is that all applications run without admin privilege by default; therefore, scenarios like web browsing and e-mail become much more secure without any changes to the applications. You cannot have "Protected Mode IE" without UAC.

So I encourage you to find it in your heart to try to love this feature. Here's the idea (which is only partially related to UAC): you want all your users to run as Standard User (or, as they're sometimes called, mere mortals). That is, they are in the local Users group of the workstation or in the Domain Users group and not in the local Administrators group of the workstation or the Domain Admins group in the domain. In short, they're just users. Additionally, if you want to throw some numbers at the managers in your corporations, the Gartner Group states that running your desktops as a Standard User can reduce total cost of ownership (TCO) by as much as 40 percent versus running that same Desktop with administrative credentials. The idea is that if the user, I mean, administrator of that local machine could just stop making all those darned changes, you would be at their desk fixing their computer a whole lot less. Get it?

So, what does UAC do? It prompts the users for credentials under specific conditions. Take a quick gander at the general UAC document on Microsoft's website here:

`http://technet.microsoft.com/en-us/library/cc772207%28WS.10%29.aspx`

And, if you like, check out this older but very geeky "internals about UAC" article from Mark Russinovich, "Inside Windows Vista User Account Control," found here:

`http://technet.microsoft.com/en-us/magazine/2007.06.uac.aspx`

(shortened to `http://tinyurl.com/as3oy2`).

Additionally, while there are some "internal, technical" differences between Windows Vista's UAC and Windows 7's UAC, they're not so spectacular that we need to think about them differently for the sake of our conversation. However, for that "inner geek" in you, I'll supply some links that describe the differences between Windows Vista and Windows 7's UAC at the end of this big ol' section on UAC. So hang tight.

There is one, kinda obvious difference between Windows Vista's and Windows 7's UAC. The most obvious change is an updated UAC interface to Windows 7, as seen in Figure 8.52, with two new UAC operating modes.

But, in practice, to *manage UAC*, both operating systems are really, really similar. Mark Russinovich's article (which I'll provide the link to later) confidently quotes the following: "Windows 7 carries forward UAC's goals with the underlying technologies relatively unchanged."

Great. So, if you've got Windows Vista or Windows 7, this section has you covered. Inside this section, we'll learn about the 10 different Group Policy controls you have at your disposal to configure it the way you want it to work.

Finally, we'll wrap up our talk on UAC with some prescriptive guidance for certain scenarios to help you configure users based on what they're trying to accomplish.

FIGURE 8.52 Windows 7's updated UAC interface

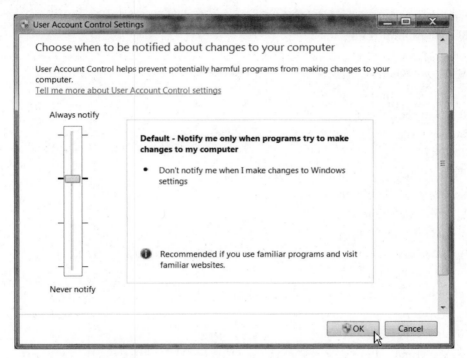

 If you're starting to develop applications for Windows 7 (or Windows Vista), here's a tip. In the past versions of Windows, we ran by default as admin and therefore developed and tested as admin, the manifestation being applications developed this way tended to not work for the Standard User. Now, the idea is that your developers will be developing and testing as Standard User by default.

Just Who Will See the UAC Prompts, Anyway?

The point of UAC is to have "administrative" type users run as mere mortals until they need to use their superpowers. To that end, you'll likely want to get a handle on just who is going to be affected by UAC prompts and have to run as mere mortals on Windows (until they elevate their credentials and use that superpower).

There are two categories of folks: anyone who's a member of some special Active Directory or local Security Accounts Manager (SAM) groups and anyone who has one of eight special rights.

Which Groups Are Affected by UAC

There are 16 accounts and related SIDs that are affected by UAC:

- Built-in Administrators
- Power Users
- Account Operators
- Server Operators
- Print Operators
- Backup Operators
- RAS Servers Group
- NT 4 Application Compatibility Group
- Network Configuration Operators
- Cryptographic Operators
- Domain Administrators
- Domain Controllers
- Certificate Publishers
- Schema Administrators
- Enterprise Administrators
- Group Policy Administrators

UAC sometimes call these users Split Token Users or Hybrid Users as they have two user tokens (nonadmin and admin). See the sidebar "How Token Filtering/Split Token Works."

Elevated Rights and SE Privileges

If the user does not belong to any of the groups listed in the preceding section but has any of the privileges listed in Table 8.4, a filtered token will be created for the user with these privileges removed. These privileges are found in the Group Policy Management Editor in Computer Configuration ➢ Policies ➢ Windows Settings ➢ Security Settings ➢ Local Policies ➢ User Rights Assignment.

You can get these rights from any level: local, site, domain, or OU. Additionally, many rights are predefined in the default Group Policy Objects (discussed in the previous chapter).

TABLE 8.4   Rights and SE Names That Generate a Filtered Token User Experience

Right	SE Name
Create a token object	SeCreateTokenPrivilege
Act as part of the operating system	SeTcbPrivilege
Take ownership of files or other objects	SeTakeOwnershipPrivilege
Back up files and directories	SeBackupPrivilege
Restore files and directories	SeRestorePrivilege
Debug programs	SeDebugPrivilege
Impersonate a client after authentication	SeImpersonatePrivilege
Modify an object label	SeRelabelPrivilege
Load and unload device drivers	SeLoadDriverPrivilege

You can check to see if a currently logged-in user has one of these privileges by typing **whoami /priv** at a command prompt.

How Token Filtering/Split Token Works

If you log in with Domain Administrator rights to a Windows XP machine, you can "do" just about anything you want, including shooting your foot off, easily. This is because if you're assigned rights at some level of Active Directory or SAM, Windows XP just lets you use them. Sounds good, until you start making a mistake while web surfing or using e-mail.

Starting with Windows Vista, things get a little more cautious. Again, the idea in modern Windows is that if you're a member of one of the special groups listed in Table 8.4, you will get a "split token." That means that in your daily life, you're running around as a mere mortal. When you need to rip off your shirt and become Superman, you can do that too—but you have to find a close phone booth, er, UAC prompt to help you with that.

So, for instance, if a user is a member of the Administrators group, the filtered token will have the Administrators group membership set to "deny only". Yep, you read that right. As they're running around as a mere mortal, anything they try to do on the system is expressly Denied.

Meanwhile, a second protection mechanism kicks in. All the machine-impacting privileges are removed from the token. Therefore, as the Domain Administrator is going about his daily life on a Windows Vista or Windows 7 machine, when he starts up things like `explorer.exe`, it's using a nonelevated process token.

You can look at this token using `whomai.exe`, which is included in Windows. First run `whoami /groups` in a command window when logged in as Domain Administrator, as shown here:

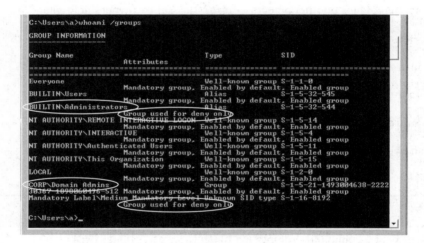

If you look closely you'll see that the BUILTIN\Administrators and the CORP\Domain Admins groups both have a special Deny token—just for them. Kooky! Again, this is reinstated once UAC prompts are satisfied.

Additionally, you can see what privileges are being used at any time with `whoami /priv`, as shown here:

```
C:\Users\a>whoami /priv

PRIVILEGES INFORMATION
----------------------

Privilege Name                  Description                              State
=============================== ======================================== ========
SeShutdownPrivilege             Shut down the system                     Disabled
SeChangeNotifyPrivilege         Bypass traverse checking                 Enabled
SeUndockPrivilege               Remove computer from docking station     Disabled
SeIncreaseWorkingSetPrivilege   Increase a process working set           Disabled
SeTimeZonePrivilege             Change the time zone                     Disabled

C:\Users\a>
```

Compare this to the whoami /priv command when run on a Windows XP machine shown here:

So, Windows XP doesn't "filter" anything. Windows goes the extra mile to strip out unused rights until you actually need them. Note that the whoami tool isn't built into Windows XP as it is in Windows Vista and later. You can load the whoami tool from the Windows XP support tools here: http://tinyurl.com/4uhnu.

Understanding the Group Policy Controls for UAC

There are 10 Group Policy controls for UAC. They are all found within Computer Configuration ➢ Policies ➢ Windows Settings ➢ Security Settings ➢ Local Policies ➢ Security Options, and all start with "User Account Control:" as seen in Figure 8.53.

Let's examine each policy setting so you can decide if you want to change the default behavior.

FIGURE 8.53   The User Account Control entries are all found under Security Options.

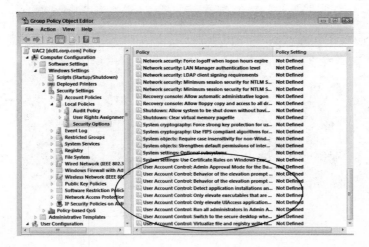

What? No Usable Local Administrator Account on Modern Windows?

By default, the Windows Vista and Windows 7 built-in Administrator account is disabled. Yep, you read that right—there is no usable built-in Administrator account on Windows. It's there; it's just disabled. Indeed, check out the following figure, where I'm simply typing **net user administrator** at a Windows command prompt. Note that the "Account active" flag is set to No.

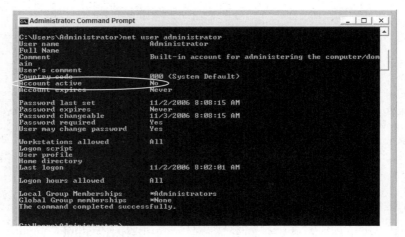

However, if you create a new Windows machine (that isn't joined to the domain), the first user you create by default has the equivalent permissions to a local administrator and all subsequent users are Standard Users—see the following figure where my first user on this fresh Windows installation is named User. Confusing, right?

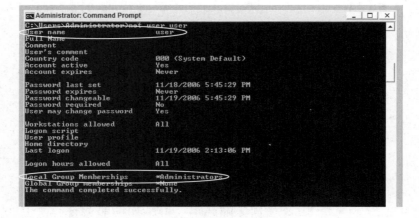

So, be careful when you give that first local user account's name and password. That first user account really has administrator rights! Yikes!

However, if, during setup, you join the domain directly, you won't have any local user accounts created, and hence, you won't have any accounts you can log onto as a local administrator. Of course, you could always log onto the Enterprise or Domain Administrator accounts (but we're talking about local accounts here).

So, what about that disabled local Administrator account? Well, again, ask yourself if you really need it. In a domain environment, you could always just log in as a Domain Administrator. And, if the machine wasn't joined to the domain during setup, you could log in with that first user. So all bases are covered.

But, if you felt like you wanted to bring back that local Administrator account, you could do so. Historically, this account has been used for pure maintenance. That's why, by default, it's not enabled and has special behavior once enabled. So before I tell you how to enable the local Administrator account, I want to pass on a big ol' cautionary note: the local Administrator account is exempt (by default) from all UAC prompts.

The behavior is the same on Windows Server 2008 if you log on with the local Administrator account or Domain Administrator account.

You won't see any prompts. If you enable the Administrator account and romp around within Windows while using it, there are absolutely no safety checks. If you wanted to change this behavior, you would manipulate the User Account Control: Admin Approval Mode for the **Built-in Administrator account** policy setting.

Again, it's not recommended that you enable the local Administrator account, but if you wanted to, the command line you would type is this:

```
net user administrator complexp@ssw0rd /active:yes
```

And again, I'm not suggesting you should run out and enable all your local Administrator accounts. But if you do have some "corporate-wide" reason to do this, it would be wise to set a complex password during machine creation time (with an answer file).

But there's another way to enable the local Administrator account. Assuming the password is set on the local Administrator account (say, via the answer file at machine creation time), you can use Group Policy to just "turn it on." You'll find the setting to turn this on in Computer Configuration ≻ Policies ≻ Windows Settings ≻ Security Settings ≻ Local Policies ≻ Security Options ≻ **Accounts: Administrator account status**.

By the way, you might be wondering what happens if your Windows XP machine is upgraded to Windows Vista. The short answer: if you have no other enabled accounts except Administrator, it will leave the Administrator account there but force it to use UAC prompting like all other accounts. Note that you cannot upgrade Windows XP to Windows 7, so the answer to "What happens in that case?" is moot.

Before we finish talking about the local Administrator account, there is one more local Administrator–related change you need to be aware of. In pre–Windows Vista, you could, if you wanted to, boot into Safe Mode logon with the *disabled* built-in Administrator account. Don't know why you'd want to, but it was possible.

Because Windows is now trying to encourage Standard Users on desktops (in businesses) and engaging parental controls (in the home), Safe Mode had to go under some security changes:

On workgroup or nondomain joined computers   If there is at least one active local Administrator account, Safe Mode will not allow logon via the disabled built-in Administrator account. But there's no issue logging in with any active Administrator account. If there are no other active local Administrator accounts, Safe Mode will allow the disabled built-in Administrator account to log on for disaster recovery. From that point, it is suggested that a new Administrator account be created before rebooting the computer.

On domain joined computers   The disabled built-in Administrator account cannot log on in Safe Mode under any circumstances. Here's where it gets tricky: if a user whose account is also in the Domain Administrators group has ever logged onto that machine before, they can log on again using Safe Mode, no problem. But what if no one from the Domain Administrators group has ever logged onto that machine? Then the computer must be started in "Safe Mode with Networking" since the credentials will not have been cached. Hopefully, Windows will not be "so broken" that networking support won't work in this case. If the machine is disjoined from the domain, it reverts back to the nondomain joined behavior.

User Account Control: Admin Approval Mode for the Built-in Administrator Account

As we've already discussed, both users and administrators have to "say yes" or provide administrator credentials.

Only admins can "say yes." Standard Users must obtain administrator credentials. Standard Users cannot just "say yes."

This prevents them from doing things that could be potentially harmful to the machine. So, this setting dictates the "Admin Approval mode" for the built-in Administrator account. What built-in Administrator account? Check out the sidebar "What? No Usable Local Administrator Account on Modern Windows?"

If you choose to enable this built-in Administrator account, this policy setting affects this account.

Enabled   By enabling this setting, the built-in Administrator will be forced to honor UAC prompts.

Disabled (default)   By default, if you choose to leave this feature disabled (the default) and log in with the local Administrator account, then that account is exempt from UAC prompts.

User Account Control: Allow UIAccess Applications to Prompt for Elevation without Using the Secure Desktop

UIAccess, or UIA, is a category of features designed to make using Windows easier for persons with disabilities. The problem is that applications that interface with the desktop might need to ask the user about security credentials, and any user needs to be able to enter the answer to UAC security prompts.

And, as it turns out, one application that many people often use is categorized as a UIA application. That's the Windows Remote Assistance application.

What happens if you try to provide remote assistance to a user by default? Well, the UAC prompts will appear on the interactive user's desktop (the person needing help) instead of the secure desktop (the person providing the help).

But if the person needing the help has the forethought, they can set up Remote Assistance with the "Allow IT Expert to respond to User Account Control prompts" option.

Here's the rub: even that check box requires the user to provide administrative credentials at that moment. So if the user is a Standard User, they can't choose to avoid seeing the credentials.

Oh, the catch-22 of it all!

That's what this policy setting is meant to help with.

Enabled (default)   If you enable this setting, the person needing help will see the UAC prompt, but the person providing help will see what the person needing help is doing. This means that the person needing help (Joe User) will need to know a local administrator account's password to get through this prompt.

Disabled   If you disable this policy setting, you don't have to worry about Joe User knowing a local administrator password in order for him to get remote help.

User Account Control: Behavior of the Elevation Prompt for Administrators in Admin Approval Mode

As stated, even if you log on as a Domain Admin to a local Windows Vista or Windows 7 box, you're still going to get UAC prompts.

Actually, if you log on with any of 15 different privileged SIDs, you'll get UAC prompts as an Admin. Or, if you log in with any of eight user rights, you're also going to see the prompts.

We saw these accounts in a list earlier in this chapter and the user rights in Table 8.4.

This policy setting controls how, when logging in as a member of one of those groups or with one of those rights, you'll see prompts.

If you're an admin, the system already knows you're an admin. It won't (by default) re-ask you to supply credentials. It will, however, ask you (essentially) to acknowledge you're about to do a potentially harmful or impactful thing, like installing an application or creating a new user.

Prompt for consent (default)   Because you're already an admin, by default you don't need to resupply your username and password; you just have to click the Continue button or use Alt+C.

Prompt for credentials   This requires an admin to reenter their username and password or provide the username and password of any other Administrator account.

Elevate without prompting   Use with caution: this will silently "say yes" to any prompt if you're logged in as an admin. Microsoft suggests that this only be used in the most secure (they call it *constrained*) environments.

User Account Control: Behavior of the Elevation Prompt for Standard Users

As expected, mere mortals have to supply some additional credentials to perform administrative tasks. When will mere mortals be asked for administrative credentials?

Prompt for credentials (default)   Users logging into nondomain joined machines will always be prompted for administrative credentials. If the user enters valid administrative credentials, the user will be permitted to continue.

Prompt for credentials on the secure desktop   Similar to the previous setting, but prompts users on the secure (grayed-out) desktop, which proves that the request is coming from UAC and not a bad guy. What's weird about this setting is, the Explain text says this is the default, but in reality the previous setting (Prompt for credentials) is set up on the multiple workstations and servers I tested. And, moreover, the default action does, indeed, seem to be what this setting says—Prompt for credentials on the secure desktop. Not exactly sure why there's a discrepancy here, but I thought I would point it out.

Automatically deny elevation requests   If users shouldn't access certain stuff, why even prompt for credentials? If you set this policy setting to "Automatically deny elevation requests," the user will simply get an "Access Denied" anytime they try to do something privileged. I discuss this a bit later in the section "UAC Policy Setting Suggestions."

This setting's Explain text says, "Default for enterprise," but it's really a "strong suggestion" for the enterprise. See the scenarios a little later for more information about why this is recommended.

User Account Control: Detect Application Installations and Prompt for Elevation

This security setting determines the behavior of application installation detection for the entire system.

Enabled (default)   Applications that start with the words *setu* (yes, that's right, *setu*, as in setup.exe, setupnow.exe, and others), *instal* (yes, again, it's *instal*), or *update* will be automatically detected by UAC and prompted for credentials. Note that the policy setting Explain text says, "Default for home," but it's really default for everyone.

Disabled   If you're using GPSI or SMS to deploy your software, this feature isn't needed. It's only required when Junior or Grandma tries to run `setup.exe` for EvilApp6. GPSI and SMS automatically work around this, so you can safely set this to Disabled here if you want to.

This policy setting says, "Default for enterprise," but it's really a "strong suggestion" for the enterprise. See the scenarios a little later for more information about why this is recommended.

User Account Control: Only Elevate Executables That Are Signed and Validated

You can set up UAC such that applications only run if they are digitally signed via a PKI (Public Key Infrastructure) and Trusted. Enterprise administrators can control the allowed applications list by populating certificates in the local computer's Trusted Root Store.

Population of this store is supported by Group Policy.

Enabled   Only applications signed by a trusted PKI certificate are permitted to run.

Disabled (default)   It doesn't matter if the application is signed via PKI.

User Account Control: Only Elevate UIAccess Applications That Are Installed in Secure Locations

We talked about UIAccess (UIA) programs when we checked out the **User Account Control: Allow UIAccess applications to prompt for elevation without using the secure desktop** setting earlier.

Again, UIAccess is a category of features designed to allow persons with disabilities to more easily use Windows. The problem is that these same applications have the potential to be places where an attacker can gain a toehold in the system and do nefarious things. So, this policy setting manages UIAccess programs and ensures that they can be run only in secure locations. This policy setting takes advantage of IL (Integrity Level) and MIC (Mandatory Integrity Control).

IL (Integrity Level) and MIC (Mandatory Integrity Control) are whole new concepts in modern Windows (and simply too deep to go into here). In short, these facilities let certain users and programs have certain rights to files based on their "trust level." An ever-so-brief overview of MIC can be found at http://tinyurl.com/y8753w, though decent online information on this subject is kind of hard to come by. One such decent, but not online, source is Mark Minasi's book *Administering Windows Vista Security: The Big Surprises* (Sybex, 2006).

Enabled (default) Specifies that an application will only launch with "UIAccess integrity" if it resides in a secure location in the file system. The secure locations in Windows are limited to the following directories:

- `\Program Files\`, including subdirectories
- `\Windows\system32\`
- `\Program Files (x86)\`, including subdirectories for 64-bit versions of Windows

Windows enforces a PKI signature check on any interactive application that requests execution with UIAccess integrity level regardless of the state of this security setting.

Disabled An application will start with UIAccess integrity *even if it does not* reside in one of the three secure locations in the file system.

User Account Control: Run All Administrators in Admin Approval Mode

This is the "master switch" for UAC.

Enabled (default) If this setting is Enabled, all UAC prompts are possible (although they might not all happen, based on other things you set). However, at least this switch needs to be Enabled. Changing this setting requires a system reboot.

Disabled If you Disable this policy, UAC and all of its supporting functionality just goes away. Not suggested.

The Security Center feature in Windows will demonstrate that the overall security of the operating system has been reduced.

User Account Control: Switch to the Secure Desktop When Prompting for Elevation

When you try to perform any administrative task, including taking remote control of a PC, you are prompted for authorization. This security setting determines whether the elevation request will prompt for the interactive users desktop or the Secure Desktop.

You might be wondering what the difference is between prompting for the *Secure Desktop* versus the *Interactive Desktop*. The Secure Desktop only allows trusted SYSTEM processes to run on it, which means that an application must have already been approved by an Administrator to be installed and run with SYSTEM privilege. The Interactive Desktop allows USER processes to run (such high-level approval isn't required to install and run USER processes). The interesting part of all this is that it only requires USER-level privilege to spoof the user into believing they are seeing and/or clicking on something that is being generated, legitimately, from Windows. Therefore, by placing the elevation dialog box on the Secure Desktop, only a highly privileged process can hope to run there, which means that the dialog box the user is seeing and interacting with is a genuine one that Windows has generated (not some bad guy hoping you'll click OK).

The Secure Desktop protects against input and output spoofing when a user interacts with the UAC elevation dialog box.

Enabled (default)   All elevation requests by default will go to the Secure Desktop. The Secure Desktop is used here as an "antispoofing" technology, so it is recommended that you leave this on.

Disabled   All elevation requests will go to the user's Interactive Desktop. In some specific cases (e.g., an enterprise that leverages Remote Assistance and doesn't allow their Standard Users the ability to approve an elevation request), it may be all right to disable this policy.

Virtualize File and Registry Write Failures to Per-User Locations

Windows Vista and later machines have a new feature called File and Registry Virtualization. The idea is that for years programmers have been told "It's okay to dump your garbage anywhere in Windows." Now, in modern Windows, it's not. But what about those poor applications? They need to keep working, too. This feature will redirect potentially harmful file and Registry writes to "okay" locations.

The idea is that some applications might try to write to profile and Registry locations they don't have access to, so a modern Windows system will redirect (or, as Microsoft calls it, *virtualize*) these writes to writable places in the profile and Registry. So, if an application tries to write application data to `%ProgramFiles%`, `%Windir%`, `%Windir%\system32`, or `HKLM\Software\`, this virtualization feature kicks in and gently places the data into the kosher places in the file system and Registry. Don't panic for now; I discuss file and Registry virtualization in detail in the next chapter.

This will happen automatically when anyone is logged in as a Standard User.

An administrator may choose to disable this feature—if she's sure she's running all modern Windows–compliant applications. But how would you really be sure?

Enabled (default)   Facilitates the runtime redirection of application write failures to defined user locations for both the file system and Registry.

Disabled   Applications that write data to protected locations will simply fail as they did in previous versions of Windows.

There is a neat round-up of File and Registry virtualization issues found in one Knowledge Base article here: `http://support.microsoft.com/default.aspx/kb/927387`.

UAC Policy Setting Suggestions

There are 10 UAC settings, which we just explored. That means you've got a lot of power to control UAC. As we stated, you really don't want to just "turn it off." You want to tune it based on your situation.

Let's examine some cases, the default behavior, and some suggested remediations.

Case 1: Enterprise Desktop: Standard User (Who Gets Help Remotely When Needed)

This is the type of user who will never need to perform an elevated or privileged administrative task. The majority of users fall into this category. If you need to help them, how will you? Likely, you'll simply use Remote Desktops and perform desktop management remotely.

Suggestion 1: Set "UAC: Behavior of the elevation prompt for Standard Users" to Disabled.   If the user should never perform an administrative task, then why present them with the opportunity? If you perform this simple change, they simply won't see the UAC prompts, and it will be denied. By performing this step, you're reducing the overall "attack surface."

Additionally, if users see the credential dialog box, it can motivate them to call the help desk and beg for a valid Administrator account. You don't want to get caught in this trap. You can eliminate this type of support call.

Suggestion 2: Set "UAC: Switch to the Secure Desktop when prompting for elevation" to Disabled.   The Secure Desktop can be disabled if the logged-on Standard User never elevates. The technology is designed to protect elevations; if the logged-on user never elevates, the Secure Desktop protection is not needed. Be sure you're positively using suggestion 1 along with suggestion 2 in this two-part tip. Otherwise, you're possibly opening up a security hole.

Case 2: Enterprise Desktop: Standard User (Who Gets "Over-the-Shoulder Help" When Needed)

In some environments, the user puts in a request, and the administrator walks over to the desk and, while the user is logged in, helps adjust or install applications. This is sometimes called "Over-the-Shoulder" (OTS) assistance. OTS assistance often takes place in doctor and lawyer offices and other smaller offices that occasionally need tuning.

Main suggestion: Set "UAC: Behavior of the elevation prompt for Standard Users" to "Prompt for credentials."   In smaller organizations it may be preferable to leave this policy enabled to facilitate administrative help without requiring the administrator to perform a Fast User Switch and log on as himself.

Case 3: Enterprise Desktop: Protected Administrator

This is the case where you've been forced into giving Sally local administrative privileges on her own machine. You don't want to do it, but you have to for some reason. This can happen if Sally is already an administrator of her Windows XP machine before you upgrade it to Windows Vista. Or, you install Windows 7 for her, and you're forced to give her administrator rights.

In UAC parlance, Sally would be called a *Protected Administrator* because she is a user who is either directly or indirectly a member of the local administrators group of the client workstation.

Main suggestion: Set all UAC policies at the default.   Windows UAC policy defaults are optimized for the Protected Administrator user account type. Do the dirty deed: give Sally the admin rights she needs (boo! hiss!). The good news, though, is that the default UAC policies will force the applications that previously ran on XP with administrative privileges to run with the equivalent privilege of a Standard User.

So now, your e-mail editor and web browser will no longer run with administrative privileges unnecessarily. Rejoice in attack surface reduction!

Case 4: Enterprise Desktop (Running Only Windows Vista "logo'd" Software)

I'm not holding my breath for this one in the near or mid-term, because I know you're going to have lots of old and crusty software that isn't "ready for modern Windows."

Suggestions: Set "UAC: Behavior of the elevation prompt for Standard Users to Automatically deny elevation requests" to Disabled.

Set "UAC: Switch to the secure desktop when prompting for elevation" to Disabled.

Set "Virtualize file and registry write failures to per-user locations" to Disabled.

If you are running applications that are designed for the Standard User, you will not use nor require the virtualization feature. This feature was designed as legacy application compatibility mitigation but comes with a price.

Applications that leverage virtualization perform a "double read" when accessing data that could potentially be in a virtualized location.

So, if the application was installed to `%ProgramFiles%\ApplicationX\` and under that folder are `FileX` and `FileY`, if during runtime ApplicationX modifies and saves `FileY`, this forces `FileY` to be virtualized to `%userprofile%\..\..\VirtualStore\Program Files\ApplicationX\FileY`.

The next time ApplicationX tries to access `FileX`, it must first look in the user "VirtualStore" as `FileX` could have potentially been virtualized. If `FileX` is not found, it will then query the "real" `%ProgramFiles%\ApplicationX\FileX`.

That's going to be a performance hit. But with these settings, you would increase performance. Again, this is only a good idea if all the applications are Windows Vista-ized, er... Windows 7-ized, er, modernized.

Case 5: Enterprise Desktop: Protected Administrator (All Applications Are Signed)

Again, this is a long-term goal for you to reach in your environment. The goal is that all applications are signed by the organization and only a restricted set of "Application signing certificates" are trusted by the client computer.

Main suggestion: Set "Only elevate executables that are signed and validated" to Enabled.   This configuration will ensure that only those applications that either ship with Windows or are explicitly signed and trusted by the organization will be allowed to run with administrative rights.

WARNING   If you invoke an elevated cmd.exe "command host," you can then launch most applications from within the command host environment, thus bypassing this policy check.

Case 6: Power User–Style User Who Shares Computers with Standard Users

In this case, you would want the power user to be prompted when they do an administrative action. Give the right credentials, then, poof! They're in. But you also want to silently deny the regular user. Don't let them even see what they shouldn't play with.

Main suggestion: Set "Behavior of the elevation prompt for administrators in Admin Approval Mode" to "Elevate without prompting."   If the user wants to gain the benefits of the "Split Token" but never see a UAC elevation dialog box, then this configuration is better than disabling UAC altogether.

Remember that when UAC is disabled, all its supporting technologies are also disabled. In most cases this is not desirable.

Case 7: Your Users Request Assistance with Windows Remote Assistance

In this case, you would want to ensure that users don't have to know a local administrator password to get help.

Main suggestion: Utilize the default and ensure "Allow UIAccess applications to prompt for elevation without using the secure desktop" is set.   This way, it's a clear path for users to ask for help and for you to provide help.

UAC Final Thoughts and References

As I stated in the introduction, UAC hasn't changed, internally, too much from Windows Vista. But if you want to get a leg up and learn what's different, here are some articles I suggest you read.

"Inside Windows 7 User Account Control," by Mark Russinovich

`http://technet.microsoft.com/en-us/magazine/2009.07.uac.aspx`

  or `http://tinyurl.com/mokz59`

"Engineering Windows 7 (UAC), Post 1":

`http://blogs.msdn.com/e7/archive/2008/10/08/user-account-control.aspx`

  or `http://tinyurl.com/3jn5g3`

"Engineering Windows 7 (UAC), Post 2":

`http://blogs.msdn.com/e7/archive/2009/01/15/user-account-control-uac-quick-update.aspx`

  or `http://tinyurl.com/9a8vrj`

"Engineering Windows 7 (UAC), Post 3":

`http://blogs.msdn.com/e7/archive/2009/02/05/update-on-uac.aspx`

  or `http://tinyurl.com/dyp9s8`

"Engineering Windows 7 (UAC), Post 4":

`http://blogs.msdn.com/e7/archive/2009/02/05/uac-feedback-and-follow-up.aspx`

  or `http://tinyurl.com/ct8wt6`

Wireless (802.3) and Wired Network (802.11) Policies

Built-in support for wireless networks was introduced for Windows XP and Windows 2003 and is now enhanced for Windows Vista and later. Additionally, Windows Vista has a Wired policy that is new and neat. And Windows 7 added a few more bells and whistles (which can be found in the same place as the Windows Vista settings).

You can see two new nodes in Computer Configuration ➢ Policies ➢ Windows Settings ➢ Security Settings ➢ **Wired Network (IEEE 802.3) Policies** and **Wireless Network (IEEE 802.11 Policies)**, as seen in Figure 8.54.

FIGURE 8.54 New nodes for Wired and Wireless policies are now available.

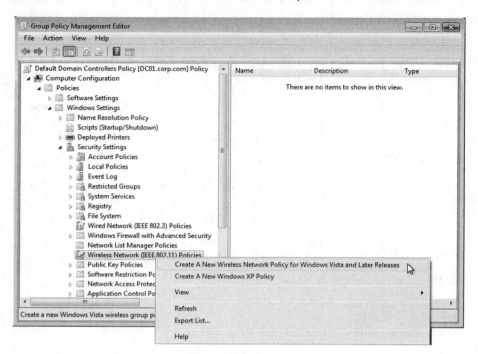

Here's the trick, though: to make the examples in this section work, you need to have an updated schema. You can get the updated schema in one of three ways:

- If you do a fresh installation of Windows Server 2008 as your first Active Directory domain.

- If you use the Windows Server 2008 or Windows Server 2008 R2 `adprep /forestprep` command, found in the `\sources` directory on the Windows Server 2008 DVD. To prepare your Windows Server 2003 domain for the introduction of Windows Server 2008 Domain Controllers, you'll also need to run `adprep /domainprep` in each domain (after the `/forestprep`, which takes care of the schema update). Additionally, you might need to run `adprep /domainprep /gpprep`. Please check Microsoft Knowledge Base article 324392 (`http://tinyurl.com/39r59e`) for additional information.

- You can manually update a Windows Server 2003 domain's schema to just support these attributes. You can find that information here: `http://tinyurl.com/yzqqumh`, in the article "Active Directory Schema Extensions for Windows Vista Wireless and Wired Group Policy Enhancements." There are two scripts you must run to make the updates: one for Wired and one for Wireless policy.

To make use of Wireless and Wired policies, you'll need to commit to one of these three steps or these policies just won't work. Note that you must be an Active Directory Schema Admin to make these changes.

So, instead of reproducing all the steps here, just go there, take the time to do this in your test lab (or get permission to do this in your real world), then come back here when you've finished.

Note that if you try to create new Wireless Network (IEEE 802.11) policies for Windows XP *without* updating the schema, these policies will succeed, because Windows XP doesn't require the updated schema. Do note, however, that this still requires the Windows Server 2003 Active Directory schema; the Windows 2000 Active Directory schema won't work.

However, if you don't have the schema update, and you attempted to create a new Wireless policy for Windows Vista or later or new Wired policy (which is Windows Vista and later–only anyway), you'll encounter what you see in Figure 8.55.

FIGURE 8.55   What happens if you try to create a new Wired or Wireless policy for Windows Vista and later without the schema update

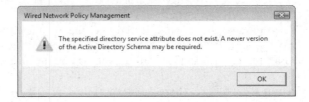

Assuming you've modified the schema as required, you're ready to move on.

802.11 Wireless Policy for Windows XP

When you right-click **Wireless Network (IEEE 802.11) Policies,** you can select "Create a New Windows Network Policy for Windows Vista and Later Releases" or "Create a New Windows XP Policy" as seen in Figure 8.54 earlier. For XP, you know which one to pick.

You can set all sorts of wireless parameters for your Windows XP or Windows 2003 computers (though it's unlikely you'll have many Windows 2003 computers with wireless cards). The policy settings themselves are beyond the scope of this book and include options such as WEP, EAP/Smartcard usage, and other scary-sounding wireless settings. However, you can learn about the controllable settings in "Securing Wireless LANs with Certificate Services." At last check it was found here: `http://tinyurl.com/yzm3tv`.

Note that your users need to be connected to the hard-wired network at least one time and download Group Policy from a Domain Controller to get the appropriate certificates for Wireless policy.

802.11 Wireless Policy and 802.3 Wired Policy for Windows Vista and Later

For Windows Vista and later, the Wireless policy has some new bells and whistles, and the Wired policy is specific to Windows Vista and later. And, for Windows 7, both the Wired and

Wireless policies have even more bells and whistles than Windows Vista. When you create a new policy for each, you'll clearly see a little subsection that houses the Windows 7–specific features that only Windows 7 clients can utilize.

However, in the new goodies for Wireless you get things like "Mixed Security Mode" (where you can configure several settings to single SSID) and "Allow and Deny Lists" (where you can dictate specifically which SSIDs they can connect and not connect to).

At last check, a good starting point for leveraging these policies (the Windows Vista and later versions, anyway) can be found here:

    http://technet.microsoft.com/en-us/magazine/2007.04.cableguy.aspx

(shortened version: http://tinyurl.com/ykfmkax).

Note that machines always need to first make contact with a Domain Controller to download Group Policy over the wired Ethernet at least one time before this Wireless policy can kick in.

Additionally, the Wired policies don't look all that exciting at first blush. But they're the backbone for Network Access Protection (NAP)—a feature for Windows Server 2008 (with Windows XP/SP3 and later clients) that will prevent rogue machines from getting on your network.

Again, while they're not shown here, there are several new Wired and Wireless policy settings for Windows 7 target computers. When you create a new Wired or Wireless policy, you won't miss 'em. They're cordoned off in a category labeled "Windows 7 policy settings."

You can also leverage Wired policy if your Cisco switch enforces 802.1x authentication. This is common in high-security environments where you want to prevent unauthorized users from plugging laptops into hot network drops. You can learn more about 802.1x authentication with Microsoft's NAP in the downloadable bonus chapter "Network Access Protection (NAP) with Group Policy" from www.GPanswers.com.

Configuring Windows Firewall with Group Policy

Windows XP/SP2 and later machines have a firewall that you can enable if you want to. Actually, Windows XP/SP2, Windows Vista, Windows 7, and even Windows Server 2008 and Windows Server 2008 R2 already have that firewall enabled.

But really, what's the point? The point of a firewall on your machine (whatever kind it is) is to allow certain kinds of traffic to pass through and certain kinds of traffic to be prevented. That's it. Nothing mysterious here about a firewall.

Starting with Windows XP/SP2, all inbound communication was filtered by a firewall. We saw this phenomenon in Chapter 2 when we tried to perform a "Group Policy Results" to our Windows XP or later client system and got an RPC error (which is the same error we'd get if the machine were off). Note that Windows Server 2003/SP1's and Windows XP/SP2's firewalls are functionally equivalent. However, Windows Server 2003/SP1's firewall is not turned on by default when the system is running. It is, however, turned on by default, initially, if you're performing an integrated (also known as *slipstreamed*) Windows Server 2003/SP1 installation, but that's another story.

But the firewalls of Windows Vista, Windows 7, and Windows Server 2008 are on by default, and thankfully, those operating systems have a brand-spankin'-new firewall and a killer updated way via Group Policy to control it. This technology is dubbed WFAS: Windows Firewall with Advanced Security.

Let me declare right now that it's simply not possible for us to go into every single thing you can do with WFAS. That's (at least) a whole book in and of itself.

My goal is to acquaint you with the Windows XP, Windows Vista, Windows 7, and Windows Server 2008 versions of the firewall vis-à-vis Group Policy. That way, when you know the underlying geeky firewall technology, protocols, encryption, certificates, and so on, you'll be ready to implement it all because your Group Policy knowledge will be solid enough to allow you to do what you want.

The other big part is helping you understand precedence order. With a lot of things in Group Policy–land, understanding why a policy (Group Policy or IPsec policy or Connection Rule Policy, and so on) takes effect is paramount to being a master troubleshooter.

Again, the Windows Firewall is a big, big topic, and you should read everything you can here:

http://technet.microsoft.com/en-us/network/bb545423.aspx

(shortened to http://tinyurl.com/5rvb62).

Before you go headlong into manipulating and changing the default firewall settings for Windows XP or Windows Vista and later, I recommend that you use caution. In other words, the firewall is, in fact, turned on by default in these operating systems for a reason.

It provides the most protection from the bad guys trying to infect and hack your Windows machines. And it makes sure you'll be mindful about opening up just the ports you want to use, even on a server—well, Windows Server 2008 Server by default, anyway.

So, if you're going to start opening ports on your machines (or kill the firewall altogether), please use these policy settings with caution.

Know what you're changing and why you're changing it.

Again, the defaults are there for a reason!

Everything Old Is New Again: The Windows XP vs. WFAS Firewall Controls

Before we get too far down the pike here, let me describe one potential pitfall about what's happened here since Windows Vista: because Windows XP (and Windows Server 2003 for that matter) already had a firewall (with one set of Group Policy controls), and now Windows Vista and later have an updated firewall (with an updated set of Group Policy controls), it can sometimes be a little confusing just what you're controlling and where you're supposed to go in the Group Policy Management Editor in order to control it.

Now there are two sets of firewall settings:

- The "older" Windows XP firewall settings (where both Windows XP and Windows Vista and later machines can embrace most of these settings)

- The "newer" WFAS settings for Windows Vista and later (which Windows XP may not know how to handle)

Indeed, in Chapter 2, we used the policy **Windows Firewall: Allow inbound remote administrative exception** when we wanted to allow the required ports on both Windows XP and Windows Vista to open up so we could perform a Group Policy Results analysis.

Yep, that one worked! But I haven't tested all the Windows XP policy settings against a Windows Vista, Windows 7, or Windows Server 2008 firewall. And, indeed, there's a more specific, targeted way to achieve the same goals with the WFAS firewall, which is found on Windows Vista, Windows 7, and Windows Server 2008.

So, my humble suggestion, before you start creating lots and lots of GPOs with Windows Firewall policies in them, is to name them as such based on which operating system they're supposed to target. Then, you have a very clearly named GPO that you can link to proper places in your hierarchy.

Therefore, I suggest you keep your GPOs separate. Have GPOs that affect only the Windows XP firewall, GPOs that affect only the Windows Vista/Windows 7 firewall, and maybe others that affect only the Windows Server 2008 firewall. In this example, you can see two GPOs linked to two OUs. We have "Sales Firewall Policy for Windows XP" and "Sales Firewall Policy for Vista / Win7 Computers" and they're only affecting the specific type of computers inside the OUs. I think, in the long run, this is the cleanest and least-confusing path.

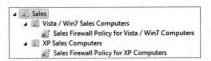

This might not always be possible, but it is by far the cleanest implementation.

The other way to specify which GPOs affect which machines is via WMI filtering (explored in detail in Chapter 4). With WMI filters you can "target" a machine based on various characteristics. Here are the WMI queries you'll need to target a specific GPO to a specific machine type.

For Vista RTM:

```
Select * from Win32_OperatingSystem Where BuildNumber=6000
```

For Windows XP:

```
Select * from Win32_OperatingSystem Where BuildNumber =2600
```

For Windows Server 2008 and Windows Vista/SP1:

These two operating systems both share build number 6001. You can use the same query to address both Windows Server 2008 and Windows Vista/SP1 machines as:

```
Select * from Win32_OperatingSystem Where BuildNumber = 6001
```

For Server 2008/SP2 and Windows Vista/SP2:

```
Select * from Win32_OperatingSystem Where BuildNumber = 6002
```

For Windows 7 and Windows Server 2008 R2:

```
Select * from Win32_OperatingSystem Where BuildNumber = 7600
```

These are just some examples. If you have alternate operating systems not listed here, be sure to use the tools in Chapter 4 to glean the `BuildNumber` for the operating system you want to target.

Manipulating the Windows XP and Windows Server 2003 Firewall

Most of the discussions in this particular section will revolve around trying to manipulate the Windows XP firewall (or Windows Server 2003 firewall, if you've enabled it).

WARNING Again, as stated, most of the techniques we'll perform here should work just fine if the target machine is a Windows Vista, Windows 7, or Windows Server 2008 machine with its new WFAS. But I haven't specifically tested each of these settings against Windows XP or Windows Server 2008. We'll explore the ins and outs of manipulating those operating systems' WFAS in the next section.

Domain vs. Standard Profiles for Windows XP and Windows Server 2003

If you dive down into the new firewall policy settings, contained within Computer Configuration ➢ Policies ➢ Administrative Templates ➢ Network ➢ Network Connections ➢ Windows Firewall, you'll notice two branches: Domain Profile and Standard Profile. You can see them in Figure 8.56.

Inside each branch, you'll see a gaggle of settings that are exactly the same. So, what gives?

When policy settings within the Domain Profile are enabled, they affect the firewall when they make contact with the Domain Controller. This is usually when a computer is at the central office and a normal logon occurs.

In Windows XP, the computer didn't need to authenticate to a Domain Controller for Domain Profile policy settings to kick in. In Windows Vista and later, authentication to a Domain Controller is required.

When policy settings within the Standard Profile are enabled, they affect the firewall when Windows *cannot* authenticate to a Domain Controller. This might happen when the user is in a hotel room, an Internet cafe, or other areas with public connectivity.

FIGURE 8.56   The Domain Profile is used when the machine can make contact to a Domain Controller. The Standard Profile is used when the machine is in someplace like a hotel room or Starbucks.

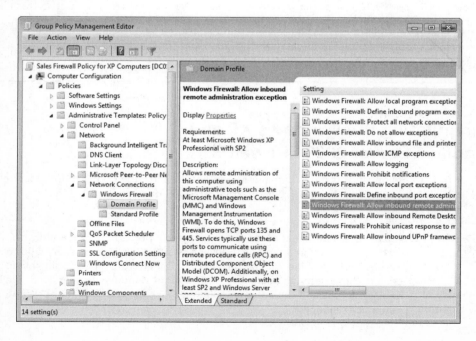

You might set up your Domain Profile settings to have additional port exceptions to be used by the central office administrative team for scanning and remote administration. And you can leverage your Standard Profile settings to ensure that the firewall is at its maximum enforcement. In short, you get to choose how strong the firewall will act in each of these circumstances.

Microsoft has a great little article on how the computer fundamentally determines if it should use the Domain Profile or the Standard Profile. Check it out here: `http://tinyurl` `.com/cao73`.

Again, these settings here are meant for the Windows XP/SP2 firewall, but they should also work if a Windows Vista/Windows 7 firewall gets these settings from a downloaded Group Policy. However, I haven't personally tested each and every one. Here are some tips if you choose to affect Windows Vista and later machines with Windows XP/SP2 settings:

- Standard Profile settings apply to both the private and public profiles for Windows Vista and later.

- If you configure the more modern "Advanced Firewall Policy" (up next), then the Standard Profile settings will stop applying. The assumption is that if the computer is getting a new policy, you must have started using the new policy model.

Killing the Firewall for Windows XP and Windows Server 2003

There might be times when you just want to outright kill the Windows XP, Windows Vista, or Windows 7 firewall. Additionally, you can prevent an inadvertent mishap should someone try to enable it on Windows Server 2003 or Windows Server 2008 if you like.

I explained this in Chapter 2, but since we're here again, let's review. Again, note that the recommended course for manipulating Windows Vista and later firewall will be discussed later, even though this technique will, in fact, work.

To kill the XP/SP2 (or later) firewall, drill down to Administrative Templates ➢ Network ➢ Network Connections ➢ Windows Firewall ➢ Domain Profile and select **Windows Firewall: Protect All Network Connections**. But here's the thing. You don't choose to *Enable* this policy. No, no. You *Disable* it. Yes, you read that right—you Disable it. Read the Explain text help inside the policy for more information on specific usage examples.

Before you do this, though, remember that it's a better idea to leave it on and just filter based on the traffic you know you want. Only kill the firewall as a last resort.

Opening Specific Ports, Managing Exceptions, and More for Windows XP and Windows Server 2003

Microsoft did a lot of the hard work for me. They've put together a stellar document about how to fully manage all aspects of your Windows XP/SP2 (and Windows Server 2003/SP1) firewall with Group Policy. By using the techniques Microsoft provides, you'll be able to have very granular control over how the firewall is used in your company (and when users are away from your company).

You can learn how to open specific ports, make specific program exceptions, turn on logging, and more.

For more information about deploying Windows Firewall, see "Deploying Windows Firewall Settings for Microsoft Windows XP with Service Pack 2" on the Microsoft Download Center website at `http://tinyurl.com/a8bfc`. Another excellent article can be found here:

`www.microsoft.com/technet/community/columns/cableguy/cg0106.mspx`

(shortened to `http://tinyurl.com/ujg25`).

Windows Firewall with Advanced Security (for Windows Vista and Windows Server 2008)—WFAS

In this section we'll take a bite-sized tour of what we can do with the updated Windows Firewall with Advanced Security (WFAS). This new item runs on Windows 7, Windows Vista, and Windows Server 2008.

WFAS's two "prime directives" in life are to:

- Block all incoming traffic (unless it is requested or it matches a configured rule)
- Allow all outgoing traffic (unless it matches a configured rule to prevent it)

As you go along in these examples, you'll see UI references to "Location" type, which can be "Domain Location," "Public Location," and "Private Location." To help you understand Network Location Types, read the article "Network Location Types in Windows Vista" here: `http://tinyurl` `.com/669qxb`. Because the Windows 7, Windows Vista, and Windows Server 2008 machines we'll be manipulating are joined to the domain, they will be considered a part of the "Domain Location" where we can control the WFAS via Group Policy.

Additionally, the IP security (IPsec) function (discussed in more detail next) is also part of WFAS (where it was a separate node of the UI in the Group Policy Management Editor for pre-Vista management stations). We'll see how this all fits together as we work through this section.

Holy Cow! Three Ways to Set WFAS Settings!

There are three different *stores* for Windows Firewall for Advanced Security policies and four different ways to make that happen:

- The Active Directory–based Group Policy you know and love
- Local Group Policy accessible via `gpedit.msc`
- By running `WF.MSC`, which opens a GUI to the "local WSAF store"

Here's where it gets confusing, so stay with me here: the store hosting rules from WF.MSC and from Local Group Policy are in fact *separate*.

If you crack open WF.MSC, you'll see that there are a number of default rules in WF.MSC (as seen here):

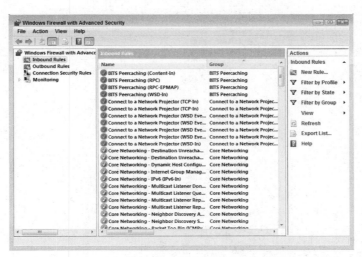

But open the Local Group Policy Editor, and you won't see those rules at all!

You can also see this behavior via the command line. The command is Netsh (then press Enter) advfirewall (then press Enter). Once inside, you can poke around. This is the command-line interface for all the goodies you're looking at in the Group Policy Editor.

By default you're poking around the "local Windows Firewall store" (the same thing you'd see when you use WF.MSC), but you can use the set store command to change focus to, say, the local GPO or even an Active Directory–based GPO. The idea is that once you've "set store" to another place, say a particular GPO, you can do everything via the command line you could do via the GUI.

Nice touch!

Getting Started with WFAS "Properties"

The first place you might want to check out on your WFAS journey is the "Properties" of the WFAS node. Now, I say "Properties" with quotes because there isn't a precise name for them. But, I'll call them "WFAS Properties" for our purposes. You find them by right-clicking over the "Windows Firewall with Advanced Security" node (with the little brick and the world icon) and selecting Properties, as seen in Figure 8.57.

FIGURE 8.57 The Windows Firewall with Advanced Security has "Group Policy–like" properties inside.

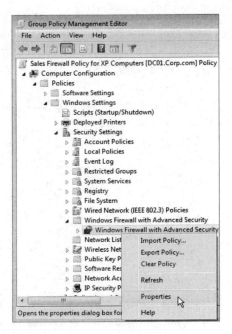

Once there, you'll have lots of settings to play with. These settings specify certain behavior types based on how the machine is connected and some IPsec settings. You can see this in Figure 8.58. However, the trick about all of the WFAS Properties settings is that they act exactly like regular Administrative Templates policies. So, recall how in all Administrative Templates policy settings there is an "Enabled," "Not Configured," and "Disabled" ability? Well, all the settings contained here work exactly the same way across multiple GPOs, if configured. You can see an example of a subproperties page in Figure 8.58 where it demonstrates "Yes," "No," and "Not Configured." Each setting also displays the default setting if you do nothing (which is a nice touch).

Again, the point is that all the settings contained at this level are just like normal, everyday, garden-variety Group Policy. If stored at the Local or domain-based levels, the regular Group Policy precedence rules will apply.

What we'll learn about *next* is a little different, because, while it uses the Group Policy interface, it's not exactly the same "Group Policy rule precedence" that you've come to know and love with the kinds of settings in here. Stay tuned—I'll explain it as we learn more and more, and then wrap up our discussion about WFAS with an overall cheat sheet to help you grasp which rules come from where and what will win.

FIGURE 8.58 Imagine that all the settings in the WFAS Properties are just like Administrative Templates settings in other areas of Group Policy.

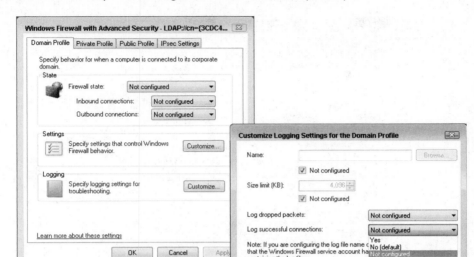

Creating New Inbound and Outbound Rules with the WFAS

WFAS is updated to support a neat-o new UI as well as some amazing under-the-hood features. Again, we simply don't have room to go over everything, so we'll have to make do with a brief tour. One important point to note is that WFAS has both inbound and outbound rules (where Windows XP's firewall had only inbound rules). You can see where to create rules in Figure 8.59 and simply right-click over the rule type to create a new rule.

Inbound Rules The goal of inbound rules is to prevent the bad stuff from reaching your machine and allow only traffic you request to reach you. This is the kind of thing most firewalls are used for.

Outbound Rules At first blush, outbound rules seem counterintuitive. Why would you ever want to restrict outbound communication, right? Well, you might want to lock down a workstation from opening connections outbound to particular services. For example, you might have a specialty workstation that is only supposed to be used as a web-browser machine. Well, you can then lock out all outbound remote ports except port 80 (HTTP) and 443 (SSL/HTTPS). This would potentially allow you to squelch a virus or malware program that was trying to "phone home" or otherwise be a baddie. (Note that this works only if you lock out remote ports. If you locked out the local ports, this trick won't work.)

FIGURE 8.59   Once you locate the Inbound and Outbound Rules nodes, you can right-click to select New Rule.

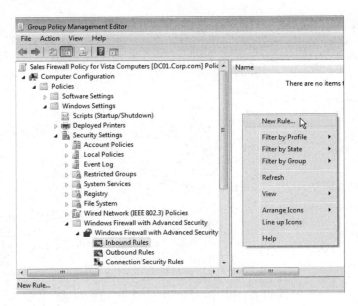

Connection Security Rules   These rules dictate if this machine is going to be able to talk to other machines at all. You can create all kinds of rules here, including only being able to talk with machines that are on the same domain, or just enable specific machine-to-machine contact. This is the new way to perform IPsec rules, though there's little mention of the word *IPsec*, actually. Additionally, there are settings here that work in conjunction with an advanced feature (which we cannot cover here) called Network Access Protection (or NAP). The idea is that if your machine doesn't meet certain criteria, then it shouldn't be allowed to talk with its other brothers and sisters. This is configured via the NAP MMC snap-in. Learn more about NAP at www.microsoft.com/nap and in a downloadable chapter from www.GPanswers.com.

WARNING   The rules you create should be ignored by pre-Vista machines (such as Windows XP). Be sure to read the sidebar "Everything Old Is New Again: The Windows XP vs. WFAS Firewall Controls."

Inbound and Outbound Rule Types

Once you've elected to create a rule, there are four rule types to choose from, as seen in Figure 8.60.

FIGURE 8.60 After creating an inbound or outbound rule, you must select the type. Most often, you'll select Predefined.

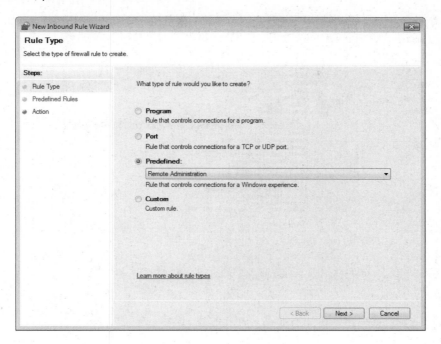

Program You can dictate which programs (specified by path and executable name) you want to allow traffic to flow between. You need to also specify an action (Allow, Block, or "Allow the connection if it is secure"). Note that the "Allow the connection if it is secure" setting requires a valid connection security configuration as well as IPsec rules deployed to handle the IPsec portion of the enforcement.

Port This is a specific rule based on TCP or UDP ports. You must also specify which ports (separated by commas). Specific ranges, say, 80–100, won't work unless individually listed with commas separating them.

Predefined This will likely be where most people spend their time. This is a collection of "well-known" services and which ports to open up if you want traffic to flow. There are some new predefined collections for some Windows 7 scenarios.

Custom This is the kitchen sink. If you want to go whole hog and tweak until you're blue in the face, this is the place for you. If you couldn't configure the settings using one of the other three ways, this is where you do it.

If you want to try this out for a WFAS machine, select Predefined, then use the pull-down to see the various Predefined options, as seen in Figure 8.61. If we want to parallel the example in Chapter 2 (which Allowed Remote Inbound Administration Exception), we could simply select "Remote Administration," as seen in Figure 8.61.

FIGURE 8.61 Use the Predefined rules to allow the kinds of "well-known" traffic your people might need.

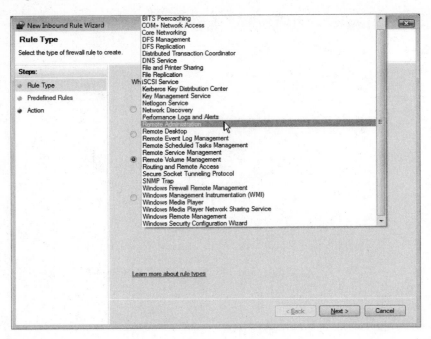

By clicking Next in the wizard, you'll zip past all the predefined rules, saving you oodles of time. Once the wizard is complete, you'll see the new inbound rule and its name, as seen in Figure 8.62. To see what that rule is really doing, just check out the Properties for each line item.

Connection Security Rules

In the previous example we leveraged an inbound rule to open up WFAS to allow a remote administration exception. And the procedure would be pretty similar if we wanted an outbound rule as well.

However, Connection Security rules are different. Connection Security rules define how and when computers authenticate using IPsec or Authenticated IP. Connection Security rules are used in establishing server and domain isolation, as well as in enforcing NAP policy.

These allow you to specify which other computers you can talk with. Again, the idea here is to prevent your target machines from talking with the bad guys.

You can see the list of available Connection Security rule types in Figure 8.63.

You can find more information on Authenticated IP at http://tinyurl .com/yelj7a and more on rule types at http://tinyurl.com/yx4rkk.

FIGURE 8.62 When the rule is complete, you'll see the results in the right pane.

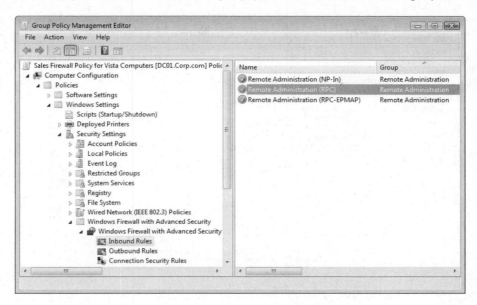

Rule Precedence

What if you have multiple WFAS rules applying? Which WFAS rule is going to win to restrict the traffic?

Additionally, what if you have multiple GPOs that affect this target machine with multiple rules? Turns out, it doesn't matter. All rules are simply "additive" among all GPOs—for the type of rule it is.

So, all inbound rules are all added up. All outbound rules are all added up, and so on. What you might care about is if a conflict exists between, say, an inbound rule and an outbound rule. Which will win there?

Again, the list of WFAS rules is merged from all sources and then processed in the order shown next from top to bottom. This rule process ordering is always enforced, regardless of the source of the rules:

Windows Service Hardening This rule restricts services from establishing connections. These are generally automatically configured out of the box so that Windows Services can only communicate in specific ways (that is, restricting allowable traffic through a specific port). However, until you create a firewall rule, traffic is not allowed.

Connection Security Rules This type of rule defines how and when computers authenticate using IPsec. Connection Security rules are used in establishing server and domain isolation, as well as in enforcing NAP policy.

FIGURE 8.63   WFAS Security Rules offer lots of flexibility.

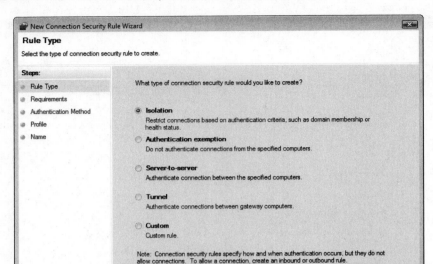

Authenticated Bypass Rules   This type of rule allows the connection of particular computers if the traffic is protected with IPsec, regardless of other inbound rules in place. Specified computers are allowed to bypass inbound rules that block traffic. For example, you could allow remote firewall administration from only *certain* computers by creating an "Authenticated bypass" rule for those computers. Or, you could enable support for Remote Assistance by the help desk *only* from the help desk computers.

Block Rules   This type of rule explicitly blocks a particular type of incoming or outgoing traffic.

Allow Rules   This type of rule explicitly allows a particular type of incoming or outgoing traffic.

IPsec (Now in Windows Firewall with Advanced Security)

The Internet Protocol security function, or IPsec for short, has a big job: securing the exchange of packets on your TCP/IP network. Its primary mission is host-to-host authentication. However, you can additionally choose to encrypt the traffic via tunneling or network encryption so others can't "spy" on the data flying by.

Maybe you have one super-important Human Resources server. And you want to ensure that no one except the Human Resources people can talk with that server. That's IPsec's job: ensuring that only the right people on the right computers can talk with the other computers you specify.

 IPsec is based on IKE. The RFCs on IKE only support the concept of *computer authentication*. Microsoft, however, has gone the extra mile and introduced an extension to IKE called Authenticated IP (AuthIP). This new feature introduces the ability to support *user* authentication *as well as* computer authentication. Additionally, the administrator can choose to use *both* user and computer authentication if desired.

IPsec General Resources

IPsec is a big, big topic, and not one we can cover in enormous detail here. However, my goal for this section is to get you up to speed on the WFAS implementation of IPsec and explain how "legacy" IPsec interacts with the "new" IPsec. So, if you're not familiar with IPsec and want to follow along, you'll have to spend some quality time at the following websites:

- www.microsoft.com/ipsec

- http://technet.microsoft.com/en-us/network/bb545651.aspx

- A great document from Microsoft titled "Introduction to Windows Firewall with Advanced Security" found at http://tinyurl.com/yx4rkk

- www.microsoft.com/windowsserver2003/techinfo/overview/netcomm.mspx (http://tinyurl.com/4x5y)

I also recommend this excellent webcast from TechEd 2006 by Steve Riley that covers both the firewall and IPsec improvements: http://tinyurl.com/yl4bw3.

Server and Domain Isolation with IPsec

IPsec, at its core, restricts who is talking to whom. Okay, great. So, armed with that knowledge, you can take it to the next level and make sure that machines you know nothing about can't talk to machines you do.

For instance, imagine a consultant comes into your business with a laptop and plugs in. Chances are, with enough poking around, he could figure out your IP address scheme. Now he's able to ping servers and see what's going on over there on machines without a firewall. And, what if he brought a virus in with him from the cold, dark, outside world? Oops, you've got a problem.

To combat this, let's assume instead you want to create "rings of protection" among machines you trust and machines you really trust. That's the idea of server and domain isolation with IPsec. You can see the general idea here in this graphic.

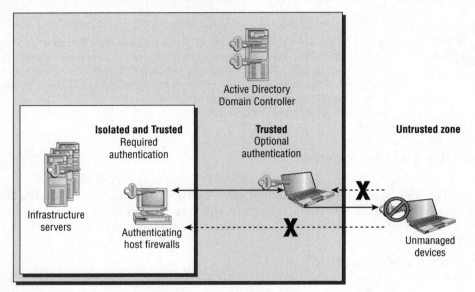

What sounds like a swell idea (and it is) can be a big project. Indeed, to protect your Windows XP, Windows 2000, and Windows Server 2003 machines from outside invaders (so they'll talk only with other machines you trust) takes about 300 pages of reading and implementing. You can find the big guide for this here:

    www.microsoft.com/technet/security/guidance/architectureanddesign/ipsec/
    default.mspx

(shortened to http://tinyurl.com/yywxas).

Again, it's something like 300 pages to do this for pre-Vista.

But if you check out:

    http://support.microsoft.com/default.aspx/kb/914841

you'll find information on the Simple Policy Update that adds more Windows Server 2003 and Windows XP IPsec support—specifically to reduce the amount of IPsec filters you need to pull this off.

In Windows 7, Windows Vista, and Windows Server 2008, it's simpler. There's a great new Microsoft document called "Step-by-Step Guide: Deploying Windows Firewall and IPsec Policies," which is found at http://tinyurl.com/2rmd7u and covers this specific topic in depth.

Getting Started with IPsec with WFAS

Here's where it starts to get a little confusing. That's because there are two types of IPsec rules. I don't know if they have "proper" names, so we'll just call them "older" and "newer" rule types.

Older rule types are found in the node Computer Configuration ➢ Policies ➢ Windows Settings ➢ Security Settings ➢ **IP Security Policies on Active Directory**.

Newer rule types are found inside the new WFAS. Specifically, again, it's Computer Configuration ➢ Policies ➢ Windows Settings ➢ Security Settings ➢ **Windows Firewall with Advanced Security**. You can see both nodes highlighted in Figure 8.64.

FIGURE 8.64   You can see both the "old" and "new" places to configure IPsec policies.

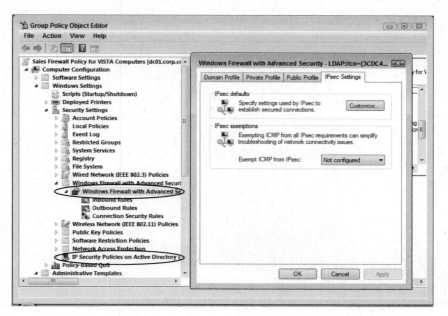

To configure "old" IPsec policies, you right-click **IP Security Policies on Active Directory** and select "Create IP Security Policy."

To configure "new" IPsec policies, you right-click **Connection Security rules** and just get started with "New Rule." If IPsec is required it will just automatically be part of that rule.

Note that advanced IPsec configurations may require some additional "global" settings. To do this, right-click **Windows Firewall with Advanced Security** and select Properties, then click the IPsec Settings tab as seen in Figure 8.64. Then, when you click the Customize button in the IPsec Settings tab, you'll have the range of additional IPsec options to play with, as you can see in Figure 8.65.

Note that the "old" IPsec policies' "Default Response Rule" is not valid for Windows Vista and later. The Group Policy editor will warn you of this if you try to create an IPsec policy using an updated GPMC management station. In short, don't mix old and new policies on the same computer.

FIGURE 8.65   Some "base" IPsec settings for a GPO can be found in the "Windows Firewall with Advanced Security" properties.

Understanding How WFAS IPsec Rules Work

There are now two types of IPsec rules that can be applied to a machine with WFAS (Windows Vista and later).

Again, we're calling these the old IPsec rules and the new IPsec rules here. The old IPsec rules are configured in the IP Security Policy Management MMC snap-in.

Old IPsec rules   These are IKE rules that support only machine-based Kerberos, x.509 certificates, and preshared key authentication. Old IKE-based rules are applied in the same way to Windows Vista/Windows 7 as they were in pre–Windows Vista operating systems: while multiple policies can be applied to a given machine, the last writer wins and there is no merging of IKE policy settings. So, if you had a policy set at the domain level and another set at the OU level, the OU level would win because there is no merging of any old IPsec rules.

New IPsec rules   Again, the new IPsec rules are created on machines with WFAS and applied to machines with WFAS (for Windows Vista and later). These rules are supported by an extension to IKE called Authenticated IP (AuthIP). As stated, a seriously good read on AuthIP can be found here: http://tinyurl.com/yelj7a. Here are some helpful tidbits as you explore the new WFAS IPsec. These (really geeky) tidbits are coming (nearly verbatim) from the IPsec team at Microsoft, so, thank them (not me) if you get a nice tip here.

- You can now leverage Interactive user, Kerberos/NTLMv2 credentials, User x.509 certificates, Machine X.509 certificates, NAP Health Certificates, and Anonymous Authentication (optional Authentication) for authenticating an IPsec connection.

- When configuring GPOs for connection security and firewall policies, you could disable the use of local firewall and Connection Security rules. That way, only the Group Policy linked to the site, domain, or OU GPOs could control the Windows Firewall behaviors. You can see where to do this in Figure 8.66 a bit later.

- Like other firewall and Group Policy rules, connection security rules are merged from all applicable GPOs (and processed according to the Rule Precedence list discussed earlier).

- Connection Security policies can be configured to create "old" (compatible) policies as well as Windows Vista and later (see the sidebar "Super-Geeky Note from the Microsoft IPsec Team #1: What's Going on Under the Hood").

- Only AuthIP policy is created for Windows Vista and later because IKE doesn't support User Authentication. Again, see the sidebar "Super-Geeky Note from the Microsoft IPsec Team #1: What's Going on Under the Hood."

- As noted earlier, Connection Security rules are merged from all applicable GPOs. However, there is a related group of settings for IPsec/Authenticated IP that manage the default IPsec behaviors that are not additive. The settings include the global authentication sets, Quick Mode and Key Exchange settings, and ICMP exemptions.

- On a WFAS client, Connection Security and IPsec rules can come from multiple GPOs. That is, all Connection Security rules on the client that make use of default auth/crypto sets will use the sets from the highest precedence GPO. If you need more flexibility, you have the three options. For authentication sets, configure the authentication through the Connection Security rule instead of using the default authentication. For Quick Mode crypto, use the command line netsh advfirewall to configure Quick Mode crypto settings on a per–Connection Security rule basis as needed. For Main Mode, only one set is supported per policy. In the case where multiple Main Mode crypto sets are received, the one from the highest precedence GPO will be applied to all Connection Security rules in the policy. There is unfortunately no way to customize the rules to use different Main Mode crypto sets.

NOTE   Honestly, these tips are more for the IPsec "superstars" out there than us normal people (me included), so don't panic if it's not 100 percent evident or relevant to your situation.

How Windows Firewall Rules Are Ultimately Calculated

Hopefully by now you understand that there are two categories of "things" that can be set by WFAS policy: properties and rules.

**Super-Geeky Note from the Microsoft IPsec Team #1:
What's Going on Under the Hood**

With WFAS, an admin can create IKE-based IPsec policies through the IP Security Policy Management snap-in. An admin can also create Connection Security rules that will be compatible with down-level IKE-based policies.

So, when the policy is created, here's what's happening under the hood:

- If no WFAS-specific features are required, the policy will be created with both a set of AuthIP (Vista and later) rules and a set of IKE rules for when the Vista (and later) system needs to connect to IKE-based 2000, XP, and 2003 systems.

- If there are WFAS-specific features (like requiring the use of a second User Authentication), then the system will *not* create pre–Windows Vista IKE rules.

What? Why not?

Simple: Since IKE on XP can't do User Authentication, there's no need to create extra policies where only Windows 7–, Windows Vista–, and Windows Server 2008–specific features are used.

See! Told you this was geeky!

**Super-Geeky Note from the Microsoft IPsec Team #2:
Get the Right Certs to Do the Right Job**

There is a particular nuance with regard to certificates that you'll need to know about before you go headlong into using IPsec and AuthIP. Again, the IPsec/AuthIP policies that are created by WFAS will use AuthIP by preference.

- If both machines are Windows Vista and later, then they'll use AuthIP to negotiate and authenticate.

- If one of the two talking machines is pre–Windows Vista, then the system will use IKE-based functionality.

- AuthIP uses SSL certs with client and/or server authentication settings configured.

- SSL certs can be client authentication or client and server authentication certs. And either should work.

What this means is that if you are constructing policies to use certificate authentication for Windows Vista and later, you'll need certificates that will work with AuthIP. That means the certificates you deploy to the clients need to be SSL certs with client and/or server authentication (depending on if you want one-way or mutual authentication).

Note that these certs differ from the standard digital certs used in Windows XP/2003.

Precedence Order for Properties

Properties are found in three ways:

- Running `WF.MSC` and right-clicking over the Windows Firewall with Advanced Security node (topmost node) and selecting Properties. This is the "local WFAS" store.
- Editing the local GPO of the machine and right-clicking over the Windows Firewall Advanced Security node and selecting Properties.
- Creating a new Active Directory–based GPO, then right-clicking over the Windows Firewall Advanced Security node and selecting Properties.

Again, these properties all act like regular Group Policy Administrative Template settings.

Now, the one thing I waited to explain until now is this: you can "block" the local WFAS store from being added to the calculations. To do this, in any GPO that has Windows Firewall settings that apply to the computer, right-click the Windows Firewall Advanced Security node and select Properties. Then, in, say, Domain Profile (or the other profiles), click Customize. Locate the Rule Merging section and select No, as seen in Figure 8.66.

This will only block a rule merge. Or, additionally, you could choose No from the "Apply local connection security rules" drop-down to block those.

However, it should be noted that you could prevent a local admin from being able to control a property just by setting it in the GPO.

Again, the default is "Yes" that local WFAS store settings (and rules) would apply. Change this only if you do not want local rules to apply. However, note that WFAS has a zillion built-in firewall rules. And, if you set this to "No," then all those rules suddenly— poof!—turn off. And WFAS's default action would be to block all incoming traffic. To change this you would need to set specific rules (I suggest "Predefined rules") to specify which inbound traffic you would allow through.

 You could export the local WFAS store first, and then import it into a domain-based one if you so choose.

Precedence Order for Rules

We've already discussed rule precedence (see the section "Rule Precedence" earlier). Even though the specific "what rule will win" aspect is pretty complicated, the overall Group Policy "rules" are simple.

FIGURE 8.66 You can block the application of the local WFAS firewall rules or local connection security rules by setting it in any Group Policy linked to the computer.

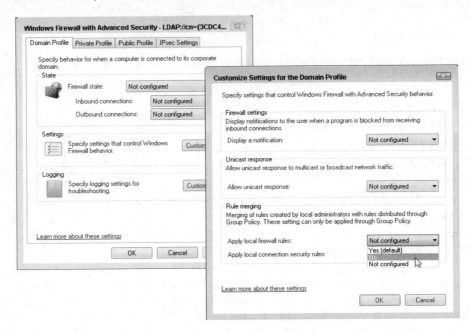

Basically, all Group Policy Objects that contain any WFAS rules are simply added up. There isn't even a concept of a "conflict" with WFAS rules, because the rules are just "separated" into buckets:

- So, all the inbound rules are added up from the local store, then all GPOs.

- Then, all the outbound rules are added up from the local store, then all GPOs.

- And all the Connection Security rules are added up from the local store, then all GPOs.

- If there's a Deny/Block policy for *any* rule, that's always going to win for that rule type.

You can, if you want, disable the local WFAS store and ignore those rules. That way, you just guarantee that Group Policy is doing all the dirty work to configure everything. In my opinion, this seems like a good way to go, so you don't have to remember if there even is a local WFAS store.

Again, you can see how to kill the WFAS local store's rule application in Figure 8.66.

One final parting WFAS tip. If you check out the local WFAS editor by clicking Start and then typing **WF.MSC** in the Start Search dialog box, you'll also have the ability to see the WFAS "monitor," which can be useful for troubleshooting.

What I Didn't Cover

Unfortunately, space limitations restrict me from delving into *all* security functions of Group Policy. Of note, two categories are missing from this Group Policy security roundup that can affect all computers:

- Certificate Services and Public Key Infrastructure (PKI)

- EFS and the EFS Recovery Policy

For More on Certificate Services and PKI

For getting a grip on Certificate Services and PKI, check out the Microsoft Press (2008) book *Windows Server 2008 PKI and Certificate Security* at:

   www.microsoft.com/MSPress/books/9549.aspx

For More on EFS and the EFS Recovery Policy

You'll find information on the Encrypting File System in Windows XP and Windows Server 2003 at http://tinyurl.com/576kx.

Additionally, see the Microsoft Knowledge Base article "Best Practices for the Encrypting File System" (KB 223316) at http://support.microsoft.com/kb/223316.

Final Thoughts

To know security, you need to know Group Policy. To that end, we've toured some of the major sights along the Group Policy security highway. From the "Default Domain Controllers Policy" and "Default Domain Policy" GPOs to Software Restriction Policies to AppLocker—a lot can be accomplished in there.

Walking up to a specific machine and applying local security sounds like a great, straightforward idea—until you have so many machines you couldn't possibly walk up to them all. This chapter covered some alternate methods for asserting your will across the network.

I covered this back in Chapter 3, but remember that most items in the security branch of a GPO will take effect, maximally, every 16 hours—even if the Group Policy doesn't change in Active Directory. This ensures that if a nefarious local administrator changed the policies on his workstation, they'll eventually be refreshed. However, recall that this "Security Background Refresh" will not affect other areas of Group Policy by default. If you want similar behavior, be sure to read Chapter 3 where I discuss the implications of the setting named **Process even if the Group Policy objects have not changed.** You can enable different sections of Group Policy to do this by drilling down in the Group Policy Management Editor within Computer Configuration ➢ Policies ➢ Administrative Templates ➢ System ➢ Group

Policy. Again, this was covered in Chapter 3. So, for fullest security and protection, reread that chapter to understand why and how to enable those settings.

When it comes to restricting software, Software Restriction Policies are fine for Windows XP and Windows Vista, but AppLocker has a real leg up. Be careful in not locking yourself out "too much" lest you'll need to revert your policies or recover your machines. Other than that—they're great.

Finally, remember that Fine-Grained Password Policy (FGPP) isn't really related to Group Policy, but there is a tie-in: if no FGPP is assigned to a user or group, the domain-wide defaults take effect. You might want to consider choosing one or the other: either keep using the Default Domain GPO to store the passwords for everyone in the domain, or consider assigning FGPPs for positively everyone in the domain. That way, you only have to troubleshoot one area if you suspect a problem.

Designing vs. Implementing

This chapter is "Implementing Security with Group Policy" because that's what we did. However, an equally challenging project is the *design* of your security policy battle plans *before* you march headlong into implementation. There are several excellent Microsoft resources, made specifically for the task of working through some examples to design security with GPOs. The oldest one is the "Common Scenarios" white paper at http://tinyurl.com/4oaks. You can also just search for "Group Policy Common Scenarios Using GPMC" on Microsoft's website.

The "Common Scenarios" white paper includes several "canned" GPOs that help you learn how to design a security policy and includes situations where computers should be Lightly Managed, Mobile, and Kiosk. Once you play with each scenario, you can decide which features you want to keep in your own environment. These GPOs aren't meant to be deployed as is (you should modify them to suit your own business), but you'll get a better handle on some security design options. A white paper is included to help you work though the scenarios. In all, I think it's an excellent follow-up once you've been through the exercises in this chapter.

There are some newer resources as well in the following guides:

- Windows Vista Security Guide (http://tinyurl.com/scpor)

- Windows Server 2008 Security Guide (part of the Security Compliance Management Toolkit Series, which is found here: http://tinyurl.com/55u5wj)

- Windows 7 Security Guide (http://tinyurl.com/5a5156) or:

  http://technet.microsoft.com/en-us/library/cc677002.aspx

At last check, these guides contain "GPOAccelerator" tools, which is a fancy way of saying "We'll create the test GPOs for you from the stuff inside the docs, and you hammer them out to fit your world." They're worth a look and are free, so that's a bonus.

9

Profiles: Local, Roaming, and Mandatory

When a user logs onto a Windows machine, a profile is automatically generated. A *profile* is a collection of settings, specific to a user that sticks with that user throughout the working experience. In this chapter, I'll talk about three types of profiles.

First is the *Local Profile*, which is created whenever a user logs on. Next is the *Roaming Profile*, which enables users to hop from machine to machine while maintaining the same configuration settings at each machine. Along our journey, I'll also discuss some configuration tweaks that you can set using specific policy settings—specifically for Roaming Profiles.

The third type of profile is the *Mandatory Profile*. Like Roaming Profiles, Mandatory Profiles allow the user to jump from machine to machine. But Mandatory Profiles force a user's Desktop and settings to remain exactly the same as they were when the administrator assigned the profile; the user cannot permanently change the settings.

Here's a little "cheat sheet" before we go much further. You need a guide to understand which operating system's profiles are compatible and which are not.

- Version 0: Windows NT

- Version 1: Windows 2000, Windows 2003, and Windows XP

- Version 2: Windows Vista and later, including Windows 7, Windows Server 2008 and Windows Server 2008 R2 (as clients)

We'll barely be talking at all about Version 0 profiles here. But we will be getting into Version 1 and Version 2 profiles. But before we get too far down the line, let's just break the bad news: if you're interested in setting up Roaming Profiles for both your Version 1 type machines and Version 2 type machines, you'll be setting up "parallel worlds." That is, you'll set up two Roaming Profile infrastructures (one for Version 1 and one for Version 2) and the two shall never meet.

If the two shall never meet, how will you share data for a user if he roams from a Windows XP to a Windows 7 machine and back again? That's the next chapter, where we take on redirected folders. So, stay tuned for that after you've successfully set up Roaming Profiles for Windows XP and Windows 7. (Again, we'll be using Windows 7 as our primary example for a Version 2 profile in this chapter, but you're welcome to use Windows Vista if you like.)

In general, your users will use desktop machines when roaming. However, users could, of course, roam to a server, like Windows Server 2003 or Windows Server 2008. Roaming Profiles will keep on working in those scenarios as well. Just remember that Windows Server 2003 is a Type 1 and Windows Server 2008 is a Type 2.

What Is a User Profile?

As I stated, as soon as a user logs onto a machine, a Local Profile is generated. This profile is two things: a personal slice of the Registry (contained in a file) and a set of folders stored on a hard drive. Together, these components form what we might call the *user experience*—that is, what the Desktop looks like, what style and shape the icons are, what the background wallpaper looks like, and so on.

The *NTUSER.DAT* File

The Registry stores user and computer settings into a file named NTUSER.DAT, which can be loaded and unloaded into the current computer's Registry—taking over the HKEY_CURRENT_USER portion of the Registry when the user logs on.

In Figure 9.1, you can see a portion of a Windows XP machine's HKEY_CURRENT_USER, specifically, the Control Panel ➢ Desktop ➢ Wallpaper setting, which shows c:\WINDOWS\web\wallpaper\Bliss.bmp in the Data column.

FIGURE 9.1 A simple Registry setting shows the entry for the wallpaper.

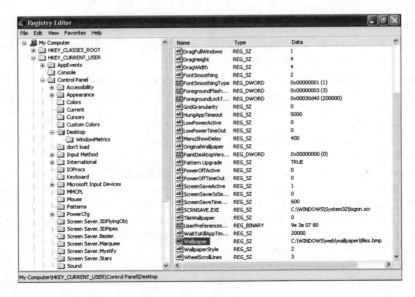

This portion of the Registry directly maps to a file in the user's profile—the NTUSER.DAT file. You'll find that many of a user's individual settings are stored in this file. Here are detailed descriptions for some of the settings inside NTUSER.DAT:

Accessories   Look-and-feel settings for applications such as Calculator, Clock, HyperTerminal, Notepad, and Paint.

Application   Settings for things like toolbars for Office applications and most newer applications.

Control Panel   The bulk of the settings in NTUSER.DAT. Settings found here include those for screen savers, display, sounds, and the mouse.

Explorer   Remembers how specific files and folders are to be displayed.

Printer   Network printer and local printer definitions are found here.

Drive Mappings   Stored, persistent drive mappings are stored here.

Taskbar   Designates the look and feel of the taskbar.

Profile Folders for Type 1 Computers (Windows 2000, Windows 2003, and Windows XP)

By default, Windows 2000, Windows 2003, and Windows XP profiles are stored in a folder under the C:\Documents and Settings folder.

Ultimately, what the user "sees" as their profile is an amalgam of two halves: their own personal profile and components from what is known as the "All Users" profile.

So, each user has a unique profile, and each user leverages a shared profile.

Understanding the Contents of a User's Profile (for Type 1 Computers)

Items in the profile folders can be stored in lots of nooks and crannies. As you can see in Figure 9.2, both visible and hidden folders store User Profile settings.

To show hidden files in an Explorer window, choose Tools ➤ Folder Options to open the Folder Options dialog box, and click the View tab. Click the "Show Hidden Files and Folders" radio button, and then click OK.

Here are the folders and a general description of what each contains.

Application Data   Used by many applications to store specific settings, such as the Microsoft Office toolbar settings. Additionally, items such as Word's Custom Dictionary are stored here. MST (Microsoft Transform) files are stored here by default. MST files modify Windows Installer applications by providing customized application installation and runtime settings. (See Chapter 11 for more information on MST files.)

FIGURE 9.2 A look inside Frank Rizzo's profile reveals both visible and hidden folders.

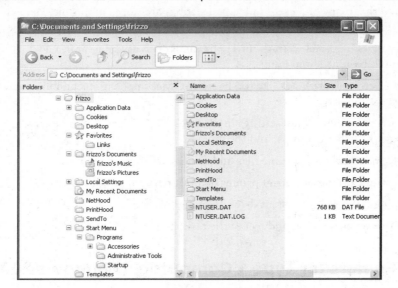

Cookies Houses Internet Explorer cookies so that pages on the Internet can remember specific user settings.

Favorites Houses Internet Explorer Favorites—the list of saved web page links.

Desktop Contains only files that users store directly on the Desktop. Special icons such as My Network Places, My Computer, and the Recycle Bin are not part of the Desktop profile.

Local Settings Contains application data specific to the user's machine, such as Internet Explorer History, temporary file storage, and other application data. This folder does not roam when Roaming Profiles are set up (see the "Roaming Profiles" section later in this chapter). Like the Application Data folder, this folder is to be used at an application vendor's discretion.

My Documents Now, users of all sophistication levels can leverage this centralized repository for their data files. The My Documents folder has the advantage that it's easily understood by end users, instead of them having to wonder about which file goes in which drive letter path. In fact, the default Office 2000, Office XP, and Office 2003 "Save as" path is to My Documents. This will come in handy, as you'll see in the next chapter. My Documents contains My Pictures, and Windows XP Profiles also contains My Music.

NetHood Contains shortcuts to network drives. Even though the NT 4 Network Neighborhood was renamed to My Network Places, the NetHood folder is still around and performs the same functions.

PrintHood Contains shortcuts to network printers; similar to NetHood.

Recent   Contains a list of the most recently used application files and user data files like .TXT and .DOC files.

SendTo   Contains icons that applications can use to tie into Explorer to allow file routing between applications, such as Outlook, and folders.

Start Menu   Contains the shortcuts and information that users see when they choose Start ➢ All Programs. Each user's Start Menu folder is different. For example, if Joe installs DogFoodMaker 4 and Sally installs CatFoodMaker 8.1, neither will see the other's icons. To allow them to see each other's icons, the icons need to live in the All Users ➢ Start Menu folder (see the next section). Note that if the application does a per-user installation, shortcuts will be present in the user's profile. If the application does a per-machine installation, the shortcuts are in the All Users profile.

Templates   Contains the templates that some applications, such as Excel and Word, use to perform conversions. Like the Application Data folder, this folder is to be used at an application vendor's discretion.

The All Users profile (for Type 1 Computers), which is found at the variable location %ALLUSERSPROFILE%, typically maps to C:\Documents and Settings\All Users.

Applications often add icons to the %ALLUSERSPROFILE%\Start Menu to ensure that all users can run them.

Again, users end up seeing the combination of their own profile plus whatever is presented in the All Users profile.

Profile Folders for Type 2 Computers (Windows 7, Windows 2008, and Windows Server 2008 R2)

As I stated in the introduction to this chapter, the profiles for Windows XP and Windows Vista (and later) are basically incompatible. For our examples, we'll be poking around Windows 7, but a Windows Vista machine is a perfectly acceptable substitute if that's what's available to you.

There might be some similarities between the two (and actually, Windows 7 goes the "extra mile" to try to help bridge the differences between the two). The items we'll be looking at here have moved from their original place in Windows XP to a new place in Windows 7—the Users folder, which is typically found hanging off of C:\. The \Users folder in Windows 7 is the equivalent of the Documents and Settings directory in Windows XP.

Additionally, again, all this information is valid for Windows Server 2008 and Windows Server 2008 R2 machines too. The same structure from Windows Vista is carried forward to Windows Server 2008, Windows 7, and Windows Server 2008 R2. However, we'll be concentrating on Windows 7 because it's what your users will mostly be logging onto.

Understanding the Contents of a User's Profile (for Type 2 Computers)

Inside the Windows Vista and later profile there are a lot of new folders and some that simply look familiar. Let's take a quick look at what's inside the Windows 7 profile.

Contacts   This is new for Windows Vista and later. This folder stores what are known as "Windows Contacts."

Desktop   Similar in function to Windows XP's Desktop (see earlier).

Documents   Was My Documents in Windows XP. Same basic function. Stores basic documents such as word documents and such.

Downloads   This is new for Windows Vista and, yes, it's there as well for Windows 7. It becomes a storage spot for users' downloads.

Favorites   Similar in function to Windows XP's Favorites (see earlier).

Links   This is where Explorer's Favorite Links are stored. You'll see these down the left pane of Explorer.

Music   Was My Music in Windows XP.

Videos   Was My Videos in Windows XP (though not officially part of the Windows XP profile).

Pictures   Was My Pictures in Windows XP.

Saved Games   This is a new folder to save users' saved games into. I'm sure network administrators everywhere are just *thrilled* about this.

Searches   This is new for Windows Vista and Windows 7, and it will save stored searches for Explorer.

AppData   Was Application Data in Windows XP. Since Windows Vista, AppData is bifurcated into two parts: Local (to the computer only) and Roaming (for the specific user). We'll be talking more about Roaming Profiles in a bit, but this part is important to understand for when we do tackle them.

The AppData\Roaming folder performs the same function as the Documents and Settings\ <username>\Application Data folder in Windows XP.

The AppData\Local folder is now meant to hold machine-specific application data that isn't supposed to roam with the user. This folder is to be the equivalent for Local Settings\Application Data in Windows XP.

The AppData\LocalLow folder is a special directory with "low integrity" rights. So files that get stored here will have a lower integrity level than in other areas of the operating system. See the sidebar "The LocalLow Folder within AppData" for more information.

The *LocalLow* Folder within *AppData*

Within a user's AppData folder, there are two obvious entries: Local and Roaming. These make sense and are used when that corresponding condition is true. However, also note the presence of a LocalLow folder.

Windows Vista and later has various ways applications can run. One way is Protected Mode, which guarantees a program will run with low rights. When running in this way, the application only has access to this portion of the User Profile. Internet Explorer in Windows Vista and later is one such application. Internet Explorer in Windows Vista and later runs in Protected Mode, so this prevents malware and other various nasties from infecting your computer, or possibly compromising user specific information.

Protected Mode uses the LocalLow profile folder.

Also note there are low-integrity folders for Cookies, History, and Favorites.

For more on integrity levels, check out Mark Minasi's book *Administering Vista Security: The Big Surprises* from Sybex (2006).

In the next section, I talk about how several Windows XP holdovers are mapped to directories within AppData.

Adjusting for Windows XP Holdovers

Even though we're exploring the Windows Vista and later profile, something interesting should be noted: Windows Vista and later profiles are set up to automatically handle older applications that are still looking for Windows XP locations. For instance, if an application wanted to expressly save something in My Documents, it would have a problem. My Documents doesn't exist anymore, right? Now, it's just Documents for Windows Vista and later. To that end, the Windows Vista and later profile has what are called Junction Points, so when an application visits My Documents it's really going to Windows Vista's Documents.

To see these pointers, we need to see the hidden files inside a Windows Vista and later profile. You can perform this by going to the user's profile and typing **dir /ah /og** (to show hidden files and to sort by directories first). You can see this in Figure 9.3.

Note that upon further inspection, the following folders appear at the top level of the profile, but really, they are placed into either AppData\Roaming or AppData\Local:

FIGURE 9.3   A view inside a Type 2 profile (dir /ah /og)

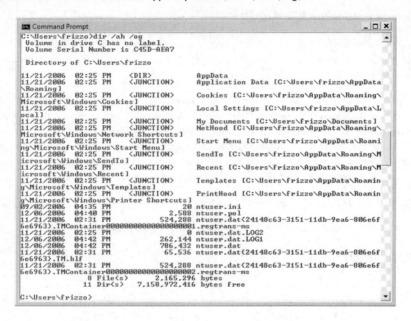

TABLE 9.1   Windows XP and later Redirected Folder names and directories

Windows XP Holdover	Linked to Windows Vista+ Folder	Directory path relative to c:\Users\{username}
My Documents	Documents	\Documents
Application Data	AppData	\AppData\Roaming
Cookies	AppData\Roaming	\AppData\Roaming\Microsoft\Windows\Cookies
Local Settings	AppData\Local	\AppData\Local
NetHood	AppData\Roaming	\AppData\Roaming\Microsoft\Windows\Network Shortcuts
Start Menu	AppData\Roaming	\AppData\Roaming\Microsoft\Windows\Start Menu
Recent	AppData\Roaming	\AppData\Roaming\Microsoft\Windows\Recent

TABLE 9.1   Windows XP and later Redirected Folder names and directories *(continued)*

Windows XP Holdover	Linked to Windows Vista+ Folder	Directory path relative to c:\Users\{username}
Templates	AppData\Roaming	\Appdata\Roaming\Microsoft\ Windows\Templates
Printhood	AppData\Roaming	\AppData\Roaming\Microsoft\ Windows\Printer Shortcuts
SendTo	AppData\Roaming	\AppData\Roaming\Microsoft\ Windows\SendTo

Curious about what those regtran-ms files are? I was! According to my sources at Microsoft, these are the Kernel Transaction Manager (KTM)-generated files. The Vista and later Registry uses KTM to avoid corruptions, so you should never see Registry corruption (with regard to profiles) anymore. Let's hope anyway.

Virtualized Files and Registry for Programs

Some applications try to do bad, bad things. And Windows XP will (usually) let them. For instance, an application could try to write program data to:

C:\program files\dogfoodmaker5\settings.ini

This DogFoodMaker application has no business writing settings there. In reality, settings should be in the user's profile, specifically in the Application Data (AppData) section (either user or machine based).

To that end, Windows Vista and later will redirect writes like this to a location where the application should be writing. Microsoft calls this redirection *virtualization—file virtualization* and *Registry virtualization*. Here's an example:

C:\users\<*username*>\AppData\Local\VirtualStore\Program Files\dogfoodmaker5

And, because multiple users could be using the same machine, a separate copy of the virtualized file is created for each user who runs the application.

Indeed, if you wanted to see these redirected files right away, Windows Explorer has its own button to see them. If there is a virtualized version of a file related to the current directory, a Compatibility Files button appears that will take you to the virtual location to view that file. In this example, you can see that someone tried to put junk in the \Windows directory.

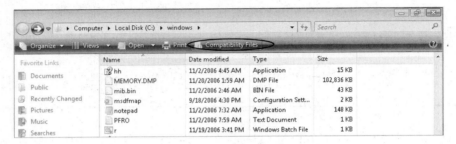

Writes to incorrect places to the Registry work the same way. Bad writes get redirected to:

HKEY_CLASSES_ROOT\VirtualStore\MACHINE or USER\SOFTWARE

This automatically takes effect if the application isn't UAC compliant. So, file virtualization doesn't affect applications that are run with full administrative rights (when, say, someone elevates it to run as an admin).

This technology is, of course, a Band-Aid. It permits pre–Windows Vista applications to run in a predictable way. But it should be considered a short-term fix rather than a long-term solution. The goal is to ensure that your application developers modify their applications so that they meet the guidelines of the Windows Vista Logo program instead of depending on file and Registry virtualization.

Note that file and Registry virtualization is disabled under some circumstances:

- File and Registry virtualization is simply not supported for Windows Vista 64-bit applications. These applications are expected to be UAC compliant and to write data to the correct locations.

- Virtualization is disabled for applications that include an application manifest with a desired execution level attribute. If you're a developer, you can learn more about application manifests here: http://tinyurl.com/ftvn5.

Additionally, note you can turn off virtual file and Registry abilities. That security policy is located in Computer Configuration ➢ Policies ➢ Windows Settings ➢ Security Settings ➢ Local Policies ➢ Security Options ➢ **User Account Control: Virtualize file and registry write failures to per-user locations**. You need to click "Define this policy setting," then select Disabled to turn it off.

One side note: Windows 7 adds the C: drive as another area for File virtualization whereas Windows Vista didn't do that. Nice update.

The Public Profile (for Type 2 Computers)

The Public profile in Windows Vista and Windows 2008 replaces the All Users concept in Windows XP and previous machines. However, it provides the same basic function: the end user's experience becomes their own profile *plus* the contents of the Public profile. Again, categories like the Desktop and Start Menu become good candidates here, because the icons you place here affect everyone.

The Default Local User Profile

The Default Local User Profile folder contains many of the same folders as any user's own Local Profile. Indeed, the Default User Profile is the template that generates all new local User Profiles when a new user logs on.

When a new user logs on, a copy of the Default Local User Profile is copied for that user to C:\users\%*username*%. As will often happen, the user changes and personalizes settings through the normal course of business. Then, once the user logs off, the settings are preserved in a personal local folder in the C:\Users\%*username*% folder.

 This Default Local User Profile is different from the Default Domain User Profile described later.

As an administrator, you can create your own ready-made standard shortcuts or stuff the folders with your own files. You can also introduce your own NTUSER.DAT Registry settings, such as a standard Desktop for all users who log onto a specific machine. In the following example, you can set up a background picture in the Default Local User Profile. Then, whenever a new user logs on locally to this machine, the background picture is displayed.

For Type 1 computers (Windows XP, Windows 2003, Windows 2000), the Default User Profile is stored in C:\Documents and Settings\Default User.

For Type 2 computers (Windows Vista, Windows 7, etc.) the Default User Profile is stored in C:\users\Default.

To set up your own Registry settings in NTUSER.DAT, follow these steps:

1. Choose Start ➢ Run to open the Run dialog box. In the Open box, type **regedit.exe** and press Enter to open the Registry Editor.

2. Select HKEY_USERS, as shown in Figure 9.4.

3. Choose File ➢ Load Hive.

4. For Type 1 computers, browse to the c:\Documents and Settings\Default User folder, shown in Figure 9.4. For Type 2 computers, browse to c:\Users\Default. You might have to specifically type in the path, as the file requester may hide it from you if you are not displaying hidden files and folders.

FIGURE 9.4   Load the NTUSER.DAT file into the Registry.

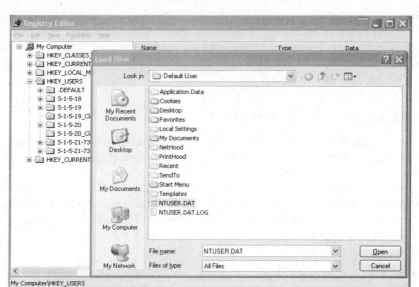

5. Select NTUSER.DAT.

6. When prompted to enter a key name, anything will work, but for our example let's use **this is a dummy key name**, and click OK. Figure 9.5 shows an example. The key name is only temporary, so its name doesn't particularly matter.

FIGURE 9.5   It doesn't matter what the temporary dummy key is called.

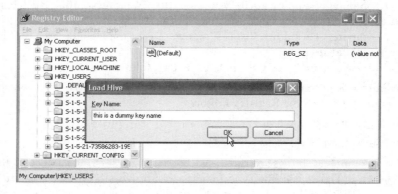

7. Traverse to any Registry key and value. In this case, we'll change all future wallpaper to Coffee Bean.bmp. To do that, traverse to Dummy Key Name ➤ Control Panel ➤ Desktop and double-click Wallpaper. If you're using Windows XP, enter the value in

this example, **c:\windows\coffee bean.jpg**, as shown in Figure 9.6. If you're using Windows Vista, enter **c:\windows\web\wallpaper\img35.tif**. Note there might already be a default image set, but you're now changing it.

FIGURE 9.6   Enter the full path where the desired wallpaper is stored.

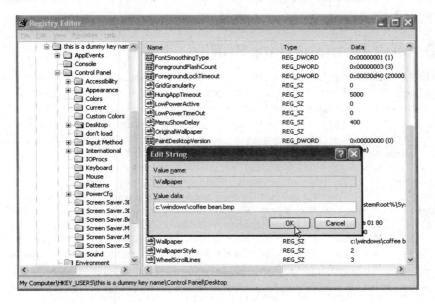

If the wallpaper file does not reside on the local system, you must alter the path to point to a server share. If the wallpaper is not present in the folder specified, no wallpaper will show up.

8. After you complete your changes, select your dummy key name, unload it by choosing` File ➢ Unload Hive, and click OK to save the changes. Again, you must highlight your dummy key name to unload the hive.

You can load the hive of any User Profile that is not currently logged on using the previously described method. This can be very useful in some situations, such as if you want to make a Registry hack as an admin on behalf of the user. Just remember to unload the hive or else you are blocking the profile.

Actually, you can also load hives from within a script (with REG.EXE). Jakob H. Heidelberg has a pretty cool article on this called "Efficient Registry Cleanup," which you can check out here: http://tinyurl.com/24dm5v.

Every time a new user generates a Local Profile, it pulls the settings from the Default Local Profile, which now has the coffee bean background picture. (Current users do not see the change because they already generated Local Profiles before the coffee bean picture was set in the default Local Profile.)

Test your changes by creating a new local user and logging on. Since this user has never logged on before, this should create a new User Profile from the default profile. See if the new user gets the coffee bean background for Windows XP and the water drop background for Windows Vista.

The Default Domain User Profile

The Default Domain User Profile is similar to the Default Local User Profile, except that it's centralized. Once a Default Domain User Profile is set up, new users logging onto workstations in the domain will automatically download the centralized Default Domain User Profile instead of using any individual Default Local User Profile. This can be a way to make default centralized settings, such as the background or Desktop shortcuts, available for anyone whenever they first log onto a machine.

WARNING   Don't create a Default Domain User Profile using Windows 2000, Windows XP, or Windows 2003 and expect your Windows NT clients to understand it. Remember: Windows NT is Type 0; Windows 2000, Windows XP, and Windows Server 2003 are Type 1; and Windows Vista and Windows Server 2008 are Type 2. Exchanging material between the types can be unpredictable.

For these examples, you'll need to create a new, mere-mortal user in the domain. In this example, we'll assume you created a user named Brett Wier.

Default Domain User Profiles for Type 1 Computers

It's easy to create a Default Domain User Profile for Type 1 computers. From any Type 1 computer, log on as Brett Wier and follow these steps:

1. Create a new, mere-mortal user in the domain. In this example, we'll create Brett Wier. From any workstation in your domain, log on as Brett.

2. Modify the Desktop as you wish. In this example, we'll use the Appearance tab in the Display Properties dialog box to change the color scheme to olive green. All you need to do is right-click the Desktop and select Properties. Then, select the Appearance tab. When you're done and back at the Desktop, create a text file, FILE1.txt.

3. Log off as Brett Wier.

4. Log back onto the workstation as the domain Administrator.

5. Click Start, and then right-click My Computer and choose Properties from the context menu to open the System Properties dialog box.

6. Click the Advanced tab, and then click the Settings button in the User Profiles section to open the User Profiles dialog box.

7. Select bwier, as shown in Figure 9.7.

FIGURE 9.7   Select Brett's entry in the User Profiles dialog box.

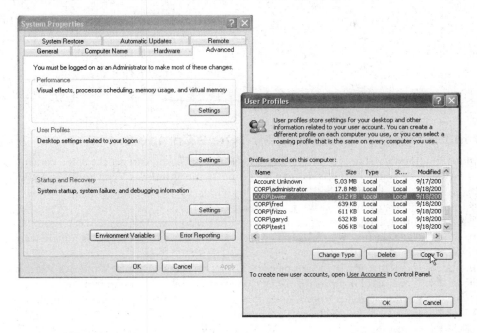

8. Click the Copy To button to open the Copy To dialog box, and in the "Copy profile to" field, enter the full path, plus the words **default user**, of the NETLOGON share of a Windows 2000 or Windows 2003 Domain Controller, as shown in Figure 2.8. In this example, it's \\dc01\netlogon\Default User. The Default User folder is automatically created.

9. Click the Change button in the Permitted to Use section, and change the default from the original user to Everyone, as shown in Figure 9.8. This lets everyone use the profile in the domain.

10. Click OK to copy the profile to the new folder and to close the Copy To dialog box.

11. Click OK to close the System Properties dialog box.

You can test your Default Domain Profile by creating a new user in the domain and logging onto any Windows XP or Windows 2000 machine. Verify that the Default Domain Profile is working by seeing if the olive green color scheme appears and that FILE1.TXT is present on the Desktop. Remember, you'll only see the magic for users who have no Local Profiles already on target machines.

FIGURE 9.8   Copy the profile you just created to the NETLOGON share of a Domain Controller. Then, click Change to allow Everyone to use the profile.

Default Domain User Profiles for Type 2 Computers

For modern computers like Windows Vista and Windows 7, you can get the same control. But here's the trick: remember how Windows XP (Type 1) and Windows Vista and Windows 7 (Type 2) profiles are incompatible?

Well, that's about to matter a whole lot, right here.

And before I proceed, I have to preface this with the following caveat: you're going to need a Windows Vista machine to complete this part of the exercise. This is a little weird, so stay with me.

First up: we need to know a certain piece of Windows magic. That is, Windows Vista and Windows 7 will only read profile directories from the network if they end in a special moniker: .v2. That's right—the directory names must have a .v2 hanging off them for Windows Vista and later to read it. So, the steps we'll perform next will be almost like what we did for Windows XP earlier, except this time, we'll provide our name with the special .v2 designation hanging off of it. Then, when users log onto Windows Vista or later machines for the first time, Windows will recognize the special directory (Default User) with the extra-special .v2 moniker and download the profile just for that operating system.

Next up: like we just learned in the XP exercise, if we want to utilize an existing local profile and utilize it in the domain, we simply use the Copy To button, right? Well, someone at Microsoft didn't get the memo with regard to Windows 7. That is, the Copy To button is present and working in Windows Vista, but totally grayed out for all local, normal users in Windows 7. What's more, the Default Profile still can be copied for some reason. Totally bizarre!

There's a very lengthy, visceral thread if you want to read about it here: `http://tinyurl.com/mzwnos`.

At the same URL (`http://tinyurl.com/mzwnos`), about halfway down into the thread, someone describes a "Windows 7 way" of performing the same task. Look for the words "I got this to work." I haven't tested it myself, but maybe it will work for you if you only have Windows 7 and no Windows Vista machine available.

But for the sake of our examples, let's assume you have a Windows Vista machine you can play with. Remember: Windows Vista and Windows 7 share the same profile structure. So there's no "penalty" for performing this on a Windows Vista machine, then using nothing but Windows 7 machines after you perform these steps (one time).

So, from a Windows Vista machine (not a Windows 7 machine) log on as Brett Wier and follow these steps:

1. Be sure you're logged onto a Windows Vista machine as Brett.

2. Modify the Desktop as you wish. In this example, go ahead and simply plop a new text file, `file1.txt`, on the Desktop, and put some fake data in it.

3. Log off as Brett Wier.

4. Log back onto the workstation as the Domain Administrator.

5. Click Start, and then right-click Computer and choose Properties from the context menu to open the System Properties dialog box.

6. Click the Advanced System Settings task, and then click the Settings button in the User Profiles section to open the User Profiles dialog box.

7. Select bwier, as shown previously in Figure 9.7. Note this figure shows Windows XP, but it should look similar in Windows Vista.

8. Click the Copy To button to open the Copy To dialog box, and in the "Copy profile to" field, enter the full path plus the default user of the NETLOGON share of a Windows 2000, Windows Server 2003, or Windows Server 2008 Domain Controller, as shown previously in Figure 9.8. In this example, it's `\\dc01\netlogon\Default User.v2`. Note that no quotes are needed (as is often the case with items that have spaces in them). You can see an example in Figure 9.9. The `Default User.V2` folder is automatically created.

9. Click the Change button in the Permitted to Use section, and change the default from the original user to Everyone, as shown previously in Figure 9.8. This lets everyone use the profile in the domain.

10. Click OK to copy the profile to the new folder and to close the Copy To dialog box.

11. Click OK to close the System Properties dialog box.

You can test your Default Domain Profile by creating a new user in the domain and logging onto any Windows Vista or Windows 7 machine. Verify that the ".v2" Default Domain Profile is working by seeing if the `FILE1.TXT` is present on the Desktop.

Remember, you'll only see the magic for users who have no Local Profiles already on target Windows Vista or Windows 7 machines. Also remember that Windows XP users will have their own Default User profiles, so this can get a little confusing.

Now that you're familiar with the files and folders that make up Local Profiles, you're ready to implement Roaming Profiles.

FIGURE 9.9   Be sure to put the .v2 extension in, because this is a Windows Vista/Windows 7 (Type 2) profile.

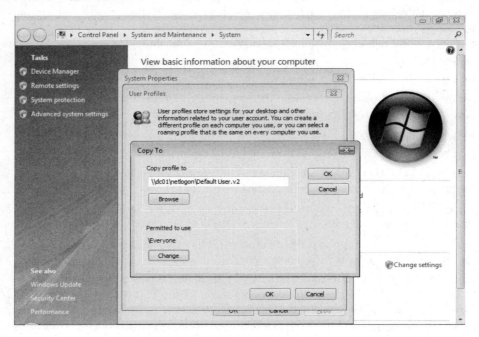

Roaming Profiles

Roaming Profiles are a logical extension to the Local Profiles concept. When users hop from machine to machine, the customized settings they created on one machine are automatically placed on and displayed at any machine they log onto.

For instance, you might have an organization in which 30 computers are at each site for general use by the sales team. If any member of the sales team comes into any office, they know they can log onto any machine and be confident that the settings from their last session are patiently waiting on the server.

Setting up Roaming Profiles for users in Active Directory is a straightforward process: share a folder to house the profiles, and then point each user's profile toward the single shared folder. By default, Roaming Profiles save a copy of the profile to the local hard drive. That way, if the network or server becomes unavailable, the user can use the last-used profile as a cached version. Additionally, if the user's Roaming Profile on the server is unavailable (and there is no locally cached copy of the Roaming Profile), the system downloads and uses a temporary Default User Profile as an emergency measure to get the user logged on with some profile.

As you'll see in the next chapter, another advantage associated with Roaming Profiles is that if a machine crashes, the most recent "set" of the user environment is on the server for quick restoration.

For those of you who threw up your hands and gave up using Roaming Profiles in Windows NT, I encourage you to try again with the newer operating systems.

For Windows 2000 and later, the Roaming Profile algorithm has been much improved since the NT 4 days. Specifically, there are three reasons why the improved algorithm is better than the old NT 4 counterpart. I know it's kind of odd in 2010 to have a book that still refers to NT 4.0. But "perception" is a weird thing. People's memories of the "bad old days" can remain and linger on, for a lot longer than we might think. Anyway, here are the main differences between then and now:

Roaming Profiles now account for multiple logins   Most people had problems when a single user logged onto multiple machines at the same time. In NT 4, the profile was preserved only from the last computer the user logged off from—potentially losing important files in the profile. Modern Windows systems don't work that way. They do a file-by-file comparison of files *before* they get sent back to the server—sending only the latest time-stamped file to help quell this problem. So, give it another go if you despaired in the past.

However, one warning should be noted. All the user's Registry settings are represented as a single file: NTUSER.DAT. Because the last writer wins, the NTUSER.DAT with the latest time stamp overwrites all others. If you make two independent changes to a setting on two different machines, you can lose one because only the NTUSER.DAT with the latest time stamp "wins."

Roaming Profiles now only pull down and push up changed files   NT 4 Roaming Profiles were on the slow side—especially over slow links. The good news about profiles from modern systems is that only new and changed files are specifically moved around the network. So, if someone logs onto the same machine over and over again, the user is not waiting for the whole gamut of profile files to be downloaded. Logging in is now faster than ever.

Better Terminal Services support for Roaming Profiles   In Windows 2000, when the user logs off a session, the system tries 60 times—about once a second by default—to tidy up the NTUSER.DAT file and send it back to the server to be housed in the Roaming Profile. Usually, it only needs one try (and about one second) to do this task. This support has been increased since Windows 2000, so see the sidebar "A Brief History of the Unloading of NTUSER.DAT and UPHClean."

A Brief History of the Unloading of *NTUSER.DAT* and UPHClean

In Windows 2000, when a profile was ready to be unloaded, it simply waited for a bit of time. If the handle was still not closed, Windows 2000 just gave up—nothing roamed and the hive was still (uh-oh) loaded. This caused profile corruption like crazy. To that end, a policy setting named "Maximum Retries to Unload and Update User Profile" can tell Windows 2000 to increase the number of tries. Bad news: there's a bug in the policy setting description that makes it seem like this policy is meant to affect Windows Server 2003 and Windows XP machines. But it doesn't. It's just for Windows 2000 machines.

In Windows XP and Windows Server 2003, the same unloading process occurs but with a little work-around. The current Registry is saved into another file, and then at logoff, roams that file to the server's NTUSER.DAT. But the problem is that the real NTUSER.DAT file on the local machine is still loaded. If, after a while the handle is closed, then the hive will be unloaded. But if the handle is *not* closed, and if the user logs on again, the hive will continue to be used.

Uh-oh. Sounds like corruption city again, right?

In this case, Roaming Profiles will not be able to update this version of NTUSER.DAT even though the server's NTUSER.DAT might be newer. So, what's the solution?

Microsoft made a download available called "User Profile Hive Cleanup Service" (or UPH-Clean), to force the handle to be closed in just this situation. It solves this exact problem and is why it's suggested for Windows Server 2003 Terminal Services. You can locate the tool at http://tinyurl.com/5of5r.

In Windows Vista and later (like Windows 7 and Windows Server 2008), this "force unload" logic is already inside the profile service itself, so this simply won't be a problem anymore. Microsoft swears that it's a guarantee that the user hive will be unloaded and therefore roam it at logoff. It is doing the same thing as Windows XP and Windows Server 2003 UPHClean, but in a much better way.

Setting Up Roaming Profiles

The first thing we need to do on our server, DC01, is to create and share a folder in which to store our profiles. In this example, we'll choose a novel name: Profiles. Normally, you'd do this procedure on a file server somewhere, not on a Domain Controller. But we'll continue on, because there's no harm here in our test lab. Again, I'll assume our server has two drives, C: and D:, and we'll perform these functions on our D: drive.

To create and share a folder in which to store Roaming Profiles, follow these steps:

1. Log onto DC01 as Administrator.

2. From the Desktop, click My Computer to open the My Computer folder.

3. Find a place to create a users folder. In this example, we'll use D:\PROFILES. After entering the D: drive, right-click and select New ➤ Folder. Name your new folder **Profiles**.

You can substitute any name for Profiles. Additionally, you can hide the share name by placing a $ after the name, such as Profiles$.

4. Right-click the newly created `Profiles` folder, and choose "Share," which opens the folder's Properties dialog box to the Sharing tab. Pull down the drop-down menu and select Everyone, and then click Add. Note that Windows Server 2003 and 2008 will default so that the share is `Everyone:Read`. Click "Share" and ensure that the share is set so that Everyone has Co-owner permissions, as seen in Figure 9.10 (left) for Windows Server 2003 and (right) for Windows Server 2008. In Windows Server 2008 R2, the permissions are called Read/Write (not shown.) Keep the rest of the defaults, and click OK. (Note that Co-owner rights are almost the same as the "Full Control" rights of yore.) Note that on Windows Server 2008 R2, the steps are slightly different. You right-click and select Share with ➢ Specific people. Then you specify the person. Finally, you're only given the choice of Read or Read/Write access.

FIGURE 9.10   Share the Profiles folder so that Authenticated Users (or Everyone) has Co-owner permissions (in Server 2003). For Server 2003, utilize at least Change control.

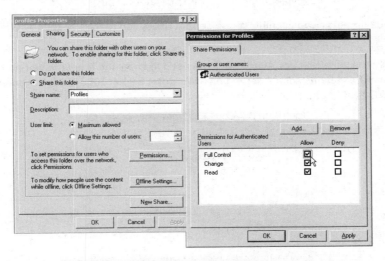

Now you need to specify which network user accounts can use Roaming Profiles. In this example, you'll specify Brett Wier. Brett will now be able to hop from workstation to workstation. When he logs off one workstation, the changes in the profile will be preserved on the server. He can then log onto any other workstation in the domain and maintain the same user experience.

Caching and Roaming Profiles

Roaming Profiles are automatically cached with their own independent algorithm. In the second figure in this sidebar, you can see the Caching button, which controls caching on a share. We'll learn about offline files and caching in the next chapter. But for now, we need to have a little side discussion about the Caching button.

Windows 2000 servers have caching turned off by default for all shares.

Windows 2003 servers have caching set up so that users can manually specify what files to keep offline.

A Windows XP machine tells you everything you need to know the first time you go to the event log when the default caching setting on a Windows Server 2003 is used in conjunction with a Roaming Profile share.

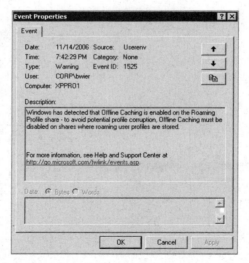

Windows XP explains that "Offline Caching must be disabled on shares where roaming user profiles are stored." To do that, click the Caching button within the Profiles share and select "Files or programs from the share will not be available offline," as seen here for Windows Server 2008.

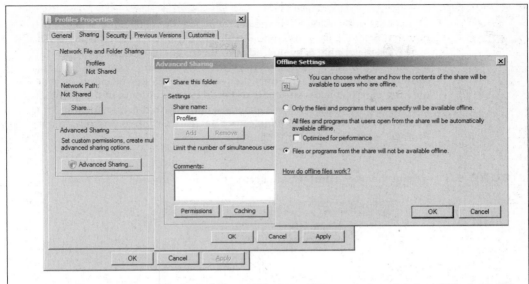

When you do, you'll see Windows XP and Windows Vista stop complaining. (Windows XP and Windows Vista complain with the same Event ID.)

For more information on this phenomenon, see the Knowledge Base article Q287566, "Offline File Caching Option Must Be Disabled on Roaming Profile." (For more on the Caching button, see the next chapter.) Additionally, do not use the Encrypting File System (EFS) on shares containing Roaming Profiles. If you do so, roaming will not work.

To modify accounts to use Roaming Profiles, you'll leverage Active Directory Users and Computers as follows:

1. Choose Start ➢ All Programs ➢ Administrative Tools ➢ Active Directory Users and Computers.

2. Expand Corp.com in the tree pane, and double-click Brett Wier's account to open the Brett Wier Properties dialog box; click his Profile tab.

3. In the Profile Path field, specify the server, the share name, and folder you want to use, such as \\Dc01\profiles\%username%. After you enter that, click OK. Then, just as a quick test, go back into the user account and look again at the Profile tab. When you do, you should see the username automatically filled in, as seen in Figure 9.11. For our purposes, you can leave all other fields blank.

4. Click OK.

The syntax of *%username%* is the secret sauce that allows the system to automatically create a Roaming Profiles folder underneath the share. The *%username%* variable is evaluated at first use, and Windows springs into action and creates the profile. Windows is smart too—it sets up the permissions on the folder with only the required NTFS permissions, so that only the user has access to read and modify the contents of the profile. If you want administrators to have access along with the user, see the information in the "Add the Administrators Security Group to Roaming User Profiles" section later in this chapter.

FIGURE 9.11 Point the user's profile path settings at the server and share name.

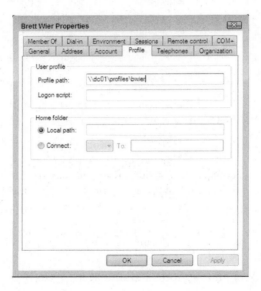

Modifying Multiple Users' Profile Paths

After you set up Roaming Profiles and get comfortable with their use, you'll likely want the rest of your users to start using Roaming Profiles as well. The Windows Server 2003/2008 Active Directory Users and Computers tool allows you to modify the profile paths of multiple users simultaneously. To do so, follow these steps:

1.   Select the users (hold down Ctrl to select discontiguous users).

2. Right-click the selection, and choose Properties from the context menu to open the "Properties for Multiple Items" (previously called "Properties On Multiple Objects") dialog box:

3. Click the Profile tab, if necessary.

4. Click the Profile path check box, and enter the path.

5. Click OK to give all the selected users the same path, making sure you use the *%username%* convention in the path you specify.

If you'd like to put on your coding hat, you can use the following sample VBScript code to run through all the users in the domain Corp.com in the Phoenix OU and change their profile path so that they have access only to their own profile folder. Upon first use by the user, the folder is automatically created, and the user is granted exclusive access to that folder.

```
Set UserContainer = getobject("LDAP://ou=Phoenix,dc=Corp,dc=com")
UserContainer.filter = array("User")

for each User in UserContainer
     Username = User.SamAccountName
     Userprofilepath = "\\Profile_server\Profiles\" & Username

     Wscript.Echo User.ProfilePath

     If User.ProfilePath = ""  Then
```

```
            User.Put "ProfilePath" , UserProfilePath
            User.Setinfo
         Wscript.Echo "Profile for user "
             & Username & " has been set to "
             & UserProfilePath & "."
     Else
         Wscript.Echo "Profile for user "
             & Username & " was already set to "
             & UserProfilePath & "."
     End if


next
```

Testing Roaming Profiles

You can easily test Roaming Profiles if you have multiple workstation machines. I suggest you log on as Brett from both a Windows XP machine (Type 1) and a Windows 7 machine (Type 2). Make sure these workstations are members in your domain.

Roaming from Windows XP to Windows XP

Log on first to the Windows XP machine. Then, make two simple changes to the profile for testing:

1. In the My Documents folder, create XPFILE1.TXT and save some dummy data inside.
2. Change the color scheme to something different—like silver.
3. Log off as Brett Wier.
4. Log onto another XP workstation as Brett Wier and make sure that XPFILE1.TXT was properly sent to the second machine and that the background has changed.

Right-click the XPFILE1.TXT and choose Properties from the context menu to see the file's properties. Take note of the path where the file is actually residing. You can compare that file's location now (the local hard drive) with the file's location after the next chapter is completed. Hopefully, by the time the next chapter is completed, the file will be magically transported to the server, and the display will demonstrate this.

Roaming from Windows 7 to Windows 7

Now, log on as Brett to a Windows 7 machine.

Then, make two simple changes to the profile for testing:

1. In the My Documents folder, create WIN7FILE1.TXT and save some dummy data inside.

2. Change the color scheme to something different—like "Windows Classic."

3. Log off as Brett Wier.

4. Log onto another Windows 7 workstation as Brett Wier and make sure that WIN7FILE1.TXT was properly sent to the second machine and that the background has changed.

Right-click the WIN7FILE1.TXT file and choose Properties from the context menu to see the file's properties. Take note of the path where the file is actually residing. You can compare that file's location now (the local hard drive) with the file's location after the next chapter is completed. Hopefully, by the time you perform all the exercises in the next chapter, the file will be magically transported to the server and the display will demonstrate this.

Additionally, notice how XPFILE1.TXT, the file created on the Windows XP machine, is not present. Again, this is because Windows 7 (Type 2 profiles) and Windows XP (Type 1 profiles) don't intermingle.

Back on the Server

If you check out what's transpired on the server, two unique directories are created for Brett, one for each type of computer he logs onto (Type 1 and Type 2), as seen in Figure 9.12.

FIGURE 9.12 On the server, a folder for each computer type has been generated.

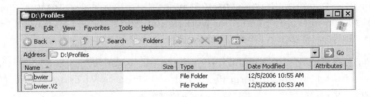

Additionally, note that even if you're an administrator, you cannot dive into Brett's profile folders. An example of this failure can be seen in Figure 9.13. This is a safety mechanism that gives Brett exclusive permissions over his personal sensitive stuff. If you want administrators to have access along with the user, see the information in the "Add the Administrators Security Group to Roaming User Profiles" later in this chapter.

Upshot of Roaming Profiles in a Mixed Windows 7 and Windows XP World

It's bad news for mixed environments. Logging onto Windows XP and then to Windows Vista or later (or vice versa) does not "share" information in any way.

As we saw, XPFILE1.txt was created (and available) only in the Windows XP profile. And WIN7FILE1.TXT was created (and available) only in the Windows 7 profile. So, Windows XP and Windows 7 profile data can never be shared.

What a bummer (on the surface at least). But don't worry; we'll overcome it.

FIGURE 9.13   Administrators cannot poke around User Profiles (by default).

To that end, if we want a "one stop shop" place for our documents, Start Menu icons, and more, we'll have to leverage the Folder Redirection mechanism in the next chapter. Not to get too far ahead of ourselves, but Folder Redirection's goal is to make various items (like the Documents of Windows 7 and the My Documents of Windows XP) point to the *same place* on a network share. That way, regardless of the kind of machine you log in with (Windows XP or Windows 7), your data will *always* be available.

So, stay tuned for that in the next chapter.

The Impact of Users Latching onto *Documents/My Documents*

Because Documents (for Windows Vista and Windows 7) and My Documents (pre-Vista) is part of the profile, there is the extra burden of lugging all the files in My Documents back and forth across the network each time a user logs on. This can have serious ramifications. Once users start using the My Documents folder, they generally don't want to stop. They place 50MB worth of PowerPoint files, 50MB of Word documents, and 50MB of Visio files in My Documents and then roam to another workstation, and they've just moved 150MB of data across the network at logon time! Ouch!

In any case, this pain can fortunately be mitigated in two ways. Windows 2000 and newer clients handle Roaming Profiles differently than their Windows NT cousin does. (Again, I think it helps to understand history as well as modernity.)

Let's imagine that we have two users: one on Windows NT and another on, say, Windows 7. Each user puts 300MB of files into the Roaming Profile. When a user on Windows NT does this, all files in the profile are copied up to the server—lock, stock, and barrel—up to the server and then back over to the target workstation every time a user logs on or off. Can you say "painful"?

Windows 2000 and later clients (like Windows 7) transfer *only* changed files up and back between the client and server. Thus, if a user transfers 60MB of data and then changes one file, only that file is sent back to be saved in the Roaming Profile. This feature is great news if a user uses the same machine day in and day out; only the changes are pushed up and back. But the usefulness of this feature breaks down any time a user roams to a computer they have never used before. In this case, the entire contents of the Roaming Profile (including Documents/My Documents) are brought down from the server.

That's why the real power comes with a key feature, Redirected Folders, which we'll explore in the next chapter.

Migrating Local Profiles to Roaming Profiles

In some situations, you might already have lots of machines with Local Profiles. That is, you didn't start off your network using Roaming Profiles, and now you have either many machines with Local Profiles or just pockets of machines with a combination of Roaming Profiles and Local Profiles. You can, if you want, maintain the user's Local Profile settings and transfer them to the spot on the server you set up earlier. You can convert a Local Profile to a Roaming Profile in two ways. Whichever option you choose, you first need to set up a share on a server.

Automatic Upload of Existing Local Profiles

In general, this step couldn't be easier. As we did earlier, on each user's Profile tab, point the profile path to \\servername\share\%*username*%, as seen earlier in Figure 9.11. The next time the user logs onto a machine with a Local Profile (and then logs off), the Local Profile is automatically uploaded to the server to become their future Roaming Profile. For most users, this is the way to go.

And, remember, profiles are zapped up to their source on the server independently. If a user has used both Windows XP and Windows Vista and later machines in the past, and then travels back to these Desktops, each computer's profile is zapped up into their own directory. Those directories can be seen in Figure 9.12, shown earlier.

But what if the same filename exists, say, on the Desktop on three machines the user has logged onto in the past? The system will automatically figure out which is the last-written file based on the file date. And that file will end up being the only copy placed in the directory. In other words, you won't see three files with the same name in the profile directory—even if it exists on three local machines.

Manual Upload of Existing Local Profiles

If the user has logged onto multiple workstations and therefore has multiple Local Profiles, you might want to guarantee that one specific Local Profile becomes the Roaming Profile for that user. The procedure is nearly identical to the one you used to create the Default Domain User Profile.

However, the problem we isolated earlier remains the same: the blasted Copy To button is grayed out for normal profiles on Windows 7. So, if you want to do this for a Type 1 profile (Windows XP), no problem. For Type 2 profiles (Windows Vista or Windows 7) you must use a Windows Vista machine, because Windows 7's Copy To button is simply grayed out and unusable for normal profiles.

To preserve a specific Local Profile and convert it to a Roaming Profile, follow these steps:

1. Log on as the Administrator to the workstation where the desired Local Profile resides.

2. Choose Start, right-click My Computer (for Windows XP) or Computer (for Windows Vista), and choose Properties from the context menu to open the System Properties dialog box.

3. For Windows XP, click the Advanced tab, or for Windows Vista, click "Advanced system settings."

4. Then in the User Profiles section, click Settings to open the User Profiles dialog box.

5. Select the Local Profile you want to convert to a Roaming Profile, and then click the Copy To button to open the Copy To dialog box, as shown in Figure 9.14.

FIGURE 9.14   In Windows XP, to move a specific profile to the server, use the Copy To dialog box.

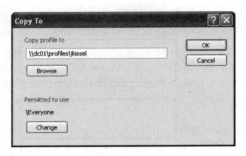

6. Enter the server name, shared folder name, and folder name of the profile storage path. In Figure 9.14, this is the path for a Type 1 computer (like Windows XP). If this were targeted for Windows Vista or Windows 7 machines, you would have to type **.v2** at the end, like \\dc01\profiles\jkissel.v2, as shown in Figure 9.15.

FIGURE 9.15   If you want to push up a Windows Vista profile, you need to add a ".v2" at the end, as seen here. These profiles will work just fine when users use Windows 7 to grab them.

7. Also, be sure to change the profile's permissions so that at least the user has access.

8. Click OK.

When you do, the user's folder is automatically created in the shared folder.

Changing the Profile Type from Roaming to Local

Mere-mortal users (those without administrative privileges) can go to the User Profiles dialog box (as seen earlier in Figure 9.7), choose their own profile, then change the profile type with the Change Type button. This will change their profile from Roaming to Local or back again and thus specify which copy of the profile (Local or Roaming) is to be used when they log on.

If a user selects Local Profile, a Roaming Profile reverts to a Local Profile. The Roaming Profile on the server stays there, but the user doesn't use it when working at this local machine. The next time the user works at this specific workstation, the changes are only saved to the Local Profile.

If the user selects Roaming Profile, and the Roaming Profile is on the server, the system determines which copy is newer. If the local copy is newer, the user is asked whether to keep or ditch the profile on the server.

Also, don't forget that for each specific user Local Profile you manually convert to a Roaming Profile, you'll need to modify the profile path (similar to that seen in Figure 9.11 earlier). Once you've done this, this user, Jimmy Kissel, can now log onto any Windows 2000 or Windows XP machine as jkissel, and this specific profile (that you just pushed up) will follow him as a Roaming Profile.

Roaming and Nonroaming Folders

Oftentimes, you'll want to get a handle on specifically what, inside the Roaming Profile, is roaming and what isn't roaming. Things are different for Windows Vista, Windows 7, and Windows Server 2008 (Type 2 computers) and Windows 2000, XP, and Windows Server 2003 (Type 1 computers). Let's check out those differences here.

Roaming and Nonroaming Folders for Type 1 Computers

Now that you have a grip on which folders constitute the profile and how to set up a Roaming Profile, it might be helpful to know a bit about what's going on behind the scenes. Remember that several folders make up our profile.

Type 1 Profile Directories That Do Not Roam

Local settings, including local machine-specific application folders and information, do not roam when Roaming Profiles are enabled. This is true for the local computer's Application Data. Some applications write information specific to the local computer here. The `Application Data` folder is located in `\Documents and Settings\`*`<Username>`*`\` `Local Settings`. Any subfolder below this folder also does not roam, including:

- `History`
- `Temp`
- `Temporary Internet Files`

Type 1 Profile Directories That Do Roam

All other folders do roam with the user.

There's an `Application Data` directory that does roam with the user. This `Application Data` folder is located in `Documents and Settings\`*`<Username>`*. This is typically a per-user store for application data, such as `Office 2000/XP/2003 Custom Dictionary`. These are the kinds of things you would want to roam with the user:

- `Cookies`
- `Desktop`
- `Favorites`
- `My Documents`
- `My Pictures`
- `NetHood`
- `PrintHood`
- `Recent`
- `Send To`
- `Start Menu`
- `Templates`

Indeed, `My Documents`, `My Pictures`, `Desktop`, `Start Menu`, and `Application Data` have an additional property; they can each be redirected to a specific point on the server, as you'll see in the next chapter.

Roaming and Nonroaming Folders for Type 2 Computers

If we crack open a Windows 7 Roaming Profile, we can see some things are similar and some things are different compared to a Type 1 profile.

Figure 9.16 shows what the profiles look like when viewed from a pre-Vista machine. Note how the "My" prefix magically appears when viewed here, even though under the hood there is no "My" prefix. You can see this in Figure 9.17 when viewed directly from a Windows 7 machine.

In order to see the contents in Figure 9.16, you need to be logged in as Brett Wier, or take ownership of the directory as the Administrator.

FIGURE 9.16   Some of the contents of a Type 2 computer are similar to a Type 1 computer. Note that when viewed on a pre-Vista machine, Type 2 profiles have the "My" prefix because they're viewed within a pre-Vista machine's Explorer.

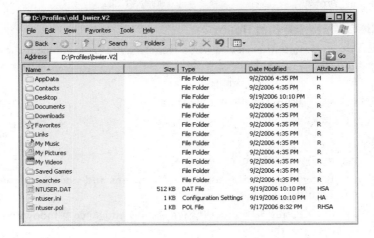

FIGURE 9.17   The same folder, when viewed directly from the command line. Note the absence of the "My" prefix for Music, Pictures, and Videos.

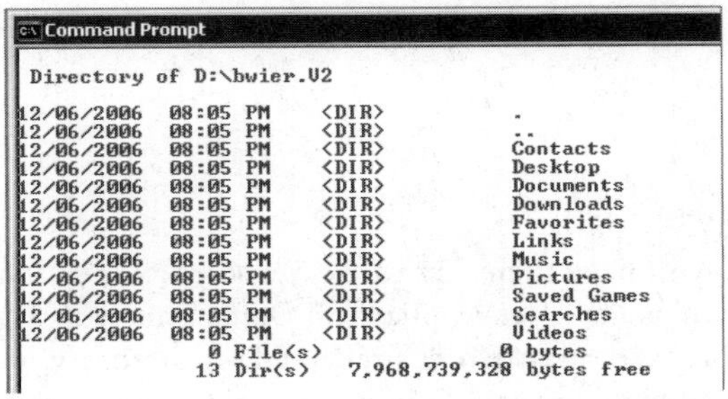

Let's get a grip on which directories roam and which don't roam.

Type 2 Profile Directories That Do Not Roam

Local settings, including local machine-specific application folders and information, do not roam, even when Roaming Profiles are enabled. The nonroaming directories will stay on each local computer in the \Users\<Username>\AppData\ directory. Inside \AppData are two directories that contain this nonroaming data: Local and LocalLow.

Any subfolders within Local or LocalLow do not roam, including:

- History

- Temp

- Temporary Internet Files

See the sidebar "The LocalLow Folder within AppData" for more information about LocalLow.

Type 2 Profile Directories that Roam

All other folders do roam with the user. When a Roaming Profile is enabled, these directories are shot up to the server and stored within a user's own private directory with their <username>.v2:

- Contacts (new for Windows Vista and later)
- Desktop
- Favorites
- Documents (was My Documents in Windows XP)
- Pictures (in Windows XP, this was under My Documents and since Windows Vista, it's at the root of the profile).
- Music (in Windows XP, this was under My Documents and since Windows Vista, it's now found at the root of the profile).
- Videos (new for Windows Vista and later machines)
- Under \Appdata\Roaming\Microsoft you will find:
  - Credentials
  - Crypto
  - Internet Explorer
  - Protect
  - SystemCertificates

Of course, your users will need their day-to-day goodies as they roam from machine to machine. This is known as Per-User Application Data. This stuff is stored within the Roaming Profile's \Appdata\Roaming\Microsoft\Windows directory. Here, you'll see lots of stuff you know and love, including the following Desktop attributes, as seen in Figure 9.18:

- Network Shortcuts
- Printer Shortcuts
- Recent
- SendTo
- Start Menu
- Templates
- Themes
- Cookies (hidden for some reason)

FIGURE 9.18   The AppData\Roaming directory in the Type 2 computer contains the only directories that will roam with the user.

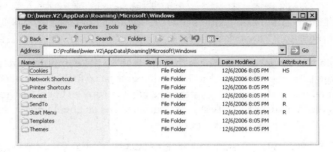

Managing Roaming Profiles

We've just been through how to set up and use Roaming Profiles. But don't leave home without these parting words about managing them day to day.

Merging Local Profile and Roaming Profile

Once a Roaming Profile is established, users can hop from machine to machine confident that they'll get the same settings. However, if a user with a Roaming Profile hops to a Windows XP machine on which they once had a Local Profile, something special happens: the previous Local Profile and the existing Roaming Profile are merged (except for the NTUSER.DAT settings). This data is then saved to the Roaming Profile folder on the server at logoff time.

This is helpful should a user have just the one copy of a critical document stored in the My Documents folder of XPPRO2. The next time he logs onto XPPRO2, that missing document will appear in his My Documents in his Roaming Profile. Oh, and you don't have to worry about overwriting existing files in the profile, either; the latest time-stamped file is preserved.

Ditto for a Windows Vista or later machine and its profile. Just remember that these profiles are considered separate (because they are).

You can prevent this behavior on Windows XP and Windows Vista (and later) machines. For information on how to do this, see the "Prevent Roaming Profile Changes from Propagating to the Server" section later in this chapter.

Guest Account Profile

Who uses the Guest account anymore? Apparently someone, because Microsoft has slightly changed the behavior of the Guest account in Windows XP and later: the profile of a guest user is deleted at logoff—but only when the computer is joined to a domain. If the Windows XP or Windows 2003 machine is in a workgroup, no guest profiles (of users in the Guests group) are deleted at logoff.

Additional System Profiles for Windows XP and Later

Windows XP and later contain two profiles that are meant to be used by newly installed services: Local Service and Network Service.

Local Service   Meant to be used by services that are local to the computer but do not need intricate local privileges or network access. This is in contrast to the System account, which pretty much has total authority over the system. If a service runs as Local Service, it appears to be a member in the local users group. When a service runs as Local Service across the network, the service appears as an anonymous user.

Network Service   Similar to Local Service but has elevated network access rights—similar to the System account. When a process runs under Network Service rights, it does so as the SID (Security ID) assigned to the computer (which in an Active Directory environment is a member of Domain Computers, and therefore also a member of Authenticated Users).

Windows XP and later automatically creates these profiles, which are basically normal but still a little special. For instance, you will not see the Local Service or Network Service in the listing of Profiles in the System Properties dialog box. You can see them in the Documents and Settings folder; however, they're "super-hidden" so that mere mortals cannot see them by default. You can see them in the top window here:

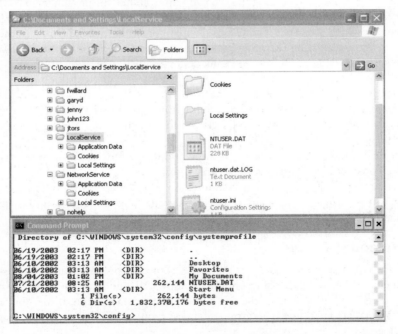

On Windows Vista and later, the Local Service and Network Service profiles have moved to the `%windir%\ServiceProfiles` directory. Windows can also load software, services, and its own profile when the computer starts up. Indeed, you see this profile in the "Log on to Windows" dialog box, in which you are prompted to press Ctrl+Alt+Del. Basically, this is the profile for when no one is logged on.

When this happens, Windows loads what is called the .DEFAULT (pronounced "dot default") profile. In Windows 2000, the .DEFAULT profile was in `c:\winnt\`*computername*, in which *computername* is the name of the computer. But applications sometimes flipped out if services tried to load portions of this part of the profile's Registry. To adjust for this, Windows XP and later plunked the .DEFAULT profile in:

`c:\windows\system32\config\SystemProfile`

Applications that leverage the .DEFAULT profile always use this Registry part, and troublesome application problems related to .DEFAULT should be quelled.

You can see the System Profile in the command prompt window in the lower half of the preceding graphic.

If the Windows XP or later computer is in a domain, and a user is a member of both the Guests and the Local Administrators group, the profile is not deleted—quite an unlikely scenario.

Cross-Forest Trusts

Roaming Profiles, like GPOs, are affected by Cross-Forest Trusts. Whether a user gets a Roaming Profile depends on the client operating system they're logged onto. (This operating-specific variance is documented in Chapter 4.) When clients log onto computers that enforce the rule, you'll get the message shown in Figure 9.19.

FIGURE 9.19 Users roaming within Cross-Forest scenarios receive this message.

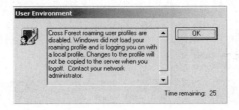

You can use a policy setting to prevent this from affecting your client computers. To do this, locate the **Allow Cross-Forest User Policy and Roaming User Profiles** policy setting by drilling down in Computer Configuration ➢ Policies ➢ Administrative Templates ➢ System ➢ Group Policy.

Manipulating Roaming Profiles with Computer Group Policy Settings

Roaming Profiles are simple to set up and maintain, but sometimes you'll want to use certain policy settings to affect their behavior. The policies you'll be setting appear in the Computer Configuration section of Group Policy. Drill down into Policies ➢ Administrative Templates ➢ System ➢ User Profiles, as shown in Figure 9.20.

FIGURE 9.20 There are many policy settings that affect profiles.

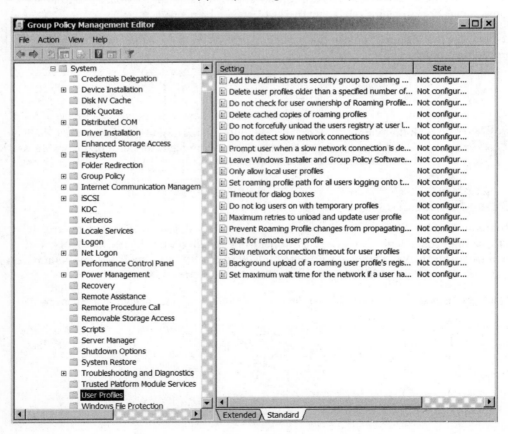

Recall that computers must be in the OU that the GPO affects (or in a child OU that inherits the setting). Or the GPO could be linked to the root of the domain and scoped to a security group that the computer is a member of.

If a user is moved to a new OU, then the user needs to log off and back on. If a machine is moved to a new OU, then the machine needs to reboot.

Before implementing any policy setting that affects Roaming Profiles, read through this section to determine if it adds value to your environment. Then, create a test OU and ensure that the behavior is as expected.

Do Not Check for User Ownership of Roaming Profile Folders

This policy setting applies only to Type 1 profiles. Specifically, Windows XP without a service pack and Windows 2000 with SP3 and earlier may have a potential security hole. If someone, such as a member of the Server Operators group, creates the user's target profile subfolder on the server, that creator is also the owner of the subfolder. When the user then pushes up their profile to the subfolder, the user isn't the only one with access to the profile; the creator/owner also has access. This could mean that the creator/owner can peer inside and get stuff they really shouldn't have.

If a client logs onto a Windows 2000/SP4 computer or later, the machine is smart enough to first check to see if the user is the only one with permissions on the folder (as seen earlier in Figure 9.13) before moving sensitive profile data up. If you enable this policy setting, you're telling newer machines to act like older machines and allow sensitive profile information to move up to the server, even if the user doesn't have exclusive access and ownership to the subfolder. Personally, I would leave this unconfigured. (You can read more about this in Knowledge Base article 327259, "Windows Server 2003 Checks for Pre-created Roaming Profile Folders When You Make a Roaming User Profile.")

Delete Cached Copies of Roaming Profiles

This is a space-saving and security mechanism that automatically deletes the user's locally cached profile when the user logs off. The default behavior is to allow files to be downloaded and pile up on each and every hard drive to which the user roams. You can enable this policy setting to (as the forest rangers say) "Leave only footprints and take only memories." Heck, you won't even be leaving any footprints.

This policy setting has two downsides, however; let's walk through two scenarios to examine these potential problems.

Problem scenario 1: Server down at login time   This policy setting is set to delete cached copies of Roaming Profiles. The user logs on, makes some changes, and logs off. The profile is automatically sent back to the server, and the footprints are washed away on the local machine.

Now, let's say that the server that houses the Roaming Profiles goes down. By default, if the user tries to log on and the server is unavailable to deliver the Roaming Profile, the locally cached copy of the profile is summoned to take its place. Once you enable this policy setting, you're severing a potential lifeline to the user if the server that houses the Roaming Profile becomes unavailable. Enabling this policy setting sweeps up after the user on the local machine at logoff. If the server goes down, the user will not get their locally cached version of the Roaming Profile because there is no locally cached version of the profile. Rather, the only profile the user will get is a temporary Local Profile that is not saved anywhere when the user logs off.

Problem scenario 2: Up and back and up and back   Again, by setting this policy setting, you're deleting all cached files. So, when the user logs back onto the same machine, all the Roaming Profile files need to get redownloaded from the Roaming Profile on the server, which means you're killing the caching inherent in the Roaming Profile system. In essence, you're making your machine act like NT 4, where the whole profile gets redownloaded at login. Note, however, that at logoff time, things should still be faster than NT 4 because you're pushing up only changes (where NT 4 would have pushed up *all* the files).

So those are the major problem scenarios. Let's take a look at a scenario where this setting is extremely useful.

This policy setting is useful in high-security environments where you need to make sure that no trace of potentially sensitive data in the profile is left behind. Be careful when using it with laptops, however, because users frequently need to use their copy of the locally cached version of the profile to get their work done. Additionally, enabling this policy setting does not prevent third-party tools from "resurrecting" deleted files inside the profile. It deletes the files but doesn't obliterate them to prevent industrious hackers from any possible recovery.

Once this policy setting is Enabled, the profile is erased only on logoff. And then it erases only profiles from machines on which users don't already have an existing cached copy! If you need to maintain a high-security environment, be sure to enable this policy setting early so that users don't have time to roam from machine to machine sprinkling copies of their profiles around (which won't get erased later by use of this policy setting).

 To use this policy setting, you'll need to disable (or not configure) the **Do not detect slow network connection** policy setting, as described shortly. If a network connection is determined to be slow, it automatically tries to grab the locally cached copy of the profile, which doesn't exist if you've enabled this **Delete cached copies of roaming profiles** policy setting.

Delete User Profiles Older Than a Specified Number of Days

This policy setting is handy, and applies only to Windows Vista and later computers.

What happens when Sally User logs onto a Windows 7 machine on the 4th floor—one time? All her profile junk gets downloaded on that machine and sits there—forever. Just eating up disk space, never to be reclaimed again. Until now.

If you enable this policy setting and specify a certain number of days, the Roaming (and Local) Profiles on that Windows 7 machine will be wiped clean—automatically. The user doesn't have to do anything. The system will automatically flush them down the, er, wherever it flushes them.

Here's a huge warning: be careful with this setting. Any data that is, say, only in a Local Profile (like the Documents folder) will be gone once the profile is wiped clean. Note that the data stored in the server-side copy of a Roaming Profile, and also any data redirected using redirected folders, is not touched. Figure 9.21 shows a before-and-after picture of how drastic profile cleanup is.

FIGURE 9.21   A typical Windows Vista computer after multiple users have logged onto it over time (left). The same Vista computer (right) after this policy kicks in within 24 hours. Note even local User Profiles are gone.

Slow Network Connection Timeout for User Profiles

Enabling this entry performs a quick ping test to the profiles server. If the speed is greater than the minimum value, the Roaming Profile is downloaded. If, however, the speed is not fast enough, the locally cached profile is used unless you've enabled the previous entry (**Delete cached copy of local profiles**). In that case, the user ends up with a temporary profile as described earlier.

> Enabling the **Do not detect slow network connection** policy setting, as described in the next section, forces anything specified in this policy setting to be ignored.

This policy setting is a bit strange: even if it's not configured, it has a default. That default speed threshold is 500Kbps; if the ping test determines that the bandwidth to the machine that houses the profiles is greater than 500Kbps, the profile is downloaded. If the ping returns a bandwidth of less than 500Kbps, the Roaming Profile is skipped, and the locally cached profile is used.

You might want to enable this policy setting and decrease the value thresholds if you want to increase the chances of a dial-up connection receiving the Roaming Profile instead of the locally cached profile. If you enable this policy setting, you'll need to manually specify both an IP ping time test and a non-IP ping millisecond test. As you can see, this setting can also affect machines that aren't using TCP/IP, but that's a pretty rare event nowadays. See the Explain text for more information if you have a non-IP situation.

 Unrelated speed tests can verify the ability to apply GPOs for both the user and computer. They are in the Group Policy Editor under Computer or User Configuration ➤ Administrative Templates ➤ Policies ➤ System ➤ Group Policy ➤ **Group Policy Slow Link Detection**.

Do Not Detect Slow Network Connections

Like the previous policy setting, this one is a little strange. If it's not configured, it still has a default; the users affected by this policy setting check the **Slow network connection timeout for user profiles** setting to see what a "slow network" actually means. If you enable this policy setting, you're disabling slow network detection, and the values you place in the **Slow network connection timeout for user profiles** policy setting don't mean a thing.

Wait for Remote User Profile

Again, even if this policy setting is not defined or disabled, there is still a default; if the speed is too slow, it will load the locally cached profile. If you enable this policy setting, the system waits until the Roaming Profile is downloaded—no matter how long it takes. You might turn this on if your users hop around a lot and the connection to the computer housing the Roaming Profiles is slow but not intolerable. That way, you'll still use the Roaming Profile stored on the server as opposed to the locally cached profile.

Prompt User When a Slow Network Connection Is Detected

When the ping test determines that the link speed is too slow, the user can be asked if they want to use the locally cached profile or grab the one from the server. If this policy setting is not configured or it's disabled, the user isn't even asked the question. If the **Wait for remote user profile** policy setting is enabled, the profile is downloaded from the server—however slowly.

For pre-Vista machines, if this policy setting is enabled, the user can determine whether they want to accept the profile from the server or utilize the locally cached profile.

For modern Windows machines, if this policy setting is enabled, the user must determine before logon time (by using a check box at logon time) to use the local or remote profile, as seen in Figure 9.22.

If this setting is not configured or disabled, the system always uses the Local Profile instead of the Remote Profile when the link is slow.

FIGURE 9.22   You can specify to allow users to download their profile over a slow network connection before they actually log on using Windows Vista or Windows 7.

If you've enabled the **Delete cached copies of roaming profiles** policy setting, there won't be a local copy of the Roaming Profile, so the user will be forced to accept the Default User Profile. If the **Do not detect slow network connection properties** policy setting is enabled, this GPO is ignored.

Timeout for Dialog Boxes

This setting only applies to Windows 2000, Windows XP, and Windows Server 2003 clients (not Windows Vista or later). If the **Prompt user when slow link is detected** policy setting is enabled, the user has a 30-second countdown to respond to whether they want to download their Roaming Profile anyway. Once this policy setting is enabled, the default value of 30 seconds can be changed. This dialog box timeout is also presented when the server that houses the Roaming Profile is unavailable, when the user logs off, or when the locally cached profile is newer than the Roaming Profile stored on the server. In all cases, the user can be prompted to determine what to do. The value you specify here is how many seconds to wait for an answer before the other policy settings make the decision for the user.

Do Not Log Users on with Temporary Profiles

This is the harshest sentence you can offer the user if things go wrong. By default, if the server is down (or the profile is corrupted), the user first tries to load a locally cached profile. If there is no locally cached profile, the system creates a TEMP profile from the Default User Profile.

However, if you choose to enable the setting, the behavior changes. If no Roaming Profile or locally cached profile is available (presumably because you've enabled the **Delete cached copies of roaming profile** policy setting), the user is not permitted to log on.

Maximum Retries to Unload and Update User Profile

As previously discussed, this policy setting is meant to assist Windows 2000 Terminal Services when trying to log users off and release their Roaming Profiles. Increase this value to increase the number of attempts made at unloading the pertinent Registry information, and update the profile when users start to complain that things aren't the same as when the last logged off (especially on Terminal Services). The current Explain text states that this policy is valid for Windows 2000, Windows XP, and Windows 2003 machines only.

But it's not.

Repeat after me: it does nothing for Windows XP or Windows Server 2003. Or Windows Vista or Windows 7 or Windows Server 2008 machines for that matter.

It's a Windows 2000–only policy setting.

Add the Administrators Security Group to Roaming User Profiles

As you saw in Figure 9.13 earlier in this chapter, only the user can dive in and poke around their personal User Profile. However, you can specify that the administrator and the user have joint access to the folder.

Oddly, this policy setting is found under the Computer side of the house—not the user. Therefore, it's somewhat difficult to implement this policy setting on a small scale, because it's sometimes a mystery as to which client machine users will log onto. If you want to use this policy setting, I recommend creating a GPO with this policy setting at the domain level to guarantee that any client computers that users log onto will be affected. Modifying this policy setting so that it affects the file server housing the profiles doesn't do anything for you. It's the target client computers that need to get this policy setting.

This policy setting *only* takes effect when new users first log onto affected client computers. Once they're on, they'll make some changes that affect the profile, and then log off. When they log off, a signal is sent back to the directory housing the profile, which then finalizes the security on the directory so that both the user and the administrator can plunk around in there.

To be especially clear, as I implied, this policy setting works only for new users—those users who don't already have a Roaming Profile. Users who *already* have established Roaming Profiles are essentially left in the dark with regard to using this—but there is a ray of light. If you want the same effect, you can take ownership of a profile and manually establish administrative access for the administrator and the user, as described in the upcoming section "Mandatory Profiles from an Established Roaming Profile."

This policy setting works with Windows 2000's Service Pack 2 and later, although the policy setting's Explain text states that it's applicable to Windows XP and Windows 2003 and later. Additionally, the policy is supported on Windows Vista and later.

Prevent Roaming Profile Changes from Propagating to the Server

As previously discussed, when a user jumps from machine to machine and lands on one with an existing Local Profile, the system merges the Local Profile as a favor to the user. The idea is that if this Local Profile has a data file, say, RESUME.DOC, that's missing in the user's Roaming Profile, this is a perfect time to scoop it up and keep it in the Roaming Profile. You can dictate specific machines for which you don't want this to happen.

In general, you set this policy setting only on computers that you are sure you don't want the merge between Local Profiles and Roaming Profiles—perhaps because the Local Profiles contain many unneeded files. With the policy enabled, changes made to the profile are lost because the Roaming Profile is downloaded from the server logoff and not merged with the Local Profile.

In case you missed it, this policy setting makes the profile work like a Mandatory Profile, so don't save anything valuable in the profile, because it is going to be lost!

This policy setting affects Windows XP and later.

Only Allow Local User Profiles

This policy setting is useful when you have set up specialty machines, such as lab machines, library machines, kiosk machines, and so on. By enabling this policy setting on the machines, you can ensure that a user's Roaming Profile doesn't get downloaded onto a particular machine.

Leave Windows Installer and Group Policy Software Installation Data

Earlier, we explored the **Delete cached copies of roaming profiles** policy setting. The idea was to "clean up" behind a user when he or she logged off. This was a great idea in theory but had an unintended consequence.

If you opt to delete Roaming Profiles at logoff time, the information regarding applications deployed via Group Policy Software Installation (explored in Chapter 11) is also lost (by default). There is a new policy that affects users on Windows XP/SP2 (or Windows 2003/SP1) or later (such as Windows Vista or Windows 7) called **Leave Windows Installer and Group Policy Software Installation Data**. Once enabled, the Group Policy Software Installation data remains on the hard drive, so subsequent logins for users are much faster.

Roaming Profile Policies

If trying to figure out all the ins and outs of Roaming Profile policies is giving you a headache, use the handy flowchart in Figure 9.23 to help you figure out what each policy setting does and how it will affect your users.

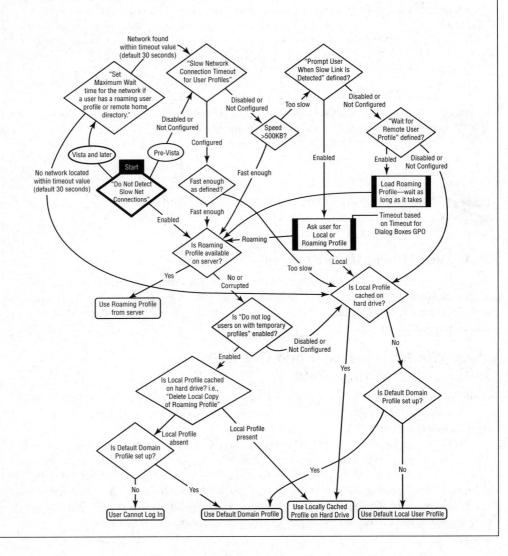

So, if you're choosing to enable the **Delete cached copies of roaming profiles** setting, enabling this one as well is probably a good idea. This policy was created to deal with the scenario where applications are deployed via Group Policy Software Installation as a full install of the application at logon time while the **Delete cached copies of roaming profiles** policy is enabled. You can find more information at `http://support.microsoft.com/ kb/828452`.

Do Not Forcefully Unload the Users Registry at User Logoff

In versions of Windows previous to Vista, the logging-off process sometimes just "hung" there. In Windows' defense, it was usually a service or something similar that kept the user's profile open. To that end, UPHClean (described earlier) was developed to help correct that problem on Windows Server 2003 Terminal Services. (See the sidebar "A Brief History of the Unloading of `NTUSER.DAT` and UPHClean.")

Now, Windows Vista and later goes the extra mile and will automatically do this.

So, the only time to enable this policy is if you think something is getting broken by this automatic process. For instance, you log on a second or third time and notice your application didn't save settings that would normally be stored in the user's Registry hives.

In other words, only enable this policy setting if you suspect some issue with the behavior of forcefully unloading the user's Registry at logoff.

This policy setting works with Windows Vista and later, including Windows Server 2008 and Windows Server 2008 R2.

Set Roaming Profile Path for All Users Logging Onto This Computer

The policy setting enables you to establish a shared User Profile path for a specific computer. Think of it as "Everyone who logs onto this computer gets the same profile."

But just because you enable this policy setting doesn't mean it's 100 percent guaranteed to be embraced. That's because other values might have precedence before this one takes effect.

Windows reads profile configurations in the following order and uses the first configured setting:

1. The Roaming Profile path specified in the Terminal Services policy setting found at Computer Configuration ➤ Policies ➤ Administrative Templates ➤ Windows Components ➤ Terminal Services ➤ Terminal Server ➤ Profiles ➤ **Set path for TS Roaming Profiles**

2. The Roaming Profile path specific in the Terminal Server user object in Active Directory Users and Computers

3. The per-computer Roaming Profile path specified (using this policy setting)

4. The per-user Roaming Profile path specified in the user object in Active Directory Users and Computers

This policy setting works with Windows Vista and later.

Set Maximum Wait Time for the Network if a User Has a Roaming User Profile or Remote Home Directory

This is a wordy policy setting, for sure, but what it does is simple: You can increase the network timeout if you know the computer may not find the network right away after a user chooses to log on. This can happen a lot in the cases where a wireless card is searching, searching, searching for the wireless access point, but, meanwhile, the user has already pressed Ctrl+Alt+Del to log on!

Ouch!

By setting this policy, the computer waits a bit first to see if the network suddenly becomes present.

If the network still isn't available (based on this value, or 30 seconds by default), the cached profile is used and the user won't have access to the network home drive.

This policy setting works with Windows Vista and later.

Background Upload of a Roaming User Profile's Registry File While User Is Logged On

Another wordy policy setting, but this one only applies to Windows 7 and Windows Server 2008 R2.

This policy is neat: it solves an interesting problem.

Remember that a user's profile is made up of a bunch of items: user data, documents, and a lot of other stuff. Arguably, the most important part of the profile is the NTUSER.DAT file— the user's portion of the Registry that is loaded in and out every time she logs on and off.

But if the user is over a slow link, maybe you don't want to move all the junk up and back and up each time. Just one trip could take a long time—even just the new files, since Windows Vista and Windows 7 only send up and back changes.

So, is there a middle ground? This policy setting's goal, when active, is to say: "Don't send up the user's data over a slow link. Send up only the NTUSER.DAT file."

Why is this a neat idea? Because you'll be able to roam to a different machine and get the same look and feel. True, the files might not be up-to-date, but, maybe you're okay with that, or using some other technique to save data files (like mapped network drives or thumb drives or something).

This policy setting might not be needed for your environment, but it's a neat idea for at least some people.

You can see how to configure it Figure 9.23.

One More Policy Setting That You Might Like

This policy setting isn't specifically profile related, but it does relate to the logon experience.

Check out **Report when logon server was not available during user logon** found in Computer Configuration (and User Configuration) ➢ Policies ➢ Windows Components ➢ Windows Logon Options. They both work the same way.

Once enabled, this policy setting displays an informative dialog box telling the user if, more or less, she's working online or offline. This can be a great first step in knowing what's going on and whether or not a problem exists.

FIGURE 9.23 Use this Windows 7–only policy setting to upload *only* the NTUSER.DAT file over a roaming profile.

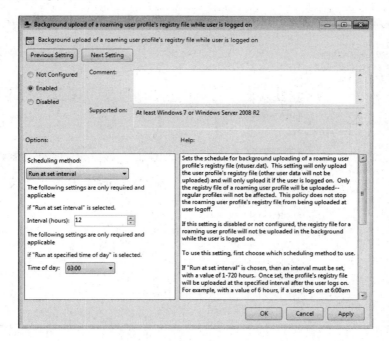

Manipulating Roaming Profiles with User Group Policy Settings

As you have just seen, most policy settings regarding Roaming Profiles are associated with the computer itself. Two policy settings, however, affect Roaming Profiles but are located on the User side of the fence: **Limit profile size** and **Excluding directories in roaming profile**. These policy settings are found under User Settings ➢ Policies ➢ Administrative Templates ➢ System ➢ User Profiles, as shown in Figure 9.24.

Limit Profile Size

This setting limits how big the profile can grow. Remember, now the My Documents folder is part of the profile. If you limit the profile size, the profile can hit that limit awfully quickly.

I recommend that you avoid using this setting unless you use the techniques described in the next chapter for redirecting folders for the My Documents folder. When that technique is applied, the redirected My Documents folder is no longer part of the profile, and the size can come back down to earth.

FIGURE 9.24   Some entries for profiles are found under the User node in Group Policy.

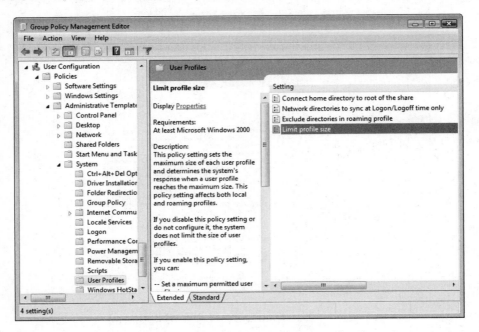

Once enabled, the setting provides three other options:

"Show registry files in the file list"   If selected, the user will see the NTUSER.DAT as part of the total calculations on space. I suggest you leave this unchecked because most users won't know what the NTUSER.DAT file is. And, by leaving it unchecked, the NTUSER.DAT file doesn't count toward the space used.

"Notify user when profile storage space is exceeded"   This option notifies the user about size infractions.

"Remind user every X minutes"   Use this setting so that it annoys the user every so often. This setting is only valid if the "Notify user when profile storage space is exceeded" box is checked, as shown in Figure 9.25.

Once this policy setting is configured, the affected users on Windows XP or Windows 2000 cannot log off until the files that compose their profile take up less than the limit. They are presented with a list of files in their profile, as shown in Figure 9.26, from which they must choose some to delete.

For Windows Vista and later machines, users get an extra notification in the notification. Windows 7 machines get a pop-up. You can see these in Figure 9.27. To see the list of files, they have to double-click the X. (You might want to mention this in your custom message.)

FIGURE 9.25   You can limit the Roaming Profile size, if desired.

FIGURE 9.26   Once the Roaming Profile size is set, users can't log off until they delete some files.

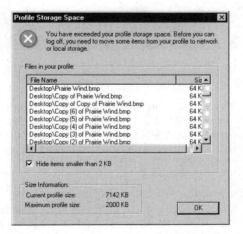

Additionally, for Windows Vista and later, users can log off, but their changes aren't synchronized back to the server. At logoff, they get greeted with the message you see in Figure 9.28. It stays on the screen for a few seconds and then goes away, allowing the next user to log on.

In general, this is a blunt instrument. The original use of this entry was for situations in which users stuffed lots of documents into their Windows NT Roaming Profile—onto the Desktop, for instance. Recall that Windows NT pushes the entire profile up and back, causing major bandwidth headaches. Indeed, because users rely heavily on the My Documents folder (which is part of the profile), there's even more reason to be concerned.

FIGURE 9.27   Windows Vista allows for a custom message in the notification area (left) and Windows 7 pops up a message for the user (right). (Yes, my message is a little silly.)

FIGURE 9.28   Users are notified their profile isn't completely synchronized.

Your roaming user profile was not completely synchronized. See the event log for details or contact administrator.

WARNING   Don't try to place disk quota restrictions on Roaming Profiles. Because applications sometimes put their own data inside the profile, users have a hard time tracking down files to delete if the quota prevented them from writing. Instead, use disk quotas on redirected folders, such as the My Documents folder.

But instead of being forced to use this policy setting as your only weapon to fight disk space usage, you have an ace in the hole; in the next chapter, you'll learn how to use Folder Redirection to redirect My Documents. You can then place a disk quota on the redirected My Documents folder.

In Windows Vista this policy setting will automatically exclude \Appdata\Local and Appdata\LocalLow directories (and all their subdirectories).

Excluding Directories in Roaming Profile

As previously stated, several folders in the profile will not roam.

For pre–Windows Vista machines, these folders are:

Documents and Settings\Username\Local Settings\Application Data

(and everything below it, including Local Settings, History, Temp, and Temporary Internet Files).

For Windows Vista and later machines, these folders are \Appdata\Local and Appdata\LocalLow and all their subfolders (like \Temporary Internet Files).

You can add additional folders to the list of those that do not roam, if you want. You might do this if you want to fix a specific file to a Desktop (if you maintain locally cached profiles). For instance, you can exclude Desktop\LargeZipDownloads if you want to make sure those types of files do not roam with the profile.

> Enter additional entries relative to the root of the profiles. For instance, if you want to add the Desktop, simply add **Desktop** (not **c:\Documents and Settings\Desktop** or anything similar), because the Desktop folder is found directly off the root of each profile.

Connect Home Directory to Root of the Share

I'm pretty sure that by the time you get to the end of this book, you won't want to use old-style "Home Drives" anymore. That's because the changes in Roaming Profile behavior and redirected folders (see the next chapter) present a better way for users to store their files. However, if you do end up using Home Drives for each user (located in the Account tab of each user account's Properties dialog box), you can specify a location for users to store their stuff. Specific environment variables typically used when setting up home directories are defined differently in NT 4 and Windows 2000 and later.

Those two environment variables, *%HOMEDRIVE%* and *%HOMEPATH%*, are automatically set when you set up, share, and assign a home directory for a user. NT 4 client computers aren't as smart as Windows 2000 computers, and they understand the meaning of the *%HOMEDRIVE%* and *%HOMEPATH%* shares a bit differently. To make a long story short, the fully qualified name path to the share isn't represented when those variables are evaluated on NT 4 clients, but it is for Windows 2000 and later clients. You can "dumb down" Windows 2000 and newer clients by applying this policy setting and making new clients act like old NT 4 clients.

> This policy is not supported on Windows Vista or later. Those operating systems *always* set %HOMEDRIVE% and %HOMEPATH% in the new way.

Mandatory Profiles

Mandatory Profiles enable the administrator to assign a single user or multiple users the same, unchanging user experience regardless of where they log on and no matter what they do. In non–mumbo-jumbo terms, Mandatory Profiles ensure that users can't screw things up. When you use Mandatory Profiles to lock down your users, you guarantee that the Desktop, the files in the profile, and the Registry continue to look exactly as they did when they were set up.

Mandatory Profiles are great when you have a pesky user who keeps messing with the Desktop or when you have general populations of users—such as call centers, nursing stations, or library kiosks—on whom you want to maintain security.

Once the Mandatory Profile is set for these people, you know you won't be running out there every 11 minutes trying to fix someone's machine when they've put the black text on the black background and clicked Apply. Actually, they can still put the black text on the black background and click Apply, and it does take effect. But when they log off or reboot (if they can figure out how to do that in the dark), the values aren't preserved. So, voilà! Back to work!

You can create a Mandatory Profile in two ways—either from a Local Profile (or locally cached profile) or from an existing Roaming Profile. I recommend creating your Mandatory Profile from a local (or locally cached) profile. By default, if you try to dive into an existing Roaming Profile folder on the server, you are denied access, as shown in Figure 9.13 earlier in this chapter. The system utilizes the *%username%* variable and automatically sets up permissions such that only the user specified can access that folder. To dive in, you have to take ownership of the entire subfolder structure first and then give yourself permission to access the folder.

In the next sections, you'll find the steps for both methods.

 If you previously set up the **Add the Administrators security group to roaming user profiles** policy setting, you won't need to worry about not being able to dive into the profile. However, the policy setting must be placed before the Roaming Profile is placed.

Establishing Mandatory Profiles from a Local Profile

The first thing to do when trying to establish the Mandatory Profile is to log on locally to any Windows XP machine as a mere-mortal user (without an existing Roaming Profile), make the modifications you want, and log off as that user.

Now that you have a local (or locally cached) profile that you want to use as your Mandatory Profile, follow these steps:

1. Log on as Administrator to the machine that houses the local (or locally cached) profile.

For Windows XP:

2. Click Start, and then right-click My Computer and choose Properties from the context menu to open the System Properties dialog box. Continue with step 4.

For Windows Vista or Windows 7 as targets, you must use a Windows Vista machine to do the dirty work. This is the same problem we saw earlier with Windows 7: The Copy To button is grayed out for normal account. So, using a Windows Vista machine:

3. Click Start, right-click Computer, and select Properties from the context menu. Then select "Advanced system settings" in the left pane.

4. For both XP and Vista, click the Advanced tab, and then click the Settings button in the User Profiles section to open the User Profiles dialog box (as seen previously in Figure 9.7).

5. Click the Copy To button to open the Copy To dialog box, and then enter the full path plus a folder for the common users, as shown in Figure 9.29. This example has \\Dc01\profiles\allnurses. The allnurses folder is automatically created under the Profiles share.

FIGURE 9.29 For Windows XP (shown at left), use the Copy To dialog box to copy one profile for many users. If you want this profile to be used for Windows Vista and later (shown at right) computers, you need to specify a .v2 extension, as seen here. Again, you need to perform the steps on a Windows Vista machine, even if your ultimate destination is Windows 7.

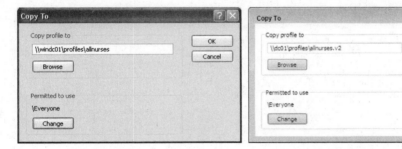

6. Click the Change button in the "Permitted to Use" section to open the "Select User or Group" dialog box and change the default from the original user to Authenticated Users. This lets everyone use the profile in the domain.

7. Click OK to actually copy the profile and to close the Copy To dialog box.

8. Click OK to close the System Properties dialog box.

Next, use Explorer to locate the share we created earlier, named Profiles. Inside the Profiles directory, you should now see the allnurses (or allnurses.v2 for Windows Vista/ Windows 7) folder. Locate the NTUSER.DAT and rename it to NTUSER.MAN, as shown in Figure 9.30.

Because NTUSER.DAT is hidden by default, you might have to change the default view options. In Explorer, choose Tools ⊁ Folder Options to open the Folder Options dialog box. Click the View tab, click the "Show Hidden Files and Folders" button, clear the "Hide File Extensions for Known File Types" check box, and click OK.

Finally, in the Properties dialog box, change the profile path of all the users who are to use the profile to \\Dc01\profiles\allnurses, as shown in Figure 9.31. Note that you do not need to specify the .v2 directory specifically for Vista users in the "Profile path" line; just enter \\Dc01\profiles\allnurses and Windows XP will use the non-.v2 directory and Windows Vista/Windows 7 will automatically find and use the .v2 directory.

Since you copied the profile to the server with permissions for Authenticated User to use, you'll also want to modify the NTFS permissions of the allnurses folder under the Profiles share to make sure it's protected. You might choose to protect the allnurses folder by setting the Permissions as shown in Figure 9.32.

FIGURE 9.30 Change a Roaming Profile to a Mandatory Profile by renaming NTUSER.DAT to NTUSER.MAN.

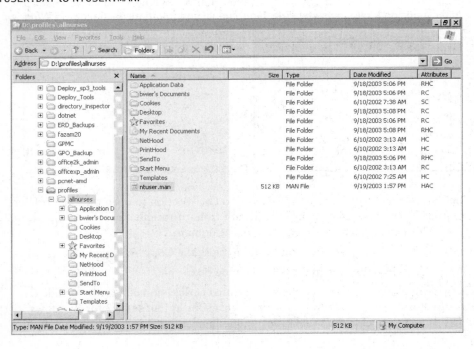

FIGURE 9.31   Point all similar users to the new Mandatory Profile.

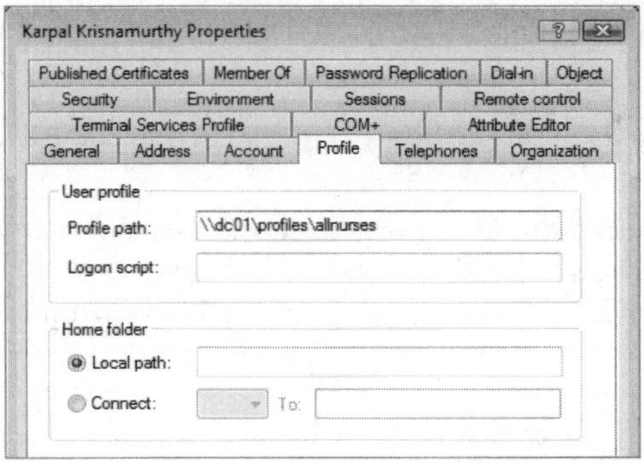

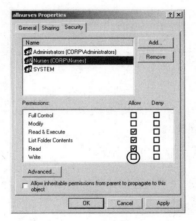

FIGURE 9.32   You can prevent people from inadvertently modifying the newly established profile.

Mandatory Profiles from an Established Roaming Profile

You might not be able to use a local (or locally cached) profile to generate the Mandatory Profile. This might be because you enabled the **Delete cached copies of roaming profiles** policy setting, and there are no locally cached profiles for you to use. In this case, you'll need to log on as Administrator on the server that houses the Roaming Profile, locate the profile folder, and take ownership of it. You can then copy the profile to another folder and have the user take back ownership of the folder. In this case, we'll take ownership of a profile for a user named garyd. To take ownership of a user's Roaming Profile, follow these steps:

1.   Log on at the server as Administrator.

2. Locate the user's profile folder, right-click it, and choose Properties from the context menu to open the User Properties dialog box.

3. Click the Security tab. You should get a message stating that the user is the only one with access to their personal folder.

4. Click the Advanced button on the Security tab to access the Advanced Security Settings dialog box. Next, click the Owner tab.

5. Select Administrator (or Administrators) from the list, click the "Replace owner on subcontainers and objects" check box (as shown in Figure 9.33), and then click OK. With Windows Server 2008, you'll have to hit the Edit button before modifying the ownership.

FIGURE 9.33 Take ownership of the folder.

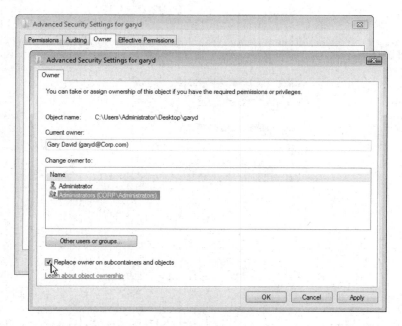

6. You will be prompted to confirm that you want to take ownership. Select Yes, and wait until you have ownership.

You can now rename the folder to a sensible name and then rename the NTUSER.DAT file to NTUSER.MAN. Last, specifically point each user account to use this new profile, as shown in Figure 9.31 earlier.

You'll then need to modify the permissions so that appropriate users only have access to the profile.

You might need to add the Administrator account or the Administrators group to the ACL of the folder and let the permissions flow downward in order to be able to see the contents. In some extreme cases, you might also need to log off and back on as Administrator to get another access token.

Forced Mandatory Profiles (Super-Mandatory)

Mandatory Profiles might not always be so—if the server is down or a user unplugs their network cable, the Mandatory Profile does not load. Indeed, the user will get the Local Default User Profile. This could be a potential security problem and possibly a violation of your corporate policy.

In instances like this, you need to determine if it's more important that a user logs on (and gets the Default Local User Profile) or that, if they don't get the Mandatory Profile, they don't get to log on at all. Microsoft calls this type of profile "Super-Mandatory." In Figure 9.30 earlier, we used a folder named `allnurses` as our Mandatory Profile folder. We can take this to the next step and ensure that no users using the `allnurses` folder can log on unless they can connect to the share on the server.

Don't forget: profiles are different for Type 1 (pre–Windows Vista) and Type 2 (Windows Vista and later). To that end, you'll need to set up Mandatory Profiles that fit for each type.

To force users who log onto Windows Vista and later to use a Mandatory Profile or lose logon capability, you need to first rename the `allnurses.v2` folder so that it has `.man.v2` instead. So, the final folder name will be `allnurses.man.v2`.

To force users to use the Mandatory Profile, or lose logon capability, simply follow these steps:

1. Create a Mandatory Profile as described earlier, including renaming the `NTUSER.DAT` to `NTUSER.MAN`.

2. For Windows XP machines, rename the entire folder from `allnurses` to `allnurses.man`. For Windows Vista machines, rename the entire folder from `allnurses.v2` to `allnurses.man.v2`

3. Change the affected users' Profile tabs to point to the new location, such as `\\Dc01\profiles\allnurses.man`, as shown in Figure 9.34.

Once the forced Mandatory Profile is introduced onto a system, the system always checks to see if the profile is available. If the forced Mandatory Profile is unavailable, the user is not permitted to log on.

Technically, you can couple a Mandatory Profile with the **Log users off when roaming profile fails** policy setting to create the same effect. However, the method detailed here is preferred.

FIGURE 9.34   You can force a Mandatory Profile if absolutely necessary.

Final Thoughts

In this chapter, you learned about the three profile types: Local, Roaming, and Mandatory.

Local Profiles alone are great—for only the smallest of environments. However, remember that there's a lot you can do to get a similar look and feel for when new users show up on the job. You can craft a Default Local User Profile, or, even better, a Default Domain User Profile.

Step up to Roaming Profiles when you have even a handful of users and you want to allow them to bounce from machine to machine and keep their look and feel. Roaming Profiles have grown up since the days of Windows NT. The algorithm to move the profiles up and back is much improved, and you should give it another try if you once gave up in frustration.

Roaming Profiles are especially useful if you want to bring users' Desktops and laptops back from the dead, as we'll explore in the next two chapters. Indeed, you can use Roaming Profiles as a handy way to upgrade users' machines while preserving their Desktops.

Remember that the Active Directory Users and Computers tool allows you to select multiple users at once and set their Roaming Profile path to a server. And, as stated earlier, there's no need to create the folder underneath the shared directory first—the system will automatically do that once the *%username%* variable is encountered.

Even though we set up Roaming Profiles for our Type 1 computers (pre–Windows Vista) and our Type 2 computers (Windows Vista and later), we still have a problem: we have no way to exchange data between the two. If someone logs onto Windows 7 and drops some music files in their profile, then they log onto a Windows XP machine, they simply won't see those music files. In the next chapter, we'll discuss Redirected Folders. The idea is that instead of saving critical data in our profile, we save it on a point on our server. That way, if we're on Windows 7 or Windows XP, we'll be able to just reach out and touch the data that lives on the server. We'll get there right around the corner.

As stated earlier, there are a lot of policy settings you can utilize to hone how profiles work. You can set up your environment to be moderately secure when using the **Delete cached copies of roaming profiles** policy setting. And you can allow joint ownership of the user's Roaming Profile directory on the server by utilizing the **Add the Administrators security group to roaming user profiles** policy setting.

Use Mandatory Profiles sparingly. With Group Policy settings available to tie down all sorts of settings, Mandatory Profiles are really only a last resort. And Forced Mandatory Profiles are a really, really last resort (if there's such a thing).

10

Implementing a Managed Desktop, Part 1: Redirected Folders, Offline Files, and the Synchronization Manager

You get Active Directory, you get Group Policy. That's the good news. The better news is how you can put your knowledge of Group Policy to use to keep your users happy. Here's the idea: easily create a consistent environment for your users no matter where they roam.

In the previous chapter, you used Roaming Profiles to kick off your journey to a consistent environment. But that only got you so far—especially if you had both Windows XP and Windows Vista (or later) machines. That's because when you roamed from Windows XP to Windows 7 (or vice versa), you didn't maintain the goodies, like the stuff you put in My Documents (for XP) and Documents (for Windows Vista and later). Each computer type became its own island.

Now, let's explore how to create a *managed desktop*. A managed desktop is one where you can create a predictable environment for your users to log into and enjoy. It's not put together with wacky applications and icons all over the place. You know what to expect when your users log on, and so do they.

In this chapter, I'll give you an overview of what a managed desktop is and show you how to implement a gaggle of its features, among them Redirected Folders, Offline Files, and the Synchronization Manager.

 Previously, the concept of a managed desktop was called IntelliMirror. It seems like the marketing folks in Redmond have put that term to pasture, though. So, we'll just refer to IntelliMirror as a "managed desktop."

In the next chapter, I'll continue creating a managed desktop with a discussion of software deployment via Group Policy. Finally, in Chapter 12, you'll see how the "circle of life" for a computer comes together with more Group Policy Preference Extensions tricks, Shadow Copies, and more.

Overview of Change and Configuration Management

Believe it or not, you're expensive. Your salary, the percentage of rent your office takes up, the software you use that helps the business run—it all costs money. Making those costs tangible is a difficult proposition. Some costs are hard to put into concrete numbers. How do you quantify the cost of sending a technician to a user's desktop when they've inadvertently set the background color, the foreground color, and the font color to black and hit the Apply button?

Accounting for these costs is a constant challenge, and bringing these costs under control is even more difficult. In the early 1990s, the Gartner Group generated a new strategy to help with this predicament and proposed a new *TCO (Total Cost of Ownership)* model. This philosophical model essentially attempted to take the voodoo out of accounting for computing services. Simply account for every nickel and dime spent around computing, and voilà! Instant accounting!

Microsoft's first foray into aligning with the TCO philosophy was back in the NT 4 timeframe with their Zero Administration for Windows (ZAW) initiative. The first major technology set based on ZAW was called the Zero Administration for Windows Kit (ZAK).

Most organizations have two types of users: those who work on one application and one application only, and those who use a few apps (but seem to never stop playing with their Desktops). With those two types of users in mind, ZAK could be run in two modes: Taskstation, in which users were locked down to one (and only one) application, and Appstation, in which users could move between several strategically selected applications. ZAK's goal was noble: reduce the user's exposure to the Desktop and the operating system. Once that was reduced, less administration would be required to control the environment.

Although ZAK was a respectable first attempt, only a few organizations really used ZAK in the way it was intended. The adoption of ZAK never quite caught on due to the intricacy of implementation and lack of flexibility. Finally, in 2007, Microsoft took down ZAK for NT 4 as a free download.

With Active Directory as the backdrop to a new stage, a new paradigm of how administrators managed users and their Desktops could be created. Enter the Active Directory version of Zero Administration for Windows—now known as Change and Configuration Management (CCM) and the (now defunct) Microsoft term *IntelliMirror*.

Again, recall that the Zero Administration for Windows program was an "initiative," not a specific technology. With Windows 2000, Microsoft renamed the ZAW initiative to Change and Configuration Management and introduced several new technologies in order to move closer to the TCO philosophy.

In accordance with the TCO philosophy, by creating a managed desktop, each step you implement tries to chip away at each of the sore points of administering your network by implementing specific technologies. Figure 10.1 shows how Microsoft envisions the Change and Configuration Management initiative and the Windows features and technologies therein.

ZAK was kind of an all-or-nothing proposition. But today with CCM, it's not like that. You can choose the steps to perform: from setting up Roaming Profiles (which you learned about in the previous chapter) to setting up Redirected Folders and Offline Files (which you'll learn about in this chapter) to deploying software (which you'll learn about in upcoming chapters).

FIGURE 10.1 This is Microsoft's picture of how to create a managed desktop (the concept formerly known as IntelliMirror).

		Features	Benefits	Technologies
Change and Configuration Management	Managed Desktop	User Data Management	Increased protection and availability of people's data "My documents follow me!"	Active Directory Group Policy Offline Folders Synchronization Manager Redirected Folders
		User Settings Management	Centrally defined environment "My settings follow me!"	Active Directory Group Policy Offline Folders Roaming Profiles
		Software Installation and Maintenance	Centrally managed software "My software follows me!"	Active Directory Group Policy Windows Installer Service
		Remote OS Installation	Fast system configuration "Get Windows working on this machine"	Active Directory DNS DHCP Windows Deployment Service

In short, you're in control of the features and functionality you want to deploy and when you want to deploy them. Although some features that I'll describe in detail here (such as Offline Files) are available when using a Windows workstation by itself, most features (such as Redirected Folders) are actuated only when you have the marriage between Active Directory and a Windows client.

Again, you built a bit of a foundation for your journey toward a managed desktop in the last chapter when you implemented Roaming Profiles. This enabled the basics of the "my documents follow me" and the "my settings follow me" philosophies. In this chapter, we'll explore the implementation of some of the other features needed to create a managed desktop: Redirected Folders, Offline Files, and the synchronization capabilities (in both Windows XP and later).

In normal use, people may call Offline Files something else—"Offline Folders" and also "CSC" (for "Client-Side Caching"). In regular use, they're all the same thing, but strictly, Microsoft documentation refers only to Offline Files and not Offline Folders. So, to be consistent, we'll also call the feature Offline Files.

Redirected Folders

Redirected Folders allow the administrator to provide a centralized repository for certain noteworthy folders from client systems and to have the data contained in them reside on shared folders on servers. It's a beautiful thing. The administrator gets centralized control; users get the same experience they always did. It's the best of both worlds.

Available Folders to Redirect

Windows XP and its newer cousins (Windows Vista and Windows 7) have different folders that are available for redirection. In Windows XP, you can set Redirected Folders for the following:

- My Documents
- My Pictures
- Start Menu
- Desktop
- Application Data

In Windows Vista and later, you can redirect the following folders:

- Contacts (not previously available in Windows XP)
- Start Menu (like Windows XP, but see the note following this list)
- Desktop (like Windows XP)
- Documents (was called My Documents in Windows XP)
- Downloads (not previously available in Windows XP)
- Favorites (not previously "redirectable" in Windows XP, but available in the Roaming Profile)
- Music (was called My Music in Windows XP)
- Videos (was called My Videos in Windows XP)
- Pictures (was called My Pictures in Windows XP)
- Searches (not previously available in Windows XP)
- Links (not previously available in Windows XP)
- AppData (Roaming) (was called simply Application Data in XP)
- And (Lord help us), Saved Games (not previously available in Windows XP)

 The Start Menu redirection support in Windows Vista and later is better than XP, because in XP, you didn't have the ability to redirect each user's Start Menu folder to a different location. You could only do it to a shared location. It wasn't as flexible as My Documents.

For each of these settings, there is a Basic and an Advanced configuration.

The idea is to set up a GPO that contains a policy setting to redirect one or more of these folders for clients and "stick them" on a server. Usually the GPO is set at the OU level, and all users inside the OU are affected; however, there might occasionally be a reason to link the GPO with the policy setting to the domain or site level.

In the *Basic* configuration, every user who is affected by the policy setting is redirected to the same shared folder. Then, inside the shared folder, the system can automatically create individual, secure folders for users to store their stuff.

In the *Advanced* configuration, Active Directory security group membership determines which users' folders get redirected to which shared folder. For instance, you could say, "All members of the **Graphic_Artists** Global security group will get their Desktops redirected to the ga_Desktops shared folder on Server 6" or, "All members of the Sales Universal security group will get their Application Data redirected to the AppData share on Server Pineapple."

Redirected *Documents/My Documents*

For our journey through Redirected Folders, we'll work primarily inside the Documents folder. All the principles that work on the special Documents folder work equally well for the other special "redirectable" folders, unless otherwise noted. At the end of this section, I'll briefly discuss why you might want to redirect some other folders as well.

In the last chapter, we explored how to leverage Roaming Profiles to maintain a consistent state for users if they hop from machine to machine. Roaming Profiles are terrific, but one significant drawback is associated with using Roaming Profiles. Recall that My Documents (for Windows XP) and Documents (for Windows Vista and later) are now part of the profile. On the one hand, this frees you from the bondage of drive letters and home drives. No more, "Ursula, put it in your U: drive," or "Harry, save it to the H: drive."

On the other hand, once the user data is in Documents/My Documents, your network will be swamped with all the up-and-back movement of data within Documents/My Documents when users hop from machine to machine—20MB of Word docs here, 30MB of Excel docs there. Multiply this by the number of users, and it'll add up fast! Not to mention that (for XP, at least) that data is synchronized at logon and logoff, and hence, the user may have to wait until it's all completed. As we learned in the previous chapter, the Roaming Profiles algorithm does its best to mitigate that, but it's still got to move the changed files.

But with Redirected Folders, you can have the best of both worlds. Users can save their files to the place they know and love, My Documents (for Windows XP) and Documents (for Windows Vista and later), and anchor the data to a fixed location, so it *appears* as if the data is roaming with the users. But it really isn't; it's safe and secure on a file share of your choice. And, since the data is already on the server, there's no long wait time when logging on or logging off.

There are two added bonuses to this scheme. Since all the Documents/My Documents files are being redirected to specific fixed-shared folders, you can easily back up all the user data in one fell swoop. Perhaps you can even make a separate backup job specifically for the user data that needs to be more closely monitored. Additionally, you can set up Shadow Copies for the disk volumes that house redirected Documents/My Documents files so users can restore their own files, if necessary. The Shadow Copies function is explored in Chapter 12.

Basic Redirected Folders

Basic Redirected Folders works best in two situations:

- Smaller environments—such as a doctor's office or storefront—where all employees sit under one roof

- In an organization's OU structure that was designed such that similar people are not only in the same OU, but also in the same physical location

The reason these simple scenarios make a good fit with the basic option is that such situations let you redirect the users affected by the policy setting to a server that's close to them. That way, if they do roam within their location, the wait time is minimal to download and upload the data back and forth to the server and their workstation.

In the following example, I've created an OU called **LikeUsers** who are all using the same local server, DC01. Setting up a basic Redirected Folders for My Documents is a snap. It's a three-step process:

1. Create a shared folder to store the data.

2. Set the security on the shared folder.

3. Create a new GPO and edit it to contain a policy setting to redirect the Documents/My Documents folder.

To create and share a folder to store redirected Documents/My Documents data, follow these steps:

1. Log onto DC01 as Administrator.

2. From the Desktop, double-click My Computer to open the My Computer folder.

3. Find a place to create a users folder. In this example, we'll use D:\DATA. Once you're inside the D: drive, right-click D:\ and select the Folder command from the New menu, then type **Data** for the name.

 You can substitute any name for Data. Some use DOCS, MYDOCS, or REDIRDOCS. Some administrators like to use hidden shares, such as Data$, MYDOCS$, or MYDOCUMENTS$. This works well, too.

4. Right-click the newly created Data folder, and choose Share, which opens the Properties of the folder, focused on the Sharing tab. Pull down the drop-down menu and select Everyone, and then click Add. Note that Windows Server 2003 and 2008 will default such that the share is Everyone:Read. Click Share and ensure that the share is set so that Everyone has Co-owner permissions, as seen in Figure 10.2 on the top. Keep the rest of the defaults, and click OK. (Note that Co-owner rights are almost the same as the "Full Control" rights of yore.) Note that on Windows Server 2008 R2, the steps are slightly different. You right-click and select Share with ➤ Specific people. Then you specify the person. Finally, you're only given Read or Read/Write access, as seen in Figure 10.2 on the bottom.

FIGURE 10.2 Share the Data folder such that Everyone has Co-owner permissions.

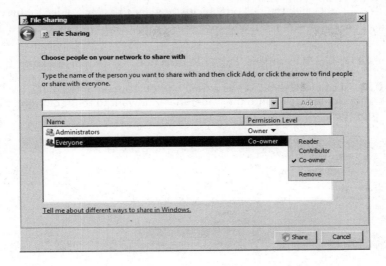

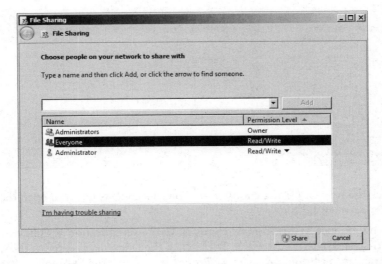

Be sure that the NTFS permissions allow write access for the users you want as well. In other words, both the Share level and NTFS permissions must allow the user to write.

Now that the share is created, we're ready to create a new GPO to do the magic. Again, you'll want to do this on your Windows 7 management station, WIN7MANGEMENT. This machine should have Windows 7 along with the RSAT tools, which contain the updated GPMC.

To set up Redirected Folders for Documents/My Documents, follow these steps:

1. In the GPMC, right-click the OU on which you want to apply Folder Redirection (in my case, the **LikeUsers** OU), and choose "Create a GPO in this domain, and Link it here."

2. Name the GPO, say, "Documents Folder Redirection," as shown in Figure 10.3.

FIGURE 10.3 The LikeUsers OU has a GPO named "Documents Folder Redirection." After drilling down into the folder that you want to redirect, right-click and choose Properties.

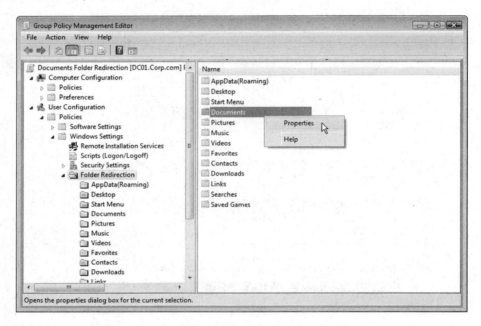

3. Right-click the new GPO, and choose Edit from the context menu to open the Group Policy Management Editor.

4. Drill down to Folder Redirection by choosing User Configuration ➢ Policies ➢ Windows Settings ➢ Folder Redirection. Right-click the Documents entry in the Group Policy Management Editor, and choose Properties to open the Documents Properties dialog box, as shown in Figure 10.4.

5. In the Setting drop-down list box, select "Basic—Redirect everyone's folder to the same location."

Don't click OK (or Apply) yet. There's more to do. If you do click OK or Apply, you're going to get a warning (which we'll talk about in the sidebar "What Happens When You Edit a GPO from an Older GPMC?" later in this chapter).

FIGURE 10.4   The Basic settings redirect all users in the OU to the same location.

The Target Tab

The "Target folder location" drop-down list box has the following four options:

Redirect to the user's home directory   Many companies use home drives for each user and have the users store all their stuff there. To set a home drive for each user, in Active Directory Users and Computers, click the Profile tab for the user and enter a path in the "Home folder" section. The idea behind this setting is that it's an easy way to help users continue to use a drive letter they already know and love, say, H: (for Home directory) in addition to the Documents/My Documents redirection. If you choose this setting, both H: and Documents/My Documents point to exactly the same place—the path you set in the Home folder section in Active Directory Users and Computers. In this book, we didn't set up home drives because Documents/My Documents redirection frees us from the need to do so. This setting is provided here only as a convenience for organizations that want to continue to use home folders. If you plan to eventually get rid of home drives in your company in lieu of just a redirected Documents/My Documents folder, my advice is not to use this setting; instead, use the Redirect to the following location setting (explored shortly). Note this setting is only available when using Documents redirection, and is not available for the other folders.

    If the user has no Home folder, this option is ignored, and the folder stays in its current location.

Share Permissions: Full Control (Co-owner),
Read/Write vs. Change (Contributor)

In the last chapter, we set up a shared folder for our Roaming Profiles. We put Contributor/ Change control on the permissions (for Windows Server 2008) or Read/Write Permissions (Windows Server 2008 R2), and this was enough. Interestingly, here, on the share that will house our Redirected Folders, we need Full Control permissions, or the Folder Redirection will fail.

So, is there a problem using Full Control, or Windows Server 2008's Co-owner rights? Is there a way to exploit an attack on a share with Full Control? Not really, unless the underlying NTFS permissions are open for an attack. Basically, as long as the root folder of the share is an NTFS folder with appropriate permissions, there is no reason to use anything other than Everyone:Full Control, or Windows Server 2008's Co-owner rights, on the share— though there's certainly nothing wrong with Authenticated Users:Full Control (or Windows Server 2008's Co-owner rights), either.

Some people used to insist on using share permissions, but it was often because they instituted the practice in the dark days of OS/2 and Microsoft's LAN Manager and got used to it (and maybe they had the "insecure" FAT file system running). The share permission is simply a security descriptor stored in the Registry entry for the share in the LanManServer entries on the server. Giving Everyone:Full Control (or using Windows Server 2008's Co-owner rights) doesn't change the permissions on the Registry entry itself, so it cannot be used as an exploit for getting a toehold on the server.

The moral of the story: have the correct NTFS permissions under the folder that contains the share. Indeed, share permissions aren't sufficient if someone gets physical access, or near-physical access, to the box—for example, via Terminal Services access.

Create a folder for each user under the root path If you plan to redirect more than just the Documents/My Documents folder (say, the Application Data or Desktop), you might want to select this option. This creates secure subfolders underneath the point you specify. As you can see in Figure 10.4 earlier in this chapter, entering \\DC01\data in the Root Path box shows an example of how all users affected by this policy setting are redirected.

In the example, you can see that Documents for a user Clair will be redirected to her own folder in the Data share. Go ahead and perform this now.

This choice might be good if you don't want to have to remember what the specific environment variables point to.

In our example, we're using DC01, a Domain Controller. You usually wouldn't do this; rather, you'd use a regular run-of-the-mill file server (as a member server, not a Domain Controller). We're doing that here simply for the sake of example.

Redirect to the following location   This option makes sense if you plan to redirect only Documents/My Documents or just one other redirectable folder.

It also makes sense if you want to leverage the maximum flexibility. This selection allows you to specifically dictate where you want the folder placed. That's because you can use environment variables here.

For instance, to use this setting, type \\DC01\data\%*username*% in the Root Path text box. Then, a subfolder for the user is created directly under the Data shared folder. This is the selection to choose when none of the others are to your liking; you have the most flexibility with this option.

 In advanced configurations, you can use this setting to (get this) co-share a Documents/My Documents folder between multiple users. Crazy! But you need to ensure that you set the right ACLs on the folder as well as enable the policy named **Do not check for user ownership of Roaming Profiles**, which is located in Computer Configuration ➤ Policies ➤ Administrative Templates ➤ User Profiles.

Redirect to the local *userprofile* location   With this option, you redirect the folder for the user back to their Local Profile. It's useful when you want to remove redirection for a particular folder without affecting the rest of the other Redirected Folders.

Don't click OK (or Apply) yet. There's more to do. If you do click OK or Apply, you're going to get a warning (which we'll talk about in the sidebar "What Happens When You Edit a GPO from an Older GPMC?").

The Settings Tab

When you click the Settings tab, you have access to additional options for Folder Redirection. The Settings tab is the hidden gem of Folder Redirection; it activates a bit of magic. Figure 10.5 shows the Settings tab for Documents.

By default, users have exclusive NTFS permissions to their directories, and the contents of their Documents/My Documents folders are automatically moved to the new directory. You can change this behavior, if desired, by making the appropriate choices on the Settings tab.

Because we're discussing My Documents (for Windows XP) and Documents (for Windows Vista and later) at this point, we'll dive into the Settings tab specifically for Documents for Windows Vista and later. However, each setting discussed here affects the other potentially Redirected Folders in exactly the same way. Let's take a look at some of the options available on this tab.

FIGURE 10.5 The Settings tab in Folder Redirection holds all sorts of magical powers!

Grant the user exclusive rights to Documents By default, this check box is checked. You're instructing the system to create a secure directory under the redirection. This check box sets NTFS permissions on that directory so that only that user can enter the directory. This keeps prying eyes, even those of nosy administrators, out of people's personal business. If you want to change this setting, uncheck the box.

Deselecting the "Grant the user exclusive rights to Documents" check box sets no additional permissions, nor does it modify the target directory permissions in any way. When the folder gets created, it inherits its parent folder permissions instead of creating its own, exclusive, non-inherited permissions. The NTFS permissions are not modified. Because Windows Server uses NTFS inheritance, newly created folders receive the same permissions as the parent folder.

If this box is checked and you do need to dig into someone's personal directory, you'll have to take ownership of the directory, as described in the previous chapter. Or, if you set it up in advance (using the information in the "How to Grant Administrators Access to *Documents/My Documents* (or Other Redirected Folder*" sidebar), you'll be able to get in whenever you want! (Again, though, you need to set it up in advance.)

Move the contents of Documents to the new location By default, this check box is selected. When you start out creating a managed desktop, Microsoft is betting that the first thing you do is set up Roaming Profiles and then move on to setting up Redirected Folders. In between those two time periods, however, users have surely created their own documents and started putting them in their Documents folder in their Local or Roaming Profile. Enabling this option magically moves (not copies) their documents from their profile (Roaming or Local) to the appointed place on the server the next time they log on.

> If users have bounced from machine to machine and sprinkled data in the local Documents folder, the files in Documents will move them to the redirected location the next time the user logs onto that machine. The only time to worry is when two files have the same name—the latest time-stamped file wins and stays on the server.

Also apply redirection policy to Windows 2000, Windows 2000 Server, Windows XP, and Windows Server 2003 operating systems   This setting gets the prize for greatest number of characters in a dialog box with just one check box. You'll only see this option when you create a GPO using a modern GPMC. You can see this highlighted in Figure 10.5. Here's what happens:

This check box turns on or off what is called (unofficially) "downlevel compatible" Folder Redirection mode. This addition helps bridge the differences between the pre-Vista and Vista and later system profile hierarchies.

If you enable this box (downlevel compatible):

- The target folder name for the Documents folder will automatically be set to My Documents; of course, you can change it to whatever you like.

- The Music and Videos folders will also automatically be redirected to the Follow the Documents folder, which means its target location will be <MyDocPath>\My Music and <MyDocPath>\My Videos. This is because pre-Vista Folder Redirection does not support individual redirection for these two folders.

- The Pictures folder, by default, will be set to follow the Documents folder. But there are some differences: since you can specify different locations in the pre-Vista system, you can do it on Vista and later as well. This means you can still change the Pictures folder to other places (including back to the Local Profile) as well.

If you disable this box (pure Vista and later mode):

- The target folder name will be Documents by default—you can still change it to other names.

- Pictures/Music/Videos will not automatically be placed within Documents as a parent. They remain where they are. You can configure them to redirect to any location you want, and the target folder name is also the new name without the "My" prefix.

The pure Vista and later mode gives the customer more flexibility; if you don't have pre-Vista systems in your environment, then it is better to use this mode.

Policy Removal   You must select one of the two settings under the Policy Removal heading. The point of having OUs is that you can move users easily in and out of them. If the user is moved out of an OU to which this policy applies, the following options help you determine what happens to their Redirected Folder contents:

Leave the folder in the new location when policy is removed If this option is selected and the user is moved out of the OU to which this policy applies, the data stays in the shared folder and directory you specified. This is the default. The user will continue to access the contents of the Redirected Folder. However, there is one potential pitfall when using this option. To get a grip on it, read the Real-World Scenario "Folder Redirection Pitfalls," later in this chapter.

Redirect the folder back to the local userprofile location when policy is removed If this check box is selected and the user moves (or the policy no longer applies), a copy of the data is sent to the profile.

If Roaming Profiles is not set up, a copy of the data is sent to every workstation the user logs onto. If you've set up Roaming Profiles, the data gets pushed back up to the server and shared folder that houses the user's Roaming Profile when the user logs off.

This setting is useful if a user under your jurisdiction moves to another territory. Once this happens, you can eliminate their junk cluttering your servers (as long as you're not the administrator of the target OU). Use this option with care, though; since the user's data isn't anchored to a shared folder, the network traffic will increase when this data roams around the network.

I recommend that you check with the target OU administrator to ensure that some Folder Redirection policy will apply to the user. This eliminates all the "up and back" problems associated with maintaining user data inside regular Roaming Profiles.

Don't click OK (or Apply) yet. There's more to do. If you do click OK or Apply, you're going to get a warning (which we'll talk about in the sidebar "What Happens When You Edit a GPO from an Older GPMC?").

Folder Redirection Pitfalls

Earlier, you learned about the "Leave the folder in the new location when policy is removed" setting when redirecting folders. However, let's work through a quick example—we'll assume that the check box is checked, and a user is being asked to use two machines.

Let's imagine the following scenario:

- There is a user Fred in the Sales OU.

- Fred uses ComputerA.

- There is a GPO linked to the Sales OU that contains a Folder Redirection policy. This policy redirects his Documents folder and has the "Leave the folder in the new location when policy is removed" setting enabled.

Fred logs onto ComputerA, and the Documents folder is redirected to \\server1\share1\ Fred\documents. As expected, Folder Redirection is working fine and dandy.

Now, let's assume Fred gets transferred to another job in Marketing, say, and his account is moved from the Sales OU to the Marketing OU. Let's assume Marketing does not have a Folder Redirection policy for Documents in place.

What happens the next time Fred logs onto ComputerA?

Well, because the GPO doesn't apply to him, the policy for Folder Redirection will be removed. However, the Documents folder is still pointing to the server, and he can see all of his data on the server. Fred clicks his Documents folder and all is well. He sees the files on the server just fine. As far as the user is concerned, nothing "changes" because "Leave the folder in the new location when policy is removed" was selected.

A week later, ComputerA catches fire. Fred gets a brand-new machine, ComputerB, which he has never logged onto before.

When Fred logs onto ComputerB, his Documents folder will be pointing to C:\ users*%username%*\Documents—not the server location as it was on ComputerA.

This makes sense: there isn't a Folder Redirection policy that affects Fred anymore. Remember—he's moved to Marketing, and they don't have a Folder Redirection policy. So, he never got the "signal" to use the server location he once did.

So, when Fred clicks Documents on ComputerB, he sees...nothing. However, Fred still has *rights* to get his files. So, if he wanted access to his files on ComputerB, he would have to navigate to \\server1\share1\%username%\documents via an Explorer window to be able to see his data.

How to Grant Administrators Access to *Documents/My Documents* (or Other Redirected Folders)

As you learned in the last chapter, it's possible to grant administrators access to the folders where users store their Roaming Profiles. In that chapter, you set up a policy setting that affects the client computers; the first time the user jumps on the computer, the file permissions are set so that both the user and the administrator have joint access. However, that's not the case with Redirected Folders.

If you want both the user and the administrator to have joint access to a Redirected Folder such as Documents, you need to perform two major steps:

1. Clear the "Grant the user exclusive rights to Documents" setting (as seen in Figure 10.5).

2. Set security on the subfolder you are sharing that will contain the Redirected Folders.

In the Security Properties dialog box of the folder you shared, select Advanced. Uncheck the "Allow inheritable permissions from parent to propagate to this object" check box. Now, remove the permissions, and then add four groups, assign them permissions, and dictate where those permissions will flow. Here's the breakdown:

Administrators   Full Control, which applies to "This folder, subfolders, and files"

System   Full Control, which applies to "This folder, subfolders, and files"

Creator Owner   Full Control, which applies to "This folder, subfolders, and files"

Authenticated Users   Create Folders/Append Data, Read Permissions, Read Extended Attributes, which apply to "This folder only" (as seen here):

This information is valid for Windows 2003 (and likely works for 2008 servers, but I didn't specifically test). And you can find more details in the Knowledge Base article Q288991. Adding these groups and assigning these permissions appears to remove the automatic synchronization of Redirected Folders, as you'll see a bit later. However, you can restore this functionality with the **Administratively Assigned Offline Files** policy setting—again, we'll explore that later.

But we have a problem. What if you've already set up Redirected Folders, and users already have their own protected subfolders? How do you go back in time and fix the ones that already were created?

It could require a bit of work, but you could take ownership of the files, and then add in the rights for both you and the user to have access to the files. Finally, for good measure, you should use the subinacl command (with the /setowner flag) to grant ownership access of the files back to the user (which will be stripped when you take ownership.)

Advanced Redirected Folders

Anything beyond the basics as previously described isn't required. However, you can set up some advanced options using the Setting drop-down list box, as shown in Figure 10.4 earlier in this chapter. Advanced Redirected Folders works best in two situations, both larger environments:

- A campus with many buildings. You'll want to specify different Redirected Folders locations that are closest to the biggest groups of users.

- More likely, a specific department that is charged with purchasing its own server and storage. In this scenario, there's usually a battle over who can store what data on whose server. With this mechanism, everyone can have his or her own sandbox.

In either case, you can still have an OU that affects many similar users but breaks up where folders are redirected, depending on the users' respective security groups. For example, we have an OU called **Sales** that contains two global security sales groups: East_Sales and West_Sales. Each Sales group needs their folders redirected to the server closest to them, either East_Server or West_Server. First, you'll want to create the shares on both the East_Server and West_Server as directed earlier. For this example, they're each shared out as Data. To perform an Advanced Folder Redirection, follow these steps:

1. Log onto WIN7MANAGEMENT as Administrator (if you haven't already).

2. Start the GPMC.

3. Right-click the OU on which we want to apply Folder Redirection, in this case the **Sales** OU, and select "Create a GPO in the domain, and Link it here."

4. Enter a descriptive name, such as "Advanced Folder Redirection for the **Sales** OU," for the GPO. Select it, and click Edit to open the Group Policy Management Editor.

5. The GPO for the OU appears. Drill down to Folder Redirection by choosing User Configuration ➢ Policies ➢ Windows Settings ➢ Folder Redirection.

6. Right-click the Documents folder in the Group Policy Management Editor, and choose Properties from the context menu to open the Documents Properties dialog box. In

the Setting drop-down list box, select "Advanced—Specify locations for various user groups." The dialog box changes so that you can now use the Add button to add security settings, as shown in Figure 10.6. Click OK.

FIGURE 10.6 Use the Advanced redirection function to choose different locations to move users' data.

7. Click the Add button in the My Documents Properties dialog box to open up the Specify Group and Location dialog box. Click Browse under Security Group Membership, and locate the **East_Sales** global security group.

8. From the "Target folder location" drop-down, choose "Redirect to the following location" and enter the UNC path of the Redirected Folder. In this case, it's **\\east_server\data\\%username%**. Click OK to close the Specify Group and Location dialog box.

9. Repeat steps 7 and 8 for the **West_Sales** global security group.

Don't click OK (or Apply) yet. There's more to do. If you do click OK or Apply, you're going to get a warning (which we'll talk about in the sidebar "What Happens When You Edit a GPO from an Older GPMC?").

When you're finished, you should have both **East_Sales** and **West_Sales** listed.

The next time the user logs on, the settings specified in the Settings tab take effect; by default, a new folder is generated specifically for each user, and the current documents in the user's Documents folder are transported to the new Redirected Folder location. Note that if the user is an inadvertent member of both groups, then the membership of the upper group wins.

What Happens When You Edit a GPO from an Older GPMC?

As I've suggested, you should be using a Windows 7 management machine to do your GPO creation. Why? Because you'll always have the full ability to edit whatever new goodies are in the Group Policy Object Editor.

And for Folder Redirection, this isn't any different. As you saw in Figure 10.3, Windows Vista and later has a lot more folders it can possibly redirect (like Links, Searches, and others listed previously) and some that are more familiar (like Start Menu and Documents).

So, whenever you click OK after editing any Folder Redirection policies on an updated GPMC, you'll always get a warning like this one:

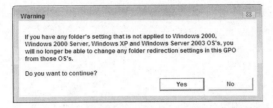

This warning is saying "You're editing this GPO on an updated GPMC. If you edit it on an older GPMC, you're going to be in for a world of hurt."

Indeed, this is true. Take a look at the same GPO when viewed on a Windows Server 2003 GPMC if you had a policy for, say, the Links folder. The GPMC on that older machine doesn't know how to interpret the settings. This makes sense: the updated GPMC has newer settings for Vista and later; older management stations don't know what to do with this information. Sometimes, the GPMC displays only the information it can. For instance, older GPMCs can still sometimes figure out what's going on in the Documents folder when it's redirected—but not always, as you can see here:

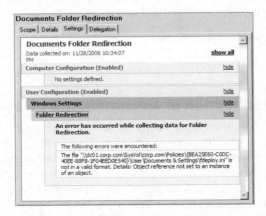

Then, if you decide to try to edit Folder Redirection policies of a GPO you created using an updated GPMC by using an older GPMC, again, it's a world of hurt. Take a look what happens when you try to make a change in, say, My Documents (if this was originally created on an updated GPMC). The system throws an "Access is denied" message—which is pretty elegant, considering the circumstances.

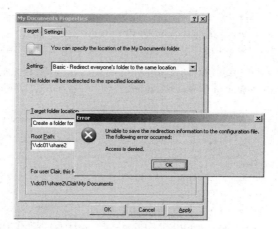

So, the message is clear: create and edit your GPOs using a modern GPMC. Don't create the GPOs using a modern GPMC and then return to the older GPMC.

In case you're interested, here's what's happening under the hood:

The updated GPMC's Folder Redirection routine writes a new file into the GPT called fdeploy1.ini that doesn't overlap with the old one (called fdeploy.ini). However, it does populate fdeploy.ini when you select downward-compatible mode. But you see this message on an older GPMC because the newer GPMC sets the "old" fdeploy.ini file that it creates for downward compatibility as Read-only in the GPT, effectively preventing the older (downlevel) GPEditor from writing to it.

It's a pretty low-tech solution, but it works.

Testing Folder Redirection of *Documents/My Documents*

In the previous chapter, you used Brett Wier's account to verify that Roaming Profiles were working properly. You did this by creating a test file, FILE1.TXT, in the My Documents folder and noting that the file properly roamed with the user when he hopped from machine to machine. Additionally, you noted that the file location was on the local hard drive in his locally cached copy of his Roaming User Profile. To see whether My Documents is being redirected, move Brett's user account into an OU that has the My Documents folder redirected as specified in either the Basic or Advanced Folder Redirection settings.

You will need to log off and back on as Brett to see the changes take effect. Group Policy background refresh (as detailed in Chapter 3) does not apply to Redirected Folders.

I'm going to do something here I haven't done yet. I'll show you the results of folder redirection on all four machines types: Windows 2000, Windows XP, Windows Vista, and Windows 7. Why? Because they're each a little different. And, yes, Windows 2000 is old, but it's good to understand *original* behavior before trying to understand *current* behavior.

Let's first see what happens when we log onto a Windows 2000 machine as Brett Wier and open My Documents. Right-click FILE1.TXT and note its location, as shown here:

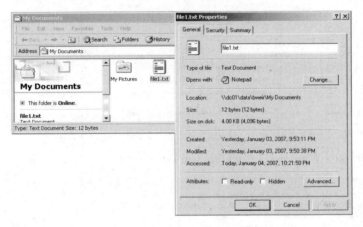

The file was automatically transported from the Roaming Profile and anchored to the fixed point on the server, in this case \\DC01\data\bwier\Documents.

If you perform the same experiment on a Windows XP machine, you'll see this:

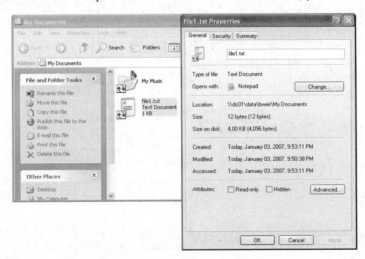

On a Windows Vista machine, you'll see this:

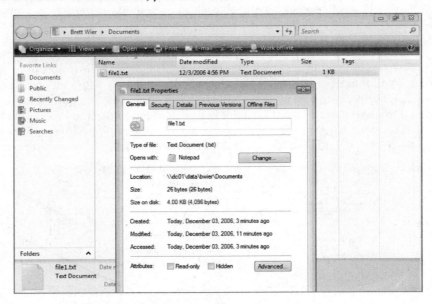

And finally, on a Windows 7 machine, you'll see this:

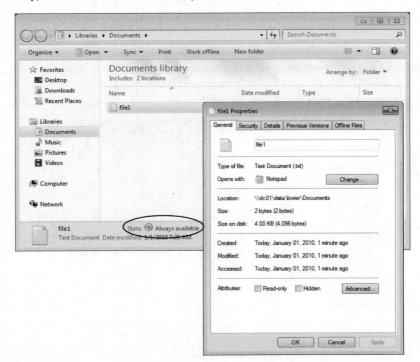

The arrows from Windows XP and later signify that you're one step closer to having a managed desktop: a feature that's already working for you—Offline Files, which I'll talk about in the next major section.

However, one point should be gleaned from these four figures. The behavior of Windows XP and later is different from that of Windows 2000. When a Windows XP or later machine uses a Redirected Folder, the entire contents are automatically cached offline. Thus, when the network is offline, your users still have total access to the files they need.

For now, however, note at least that even between Windows Vista and Windows 7, the UI has changed to show users whether or not Offline Files are engaged, as seen in the Windows 7 figure, circled.

Stay tuned for Offline Files, where we'll discuss how to put this knowledge to good use.

 You will not see the arrows if you performed the procedure in the "How to Grant Administrators Access to Documents/My Documents (or Other Redirected Folders)" sidebar earlier in this chapter. However, you will see these arrows if you follow these instructions in the "Administratively Assigned Offline Files" section later in this chapter.

Redirecting the Start Menu and the Desktop

The Start Menu and Desktop might seem like weird items to redirect. However, in some cases, you might want to.

One case is in a common computing environment—such as a nursing station, library computer, or kiosk—where you want to make sure the same Start Menu and/or Desktop is always presented. Then, you can lock down the target location of the redirected items to ensure that they cannot be changed.

In cases like these, you specify a shared folder with Read-only access for the Security group who will use it and Full Control for just one person who can change the Start Menu or Desktop (such as a fake account that no one uses within that Security group). That way, no one in the affected group can normally change the common Start Menu or Desktop except for the administrative user of the bogus account you created, who has Full Control permissions over the share.

Instead of using the *%username%* variable, you fix the redirection to a specific shared folder and directory, as shown in Figure 10.7. Since all users are to use the same settings, there's no need to use *%username%*. Indeed, because you're locking the shared folder down as Read-only for the Security group, the username is moot.

You could also argue that redirecting the Desktop is good for those who have users who think the Desktop is a perfect dumping ground for big documents. If you redirect the Desktop, you're reducing the size of the Roaming User Profile. It's up to you if you want to explore this option.

FIGURE 10.7   Use one static path to ensure that all Desktops receive the same setting.

You'll find additional Group Policy settings regarding the configuration of the Start Menu in User Configuration ➢ Policies ➢ Administrative Templates ➢ Start Menu & Taskbar.

Redirecting the *Application Data*

Because application designers can decide what to put in the Application Data folder in the profile, an administrator never knows what size this folder could grow to. By redirecting the Application Data folder, files—such as custom dictionaries or databases—can be firmly planted on the server instead of having to go up and back with each logon with the Roaming Profile.

In Windows XP, there are some potential downsides to redirecting Application Data. One potential downside is that this folder contains the user's private PKI (Public Key Infrastructure) keys. If you use Windows XP and redirect this folder to a server, the keys are available to anyone with access to those files on the server. This isn't necessarily a security breach, because the keys are encrypted with a hash of the user's password and other elements, but take special precautions just in case.

The real danger in redirecting Application Data for Windows XP shows up when users need to decrypt Encrypting File System (EFS) files. To do so, they need access to their private PKI keys. If you've redirected Application Data to the server, and the server goes down or the user's computer goes offline, how will users get their keys to decrypt their EFS files?

- Well, in Windows 2000, this was a big problem by default. Remember, Windows 2000 machines don't automatically make Redirected Folders always available offline. So, in the case of Windows 2000, the keys are cached in memory until they are cleared out by reboot.

- If the client is a Windows XP machine, the EFS files are cached offline automatically. The only issue would be if someone turned off offline caching of files. If offline caching is turned off and the `Application Data` is redirected, and the computer is off the network, the user most likely wouldn't be able to access his or her encrypted files.

- In Windows Vista and later, things have changed even further. When you redirect the `Appdata\Roaming` folder, the following folders are not redirected to the server: `Appdata\Roaming\Microsoft\` with subdirectories `Credentials`, `Crypto`, `Protect`, and `System Certificates`. So, previous worries about where the keys are and who has access to them are reduced.

The final note here is that because Microsoft applications use the `Application Data` folder to store their settings data, this folder is heavily accessed (for example, by Outlook). Redirecting the folder, especially if it's not cached, can be painful from a performance perspective. (Note, however, that Windows XP and later should automatically cache this folder when redirected.)

Group Policy Setting for Folder Redirection

There are only a handful of settings that control Folder Redirection. They're located in Computer *and* User Configuration ➤ Policies ➤ Administrative Templates ➤ System ➤ Folder Redirection. If there's a conflict between the User and Computer side, the Computer side will win.

Do Not Automatically Make Redirected Folders Available Offline (User Side Only)

As you're about to discover, Windows XP and later go the extra mile and automatically cache every scrap of data you have in, say, `Documents/My Documents` (or any other Redirected Folder). The idea is that if you're offline, you might need the data on the road. (Don't worry; we'll get to this in excruciating detail soon.)

This setting lets you disable that behavior. You might want to do this if you have laptops that travel to places with slow links because all of the user's data will be downloaded over that slow link. See the section "Using Folder Redirection and Offline Files over Slow Links" later in this chapter.

In versions prior to Windows Vista, this was an Offline Files policy. It is now a Folder Redirection policy. Why the change? There was no Offline Files API prior to Vista, so a feature like Folder Redirection had no way to pin a folder into the CSC cache. Now that Offline Files has an API, Microsoft chose to move this "decision" to pin files over to Folder Redirection. Now, Folder Redirection decides whether or not it should pin the Redirected Folder. It becomes a much cleaner solution under the hood.

Because this policy is a User-side policy, it becomes difficult to implement on a system-wide level.

Use Localized Subfolder Names When Redirecting *Start* and *My Documents* (Both User and Computer)

This setting is one that you might consider using in a multilingual corporate environment. However, it's quirky.

The policy affects only legacy subfolders of My Documents (My Music, My Pictures, and My Videos) and the Start Menu subfolders. This policy *does not* affect the root Documents or Start Menu folders.

It supports the legacy scenario where users may be sharing data between a multilingual Windows Vista and later machine and a localized Windows XP machine. In that scenario, the legacy folder structure is preserved. The subfolders like My Music also map correctly to the localized name on the localized downlevel OS. The supported scenario is only when the user goes across the same languages—that is, Vista (and later) French to XP Localized French (but *not* across languages).

 This policy setting affects only Windows Vista and later.

Troubleshooting Redirected Folders

Occasionally, Folder Redirection doesn't work as it should. Or maybe it does. We'll check out some cases in which it appears not to be working but really is.

Windows XP (and Later) Fast Boot and Folder Redirection

If you see the message in Figure 10.8, you might initially think that Folder Redirection isn't working as it should. This event tells us that by default, Fast Boot is enabled in Windows, and Folder Redirection will not take effect until the next logon.

With the default (that Fast Boot is enabled), Basic Folder Redirection needs two logons to take effect and Advanced Folder Redirection needs three logons to take effect (see Chapter 3 for more information).

Permissions Problems

Be sure that the user has access to the folder; specifically, make sure that the share you use for Folder Redirection is set so Authenticated Users has Full Control. Without it, you might encounter Event ID 101, as shown in Figure 10.9 (left) for Windows XP. Another common Windows XP event for security problems is Event 112: "The security descriptor structure is invalid." Again, the idea is that there are some permissions problems—usually share-level permissions where Authenticated Users weren't set up properly for Full Control (or Co-owner).

FIGURE 10.8   Fast Boot in Windows XP (and later) can delay Folder Redirection until multiple reboots.

You can see a similar error for Windows Vista and later, but with event ID 502, as shown in Figure 10.9 (right).

FIGURE 10.9   Windows XP (left) and Windows 7 (right) require that the user has permissions to write to the share you set up. The event IDs are different, but the results are the same.

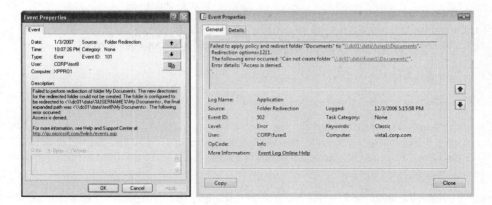

Use *GPResult* for Verification

First, make sure the user is being affected by the GPO you set up that contains your Folder Redirection policy. Use the GPResult tool we explored in Chapter 7. Figure 10.10 shows a snippet from the output of GPResult /R /v on Windows 7 when Folder Redirection is working.

FIGURE 10.10   GPResult can help you determine if Folder Redirection is working.

```
Folder Redirection
-----------------------
    GPO: Documents Folder Redirection
        KeyName:       InstallationType:  basic
            Grant Type:          Exclusive Rights
            Move Type:           Contents of Local Directory moved
            Policy Removal:      Leave folder in existing location
            Redirecting Group:   N/A
            Redirected Path:     \\dc01\data\%USERNAME%\Documents
```

If no Folder Redirection policy displays in the output when you run GPResult /v, chances are the user is not being affected by the policy. Check to see if the user has permissions on the GPO for both Read and Apply Group Policy. If he or she is getting the GPO as indicated via GPResult /v, also make sure that the target server is still available, that the share is still shared, and that the user has rights to write to that share and folder. Last, make sure the user isn't hitting a disk quota on the volume on which the shared folder resides, as this can generate mixed results.

Enabling Advanced Folder Redirection Logging

Folder Redirection can provide a detailed log should the event log and GPResult not turn up what you're looking for. The procedure for this is different for pre-Vista vs. Windows Vista and later machines.

Turning on Advanced Folder Redirection Logging for Pre-Vista

For pre-Vista machines (like Windows XP), you'll modify the Registry, which will create a log file for the Folder Redirection process. To do so, you need to modify the Registry as follows:

HKLM\Software\Microsoft\Windows NT\CurrentVersion\Diagnostics

If the Diagnostics key doesn't exist at the end of this Registry path, you'll need to create it. Then, add a new Reg_DWORD of FdeployDebugLevel and set it to 0f in hex or 15 in decimal.

Once you do this, you can find the log file at:

%windir%\debug\usermode\fdeploy.log

Only the administrator can read the log file, so you have two options. First, you can log off as the user and log back on as the local administrator to read the log file in action. Alternatively, you can use the runas command to view the log as an administrator while you're still logged in as the user.

Turning on Advanced Folder Redirection Logging for Windows 7 Machines

Perform the same steps as the previous section for Windows Vista and later. However, you don't find the log in a file. Just log off and log on, and in the Application log in Event Viewer, look for "Folder Redirection" events.

Offline Files and Synchronization

We've mitigated the amount of traffic our network will have to bear from Roaming Profiles by implementing Redirected Folders—especially for My Documents (for Windows XP) and Documents (for Windows Vista and later). But we still have another hurdle. Now that we're anchoring our users' data to the server, what's to happen if the server goes down? What happens if our network cable is unplugged? What if our top executive is flying at 30,000 feet? How will any of our users get to their data? The answer, in fact, comes from another feature—Offline Files.

The Offline Files feature seeks to make files within shares that are normally accessed online available offline. You can be sitting under a tree, on an airplane, in a submarine—anywhere—and still have your files with you.

Here's a brief overview of the magic: once you enable a particular share to support the function, the client's Offline Files cache maintains files as they're used on the network. If the share is redirected, as we did in the previous section, Windows XP and later will automatically cache all the files within that share. No action or setup needed.

What's the payoff? When users are online and connected to the network, nothing really magical happens. Users continue to write files on the server as normal. However, in addition to the file writes at the server, the file writes additionally get reflected in the local cache too, as a protection to maintain the files in cache. Moreover, reads are satisfied from the client, thus saving bandwidth.

You can use Offline Files for any share you like and practically guarantee that the data users need is with them. Again, as we've noticed, Windows XP and later already seem to do something special when you're using Redirected Folders. That is, when these operating systems notice that a user's folder is redirected, they'll automatically make that data available offline for that folder.

Additionally, it's certainly possible to use Offline Files for public "common" shares. For example, an administrator can set up shares for customer data, and a server can have a "general repository" from which multiple users can access files. We'll see how this works around the bend (especially when two people change the same file). Sounds bad, but it's not crazy-bad.

We'll also explore the differences in Offline Files between Windows XP and the newer cousins, Windows Vista and Windows 7.

So, for these examples, if you want to follow along, create a share called Sales on \\DC01. You wouldn't normally stick shares on your Domain Controller, but for our working example here, it'll be just fine. Additionally, stick 10 text files—salesfile1.txt through salesfile10 .txt—in there, so you can watch the reaction as various flavors of Windows try to touch these files. Finally, map a network drive over to \\DC01\sales from your test machines (Windows XP and, say, Windows 7).

WARNING   There are three shares that you should not place Offline Files on. Don't use Offline Files with the SYSVOL or the NETLOGON share. Nor should you use Offline Files with the Profiles share you created in the last chapter (more on this later).

Making Offline Files Available

When you set up any shared folder on your server, you'll be able to set up the Caching parameters. In Windows Server 2008 and Windows Server 2008 R2, you find the Caching button by clicking over the share, clicking Advanced Sharing, and then clicking the Caching button, as seen in Figure 10.11.

FIGURE 10.11   Four offline settings for caching behaviors are available in Windows Server.

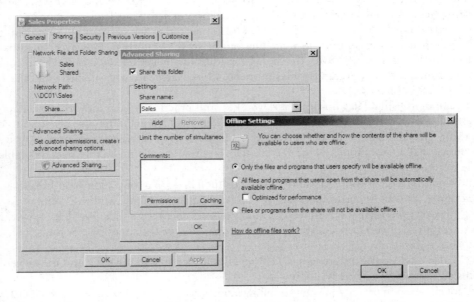

The default setting, "Only the files and programs that users specify will be available online," may not be the most efficient setting for this feature. The four settings are described in the following sections.

Only the Files and Programs that Users Specify Will Be Available Offline

With this setting, users must specify which files they want to keep with them offline. They can do this in the Documents/My Documents folder by right-clicking a file (or, more commonly, a folder) and choosing "Make Available Offline" in Windows XP (see Figure 10.12, top) or

"Always available offline" in Windows Vista and later (see Figure 10.12, bottom) from the context menu. The unofficial term for this is *pinning* a file, but you won't see that term in any official Microsoft documentation. Users can pin as many files as they like; the number of files is limited only by the size of their hard drive (in Windows XP) or, in Windows Vista and later, this can be imposed by a hard "max space" limit via Group Policy (explored a little later).

FIGURE 10.12   Users can pin files by right-clicking them and making them available offline for Windows XP (top) and Windows 7 (bottom).

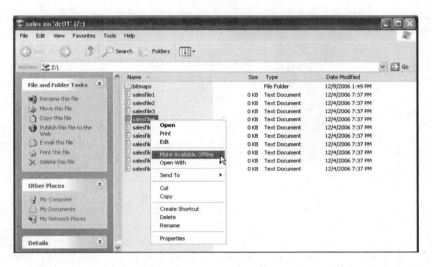

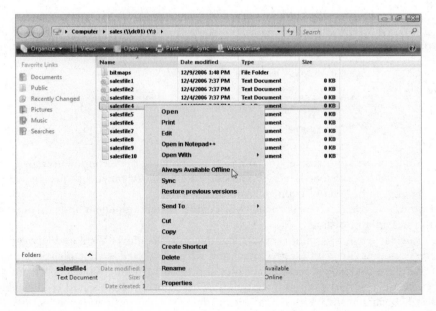

If a Windows XP user chooses to pin individual files manually, the Offline Files Wizard asks some simple questions (see Figure 10.13). This wizard runs only the first time a user pins one or more files, and each user on a computer who pins files from that computer walks through the wizard once. As stated, in Windows Vista and later, the command is slightly different, and there is no wizard. It just does it—short and sweet. (Note, however, that in Windows 7, you need to refresh the folder to see the icons.)

FIGURE 10.13   The Windows XP Offline Files Wizard asks if the user wants to synchronize upon logon and logoff (in Windows XP, usually a pretty good idea).

In pre-Vista, a balloon announces changes in Offline Files cache state, although a user who does not enable reminder balloons will still see the initial state change balloon tips. Once the wizard is finished, the pinned files are automatically brought down into the local cache. Users get a little graphical reminder attached to the pinned file's icon, as shown in Figure 10.14.

FIGURE 10.14   Pinned files can easily be recognized by their yin-yang (left) or "round-trip" (right) icon.

Vista and Windows 7 pinned file | Windows XP's pinned file

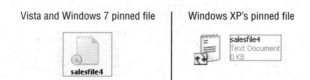

The reminder is an unobtrusive yin-yang icon symbolizing the harmony users will feel knowing their files are safe on the server and cached locally. Or maybe it's just two arrows showing the file can be "round-tripped." You be the judge.

If you want, you can disconnect the network cable to your test client and still access any file that's now available offline.

As you saw earlier in this chapter, users logging onto Windows Vista and later with redirected Documents (or Windows XP machines with redirected My Documents) folder already have these yin-yang icons on their files and folders. Again, Windows XP and later do a little extra magic and guarantee that all files in important Redirected Folders (such as the redirected Documents/My Documents) are available wherever the user roams.

All Files and Programs that Users Open from the Share Will Be Automatically Available Offline

If you plan to use Offline Files for "regular shares" (as opposed to, say, redirected Documents), you might want to select this option. When users access any files in a share with this setting, the files are copied and stored in a local cache on the workstation.

In Windows XP, by default, 10 percent of the C: hard-drive space is used to maintain files in a first in/first out fashion.

For Windows Vista and later, that default is changed to 25 percent of free disk space when the drive cache is first created. This could mean that if you have only a little space left when the drive cache is created, it won't be 25 percent of the drive.

Before turning this on for any share or shares, be sure to read the section "It's Not Offline Files—It's Explorer!" a bit later in this chapter to understand how turning this on could be a potential headache. Additionally, you might not want to go "automatic" and make things more manual. This strategy can be a good thing. I explore this option in the upcoming sidebar "Autocache vs. Administratively Assigned Offline Files" a bit later.

Later in this chapter, in the "Manually Tweaking the Offline Files Interface for Windows 7 Machines" section, you can see this "25 percent of available disk space" formula in action. In Figure 10.33, you'll see that my offline cache size is only 15.2 percent. This number was calculated because it was 25 percent of free disk space at that time.

For example, let's say you're using Windows XP and have a 1GB C: partition. In this case, 100MB of data flows in and out of your cache. Let's also say that you have 11 files, each 10MB in size, named FILE1.DOC through FILE11.DOC. You consecutively click each of them to open them and bring each into the cache. FILE1.DOC through FILE10.DOC are maintained in the cache until such time as FILE11.DOC is read. At that time, since FILE1.DOC was first in the cache, it is also the first to be flushed from the cache to make way for FILE11.DOC.

The files are ejected in a background thread called the CSC Agent. The agent periodically makes a pass over the cache removing autocached files as necessary. If a Write operation grows the cache size beyond the established limit, it doesn't immediately evict the least recently used autocached file. The CSC Agent is only periodically brought into memory for execution.

Additionally, files can be pinned, as they were in the "Only the files and programs that users specify will be available online" option. Pinned files don't count toward the cache percentage in Windows XP, but *do* count toward pinned cache size in Windows Vista and later.

In all cases, though, pinned files are exempt from being flushed from the cache and are protected, and thus "always available" to your users when working offline.

Although it's tempting, do not use Automatic Caching for Documents for the share that houses the Roaming Profiles you set up in Chapter 9. See the next section, "Files or Programs from the Share Will Not Be Available Offline" for the reasons.

Files or Programs from the Share Will Not Be Available Offline

If you choose this option, no files are cached for offline use, nor can they be pinned. This doesn't prevent users from copying the files to any other place they might have access to locally or to another network share they have access to that does have caching enabled.

Another Option: Optimized for Performance

This option's name is highly misleading. The idea is to use this setting for read-only files that you want available offline and in the cache, such as executables. According to Microsoft, this setting does a "version check" instead of creating a handle on the server if the access is read-only. Since there is no server handle, the system tries to use the local version first to save bandwidth when it can use either the locally cached version or the network version.

Upon performing a network trace of the interaction of Optimized for Performance, there seems to be no discernible difference between it and "All files and programs that users open from the share will be automatically available offline." Therefore, use "All files and programs that users open from the share will be automatically available offline" (or Automatic Caching for Documents) whenever possible.

Inside Windows XP Synchronization

Now, we want to spend a little time understanding what's going on in synchronization land. Here, we'll explore Windows XP's synchronization engine. Then, we'll take some time and explore the Windows Vista and later synchronization engine.

Inside the Windows XP Offline Files and Synchronization Manager Interface

Most people would start out by exploring Tools ➢ Folder Options and selecting the Offline Files tab. You can see this in Figures 10.15 and 10.16.

FIGURE 10.15   The Folder Options item on the Tools menu is the first place to start your Offline Files configurations.

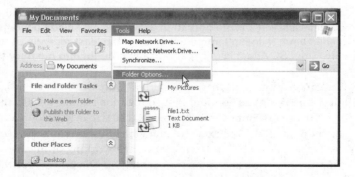

FIGURE 10.16   The default options for Offline Files on a Windows XP Professional machine. Only administrators can change all the options.

Indeed, this is where Offline Files live in Windows XP. But this is only half of where the synchronization magic in Windows XP *occurs*. That's because, in Windows XP, the Offline Files handler is used as a snap-in for a component called the Synchronization Manager. The Synchronization Manager is a framework for plug-ins such as Offline Files to use. The other half of the magic is in the Synchronization Manager itself.

You can open the Synchronization Manager (the Items to Synchronize dialog box, which is shown in Figure 10.17) in two ways:

- From the Desktop, choose Start ➢ All Programs ➢ Accessories ➢ Synchronize.

- In Explorer, choose Tools ➢ Synchronize.

Users can specifically choose which plug-ins they want to use, such as Offline Files or Offline Web Pages, as shown in Figure 10.17. For each plug-in, they can select which data (such as shares) they want the Synchronization Manager to handle. Additionally, the buttons in this dialog box perform the following functions:

Synchronize   Forces the Synchronization Manager to pop into the foreground and start the synchronization process.

Properties   Allows the user to open the Offline Files folder to view the files in the local cache. Same as the View Files button shown earlier in Figure 10.16.

Setup   Allows you to refine how synchronization is controlled. You can see the result in Figure 10.18.

FIGURE 10.17 Users can select specific shares on which to synchronize items.

FIGURE 10.18 The Synchronization Manager is a framework for snap-ins such as Offline Files and Offline Web Pages.

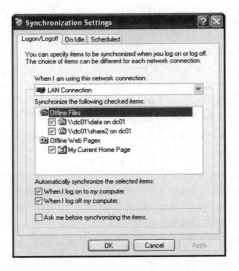

Here, a user can specify which Synchronization Manager snap-ins to use. In this case, the Offline Files snap-in is selected (with two entries), and the Offline Web Pages is also selected. The other entries on the Logon/Logoff tab that need specific attention are the "When I log on to my computer" and "When I log off my computer." These entries co-interact with the Offline Files "Synchronize all offline files when logging on" and "Synchronize all offline files before logging off" as in Figure 10.16 earlier in this chapter. Now, we'll take some time to explore that interaction.

Understanding Offline Files and Synchronization Manager Interaction

Offline Files has two possible synchronization modes: Quick Sync and Full Sync. Here's how each works:

Quick Sync   At logon, the files that were modified in the local client cache are pushed up to the server. At logoff, only the files that the user actually opened on the server are brought down into the local cache.

Full Sync   At logon, *all* the files the user has in cache are synchronized with the copies on the server. Updated files on the server also come down into the cache. Also, if the user is caching an entire folder, those files come down into the cache. At logoff, the same occurs. That is, all the files the user has in cache and any new files on the server are synchronized in the cache.

For Full Sync, we're mainly concerned with the two options: "Synchronize all offline files when logging on" and "Synchronize all offline files before logging off." The key word to focus on in these options is *all*. You can see these settings in Figure 10.16 earlier in this chapter. Checking either of these options (or both) directs the Offline Files handler to utilize the Synchronization Manager to synchronize *all* content.

The Synchronization Manager settings (seen in Figure 10.18) control how the Synchronization Manager responds to the logon and logoff conditions on the computer. If these check boxes are *not* checked, *no* Synchronization Manager activity occurs at the corresponding time. These settings apply equally to all handlers registered with Synchronization Manager—not just the Offline Files handler.

So that's how they work together: the two dialog boxes' settings are interdependent for how Offline Files will synchronize. Indeed, if the corresponding Synchronization Manager setting is *not* enabled, the Offline Files setting has no effect.

Table 10.1 describes the behavior at logon. Table 10.2 describes the behavior at logoff.

TABLE 10.1   Logon Behavior with Synchronization Manager Settings and Offline Files Settings

Synchronization Manager Setting "When I log on to my computer"	Offline Files "Synchronize all offline files when logging on"	Resulting Behavior
Off	Off	No sync activity at logon
Off	On	No sync activity at logon
On	Off	Quick Sync at logon
On	On	Full Sync at logon

TABLE 10.2   Logoff Behavior with Synchronization Manager Settings and Offline Files Settings

Synchronization Manager Setting "When I log off my computer"	Offline Files "Synchronize all offline files before logging off"	Resulting Behavior
Off	Off	No sync activity at logoff
Off	On	No sync activity at logoff
On	Off	Quick Sync at logoff
On	On	Full Sync at logoff

Unfortunately, there is little coordination between the Synchronization Manager and Offline Files user interfaces. However, there is one small interaction: if you enable Offline Files' "Synchronize all offline files when logging on" or "Synchronize all offline files before logging off," Windows automatically enables the corresponding Synchronization Manager setting. The opposite is not true.

People often think there is more coordination between Windows XP's Offline Files and Synchronization Manager than there really is. It's not uncommon for people to think that Synchronization Manager *is* Offline Files. Synchronization Manager is simply a place to host various synchronization plug-ins (such as Offline Files), a place where those plug-ins can display their items, and a place for users to select specific items for synchronization at specific times (and in response to specific events).

Inside Windows 7 File Synchronization

The Windows XP synchronization engine was good, but it could have been better. The Windows Vista and later (like Windows 7) File Synchronization was rewritten in several ways to try to address some of the shortcomings of the Windows XP version.

Better Handling of Downed Shares

If a user was using a Windows XP machine and was leveraging several offline-enabled shares, and one network share went down, XP always thought the whole server went down. So, the upshot was that other shares (that you likely didn't set to be available offline) were then suddenly also not available. Again, that server itself really never went down—just one share on that server. While bad, it doesn't sound *that* bad on first blush. But if you were using a domain-based DFS (Distributed File System), this could be a major problem—especially if you put your redirected My Documents folder in a domain-based DFS. If even one share in the DFS went offline, XP would assume the whole caboodle wasn't available.

In Windows Vista and later, things get smarter. If one share goes down, it doesn't assume (thankfully) that the whole server up and died. It just transitions that one share to offline and keeps trying the other shares. Same with domain-based DFS shares. If you can't access one, it doesn't assume the whole DFS up and died—it will make just the parts that appear offline to be available offline.

For more information on DFS, check out Microsoft's Distributed File System Technology Center at `http://tinyurl.com/9p7uh`.

Better Handling of Synchronization

Synchronizing files gets much smarter in Windows Vista and later. In Windows XP, you had to close *all* your open files (handles, really) in order for synchronization to start. In Vista and later, it's supposed to be "absolutely seamless," to quote a Microsoft person. Since Vista, changes are just synchronized in the background, and the user doesn't notice anything has happened. Of course, a file cannot be synchronized while it is held open for write. All files need to be closed, and then they're automatically synchronized.

Also, modified files, or files currently in conflict, continue to stay offline while all other files and folders are transitioned online. The conflicting files are transitioned online after the conflict is resolved.

No More Logon/Logoff Syncing Files Dialog Boxes

On Windows XP, when you log off your machine, you'll see your files synchronizing (provided "sync at logoff" was turned on). This was often confusing for a new user who had no training about what was going on. In Windows Vista and later, there are no more synchronization dialog boxes during logoff (or logon, for that matter). In fact, there's no more synchronization at logoff. I make note of this in case you have some reliance that absolutely guarantees that your files need to be synchronized at logoff in Windows Vista and later as they were in Windows XP.

Better Transfer Technology

In Windows XP, the following file types cannot be cached:

- `.PST` (Outlook personal folder)
- `.SLM` (Source Library Management file)
- `.MDB` (Access database)
- `.LDB` (Access security)
- `.MDW` (Access workgroup)
- `.MDE` (Access compiled module)
- `.DB?` (everything that has the extension `.DB` plus anything else in the third character, such as `.DBF`, is never included in the cache)

In Windows Vista and later, those limitations are out the window. Not only is there a brand-new algorithm to help determine which files and directories are different, but also this same technology sends over *just the changed data* in a file. So, previous limitations on the types of files are gone. The new technology is called *Bitmap Differential Transfer* (BDT). BDT is so amazing, it keeps track of what *disk pages* of the files have changed. So, if you change 2 bytes in a 2GB file, only that block of data is sent to the server, instead of the whole 2GB.

And, did you catch that Outlook .PST files are no longer unsupported? That is, you can use Offline Files with 2GB .PST files, and Microsoft will support you.

In my opinion, that's worth the price of upgrading past Windows XP right there.

The BDT technology only works (right now) when you change a file on the *client* and want to sync it back to the *server*. This is fine, as this is the usual case. However, should someone work directly on a file on the server (and hence, your file on Windows Vista and later is out of date), sadly, the entire file is pulled down to the client. BDT can't send just the changed bytes.

The other BDT limitation is that it isn't effective on *new* files. All of the new files are synchronized back to the server. And this can be a pitfall, because some applications (like Microsoft Word) insist on creating new files sometimes—even though you're editing what *feels* like the same .DOC file. There is a good blog entry here:

https://blogs.technet.com/filecab/archive/2006/07/11/441131.aspx

---

What's Really Happening in the Background on Windows 7?

The Offline Files service automatically synchronizes files in several scenarios:

- If the user is working online, every five minutes, the service "fills" in any sparsely cached files. This helps reduce the chance of transitioning offline and sparse files becoming unavailable to the user.

- Approximately one minute after user logon, the Offline Files service performs a full two-way synchronization of all content cached by that user. This is essentially the "logon sync" that was prominent in XP.

- Whenever a share transitions from offline to online, the Offline Files service performs a full two-way synchronization of that scope for each logged-on user.

Because of these background activities, the need to sync at logoff is reduced (since Windows XP). Since sync-at-logoff is not officially exposed in either the Offline Files or Sync Center UI, a user must manually sync using Sync Center before logging off if they wish to ensure that they have (in their local cache) all of the latest content from the server(s).

Better User Interface Design and Experience

Windows Vista and later doesn't show a pop-up and tell the client he's now offline. This is good. We don't need to scare the users any more than usual. Because the experience is now "seamless," there's nothing that needs to be said to the user. However, if you select an offline folder (such as the Sales share) and then click on some whitespace within the folder, you'll see a status in the bottom left, as shown in Figure 10.19.

Additionally, users can choose if they want to manually work offline (as also seen in Figure 10.19). A user might choose to do this if the connection to the server is slow or unreliable, or maybe it's an expensive connection or he or she just wants to test the offline experience.

There's no pop-up window at logoff telling users anything about the offline synchronization—because there is no synchronization at logoff. Synchronization is just quietly happening in the background. The downside, as stated earlier, is that Windows Vista and later might not have all the files synchronized when a user logs off if synchronization hasn't recently occurred.

FIGURE 10.19   Windows 7's Offline Files User Interface isn't as "in your face" as Windows XP's.

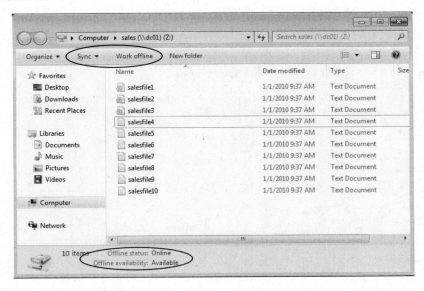

Windows Vista and later also has a new Sync Center (reborn as the next generation of the Sync Manager from Windows XP). It's a complete redesign/rewrite, but it serves the same function. This Sync Center can be found from the Control Panel or by typing **Sync** on the Find bar in Windows 7, as seen in Figure 10.20.

The idea of the Sync Center is that it's a common user interface where all files and devices can get synchronized. So, expect things like handheld devices and other synchronizing things to make their way here. I don't know if this will end up being a nice unified experience or kind of a "catchall" place for anything in Windows and later that synchronizes. You can see the Sync Center in Figure 10.21.

FIGURE 10.20   Finding the Sync Center in Windows 7

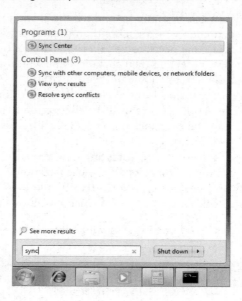

FIGURE 10.21   The new Windows 7 Sync Center

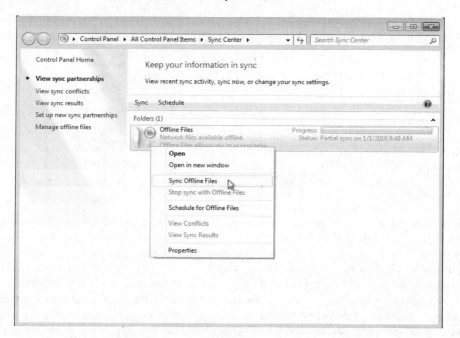

We'll explore more of the options here in the upcoming section "More to Tweak in Windows 7: Offline Files Sync Schedule."

Better Offline Experience (Unified "Namespace" View)

Here's a common problem scenario with Windows XP. Let's assume Xavier chose to make three files out of ten available offline. When Xavier's computer went offline, the three files Xavier chose to keep offline were, of course, still there for Xavier to play with. However, the remaining seven files (which he didn't choose to make available offline) simply—poof!—disappeared. This behavior could be confusing for users who weren't sure what the heck was going on. Windows Vista and later now introduces "ghosting" (which has nothing whatsoever to do with a product by Symantec).

Let's take the same scenario for Seven on her Windows 7 machine. If she chooses to make those files Always Available Offline, as in Figure 10.22, then she gets a different experience. Windows Vista and Windows 7's Offline Files Ghosting will show the seven files "ghosted," as shown in Figure 10.23. Ghosts are namespace holders; they are visually different and are grayed out, plus they have an X icon overlay showing that they're not accessible. The files are on the server, but because they're only on the server, Seven can't access the files until she reconnects and makes them available offline.

FIGURE 10.22   Before Seven goes offline, she pins `salesfile1.txt`, `salesfile2.txt`, and `salesfile3.txt`.

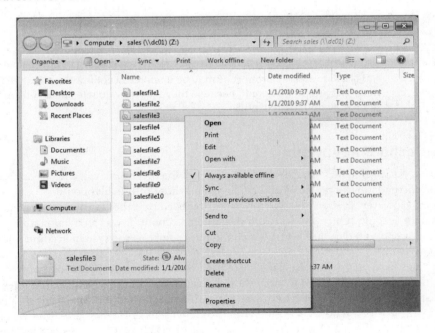

FIGURE 10.23   Files that are not available show a "ghosted" icon with a little "X," and when you select a ghosted file, the bottom status bar changes to show "Offline Availability: Not available."

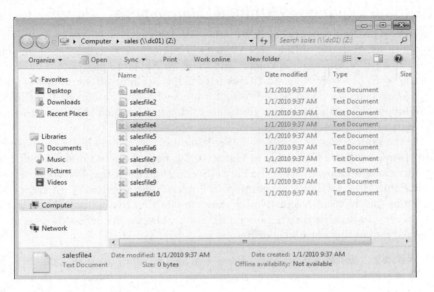

 The "Offline availability" status of "Not available" is an additional cue to the user that the file is not available for use. Note that these "Offline availability" and "Offline status" properties may be enabled as columns in the shell folder view. They're off by default because they take up valuable space, but some users may find them useful.

Better Cache Encryption

In Windows XP, offline files had the ability to be encrypted. This way, if the laptop was stolen and the bad guy rooted around the file system, those offline files couldn't be seen in the clear. However, it wasn't long before it was realized that the encryption was based on the system account. Once you hijacked the system account, it was a trivial matter to see inside this encrypted cache. Just run a command prompt as the system account and—poof!—you're in!

First things first: you should be using some kind of full drive encryption on your machine (like BitLocker for Windows 7) should it get stolen. But there's also an interesting part of offline files—the cache of offline files can be encrypted too. In Windows Vista and later, offline files are now encrypted with the credentials of the first user who wants to encrypt a file. Using the user certificate is more secure (as hacking the system account is trivial), and this has a side benefit where multiple users of the same machine cannot see one another's encrypted cached files. However, this has a negative side detractor. What if Xavier and Seven both have access to an encrypted file on a file server? Actually, this isn't a big deal if both Xavier and Seven are online using different systems. XP and later all have provisions for multiple certificates to be inside a file, allowing both users access to the file.

The problem comes in if Xavier or Seven wants to use that file while offline, and they both use the same Windows 7 laptop. Here's where it gets sticky. If you choose to enable encrypted offline cache in Windows Vista and later, you cannot share the same encrypted file with another user *on the same machine* (when that file transitions to offline). Only the user who initially encrypted the file can access that file when offline. The file is encrypted using only one certificate, and that is the reason why multiple users cannot access them offline.

Again, this isn't a problem when Xavier and Seven are online (and use the same Windows Vista or Windows 7 laptop)—both users can continue to access the server version from the same client and get in using their certificate.

So, you could argue that with full disk encryption (like BitLocker) you wouldn't need to encrypt the offline files cache—and you'd be right. But it's interesting to know this is there as you come across it in the user interface.

Other Random New Goodies for Windows 7

Here's a smattering of additional goodies you get with Offline Files in Windows Vista and later:

- One of the key problems with Windows XP's Offline Files feature was that it was never quite sure whether or not you were using a slow link. That is, if you had connectivity but the connection was slow, Windows XP would still use the file over the network rather than just use the copy it had cached locally. This would get really, really bad if you had lots of files over the network and even just looked at a thumbnail view (in Windows XP). The whole file would be downloaded. In Windows Vista and later, this can change. It's not changed by default, but see the section a little later "Using Folder Redirection and Offline Files over Slow Links."

- Offline Files in Windows Vista and later is much smarter about detecting a slow-link condition—but only if you "explain" to Windows Vista (or Windows 7) what a slow link is; more on this later. And, during a slow link, it will simply transition to working offline. However, a user can, if desired, manually initiate a sync in the Sync Center. Finally, the user may force a transition to online mode if desired.

- You can, if you want, write your own scripts to manage the offline cache. Basically, all Offline Files functionality is scriptable and/or available via APIs. For instance, you could write a script to delete all files in cache, or initiate a sync, and other goodies as you wish. (See the sidebar "Power Admins Rejoice: Scripting Offline Files" a little later). See the note after these bullet points for some additional geeky info about scripting.

- Windows XP had a 2GB maximum Offline Files limit. That limit is gone with Windows Vista and later.

- In case you missed it before, Windows Vista and later machines send only the changed bits back to the server—not the whole file. This is via the Bitmap Differential Transfer

(BDT) protocol. And, this new BDT magic works with (get this) any SMB server share back as far as Windows 2000 server! That's right. You don't need a Windows Server 2008 machine to take advantage of this. Your Windows Vista and later clients do all the magic on their own.

Not to get too geeky, but the script support is implemented as a Windows Management Instrumentation (WMI) provider. You can learn more about the Win32_OfflineFiles class by looking here: http://tinyurl.com/yezar8j.

Roaming Profile Shares and Offline Cache Settings

You should not use any caching with shares for Roaming Profiles. If any caching is enabled for profiles, Roaming Profiles can fail to act normally. Roaming Profiles has its own "internal" caching that is incompatible with Offline Files caching.

The correct choice for Roaming Profile shares is to select "Files or programs from the share will not be available offline" for shares on Windows 2003 and Windows 2008.

The Windows 2003 caching default is to select "Only the files and programs that users specify will be available online." This setting is not ideal, as there might be a way for users to get into the contents of their profile and make portions available offline.

If you did set up a profile share in the last chapter, go back to that share and ensure that the share is set to disallow all caching.

Handling Conflicts

But a potential problem lies in these public "common" shares: what if someone on the road and someone in the office change the same document? In that event, the Windows XP Synchronization Manager or Windows Vista and later Sync Center will handle conflict resolution on behalf of the Offline Files component.

When conflicts occur on a Windows XP machine, a user sees what's shown in Figure 10.24. As you can see, the user can inspect the contents of each version of the file, although that's usually not much help because there's no "compare changes" component to this resolution engine, and there's no way to "merge" the documents. But you can paw through the file yourself if you can remember where the last change was. It's not much, but it's a start.

In general, the Offline Files handler is fairly smart. If a file is renamed on either side (network or local cache), the engine wipes out the other instance of the file (because it thinks it's been deleted) and creates a copy of the new one. Hence, it appears a rename has occurred.

FIGURE 10.24   The Windows XP conflict-resolution engine pops up when there's a conflict. It helps users decide which version of a file they want to keep.

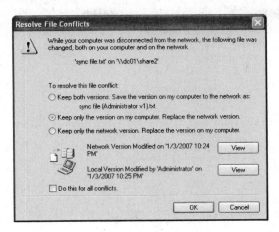

In Windows Vista and later, if a file changes both on the server and on the client, you'll get a message like the one in Figure 10.25 when you start to work online again. Then, a similar conflict-resolution experience can be seen in Figure 10.26, where the user can click the Resolve button. Finally, the user can make a choice of how to deal with the conflict, as you can see in Figure 10.27.

FIGURE 10.25   When Windows Vista or later connects up and recognizes a file has changed on both the server and the client, you'll get this message.

FIGURE 10.26   Use the Sync Center's Resolve button to handle conflicts.

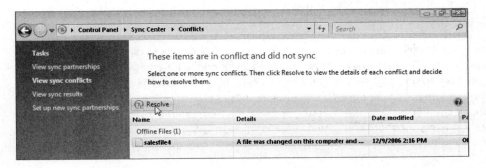

FIGURE 10.27 Windows Vista or later shows you your options to resolve a conflict.

Client Configuration of Offline Files

You might want to default your shares to "All files and programs that users open from the share will be automatically available offline"—also known as Autocache. We're about to explore what happens if you leverage Autocache, but before we dive into it, be sure to read the sidebar "Autocache vs. Administratively Assigned Offline Files."

Autocache vs. Administratively Assigned Offline Files

I've suggested that you simply enable "All files and programs that users open from the share will be automatically available offline" for every share. In retrospect, I think I could have given you better advice.

Here's why.

Once that setting is enabled on a share, *everyone* who connects to this share will auto-cache the files. So, for instance, if you set Autocache on the Sales share, an errant Human Resources person just poking around and opening up that share will start to stream those Sales files into the cache—even if that person doesn't plan on using them. Sure, eventually, those files will be ejected after nonuse, but why get the user into a situation where he's merely looking at a share and then downloading all the junk in it? (Of course, it isn't junk to the Sales guys—but the HR person certainly doesn't care about it much.)

A better approach is to specify that Sales guys need to autocache the Sales share. And you can't do that directly in the share. To do that, you'll need a policy setting named **Administratively Assigned Offline Files**. Now, before I get too far ahead of myself, I will say that enabling this policy setting takes work. That is, every time you create a new share for the Sales guys, you'll have to edit the GPO and specify the additional share. That way, only the Sales guys will autocache the Sales shares. Ditto for HR and other folks around your Active Directory.

So, setting Autocache on all your shares (except the Profiles share) sounds like a good thing—but it's a better thing (if you can keep on top of it) if you hone in on the focus of *who* autocaches *which* shares with **Administratively Assigned Offline Files,** explored a bit later in the text.

If you do decide to use Autocache, you can configure clients to use Offline Files with the aforementioned setting in three ways:

- Take the "do nothing" approach.
- Run around to each client and manually specify settings.
- Use Group Policy (insert fanfare music here).

This section explores the options clients can set on their own computers (or with your assistance). Then, in the later sections, "Using Group Policy to Configure Offline Files (User and Computer Node)" and "Using Group Policy to Configure Offline Files (Exclusive to the Computer Node)," we'll explore the broader scope of GPOs to see what sort of configuration we can do.

Another option is that you can script your changes via the Offline Files WMI provider described earlier. Of course, that only works for Windows Vista and later clients.

The "Do Nothing" Approach

If you do absolutely nothing at all, your clients will start to cache the files for offline use the first time they touch files in a share. This is called autocaching. The underlying Offline Files behavior is the same for all versions of Windows. However, as expected, some subtle differences can be found in each.

Windows Server 2003 and Windows Server 2008 acting as client computers are not enabled to cache files; this feature is specifically disabled in the operating system but can be turned on if desired. See the sidebar "Offline Files for Windows Server."

Keep this difference in mind if you plan to enable caching for your shares to use Offline Files. In the examples in this section, we have a share called Sales, which contains some important files for our Sales users. For this example, again, ensure that the "All files and programs that users open from the share will be automatically available offline" caching option is set on the share on our server.

Windows 2000 Reaction to Enabling Caching on Shares

Wanda is using her Windows 2000 laptop. (Okay, I know she isn't anymore, but just go with me to help with understanding the differences.) She maps a drive to the Sales share (which maps as E:, as shown in Figure 10.28). When she uses Explorer to view the files on E:, she sees one she needs (`customer1.doc`) and double-clicks it to open it (as you can see in the bottom-right window in Figure 10.28). The file is now placed inside the Offline Files cache.

FIGURE 10.28   The files in the Offline Files folder cache are only those that Wanda (on her Windows 2000 laptop) has actually used.

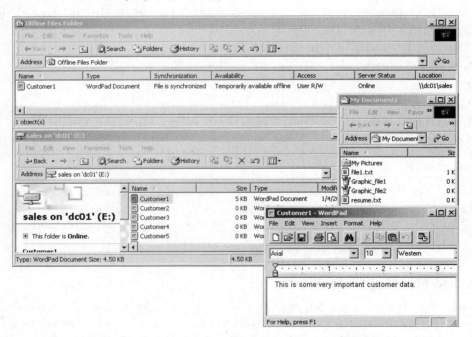

To see which files are within the file cache, Wanda chooses Tools ➢ Folder Options ➢ Offline Files ➢ View Files to open the topmost window in Figure 10.28. I'll discuss selecting View Files next, in the "Windows XP Reaction to Enabling Caching on Shares" section.

Wanda continues, using several documents in her redirected My Documents folder. Only the files she specifically opens will automatically be placed in the cache. She logs off and goes home.

Windows XP Reaction to Enabling Caching on Shares

Wanda's co-worker, Xena, is using a Windows XP laptop to do similar work. She maps a drive to the Sales share (which maps as Z:, as shown in Figure 10.29). When she uses Explorer to view the files on Z:, she sees one she needs (hello1.doc) and double-clicks it to open it. That file is immediately placed inside the Offline Files cache. It is now marked "Temporarily available offline."

FIGURE 10.29 An Offline Files folder in Windows XP shows much more activity than an Offline Files folder on a Windows 2000 machine.

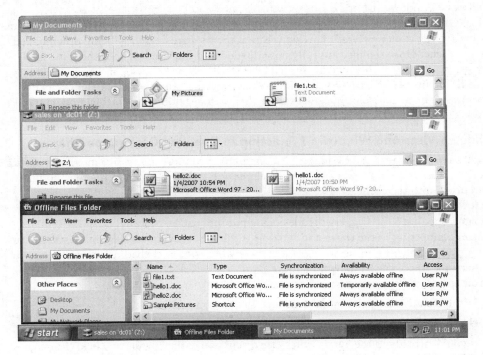

To see which files are in the file cache, Xena chooses Tools ➢ Folder Options ➢ Offline Files ➢ View Files to open the topmost window (in Figure 10.29).

Additionally, as shown earlier in this chapter, any files in redirected My Documents have the yin-yang/round-trip icons. This icon means that any file in a Redirected Folder is guaranteed to always be available offline (that is, pinned). What's interesting is that you can see the same icon demonstrating the file is round-tripped in two places: in a document in My Documents (file1.txt) and also in the Offline Files Folder window. The file will be listed as "Always available offline." The other files within the redirected My Documents are present within the Offline Files Folder window, but are simply not displayed in Figure 10.29 due to space constraints.

When Xena then uses Explorer to open Z: to see the Sales files, she sets into motion a flurry of events that are particular to Windows XP. That is, as soon as Explorer touches the rest of the files in the Sales share, they begin to download and are *automatically placed in the offline cache.* Again, Xena didn't click each of the files in the Sales share; rather, she only opened an Explorer window. This behavior is specific to Windows XP (and not to Windows 2000). The Explorer in Windows XP is different from that in Windows 2000. Specifically, Windows XP Explorer performs an actual "file touch" to retrieve additional information, such as the file's Summary information or, for instance, when it tries to create a mini-view of a graphic. This "file touch" occurs only in Explorer's Thumbnails view in Windows XP, not in List or Details view.

The Offline Files window may occasionally display that a particular file's status is listed as "Local copy is incomplete." This signals that the files are currently being downloaded into the cache. Once the files are fully downloaded and the window refreshed, the field changes to "File is synchronized," as seen next to the file hello1.doc in Figure 10.29.

Additionally, note that Xena can pin any file from the Sales share that she wants to guarantee to be available offline. She's done this with hello2.txt, which is now marked "Always available offline."

Windows Vista and Windows 7 Reaction to Enabling Caching on Shares

Windows Vista is similar to Windows XP (perhaps even more aggressive in what it caches). That's because just about every view in Explorer will trigger a touch to the file and make it zoom down into the cache.

However, Windows 7's Explorer seems to have "calmed down," because it seems now that only opening a file triggers the files being put into cache. Hooray!

After connecting to the share and looking at the files via Explorer (Windows Vista) or opening a specific file (Windows 7), you can see which files it cached. It's more than a little cumbersome to see the list of offline files.

You have three options to see what's happened:

- In the Details view, add in the column "Offline availability."

- On the Start menu, type **Offline** and select "Manage offline files."

- If you're already in the Sync Center (see discussion earlier), you can click "Manage offline files," as seen in Figure 10.21.

 Control Panel also has a search bar. You can type **offline** there and it will take you to the Offline Files Control Panel applet.

Then, you can click through and hit the button "View your offline files." You'll see a screenshot of this a bit later in Figure 10.32.

Then, click through the Mapped Network Drives and find Sales. Tucked away in the far right is a column labeled Offline Availability (though you might have to move around the columns a bit). In Figure 10.30, you can see the Offline Availability column.

FIGURE 10.30   The Windows Vista and later Offline Availability column shows you the status of your files.

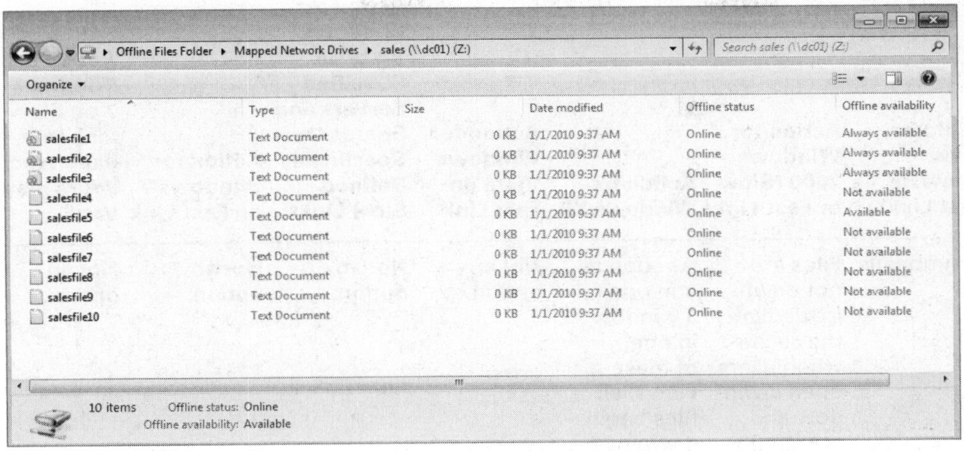

It's Not Offline Files—It's Explorer!

Yep, you just saw different behaviors from different operating systems. What is going on underneath the hood?

As I alluded to, Explorer is to blame as the prime culprit of the different behaviors (or at least the first place you'll want to look). In Windows XP, the Thumbnails view in Explorer is quite rigorous and will try to bring down the whole file (even if it's not opened.) Really, anytime the file is opened for a read, it's put in the cache.

On the surface, you might think this behavior of Windows XP's Explorer's Thumbnails view is a good thing. Sure, it's silently caching files; indeed, how could this be a bad thing? Because if Wanda puts a 100MB file in the Sales share, Xena will be forced to download it. That's bad—especially if Xena comes in over a slow link. We'll explore at a detailed level what happens over a slow link in the "Using Folder Redirection and Offline Files over Slow Links" section coming right up.

Windows Vista is no picnic, either. It doesn't have "thumbnails" but it does have various other modes. And, again, simply looking at a list of files in those modes will bring down the files.

But, for now, Table 10.3 has a sneak preview of what we're going to find. Table 10.3 shows specifically what happens with Windows 2000, Windows XP, Windows Vista, and Windows 7 when Offline Files is used over fast and slow links.

The good news is that Windows 7's Explorer doesn't seem to trigger the download in the same way that all the versions before it did. So merely clicking on the file, or doing a search for the file, doesn't (thankfully) bring all those files down into the Windows 7 cache.

TABLE 10.3 How Windows Explorer Reacts to Caching with Offline Files

Explorer View (Slow or Fast Link)	Action for Windows 2000 (Slow or Fast Link)	Action for Windows XP	Action for Windows Vista on Fast Link	Action for Windows Vista on Specified Servers and Shares Over Specifically Defined Slow Links	Action for Windows 7 on Fast Link	Action of Windows 7 on Slow Link (my experience; yours may vary)
Thumbnails	Files are not downloaded into the cache when users open a window and are simply looking at the files. However, as soon as the file is clicked, it is downloaded into the cache.	As soon as you open a window in one of these views, all files begin downloading into the cache.	Not an option.	Not an option.	Not an option.	Not an option.
Tiles	Not an option.	Files are not downloaded into the cache when a window is open and users are simply looking at the files. However, as soon as the file is clicked, it is downloaded into the cache.	Not an option.	Not an option.	Surprisingly, files are not downloaded into the cache unless specifically opened.	Files are not available unless they are cached.

TABLE 10.3   How Windows Explorer Reacts to Caching with Offline Files *(continued)*

Explorer View (Slow or Fast Link)	Action for Windows 2000 (Slow or Fast Link)	Action for Windows XP	Action for Windows Vista on Fast Link	Action for Windows Vista on Specified Servers and Shares Over Specifically Defined Slow Links	Action for Windows 7 on Fast Link	Action of Windows 7 on Slow Link (my experience; yours may vary)
List	Files are not downloaded into the cache when a window is open and users are simply looking at the files. However, as soon as the file is clicked, it is downloaded into the cache.	Files are not downloaded into the cache when a window is open and users are simply looking at the files. However, as soon as the file is clicked, it is downloaded into the cache.	As soon as you open a window in one of these views, all files begin downloading into the cache.	Files are not downloaded into the cache unless specifically opened.	Files are not downloaded into the cache unless specifically opened.	Files are not available unless they are cached.
Details	Files are not downloaded into the cache when a window is open and users are simply looking at the files. However, as soon as the file is clicked, it is downloaded into the cache.	Files are not downloaded into the cache when a window is open and users are simply looking at the files. However, as soon as the file is clicked, it is downloaded into the cache.	As soon as you open a window in one of these views, all files begin downloading into the cache.	Files are not downloaded into the cache unless specifically opened.	Files are not downloaded into the cache unless specifically opened.	Files are not available unless they are cached.

TABLE 10.3 How Windows Explorer Reacts to Caching with Offline Files *(continued)*

Explorer View (Slow or Fast Link)	Action for Windows 2000 (Slow or Fast Link)	Action for Windows XP	Action for Windows Vista on Fast Link	Action for Windows Vista on Specified Servers and Shares Over Specifically Defined Slow Links	Action for Windows 7 on Fast Link	Action of Windows 7 on Slow Link (my experience; yours may vary)
Large Icons (or Windows Vista+ Extra Large Icons, Large Icons, or Medium Icons)	Files are not downloaded into the cache when a window is open and users are simply looking at the files. However, as soon as the file is clicked, it is downloaded into the cache.	Not an option.	As soon as you open a window in one of these views, all files begin downloading into the cache.	Files are not downloaded into the cache unless specifically opened.	Files are downloaded into the cache when viewed as large or extra large icons. Files are not downloaded into the cache when viewed as medium icons.	Files are not available unless they are cached.
Small Icons	Files are not downloaded into the cache when a window is open and users are simply looking at the files. However, as soon as the file is clicked, it is downloaded into the cache.	Not an option.	As soon as you open a window in one of these views, all files begin downloading into the cache.	Files are not downloaded into the cache unless specifically opened.	Files are not downloaded into the cache unless specifically opened.	Files are not available unless they are cached.

Running Around to Each Client to Tweak Offline Files and the Synchronization Manager

If you wanted to, you could teach your users how to manage Offline Files themselves. (I'll wait a minute or two until the laughter stops.) Okay, maybe not, but if you ever needed to manage a computer that was using Offline Files but not using Group Policy, here's how you'd do it.

Manually Tweaking the Offline Files Interface for Pre-Vista Machines

As you saw, our old friend, Windows XP, has a baseline interaction with the synchronization of files. Optionally, you can manually configure your clients for some additional features of Offline Files and the Synchronization Manager. Earlier, I described the synchronization mechanism of Offline Files as a "plug-in" for the Synchronization Manager. When you want to change the client-side behavior of how Offline Files works, you need to fundamentally understand this concept.

Since Offline Files is one entity and the Synchronization Manager another, they have two separate interfaces. Because they're independent entities, some pieces work independently; however, Offline Files has a plug-in to the Synchronization Manager, so they are also interdependent. To get an idea of how these two components work separately and together, you first need to locate their interfaces and see what goodies each has. You then need to know how they interact.

To manually tweak the Offline Files behavior, you'll need to get to the Offline Files interface. This is different for pre-Vista compared with Windows Vista and later machines.

To tweak the settings for, say, a Windows XP machine, open the My Documents folder, and choose Tools ➢ Folder Options to open the Folder Options dialog box, as seen previously in Figure 10.15. In this case, we're using the My Documents folder, though any Explorer window returns the same results. As stated, 10 percent of the C: drive is configured to hold the cache, as you saw in Figure 10.16.

On the Offline Files tab, click the Enable Offline Files check box to display the other options (as follows), which the user can configure.

Synchronize All Offline Files When Logging On   This setting is available only for Windows XP, and the user can change it. This entry co-interacts with the Synchronization Manager's similar entries, "When I log on to my computer" and "When I log off my computer." I talked more about this in the earlier section, "Understanding Offline Files and Synchronization Manager Interaction."

Synchronize All Offline Files Before Logging Off   The user can change this option. This entry co-interacts with the Synchronization Manager's similar entries, "When I log on to my computer" and "When I log off my computer." I talked more about this in the section, "Understanding Offline Files and Synchronization Manager Interaction."

Display a Reminder Every X Minutes   When this box is selected (and a number is entered), users get a little pop-up balloon explaining that the connection to the machine where the files are stored has been severed. This is another win-lose area. On the one hand, if this option is selected, your users are well informed that the network has gone down. On the other hand, your users are well informed that the network has gone down, and they will probably call you, complaining. (This is because every new dialog box a user encounters automatically means that you need to be called, but I digress.) You can leave this option on or off here or use Group Policy to turn it off (as you'll see a bit later). Figure 10.31 shows a special case for balloon reminders that cannot be turned off. This occurs when the state changes.

FIGURE 10.31   Pop-up balloons inform your users that they have lost connectivity to the network.

Create an Offline Files Shortcut on the Desktop   Enabling this option displays a shortcut on the Desktop, the same as if you were to click the View Files button in the Folder Options dialog box. I'll discuss View Files in a moment.

Encrypt Offline Files to Secure Data   Only administrators of the machine can choose this setting. Administrators everywhere should be running to enable this setting. This is one of the major benefits for putting Windows XP on desktops, and especially on laptops. That is, if the user uses EFS (Encrypting File System), the files stored in the offline cache are also encrypted. In Windows 2000, this was a major security hole. Specifically, if the laptop were stolen, the bad guy wouldn't be able to get to the encrypted data files on the hard drive, except for those still preserved in the Offline Files cache. With just a little know-how, this was a major exploit. Did I mention how major this is? Be sure to select this check box (or use a GPO to ensure the policy setting is delivered to all your Windows XP and Windows 2003 machines). The bad news is that even with this nice plug, an attack is still possible on EFS. See two articles: `http://tinyurl.com/2vdfwm` and `http://tinyurl.com/2v668u`. (Note that these articles may look a little funny because I've linked to their Internet archives, as the original articles are no longer available.) For Windows Vista and later, use BitLocker for whole drive encryption, which, so far, doesn't have any decent attack vectors.

Amount of Disk Space to Use for Temporary Offline Files   This slider goes from 0 percent to 100 percent of your C: drive. The default is 10 percent. Again, only files set up to use "All files and programs that users open from the share will be automatically available offline" use this setting. Files that are manually pinned are not counted toward the percentage specified here; they are always available. You can change this percentage using Group Policy, as you'll see a bit later. Due to a limitation in the way Windows XP was written, a maximum of only 2GB of disk space can be used.

The following three additional option buttons are certain to scare away even the most fearless of end users. You just click each of the following three buttons, which give you more stuff to play with:

Delete Files   This opens up the Confirm File Delete dialog box. Users run in terror when they see the word *Delete*. Because of this, there's a good chance that they won't go poking around here. Indeed, nothing actually gets deleted other than the files in the local cache. Files on the server stay on the server.

Note that if you Ctrl+Shift when clicking Delete, it completely reinitializes the offline cache, which might help with any specific corruption issues on your Windows XP and later machines.

View Files   Clicking this button opens up the Offline Files Folder window and lets you peek into the local cache, as shown in Figures 10.28 and 10.29 earlier in this chapter. Files that are pinned are represented as Always Available Offline. Those that are just in the cache for now are listed as Temporarily Available Offline. This interface is similar to Explorer; it's really Explorer with rose-colored glasses on to make sure that the under-the-hood manipulations of the local cache are properly handled. The local cache is stored in the hidden directory `C:\windows\CSC`. Do not use Explorer or a command prompt to poke around there. The best way to manipulate locally cached files is through the View Files GUI.

This CSC directory is not created until Offline Files are enabled on your Windows XP machine, and Offline Files cannot be enabled without turning off Windows XP's Fast User Switching functionality. However, all of this happens automatically when you join a Windows XP Professional machine to the domain.

Also note that Offline Files are not available for Windows XP Home Edition.

Advanced   This opens up the Offline Files—Advanced Settings dialog box. In this scary dialog box, you can specify what happens if a computer becomes unavailable. You can prevent the user of this workstation from accessing files in the local cache should the corresponding server go down. To be honest, I don't know why on earth you would ever do this, except for some wacky security concern. This is on a per-server, not per-share basis, so be especially careful if this user has many shares on one particular server.

Offline Files for Windows Server

By default, Offline Files is enabled only on the workstation versions of the operating system.

On Windows 2003 servers, you specifically enable it (either via Group Policy or manually, as seen in the section, "Manually Tweaking the Offline Files Interface for Pre-Vista Machines," and in Figure 10.16). The idea is that this function is largely used when mere mortals log on to their Desktop systems—not when administrators log onto servers. However, it can be manually enabled.

If you intend to use Offline Files when logged onto Windows 2003, you must (oddly) disable Remote Desktop. To do so, right-click My Computer and choose Properties from the context menu to open the System Properties dialog box. In the Remote tab, ensure that "Allow users to connect remotely to this computer" is cleared. Of course, this will disable Remote Desktop connections, but it will allow you to utilize Offline Files while logged onto Windows 2003 systems.

Note that this problem between Terminal Services and Offline Files no longer exists since Vista. All of the interlock UI between the two features has been removed.

Offline Files is also disabled on Windows Server 2008 by default, but can be enabled via the Offline Files Control Panel applet. However, you'll also need the Desktop Experience Feature installed using Server Manager. Without the Desktop Experience feature, there is no access to the Sync Center UI.

Manually Tweaking the Offline Files Interface for Windows 7 Machines

Again, if you needed to manually tweak Offline Files for Windows Vista and later (like Windows 7), here's how you'd do it. There's an Offline Settings icon hiding in the Control Panel. There are two ways to find it:

- In "regular" view, click under Network and Internet, then select Offline Files.
- In Classic View, you can see Offline Files just sitting there among the other icons.

Once you've made your selection, you'll note there are four tabs, as seen in Figure 10.32:

General   On the General tab, you can select Disable Offline Files, which, when presented with local administrator credentials, will do just that.

You can also open the Sync Center (previously discussed) or view all the files from all shares that are available offline.

FIGURE 10.32   You can manually turn off Offline Files with local administrator credentials.

Disk Usage   The Disk Usage tab has two main items: changing the disk usage limits and flushing the cache with Delete Temporary Files. This only deletes any unpinned files from the cache. You can see this in Figure 10.33.

FIGURE 10.33   You can use the sliders to manage your hard-disk usage.

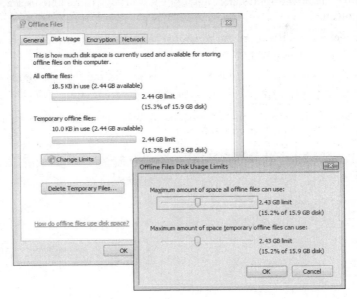

In Windows XP, the space used by pinned files was excluded from the cache-space-usage calculation. This meant a user could pin files until he was out of hard drive space. In Windows Vista and later, both pinned files and automatically cached files must fit neatly into a container size you specify. The first slider (shown in Figure 10.33) is the total space that all offline files will use on this machine (including pinned files). The lower slider is just for automatically cached files. You can use Group Policy to guarantee these numbers via the policy setting Limit disk space used by offline files (for Windows Vista and later only).

Encryption   This tab literally has only two buttons on it: Encrypt and Unencrypt. Here, in the user interface, a user can do this manually. You'll also see later that Offline Files supports a Group Policy setting (Encrypt the Offline Files cache) that causes the cache to become encrypted.

I described this already, but here's the breakdown: when that policy setting is enabled, or the Encrypt button is clicked, the Offline Files service performs the encryption automatically on behalf of the first user who logs on, shortly after he logs on. But what if multiple users use the same Windows Vista and later machine, say, as a traveling laptop?

If User 1 encrypts the redirected Documents folder, everything is hunky-dory for any user on a particular Windows Vista and later machine. So, User 2, User 3, and so on who are on the same machine will have no problems accessing that file. That is, provided the file is network-accessible. But, when the machine is offline, User 1 (the one who encrypted the file cache) will be the only user who can access those Offline Files while offline.

That's a subtle behavior, but it may be important if you share a specific laptop, encrypt the offline files that reside on a public share, and expect everyone to be able to read it when those users are offline.

Network　The Network tab allows you to choose how often you want to verify you're working on a fast or slow connection.

In Figure 10.34 (left) you can see Windows Vista's Network tab. On the right, you can see Windows 7's Network tab.

FIGURE 10.34:　You can see the differences between the Windows Vista (left) and Windows 7 (right) Offline Files Network tabs.

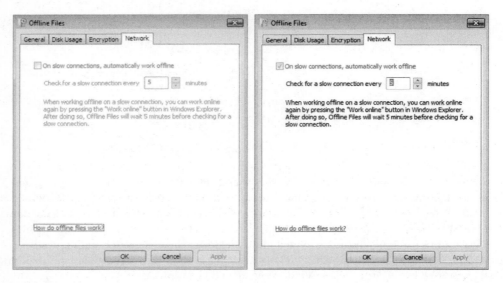

In both cases, you'll see "On slow connections, automatically work offline." And, in both cases, that check box is grayed out. However, on Windows Vista, the checkmark is unchecked, and on Windows 7, the checkmark is checked. And what's weirder is that not even an administrator can modify the setting.

For Windows Vista, this check box in this tab is *only* available when the Windows Vista–specific policy setting Configure slow link mode is set. Once the check box is selected (by the policy being Enabled), the remainder of the controls will be enabled.

One more note here: this setting is a bit irregular. Once the policy setting is Enabled (which enables the controls), *any* user of the client is allowed to change that time value setting. And that time value affects *all* users of the client computer. The rationale is that the setting must be per-machine to correspond with the per-machine cache, but any user of the client should be able to set it.

And because on Windows 7, the checkmark is automatically checked, all Windows 7 users on the same machine can optionally manually change how often the machine looks for a slow connection.

But here's the trick about slow connections: you have to be ridiculously specific to Windows Vista and later machines and explain to it (like to a two-year-old) exactly what servers and what shares and what speeds constitute a slow network connection. Well, a little less so with Windows 7; it uses one parameter, link latency, to determine if a link is slow. Link latency is, more or less, the "round-trip time" it takes for a packet to go back and forth. It's a pretty coarse measurement, which we'll talk about a little later.

So, even though Windows Vista automatically transitions to an offline state on a slow connection, you have to explain just what that slow connection is. That's not really changed with Windows 7, but it does use that one measurement, link latency, to make a snap judgment about the link speed.

The policy setting you'll use to teach both Windows Vista and Windows 7 what defines a slow link is called **Configure slow link mode** (which is a setting in Windows Vista and later). I'm telling you this so you don't get confused with the unfortunately named **Configure Slow link speed** (which is a Windows XP–only setting).

More to Tweak in Windows 7: Offline Files Sync Schedule

Again, the Sync Center is where users can go to see what has synchronized or to manually kick off a synchronization. There are, however, some tweakable features.

I've already expressed how Windows Vista and later positively does not synchronize files at logoff (whereas Windows XP did). However, you can specify some options for the user in order to dictate when Offline Files performs its syncing.

In the Sync Center, click the Schedule button, as seen in Figure 10.35. When you do, you'll be presented with the "Which items do you want to sync on this schedule?" dialog box, also shown in Figure 10.35. The check box called "Sync item name" is intended for selecting All or Nothing, but a minor bug seems to be involved, so clicking anywhere in the list field clears the list selections.

Yes, they just disappear—strange. Anyway, select the partnership and click Next.

Next, you'll be asked "When do you want this sync to begin?" and you can choose "At a scheduled time" or "On an event or action." (This screen isn't shown here in the book.) You can see the options for "At a scheduled time" in Figure 10.36 (with its "More scheduling options" dialog box, also shown). You can see the options for "On an event of action" in Figure 10.37 (with its "More scheduling options" dialog box shown).

Again, these are optional settings for each Windows Vista and later machine. The bad news is that there is currently no direct way to dictate these settings using Group Policy.

FIGURE 10.35   The Windows Vista and later Sync Center has options you can set for each item under Schedule.

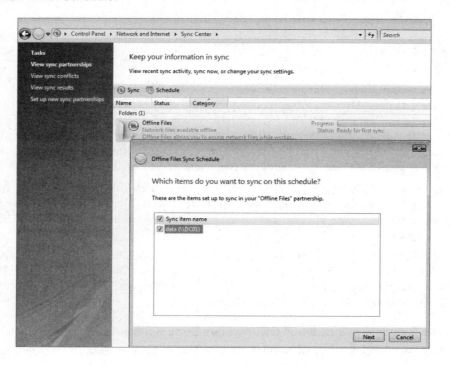

FIGURE 10.36   The time-based schedule synchronization options.

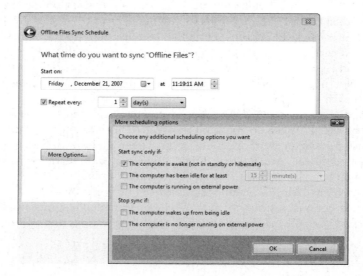

FIGURE 10.37   The action-based schedule synchronization options.

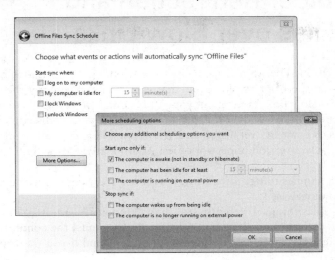

Power Admins Rejoice: Scripting Offline Files

I've got good news and bad news for you admins out there. That is, if you want to do a lot of ultra-geeky command line–only stuff with Offline Files (properly known as Client-Side Caching), there's a great tool.

Good news: the tool is free.

Bad news: the tool only works with Windows XP (not Windows Vista and later yet) and is only available if you call Microsoft PSS.

Did I mention the tool is free? If you call PSS and reference KB article 884739, they'll just mail it to you—no questions asked. Check out all the geeky fun at http://support .microsoft.com/kb/884739.

There likely won't be a Windows Vista and later version of the CSCCMD.EXE command-line tool. And, even if there were, the Offline Files scripting and programming interfaces provide much more flexibility (and capability) than CSCCMD.EXE. Microsoft's goal is to help you move toward using scripts.

Most administrators will want to use the WMI scripting interface found here:

    http://msdn.microsoft.com/en-us/library/cc296091(VS.85).aspx

Note that these programming and scripting interfaces work only for Windows Vista and later.

Using Folder Redirection and Offline Files over Slow Links

In Windows XP, Offline Files thinks a slow link is 64Kbps. Since no analog modem is going to achieve that speed, every old-school dial-up-with-a-modem user theoretically will be coming in over a slow link. How about your VPN connections from hotel rooms? Are those faster than 64Kbps, or slower? It depends on how fast your connection is.

So when XP users come in over a slow link (less than 64Kbps), the system automatically uses their locally cached version of network files. Additionally, files will not sync when users log on.

Windows Vista handles things differently. It assumes every connection to a share is a fast link until told otherwise.

Windows 7 handles things differently still than Windows Vista. It assumes that if the "latency" of a connection is less than 60ms, only *then* must the connection be slow. You'll see how to change these defaults right around the bend if you want to manage users' experiences.

When using Offline Files over a slow link, you need to consider the consequences of, say, a private folder like a redirected Documents/My Documents, as well as a regular share, like our Sales share.

The "normal case" is easy. That is, someone has already been to the main office, received a GPO that says "Use Folder Redirection for your Documents/My Documents folder," and the system automatically creates a copy of the files in the Offline Files cache. Then, when traveling with a Windows XP, Windows Vista, or Windows 7 machine, the computer simply uses the local copy before using the network. Again—that's the super-easy, most-used case for Redirected Folders plus Offline Files.

The hard stuff happens when we are using "regular shares": the not-so-usual case if we use Folder Redirection for stuff *other than* My Documents, the Desktop folder, and the other special folders.

What happens then?

Or, what happens if we just show up in another country over a slow link with a totally new laptop, without any data in our Offline Files cache?

In this section, we cover those hard cases. And the bad news is that you will see different behaviors for Windows 2000, Windows XP, Windows Vista, and Windows 7.

They all have different reactions to slow links with regard to Offline Files.

Now, here's a big ol' warning for this whole "Using Folder Redirection and Offline Files over Slow Links" section. I was able to test some, but not all, configurations between Windows clients and fast and slow–link scenarios. I'm going to describe what should happen, but your experiences may vary. Offline Files does have a (well-earned) reputation for having odd and sometimes unexpected behaviors. My goal here is to document what I know *should* happen, even if it doesn't always happen that way for you.

Synchronizing over Slow Links with Redirected *My Documents*

The first place you can run into trouble is if the user has never synchronized on a particular machine. For example, Charles is a member of the Marketing group. He's given a generic "workgroup" laptop to take to an emergency meeting in China. But Charles doesn't synchronize with the fast LAN before he runs out the door to catch his plane. Of course, he won't have any files while he's on the long flight to China.

But worse, when he gets to China and uses a slow link to dial or VPN, what is going to happen? Will it be a long login time for Charles? What will he see and what won't he see?

It depends on what laptop Charles grabbed before he left for his trip to China:

Windows XP Laptop   The default behavior of Folder Redirection is to not engage Folder Redirection over a slow link (see Chapter 3). So Charles won't see anything in his My Documents folder when in China (over a slow link).

Windows Vista Laptop   Again, Folder Redirection won't "kick in" over a slow link.

Windows 7 Laptop   Same thing. If the link is slow, then no-go for Folder Redirection.

Okay. So it didn't really depend on what laptop Charles grabbed before he ran out of the office. The reason why Charles couldn't see his My Documents is that Group Policy, the engine, won't process Folder Redirection directives when the Group Policy engine learns that the link speed is less than 500Kb. We learned in Chapter 3 about the Group Policy engine and how it won't process many items over a slow link, including Group Policy Software Installation directives, Folder Redirection directives, and others.

Now, what is true, in all cases, is that Charles could just map a network drive over to his Documents/My Documents and grab the files he needed that way. That would totally work, and, hence, Charles is no longer in the cold.

Again, to be super clear, we're talking about a unique case: Charles has a totally new laptop, and he's using it over a slow link for redirected My Documents. Arguably, this doesn't happen that often.

So, what if you wanted Charles to automatically "work" with this weird case, and ensure he is able to get to his redirected Documents/My Documents the very first time?

If you'd like to make redirected Documents a reality over slow links (for users who have never synchronized with the LAN), you'll need to set up a GPO that affects target computers.

You'll set up a GPO that enables the policy under the Computer Configuration ➤ Policies ➤ Administrative Templates ➤ System ➤ Group Policy ➤ **Folder Redirection policy processing** policy setting and, inside, set it to "Allow processing across a slow network connection."

A-ha! So this setting will now tell our Windows XP and later machines, "Go ahead and do that Folder Redirection thing, even over a slow link, even if I have never synchronized before."

So, again, if you don't enable this policy setting, users won't see their files in Documents/My Documents if they use a slow connection.

The only time they would see stuff in Documents/My Documents is if they have already performed a synchronization with the Synchronization Manager before they left for the trip.

Whew. Complicated!

Now, let's assume you had the forethought to enable the Folder Redirection policy processing policy setting and, inside, set it to "Allow processing across a slow network connection."

What happens now when Charles starts up for the first time in China? And what happens if Charles has 1.5GB of stuff in his Documents/My Documents folder? Now, it depends on what laptop he grabbed and how slow the link is.

Windows XP laptop (and link speed greater than 64k)   If the laptop is XP, and the link Charles gets is greater than 64k, the XP machine thinks the link speed is "fast enough." That's right: 64kbps is "fast enough" to be considered fast for XP. And because of that, XP attempts to download and to make every file available offline.

Windows XP laptop (and link speed less than 64k)   Now, Offline Files thinks the speed is "too slow." And Charles won't download all his 1.5GB of files over a slow link. Charles should have access via Folder Redirection to see all the files in the redirected share.

Windows Vista laptop (any link speed—fast or slow)   By default, Windows Vista doesn't know what "slow links" are. So, Vista just believes everything is "fast." Charles downloads his 1.5GB of Documents junk from the server when using a slow connection on a Windows Vista laptop. Note: you could have taught Vista what a slow link was (which you'll learn about in a bit). And this would have been nice, if you had set it up in advance. But you didn't. So, 1.5GB of stuff comes down the pipe, regardless of the link speed.

Windows 7 laptop (regardless of link speed)   Even though Windows 7 is able to detect one slow parameter automatically (latency), it doesn't matter. Upon the first connection to a slow share, all the files come down anyway—even over a slow network. That way, users have 100 percent of their files the first time, even over a slow network. This is by design.

Ow. Do we really want 1.5GB of stuff coming down slow links, or "just fast enough" links? Maybe or maybe not. Again, this all happened because we set Folder Redirection's "Allow processing across a slow network connection."

There's a way to prevent the behavior. If you want to enable a user's access to Folder Redirection (using the "Allow processing across a slow network connection" setting we talked about) but disable the downloading of gigabytes of files for Offline Files, the answer is simple.

In the upcoming section, "Using Group Policy to Configure Offline Files (User and Computer Node)," see the discussion on the policy setting **Do not automatically make redirected folders available offline**, which will return Windows XP and later (like Windows 7) to the older "Windows 2000–style" behavior. That is, redirected folders like Documents/My Documents will be prevented from downloading.

That way, the bandwidth your Windows users utilize when dialing up/VPN-ing in won't get crushed—ever—when using slow connections with Redirected Folders.

Remember, though, that unless the user copies the files he needs locally or manually pins them, the files in Documents will not be available offline.

Now that we've got a grip on how to deal with Folder Redirection and Offline Files for the special folders like Documents/My Documents, let's move on to Folder Redirection and Offline Files for "regular shares."

Synchronizing over Slow Links with Regular Shares

Let's look at another example. Harold, Walter, Xavier, Victoria, and Seven are members of the Sales group.

- Harold stays put in the home office and works on a desktop machine.

- Walter has a Windows 2000 Professional laptop.

- Xavier has a Windows XP laptop.

- Victoria has a Windows Vista laptop.

- Seven has a Windows 7 laptop.

Walter, Xavier, Victoria, and Seven are sometimes in the office and sometimes on the road. When in the home office, all employees plunk files into the share \\east_server\ salesfigures, which is configured to use "All files and programs that users open from the share will be available offline." They all use the Frankfurt.doc file. Both Walter and Xavier normally synchronize their computers every time they log off, grabbing the latest version of Frankfurt.doc. And because Victoria is using Windows Vista, her files are automatically synchronized in the background. Same with Seven on Windows 7.

Walter, Xavier, Victoria, and Seven leave for Frankfurt, Germany, to woo a prospective account. During the time that Walter, Xavier, and Victoria are on the plane, Harold (who's back in the office) modifies the Frankfurt.doc file with up-to-the-minute information on their prospective customer. Walter, Xavier, Victoria, and Seven all get drunk on the plane ride over and sleep the entire way. They don't even crack open their laptops to look at the Frankfurt.doc file. In short, they don't modify their copies on the laptops; only Harold modifies a copy at the home office.

Walter, Xavier, Victoria, and Seven check in to the same hotel (different rooms) and dial up/VPN the home office. They all want to ensure that the latest copy of Frankfurt.doc on the server is downloaded to their laptops to present to their client in the morning.

Windows 2000 Offline Files over Slow Links

When Walter connects, he's coming in over a slow link. Room service arrives just as he connects, and he forgets that he's logged on. An hour passes, and Walter remembers that he's in over an expensive, slow connection! Frantically, Walter disconnects. Even with that hour-long connection, Walter does not receive any updated files via Quick Synchronization. Unfortunately, he will end up looking like a jerk in tomorrow's meeting.

Walter has four choices if he wants to get the latest copy of the file from the server:

- Manually copy the file from the share to a place on his local computer. (How quaint.)

- Right-click the file in the share and pin it with Make Available Offline. The file is now permanently available offline.

- Double-click the file to open it. Then, the synchronization field changes to "Temporarily available offline" (though it should be already), and the Modified field is updated to the current time stamp from the server. The file is then updated in the cache.

- Manually force a synchronization over the slow connection to synchronize any pinned file or file already in the cache, including Frankfurt.doc.

Windows XP Synchronization Manager over Slow Links

Xavier dials the office as well. Room service arrives just as he connects, and, like Walter, he forgets that he's logged on. If Explorer in Windows XP is set up to display files in Thumbnails mode, Explorer is actually opening the files. Because Frankfurt.doc is opened, it naturally makes its way into the cache. You can see this by peering into the Offline Files folder (shown in Figure 10.38); its status is changed to "Local copy is incomplete."

FIGURE 10.38   Compared to Windows 2000, Windows XP's Explorer is more vigorous in actually touching and opening files; hence, they are downloaded into the cache.

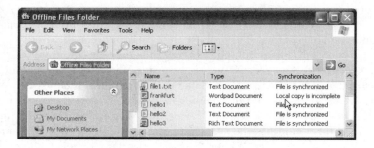

Some time later, the Synchronization column for Frankfurt.doc will change to "File is synchronized." Here's the upshot:

- Files aren't just automatically downloaded because it's Windows XP. They're downloaded because Explorer's Thumbnails view touches the files.

- All other files in the share that Xavier has used will try to update via Quick Synchronization (if Xavier hasn't updated the files himself on his laptop).

- As soon as Xavier uses Explorer to examine the files in the share with Windows XP's Thumbnails view, all the files in the share will try to be downloaded over the slow link. This could be painful.

Xavier's computer is connected over a slow, expensive connection. And now he's downloading the Frankfurt.doc file (small) and any other (potentially very, very large) file that is now on the share. This could be a major problem if Xavier just wants that one file fast. Poor Xavier is after just the Frankfurt.doc file that Harold modified. Xavier has some options while using the slow connection:

- Wait long enough, and Frankfurt.doc will automatically download in the background. Again, this happens because in Windows XP, Explorer opens the file in Thumbnails view.

- If Xavier is using Thumbnails view, then, if he just waits long enough, then all files on the share will synchronize automatically. Again, this happens because in Windows XP, Explorer opens the file in Tiles or Thumbnails view. However, files Xavier might not care about are also being synchronized.

- Double-click the file to open it. The Synchronization column then immediately changes from "Local copy is incomplete" to "File is synchronized."

- Manually copy the file from the share to a place on his local computer.

- Right-click the file in the share and pin it with Make Available Offline.

- Manually synchronize `Frankfurt.doc` and all other files in the share. This spawns the Synchronization Manager to help ensure that Xavier has the latest file and also helps if any conflicts arise.

Windows XP's Synchronization Manager State Transitions

Mobile users access their locally cached versions of files. They then return to the office and dock their systems—without a new logon or logoff. This is called a *state transition*. When a state transition occurs, the system evaluates several criteria to decide if it should keep working offline (using the files in the local cache) or start working online (using the files on the network).

A successful transition to an online state requires the following:

- All offline files in the local cache must be closed.

- The connection must be greater than 64Kbps (by default).

If either of these requirements is not met, the user will still be using the locally cached version of the file—even if the network share is theoretically usable across the network.

Again, if this user wants to use a fast connection instead of the locally cached files, he or she can choose Start ➢ All Programs ➢ Accessories ➢ Synchronize to kick-start the connection, or click the little computer icon in the notification area.

To get the latest files in the share, the user needs to synchronize again by choosing Start ➢ All Programs ➢ Accessories ➢ Synchronize. If the connection is determined to be a fast connection, changed files are automatically added to the cache for recurring synchronization.

Sometimes, an automatic state transition does not function as it should. In this case, users are advised to log off before docking. Once they are docked and network connectivity is established, logging on causes a normal synchronization cycle. Sometimes automatic state transition functions as it should, but a little slower than expected. Don't forget that Microsoft Office isn't the only application that can keep files open. Other day-to-day productivity applications you deploy for users can keep files open, and, hence, a state transition does not occur.

Moving the Client-Side Cache for Windows XP and Windows 7

You might find a reason to change the original placement of the CSC folder. For instance, you might have some PCs with two (or more) physical hard drives. Perhaps you're running out of space on the C: drive, or maybe you just want to tune a machine's performance by splitting the duties over two hard drives.

You can use the Cachemov.exe utility in the Windows Resource Kit. Simply run Cachemov.exe on the workstation that has multiple hard drives. When you are done, you have a choice as to where to move the C:\%windir%\CSC, as shown here:

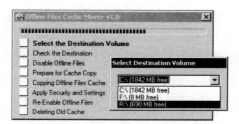

You can also use Cachemov.exe to execute batch-style in a logon script. If you want to affect multiple computers, you can run Cachemov.exe –unattend d:\, in which d is the drive to which the new CSC folder will move. Cchmvmsg.dll needs to be in the path when running Cachemov.exe in unattended mode. This tool is not available in the Windows Server 2003 Resource Kit but seems to work fine with Windows XP. Use at your own risk.

Cachemov.exe won't work on Windows Vista and later. There is a procedure to move the cache for Windows Vista. You can check out KB article 942960 at http://tinyurl.com/yl7orzy. This might work on Windows 7, too, but I haven't tested it out.

Windows Vista's Synchronization Engine over Slow Links

Victoria dials up just like Walter and Xavier. Will Frankfurt.doc automatically come down over the slow link (and the other potentially large files in the share)? By default, yes, if she looks at the share in any view that "touches the files." (See Table 10.3 earlier.)

But here's the weird part about Windows Vista (and Windows 7, for that matter). It's got the built-in intelligence to understand and recognize a slow link. But, by default, Windows Vista will simply act like Windows XP and bring down every stinkin' file you look at (even with a File List view in Explorer) over a slow link.

Ouch.

The good news is that you can control this. You simply have to tell Windows Vista which shares you want to throttle. The goal is to tell your Windows Vista clients which servers and shares should be cached over a slow link.

Windows 7's Synchronization Engine over Slow Links

Seven dials up just like Walter, Xavier, and Victoria. Will `Frankfurt.doc` (and the other potentially large files in the share) automatically come down over the slow link?

The answer is maybe. But, under most normal circumstances, the answer is no.

If Seven looks at the share in Large or Extra Large icon view, then, yes, she's officially "touched the files" and it comes down. If Seven looks at the share in List or Small Icon view, then Windows 7's Explorer doesn't seem to officially "touch" the file to bring it down.

Why does Windows 7 have more brains than Windows Vista? It has two additional things going for it, whereas Windows Vista would fall down:

- Windows 7's Explorer is less intense about when it pulls down a file. See Table 10.3. Again, only when viewing files with Large or Extra Large icon views is that considered a "touch."

- Windows 7 actually has the same "basic smarts" about slow links that Windows Vista has. But Windows 7 has those smarts turned *on*, while Windows Vista's smarts are turned *off* by default.

Now, it is possible that Windows 7 could make a "snap judgment" call and say, "Actually, pal, the link *is* fast. Even though *you* think it's slow, *I* can tell the link is really fast."

So, what does Windows 7 "know" that Windows Vista doesn't know? Windows 7 checks out the "latency speed" of the line. Latency is, more or less, the round-trip time that a ping packet takes. If that round-trip speed is 60ms or less, the link is considered "fast." If it's 60ms or more, then it's considered "slow."

Latency is kind of a weird measurement to bank on, though. Technically, your link could be 30Kbps (half the speed of a dial-up modem), but the latency could be super-zippy. Windows 7 will then cheerfully interpret that type of connection as a "fast connection" and download all the files. Not so smart after all. But you can teach them (both Windows Vista and Windows 7).

Meanwhile, Windows 7 has another trick up its sleeve.

When a link is determined to be "slow" (we'll talk about how to change the definition of what "slow" means next), the share will transition to be "offline." However, unlike Windows Vista, Windows 7 will still try to synchronize the data in the background—every 360 minutes (with a 0–60 minute random offset).

The share transitions to "offline" because you're saying, "Look, User, if you try to grab huge files from my dog-slow network, it's going to hurt everyone. So, I'll just turn that share 'off' to you, until you're on a fast connection again."

But what happens if a user then makes changes to the local version of the file (say, she gets 10 new emails in a big PST file)? Well then, you'll want to make sure that those changes (and only those changes) are delivered to the server for safekeeping (and merged with the original file).

So, Windows 7 has this superpower. It will automatically sync up all the new stuff in the background every 360 minutes or so—even over a slow link. That way, users won't auto-download big new files from the "offline" share, but they will auto-upload any small changes from the documents they already have in their cache.

This new Windows 7 behavior is configurable via Group Policy using the **Configure Background Sync** policy setting, as you'll see in the next section.

You may be asking yourself, "What if a user needs to get to a new (big) file on a share? Can he do that, even though the share now appears to be offline?" Yes. I'll show you how to do that in a second with the "Work Offline/Work Online" button (available on both Windows Vista and Windows 7).

Teaching Windows Vista and Windows 7 How to React to Slow Links

Let's recap:

- Windows Vista thinks all links are fast until you teach it otherwise.

- Windows 7 thinks that all links are fast unless the link's latency is less than 60ms.

These facts of life are not ideal. You might want some shares on certain servers to act as "fast"—always—and yet other shares on specific servers, as "slow"—always. Or some shares to act as fast under certain conditions and slow under other conditions.

You need to teach your Windows Vista and Windows 7 machines four things:

- The name of the server with the share(s)

- The name of the share(s)

- What constitutes a slow link (speed)

- What constitutes slow latency (round-trip time for ping)

Once your Windows Vista or Windows 7 client "gets" this, it starts being *much* smarter about not downloading humongous files over slow links (as Windows XP would).

You do this with the **Configure slow-link mode** policy setting located in Computer Configuration ➢ Policies ➢ Administrative Templates ➢ Network ➢ Offline Files, as seen in Figure 10.39. Figure 10.40 shows an example of how to precisely set up one server's characteristics; you can see \\server1 and share1 being set to a slow link speed of 600Kbps and Latency of 50ms.

So, when should you use throughput or latency thresholds?

Well, this policy can be set to use *either* throughput *and/or* latency thresholds. So, you can decide to use throughput, latency, or both.

What should you use? Throughput, latency, or both? The short answer is: both. In our example, Victoria wasn't pushing anything up to the server. She merely viewed the share, and—*blammo!*—tons of stuff she wasn't really interested in came streaming down the slow link. Likewise, Seven on Windows 7 could have a dog-slow link but peppy latency. Again, Windows 7 (unfortunately) sees that as "A-OK" and *blammo!* again (if, say, she used Large Icons to view the files).

FIGURE 10.39   The Settings description doesn't express this, but you can specify a single lone * (asterisk) to turn on slow-link mode for all shares on all servers.

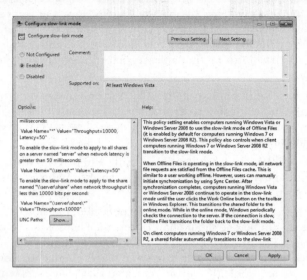

FIGURE 10.40   Specify Throughput = 600000 for 600Kbps and Latency = 50 for 50ms, for instance, to define your slow link threshold. Note, all paths should have an ending slash (\) and asterisk (*) even if you're just specifying one server and one share.

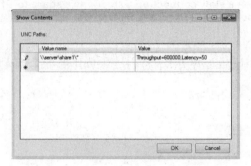

So, can either Victoria or Seven at least get to the Frankfurt.doc file? I'm afraid to say the answer is maybe. During my testing, here's what I found (your mileage, as well as Victoria's and Seven's mileage, may vary):

- If Victoria was really connected to a \\server\share (that is, a specific server and a share on that server) and used a slow link (but was still connected, nonetheless), in my testing, I found that she sometimes had access to the file, and sometimes she was blocked from getting the file. This is because the file was changed on the server. Since the share had transitioned to Offline, and I didn't have an up-to-date copy of the file, she couldn't access the changed file.

- If Victoria really wants to get that file, she can click a special UI feature in Explorer labeled "Work Online" for that particular share. That's right. Victoria can override Windows Vista and just say "Hey, I know the share is slow, and you've taken it offline. I get that. But I need my stuff. Make it so I can *Work Online.*" Of course, the bad news is that all the goo on the share she doesn't particularly care about will come streaming down (slowly) over that slow link. But at least Victoria can get access to the file she needs, right now.

- Seven gets the same "Work Online" ability that Victoria has, except the news is better. If she clicks Work Online for that particular share, then only files she touches (or files she views using Explorer's Large or Extra Large icon view) will come down. This is better than Windows Vista.

- If, however, a user like Victoria or Seven was really 100 percent offline (e.g., Victoria never got a chance to dial in back to the office), then she retains the last known copy of the file in cache (as might be expected).

So, the takeaway is that if a user like Victoria is connected, but slowly, she might not get access to the files she thinks she should have access to. That's going to be a tough one to explain to your users, I think. So, you may want to plan to show them how to transition shares to Online status if you choose to declare some shares eligible for slow-link status. In Figure 10.41, you can see where the button is located that your users will need to learn to click. You can also see some files "ghosted" (with the little "X" indicator) because they aren't in the cache (and, hence, not available for use) and those files that are available for use (not ghosted).

FIGURE 10.41 When a slow connection transitions a share to Offline, only files already in the cache are accessible. To access files on the server over a slow link, select "Work online."

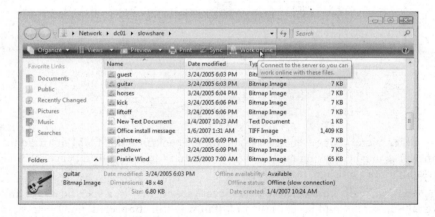

So, to use this policy setting, you add additional items for each server and share combination you needed to define individually. Or, you can also perform this operation en masse based on specific servers or, heck, have all Windows Vista and later clients react to all servers the same way.

Table 10.4 gives you some examples of values you might want to specify using the **Configure slow-link mode** policy setting when entering in the "Enter the name of the item to be added" block and the "Enter the value of the item to be added" block, and what the result would be if you used these suggestions.

Once you're done, Windows Vista clients will only download files into cache when files are actually opened up. This will speed up their normal day-to-day connection because they're not downloading files into cache that they don't need.

Now, again, Windows 7 clients have a little something special going on at this point. When a share goes slow, then is taken "offline," Windows 7 will still try to synchronize the data in the background—every 360 minutes (with a 0–60 minute random offset.)

To recap, the idea is a good one. If you made changes to the local version of the data (say, a PST, database file, or even just a Word doc), you'll want to make sure that those changes (and just those changes) make it up to the server for safekeeping. So, Windows 7 automatically syncs the changed bits in the background every 360 minutes or so. This is configurable via Group Policy, as you'll learn in the next section.

 None of the **Configure slow-link mode** values require quotes, which can be confusing if you read the Explain text in the policy setting.

TABLE 10.4   Configure Slow-Link Mode Policy Setting Examples

The "Enter the name of the item to be added" Block	The "Enter the value of the item to be added" Block	Result of These Settings
\\server1\share1*	Throughput = 600000, Latency = 50	Only \\server1\share1 would react for Windows Vista+ clients affected by this policy setting. The share will automatically transition to offline if the speed is less than 600Kbps or the latency is less than 50ms.
\\server1*	Throughput = 128000	All shares on \\server1 would react for Windows Vista+ clients affected by this policy setting. The share will automatically transition to offline if the speed is less than 128Kbps. Note that Windows Vista+ clients affected by this policy would not test for latency.

TABLE 10.4   Configure Slow-Link Mode Policy Setting Examples *(continued)*

The "Enter the name of the item to be added" Block	The "Enter the value of the item to be added" Block	Result of These Settings
**	Throughput = 400000, Latency = 20	All shares on all servers would react for Windows Vista+ clients affected by this policy setting. All shares would automatically transition to offline if the speed were less than 400Kbps or the latency were less than 20ms. Note the trailing star (*) at the end of the expression to signify all shares.
**	Latency = 30	All shares on all servers would react for Windows Vista+ clients affected by this policy setting. All shares would automatically transition to offline if the latency were 30ms. Note the trailing star (*) at the end of the expression to signify all shares.

A good blog entry on the **Configure slow-link mode** policy setting can be found at http://tinyurl.com/ydoekex.

Using Group Policy to Configure Offline Files (User and Computer Node)

Asking users to configure their own Offline Files settings can be—to say the least—confusing. This isn't the fault of Microsoft—there are just a lot of options to play with. The good news is that most Offline Files settings can be delivered from up on high.

The policy settings for the Offline Files are found in two places in the Group Policy Management Editor. Some settings affect users specifically. To get to those settings, fire up the Group Policy Management Editor and traverse to Computer Configuration ➢ Policies ➢ Administrative Templates ➢ Network ➢ Offline Files, as shown in Figure 10.42.

Nearly all the same settings are also found in the User side of the house, at User Configuration ➢ Policies ➢ Administrative Templates ➢ Network ➢ Offline Files, as shown in Figure 10.43.

FIGURE 10.42   You'll find a slew of Offline Files options under the Computer node.

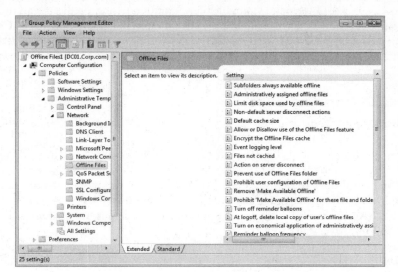

 There are no policy settings for the Windows XP Synchronization Manager or the Windows Vista and later Sync Center.

These settings give you flexibility in how you configure Offline Files. You can mix and match—within the same GPO or from multiple GPOs. The general rule is that if both computer and user settings are specified on the target, the computer wins.

FIGURE 10.43   Many Offline Files options can also be found under the User node.

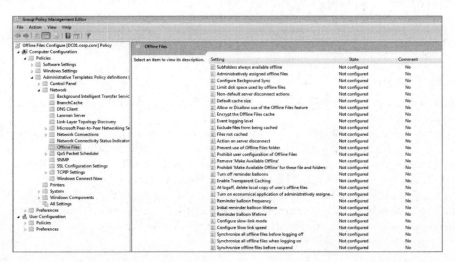

In this section, I'll briefly detail what each Offline Files policy setting does. Since most of the policies overlap in both User and Computer configuration nodes, I'll discuss all the User and Computer configuration settings and then focus on those that apply only to the Computer configuration settings.

Note that I will be discussing them in a slightly different order than what's shown in Figure 10.43.

Configure Background Sync

Configure Background Sync is a new policy for Windows 7 (or Windows Server 2008 R2) clients.

This policy setting picks up where we left off in the last section, "Teaching Windows Vista and Windows 7 How to React to Slow Links."

Again, Windows 7 does something under the hood that Windows Vista didn't do. By default, Windows 7 will synchronize any link, even if Windows 7 has determined the link is a "slow link." And the idea is that you'll want to keep local files updated with the server, even on a slow link, "every so often."

Although it's true that most of the time, the changes will originate from the laptop and need to be saved to the server, there are also going to be times when the data on the server has changed and it needs to update the laptop. Background Synchronization is indeed a two-way sync.

Remember: when changes go up to the server, they're quick, because only the changed blocks are uploaded. However, changes from the server *down* to the laptop could be slower, because in those cases, the whole file needs to come down.

This process happens every 360 minutes, by default, with a random offset of 0–60 minutes. You can change the definitions using this policy setting.

Additionally, there's an (almost secret) check box in this policy setting: "Enable Background Sync for shares in user selected 'Work Offline' mode," as seen in Figure 10.44. This setting also ensures that when users manually flip a share to "Offline" (see Figure 10.41), those shares are *also* synchronizing changed data as well.

Using this policy setting is likely a good idea for most environments, but it's your call.

Note that every user on a Windows 7 machine is affected by this policy setting, because it affects the Computer side.

Enable Transparent Caching

Another new policy for Windows 7 (and Windows Server 2008 R2) clients is **Enable Transparent Caching**.

This policy is another Windows 7 optimization, but it must be enabled for it to work. In short, if you enable the **Enable Transparent Caching** policy setting, Windows 7 will create a local cache of files that users use often. If the link is slow, it will not use the slow network to read the file the user wants, but instead use the local, secret copy it created.

In a way, this is kind of like Offline Files for files that you haven't specifically specified be available temporarily (via share settings) or permanently available online (via pinning a file).

This policy is a nice catchall for all sorts of file types, and I cannot see a good reason not to have it enabled at all times.

FIGURE 10.44 Use this policy setting to configure Windows 7's slow-link background sync.

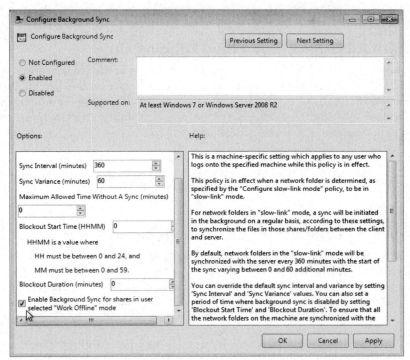

Once again, this policy setting uses network latency as the speed verification—which could be a pitfall. Again, you can have very low speeds but perfectly decent network latency, so you may want to test this out.

Note that the value appears to be requested in milliseconds, like "60" for 60 milliseconds. But when you go to enable this policy setting, it defaults to 32,000 milliseconds (32 seconds), which is the maximum possible time to wait before giving up. This behavior is just a bug in the UI of the policy setting. Just put in the number of milliseconds that's appropriate.

A little side note: my friends on the Offline Files team at Microsoft wanted me to tell you that their ideal value for this setting has tested out to be 35ms for most networks.

I was unable to test this setting in the writing of this book, so use at your own risk.

Prohibit User Configuration of Offline Files

If the **Prohibit user configuration of Offline Files** policy setting is enabled, users on the target client computer embrace the default Offline Files settings and won't be able to change them. Indeed, this happens by the forceful removal of the Offline Files tab normally found in the Folder Options dialog box, as you saw in Figure 10.16 earlier in this chapter.

This policy setting does not apply to Windows Vista and later machines.

Synchronize All Offline Files When Logging On

Enabling **Synchronize all offline files when logging on** grays out the "Synchronize all offline when logging on" check box in the Offline Files tab in the Folder Options dialog box (as seen in Figure 10.16) on the target machine, so the user can't change it. Be sure to read the section, "Understanding Offline Files and Synchronization Manager Interaction," earlier in this chapter to understand how this setting works.

 This policy setting does not apply to Windows Vista and later machines.

Synchronize All Offline Files Before Logging Off

Enabling **Synchronize all offline files before logging off** grays out the "Synchronize All Offline Files before Logging Off" check box in the Offline Files tab in the Folder Options dialog box (as seen in Figure 10.16) on the target machine, so the user can't change it. Again, the earlier section "Understanding Offline Files and Synchronization Manager Interaction" helps you understand how this setting works.

 This policy setting does not apply to Windows Vista and later machines.

Synchronize Offline Files Before Suspend

Enabling the **Synchronize offline files before suspend** setting ensures that a full synchronization occurs before the user suspends or hibernates the machine (which usually means the user will undock it or otherwise take it offline). The operating system must know about the change, and this will not work if you just close the lid on a laptop.

 This policy setting does not apply to Windows Vista and later machines.

Action on Server Disconnect

If the policy setting **Action on server disconnect** is enabled, you can select one of two options from the Action drop-down list box. This is analogous to the Advanced dialog box mentioned earlier in the section, "Manually Tweaking the Offline Files Interface for Pre-Vista Machines."

In a nutshell, you can allow normal operation of Offline Files or cease the use of Offline Files if the server goes offline. Again, avoid using this function, as it essentially defeats the whole purpose of Offline Files.

 This policy setting does not apply to Windows Vista and later machines.

Non-default Server Disconnect Actions

Non-default server disconnect actions is similar to the previous policy setting. It corresponds to the Exception List, which is revealed after clicking the Advanced button—again, found in the Folder Options Offline Files tab. Whereas the previous policy setting specified the defaults for all servers, this policy setting specifies settings for specific servers.

Settings enabled here override those in the **Action on server disconnect** policy setting as well as any other policy settings set for the target systems. When **Non-default server disconnect actions** is enabled, the Exception list is removed to prevent users from making changes.

When you configure the Computer or User option of this policy setting, the box's radio buttons above the Exception list are gray, but the Exception list itself is not. You can add any computers you desire, but they will not take effect with the policy setting in place.

This policy setting is a bit wacky: the setting will take effect on refresh, but the radio buttons don't show the actual setting until you reboot. My testing proved that a reboot was necessary for both Computer and User option settings to display in the interface. Also, when the User and Computer configurations conflict, the least restrictive setting takes precedence. If the Computer policy says you can't see the server when offline, but the User configuration says you can, you will be able to see the Offline Files when offline.

To configure this policy setting, choose Enable ➢ Show ➢ Add to open the Add Item dialog box. In the "Enter the name of the item to be added" field, type the name of the server that you want to have an explicit setting, such as **MysteryServer**. In the "Enter the value of the item to be added" field, enter either a **1** to keep the users offline or a **0** to keep them online, as shown in Figure 10.45. Click OK to add the server as an exception, click OK to close the Show Contents dialog box, and close the **Non-default server disconnect actions** policy setting.

 This policy setting does not apply to Windows Vista and later machines.

Remove 'Make Available Offline'

Enabling the **Remove 'Make Available Offline'** policy setting prevents users from pinning files by right-clicking them and selecting Make Available Offline. Files are still cached normally as dictated through other policies or by the defaults. Additionally, enabling this policy setting will not unpin already pinned files. Therefore, if you think you might not want users pinning files, you'll need to turn this setting on early in the game, or you'll be forced to run around from machine to machine to unpin users' pinned files.

FIGURE 10.45   Use this feature to prevent users from using a specific server's files when offline.

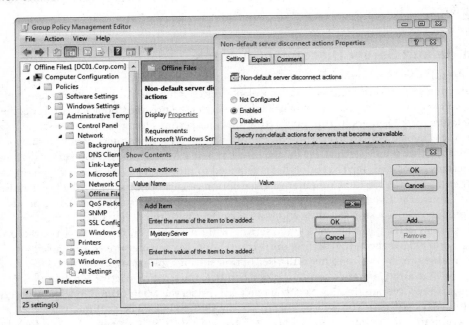

Enabling this setting does not interfere with either the Automatic Caching for Documents or the Automatic Caching for Programs setting on shared folders (as described earlier). Those files are not permanently cached (pinned).

Prevent Use of Offline Files Folder

The **Prevent use of Offline Files folder** setting prevents users from clicking the View Files button in the Folder Options dialog box. Once this option is set, users may not know which files are currently available in the cache or always available in the cache.

   This policy setting does not apply to Windows Vista and later machines.

Administratively Assigned Offline Files

Administratively assigned offline files is arguably the most useful setting in the bunch. Recall that Windows XP and later will automatically pin all files in Redirected Folders.

But what about other shares? If you want to ensure that non-Redirected Folders are *also* always available offline, this policy setting is your new best friend.

Remember, though, that in Windows XP, since these files are pinned, they are exempt from the percentage cache used (10 percent by default). That is, all files that are pinned are guaranteed to be available on the hard drive if the user transitions to offline. You can use the **Administratively assigned offline files** policy setting to force specific files or folders to be pinned, as seen in Figure 10.46.

The next time your users get this policy setting assigned, all the files affected will be pinned. Every newly created file will be pinned, as well, as shown in Figure 10.47.

So, again, the reason I find this policy setting so useful is that you can ensure that the vice president of sales always has her sales figures available. This is useful when network connectivity is spotty or absent (like on airplanes). In short, you can look like a superhero because you thoughtfully pinned these important files—and they didn't have to do any thinking at all. The files were just "there." Magic.

FIGURE 10.46   Use the **Administratively assigned offline files** policy setting to force specific files or folders to be pinned.

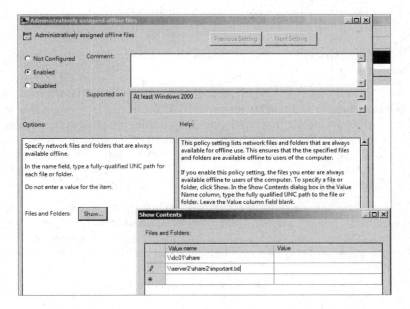

Turn Off Reminder Balloons

This setting, **Turn off reminder balloons**, corresponds to Enable Reminders in the Folders Options dialog box. Again, you might want to disable the balloons, because they may only serve to spook the herd. See Figure 10.31 earlier in this chapter for an example of a reminder balloon (though that particular balloon cannot be removed). Enabling this policy setting disables the balloons. Disabling this policy setting prevents users from disabling the balloons.

FIGURE 10.47   All files and folders specified by the (bold) **Administratively assigned offline files** policy setting are now pinned. You can see this by looking at the "State" at the bottom after clicking any file.

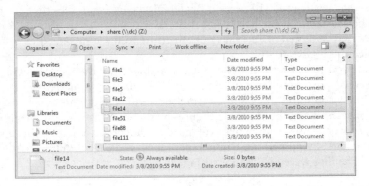

    This policy setting does not apply to Windows Vista and later machines.

Reminder Balloon Frequency

By default, balloons pop up every 60 minutes to remind users that they are working offline. Enabling **Reminder balloon frequency** and setting a time in the spin box sets that frequency and prevents the user from changing it. Disabling the policy setting keeps the default (60 minutes) and prevents users from changing the defaults.

This policy setting does not apply to Windows Vista and later machines.

Initial Reminder Balloon Lifetime

The first balloon that pops up lasts 30 seconds. Use this setting to specify how long the first balloon stays up. Enabling the **Initial reminder balloon lifetime** policy setting and entering a time in the spin box sets that duration and prevents the user from changing it. Disabling the policy setting keeps the default (30 seconds) and prevents users from changing the defaults.

This policy setting does not apply to Windows Vista and later machines.

Reminder Balloon Lifetime

After the first balloon pops up, consecutive balloons pop up every 60 minutes by default (or for whatever value is configured in the **Reminder balloon frequency** policy setting) for a total of 15 seconds each, as defined by the **Reminder balloon lifetime** policy setting. Enabling this policy setting and entering a time in the spin box sets that duration and prevents the user from changing it. Disabling the policy setting keeps the default (15 seconds) and prevents users from changing the defaults.

This policy setting does not apply to Windows Vista and later machines.

Event Logging Level

Event logging level is a good debugging feature if users complain, er, report that their synchronizations are failing. Enable this policy setting, and enter a value of 0, 1, 2, or 3:

- Level 0 records an error to the Application log when the local cache is corrupted.

- Level 1 logs the same as level 0, plus an event when the server that houses the offline file disconnects or goes down.

- Level 2 logs the same as level 1, plus an event when the computer affected by this policy setting disconnects.

- Level 3 logs the same as level 2, plus an event when the corresponding server gets back online.

Figures 10.48 and 10.49 show examples of notifications when a server becomes available again. Remember, these logs appear in the log at the workstation, not at the server.

FIGURE 10.48   The workstation log shows that the server is available.

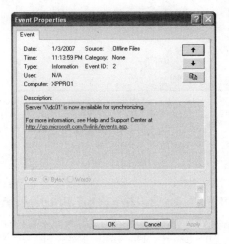

This policy setting does not affect Windows Vista and later. For Windows Vista and later Sync Center troubleshooting, see the section, "Troubleshooting Sync Center," later in this chapter.

Prohibit 'Make Available Offline' for These File and Folders

Okay, so there's a grammar problem in the name of this policy setting, but it's still useful. If you want to allow most users to pin files in a share, but ensure that certain users can't pin files in a share, **Prohibit 'Make Available Offline' for these file and folders** is the policy setting for you. After you enable this setting, just add the full UNC (Universal Naming

Convention) path to the share or share and file you want to block from being pinned. For instance, if you want to block \\DC01\sales from being pinned, enter it in this policy setting and then ensure that it applies to the appropriate users.

FIGURE 10.49   The workstation log shows state transitions in relation to the server.

    This policy setting applies only when users are using Windows XP.

Do Not Automatically Make Redirected Folders Available Offline

I get several emails a month asking me how to prevent Windows XP from pinning all files in Redirected Folders such as Documents. Here it is: ensure that it affects all the users you want. Of course, this trick should work for Windows Vista and later as well.

Actually, the **Do not Automatically Make Redirected Folders Available Offline** policy isn't found (anymore) in Computer Configuration ➢ Policies ➢ Administrative Templates ➢ Network ➢ Offline Files. In Windows Vista and later, it's been moved to User Configuration ➢ Policies ➢ Administrative Templates ➢ System ➢ Folder Redirection (and we discussed it earlier). But I'm bringing it up again here because this policy does directly relate to Offline Files—even though it's been moved to the Folder Redirection section.

Because this policy is a User-side policy, it becomes difficult to implement on a system-wide level. See the upcoming section, "Turning Off Folder Redirection's Automatic Offline Caching for Desktops," which describes how to use the **Do not Automatically Make Redirected Folders Available Offline** policy setting by strapping on a set of fangs.

Using Group Policy to Configure Offline Files (Exclusive to the Computer Node)

As we just explored, most policy settings for Offline Files are duplicated in both the User and Computer halves of Group Policy. But several settings appear only on and apply only to the Computer half.

Allow or Disallow Use of the Offline Files Feature

The **Allow or Disallow use of the Offline Files feature** policy is the "master switch" for Offline Files. This policy can affect Windows XP and later. Once a machine embraces this policy setting, a reboot is required. Disable (yes, disable) this policy setting and you effectively turn off Offline Files. Note that a restart is required.

In Windows XP, this policy setting is similar to the **Prohibit user configuration of Offline Files** setting discussed in the previous section. Once that policy setting is enabled, the Offline Files feature is active, and users cannot turn it off or change the settings. If **Allow or Disallow use of the Offline Files feature** is enabled, Offline Files is enabled, but users can change the settings. If no additional GPOs are defined, the defaults are used. Once this policy setting is disabled, the target machine's Offline Files tab in the Folder Options dialog box (seen in Figure 10.16) has grayed-out check boxes, and Offline Files is disabled.

Recall that Offline Files is enabled only for workstation machines. It's disabled for servers by default. You can use the **Allow or Disallow use of the Offline Files feature** policy setting to your advantage to turn on Offline Files on all your Windows Server 2003 or Windows 2008 computers easily—not that you would need to, as it's highly unlikely your servers will often be offline. Note that Windows Server 2003 requires that Remote Desktop Connections be *disabled* in order for Offline Files to function. See the sidebar, "Offline Files for Windows Server," earlier.

 If you enable this feature, it should kick in right away (when the background refresh interval hits). However, disabling this feature is another story. If one or more files are open in the cache when you try to disable the feature, that disable operation will fail; a reboot is required. You can experience the same behavior when trying to disable the feature through the user interface.

Default Cache Size

The **Default cache size** policy setting corresponds to the "Amount of disk space to use for temporary online files" slider in the Offline Files tab in the Folder Options dialog box, as shown in Figure 10.16 earlier in this chapter. You can control what percentage of the C: partition is available for automatic caching.

If you enable this policy setting, you must enter a whole number that represents what percentage of the partition you will be using. If you want to use 31 percent, enter **3100**. (The total range begins at 0 percent, then can be set to 100 or 1 percent, and ends at 10,000 or 100 percent.) This setting is then locked in, and users can't change it. If you disable this policy setting, the default cache-size of 10 percent of the hard drive space is locked in, and users can't change it. Remember that the XP Offline Files cache has a maximum size of only 2GB. Since this policy setting works with a percentage value, it can be difficult to know if that percentage exceeds 2GB on any target volume.

This policy setting applies to Windows 2000, Windows XP, and Windows 2003 computers only.

You might need to reboot the target machine for this policy setting to take effect. It does not always work when a background refresh is kicked off.

Files Not Cached

By default, for Windows XP, several file extensions cannot be cached, due to their sensitive nature. Microsoft is concerned that especially large files will be shuttled up and back with just 1 byte changed. Therefore, the synchronization is hard-coded not to cache certain file extensions, most notably databases. That is, for extra protection, Microsoft prevents databases from being cached. The following file types cannot be cached:

- .PST (Outlook personal folder)
- .SLM (Source Library Management file)
- .MDB (Access database)
- .LDB (Access security)
- .MDW (Access workgroup)
- .MDE (Access compiled module)
- .DB? (everything that has the extension .DB plus anything else in the third character, such as .DBF, is never included in the cache)

If you enable the **Files not cached** policy setting, you can add to this list. For instance, you can add your own file types in the form of *.DOC, *.EXE, and *.JAM to also eliminate the caching of only .DOC, .EXE, and .JAM files. In my testing, there appears to be no way to allow the caching of the hard-coded database files listed earlier. If users try to synchronize any of these file types, the Synchronization Manager balks with a "Files of This Type Cannot Be Made Available Offline" message. Windows XP/SP2 adds the capability to turn off the error every time users log synchronize. Although it is basically a manual endeavor, the hacks are described in KB 811660 in the section, "Exclusion Error Suppression."

This policy setting applies to Windows 2000, Windows XP, and Windows 2003 computers only. The next policy setting is valid for Windows 7.

Exclude Files from Being Cached

Exclude files from being cached is very similar to the policy setting before it, except that this one is valid on Windows 7.

So, to recap:

Files not cached (the previous policy setting) is valid for Windows XP, 2003, and the like.

Exclude files from being cached is valid for Windows 7 and Windows Server 2008 R2 as clients.

What about Windows Vista? Sorry, Windows Vista. You're left out of the fun here. You'll cache every file type.

So, if you have Windows 7 machines, and you want them to exclude all *.JAM and *.LSR files, just add them to this policy setting as a list with semicolons separating them.

At Logoff, Delete Local Copy of User's Offline Files

The **At logoff, delete local copy of user's offline files** policy setting sort of defeats the purpose of using Offline Files in the first place. Its main purpose is for logon use at a kiosk-style machine. That is, users log on for a bit and then log off. You'll want to ensure that their Offline Files are cleaned up behind them. Another reason I can see using this policy setting is to prevent files from being lifted off a user's hard drive. Theoretically, you can do this by digging around in the C:\windows\CSC folder. Even if the files are deleted at logoff, a good hacker could theoretically get the files back via an "undelete" program of some type.

Moreover, this policy setting doesn't guarantee a synchronization before it wipes the local cache clean upon logoff. Therefore, I strongly recommend that if you use this policy setting, you pair it with the "Synchronize all offline files before logging off" option (seen in Figure 10.16), which will save your users' bacon. Avoid using this option unless you have some workstation that needs extra security and is infrequently used, and you don't mind if the occasional file gets lost when using it.

If protection is what you're after, and you use EFS setup for your laptop users, a better option (for Windows XP machines only) is to use the **Encrypt the Offline Files cache** policy setting, discussed shortly.

The **At logoff, delete local copy of user's offline files** policy setting does not apply to Windows Vista and later machines.

Subfolders Always Available Offline

The **Subfolders always available offline** policy setting is useful if you want to ensure that all subfolders are also available offline. Essentially, it prevents users from excluding the ability to cache subfolders and makes subfolders available offline whenever their parent folder is made available offline. Any new folder a user creates under cached subfolders is automatically cached and synchronized when the parent folder is scheduled for synchronization.

This policy setting applies only to Windows XP.

Encrypt the Offline Files Cache

If you have EFS set up for your laptop users, enabling **Encrypt the Offline Files cache** is a good idea. By default, even files stored in an encrypted format on shares were not protected in the Windows 2000 file cache. With Windows XP, they can and should be.

This policy setting applies only to Windows XP (regardless of all the notes in the policy setting's Explain text "Requirements").

Configure Slow Link Speed

Recall that the Synchronization Manager in Windows XP thinks a slow link is 64Kbps. When a user comes in over a slow link (less than 64Kbps), the system automatically uses his locally cached version of network files. Additionally, the foreground Synchronization Manager does not run. You can change the definition of the speed of a slow link using **Configure slow link speed**, but only for Windows XP and Windows 2003 clients.

This policy setting applies only to Windows XP and Windows 2003 computers.

Configure Slow-Link Mode

We explored **Configure slow-link mode** earlier in the sections "Windows Vista's Synchronization Engine over Slow Links" and "Windows 7's Synchronization Engine over Slow Links." Check out those sections for detailed usage examples.

This policy setting applies only to Windows Vista and later.

Turn On Economical Application of Administrative Assigned Offline Files

Read the name of the policy setting again. Then forget it.

It should have been called **Turn *off* economical application of administrative assigned Offline Files.** Yes, off.

Synchronization Manager Limitations in Windows XP

You might see some weird behavior if a single computer is shared among multiple people. You can see this behavior in the following example.

You've configured two GPOs that redirect My Documents to two different locations: \\ WS03ServerA\UserDocs and \\WS03ServerB\UserDocs. Link the first GPO to OU-A and the second GPO to OU-B. OU-A contains Fred, and OU-B contains Robin.

Fred logs on and verifies that the My Documents redirection has taken effect by looking at the path in the Properties dialog box. If Fred opens the Synchronization Manager after creating or modifying a file in \\WS03ServerA\Data, he sees the \\WS03ServerA\UserDocs UNC in the synchronization list. When he logs off, he sees the synchronization happen for this UNC.

Now, Robin logs onto the same Windows XP workstation and verifies that My Documents redirection has taken effect. When Robin opens the Synchronization Manager, she sees the \\WS03ServerA\UserDocs UNC and the \\WS03ServerB\UserDocs UNC in the synchronization list. When she logs off, she sees both paths attempting to perform a synchronization.

You can take this to extremes, too. Try to configure five users in five different OUs with five different GPOs, each redirecting My Documents to one of five different servers. As each user logs onto a single Windows XP Desktop, the UNC path for that user is added to the UNC paths for the other users in Synchronization Manager.

So, what should you do? Allow only your laptop users to use offline caching. You can configure a GPO to prohibit offline caching for desktops and leave it enabled for laptops. Since laptop users don't tend to share their machines often, they don't build up many synchronization links. The workaround for those users is to open the Synchronization Manager and uncheck all UNC paths except their own. But no user is going to do this.

After you have Windows XP/SP2 installed on the client, you have another option. You can leverage the tips in KB 811660, which explains how to perform several new feats of magic. One of the sections in the article describes how you can "Prevent admin pinning of files for nonprimary users." Hence, when logging out, the main user of the machine will no longer resync the other user's settings. Here's the bad news, though: there are no Windows XP/SP2 policy settings to help you. It's basically a manual endeavor to enter in the hacks described in KB 811660.

The caching of permissions on directory entries in the Offline Files cache has improved this situation significantly in Windows Vista and later.

Here's the history of this setting. Recall that you can use the **Administratively assigned offline files** policy setting to guarantee a share be offline for a user. This is great, except that with Windows XP, people found that their servers were experiencing very high file loads when users would log onto their clients (that is, at 9 a.m.). What was happening was that each client was trying to process his or her **Administratively assigned offline files** policy. Windows XP/SP2 had a Registry punch (found in KB 830407) to ease this problem. It was called "economical administrative pinning." Once it was enabled, any client with this behavior would perform the full pinning operation *only* if the top-level folder was not yet pinned in the Offline Files cache.

The result is that when the policy is processed once, subsequent logons to the server do not jam the server up.

This behavior was added and turned on, by default, in Windows Vista and later. However, the policy title really should be **Turn *off* economical application of administratively assigned Offline Files**. Once this policy setting is Disabled (yes, Disabled), the policy setting reverts back to pre–Windows XP/SP2 behavior.

 This policy setting applies only to Windows Vista and later.

Limit Disk Space Used by Offline Files

In Windows XP, files expressly pinned weren't counted toward Offline Files usage. In Windows Vista and later, with the **Limit disk space used by Offline Files** policy setting, you can dictate how many megabytes you want to set aside for *all* Offline Files—those automatically cached and those pinned.

There are two settings here:

- One for total size of Offline Files (including those that are pinned)
- One for the size of autocached files

The Group Policy interface allows you to set the second number higher than the first—but that setting isn't possible in real life. Indeed, if you go back to Figure 10.33 you'll see the sliders for this setting in the interface. If you try it out, you'll notice you can't slide the second slider past the first. That's because you can't have a size bigger than the "Maximum amount of space all offline files can use." If you do that, the second number will automatically be set to the first number.

 This policy setting applies only to Windows Vista and later machines.

Troubleshooting Sync Center

The event log in Windows Vista and later is a deep and rich place. To that end, there are two places in particular to go when troubleshooting Sync Center problems.

Enabling the Offline Files Log

The Offline Files log file is located in Event Viewer ➢ Applications and Servers Logs ➢ Microsoft ➢ Windows ➢ Offline Files. Once there, dive one level deeper into the Operational log. In Figure 10.50, you can see a Windows 7 event from the OfflineFiles Operational Log.

FIGURE 10.50   Information found in the OfflineFiles Operational Log. To see data here, you must enable the log first.

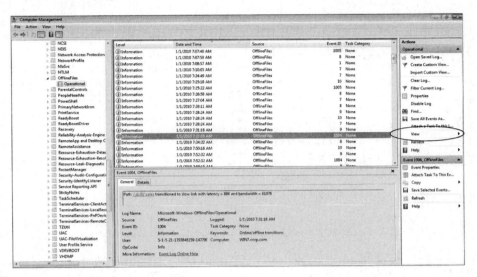

The events you'll find here are mostly the successful or unsuccessful startup/shutdown of the Offline Files feature as well as online/offline transitions. In the events (like what's seen in Figure 10.50), you can see the speed at which the machine believes the link is in terms of latency and bandwidth.

Note that the Offline Files Operational log isn't enabled by default on Windows Vista. You need to right-click over the word "Operational" and select "Enable log."

Enabling the Sync Log

There is also a Sync Log, but you need the super-secret entry key to know it's there. The thing to know how to do is called Show Analytic Channels, and here's how to do it.

As shown previously in Figure 10.50, the rightmost pane of the Computer Management Console's log view contains a View action. Click that View option and select "Show Analytic and Debug Logs." You can see "View" highlighted in Figure 10.50 for quick reference. Once you do, you'll then be able to find the Sync Log hiding under Microsoft ➢ Windows ➢ Offline Files. Right-click Sync Log and you can click the Enable item.

This is an analytic channel that reports sync activity *as it is happening* in the Offline Files service. It is not intended for use by end users, but should prove valuable to administrators to gather specific information about what's going on. (Microsoft PSS could ask you for this information, too.)

When that log is enabled, log entries appear for items that are being synchronized within the service. This means that any item synchronized by the service will be reported, not only items synchronized through Sync Center. You can see one of these events in Figure 10.51.

FIGURE 10.51   You can get blow-by-blow details of what is being synced via Offline Files.

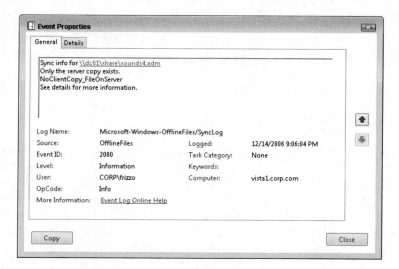

If you open one of these sync events to the Details tab in the Event Viewer, you can see the XML format containing the details; then, you can buy your favorite scripting pal some lunch to make some killer reports for you based on the XML data!

Turning Off Folder Redirection's Automatic Offline Caching for Desktops

I've never met a policy setting I didn't like. But I have met a few that missed their calling. The policy setting at User Configuration ➢ Policies ➢ System ➢ Folder Redirection ➢ **Do not Automatically Make Redirected Folders Available Offline** has missed its calling.

What on earth am I talking about?

Well, let's take a minute and analyze the normal function of Offline Files: its primary mission is to maintain files when you're not on the network so you can keep working. Super. So, what kinds of computers are off the network a lot? Laptops, of course. And desktops generally *stay* on the network.

Assuming your laptops represent 10–30 percent of your workforce, do you need those files automatically cached on *every* machine in your enterprise like the remaining 70 percent of your desktops?

Why should you care about turning it off?

Because, depending on whom you ask, it could be a security risk. Do you want cached copies of your precious documents on every machine to which your users roam? Likely not. Isn't putting your user's documents on every desktop they roam to a security risk? In a way, yes!

Sure, you could encrypt the Offline Files using EFS or BitLocker, but, let's face it, most people simply don't use EFS today. And while BitLocker looks promising, its deployment isn't widespread. And, even then, if BitLocker is implemented, it's most likely not on the desktop computers but, rather, laptops (because it's usually only laptops that have the special Trusted Platform Module [TPM] chip needed for BitLocker—but I digress).

Finally, let's not forget that every time a user roams to a desktop, he's just wasting space on the local hard drive. Remember, desktops are *normally* connected to the network just fine. Do they need *another* copy of their documents clogging up the local disk when they roam and Redirected Folders autocaches your documents?

So, in my analysis (and I'm just one guy with an opinion here), Offline Files doesn't make sense on a well-running network where your desktops and servers are on a fast LAN. Let me be clear: it won't hurt anything, either. But with files flying around everywhere, being sprinkled from desktop to desktop, it can be a security risk, waste space, and promote unnecessary synchronization and bandwidth.

Let me be a zillion percent clear: I positively love this feature for my *laptops*. I'm just not that wild about it for my *desktops*. However, I likely would keep it on my desktops if I were connected to servers on a slow WAN, like a branch office (especially if that WAN link was flaky).

So, my first thought when I read the name of this policy setting (**Do not Automatically Make Redirected Folders Available Offline**) was "A-ha! They're thinking what I'm thinking! There's a policy setting that enables me to turn it off for desktops!"

Except that's not how this policy setting works. This policy setting is not on the Computer side; it's on the User side. So, inherently, it cannot simply be put in a GPO and linked to, say, the Desktops OU to turn it off.

With this policy setting, you can only say, "The users in Sales don't automatically make their Redirected Folders available offline." But that's not the point, is it? You want the Sales folks to cache their documents on their laptops but *not* cache them on the various desktops they roam to (especially if they're public computers).

Now, cracking open the underlying ADMX file, I learned that the Registry key for this policy setting is a value called:

```
HKEY_Current_User\Software\Policies\Microsoft\Windows\NetCache
```

and it sets a REG_DWORD of DisableFRAdminPin to 1.

And then, it came to me in a dream: if I could somehow apply this policy setting (or the underlying Registry setting) to only my desktops, then, bam! I could turn off Offline Files for desktops (which would leave it on for laptops) and I would get the effect I wanted! I needed to find a way to drop a *user-based* Registry item onto specific *computers*.

Let me jump to the end of the story and tell you what I found when I applied this policy setting (or the underlying Registry entry) on Windows XP and Windows Vista and later machines.

Turns out, when I did this, Windows XP and Windows Vista and later didn't react the same way to it. Here's what I found, with Jakob Heidelberg, the technical editor of the previous edition, to back me up (your mileage may vary):

When we applied the Registry value to Windows XP   Windows XP just eats the policy setting (or Registry value) and, bang! Offline Files goes out like a light. It's awesome. If you've never told Windows XP to try to use Offline Files, you'll be 100 percent successful immediately: Windows XP just won't try to use Offline Files with Redirected Folders.

However, there's a catch. If you have the Registry tweak set, and the desktop goes offline for some reason for a period of time (you experience a network failure or the server goes offline, for instance), *and* the user creates or edits a document while offline, that document will be synchronized the next time the client is online (which is good). However, it will also stay in the local cache from that point.

That's not what we wanted. However, since we're talking about desktops (and they're usually online all the time), this shouldn't happen too much.

Now, with a little extra elbow grease and magic, you might be able to flush the cache using CSCCMD.EXE (see the sidebar "Power Admins Rejoice: Scripting Offline Files"), but you're on your own for that.

When we applied the Registry value to Windows Vista and Windows 7   Windows Vista and Windows 7 react kind of like Windows XP to the policy (or Registry addition), but it gets a little better.

The next time you log on, those redirected files are flushed from the local cache forever. So, with Vista and Windows 7, you will be sure no Offline Files are stored locally once the policy setting (or Registry item) is set.

You may have to perform one more sync via Sync Center to get the flush to occur. Whew. Figuring all that out made both Jakob's and my head spin! Be sure to test our findings out thoroughly in your environment before you roll out one of our proposed plans in a widespread way. Now, once we know the predicted behavior, how do we get user-based policy setting (or underlying Registry entry) applied to *just* our desktops?

There are three ways to get this setting applied just on desktops (that is, turn it off just for desktops) but leave it on for laptops. Here are the three tricks I have up my sleeve:

- Create a custom WMI Filter to apply to a GPO (with the policy setting contained within it).
- Use Group Policy Preference Extensions to jam in the same Registry value that the policy setting would, but ensure that only users on desktops get the setting.
- You can use PolicyPak to deploy the setting, and use its "Switched Mode" to specifically get it to people on particular computers.

Figure 10.52 shows an example of what happens after a user logs onto a Windows Vista or later desktop after we make our setting. You can see that synchronization has been turned off, but folder redirected files are still stored on the server but not cached to the desktop (no little yin-yang symbols on the file icons).

Any of these will work, so, let's get started!

If you've figured out a more creative or alternate way to do this, let me know, and I'll include it in a GPanswers.com newsletter.

FIGURE 10.52   Documents are still redirected to the server, but for users on desktops, you can avoid the synchronization (copy) to the local computer.

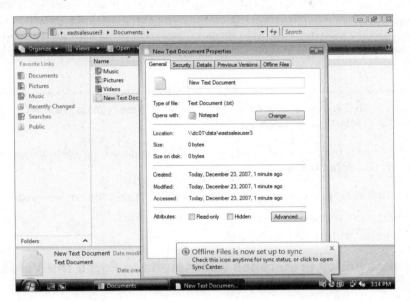

Using WMI Filters to Forcibly Apply This Setting Specifically to Desktops

This technique assumes you understand how to create WMI filters. If you need a refresher, please check out Chapter 4, where I cover it in depth.

Here are the short steps you'll need to forcibly disable Redirected Folders from automatically making the contents offline on desktops:

1. Create a new GPO that Enables the **Do not Automatically Make Redirected Folders Available Offline** policy. You don't need to configure any other settings in the GPO.

2. Link the GPO to OUs containing user accounts. Again, please, please read my warnings about how WMI filters can slow you down in Chapter 4.

3. Create a WMI filter that determines if a machine meets certain criteria. My suggestion is to check to see if it's a desktop (and not a laptop).

    ▪   If it's a desktop, then the users on those desktops will successfully embrace this GPO (and the adjusted synchronization behavior as described earlier will be performed).

    ▪   If it's not a desktop, then the standard behavior to sync Redirected Folders will continue (this is what we want).

All you need is a sample WMI query (once you've learned the basics). This query will work a lot of the time (although perhaps not all of the time):

```
Select * From Win32_PhysicalMemory Where FormFactor != 12
```

This query returns `True` on computers that do not have SODIMM form factor memory and `False` on computers with SODIMM form factor memory. The assumption is that pretty much all laptops will have this style memory and that your desktops will not. While it's true some desktops do use SODIMM memory, most don't—so it's a pretty good bet, and will work a high percentage of the time. We've tested this out and it seems to work for most cases.

To learn more about the `Win32_PhysicalMemory` class, visit `http://tinyurl.com/2hq6e6`.

How did we figure out this query? Hats off to Jakob for launching a worldwide search for the answer. Check out the thread at:

```
http://heidelbergit.blogspot.com/2008/02/wmi-filter-contest-are-you-
knight-in.html
```

(shortened to `http://tinyurl.com/yvpshy`).

Using Group Policy Preference Extensions to Force the Value (Just for Users on Desktops)

Because we can't just apply the policy setting to the User side, we need to get tricky. Again, the underlying Registry entry for the policy setting is:

```
HKCU\Software\Policies\Microsoft\Windows\NetCache
```

and it sets a `REG_DWORD` of `DisableFRAdminPin` to 1.

We need to get this to our desktops.

Now, the Registry entry itself can't figure out if the user's machine is a desktop or laptop. But with some of our Group Policy Preference Extensions superpowers, we can set the same Registry value and ensure that it *only* affects machines that are desktops!

So, create a GPO and link it to your user population. Then, use the Registry Extension on the User side to specify the Registry value, as seen in Figure 10.53.

However, at this point, you need to target the value so only users logged onto desktops get the preference setting containing the Registry entry. In Figure 10.54, you can see my suggested target. In short, I'm saying three things must be true for it to be a desktop:

- It is not a laptop (because the hardware profile says so).
- It has no battery.
- It has no PCMCIA slots.

Again, this might not be perfect in all situations, but it should suffice for most.

Alternatively, if all of your desktops had the word *Desktop* or some other distinguishing factor in the name, you could use a query like the one shown in Figure 10.55.

FIGURE 10.53 This is the same Registry entry that Do not Automatically Make Redirected Folders Available Offline would put in place.

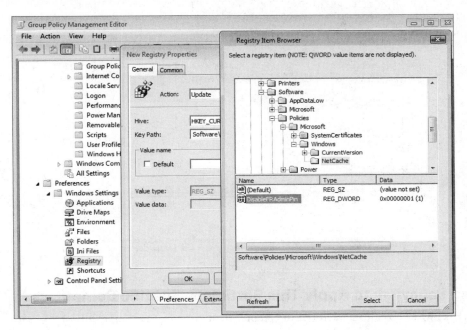

FIGURE 10.54 If you use this query, it will usually determine that your machine is a desktop and not a laptop.

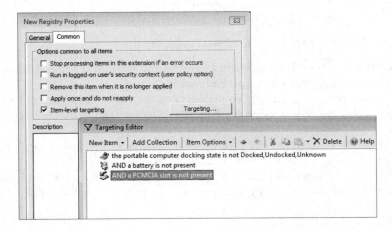

FIGURE 10.55   If you have a uniform naming convention for your desktops, this job is even easier.

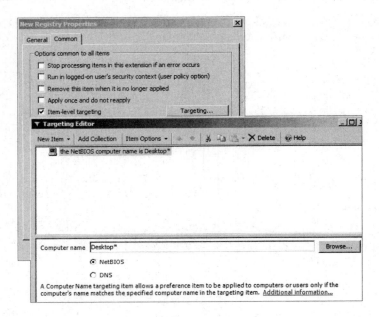

Using PolicyPak to Apply This Setting to Specific Computers

PolicyPak, which you learned about in Chapter 6, enables you to dictate all sorts of settings to your clients' machines. Indeed, one of PolicyPak's superpowers is to enable you to target User-side settings to all users on a specific machine. PolicyPak calls it "switched mode."

PolicyPak can simply process user settings for every user on a specific computer, if that's what's needed. And that's precisely what's needed in this case.

You want to deliver the Registry value of

```
User\Software\Policies\Microsoft\Windows\NetCache
```

and set a REG_DWORD of DisableFRAdminPin to 1. And you want to set it up so all users on a particular gaggle of computers (desktops) embrace it.

PolicyPak to the rescue. Just create your PolicyPak the way you learned in Chapter 6. Put the setting into a check box using the PolicyPak Design Studio, and then compile your project.

Create a GPO that's linked to your desktops. Then, deploy the Registry setting to the Computer side, like what's seen in Figure 10.56.

Now, you've done it. You've linked a GPO to your desktops, which will deploy a User-side policy setting. And whenever any user logs onto those desktops, PolicyPak will deliver the setting.

FIGURE 10.56   PolicyPak enables you to deliver User-side settings (top) to your computers (bottom).

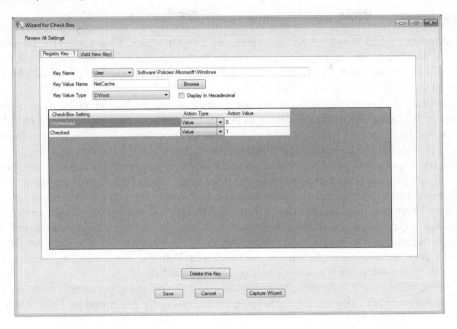

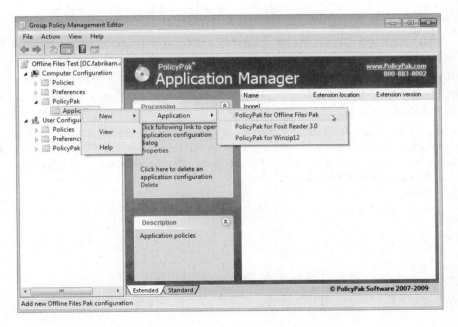

Final Thoughts

In the previous chapter, you set up Roaming Profiles. But there was a problem. If you had both Windows 7 and Windows XP machines, you wouldn't "see" files, say, in the Documents folder in Windows Vista and later show up in the My Documents folder on Windows XP. Here, you set up Redirected Folders, which anchored My Documents (for Windows XP) and Documents (for Windows Vista and later) to the same place.

This strategy gave you several key features: a centralized backup place for critical files, the ability for users' Documents contents to be available on any workstation, and the ability to mitigate the generated traffic caused by Documents being located within the profile. By default, the Documents folder is located within the profile.

You also set up Offline Files so that files work offline as though they were online. You used Group Policy to specify how your users and computers would use this function. Recall that Documents/My Documents is already automatically pinned if you use Windows XP and Windows Vista and later. But Windows Vista thinks everything is "fast" until you expressly tell it what servers (and optionally shares) it should check to see if it's slow. Windows 7 does a little better, because it automatically uses latency to determine if a link is slow or not, but it's not a great measurement. Be sure to use the Group Policy settings we explored in this chapter to hone how both Windows Vista and Windows 7 work.

If you're still using Windows XP/Service Pack 2 or 3, you should note that there are some additional hacks you can perform to squelch some noise generated by Offline Files (see KB 811660) during logoff.

If you just can't get enough information on Offline Files, be sure to check out the following resources:

- "What's New in Offline Files for Windows Vista," at http://tinyurl.com/2moatb.
- "Changes to Offline Files in Windows Vista" (written by me), in *TechNet Magazine*: http://tinyurl.com/2zkk8p.
- "Changes to Offline Files in Windows 7" (coming soon as of this writing). Look for it on Microsoft.com's TechNet resources (not the magazine) website.

Creating a managed desktop isn't easy; there's a lot to configure. And you're well on your way to making your Windows life more livable. In the next chapter, we'll continue our desktop management story. We'll learn how to distribute software to our users and computers. So, turn the page and get started!

11

The Managed Desktop, Part 2: Software Deployment via Group Policy

Two chapters ago, I discussed and implemented the first big feature of getting your managed desktop story in gear: Roaming Profiles. Once Roaming Profiles are enabled, users can roam from machine to machine, comfortable that their working environment will follow wherever they go.

In the last chapter, I discussed and implemented more features to get your managed desktop handled. First, we tackled Redirected Folders, which took Roaming Profiles one step further and anchored the user's Documents or My Documents folder to a share on a server. We then used the Group Policy settings on Offline Folders and the Synchronization Manager to ensure that certain files are always available in the cache if our connection to the server goes offline or if the server itself goes offline.

We're well on our way to implementing a fully managed desktop. We want our users to roam freely across our entire environment and take all their stuff with them. But we're missing a fundamental piece of the equation: how can we guarantee that a specific application is ready and waiting for them on that machine? What good is having your user data follow you if an application needed to access the data isn't available? That's what we're going to handle in this chapter.

NOTE This chapter is all about "deploying and installing" software to the desktop. However, there is an alternate Microsoft technology, called Microsoft Application Virtualization (App-V), which, well, doesn't install software at all. It's a newer technology that enables administrators to deploy software without actually having it installed. For more information on App-V, see our three downloadable bonus chapters at www.GPanswers.com/book.

Group Policy Software Installation (GPSI) Overview

Without any third-party software distribution mechanism, such as SCCM 2007 (what was known as SMS) or Altiris (or something similar), most environments require that you spend a lot of your time running from desktop to desktop. In a typical scenario, a user is hired and fills out the human resources paperwork, and a computer with the standard suite of software is dropped on his or her desk.

Usually, this machine comes from some sort of "deployment farm" in the back office, where scads of machines are imaged (a la Symantec's Ghost) by the scores. Or maybe the team is using Microsoft deployment techniques, like the Microsoft Deployment Toolkit (MDT) to blast images out there.

The user then starts to surf the Internet—er, I mean—get to work. Soon enough, it's discovered that the user needs a specific application, and a desktop technician is dispatched to fulfill the user's request for new software. When the desktop technician arrives, he either loads the user's special software via the CD drive or connects to a network share to pull down the software.

That's a lot of manual labor; let's make the pain stop.

Group Policy Software Installation (GPSI) is the next big feature we'll set up. This feature allows users to automatically pull applications through the network. GPSI further chips away at the workstation maintenance total cost of ownership (TCO).

There are essentially four steps to going from 0 to 60 in four seconds when it comes to deploying software with GPSI features:

1. Acquire a software setup package with an .MSI extension.

2. Share and secure a software distribution shared folder.

3. Set up a GPO to deliver the software.

4. Assign or Publish the software.

We will approach each of these steps in our software configuration journey in the next few pages.

Before we get too far along, I want to clear up a terminology misnomer. Specifically, many people incorrectly refer to the Group Policy Software Installation mechanism using the lone word *IntelliMirror*. As you might have noticed, we haven't included it in the book's title because the word IntelliMirror isn't being used very much. I think this is why: IntelliMirror (the concept) was just one piece of the managed desktop story, whereas Group Policy Software Installation is only one of those pieces. Anyway, the term IntelliMirror has come and gone, but the idea of a *managed desktop* is here to stay.

Software installed this way—via Group Policy—is referred to in many Microsoft documents as *managed* software. Group Policy can perform what is generically known as an *advertisement* of software, and the Windows Installer Service picks it up and runs with it to perform the installation. Let's get started by understanding the Windows Installer Service.

Now, I'm guessing that some large percentage of people are flipping to this chapter to find out how to deploy "the big one"—Office—to their client machines using Group Policy. That's great. I'm going to show you how to do that. But I have to begin by explaining exactly how we're going to address the problem that is Microsoft Office:

Office 2003 is "normal"   We'll be using Office 2003 as our "working example" throughout the chapter. This will get you familiar with the normal constructs of GPSI. We'll cover .MSI files, how to create what's known as "transform files" (.MST files), how to patch .MSI files, and a whole lot more.

The material you learn here will be valid for 99 percent of the software packages out there, except (mostly) for its newer siblings: Office 2007 and Office 2010

Note that for our working examples in the chapter, you could also substitute Office 2000 and Office XP for Office 2003, as all three of those packages are "normal"

Office 2007 is "abnormal"   Although it's true that Office 2007 can be forced to be deployed using GPSI, it's "abnormal." In short, you cannot use the "normal" constructs to deploy Office 2007, in the same way you will learn about for Office 2003.

Office 2010 is "double abnormal"   Although it's possible (barely) to deploy Office 2007 using GPSI, with Office 2010, it's not possible at all.

So for Office 2007 and Office 2010, I'll have a section near the end of the chapter that specifically talks about each of these versions (because they're different.)

The point, however, is that I would suggest you learn all the "normal stuff" using Office 2003. Then, take a big deep breath, clear your head, and learn all the Office 2007/Office 2010 weirdness.

The good news is that we will be able to deploy Office 2007 and Office 2010 using Group Policy. The bad news is that we won't be able to do it in the "normal way."

So, to get started, you'll learn all the "normal stuff" using Office 2003 as our prime example. Then, we'll spend some quality time specifically addressing Office 2007 and Office 2010, our oddballs.

The Windows Installer Service

A background service called the *Windows Installer Service* must be running on the client for the software deployment magic to happen. The Windows Installer Service can understand when Group Policy is being used to install or revoke an application and react accordingly. The Windows Installer Service has a secret superpower; it can run under "elevated" privileges. In other words, the user does not need to be a local administrator of the workstation to get software deployed via Group Policy.

So, the Windows Installer Service installs the software with administrative privileges. Once installed, however, the program is run under the user's context.

Windows Installer can install applications via *document invocation* or *auto-install*. Windows Installer is automatically started when you choose a specific extension or extensions. For instance, if you are e-mailed a file with a .PDF extension, and then double-click to open it (but don't yet have Acrobat Reader installed), the Windows Installer Service can be automatically invoked to bring down Adobe Acrobat Reader from one of your servers. This is described in more detail in the "Advanced Published or Assigned" section, later in this chapter. Additionally, Windows Installer can determine when an application is damaged and repair it automatically by downloading the required files from the source to fix the problem.

You might have heard the phrase "advertising a package" or, in short, an advertisement. An advertisement is a generic term that means software is "offered" by Active Directory to the client machine. But the client has three ways to accept that advertisement. You'll see later that the shortcut can be selected, which will download the application (that's one way). Another way is to click a file extension that is registered for GPSI (we already mentioned this one), and, finally, you can invoke an advertised COM object (which we won't be discussing here).

Understanding *.MSI* Packages

About 99 percent of the magic in software deployment with Group Policy is wrapped in a file format called .MSI. The .MSI file has two goals: to increase the flexibility of software distribution, and to reduce the effort required to make new packages. When a software application is rolled out the door, files in the .MSI format are often "standard issue" (though sometimes they are not). For instance, every edition of Office since Office 2000 has shipped as a .MSI distribution.

On the surface, .MSI files appear to act as self-expanding distribution files, like familiar, self-executing .ZIP files. But under the surface, .MSI files contain a database of "what goes where" and can contain either pointers to additional source files or all the files rolled up inside the .MSI itself. Additionally, .MSI files can "tier" the installation; for instance, you can specify, "Don't bother loading the spell checker in Word, if I only want Excel." Sounds simple, but it's revolutionary.

Moreover, because .MSI files are themselves a database, an added feature is realized. The creator of the .MSI package (or sometimes the user) can designate which features are loaded to the hard drive upon initial installation, which features are loaded to the hard drive the first time they are used, which features are run from the CD or distribution point, and which features are never loaded. This lets administrators pare down installations to make efficient use of both disk space and network bandwidth.

With .MSI files, the bar is also raised when it comes to the overall management of applications. Indeed, two discrete .MSI operations come in handy: Rollback and Uninstall. When .MSI files are being installed, the entire installation can be canceled and simply rolled back. Or, after an .MSI application is fully installed, it can be fully uninstalled. You are not guaranteed exactly the same machine state from Uninstall as you are with Rollback, however. The GPSI features in Active Directory are designed mainly to integrate with the new .MSI file format. There is other legacy support, as you'll see later.

Utilizing an Existing *.MSI* Package

As stated, lots of applications come as .MSI files. Some are full-blown applications, such as Office 2000 and later. Others are smaller programs that you might use a lot, such as the GPMC (Group Policy Management Console) or the .NET Framework. All these aforementioned applications come as an .MSI. Be forewarned: just because an application comes as an .MSI doesn't necessarily mean it can always be deployed via GPSI; however, that's a pretty good indication. Yet, even though versions of the Norton AntiVirus client shipped as an .MSI, it wasn't installable via GPSI until version 9. Ditto for Adobe Acrobat. Until Acrobat version 7, the Reader Program didn't ship as an .MSI, but the full version did. But even though earlier versions of Adobe Acrobat shipped as .MSI files, they simply weren't deployable via GPSI.

Additionally, some .MSI applications (such as Office 2000, Office XP, and Office 2003) can be deployed to *either* users or computers. However, some applications, such as the older, Windows XP-based GPMC.MSI and the .NET Framework's .MSI, can *only* be deployed successfully to computers.

You'll want to check with the manufacturer of the .MSI file to understand how it needs to be installed. The .MSI files that can be deployed via GPSI usually come in three flavors:

- Some .MSI packages are just one solitary file, and they come ready to be deployed. The original GPMC and the Windows 2003 Administration tools (Adminpak.msi) are examples in this category. (In Figure 11.1, you can see what happens if you try to deploy the older GPMC to a user account.)

- Some .MSI packages have one file to "kick off" the installation. Then, there are a gaggle of other files behind it. The .NET Framework (netfx.msi) and service packs (update.msi) are examples in this category.

- Other .MSI files need to be "prepared" for installation. Usually, these applications are more complex. Office 2000, Office XP, Office 2003 (but not Office 2007 or Office 2010), and Microsoft TechNet are examples in this category.

Many people want to deploy big applications, such as the Office suite. Again, for the majority of this chapter, I'm going to be using the older Office 2003, because it's very "normal" in the way it's deployed. And, by learning Office 2003, you'll be able to take the knowledge and deploy many other applications (just not Office 2007 or Office 2010, sadly).

So, for these examples, I'll assume you have a copy of Office 2003. Note that only the Enterprise versions of these applications are guaranteed to work using GPSI. Other editions, like Home and School, may not work properly deployed via GPSI.

FIGURE 11.1   The original XP version of the GPMC isn't meant to be deployed to users using GPSI. Indeed, when I hit OK, I just go into an endless loop!

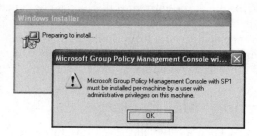

Setting Up the Software Distribution Share

The first step is to set up the software distribution shared folder on a server. In this example, we'll use DC01 and create a shared folder with the name of Apps. We want all our users to be able to read the files inside this software distribution share, because later, we might choose to create multiple folders to house additional applications' sources. Later, we'll also create our first application subfolder and feed Office 2003 into its own subfolder.

To set up the software distribution shared folder, follow these steps:

1. Log onto DC01 as Administrator.

2. From the Desktop, click My Computer to open the My Computer folder.

3. Find a place to create a Users folder. In this example, we'll use D:\APPS. Once you've opened the D: drive, right-click D: and select the Folder command from the New menu; then, type **Apps** as the name. (You can substitute any name for Apps.)

4. Share the Apps folder so that Everyone has Read access. Note that the Domain Users group isn't sufficient here, because computers also must have access. The procedure for this is slightly different for Windows Server 2003, Windows Server 2008, or Windows Server 2008 R2. While you're in the Permissions for the Apps dialog box, also ensure that the Administrators group has Full Control permissions on the share.

You can use Share permissions, NTFS permissions, or both, to restrict who can see which applications. The most restrictive permissions between Share level and NTFS level permissions are used. Here, at the Apps share, you want everyone to have access to the share. You'll then create subfolders to house each application and use NTFS permissions to specify, at each subfolder level, which groups or users can see which applications' subfolders.

Again, in this example, we're using a simple share on a simple server. Here, we'll be installing from a Domain Controller in our examples, which you wouldn't normally do in real life, but it's okay for our examples. Indeed, the best thing to do is to use Distributed File Systems (DFS) Namespaces to ensure that users can get to this share from another server, even if this server is down. DFS Namespaces is beyond the scope of this book, but read the sidebar "Normal Shares vs. DFS Namespaces."

It's a good idea to exclusively use DFS Namespaces for package installation points. This is because if you move a package, you will likely cause a product reinstallation on your target machines. This happens whenever the original source location changes. By using DFS Namespaces, you can avoid this problem.

Setting Up an Administrative Installation (for *.MSI* Files that Need Them)

As stated, not all .MSI files are "ready to go"; some need to be prepared. To prepare Office 2000, Office XP, and Office 2003, you must perform an *Administrative Installation* of its .MSI file. In this procedure, the system will rebuild and copy the .MSI package from your CD-ROM source to a destination folder for use by your clients. While the package is being rebuilt, it injects the serial number for your users and other customized data. Again, to be clear, not all .MSI packages must be prepared in this manner. Be sure to check your documentation.

Neither Office 2007 nor Office 2010 requires this Administrative Installation step (see the section "Deploying Office 2007 and Office 2010 Using Group Policy," later in the chapter).

To perform an Administrative Installation of Office 2000, Office XP, or Office 2003, you'll use the msiexec command built into Windows 2000 and Windows 2003. The generic command is msiexec /a *whatever*.msi. For Office XP, the command is msiexec /a PROPLUS.MSI. For Office 2003, the command is msiexec /a PRO11N.MSI.

When you run this command, Office is not installed on your server (or wherever you're performing these commands). This can be confusing, as the Office Installation Wizard is kicked off, and it will write a bunch of data to your disk. Again, to be clear, an Administrative Installation simply *prepares* a source installation folder for future software deployment.

The Office Installation Wizard will show that it's getting ready for an Administrative Installation, as shown in Figure 11.2.

Your next steps in the Installation Wizard are to specify the organization and the installation location and to enter the product key. For the installation location, choose a folder in the share you already created, say, D:\apps\office2003distro. Be sure to enter a valid product key, or you cannot continue. The next screen asks you to confirm the End-User License Agreement. Finally, the Administrative Installation is kicked off, and files are copied to the share and the folder (as shown in Figure 11.3).

Note that not every application requires any "preparation" for an Administrative Installation like Office 2003.

Many applications are "ready to rock" with no preparation necessary. In those cases, I suggest you just create a subdirectory under APPS, based on the package name, and dump the installation files to that directory. Even more ideal is to have a version number within each application's directory to further segregate.

You'll have to check with each package manufacturer to see whether or not an administrative installation is required.

FIGURE 11.2   You need to perform an Administrative Installation to prepare a source installation folder for Office.

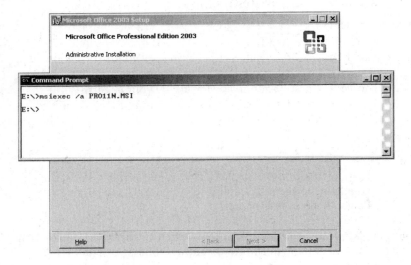

FIGURE 11.3   The files are simply copied to the share; Office isn't being installed (despite the notification that it is).

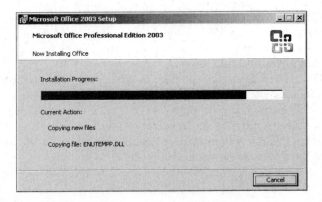

About Underlying Share Permissions

When you set up shared folders, also lock them down with NTFS permissions to prevent unauthorized users from accessing the installations. Even though GPSI can *target* specific users, it makes no provisions for security. Rather, if your users discover the distribution shared folder, they'll have the keys to the candy store unless you put security on the shared folder or, even better, utilize NTFS permissions as a deadbolt on the lock.

You can expose or hide your shared folders; to hide them, add a $ (dollar sign) to the end of the share name. You can have one shared folder for each package or one shared folder for all your software with subfolders underneath, each with the appropriate NTFS permissions.

I do not recommend (nor is it possible) that you dump all the installations in one shared folder without using subfolders. Using subfolders lets you differentiate between two applications that have the same name (for example, Setup.msi) or two versions of the same application (Office 2003 and Office XP).

Creating Your Own *.MSI* Package

It's great when applications such as Office 2003 come with their own .MSI packages, but not every vendor supplies .MSI packages. You can, however, create your own .MSI packages to wrap up and deploy the software you've already bought that doesn't come with an .MSI package.

Some of the popular ones are

- WinINSTALL from Scalable Software:

  www.scalablesoftware.com/WinINSTALL_LE.aspx

- Symantec/Altiris Wise Package Studio:

  http://tinyurl.com/2wexqw

- Flexera AdminStudio:

  http://tinyurl.com/yc27wbt

The general steps for using a repackaging tool are as follows:

1. Take a snapshot of a clean source machine.

2. Run the current setup program of whatever you want to wrap up.

3. Fully install and configure the application as desired.

4.   Reboot the machine to ensure that changes are settled in.

5.   Take a snapshot again, and scour the hard drive for changes.

Once the changes are discovered, they're wrapped up into an .MSI file of your choice, which you can then Assign or Publish.

Due to page count, I can't go into the ins and outs of creating your own .MSI files. However, I have two options for you. First, you can take a look at my book *Windows 2000 Group Policy, Profiles, and IntelliMirror* (Sybex, 2004), which includes the step-by-step process. Or, you can check out another resource that demonstrates this process with free and "pay" tools: *The Definitive Guide to Windows Installer Technology for System Administrators* (which is free and which I co-wrote) is available at:

    http://nexus.realtimepublishers.com/dgwit.php

The third-party tools have some fairly robust features to assist you in your .MSI package creation. As I stated, the .MSI format lets you detect a damaged component within a running application. This feature is called *keying* files for proper operation. For example, if your Ruff.DLL gets deleted when you run DogFoodMaker 7, the Windows Installer springs into action and pulls the broken, but keyed, component back from the distribution point—all without user interaction.

Additionally, if you're looking for some heavy-duty .MSI training, consider my pal Darwin Sanoy, who can be found at:

    http://desktopengineer.com/windowsinstallertraining

(Let him know I sent you.)

Assigning and Publishing Applications

Once you have an .MSI package on a share, you can offer it to your client systems via Group Policy. GPSI is located under both Computer and User Configuration directories and then Policies ➢ Software Settings ➢ Software Installation. Before we set up our first package, it's important to understand the options and the rules for deployment. You, the administrator, can offer applications to clients in two ways: *Assigning* or *Publishing*.

Assigning Applications

The icons of Assigned applications appear in the user's Start Menu. More specifically, they appear when the user selects Start ➢ All Programs. However, colloquially, we just say that they appear on the Start Menu. You can Assign applications to users or computers.

What Happens When You Assign Applications to Users

If you Assign an application to users, the application itself isn't downloaded and installed from the source until its initial use. When the user first clicks the application's icon, the Windows Installer (which runs as a background process on the client machine) kicks into high gear, looks at the database of the .MSI package, locates the installation point, and determines which components are required.

Assigning an application saves on initial disk space requirements since only an application's entry points are actually installed on the client. Those entry points are shortcuts, CLSIDs (Class Identifiers), file extensions, and, sometimes, other application attributes that are considered .MSI entry points.

Once the icons are displayed, the rest of the application is pulled down only when necessary. Indeed, many applications are coded so that only portions of the application are brought down in chunks when needed, such as a help file that is only grabbed from the source when it's required the first time.

When portions of an application are installed, the necessary disk space is claimed. The point is that if users roam from machine to machine, they might *not* choose to install the Assigned application, and, hence, it would not use any disk space. If users are Assigned an application but never get around to using it, they won't use any extra disk space. Once the files are grabbed from the source, the application is installed onto the machine, and the application starts. If additional subcomponents within the application are required later (such as the help files in Office 2003 Word, for example), those components are loaded on demand in a *just-in-time* fashion as the user attempts to use them.

What Happens When You Assign Applications to Computers

If the application is Assigned to computers, the application is *entirely* installed and available for all users who use the machine the next time the computer is rebooted. This won't save disk space, but will save time because the users won't have to go back to the source for installation.

Publishing Applications

The icons of Published applications are placed in the Add or Remove Programs folder in Control Panel in Windows XP, or in the "Install a program from the network" window in Windows Vista or Windows 7, as seen in Figure 11.4.

You can Publish to users (but not computers). When you Publish applications to users, the application list is dynamically generated, depending on which applications are currently being Published. Users get no signals whatsoever that any applications are waiting for them in Control Panel.

Once the application is selected, all the components required to run that application are pulled from the distribution source and installed on the machine. The user can then close Control Panel and use the Start Menu to launch the newly installed application.

FIGURE 11.4   Windows Vista and Windows 7 applications can be Published in the (very) hard to find "Install a program from the network," as seen here.

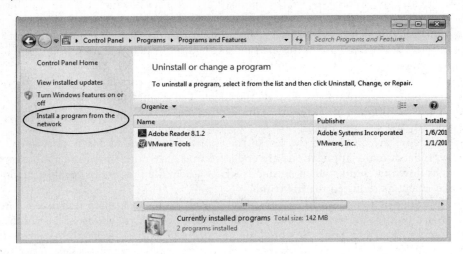

By default, the icons of Assigned applications are also placed in the Add or Remove Programs folder (or "Install a program from the network") for download. In other words, by default, all Assigned applications are also Published. The "Do Not Display this Package in the Add/Remove Programs Control Panel" option is unchecked by default; therefore, the application appears in both places by default upon Assignment. (I'll discuss this option in the "Advanced Published or Assigned" section.)

 Published apps are also advertised to be run automatically via document invocation (again, also known as auto-install).

Rules of Deployment

Some rules constrain our use of GPSI, regardless of whether applications are Assigned through the Computer or User node of Group Policy. As just stated, the icons of Assigned applications appear on the Start Menu, whereas the icons of Published applications appear in the Add or Remove Programs folder (or "Install a program from the network"). With that in mind, here are the deployment rules:

Rule 1   Assigning to computers means that anyone who can log onto machines affected by the GPO sees the Assigned application on the Start Menu. This is useful for situations such as nursing stations. You can also Assign applications to users in the GPO, which means that whenever users roam, their applications follow them—no matter which machine they reside at physically.

Rule 2   You can't Publish to computers; you can only Assign to computers within a GPO.

Why the funky rules? Although I have no specific confirmation from Microsoft, I'll make an observation that might help you remember these rules: most users can use the Start Menu to launch applications. Therefore, Assigning applications to users makes sense.

Additionally, since applications Assigned to computers apply to *every* user who logs onto a targeted machine, the users in question can also surely use the Start Menu to launch the Assigned applications. But using Published applications takes a little more computer savvy. Users first need to know that applications are Published at all and then check the `Add or Remove Programs` folder (or "Install a program from the network") to see if any applications are targeted for them. A specific user might know that applications are waiting for her, but it's unlikely that all users using a computer would know that. In any event, just remember the following rules:

- You can Assign to users.
- You can Assign to computers.
- You can Publish to users.
- You cannot Publish to computers.

Since this level of sophistication isn't really the norm, I bet Microsoft avoided providing Publishing capabilities for computers because there is no guaranteed level of sophistication for a specific user of a specific computer.

Package-Targeting Strategy

So far, we've set up our software distribution shared folder, prepared the package to the point of distribution, and (optionally) tied it down with NTFS permissions. Now, we need to target a group of users or computers for the software package. Here are some possible options:

- Leverage an OU for the users you want to get the package, move the accounts into this OU, and then Assign or Publish the application to that OU. Whenever members of the OU log on, the application is available for download. Each user can connect to the distribution source and acquire a copy of the installation. This is best for when your users are mostly using desktops. Because desktops are connected to the network, the just-in-time fashion of the download really makes sense here.

- Leverage an OU for the computers that you want to get the package, and then Assign the application to the computers in that OU. When the computer is rebooted, then, whenever any user logs onto the targeted machines, the application is fully downloaded and ready to go. This isn't true for every application (like Office 2007, shown later). But it is true for just about everything else. This is best if you have a gaggle of laptop users. You'll want to ensure that the entire application is loaded before users go on the road with their machines. This strategy is ideal for this scenario.

- Assign or Publish the application at the domain or OU level, and then use GPO Filtering with Security Groups (see Chapter 2). This is a more advanced technique, but can be very useful when you want to give someone only the ability to modify group memberships, and (by modifying the group membership) also deploy software to a group of users (or even computers).

- Assign or Publish the application at the domain or OU level, and then use WMI (Windows Management Instrumentation) Filtering based on specific information within machines. (See Chapter 4 in the "WMI Filters: Fine Tuning When and Where Group Policy Applies" section.) This is most useful if you want to strategically target machines based on very specific criteria. For instance, "Only deploy this software to users with 2GB of RAM and hotfix Q24601."

 There's also the ability to permission individual packages within a GPO for more fine-grained targeting. Check out the Security tab for each package.

We could use any of these methods to target our users. The first two options are the most straightforward and most common practice. In our first example, we'll leverage an OU and Assign the application to our computers. We'll use the **Human Resources Computers** OU and Assign them Office 2003.

Normal Shares vs. DFS Namespaces

The GPSI features are like the postal service; they're a delivery mechanism. Their duty is to deliver the package and walk away. But it's something of a production before that package is delivered into your hands, and that's what we'll tackle in the next section.

Before we get there, however, you need to prepare for software distribution by setting up a *distribution point* to store the software. You can choose to create a shared folder on any server—hopefully, one that's close to the users who will be pulling the software. The closer to the user you can get the server, the faster the download of the software and the less saturated your network in the long run.

In a nutshell, GPSI delivers a message to the client about the shared folder from which the software is available. However, if you are concerned that your users will often roam your distributed enterprise, you can additionally set up DFS Namespaces.

DFS Namespaces is the *Distributed File System* technology that, when used in addition to Active Directory Site Topology definitions, can automatically direct users toward the share containing the software closest to them. The essence of DFS Namespaces is that it sets up a front-end for shared folders and then acts as the traffic cop, directing users to the closest replica. To explore DFS technology, visit www.microsoft.com/dfs.

DFS Namespaces has an extra huge benefit over using normal shares. If a normal share on a normal server goes down (and the client application needs a repair), the client can just find another node (the next closest node) on the network that contains the software. Or, if you want to repurpose that server for something else, you don't have to worry about the gruesome problem of removing the software from everywhere, putting the share on the new server, and redeploying the application. With DFS, you just add a server with the share contents and change a few pointers around on the back-end.

But what if you're in one of these two traps already? Is there hope to move from a "one, server" GPSI deployment to something more robust? Yep! And that, my friends, is what my Newsletter #19 is all about on GPanswers.com. It's called the File Server Migration Toolkit (FSMT). The FSMT can move files from an existing server to another server. And, here's the magic: it can tell the new server to take on the additional name of the old server. So, your clients never know anything has changed under the hood. Really neat stuff (and it uses DFS technology to do the magic). Again, check it out in Newsletter #19.

Creating and Editing the GPO to Deploy Office

We are now ready to create our GPO and Assign our application to our users. In this example, we'll Assign Office 2003 to computers, but this procedure works for just about every application that's "Group Policy deployable." Again, Office 2007 and Office 2010 break the rules, so learn now with Office 2003—and you'll be good to go for almost all applications (except Office 2007 and Office 2010).

Open the GPMC, and then follow these steps:

1. To create a GPO that deploys Office 2003 to the **Human Resources Computers** OU, right-click the OU and choose "Create a GPO in this domain, and Link it here" from the context menu to open the New GPO dialog box. Enter a descriptive name in the New GPO dialog box, such as **Deploy Office 2003** (**to computers**). The GPO should now be linked to the **Human Resources Computers** OU.

2. Right-click the link to the GPO (or the GPO itself), and choose Edit from the context menu to open the Group Policy Management Editor.

The software distribution settings are found in both Computer Configuration and User Configuration, as shown in Figure 11.5.

For this first package, we will Assign the application to the computers in the **Human Resources Computers** OU.

1. Choose Computer Configuration ➢ Policies ➢ Software Settings.

2. Right-click "Software installation" and choose New ➢ Package, as shown in Figure 11.5, to open the Open dialog box, which lets you specify the .MSI file.

Do not—I repeat—do not use the Open dialog box's interface to click and browse for the file locally. Equally evil is specifying a local file path, such as D:\apps\office2003distro\pro11n.msi. Why is this? Because the location needs to be from a consistently available point, such as a UNC path. Entering a local file path prevents the Windows Installer at the client from finding the package on the server. Merely clicking the file doesn't guarantee that the package will be delivered to the client. Again—entering the full UNC path as shown in Figure 11.6 is the *only* guaranteed method to deliver the application to the client.

You will need to specify the full UNC path on the shared folder for the application. Let me say that again: you will need to specify the network path, not the "local" path, or the installation will fail.

Earlier, we put our Office 2003 Administrative Installation inside the APPS share on the DC01 server inside the OFFICE2003DISTRO directory. If you take a look at the Office 2003 media, you'll note there are lots of .MSI files that might work. However, there is only one that is meant for GPSI distribution. The precise name will vary depending on the version of Office 2003 you have. In my case, I have Office 2003 Professional Edition. The file that I'll need to deliver using GPSI is named Pro11.msi. Therefore, the full UNC path to the application is \\DC01\apps\OFFICE2003DISTRO\Pro11.MSI, as shown in Figure 11.6.

FIGURE 11.5   Right-click the GPSI settings to deploy a new package.

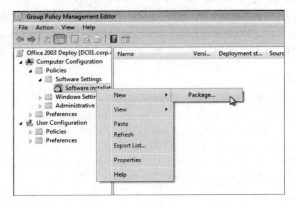

FIGURE 11.6   Always use the full UNC and never the local path when this dialog box requests the file.

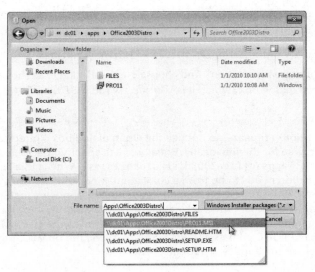

Before You Ramp Up, Let's Talk about Licensing

A FAQ I get when I teach my Group Policy Intensive course is this: "If I use GPSI to deploy applications to my users, how does this affect my licensing agreements with Microsoft or other software vendors?" The next most frequently asked question about GPSI is this: "If I use GPSI to do mass rollouts, how can I keep track of licensing for reporting during audits?" Bad news on both fronts, friends.

Occasionally, the Microsoft technology doesn't work in lockstep with usable licensing agreements. Specifically, if you use GPSI as your mechanism to get software to the masses, you need to be especially careful with your Microsoft licensing agreements or any other licensing agreements. When you deploy any software via GPSI, you have the potential to load the software on a machine and make it available to any number of users who can log onto that machine. As I discussed, using GPSI to deploy to computers gives everyone who logs onto the machine (via the domain) access to the icons on the Start Menu. And, if you target users, whether the application is available only for that user depends on the application. For instance, a well-written .MSI, say, Office XP, prevents users who aren't Assigned the application from using it; but other .MSI applications (especially those you create with third-party tools) may not. And when you use GPSI to deploy an application to, say, users in an OU, you won't know how many users accept the offer and how many users don't end up using the application.

With that in mind, GPSI is a wonderful mechanism for deploying software. But in terms of licensing and auditing, you're on your own. My advice is that if you're planning to use GPSI for your installations, check with each vendor to find out the vendor's licensing requirements when you Assign to users and Assign to computers.

Remember: you have a large potential for exposure by doing a GPSI to users and/or computers; protect yourself by checking with your vendor before you do a mass deployment of any application in this fashion. Additionally, it's important to remember that there is no facility for counting or metering the number of accepted offers of software for auditing purposes.

That's where Microsoft's SCCM 2007 is supposed to come into play to help you determine "who's using what."

Finally, if you're looking for an all–Group Policy solution to help mitigate these (and other) problems, check out Specops Software's Specops Deploy (www.specopssoft.com). But stay tuned—more on that later.

Once the full UNC path is entered, a dialog box will appear, asking which type of distribution method we'll be using: Assigned or Advanced. Published will be grayed out because you cannot Publish to computers.

For now, choose Assigned and click OK. When you do (and you wait a minute or two), you'll see the application listed as shown in Figure 11.7. Hang tight—it'll show up.

FIGURE 11.7   The applications you assign are listed under the node you chose to use (Computer ➢ Software installation or User ➢ Software installation).

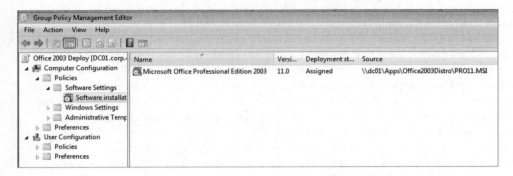

Understanding When Applications Will Be Installed

Once you've Assigned or Published an application, you'll need to test it to see if it's working properly. Here's how users and computers should react:

- Applications Published to users on any operating system should show up right away in Control Panel. No reboot or log out (and log back in) should be required, but you might have to refresh the Add or Remove Programs folder (or "Install a program from the network"). An application isn't installed until a user specifically selects it or the application is launched via *document invocation* (also called *install-on-first-use* or *advertisement*). Recall that document invocation allows the application to be installed as soon as a file associated with the application is opened.

- Applications Assigned to users on Windows 2000 or Windows 2003 computers should show up on next logon on the Start Menu. Applications Assigned to Windows 2000 or Windows 2003 computers should install upon next reboot. All users logging onto those computers will see the icons on the Start Menu.

- If you're deploying to users on Windows XP or later, you need to know whether Fast Boot is turned on. Recall from Chapter 3 that Fast Boot is enabled by default for Windows XP and later, and you will need to explicitly turn it off. To review:

  - If Windows XP or later Fast Boot is enabled and you Assign applications to users, it will take two logoffs and logons for the icons to appear on the Start Menu.

- If Windows XP or later Fast Boot is enabled and you Assign applications to computers, it will take two reboots before the assignment is installed. Afterward, icons appear for all users on the Start Menu. If you want to turn off this behavior for Windows XP and later, you can do so. Just check out Chapter 3 to learn how.

- Note, however, that Windows XP and later Fast Boot is always off if a Roaming Profile is used.

You'll need to adjust the deployment properties before certain applications will deploy properly to users. (More on this in the "Advanced Published or Assigned" section later in this chapter.)

Testing Assigned Applications

Before you go headlong and try to verify your deployment of Office 2003, first verify that a machine is in the **Human Resources Computers** OU, and then reboot the first test machine in the OU.

If you're Assigning an application to a Windows XP machine, you'll see this during startup, as shown in Figure 11.8.

If you're Assigning an application to a Windows Vista or Windows 7 machine, by default, you won't see anything during startup except a "Please wait..." and a lot of disk activity. However, if you enable the policy setting **Verbose vs normal status messages** located within Computer Configuration ➢ Policies ➢ Administrative Templates ➢ System, you'll see more information during startup, such as the application's title, as seen in Figure 11.9.

FIGURE 11.8 Applications Assigned to computers install completely upon reboot.

FIGURE 11.9 If you enable the Verbose vs normal status messages policy setting to affect your Windows Vista or Windows 7 machines, you'll see the name of the software installing instead of a lousy "Please wait..." message.

Installing managed software Microsoft Office Professional Edition 2003...

Go ahead and get a cup of coffee while this is installing. It takes a while. Really. Go ahead. I'll wait.

Once the application is fully installed, you can log on as any user in the domain (or the local computer) and see the application's icons on the Start Menu, as shown in Figure 11.10.

FIGURE 11.10   The Office icons and program names will appear on the Start Menu (more specifically on the Start ➤ All Programs menu).

If you're deploying Office 2003 (or earlier), the icons will show up right away on the Start Menu for all users who log in. Again, note, you won't get this same, predictable behavior for Office 2007, which we'll discuss later.

When the installation is complete, you'll see your newly installed items on the Start ➤ All Programs menu. These are nicely highlighted for Windows XP and Vista. But on Windows 7, as shown in Figure 11.10, the highlighting seems to have gone away. Note, on Windows 2000, the icons are also not highlighted.

I guess everything old is new again.

At this point, any user can select any Office application, and the application is briefly prepared and then displayed for the user.

Stay tuned for more information on Assigning and Publishing .MSI applications (particularly to users). For now, let's switch gears and look at another deployment option.

Understanding *.ZAP* Files

Using .MSI files is one way to distribute software to your computers and users, but one disadvantage is associated with this process: you must actually have an .MSI package that you deploy. Indeed, some applications don't come with .MSI packages, and repackaging them with a third-party tool doesn't always work as expected. If you already have your own Setup.exe (or similar program), you can leverage a different type of installation: .ZAP files, which invoke your currently working Setup.exe program.

Sounds great—but there is a downside: .ZAP files are not as robust as .MSI files. This "unrobustness" comes in several forms:

- They do not take advantage of the Windows Installer, and therefore, they are not self-repairing should something go awry on the client.

- You can Publish but can't Assign .ZAP files. Their icons are available only in Control Panel, and the application is installed all at once. And since .ZAP files are always Published, they can only be Published to users, not computers.

- The user is in full control of the install, unless you've magically scripted Setup.exe. This can create trouble for end users (and for you).

- The .ZAP files run with the user's privileges. They cannot run with elevated privileges. Again, only .MSI applications (not .ZAP files) automatically run elevated even for non-privileged users once deployed via GPSI.

Like .MSI files, .ZAP files (and their corresponding setup executables) can also be automatically invoked when a specific extension (or set of extensions) is chosen via *document invocation* (also called *auto-installer*). Auto-install is described in more detail in the "Advanced Published or Assigned" section, later in this chapter.

Creating Your Own *.ZAP* File

A .ZAP file resembles an .INI file: it is a simple file created with a text editor such as Notepad, and it has headings and values. Instead of repackaging WinZip 8 with WinINSTALL (or any of the third-party applications), you can simply create a .ZAP file for a WinZip 8 setup executable, WinZip80.exe.

A sample WinZip 8 .ZAP file might look like this:

```
[Application]
FriendlyName = "Winzip 8.0 ZAP Package"
SetupCommand = "WINZIP80.exe"
DisplayVersion = 8.0
Publisher = WinZip Computing

[EXT]
.ZIP=
.ARC=
```

Let's briefly break down each entry. The [Application] heading is required, and the only other required elements are the FriendlyName and the SetupCommand, which are self-explanatory.

The entry pointed to the `SetupCommand` should be in the same folder as the `.ZAP` file itself. If it isn't, you can use UNC paths to specify, such as

```
SetupCommand = "\\DC01\winzipsource\winzip8.exe"
```

Everything else is completely optional but might help you and your users sort things out. The [EXT] heading can list the file extensions that can fire off this particular `.ZAP` installation and the corresponding `WINZIP80.exe` setup executable. Listed in this sample file are `.ZIP` and `.ARC`, but you can also add file types such as `.TAR` and `.Z`. The [EXT] heading is not required and may not even be desired, depending on the application and its setup routine.

Publishing Your Own *.ZAP* File

If you want to Publish your own `.ZAP` file, you'll need to bring all the steps you've learned together:

1. Place the setup executable (in this case, `WINZIP80.exe`) in a subfolder (say, `WINZIPSOURCE`) underneath a shared folder (in this case, `APPS`).

2. Lock down the `WINZIPSOURCE` subfolder with NTFS permissions.

3. Create the `WINZIP8.zap` file as directed earlier using Notepad.

4. Copy the `.ZAP` file to the distribution subfolder (`WINZIPSOURCE`).

5. Finally, distribute (Publish) the `.ZAP` package to your users.

Testing Your *.ZAP* File

Test your `.ZAP` file and distribution point by logging onto a workstation to which the GPSI policy applies. Open the `Add or Remove Programs` folder in Control Panel (or "Install a program from the network"), and click Add New Programs in the column on the left, as shown in Figure 11.11. The application should appear in the list of programs available to add, named according to the entry in the `FriendlyName` field that you specified in the `.ZAP` file.

FIGURE 11.11 ZAP files are always Published to Control Panel (XP shown).

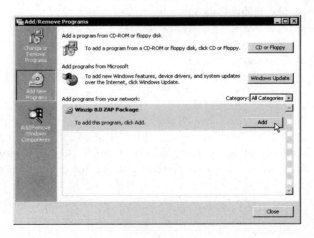

Once you've selected it and clicked Add, the WinZip setup program will launch and can be set up in any desired fashion.

> Alternatively, you can double-click either a .ZIP or an .ARC file to automatically launch the .ZAP file setup application via document invocation (also known as auto-install).

Testing Publishing Applications to Users

You can also test Publishing applications before continuing. Recall that the icons of Published applications appear in the Add or Remove Programs folder (or "Install a program from the network") in Control Panel. However, the usefulness of Published applications is minimal, which is why it's relegated to such a small section for discussion. Users must be specifically told there's something waiting for them, hunt it down themselves, and install it. And, applications can only be Published to users, not computers; so a user who is getting a Published application must be logged in.

To test this for yourself, simply select Publish when adding a new application, or right-click an existing package Assigned to users and choose Publish from the context menu.

To see a Published application in action on a Windows XP or Windows 2000 machine, follow these steps from a client who is receiving a Published application:

1. Choose Start ➢ Control Panel ➢ Add or Remove Programs to open the Add or Remove Programs applet in Control Panel.

2. Click the Add New Programs button to display those applications that have been Published for the user, as seen previously in Figure 11.11.

3. Ask the user to click the Add button next to the application, and it will be fully loaded on the machine.

The applications will then appear on the Start ➢ All Programs menu, as seen previously in Figure 11.10, ready to be utilized.

To see a Published application in action on a Windows Vista or Windows 7 machine, follow these steps:

1. Choose Start ➢ Control Panel ➢ Programs ➢ Get Programs ➢ Install a program from the network.

2. Select the application and select Install, as shown in Figure 11.12.

A Published application needn't be fully relegated to lying dormant until a user selects it. Indeed, the default is to specify that the application automatically launch via document invocation (also known as auto-install) as soon as an associated file type is opened. In this way, you can have the application available for use but just not have the application's icons appear on the Start Menu as you do when you Assign it. However, you can turn off document invocation by clearing the "Auto install this application by file extension activation" check box as specified in the section, "The Deployment Options Section," a bit later.

FIGURE 11.12   A Published application in Windows Vista and Windows 7 can be seen in Control Panel.

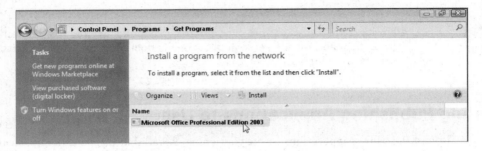

 You'll need to adjust the deployment properties before certain applications will deploy properly to users. (More on this in the "Advanced Published or Assigned" section later in this chapter.)

Application Isolation

In many circumstances, applications are *isolated* for their intended use. Here are some examples:

- Users do not share Assigned or Published applications that an administrator has set up. For instance, User A is Assigned an application and installs it. User B can use User A's machine, but is not Assigned the application via Group Policy. Therefore, when User B logs onto that machine, User B does not see the Assigned icons for User A.

- Users require their own "instance" of the application. If User A and User B are Assigned the same application, each user must contact the source and perform a onetime per-user customization that some applications require. In most circumstances, this will not double the used disk space, and the time for installation for the second user is not very long because portions of the application are already installed for User A.

- If two users are Assigned different applications that register the same file types, the correct application is always used. For instance, Joe and Dave share the same machine. Joe is Assigned Word 2000, and Dave is Assigned Office XP. When Joe opens a .DOC file, Office 2000's Word 2000 launches. When Dave opens a .DOC file, Office XP's Word 2002 launches. I even tried deploying Office 2007 to the computer and Office 2003 to a user, and the user side won. But, Office 2007's icons were available for selection, of course, via the Start Menu.

- Depending on the .MSI application, users might not be able to go "under the hood" and select the .EXEs of installed programs. For instance, if User A is Assigned an application, User B (who is not Assigned the application) cannot just use Explorer, locate the application on the hard drive, and double-click the application to install it. This is not a hard-and-fast rule and is based on how the .MSI application itself is coded. In Figure 11.13, you can see what happens when a user who is not specifically Assigned Office 2000 (yes, Office 2000) tries to run `Winword.exe` from Program Files. However, I tried this again with Office 2003, and, well, it let me run it just fine as another user.

FIGURE 11.13   Some applications prevent users from just clicking the actual .EXE of the installed file. Again, this behavior is entirely application-specific.

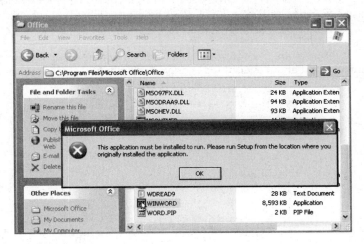

- Users can uninstall applications that they have access to in the Add or Remove Programs folder (or "Uninstall or change a program" in Windows Vista and later parlance). This has a two-part implication. First, by default, all Assigned applications are also Published, and thus, users can remove them using the Add or Remove Programs folder. The icons for the applications will still be on the Start ➤ All Programs menu the next time the user logs on. The first time the user attempts to run one of these applications by choosing Start ➤ All Programs ➤ *application*, the application reinstalls itself from the distribution point. The second implication deals with who, precisely, can remove Assigned (or Published) applications. First, users cannot delete applications that are directly Assigned to computers. Next, users cannot delete applications that aren't directly Assigned to their user account.

Office 2000 and later can prevent users from just clicking their installed .EXEs. These applications use .MSI APIs to verify the application state. For more information about how an application can become "installer aware," see http://tinyurl.com/ybehoc2.

Advanced Published or Assigned

When you attempt to Publish or Assign an application to your users or computers, you are given an additional selection of Advanced. If you didn't choose Advanced when you initially deployed the application, that's not a problem. You can simply right-click the package and choose Properties from the context menu to open the Properties dialog box. The only option that is not available in this "after the fact" method is the ability to add Microsoft Transform Files, which I'll describe in the section, "The Modifications Tab," later in this chapter.

The Properties dialog box has six tabs: General, Deployment, Upgrades, Categories, Modifications, and Security. In Figure 11.14, the Properties dialog box is focused on the Deployment tab, which is discussed in detail in this section.

FIGURE 11.14 These are the options on the Deployment tab when Assigning to computers. Note how just about everything is grayed out when Assigning to computers.

The General Tab

This tab contains the basic information about the package: the name that is to be displayed in the Add or Remove Programs folder (or "Install a program from the network"), the publisher, and some language and support information. All this is extracted from the .MSI package.

Under the General tab, you'll find another little goodie: you can specify the URL of a Web page that contains support information for the application. For instance, if you have specific setup instructions for the user, you can place the instructions on a page on one of your intranet servers and include the URL with the package. The client's Add or Remove Programs folder displays a hyperlink to the URL next to the package. Although .ZAP files also display this information, you can't configure these files once they are Published.

The Deployment Tab

This tab, as shown in Figure 11.14, has three sections: "Deployment type," "Deployment options," and "Installation user interface options." There is also an Advanced button at the bottom of the tab. Which options on the Deployment tab you choose depends on how you want to deploy the application and whether you are Assigning to computer or Assigning or Publishing to users. Figure 11.14 earlier shows the options when you're Assigning to computers.

Figure 11.15 shows the options on the Deployment tab when Assigning an application to users. You'll notice that many more options are available than when Assigning to computers. The options in the "Installation user interface options" section are critical, and you will likely need to change them before applications are correctly Assigned or Published to users.

FIGURE 11.15   These are the options on the Deployment tab when Assigning or Publishing to users.

The Deployment Type Section

The options in this section let you instantly change the deployment type from Published to Assigned, and vice versa, and are available only when you are deploying applications to users. When you are deploying applications to computers, Assigning is the only option. If you're deploying to user accounts, you can also change the deployment type by right-clicking the package definition. You can see a package definition of an application in the

Group Policy Management Editor dialog box in Figure 11.7, earlier. Then, you can select the deployment type, Assign or Publish, from the context menu.

The Deployment Options Section

This section has four check boxes:

Auto-install this application by file extension activation   When .MSI applications are Published or Assigned (or .ZAP packages are Published), each of their definitions contains a list of supported file types. Those file types are actually loaded inside Active Directory.

When a GPO applies to a user or a computer and this check box is selected, the application is automatically installed based on the extension. This is, essentially, application execution via document invocation. Note that this option is always automatically selected (and cannot be unselected) if you Assign the application. That is, document invocation is only optional when Publishing.

Document invocation is most handy when new readers and file types are released, such as Adobe Acrobat Reader and its corresponding .PDF file type. Simply Assign or Publish an application with this check box enabled, and Acrobat Reader will be automatically shot down to anyone who opens a .PDF file for the first time. This check box is selected by default when you are Assigning applications to users or computers.

Uninstall this application when it falls out of the scope of management   GPOs can be applied to sites, domains, or OUs. If a user is moved out of the scope to which this GPO applies, what happens to the currently deployed software? For instance, if a user or computer is moved from one OU to another, what do you want to happen with this specific software package? If you don't want the software to remain on the workstation, click this check box. Remember—the applications aren't removed immediately if a user or computer leaves the scope of the GPO. As you'll see shortly, computers receive a *signal* to remove the software. (This is described in the "Removing Applications" section, later in this chapter.)

Do not display this package in the Add/Remove Programs control panel   As mentioned, icons and program names for Assigned applications appear in the Start ➤ All Programs menu, but, by default, they also appear as Published icons in the Add or Remove Programs applet in Control Panel. Thus, users may choose to install the application all at once or perform an en masse repair. However, the dark side of this check box is that users can remove any application they want. To prevent the application from appearing in the Add or Remove Programs folder or "Install a program from the network," select this check box. When the application is then earmarked for being Published, the application is available only for loading through document invocation.

Install this application at logon   This option is new and applies only to Windows XP and later clients. See the section, "Using Group Policy Software Installation over Slow Links," later in this chapter for a detailed explanation.

The Installation User Interface Options Section

Two little, innocuous buttons in this section make a world of difference for many applications when Assigning or Publishing applications to users. Some .MSI packages can recognize when Basic or Maximum is set and change their installation behavior accordingly. Others can't. Consult your .MSI package documentation to see if the package uses this option and what it does.

Assigning applications like Office 2003 to users can be disastrous if you retain the default of Maximum. Instead of the application automatically and nearly silently loading from the source upon first use, the user is prompted to step through the Office 2003 Installation Wizard (the first screen of which is shown in Figure 11.16).

FIGURE 11.16   The default of Maximum results in many applications (like Office 2003) no longer being a silent install.

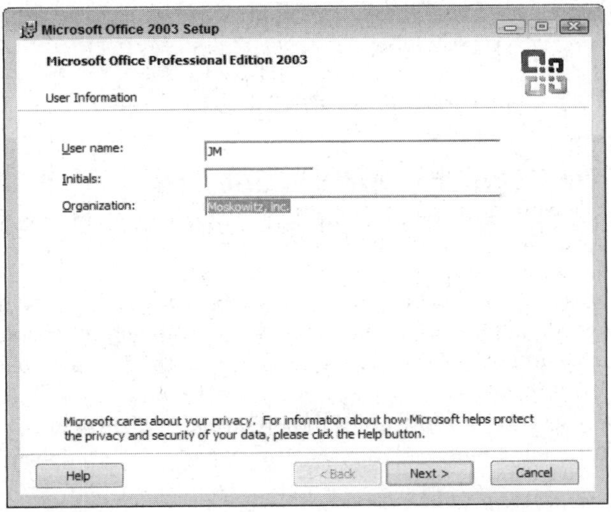

Simply choosing Basic remedies this problem: Office 2003 is magically downloaded and installed for every user targeted in the OU. Why is Maximum the default? I wish I knew. For now, if you're Assigning applications to users, be sure the Basic check box is checked. For information about how to change the defaults, see the "Default Group Policy Software Installation Properties" section later in this chapter.

The Advanced Button

Clicking the Advanced button opens the Advanced Deployment Options dialog box, as shown in Figure 11.17. This dialog box has two sections: "Advanced deployment options" and "Advanced diagnostic information."

FIGURE 11.17   The options in the Advanced Deployment Options dialog box in Windows Server 2003

The Advanced Deployment Options Section

In the modern GPMC, this section has three options, and in the old GPMC, it has four options:

Ignore language when deploying this package   If the .MSI package definition is coded to branch depending on the language, selecting this option can force one version of the language. Normally, if the language of the .MSI package doesn't match the language of the operating system, Windows will not install it. The exceptions are if the application is in English, if the application is language-neutral, or if this check box is checked. If there are multiple versions of the application in different languages, the .MSI engine chooses the application with the best language match.

Remove Previous Installs of This Product for Users, If the Product Was Not Installed by Group Policy-Based Software Installation (old versions)   If you use a really old version of the Group Policy editor, you'll see this option. However, in Figure 11.17, there is just an empty hole. For each .MSI application, a unique product code (which is shown in Figure 11.17) is embedded in the .MSI. If your users somehow get their own copy of the .MSI source, and the product code matches the .MSI application, they can forcibly uninstall their copy before loading the copy you specified.

This can come in handy if the folks in your organization run out to the local big-box store and buy a version of a program you weren't ready to deploy using Group Policy—say, Office 2003. If users acquire and install their own copy of Office 2003 before you're ready to officially deploy it using Group Policy, you can forcibly remove the copy they install. Once you are ready to deploy Office 2003 using Group Policy, be sure to select this check box to remove all copies of Office 2003 that you did not deploy using Group Policy. The copy you're shooting down from on high will then be installed. In this way, you can ensure that all copies you deploy using Group Policy are consistent, even if your users try to sneak around the system.

This works because the unique product code you're sending via Group Policy matches the product code of the .MSI package the user loaded on the machine. The Office 2003 you deploy is essentially the same as the Office 2003 they deploy. The product codes match, and the application you deliver wins if you select this check box.

Why is this option absent from the later versions of the Windows 2000 tools or the Windows Server 2003 version of the Adminpak tools? Because this default behavior is set "on" from Windows 2000 Service Pack (SP4) and later. This procedure is performed automatically and is no longer required as an option.

Even if you repackage your own applications (such as WinZip, Adobe Acrobat Reader, and so on) using a third-party tool (such as WinINSTALL), a product code is automatically generated when the package is created, However, if you deploy those repackaged applications with Group Policy (in conjunction with this check box in Windows 2000), this procedure does not remove copies of applications that users installed with Setup.exe-style programs. It removes only applications on the target machine that have an .MSI product code.

Make this 32-bit X86 application available to Win64 machines   Modern 64-bit clients ignore this setting. I tested it with Windows XP 64 and Windows 7 64 bit, and this setting didn't matter—on or off. It was used for older computers, like Windows Server 2003 targets.

Include OLE class and product information   I've never needed this switch, but here's the idea: if the application you're deploying uses COM classes, and that COM class is triggered, then the application is pulled down automatically. Again, I never needed it. Check with your application vendor to see if you need this switch.

The Advanced Diagnostic Information Section

You can't modify anything in this section, but it does have some handy information.

Product code   As mentioned, if the unique product code of the application you are deploying matches an existing installed product, the application will be removed from the client.

Deployment count   A bit later in this chapter, you'll learn why you might need to redeploy an application to a population of users or computers. When you do, this count is increased. See the section, "Using MSIEXEC to Patch a Distribution Point," a bit later for more information.

Script name   Whenever an application is Published or Assigned, a pointer to the application, also known as an .AAS file, is placed in the SYSVOL in the Policies container within the GPT (Group Policy Template). The .AAS files are application advertisement script files and are critical to an application's ability to install on first use. This entry shows the name of the .AAS file, which can be useful information if you're chasing down a GPO replication problem between Domain Controllers.

The Upgrades Tab

You can deploy a package that upgrades an existing package. For instance, if you want to upgrade from Office XP to Office 2003, you can prepare the Office 2003 installation (as we did earlier) and then specify that you want an upgrade, which can be either mandatory or optional.

 There is no Upgrades tab for .ZAP package definitions.

Moreover, you can "upgrade" to totally different programs. For instance, if your corporate application for .ZIP files is WinZip but changes to UltraZip, follow these steps to upgrade:

1. Create the UltraZip .MSI package, Assign or Publish the application, open the Properties dialog box, and click the Upgrades tab.

2. Click the Add button to open the Add Upgrade Package dialog box, as shown in Figure 11.18.

3. In the "Package to upgrade" section, select the package definition (in this case, WinZip 8). Note that WinZip doesn't specifically appear in our example in Figure 11.18; it's just the dialog box.

FIGURE 11.18   Use the Upgrades tab to migrate from one application to another.

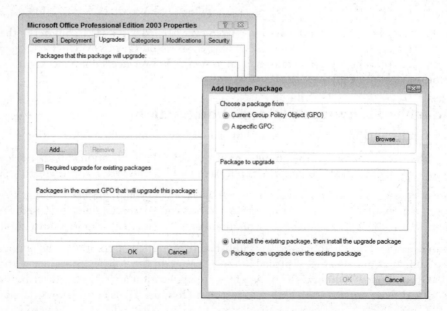

Although you can click the Browse button to open the Browse dialog box and select another GPO for this to apply to, it's easier to keep the original package and upgrade in the same GPO scope.

4. Use the options at the bottom of the Add Upgrade Package window to choose either to uninstall the application first or to plow on top of the current installation, and then click OK.

5. Back in the Upgrades tab, check the "Required upgrade for existing packages" check box and click OK to force the upgrade.

If the "Required upgrade for existing packages" check box is cleared, users can optionally add the program using the Add or Remove Programs applet in Control Panel. This can cause grief for some applications, such as Office 2003 and Office XP, if they're together on the same machine. Moreover, if the check box is not checked, the old application is started whenever an associated file extension (such as .DOC) is invoked.

It is best if your package is specifically written to upgrade earlier (or different) products; sometimes, it may not actually remove the previous application.

When Assigning to computers, the "Required upgrade for existing package" check box is always checked and not available for selection.

The Categories Tab

The Categories tab allows administrators to give headings to groups of software, which are then displayed in the Add or Remove Programs applet in Control Panel. Users can select the category of software they want to display and then select a program within the category to install. (In Figure 11.11 earlier, look above the mouse cursor, which shows the Category drop-down box.)

For example, you might want to create the category Archive Programs for WinZip and UltraZip and the category Doc Readers for Adobe Acrobat Reader and GhostScript. If you want, you can list a package in multiple categories. You can also create categories. For information on how to do so, see the "Default Group Policy Software Installation Properties" section later in this chapter.

The Modifications Tab

The Modifications tab is used to support Microsoft Transform Files (.MST) files, or just Transform Files for short. Transform Files are applied on current .MSI packages either to filter the number of options available to the end user, or to specify certain answers to questions usually brought up during the `.MSI` package installation.

Each vendor's `.MST` transform-creation program is unique. Ask your application vendor if a transform-generation utility for your package is available. If not, you might have to step up to a third-party `.MSI`/`.MST` tool, such as Symantec Wise Package Studio or AdminStudio by Flexera. Some applications, such as Office 2000, Office XP, and Office 2003, come with their own `.MST` generation tool.

Handy! But, again, that situation is unique. Often, vendors just assume you will be able to use an `.MST` transform-creation program to create MSTs.

> Office 2007 does not ship with an MST-generation tool. See the section, "Deploying Office 2007 and Office 2010 Using Group Policy," later for more information.

In Figure 11.19, you can see I've loaded an `.MST` file named `NOMSACCESS.MST`. This `.MST` will prohibit the use of Microsoft Access 2003 from Office 2003 but allow all other functions of Office 2003 to run.

The Modifications tab is available for use only when Advanced is selected when an application is to be initially Published or Assigned. If a package is already Published or Assigned, the Modifications tab is not usable. As you can see in Figure 11.19, all of the buttons on the Modifications tab are grayed out. Again, this is because the `.MST` file was loaded at package deployment time, and afterward, there is no way to add or remove `.MST` files after deployment. We'll reiterate and reexamine this issue a bit later.

FIGURE 11.19   You can only add `.MST` files during the package definition.

There is no Modifications tab for .ZAP package definitions because Transform Files apply only to .MSI files.

You might be wondering how you can create your own .MST files for Office—and that's what the next section is about. After you're done, you'll have the chance to load your .MST file to test it out.

 Neither Office 2007 nor Office 2010 uses Transform Files, and hence, you wouldn't use the Modifications tab. Office 2007 and Office 2010 have their own wacky way of describing settings during installation time. See the section, "Deploying Office 2007 and Office 2010 Using Group Policy," later.

Using the Office *.MST* Generation Tool

You can deploy Office 2000, Office XP, and Office 2003, for instance, whole hog by using their included .MSI package. Indeed, you saw this earlier. All applications of Office were available when our users chose to use Office. But what if we didn't want, say, Microsoft Access available to our users? Or what if we want to adjust an Office property at a global level?

Using the Custom Installation Wizards from the Office Resource Kit, you can create an .MST file that can limit which options can be installed, as well as specify all sorts of custom options, including the default installation path, the organization name, the custom Outlook behavior, and more. The tool has the same name in all three versions of Office (but the application is unique to each). Table 11.1 shows you where to find the downloads.

TABLE 11.1   Location of Office Resource Kit Downloads

Office Version	Where to Find the Resource Kit
Office 2000	http://office.microsoft.com/en-us/ork2000/default.aspx
Office XP	http://office.microsoft.com/en-us/orkxp/default.aspx
Office 2003	http://office.microsoft.com/en-us/ork2003/default.aspx
Office 2007	http://tinyurl.com/vf9e3 (goes to the Microsoft website). But there is no tool to create .MST files for Office 2007. We'll learn later that you create .MSP files (yes, .MSP files) with setup /admin. (See "Deploying Office 2007 and Office 2010 Using Group Policy.")
Office 2010	Not available as of this writing. Office 2010 is like Office 2007 in that the Office Customization Tool (OCT) is built in by simply running setup /admin. It also spits out .MSP files.

The procedure to create an .MST is straightforward but quite long, and I simply don't have room available to dedicate to each and every step. In this example, I'll assume you're using the Office 2003 Custom Installation Wizard (CIW). Here is the basic overview:

1. Choose Start ≻ All Programs ≻ Microsoft Office Tools ≻ [*the version of the tool you loaded*] ≻ Custom Installation Wizard to start the CIW.

2. Tell the CIW where your administrative installation of that version of Office is. Remember, you created an administrative installation of Office 2003 in the section, "Setting Up an Administrative Installation (for .MSI Files that Need Them)," earlier in this chapter.

3. Give your .MST file a creative name, for example, nomsaccess.mst.

4. Continue to follow the wizard's instruction, choosing your specific installation options. In this example, on screen 7 (of 24), as shown in Figure 11.20, we'll tell Office 2003 that we don't want Microsoft Access available to users.

FIGURE 11.20   Use the CIW to choose the options you want and create the .MST file.

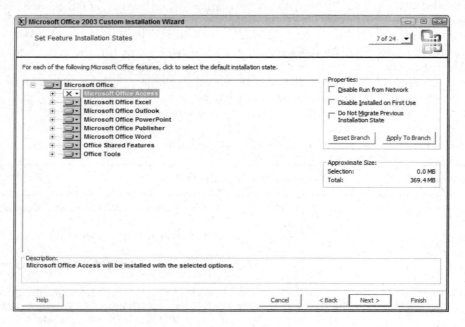

5. At the final screen, click Finish and save the .MST file to a handy location.

As the CIW presents the final wizard screen, it will give you information about how to run the .MSI file along with the .MST file manually. But you can ignore this because you're about to use the .MST file in a Group Policy Software Installation GPO.

Applying Your .*MST* File to the Installation

As previously stated, you can add .MST files only when you're initially Assigning or Publishing a package. .MST files are valid, say, for Office 2003, but, it turns out, like I said, Office 2007 doesn't support them. See the upcoming section, "Using GPSI and Customizing Office 2007 Deployments," for the details.

You performed these steps earlier in the "Creating and Editing the GPO to Deploy Office" section, as shown in Figure 11.5. When you follow those steps, the "Select deployment method" dialog box will appear. Afterward, follow these steps:

1. In the "Select deployment method" dialog box, click Advanced to open the Properties dialog box.

2. Click the Modifications tab, and click Add to open the Open dialog box.

3. In the "File name" field, enter the full UNC path of the .MST file, such as

   \\DC01\apps\office2003distro\nomsaccess.mst

 The .MST file needn't be in the same location as the .MSI distribution, as long as the path is available via the UNC name.

---

4. Click OK.

Your screenshot should be similar to what is seen in Figure 11.19 in the section, "The Modifications Tab."

Once you click OK, the .MST file will be locked in and cannot be changed. You have only two options if you are unhappy with the .MST file:

- Remove the package and deploy it again.

- Create an upgrade package as described earlier.

Removing the entire Office suite and reinstalling it can be a pain for your users, so if you want to deploy Office with (or without) .MST files, be sure to test in the lab before you start your deployment.

The Security Tab

Individual applications can be filtered based on computer, user, or Security group membership. For instance, if you Assign Office 2003 to all members of the **Human Resources Users** OU, you set it up normally, as described earlier.

 If a user who happens to administer the application in the GPO is not given Read access, that user will no longer be able to administer the application. Therefore, don't use filtering based on user or Security group membership on the administrators of the application.

What's with the Move Up and Move Down Buttons in the Modifications Tab?

If you wanted to, you could add multiple .MST files before clicking the OK button to lock in your selection. You can see this ability and the move up and move down buttons in Figure 11.19. But why would you do this?

Multiple, autonomous administrators can individually create .MST files and layer them so that each Transform File contains some of the configuration options. These files are then ordered so that the options are applied from the top down. If configured options overlap, the last-configured option wins.

However, in my travels, I haven't seen administrators choose to add multiple .MST files for the same .MSI. Typically, only one .MST file is used, as we did in the previous example.

If, however, you want to exclude a specific member, say, Frank Rizzo, you can deny Frank Rizzo's account permissions to Read the package. A better strategy is to create a Security group—say, DenyOffice2003—and put the people not allowed to receive the application inside that group. You can then set the permissions to Deny the entire Security group the ability to read the package, as shown in Figure 11.21.

FIGURE 11.21   Use the Security tab to specify who can and cannot run applications.

Default Group Policy Software Installation Properties

Each GPSI node (one for users and one for computers) has some default installation properties that you can modify. In the Group Policy Management Editor, simply right-click the GPSI node and choose Properties from the context menu, as shown in Figure 11.22, to open the "Software installation Properties" dialog box (also shown in Figure 11.22), which has four tabs: General, Advanced, File Extensions, and Categories.

FIGURE 11.22   Use the GPSI Properties dialog box to set up general deployment settings.

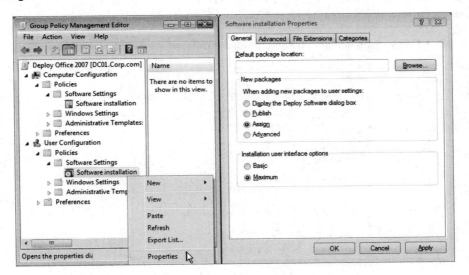

The General Tab

Most settings on the General tab are self-explanatory. Note that you can specify a default package location, such as \\DC01\apps, so that you can then use the GUI when adding packages. Avoid using direct paths such as C:\apps\ since C:\apps probably won't exist on the client at runtime.

You can also specify the behavior of what happens when you add in new packages (and the Assign action is chosen). That is, a collection of defaults you specify is automatically selected.

Last, you can establish the critical setting of either Basic or Maximum here (when Assigning applications to users). The bummer is that these default setting changes are local only for this specific GPO: the next GPO you create that uses GPSI will not adhere to the defaults you set in this GPO.

The Advanced Tab

The Advanced tab, as shown in Figure 11.23, allows you to set default settings for all the packages you want to deploy in this GPO. You saw settings with similar names earlier in the Advanced Deployment Options dialog box (Figure 11.17). The Advanced tab contains the following options:

Uninstall the applications when they fall out of the scope of management I'll discuss this setting in the "Removing Applications" section later in this chapter.

Include OLE information when deploying applications Again, an application might have COM components called by some other action. Selecting this check box will auto-download the deployed application if the trigger occurs.

The "32-bit applications on 64-bit platforms" section Again, the options in this section seem to do nothing on modern 64-bit systems.

FIGURE 11.23 You can set up some default settings for new packages in this GPO.

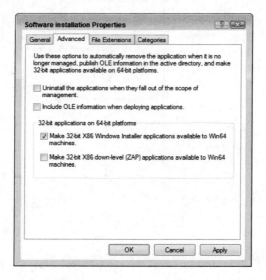

The File Extensions Tab

As stated earlier, you can install and start applications by double-clicking or by invoking their document type. For instance, double-clicking a .ZIP file can automatically deploy a Published or Assigned WinZip application. The correspondence of a file type to a package is found in either the .ZAP file definition or the .MSI file database. Once the application is set to be deployed, the file types are automatically entered into Active Directory.

Occasionally, two Published or Assigned applications are called by the same file extension. This can occur if you're upgrading a package from, say, WinZip to UltraZip, and both are using the .ZIP extension, or if you're upgrading from Office XP to Office 2003 and both Word applications use the .DOC extension.

In those cases, you need to specify which extension fires off which application. To do so, follow these steps:

1. In the "Software installation Properties" dialog box, click the File Extensions tab.

2. Click the "Select file extension" drop-down list box, and select the extension to display all the applicable Assigned or Published applications in the Application Precedence list.

3. Select an application, and then click the Up or Down button to change the order.

The Categories Tab

Categories is a domain-wide property that puts Published or Assigned software into bite-sized chunks, instead of one giant-sized alphabetized list in the Add or Remove Programs folder or "Install a program from the network" window. As noted earlier, you might want to group WinZip and UltraZip in the Archive Programs category or put Adobe Acrobat Reader and GhostScript in the Doc Readers category. On this tab, simply click the Add button to enter the names of the categories in the "Enter new category" dialog box.

Therefore, if possible, select one administrator to control this property, set it up to be centrally managed, and then use the Properties dialog box to associate a package with a category or categories.

Removing Applications

You can remove applications from users or computers in several ways. First, under some circumstances, users can manually remove applications, but as an administrator, you hold the reins. Therefore, you can set applications to automatically or forcibly be removed.

Users Can Manually Change or Remove Applications

If an application is Assigned (and also Published) to users, they can use Control Panel to change the installed options or remove the application to save space. However, Microsoft's position is that this ability provides the best of both worlds: the user can remove the application's installation (and save space), but since the application is Assigned, the icons and program names are always forced to appear on the Start ≻ All Programs menu.

But, in practice, I've found that this is a bad thing. Users can remove their applications and then go on the road with their laptops. What happens when users actually need those applications? Uh-oh. You get the picture. Again, you may wish to prevent users from being able to change this setting if you have users who like to poke around a lot.

Note, however, that applications Assigned to the computer cannot be changed or uninstalled by anyone but local computer administrators. This is a good thing.

Automatically Removing Assigned or Published *.MSI* Applications

Applications can be automatically uninstalled when they no longer apply to the user. Earlier, in the "Advanced Published or Assigned" section, you saw that in the Deployment tab of the "Software installation Properties" dialog box you can check the "Uninstall this application when it falls out of the scope of management" check box (Figure 11.15). You can specify that the application is to be uninstalled if any of the following occurs:

- The user or computer is moved out of the OU to which this software applies.
- The GPO containing the package definition is deleted.
- The user or computer no longer has rights to read the GPO.

The software is never forcibly removed while the user is logged onto the current session, but is removed a bit later in the following manner:

- Applications Published to users are removed upon next logon.
- Applications Assigned to users are removed upon next logon.
- Applications Assigned to computers are removed upon next reboot.
- Applications Assigned to computers that are currently not attached to the network are removed the next time the computer is plugged into the network, rebooted, and the computer account "logs on" to Active Directory.
- Applications Assigned or Published to users on computers that are currently not attached to the network are removed the next time they log on and are validated to Active Directory.

In these cases, the software is automatically removed upon next logon (for users) or upon next reboot (for computers). For example, Figure 11.24 shows what happens when a computer is moved out of an OU and then rebooted. Moving users and computers in and out of OUs might not be such a hot idea if lots of applications are being Assigned.

These rules assume Fast Boot is not enabled—that you've specifically *disabled* Fast Boot. If Fast Boot is enabled (the default), these rules don't apply; expect two logons or two reboots for the change to take effect.

Here's one final warning about the automatic removal of applications: GPSI cannot remove the icons and program names for the application if the GPO has been deleted and the user has a Roaming Profile and has roamed to a machine after the application was uninstalled. In this case, there is not enough uninstall information on the machine, and therefore, the icons and program names will continue to exist, though they will be nonfunctional.

FIGURE 11.24   Applications can be set to uninstall when they fall out of scope of management.

Forcibly Removing Assigned or Published *.MSI* Applications

You have seen how applications can be automatically removed from users or computers when the user or computer object moves out the scope of management. But what if you want to keep the user or computer in the scope of management and still remove an application? You can manually remove Published or Assigned applications. To do so, simply right-click the package definition, and choose All Tasks ➤ Remove, as seen in Figure 11.25. This will open the Remove Software dialog box. The options presented in this dialog box depend on whether you deployed .MSI or .ZAP applications.

FIGURE 11.25   You can revoke deployed applications by selecting Remove.

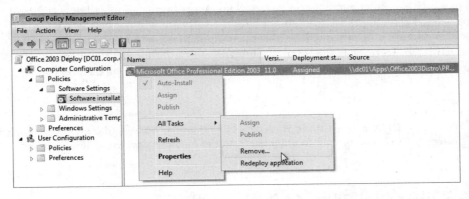

If you are removing an .MSI file, you have two options, as discussed in the next sections.

Immediately Uninstall the Software from Users and Computers

If you choose the option "Immediately uninstall the Software from Users and Computers," then all connected computers receive a signal to uninstall the software, and they follow the rules for uninstalling you learned in the previous section.

The signal to remove an application (such as Office XP) lives in the actual GPO definition. Therefore, if you're looking for success in the forcible removal of applications, don't delete the GPO right after selecting this option. If you do, the signal to remove the application won't be available to the workstations. Rather, remove the application, and leave the GPO definition around for a while to ensure that the computers get the signal to remove the software. If you remove the GPO before the target user receives the signal (upon next logon) or the computer receives the signal (upon next reboot), the application is orphaned on the Desktop and must be manually unloaded via Control Panel or by some other means (for instance, MSIEXEC, as described later in this chapter).

This is a second warning in case you overlooked the ominous message in the previous paragraph: if you remove the GPO definition before a target user or computer receives the signal, the application is orphaned on the Desktop. You can, however, likely get out of this trap if the application was specified with the "Uninstall this application when it falls out of the scope of management" check box. You can move the user or computer out of the scope of management to remove the application and then bring it back in when the application removal is completed. It's a bit rough, but it should work.

Allow Users to Continue to Use the Software, but Prevent New Installations

When you remove applications using the option, "Allow users to continue to use the software, but prevent new installations," current installations of the software remain intact. Users to which this edict applies, however, will no longer be able to install new copies of the software. Therefore, those who do not have the software will not be able to install it. Those who do have it installed will be able to continue to use it.

The self-repair features of the Windows Installer will still function (for example, if Winword.exe gets deleted, it will come back from the dead), but the application cannot be fully reinstalled via Control Panel.

Once you use this option, you will no longer be able to manage the application and force it to uninstall from the machines on which it is installed.

Removing Published *.ZAP* Applications

You have only one option for removing .ZAP applications. When you right-click the package definition and select Remove (as seen in Figure 11.25), you'll have to answer but one question: "Remove the Package but Leave the Application Installed Everywhere It Is Already Installed?"

Remember that since the .ZAP file really calls only the original Setup.exe program, ultimately, Setup.exe is in charge of how the application is uninstalled. Therefore, once applications are deployed using .ZAP files, the power to forcibly uninstall them is out of your hands.

Troubleshooting the Removal of Applications

Sometimes, applications refuse to leave the target system gracefully. Usually, this is because an application has been Published or Assigned, and the user has "double-dipped" by throwing in the CD and installing a program on top of itself. Sometimes, the Windows Installer becomes confused. When you then try to remove the application from being Published or Assigned, the application doesn't know what to do.

If an application refuses to go away (or you're left with entries in the Add or Remove Programs applet in Control Panel), you have two tools at your disposal: the Windows Installer CleanUp utility (also known as MSICUU) and MSIZAP. Both utilities are now available at Microsoft's download site. Both do essentially the same thing: they manually hunt down all Registry settings for an application and delete them. This action of deleting the Registry settings usually removes all vestigial entries in the Add or Remove Programs applet in Control Panel, but you will usually have to clean up the files that were left behind (if any).

Windows Installer CleanUp Utility (MSICUU)   This tool has a GUI. Programs displayed in the Installed Products list, as shown in Figure 11.26, are the same as those in the Add or Remove Programs applet in Control Panel. At last check, the tool was available at http://support.microsoft.com/kb/290301.

MSIZAP   MSIZAP is a command-line tool with a similar function. You must specify an .MSI product code (GUID) to hunt down and destroy. At last check, you can find additional references and download MSIZAP at http://tinyurl.com/2kobm3. However, you'll have to download and install the monstrous Windows Installer SDK just to get it.

FIGURE 11.26   The MSICUU program in the Support Tools can whack entire programs off your system.

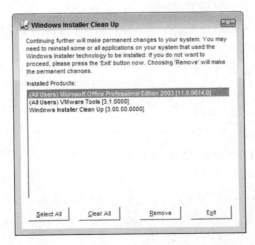

Using Group Policy Software Installation over Slow Links

First things first: applications Assigned to computers cannot ever be installed over a slow dial-up link or a VPN (virtual private network) connection. Why? Because the computer must see the network, log onto it, and then start to download the program. If you're using a dial-up or other slow connection, manual intervention to connect to the network must be involved. Therefore, in general, no applications Assigned to computers will ever install unless the computer is connected to the LAN.

 I say "in general" in the previous sentence because it does depend a bit on your VPN technology. For instance, you could have a hardware VPN, separate from the client, and a computer assignment could work over that should a slow link not be detected. Indeed, Microsoft's newest "VPN-less" technology DirectAccess might be able to overcome this limitation. I have not set up DirectAccess yet myself to test this theory.

However, when applications are Assigned or Published to users (not computers), it's a different story. When users connect via a slow link, they will not see new Assignment offers. By default, only users connected at 500Kbps or greater will see new Assignments on the Start ➤ All Programs menu. This is a good thing, too, as you wouldn't want someone dialing in over a 56Kbps modem to try to accept the offer of Office 2003.

You can change this behavior by modifying the GPO at Computer Configuration ➤ Policies ➤ Administrative Templates ➤ System ➤ Group Policy ➤ **Software Installation Policy Processing**, as shown in Figure 11.27.

FIGURE 11.27   Use Group Policy to change the default slow-link behavior.

Checking the "Allow processing across a slow network connection" check box forces all clients, regardless of their connection speed, to adhere to the policy setting. If you want to be a bit less harsh, you can change the definition of a "slow link" and modify the **Group Policy Slow Link Detection** policy setting. After you enable the policy setting, set a value in the "Connection speed (Kbps)" spin box.

One word of warning with regard to slow links: users who are Assigned or Published applications can find other ways to install applications over slow links. First, they can trot out to the Add or Remove Programs applet and select the application. Sure, the offer isn't displayed on the Start ➢ All Programs menu, but it's still going to be available in the Add or Remove Programs applet in Control Panel. To prevent this, select the "Do not display this package in the Add/Remove Programs control panel" check box, which is found in the Deployment tab of the application's Properties (see Figure 11.15).

Last, check out this scenario. Imagine that while on a fast link, a user named Wally accepts the offer for Excel. Super-duper—Excel is now installed. Now, Wally is VPNed in (on a slow link) and receives a Word document in e-mail. And Wally hasn't yet installed Word. Look out! Because .DOC is a registered file type for Microsoft Office, Word will attempt to install over a slow link (if Assigned to a user).

This happens because Wally has accepted the "offer" for Office (he got Excel over a fast link) and now selects to get Word via document invocation. To prevent this, simply clear the "Auto-install this application by file extension activation" option in the Deployment tab in the Properties dialog box of the application (again, see Figure 11.15).

As I stated earlier, users who have dialed up or VPNed over a slow link will not see *new* Assignment offers. The key word here is *new*.

However, this wasn't Wally's problem. He wasn't accepting a new offer over a slow link; rather, Wally had already accepted an offer before he left and VPNed in. If something like that should occur, you'll see something like this:

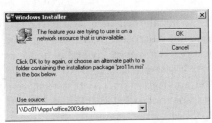

What you're seeing here is the user being asked where the installation source is—even if he's not connected to the network. Not great, because users (a) don't have a connection to the network and (b) wouldn't know the location or (c) know what to type in even if they knew the location (usually).

The best way to handle this is to simply avoid the problem entirely.

So, we could have prevented Wally's problem if the application were already fully installed. But I already said that when you Assign applications to users, the .MSI file is downloaded in chunks—not all at once—which is precisely why Wally had problems when he tried to download Word. He had the "chunk" for Excel, but not for Word. Therefore, he needed to reach the original source for a download.

There are two ways to solve this problem:

Assign applications to computers (laptop OUs)   Again, if you Assigned the application to the OU where Wally's laptop lived, the next time he rebooted, he would have the full installation of Office 2003, thus preventing the issue.

Leverage the "Install this application at logon" option   If you take a peek back in Figure 11.15, you'll see the option, "Install this application at logon." What it should say is "Install this application, in full, for the user if the machine is Windows XP or later." The idea is that whenever Wally logs onto a new machine, he will be force-fed the entirety of the application. Then, he'll be sure to have it on his laptop. Again, this setting is only available when assigning applications to users.

If the user opens the Add or Remove Programs folder (or the "Install a program from the network" window) and manually uninstalls the application, neither the logon script nor the "Install this application at logon" setting will kick back into high gear and install the application. This might be a big deal if your users fool around trying to add or remove stuff. You might also want to select the "Do not display this package in the Add/Remove Programs control panel" check box, also on the Deployment tab in the Properties dialog box.

Managing *.MSI* Packages and the Windows Installer

Users might occasionally want to install their own .MSI packages. Those packages can come on CDs from software vendors, like Microsoft (with .MSI packages such as Office 2003). Or perhaps you have .MSI applications that you've created in house using a third-party "wrap-up" tool like WinINSTALL or Wise Installer.

To manually install an .MSI application on a workstation, you can either double-click the application or use a command-line tool called MSIEXEC to kick off (or repair) the installation.

This section explores the options when manually installing existing .MSI packages that you've deployed via Group Policy. As you've learned throughout the chapter, most of the things we need in order to deploy applications can be performed using the GPSI GUI. However, some functions are available only in the command-line tool.

Inside the *MSIEXEC* Tool

MSIEXEC is a command-line tool, which helps you get applications installed.

You can use MSIEXEC in several ways, but here, we're going to look at how to use it to manage existing .MSI packages. Indeed, you can use MSIEXEC to script an installation of an .MSI package at a workstation, but why bother? You're already using the power of Group Policy. However, you might need to check out how an installation works by hand or enable additional logging for deeper troubleshooting. Or you could trigger a preemptive repair of an application at specific times. You can even use MSIEXEC to remove a specific application.

You can also use MSIEXEC as a maintenance tool for existing packages on distribution points. We'll explore a bit of both uses.

Instead of diving into every MSIEXEC command, I'll highlight some of the most frequently used. Indeed, you may never find yourself using MSIEXEC unless specifically directed to do so by an application vendor's Install program.

Using *MSIEXEC* to Install an Application

The first function of MSIEXEC is to initiate an installation from a source point. This is essentially the same as double-clicking the .MSI file, using the /I switch (for Install). The syntax for your application might be as follows:

```
Msiexec /I \\DC01\apps\yourapp.msi
```

Using *MSIEXEC* to Repair an Application

You can script the repair of applications by using MSIEXEC with the /f switch and an additional helper switch, as indicated in the Windows help file. For instance, you might want to ensure that Pro11n.msi (Office 2003) is not corrupted on the client. You can do so by forcing all files from inside the Office 2003 .MSI to be reinstalled on the client. Use the following command from the client (which overwrites older or equally versioned files):

```
Msiexec /fe \\DC01\apps\office2003distro\pro11.msi
```

If you want to ensure that no older version is installed, you can execute the following command:

```
Msiexec /fo \\DC01\apps\office2003distro\pro11.msi
```

Again, be sure to consult the Windows help file for the complete syntax of MSIEXEC in conjunction with adhering to your specific application vendor's directions.

Using *MSIEXEC* to Patch a Distribution Point

You can also use MSIEXEC to *patch*—that is, to incorporate vendor-supplied bug fixes and the like to the code base of an existing package. The vendor supplies the patches by using an .MSP file, or *Microsoft Patch* file. Office XP's service packs, for instance, come with several .MSP files that update the original .MSI files.

Office 2003 has multiple service packs. You can download the latest one (SP3) from http://support.microsoft.com/kb/923618. It contains mainsp3.msp, owc11sp3.msp, and owc102003sp3.msp.

Microsoft seems to have changed their tune midway with this technology. In some instances, you needed to apply each successive service pack's .MSP files to be sufficiently protected. However, Office XP's Service Pack 3, for instance, expressly states that it contains all the fixes contained within all previous service packs. So, be sure to read your manufacturer's instructions on whether or not to install every .MSP file from every update, or if you can make do with just the most recent.

Throughout this chapter, we've leveraged our Office 2003 administration point. We'll continue with that trend. In the following example, the Office 2003 distribution, located at \\DC01\apps\office2003distro, is to be patched with the MAINSP3.msp patch that comes with Office 2003 Service Pack 3. The resulting log file will be called logfile.txt.

Because each vendor may have a different way of patching, be sure to check out the Readme file that comes with the patch files.

The following command line is written as directed from the Office 2003 SP3 whitepaper:

```
Msiexec.exe /a \\<path>\PRO11n.MSI /p
    \\<path>\MAINSP3.msp SHORTFILENAMES=True
    /qb- /Lv* c:\Logfile.txt
```

Again, you'll have to run the command for each and every included patch file to update an Office 2003 distribution point to SP3. However, the good news is that included in the download are all updates that were contained in the previous service packs. So, at least you don't have to download and install Office 2003 to SP1, or SP2, for that matter. Just install all the patch files in SP3, and you're good to go.

Note the following important point: once the .MSI is patched, all your users (or computers) need to reinstall the application. The underlying application has changed, and the client system doesn't know about the change until you tell it. You can see how to redeploy an application in Figure 11.28. Again, this is only required after an .MSI source is patched.

Users also need to do this because of what is termed the "client-source-out-of-sync" problem. Until the client reaches and reinstalls from the updated administrative image, it won't be able to use the administrative image for repairs or on-demand installations. This is because a source location is validated by the Windows Installer before use. The criteria for validation are the name of the package file and the package code (seen as a GUID) of the package. When you patch the administrative image, you change the underlying package code GUID. Thus, the client needs the recache and reinstall in order to pick up the updated package code information.

FIGURE 11.28   Once you patch an .MSI source, be sure to select "Redeploy application."

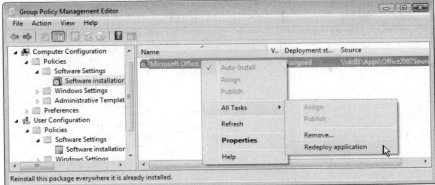

So, specifically, after you patch a distribution point (or otherwise change the underlying .MSI package in a distribution point), you need to right-click the offer and choose All Tasks ➢ Redeploy application, as shown in Figure 11.28.

 Microsoft has some Office 2003 upgrade guidance at http://tinyurl.com/2qce97.

Affecting Windows Installer with Group Policy

You can use several policy settings to tweak the behavior of the Windows Installer. Most tweaks do not involve how software is managed or deployed via GPSI because there's not much to it. You deploy the application, and users (or computers) do your bidding. Rather, these settings tweak the access the user has when software is not being Assigned or Published.

There are two collections of policy settings for the Windows Installer; one is under Computer Configuration, and the other is under User Configuration. As usual, to utilize these policy settings, just create a new GPO, enable the policy settings you like, and then ensure that the corresponding user or computer account is in the scope of management of the GPO.

Computer-Side Policy Settings for Windows Installer

To display the settings in Computer Configuration, as shown in Figure 11.29, choose Computer Configuration ➢ Policies ➢ Administrative Templates ➢ Windows Components ➢ Windows Installer.

FIGURE 11.29   Use Group Policy to affect the Windows Installer settings.

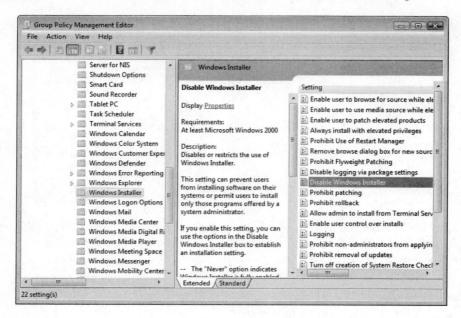

Disable Windows Installer

Once enabled, the **Disable Windows Installer** setting lets you specify one of four options:

Not Configured   Uses the settings at a higher level.

Enabled/Never   Always keeps the Windows Installer active.

Enabled/For Nonmanaged Apps Only   Turns off the Windows Installer when users try to manually install their own applications. This is useful if you want to guarantee no foreign .MSI packages are making it through the doors. This option permits users to install only those programs that a system administrator Assigns or Publishes.

Enabled/Always   Essentially turns off all methods (managed and unmanaged) for loading .MSI packages.

These options specify settings only for .MSI packages—not other programs that users can install, such as those from SETUP.EXEs and the like.

Always Install with Elevated Privileges

Deploying applications with GPSI is awesome: we do all the work with .MSI files, and we don't have to worry about users having administrative privileges. As we've already seen, we can deploy applications to users, and have the system take care of the installation in the system context (not the user context).

And, what's more, mere mortals cannot just download an .MSI application and necessarily expect it to install correctly. Many .MSI applications will fail installation if attempted in the user context. You can, however, bypass the normal security mechanism so that users can install .MSI files by enabling this policy setting. You'll need to do the same with the corresponding policy setting in the user configuration, as discussed in the "User-Side Policy Settings for Windows Installer" section in a moment.

But I would argue that the **Always Install with Elevated Privileges** setting is evil. That's because once enabled, a nefarious user would need only to create a small .MSI with a custom action to add herself to the local admin's group, and, well, that would be a problem. Avoid this entry (and its User-side cousin) at all costs.

If you are deploying .MSI applications with Group Policy, you need not use and enable this setting.

Prohibit Rollback

As stated, .MSI files can be "rolled back" during the actual installation of the application. For instance, a user can click Cancel during an installation, or the computer could suddenly be turned off.

If you enable the **Prohibit Rollback** policy setting, you're effectively telling the system not to maintain "backup files" in the case of an on-the-fly rollback. Since a rollback can be initiated during the actual installation, a "fractured" and, hence, nonworking program could remain on the system.

Personally, I would never use this policy setting.

Remove Browse Dialog Box for New Source

Recall that, at any given point, only the components required to run an .MSI application are actually downloaded. For instance, the help files in Word are downloaded the first time they are used from the installation source (usually the server), not necessarily the first time Word runs. But what happens if you move the source?

When you move an application from one shared folder to another, the application can become confused, and users need to specify a different installation point to get to the source. By default, users can browse to any source.

If you enable the **Remove Browse Dialog Box for New Source** setting, users are only allowed to use specific sources.

Prohibit Patching

If users can install some .MSI applications under their own security context, by default, they can also patch their own .MSI files with .MSP (Microsoft Patch) files by using the MSIEXEC command-line application. Enabling the **Prohibit Patching** setting prevents users from patching even their own installed .MSI applications.

Prohibit Flyweight Patching

The **Prohibit Flyweight Patching** setting is new when a GPO is created from a Windows 7 management station. However, it is valid on machines that have Windows Installer 3. Windows Installer 4 is not required.

If you enable this setting, you're instructing the engine to be meticulous during its patching of applications. If you disable this setting (or leave it Not Configured), you are telling the system to utilize a faster algorithm when patching is needed.

Disable IE Security Prompt for Windows Installer Scripts

Recall that users can manually install .MSI applications from a CD or a shared folder or a Web page. The default behavior before executing any downloaded application via Internet Explorer is to warn the user about potentially damaging content. Enabling the setting **Disable IE Security Prompt for Windows Installer Scripts** squelches this warning.

This scenario should be rare, because normally, you Publish or Assign applications in order to install them to your users' Desktops. At times, however, some applications may be best suited for downloading via Internet Explorer, and, hence, a warning message could appear and frighten your users.

Enable User Control over Installs

When an administrator Publishes or Assigns applications, all the settings specified in the .MSI application are forced upon the user. Sometimes, this behavior is undesirable. For example, you might want to let the user specify the destination folder or decide which features to download. If you enable the **Enable User Control over Installs** setting, you grant users the ability to change the default .MSI application settings.

Enable User to Browse for Source While Elevated

When an administrator Publishes or Assigns applications, all the settings specified in the .MSI application are forced upon the user from the installation point the administrator specifies. Sometimes, this behavior is undesirable because the user knows of a closer source to the application in his or her branch office. In cases like this, you might want to let the user specify the source to locate a closer source point. If you enable the **Enable User to Browse for Source While Elevated** setting, you grant users the ability to change the default .MSI source location.

WARNING   Once users are affected by this policy setting, they can basically browse anywhere they like, including the local system. If you have locked down the Desktop to prevent such behavior, enabling this setting could be a potential security hole during .MSI application install times.

Enable User to Use Media Source While Elevated

When users install .MSI packages under their own security context, they can choose whatever source they desire for the software. But when you, the administrator, Assign or Publish an application, you are essentially dictating the source of the .MSI file. If you enable the **Enable User to Use Media Source While Elevated** setting, you permit the user to choose a non-networked source, such as a CD or floppy drive, from which to install a program you specify. Enable this setting only if the **Enable User to Browse for Source While Elevated** policy is enabled.

Enable User to Patch Elevated Products

By default, only the administrator who Assigns or Publishes the application can use an .MSP file (in conjunction with MSIEXEC) to patch a program. If you enable the **Enable User to Patch Elevated Products** setting, users can use MSIEXEC to patch their local versions of Published or Assigned applications.

Allow Admin to Install from Terminal Services Session

By default, administrators using the Terminal Services Remote Administration Mode on Windows 2000 or Windows Server 2003 are prevented from installing additional Published or Assigned applications.

If you want Administrators to be able to install .MSI applications while logged in via Terminal Services session, just enable the **Allow Admin to Install from Terminal Services Session** setting so that servers and Domain Controllers download the setting and, hence, reverse this default.

Cache Transforms in Secure Location on Workstation

Recall that you can specifically customize an .MST file to hone an .MSI application. Transform Files are applied on .MSI packages either to filter the number of options available to the end user or to specify certain answers to questions, usually raised during the .MSI package installation.

Once a user starts using an .MSI application applied with an .MST file, that .MST file follows them in the Roaming Profile—specifically, in the Application Data folder, as described in Chapter 2. You can change this default behavior by enabling the **Cache Transforms in Secure Location on Workstation** setting, which takes the .MST file out of the Roaming Profile and puts it in a secure place on the workstation. On the one hand, this closes a small security hole that sophisticated users might use to hack into their own .MST files in their profiles. On the other hand, users are forced to return to the machine that has their .MST files in order to additionally modify their application.

Avoid using this setting unless specifically directed to do so by your application vendor, a security bulletin, or Microsoft.

Logging

Applications Assigned or Published using Windows Installer do not provide much information to the administrator about the success of their installation. By default, several key tidbits of information are logged about managed applications that fail. The log files are named .MSI*.LOG; the * represents additional characters that make the log file unique for each application downloaded.

Per-computer logs are in C:\windows\temp and per-user logs are in %temp%.

Thus, centralized logging and reporting is an arduous, if not impossible, task for anything more than a handful of users who are using Windows Installer. For additional logging and reporting, Microsoft recommends their Systems Management Server, as described in the section "Do You Need a 'Big' Management Tool for Your Environment?" later in the chapter.

To add logging entries, *modify the* **Logging** setting. Some settings that might come in handy are Out of Memory and Out of Disk—two common reasons for Windows Installer applications failing to load.

 You can also turn on Application Management debugging logs by manually editing the Registry of the client machine. Simply run regedit or regedt32 and edit the following key: HKEY_LOCAL_MACHINE\Software\Microsoft\ Windows NT\CurrentVersion. Create a key called Diagnostics, and then add a Reg_DWORD value called AppMgmtDebugLevel and set it to 4b in hexa- decimal. You'll then find a log in the local %windir%debug\usermode folder named appmgmt.log, which can also aid in finding out why applications fail to load.

Prohibit User Installs

On occasion, an administrator might dictate that a user is Assigned Office 2003, and another administrator dictates that a computer gets Office 2003 (but perhaps without Microsoft Access). What if the user who is Assigned Office 2003 sits down at a computer that is Assigned Office 2003 without Access? Which one wins? The application (and settings therein) Assigned to the user takes precedence.

The **Prohibit User Installs** policy setting has three options (once enabled): Allow User Installs, Hide User Installs, or Prohibit User Installs. Computers that are affected by Hide User Installs display only the applications Assigned to the computer. However, users can still install the applications Assigned to them using the Add or Remove Programs applet in Control Panel (thus overriding the applications Assigned to the computer).

If you set **Prohibit User Installs**, the user won't get the applications Assigned to him on the machines to which this policy setting applies. And the user cannot load Assigned applications to his user account via the Add or Remove Programs folder or "Install a program from the network." If he does so, he'll get an error message. If this policy setting is set somewhere else, you can also return the default behavior by setting Allow User Installs.

This policy setting can be especially handy in Terminal Services sessions or kiosk settings (for example, lab machines) where you want all users of the machine to get the applications Assigned only to computers (not to users).

This setting is valid for Windows XP and Windows 2000 machines (with Windows Installer 2 or later loaded). See the section, "The Windows Installer Service," earlier in this chapter.

Turn off Creation of System Restore Checkpoints

On a Windows XP machine and later, a System Restore Checkpoint is created when users load their own .MSI files, unless there is no user interface. The .MSI system creates System Restore Checkpoints on first installation and uninstall. System Restore Checkpoints are not created when deploying (or repairing) applications via GPSI.

Enable the **Turn off Creation of System Restore Checkpoint** setting if you want to ensure that no System Restore Checkpoints are created when .MSI files are loaded.

Note, however, that this setting is only valid on Windows XP machines.

Prohibit Removal of Updates

Windows Installer 3 and later has new technology to help roll back patches once installed. If you enable the **Prohibit Removal of Updates** policy, no one can remove software updates and patches once installed—not even an administrator. You might want to do this if your environment has special security requirements—that is, if, by unloading a patch, you might be putting the system and your company in harm's way, you might want to enable this setting. This will ensure that no one can uninstall installed patches.

If this policy setting is disabled, a user can remove updates from the computer if that user has been granted privileges to remove the update. This all depends on how the patch was deployed. Read the Explain text on this policy setting for more information.

This setting is valid only on machines that have Windows Installer 3 and later.

Enforce Upgrade of Component Rules

Windows Installer 3 can be stricter about how applications allow themselves to be updated, via .MSP files, for example. That is, some .MSP files can perform some no-no's that could inadvertently render an application to malfunction once updated.

The Explain text of the **Enforce Upgrade of Component Rules** policy setting describes two of these no-no's: when an .MSP changes the GUID of a function, and when a new component is added in the wrong place of the .MSI tree. These have to do with the way an .MSI file is represented internally to the system. If these things are changed, the application could fail to function.

To that end, enabling this policy setting forces the .MSI engine to ensure that certain safeguards are in place and that the .MSP file doesn't perform these no-no's.

If you disable **Enforce Upgrade of Component Rules**, Windows Installer is allowed to perform these no-no's.

This setting is valid only on machines that have Windows Installer 3 and later.

Prohibit Nonadministrators from Applying Vendor Signed Updates

When a patch comes out from an application vendor, how do you want to handle it? Application vendors can come out with patches that only the administrator can install—or conversely, they can come out with patches that, theoretically, even the user should be able to install. And these patches are digitally signed, so you can be sure that they're not coming from EvilSoftware, Inc. You can then allow users to just patch their own applications, but this approach is likely fraught with peril.

However, the **Prohibit Nonadministrators from Applying Vendor Signed Updates** policy setting controls just that. If you enable it, you're forcing only administrators to install updates that have been digitally signed by the application vendor.

If you disable this policy setting, mere-mortal users can install these nonadministrator updates without administrative access.

This setting is valid only on machines that have Windows Installer 3 and later.

Baseline File Cache Maximum Size

Don't you just hate it when you're asked for the original installation media when an update is available? In theory, this is silly: the application is already installed on your hard drive, so why on earth do you need the original media?

Well, with Windows Installer 3, the **Baseline File Cache Maximum Size** policy setting tries to fix that. It sets the percentage of disk space available to the Windows Installer "baseline file cache." The idea is that you can have these required files hanging around, ready for whenever an update is ready to go. Then, when the original source is needed, it goes to the baseline file cache and doesn't ask for the original installation source.

If you enable this policy setting, you can then modify the maximum size of the Windows Installer baseline file cache. Note that if the baseline cache size is set to 0, Windows Installer cannot store new files. Previously stored files will stay in place (until the application that uses it is uninstalled), but new applications (if loaded in the future) cannot store information here. Windows Installer will stop populating the baseline cache for new updates. The existing cached files will remain on disk and will be deleted when the product is removed.

Setting the baseline cache to 100 means "Use as much space as you need!"

By default, 10 percent of the hard drive is used for this purpose. Disabling **Baseline File Cache Maximum Size** forces the value at 10 percent.

This setting is valid only on machines that have Windows Installer 3 and later.

Prohibit Use of Restart Manager

The Restart Manager is a very cool new addition to Windows Installer 4. The idea is that applications can basically save their currently open files, get upgraded, and then present the saved document in the newly upgraded program. I saw a demo of this and it blew my socks off. This policy setting controls the Restart Manager. Why you would want to turn this neat thing off is a mystery to me; so leave it on unless instructed not to.

The **Prohibit Use of Restart Manager** setting is valid only on machines that have Windows Installer 4 or later (like Windows Vista, which has it installed by default) and Windows 7 (which has Windows Installer 5).

Disable Logging via Package Settings

This is another Windows Installer 4–only feature. .MSI packages can choose to log their own actions if the property is turned on within the package.

With the **Disable Logging via Package Settings** policy setting, you can let that behavior stand or turn it off.

Again, this setting is valid only on machines that have Windows Installer 4 or later (like Windows Vista, which has it installed by default) and Windows 7 (which has Windows Installer 5).

User-Side Policy Settings for Windows Installer

To display the Group Policy settings that affect the Windows Installer, as shown in Figure 11.30, choose User Configuration ➤ Policies ➤ Administrative Templates ➤ Windows Components ➤ Windows Installer. These settings affect the behavior of the users in the scope.

Always Install with Elevated Privileges

Enabling the **Always Install with Elevated Privileges** policy setting allows users to manually install their own .MSI files and bypass their own insufficient and lowly user rights in order to correctly install applications. Some applications install correctly in the users' context, but many don't.

FIGURE 11.30   The Windows Installer user settings.

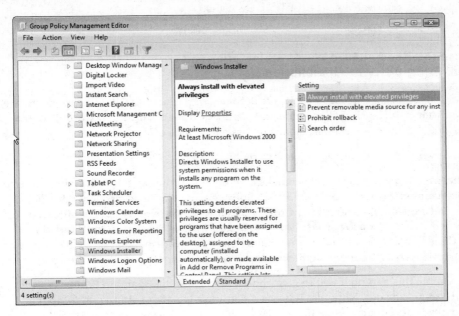

Avoid this setting! Again, users can write their own MSIs, which enable them to "be the bad guy." Don't open up this security hole!

If you don't wish to heed my warning, you still need to set the corresponding setting in the Computer half, as noted in the "Computer-Side Policy Settings for Windows Installer" section earlier.

Prevent Removable Media Source for Any Install

If you enable the **Prevent Removable Media Source for Any Install** setting, which works only for .MSI applications, users cannot install applications under their own context from removable media. Rather, only administrators can install applications, or applications must be Published or Assigned for users to use them. This prevents users from running down to the computer store, obtaining the latest version of a program, and installing it via CD.

Prohibit Rollback

See the **Prohibit Rollback** policy setting in the "Computer-Side Policy Settings for Windows Installer" section earlier.

This setting is found in both User Configuration and Computer Configuration. Recall that computer settings have precedence over user settings.

Search Order

By default, applications that are Published or Assigned using the Windows Installer search their original location for updates or repairs. If that original location is not available, the application tries other locations.

The **Search Order** policy setting allows you to specify any or all of the following locations: network, removable media, or URL (website).

**One for the Road—Leave Windows Installer and
Group Policy Software Installation Data**

Back in Chapter 9, we discussed a specific problem with regard to GPSI and roaming user profiles. That is, if you choose to enable the **Delete Cached Copies of Roaming Profiles** policy setting, the machine "cleans up" as a user logs off.

This has an unintended consequence with regard to GPSI.

Specifically, if the Roaming Profiles data is deleted at logoff time, the information regarding applications deployed via Group Policy Software Installation is also lost (by default). To that end, you should enable a new policy that affects users on Windows XP/SP2 or later called **Leave Windows Installer and Group Policy Software Installation Data**. Once that policy is enabled, the Group Policy Software Installation data remains on the hard drive, so subsequent logins for users are much faster.

Again, enable this setting if you're also choosing to wipe the Roaming Profile away when the user logs out. Note that it is not a Windows Installer setting per se, so it's located in a different area. Specifically, you'll find the policy you need at Administrative Templates ➢ System ➢ User Profiles ➢ **Leave Windows Installer and Group Policy Software Installation Data.**

If you're interested, this problem is specifically discussed in Knowledge Base article 828452, "An Assigned Package Is Reinstalled Every Time Clients Log on to the Domain."

Deploying Office 2007 and Office 2010 Using Group Policy

In the previous examples, we used Office 2003 as the "main example" of how to deploy software, in the normal case. By normal, I'm talking about, well, normal stuff:

- MSI files for deployment. Using `msiexec /a <filename.msi>` to prepare installations in some cases, like Office 2003.

- MST files for transforming applications. In the case of Office 2003, we created a `nomsaccess.mst` to prevent our users from receiving Microsoft Access.

- MSP files for patching applications.

It all makes "sense." Rather, *made* sense. Until Office 2007 came along. Again, to be clear, the stuff you learned earlier in this chapter is indeed valid for most applications under the sun.

For some reason, the Office 2007 and now Office 2010 teams decided not to follow the rules. Let's see how we can work around this limitation and use Group Policy in some form to deploy either Office 2007 or Office 2010.

Let me jump to the end of the story. You can deploy Office 2007 (barely) using GPSI. We'll explore that option, almost a "non-option" here. Then, I'll jump into Office 2010, which doesn't change the game very much, except that it eliminates all possibility of using GPSI.

In both cases, to perform the install correctly using Group Policy, we'll be using Group Policy with computer startup scripts.

That's the deal, so let's check it all out.

Office 2007 and Group Policy

If you wanted to try to deploy Office 2007 using Group Policy Software Installation, you could do what we did earlier with Office 2003: put your Office 2007 Administrative Installation inside the APPS share on the DC01 server inside the OFFICE2007SOURCE directory.

You'll similarly deploy the .MSI—the precise name will vary depending on the version of Office 2007 you've got. It's the results that are very odd.

Microsoft put together this thoughtful guide on deploying and managing Office 2007 using Group Policy: http://go.microsoft.com/fwlink/?LinkID=94264.

What Happens When You Assign Office 2007 to Users?

In short: it doesn't work. Why not? The Office 2007 .MSI files are (apparently) written to be more "modular." And, in doing so, they couldn't guarantee that one .MSI would be able to call another .MSI when initiated as a user install. It works as a Computer-side install, but not a User-side.

This deployment to a user has worked since Office 2000 but is simply not available as an option to Assign Office 2007 to users.

If you try it, the applications' icons install on the Start Menu. However, when you try to run an application, you get the error message shown in Figure 11.31.

So, long story short—don't deploy Office 2007 to your users. It just won't work. It's an application that only works when Assigned to Computers.

What Happens when you Assign Office 2007 to Computers?

Here's where it gets weird. So stay with me.

FIGURE 11.31   What happens when you try to deploy Office 2007 to a user account via Group Policy Software Installation.

If you've just Assigned Office 2007 to a Windows Vista computer or Windows 7 computer, the first user who uses Office 2007 on that computer needs to wait (a long time)! When I deployed Office 2007 to Windows Vista or a Windows 7 computer and then immediately logged in as Frank Rizzo when the Ctrl+Alt+Del prompt was available, I got what's seen in Figure 11.32.

Strangely, the message basically states that Office 2007's setup isn't compatible with Windows Vista or Windows 7. How odd. If we can get past that, we can see that what's happening behind the scenes is that Office 2007 is *still* setting up. If you click "Show me the message" (which would be better if it said "Show me the money," in one guy's opinion), you'll see what's going on under the hood (see Figure 11.33).

FIGURE 11.32   Users don't see all of Office 2007's icons until it has finished deploying itself in the background.

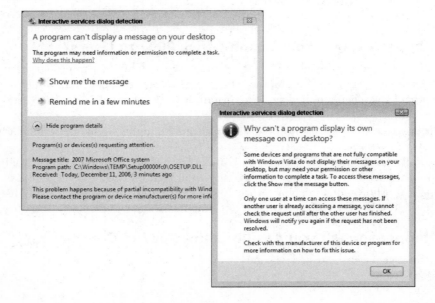

FIGURE 11.33   You can watch Office 2007's display progress when installed via GPSI on a Windows Vista or Windows 7 machine.

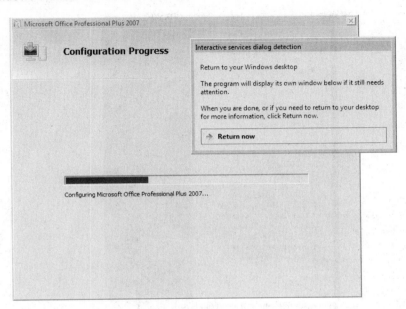

Eventually, the Office 2007 installation routine does finish. Or, if I had chosen not to immediately log in as Frank Rizzo, say, by getting a cup of coffee (maybe two) before logging in, Office 2007 would have completed on its own in the background. But, yes, you're reading this right: Office 2007 continues to install in the background even after you log in if you don't wait long enough.

This "extra setup time" after a user logs on is new for Office 2007 and not very welcome, in my opinion. And it seems that multiple users sometimes have to sit through at least some installation time to get Office 2007 configured the first time.

Once Office 2007 is fully installed, it is more or less ready to go, as seen in Figure 11.34.

Using GPSI and Customizing Office 2007 Deployments

Again, what we just saw—deploying Office 2007 using Group Policy Software Installation—performs only the most basic setup of Office 2007.

If you have a custom Office 2007 environment with bells and whistles, and you want it "your way," there's a lot more that has to be done.

Office 2007 doesn't seem to use Transform Files, and therefore, you wouldn't use the Modifications tab. Office 2007 has its own wacky way of describing settings during installation time. And the Custom Installation Wizard tool that you download? That's gone, too.

FIGURE 11.34   The Office icons and program names will appear on the Start Menu (more specifically, on the Start ➢ All Programs menu).

So, what does it take to perform an Office 2007 customized deployment? Customization and deployment happen in four steps.

Step 1: Create a `config.xml` file   This file is to be placed in the root directory of the installation location so certain parameters can be set when the computer gets the Assignment. There is a document from Microsoft that has steps for producing a `config.xml`. This document, located at `http://tinyurl.com/utaf4`, shows all the available options normally available in a `config.xml` file. But here's the trick: the document on Microsoft's site was removed, so I'm linking to a Google-cached version of it that tells the whole truth. The available configurable elements are pitiful for Group Policy installations—only four options can be set (Installation Location, Options and Features, Product Key, and Languages). (One person on the `GPanswers.com` forum also suggested that Company might work, too.) This affects every installation you use from this particular source. So, in our examples, we used the `Office2007Source` directory to perform our deployment to our client computers. If we deployed to Sales, Marketing, Human Resources, and Facilities, all these people would get these same four options because our `config.xml` file is rooted to this source. If you're only going to customize with `config.xml` files (to deploy to various categories of computers with different requirements), then you will need to maintain a separate install location for each group of computers.

Step 2: Create a custom `.MSP` File   The `config.xml` file in Step 1 can only take us so far—not very far at all when it comes to customization. However, the tool to create more Office customizations is built into the Office 2007 setup tool. Simply run `setup.exe /admin`, and—poof!—instant customization tool. (Nice touch!) Note that trial and non-Enterprise versions will not show the customization tool.

So, take a deep breath, read the next two steps, then scream out the nearest window. You might expect this new Office 2007 customization tool to produce `.MST` files like all the previous versions of Office before it.

Nope.

It produces `.MSP` files. A document at `http://tinyurl.com/39ru47` describes the way to produce `custom.msp` files.

`.MSP` files? Does that mean we can't use the Modifications tab to deploy our customization? That's exactly what it means.

Step 3: Deploy your `.MSI` file using GPSI   No big deal here. You're just using the information in this chapter to get Office 2007 installed. Remember, it only Assigns to the computer. At this point, it should pick up the `config.xml` configuration changes you made in Step 2.

Step 4: Patch your target machines   Now that you've installed Office 2007 to your zillions of machines, here's the painful part. Use a logon script, batch file, or manually walk around to each machine to have it embrace your `.MSP` customization. Use the same information found in the earlier section, "Using `MSIEXEC` to Patch a Distribution Point." However, you don't update the distribution point—instead, you patch the specific machines individually.

Ow. That means you cannot use GPSI as a "unified" way of delivering Office 2007 and also customize it. This makes me spittin' mad, because Group Policy is *the way* to do oh-so-much goodness in the world.

Office 2007 and Office 2010 via Group Policy—Another Way?

What I've just described is likely your best option for deploying a custom installation of Office 2007 if you positively must deploy using GPSI. It isn't pretty. And there is another way.

The Office team suggests that you use a technology (any technology) that allows you to run the `setup.exe` program from Office 2007, because the `setup.exe` will call all the `.MSI` files it needs for the installation you desire.

Earlier, you learned about `.ZAP` files in the "Understanding `.ZAP` Files" section. Recall that `.ZAP` files just run the underlying `setup.exe` of an application. Well, Office 2007 has a `setup.exe`. And if you put your `.MSP` files (that you created by running `setup /admin`) in the `Updates` directory on your distribution source, and then deploy using a `.ZAP` file, you should be able to install a customized Office 2007 in one fell swoop.

But don't forget—`.ZAP` files make the application's installation icons appear only in the Add or Remove Programs applet in Control Panel (or "Install a program from the network"). And `.ZAP` applications aren't manageable. So, if you wanted to update Office 2007 later with more patches, you'd basically be asking the user to handle it on her own.

As you already learned in the "Removing Published `.ZAP` Applications" section, once you've deployed an application using a `.ZAP` file, you have no way to upgrade it or revoke it. Once you've deployed it, consider it gone and basically "unmanaged" using Group Policy.

So, what's the *ideal* answer?

Well, if you read through the haze of Microsoft's Office 2007 deployment documentation, they seem to be banking on everyone using Microsoft SCCM 2007 (my thoughts on that later). But, in a nutshell, sorry, Microsoft—bad call on this one.

The "Right" Answer for Office 2007 and Office 2010 Deployment (Using Group Policy)

The Office 2010 deployment story using Group Policy doesn't get any better than Office 2007. You could argue it gets worse. There is no longer any possible way to deploy Office 2010 via Group Policy (outside of third-party tools like Specops Deploy).

I found this plucky little document, "Deployment Options for Microsoft Office 2010," here: `http://tinyurl.com/yfredq2`.

In short, there's a PDF, Visio, and XPS document showing Microsoft's sanctioned ways to deploy Office. Yes, Group Policy is on the list, but it's the same way as Office 2007: Group Policy using Startup Scripts.

Just for fun, I tried deploying Office 2010 using Group Policy Software Installation. No dice. There's a single error message in the event log with a non-obvious message about the failure.

Great.

So, here are the official steps (which will work for both Office 2007 and Office 2010). This is my suggested method for deploying, since the other options are so poor.

Step 1: Create a `config.xml` file   We saw the Office 2007 version of this earlier. It's the same idea in Office 2010. It's used when clients initially install Office 2010. You can set the installation to be silent, for instance.

At last check, the `config.xml` file for Office 2010 was documented here:

> `http://technet.microsoft.com/en-us/library/cc179195%28office.14%29.aspx`

(shortened to `http://tinyurl.com/ye4sorx`).

Step 2: Create a custom `.MSP` file   Like Office 2007, the Office 2010 `config.xml` file in Step 1 can only take us so far. Again, to create more Office, simply run `setup.exe /admin`, and—voilà!—the Office 2010 customization tool.

At last check, the Office Customization Tool (OCT) can be found here:

> `http://technet.microsoft.com/en-us/library/cc179097%28office.14%29.aspx`

(shortened to `http://tinyurl.com/ybtkxen`).

Again, it produces `.MSP` files.

Step 3: Place your `.MSP` in the updates folder   At installation time, you can have clients embrace the customizations you set in Step 2. Simply put the `.MSP` file in the Updates folder on the network installation point of Office.

Step 4: Use startup scripts to deploy Office 2007 or Office 2010　Use this suggested startup script to kick off your Office 2007 or Office 2010 installation:

```
http://go.microsoft.com/fwlink/?LinkID=94264
```

You can use the script to ensure that you're selecting the proper `config.xml` file you created in Step 1.

Optional: Re-patch your target machines　You can always create an `.MSP` file for a machine or two using the OCT. For instance, maybe you want just one or two machines not to have Microsoft Access 2010.

After creating the `.MSP` file, use the information about `msiexec /p` I detailed in the section, "Using MSIEXEC to Patch a Distribution Point." However, you don't update the distribution point—instead, you patch the specific machines individually.

You'll likely need another startup script to figure this out if you want to target specific machines.

If you've found a creative way to work around these Office 2007 or Office 2010 issues, I want to hear about it. Be sure to e-mail me at `jeremym@moskowitz-inc.com` and let me know your best techniques for deploying a customized Office 2007 or Office 2010 installation using Group Policy.

Do You Need a "Big" Management Tool for Your Environment?

Microsoft's Systems Management Server (SMS) is a big deal in corporations around the world. The newest iteration isn't called SMS 4, but rather, System Center Configuration Manager 2007 (SCCM 2007). However, because I'm an old-school kind of guy, I'll just call it SMS in this brief discussion.

SMS costs an arm and a leg, has a thoroughly esoteric licensing scheme, and requires a client component on every Windows PC and server on your network. But if you can get over these drawbacks, it houses a pretty amazing collection of core features:

- Software and Hardware Inventory
- Remote Control
- Software Metering
- Software Deployment
- Operating System Deployment
- Patch Management
- System Health Validation

Most of these features would be a welcome addition to any managed environment.

There are, of course, other management systems that don't ship from Microsoft. Companies like Symantec and LANDesk make their living selling similar tools. These all have one thing in common: more moving parts on your client and, usually, additional servers and components to move things around. They get the moniker of "Enterprise Management Systems" because they scale pretty well.

But what's also true about these tools is that they don't, fundamentally, use the Group Policy infrastructure that's already there. In other words, the "moving parts" to Group Policy are already installed on every client computer.

So, the question often comes up: do I need a "big" management tool if I'm already using Group Policy? To answer this question, we'll do a brief, head-to-head comparison: Microsoft SMS versus Stock Group Policy. However, when available, I'll also mention some third-party tools that hook right into Group Policy—leveraging the "moving parts" you already have deployed.

SMS vs. GPOs: A Comparison Rundown

Each feature of SMS is meant to chip away at that golden nugget of Total Cost of Ownership. I often get asked which has more power, SMS or Group Policy. Let's take a look at how SMS stacks up against the stuff we get in the box—all the stuff we've looked at so far.

Hardware and Software Inventory

Hardware inventory and software inventory are two critical elements that administrators need to keep in touch with what's currently out there in their environment. With this information in hand, they can rein in rogue installations of software and hardware.

Without SMS, once software is added via GPSI (or by hand, or otherwise), there is no native way, using just Active Directory with GPSI, to know who has installed what software. Although using GPSI to set up an OU, a package, and an Assignment is a pretty good yardstick for measuring what's out there, you're never certain until an actual inventory of the machine is performed.

No hardware or software inventory is built into Windows. You could build your own WMI scripts to pull out the hardware and software inventory data you want, but in doing so, you'd go insane. So, installing SMS would seem like a slam dunk.

It should be noted, though, that a nice pay tool is available that hooks into Group Policy to do this function. It's called Specops Inventory (`www.specopssoft.com`). So, if you wanted to do this function with Group Policy, it's now an even playing field. Hardware and Software Inventory, the most popular part of SMS, is not available à la carte: you have to buy the entire SMS product to get this most requested feature. With a product like Specops Inventory, you're able to just buy the functionality you need.

Remote Control

The Remote Control feature is Microsoft's version of Symantec's pcAnywhere, but it is extremely lightweight and takes up almost no disk space. However, having a program such as SMS that specifically contains Remote Control is becoming less important. You can implement remote control on the cheap with various other options. In Windows 2000, you can use NetMeeting, which is workable, if not optimal. Or you can use the 100 percent–free multiplatform VNC from www.realvnc.com.

Additionally, Windows XP and later machines have quite decent remote control built in via Remote Assistance facilities. Terminal Services has its own version of Remote Control called "shadowing."

So, although Remote Control is a great feature, it isn't as important as it used to be.

So, who wins in this category? SMS or "in the box"? It's a tie.

Software Metering

The Software Metering component has two methods of operation:

Lock Out　This method (only available in SMS 2 and dropped from SMS 2003 and later) is for strict license compliance. With this option, you can lock out users from applications if the number of licenses dries up across the environment. For example, if you purchased only 25 copies of DogFoodMaker 4.5, the 26th person cannot run it.

Log Only　This version doesn't lock users out of applications; rather, it simply logs the number of copies in use. This is useful for gauging licensing compliance, but not quite as intensive as the Lock Out method.

Without SMS, there is no way to gauge who's using what or to force users into compliance. Winner: SMS (if you really need this feature at all).

Operating System Deployment

Group Policy itself doesn't have operating system deployment as a feature. But, even free tools like the Microsoft Deployment features handily perform that job.

And, while the process to kick-start an installation isn't 100-percent hands off, it's pretty close.

The SMS Operating System Deployment can hook into the Microsoft Deployment features to make the whole operation completely hands-free. If this 100-percent hands-off capability is something you need, then the SMS (or SCCM) version is great.

But most people don't need 100-percent hands-off deployment. They just need a way to make the process smooth. Is it smoother with or without 100-percent hands-off?

That's debatable. But if I had to pick a winner here, I'd say SMS. In the end analysis, if you needed 100-percent hands-off, the only way to get it is via SMS.

You could also argue that the Microsoft Deployment Toolkit, a free download from Microsoft, might be just the free thing you need to ease the pain of deploying Windows clients and servers.

If we're strictly comparing SMS and Group Policy, then SMS wins here. But the third-party Group Policy add-ons and Microsoft freebies make it a close race.

Software Deployment

The Software Deployment feature does overlap with the Active Directory feature of GPSI. As we explored in this chapter, Group Policy has a decent set of features when it comes to deploying software to clients.

In my first book, *Windows 2000 Group Policy, Profiles, and IntelliMirror,* I said that "SMS's Software Deployment features trounce the built-in features of Active Directory." I don't know if I would still agree with that. SMS does have quite a robust deployment mechanism, and one reason is that it can leverage the WMI query data to target to machines' CPU speeds, amount of RAM, BIOS revision, and so on. But we just did the same thing several pages ago with our Windows XP clients, so GPSI is certainly catching up!

Several facets of SMS software deployment are better than the GPSI. Specifically, SMS can do the following that GPSI cannot:

- Deploy software to users or computers any time of the day or night—not just on logon or reboot.

- Compress the application and send it to a distribution point close to the user. Even if we set up GPSI with DFS Namespaces, we cannot do this. However, the replication that DFS Namespaces uses, called *DFSR,* does have the superpower of only sending over the changed bytes if possible (and that's really sweet).

- Once a machine is targeted for a delivery and the package is received, the machine can send back detailed status messages describing success or failure of the transaction.

- Dribble the applications to clients over slow links without slowing down the connection. Only when the software is fully downloaded is the install initiated.

- Get detailed, central logs about which users or computers did or did not get the package.

So, against Group Policy alone, SMS wins in this category. However, with a little elbow grease, you can get an amazing amount of mileage out of GPSI—even in large environments. The big hit Group Policy takes in GPSI seems to be that the Office team basically abandoned GPSI as a viable deployment method for Office 2007 and Office 2010.

However, those guys at Specops Software have another product that competes here, and, you guessed it—it hooks right into Group Policy. It's called Specops Deploy (www.specopssoft.com). And it overcomes some of the thorniest problems that Group Policy out of the box cannot solve. Specops Deploy can:

- Deploy .MSIs and .EXEs to client computers or users (where normal GPSI only targets .MSIs)

- Target based on time of day

- Deploy applications without requiring a reboot

- Use the Background Intelligent Transfer Service (BITS) protocol to dribble applications to clients over slow links

- Give you detailed reports about which machines and users received the software and which ones didn't

So, for SMS versus "naked" Group Policy, SMS wins.

But add a moderately priced third-party tool that hooks directly into Group Policy, and it's a much closer horse race.

Patch Management

SMS also has good patch management support, which is just a customized extension of its Software Deployment feature. You can target specific machines with specific patches. Once the patches are received, you can dictate how to react: wait for reboot, reboot now, and so on.

However, Microsoft has Windows Server Update Services (WSUS), found here:

```
http://technet.microsoft.com/en-us/wsus/default.aspx
```

WSUS is okay for most organizations, and it's in a slick interface. WSUS is controlled by policy settings on the client side—very neat, indeed.

Winner? SMS, by some margin. But from WSUS 3.0, updating clients has never been easier: it has detailed feedback, a cool admin interface, computer groups, and useful reports, and it's almost fun just sitting there controlling the patch level of your clients and servers.

GPSI and SMS Coexistence

So, who wins?

If we're talking about SMS versus "naked" Group Policy, then, yes, I'm forced to admit it—SMS does have more raw power. However, I would argue that with a little finesse, you can squeeze quite a lot out of the desktop management tools you have come to learn about with Group Policy. Add a third-party tool or two to Group Policy, and you've got some serious competition—with a very lightweight back-end infrastructure.

Some organizations use either GPSI or a "big" management tool for software deployment. And some use both. Although no two organizations ever do anything exactly the same way, there does seem to be a general trend in those places where SMS and GPSI coexist.

In cases where using GPSI or SMS is a toss-up, GPSI is generally used to deploy smaller applications that need to be rapidly fired off due to document invocation. For example, if a user is sent an Adobe Acrobat .PDF file via e-mail, but doesn't have Adobe Acrobat Reader, double-clicking the document automatically installs the application on the machine.

SMS, on the other hand, is typically used to deploy larger applications, such as the Office suite, when you need definitive feedback about what went wrong (if anything). This philosophy provides a good balance between the "on demand" feel of GPSI and the "strategic targeted deployment" feel of SMS.

As you've seen, most of the features do not overlap, making a bigger management tool, like SMS, a solid addition to any medium-sized or large environment. However, before you invest in a bigger management tool, be sure to check out the kinds of add-ons available that hook directly into Group Policy and can match the feature set. And, again, you can get those features à la carte.

Final Thoughts

In this chapter, we inspected Software Installation using Group Policy, or just GPSI for short. GPSI works with Active Directory and Windows clients. Use WSUS for patch management because patches to Windows are not deployable using GPSI.

In order to make the most of GPSI, you need to leverage .MSI applications. You can either get .MSI applications from your software vendor, or wrap up your own with third-party tools (listed in this chapter and also in the book's Appendix and "Solutions Guide" on this book's website).

Share a folder on a server you want to send the package from. Plop the application in its own subfolder, and use both share and NTFS permissions to crank down who can read the executables and install files. Remember, though, that not all .MSI applications are ready to be deployed. Some are indeed ready to go (like the .NET Framework), others require an Administrative Installation (like Office 2003), and still others ship as .MSI files but cannot be deployed via GPSI (such as older versions of Adobe Acrobat Writer).

Once you have your package, you can Assign or Publish your applications.

Assign applications when you want application icons to appear on the Start ➤ All Programs menu; Publish applications when you want users to dive into the Add or Remove Programs folder or the "Install a program from the network" window to get the application. You can leverage Microsoft Transform Files (.MST files) to hone an .MSI and customize it. (Note that neither Office 2007 nor Office 2010 uses .MST files.) You can patch existing .MSI applications with Microsoft Patch Files (.MSP files), but afterward, you need to redeploy the application.

Try not to orphan applications by removing the GPO before the target computer gets the "signal" upon the next reboot (for computer) or logon (for user). If you think you might end up doing this, it's best to ensure that the "Uninstall this application when it falls out of the scope of management" check box is checked, as seen in Figure 11.15.

Use the material in Chapter 4 (on creating WMI filters) to change the scope of management for when a GPO will apply. You can use WMI filters for any GPO you create—not just ones that leverage GPSI. However, the most common use for WMI filters is usually for GPOs that leverage GPSI. Don't forget that Windows 2000 clients don't honor WMI filters (the policy will just apply, no questions asked). Additionally, Windows XP and later clients set to evaluate a WMI filter will take some extra processing time for each filter they need to work through. Be sure to test all your WMI filters in the test lab first.

On the downside, Office used to be "normal." It used .MSIs, .MSTs, .MSPs … all in the normal way. Then, one day, with Office 2007, it all changed. And Office 2010 keeps that new (rotten) tradition. At least, now, you know what is and is not possible.

Additionally, Darren Mar-Elia, on his GPOguy.com website, has a free tool called GPSIViewer that provides a nifty list view of all deployed applications in a domain and has some printout and .CSV reporting capability, as well. Check it out at http://tinyurl .com/yb7a9rg.

12

Finishing Touches with Group Policy: Scripts, Internet Explorer, Hardware Control, Deploying Printers, and Shadow Copies

We've come a long way so far in this book.

We've got Group Policy handled. We've set up Roaming Profiles, Redirected Folders, and Offline Files. We've deployed software using Group Policy Software Installation.

We've made a pretty big cake—but no frosting. Now, it's time for the finishing touches.

In this chapter, we'll cover five big topics to round out your desktop experience:

Scripts   You can deploy startup, shutdown, logon, and logoff scripts. And there are three ways to do it.

Internet Explorer   You can deploy settings to your favorite (er, maybe not-so-favorite application). And, amazingly, there are three ways to do it.

Restricting Access to Hardware   Want a way to ensure that only the hardware you sanction gets onto your network? Well, giddy-up!

Setting Up Printers   The Group Policy Preferences have some special ability to help with printer management. I'll show you the ropes.

Implementing Shadow Copies   How long does it take you to recover a user's file if he deletes it? If the answer is "over 30 seconds," you'll want to learn how to implement Shadow Copies.

So, let's get started with the finishing … touches, that is!

Scripts: Logon, Logoff, Startup, and Shutdown

Users have always been able to get logon scripts. Windows NT 4 provided User Manager for Domains to assign logon scripts, and Windows 2000 and later domains may use Active Directory Users and Computers to assign logon scripts in much the same way.

However, you can step up to the next level using Group Policy and get more than just logon scripts:

- Users can get logon and logoff scripts.
- Computers can get startup and/or shutdown scripts.

And, the best part is, you're not limited to old DOS-style batch files. Scripts deployed via Group Policy can use DOS-style .BAT or .CMD scripts, VBScript (.VBS files), or JavaScript (.JS files), or even executables.

Also, you can also use PowerShell (.PS1) scripts when your target machine is Windows 7 or later. As you'll see, however, there are some caveats to delivering PowerShell scripts via Group Policy.

Non-PowerShell-Based Scripts

In this section, we're going to explore all the non-PowerShell ways to deploy scripts. Look at the list in the previous section; most people use .VBS or DOS-style batch files.

In these examples, I'll use basic DOS-style .BAT commands to explain the concept. First is an example of a script that displays "Hello World" and then pauses for a key press before removing the files from the *%temp%* folder.

In Notepad, create the following file:

```
Echo "Hello World."
Pause
Del /Q /S %temp%
Pause
```

Okay, my example is kind of lame. In the real world, you can do all sorts of things, like automatically fire up Excel at logon, or kick off a full-drive sweep of your virus scanner at shutdown. We're going to keep it simple for these examples.

To use scripts with Group Policy, users must be in the site, domain, or OU linked to a GPO that contains a logon or logoff script. As the name of the script implies, users execute the script only at logon or logoff. Computers must also be in the site, domain, or OU linked to a GPO that contains a startup or shutdown script, which they run only at startup or shutdown.

User and computer scripts delivered via Group Policy do not run "visibly" to the user, which prevents users from canceling them. Scripts run silently in the background unless there is a problem. At that point, you have to wait until the script times out (10 minutes by default). I'll show you a bit later how to expose the scripts to run visibly.

Startup and Shutdown Scripts (Non-PowerShell)

The Startup and Shutdown script settings are found under the Computer Configuration ➢ Policies node in the Windows Settings ➢ Scripts (Startup/Shutdown) branch. You can get your proposed script into the proper GPO in many ways; however, I think I have found the ideal way, as follows:

1. Once you're in the Group Policy Management Editor, drill down to the Scripts (Startup/Shutdown) node and double-click Startup. The Startup Properties dialog box will appear.

2. Click the Add button to open the Add a Script dialog box.

3. In the Script Name field, you can enter a filename or click Browse to open the Browse dialog box, shown in Figure 12.1.

FIGURE 12.1   You can create .BAT or .VBS files on the fly with this little trick.

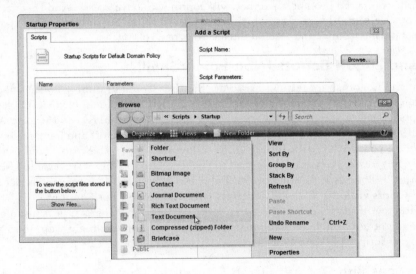

4. To create a new file, right-click in the Browse dialog box, and choose New ➢ Text Document, for example.

5. Enter a name for the file, such as **myscript.bat**.

6. When asked if you want to change the file extension, click Yes, right-click the file, and choose Edit from the context menu to open Notepad.

7. Type your script, and save the file.

8. Select the new file as the proposed script.

   Again, the computer account must be in an OU with a linked GPO that contains a script. However, don't reboot yet. By default, you won't see the script run. And, since our script contains a Pause statement, your users will wait a really long time before the script times out. To allow the script to be visible (and enable you to press any key at the pause), enable a policy setting that also affects the machine. Traverse to Computer Configuration ➤ Policies ➤ Administrative Templates ➤ System ➤ Scripts, and select either **Run startup scripts visible** or **Run shutdown scripts visible**, or enable both options. Note that, oddly, in Windows Vista and later, neither of these policy settings will do anything unless you also force the scripts to run synchronously.

Next, it's important to understand the context in which startup and shutdown scripts run. Specifically, they run in the LocalSystem context. If you want to connect to resources across the network, you'll need to ensure that those resources allow for computer access across the network (not just user access), because the script will run in the context of the computer account when it accesses network resources (such as the Domain Computers group).

Lastly, be careful in granting users the ability to see logon or startup scripts visible. This is because when the script is running, it is running with administrative credentials. So, if there is anything the user might be able to do that halts the script processing and then *remain* in the command prompt, then they will continue to have access. And that access is local system access, god-like access, which is not a good thing. So, only show the startup or login scripts during testing, and rescind during your real rollout.

Logon and Logoff Scripts (Non-PowerShell)

The Logon and Logoff script settings are under the User Configuration ➤ Policies node in the Windows Settings ➤ Scripts (Logon/Logoff) branch. If you're implementing new logon scripts, I suggest you follow the steps in the previous section. Again, the user must be in an OU with a linked GPO with a script. However, don't log off and log back on yet. By default, you won't see the script run. To allow the script to be visible (and enable you to press any key at the pause), you need to enable a Group Policy. Traverse to User Configuration ➤ Policies ➤ Administrative Templates ➤ System ➤ Scripts, and select either **Run logon scripts visible** or **Run logoff scripts visible**, or enable both options.

Logon and logoff scripts run in the user's context. Remember that a user is just a mere mortal and might not be able to manipulate Registry keys that you might want to run in a logon or logoff script.

Script Processing Defaults (and Changing Them)

One final note about scripts before we move on: different scripting types run either synchronously or asynchronously. Here's the deal:

Logon scripts run asynchronously by default   By default, logon scripts run asynchronously. That is, all scripts at a certain level will fire off at the same time. There is no precedence order for scripts at the same level, and there is no knowing which script will finish before another. If you want to change this behavior to help "link" one script after another, you have to tell the client computer to run the scripts *synchronously*. If you want to change this (and many times, you'll want to), then find Computer Configuration ➤ Policies ➤ Administrative Templates ➤ System ➤ Scripts, and enable Run logon scripts synchronously.

Bizarrely, there is also a setting that does exactly the same thing located on User Settings ➢ Policies ➢ Administrative Templates ➢ System ➢ Scripts ➢ Run logon scripts synchronously. Again, recall that if there's a conflict between these settings, the ones that affect the computer will "win."

Startup scripts run synchronously by default   By default, startup scripts run synchronously: all scripts are processed from lowest to highest priority order. Then, each script is run—consecutively—until they're finished. This usually makes the most sense, so I tend to leave it as is. However, if you want to change it, then locate Computer Configuration ➢ Policies ➢ Administrative Templates ➢ System ➢ Scripts, and enable Run startup scripts asynchronously.

Group Policy scripts time out in 10 minutes   As stated, if a script just hangs there, you'll have to wait a whopping 10 minutes for it to time out. You can change this with the policy setting found at Computer Configuration ➢ Policies ➢ Administrative Templates ➢ System ➢ Scripts called Maximum wait time for Group Policy scripts.

Old-school logon scripts run "visible"   If you use Active Directory Users and Computers to assign a user a logon script, those scripts will be visible to the user. If you want to hide old-school logon scripts from users while they run, you can change this with the policy setting found at User Settings ➢ Policies ➢ Administrative Templates ➢ System ➢ Scripts ➢ Run legacy logon scripts visible.

Also, before we move on, let's take a second to talk about "perceived slow" performance when scripts are used with Group Policy. In previous chapters, I suggested you might want to make your Windows machines act like Windows 2000. That is, use the **Always wait for the network at Startup and Logon** policy setting, which throws Windows into "synchronous" processing mode. There can be a problem with this approach: it can affect you if you have laptops that are not always on the network at bootup. This *can* cause slower performance. Imagine you have traveling users on laptops with startup and login scripts. By default, the scripts are stored on the Domain Controller. So, during bootup or login time, the laptop tries to connect to the Domain Controller for the script. You may want to dictate to the client to use a local path (like c:\scripts\blah.vbs) instead of the default, which will go to the server. Ensure that the script is contained within a path that clients cannot write to, or they could do nefarious things to the system by replacing the script (which runs as System).

Don't Panic: What to Do If Login Scripts with Network Drive Mappings Aren't Working as Expected with Windows Vista

Let's assume you have a share called "share" on DC01. Now, let's assume you have a simple login script within a GPO linked to, say, the **Human Resources Users** OU. And this simple script did the following:

- Cleared out any mapped drives
- Said "Hello World"
- Mapped a letter (s:) as a network drive to \\dc01\share
- Paused for a key press before finishing

It would look like this:

```
net use * /d /y
Echo "Hello World."
net use s: \\dc01\share
pause
```

Try this script as a logon script for a user using a pre–Windows Vista machine, and it works great. The drive letter maps at logon time, and the user can use it as long as he wants.

Try this script as a logon script for a user using a Windows Vista machine, and, well, you're going to have some issues, as shown in Figure 12.2.

FIGURE 12.2   Login scripts run fine on Windows Vista, but a mapped network drive will be inaccessible to the user.

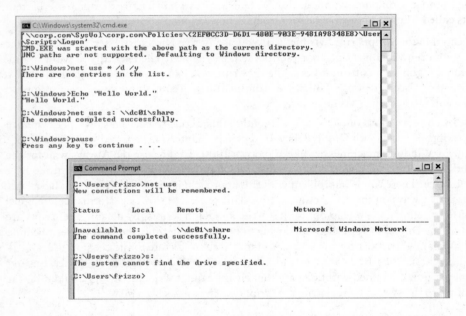

Wait—this gets even weirder. During my testing of Windows Vista, I tried logging out and logging in again, and it totally worked (as seen in Figure 12.3). Here's the thing: the correct behavior is that it's not *supposed* to succeed at all. It's spelled out right here: http://support.microsoft.com/kb/937624.

Here's the kicker: I can't explain why it does sometimes succeed on the second login.

It's not supposed to succeed because User Account Control is kicking in. So drive mappings from a higher-privilege user shouldn't be able to be leveraged from mere-mortal user accounts. (Again, I'm not sure why it succeeds on the second try sometimes. It's not supposed to.)

In short, I'm guessing that you won't ever want it so that the user can't have access to mapped drives. And with these two tips, you can make the behavior the same as in Windows XP.

FIGURE 12.3   The second time's a charm when logging in with login scripts.

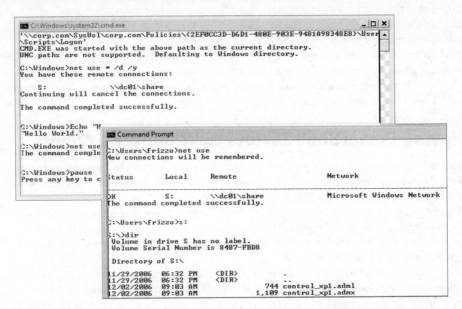

Note that, in my testing of Windows 7, I found no problems at all. Windows 7 worked like XP. They just magically mapped drives, no problems, no remediation required. Now, my experience doesn't mean you won't have issues. It just means I didn't.

Next up are the suggested methods if you do see a problem with Windows Vista (very likely) or Windows 7 (unlikely).

Vista Logon Script Remediation 1

You can set a Registry value on your Windows Vista machines so that it doesn't matter how the network drives are mapped. They'll be accessible by every user. Again, this has to be done on the target machine. Set HKLM ➤ Software ➤ Microsoft ➤ Windows ➤ CurrentVersion ➤ Policies ➤ System ➤ EnableLinkedConnections (REG_DWORD) to 1.

Adding this Registry value or changing its value back to 0 requires a reboot. By default, the Registry value doesn't exist on the system, and therefore, the linked connections are *not* added.

Note that creating EnableLinkedConnections and setting it to 1 is not officially supported in Windows Vista. Only the second method (described next) is fully supported.

Vista Logon Script Remediation 2

We've referenced the Microsoft document "Deploying Group Policy Using Windows Vista" before. It can be found here: http://tinyurl.com/yenok6.

Inside, there's the section "Group Policy Scripts Can Fail Due to User Account Control." There's a script located in the appendix that you run. This script then calls your login script and, in doing so, will bypass this issue.

But it does so in a not-very-pretty way. It submits your login script to be run as a scheduled task. So, in short, it'll take a moment (maybe more) for your login script to run. Note that you could edit the script to remove the information messages that the script is being sent to the Task Scheduler.

When I tried to use this method (using the exact provided steps), there was a problem. That's because the document didn't specify to type in the whole path of your login script as a parameter. Therefore, when the Task Scheduler tried to run it, it simply failed. I reported this issue a while ago, but the docs seemingly haven't changed.

Deploying PowerShell Scripts to Windows 7 Clients

Until recently, there was no great in-the-box way to deliver PowerShell scripts to target machines. However, Windows 7 and Windows Server 2008 R2 machines can accept PowerShell as scripts via Group Policy.

In Figure 12.4, we can see the properties of the Logon script dialog box found under User Configuration ➤ Policies ➤ Windows Settings ➤ Scripts (Logon/Logoff). Similar settings for the computer are found in Computer Configuration ➤ Policies ➤ Windows Settings ➤ Scripts (Startup/Shutdown).

You can add in the script here. PowerShell scripts must have the extension .PS1 or they will fail to execute on the client. Note that even PowerShell version 2 scripts have the extension .PS1, which, in my opinion, is kind of confusing. Meanwhile, the good news is that there's no reason most PowerShell version 1 scripts shouldn't work on PowerShell version 2 hosts, like Windows 7—unless they're using a specific PowerShell version 1 construct.

FIGURE 12.4 Group Policy can deploy PowerShell scripts.

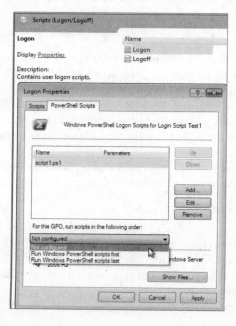

You can decide if you want this PowerShell script to run before or after regular (non-PowerShell) scripts. This setting can be performed on a per-GPO basis (seen here). Or, you can have an overarching policy setting for logon, logoff, startup and/or shutdown scripts with policy settings located at User Configuration ➢ Policies ➢ Windows Settings ➢ Administrative Templates ➢ System ➢ Scripts ➢ **Run Windows PowerShell scripts first at user logon, logoff**. And, on the Computer side, there's **Run Windows PowerShell scripts first at user startup, shutdown**. Again, the idea is that you might set one of these overarching policies first as a general case but then make an exception right in the script, as seen in Figure 12.4.

Managing Internet Explorer with Group Policy

There's Internet Explorer 6, Internet Explorer 7, and now, Internet Explorer 8. And you need to know how to control them. And that's where it gets a little confusing because there are lots of areas in Group Policy that look like they can do the job. In this section, we'll explore the places you can control Internet Explorer via Group Policy.

Internet Explorer 7 comes with Windows Vista. However, it should be noted that Internet Explorer 7 is technically labeled by Microsoft as a "required" upgrade for your existing Windows XP machines. So this tip might be too late for you. But, if you want to "block" Internet Explorer 7 from being laid down upon your existing Windows XP machines, you can "block" it. It's called the "Toolkit to Disable Automatic Delivery of Internet Explorer 7" and is found here: http://tinyurl.com/fh3bv.

The three big things we'll talk about are as follows:

- Internet Explorer Maintenance Policy (which mostly controls Internet Explorer 6)
- Internet Explorer 6, 7, and 8 Group Policy Preferences control
- Internet Explorer 7 and 8's built-in policy-based control from a Windows 7 management station

Internet Explorer Maintenance (IEM) and Group Policy Preferences Settings

Both Internet Explorer Maintenance (IEM) and Group Policy Preferences have the same job: set preferences for things. The definition here for preferences is "suggestions for how users should use Internet Explorer, but they don't need to keep your changes."

You set Internet Explorer Maintenance settings for users by traversing down to User Configuration ➢ Policies ➢ Windows Settings ➢ **Internet Explorer Maintenance**.

You set Internet Explorer preferences settings for users by traversing down to User Configuration ➢ Preferences ➢ Control Panel Settings ➢ Internet Settings and selecting a new preference item for Internet Explorer 5, 6, 7, or 8.

So, if you set a preference for the Internet Explorer home page to be www.GPanswers.com, that's great! You can see IEM settings in Figure 12.5 where I've set the home page URL to www.GPanswers.com. Ditto in Figure 12.6, where I'm using Group Policy Preferences to set the home page to www.microsoft.com.

FIGURE 12.5   You can set preferences using Internet Explorer Maintenance.

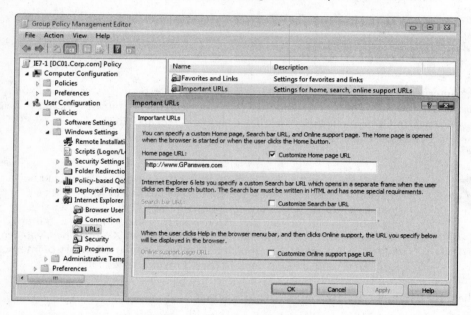

You first question might be, "Which one 'wins' if they're set inside the same GPO?" The answer is Group Policy Preferences. If you need a review on why that's the case, check out Chapter 5 in the section, "The Longer Answer: Understanding CSE Timing and Overlap."

But here's the trick (again) about IEM and Group Policy Preferences settings: there's nothing specifically saying the user can't open up Internet Explorer, access the options of the browser, and set whatever settings she wants *in place* of your preferences. In Figure 12.7, a user affected by this policy can just fire up Internet Explorer 7 on Windows Vista and change the home page to whatever she wants.

A complete rundown of all the Internet Explorer Maintenance mode settings is beyond the scope of this book. Again, you'll find all sorts of gizmos to play with that control Internet Explorer: home page settings, proxy settings, security zone settings, favorites, and so on. However, not all IEM settings will affect Internet Explorer 7 or 8, as shown in Figure 12.8.

FIGURE 12.6   Group Policy Preferences Internet Explorer settings.

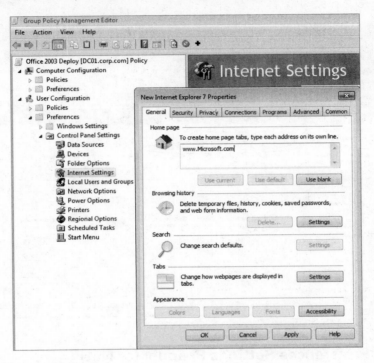

FIGURE 12.7   Users can change the preferences set in Internet Explorer Maintenance to whatever they want.

FIGURE 12.8 Some Internet Explorer Maintenance settings are not going to work for Internet Explorer 7 or 8.

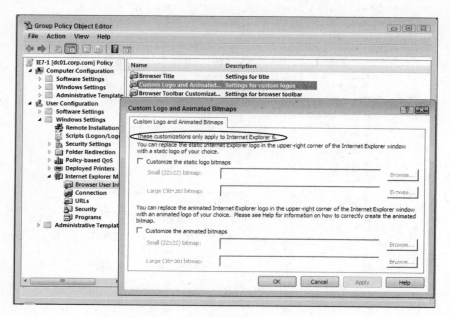

Making IE Preferences Settings Reapply (or Not)

If you choose to use Group Policy Preferences or IEM settings, you should also learn how to do one special trick: make your settings reapply if you want, or apply only once.

My suggestion is that you migrate your IEM settings to Group Policy Preferences if at all possible. But, in case you can't do that, here's the rundown of how to make each one reapply settings or apply only once.

Reapply/Not Reapply IEM Settings

There are two modes you can use to deploy Internet Explorer Maintenance settings:

Mandatory mode In Mandatory mode, the setting acts like other Group Policy settings: your desires are forced on your client machines. If users change them, the settings are reapplied. Using this mode is helpful when you want to pseudo-guarantee important options, such as security settings and proxy settings.

Mandatory mode is always set "on" by default, but needs another switch to make it fully functional. You'll need to locate the **Internet Explorer Maintenance Policy Processing** policy setting (located in Computer Configuration ➢ Policies ➢ Administrative Templates ➢ Group Policy). Inside that setting, there's a check box labeled "Process even if Group Policy Objects have not changed." Again, nothing specifically prevents users from changing these values, but once that setting is selected, when a foreground or background refresh is triggered, the values should be returned.

Preference mode   Even though IEM is set in Mandatory mode, again, it still only works like a preference because the second switch isn't set. You can, however, always force IEM into Preference mode.

The idea is that you can deliver the setting one time, and then never again. This would be good for users you want to give some degree of liberty to (for example, developers) but want to encourage to use your preferred settings. To set IEM into Preference mode, right-click the IEM node and select Preference Mode, as seen in Figure 12.9.

FIGURE 12.9   IEM can be forced into Preference mode, where it delivers the setting one time and never again.

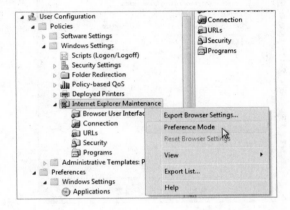

If the two modes are confusing, here's the cheat sheet: Preference mode applies only once, and then never again, while Mandatory mode will always reapply (like normal policy, but on steroids, because it won't care if the version has changed). Additionally, Mandatory mode requires that you flip the "Process even if Group Policy Objects have not changed" setting on for it to reapply.

The Internet Explorer Maintenance interface is a little goofy. For some items (such as customized program settings), you'll import the settings from the machine on which the Group Policy Management Editor is running. Additionally goofy is that once you make a change to Preference mode, you cannot return to Mandatory mode without wiping out all your settings (via the Reset Browser Settings option). You can learn more about the IEM by visiting http://tinyurl.com/yfabwk9.

Reapply/Not Reapply IE Group Policy Preferences Settings

As you learned in Chapter 5, all Group Policy Preferences items automatically reapply if users try to change them.

To change the behavior, inside the Group Policy Preference item, select the Common tab and then select "Apply once and do not reapply," as seen in Figure 12.10.

For more information on this procedure, again, check out Chapter 5 in the "Apply Once and Do Not Reapply" section.

FIGURE 12.10   Select "Apply once and do not reapply" to have your IE preferemces settings delivered only one time.

 Windows 2003 allows for what is known as "Internet Explorer Hardening," which is meant to prevent rogue Active X controls and the like from applying. Active X controls are little pieces of code that enhance the Internet Explorer experience but could be used maliciously. Microsoft has a great reference on the subject at http://tinyurl.com/54wwd. You can also search Microsoft's website for "Internet Explorer Enhanced Security Configuration."

Internet Explorer's Group Policy Settings

You're using a Windows 7 management station, right? Of course, right, because you read Chapters 1, 2, 3, 5, and 6. But if, for some reason, you're not (and you're using, say, a Windows XP or Windows Server 2003 management station), you might need to control the new goodies in Internet Explorer 7. If you need to do that, you'll must get the ADM files for Internet Explorer 7 to load on your management station. To do so, go to http://tinyurl.com/ynjyry (which expands to a Microsoft download) to get them. Then, use the information in Chapter 7 to import an ADM template.

Internet Explorer Settings Warning

As stated, configuring the Internet Explorer settings can be a bit wacky. There's one more wacky piece that makes them sometimes very difficult to work with. Some policy settings within Internet Explorer are "sticky." That is, they don't act like regular policy settings that just revert to some default when they don't apply.

If you set up Internet Explorer Maintenance policies at multiple levels in Active Directory, you'll want to test to see the "merging" of your policy settings. Some Internet Explorer Maintenance policy settings "merge," and others do not—it depends on what you are setting up. Proxy settings, for instance, do not merge; the last applied policy "wins." However, this is not true for the "Trusted Sites" configuration settings. These policy settings *will* merge. Again, be sure to test your GPOs with Internet Explorer Maintenance policies to verify whether or not your specific policy settings merge.

The one that comes to mind is the Internet Explorer Maintenance proxy server setting (mentioned earlier). If you later choose to work without a proxy server and kill the GPO, the proxy setting you set sticks with all your clients. It doesn't peel off the setting. This is a major hassle and one that has no great fix.

I retested this with Windows Vista's Internet Explorer 7, and, sure enough, they fixed it. But previous versions of the operating system aren't so fortunate.

I've heard reports of other Internet Explorer settings being sticky, but in my testing, the proxy setting is the only one I've witnessed being sticky. In short, before rolling out Internet Explorer settings (of any kind), you should also ensure that the settings you roll out are nonsticky. Or, if they are sticky, be sure to have a back-out plan to remediate the stickiness if you need to.

But wait. You say you are using a Windows 7 (or Windows Server 2008 R2) management station? Then, good news for you—the work is already done. The controls for Internet Explorer 7 are already in the box. Nothing to download, nothing to worry about.

The point of the Group Policy settings found in (User and Computer Configuration) ➢ Policies ➢ Administrative Templates ➢ Windows Components ➢ Internet Explorer ➢ Internet Settings, and in (User and Computer Configuration) ➢ Policies ➢ Administrative Templates ➢ Windows Components ➢ Internet Explorer is to guarantee settings.

In contrast, preferences (what we just saw earlier) "suggest" a setting; the Group Policy's policy settings "guarantee" it. Be sure to read both the Explain text for each Group Policy setting and the requirements. Not every setting is valid for both Internet Explorer 6 and 7, and/or 8, so be sure to read and test.

Do You Know about the Internet Explorer IEAK?

The IEAK (Internet Explorer Administration Kit) is used to set preferences or just to configure a stand-alone Internet Explorer machine. Sure, you'll usually want to use Group Policy in an Active Directory environment to set true policies (and lock down settings). But the IEAK uses a file type called .INS to set preferences. The IEAK can be downloaded here:

> www.microsoft.com/technet/prodtechnol/ie/ieak/default.mspx

The IE 8 IEAK can be found here:

> http://technet.microsoft.com/en-us/ie/cc889351.aspx

Once your .INS file is created, you can package it in a custom iesetup.exe, which can be used for deployment. Again, you'll usually not want to use the IEAK for domain-joined machines, as you've got the power of Group Policy to do that for you.

It's true, however, that the IEAK settings and Group Policy settings are darn close in similarity. But there are a few things that can be done *only* using IEAK that cannot be done through Group Policy. Two examples are the ability to set default feeds and the default search provider, which are only available in the IEAK.

But you might be asking yourself, "Which would 'win' if both applied?" The short answer is, "Whichever technology gets applied last."

So, if you start off with IEAK settings, those settings are applied.

If you later change to using Group Policy settings, those are applied.

In short, the advice is as follows:

- If you want to guarantee settings, and *can* use Group Policy to do so, you should strive to use Group Policy.

- If you haven't checked out the IE Group Policy Preference Extensions (explored in Chapter 5), you should try that next.

- Finally, only if you must, try the IEAK last.

For more information on the IEAK, check out this swell article in *TechNet Magazine*: http://tinyurl.com/ytuwnt, and this IE 8 IEAK blog entry: http://tinyurl.com/yjvfmbv.

Restricting Access to Hardware via Group Policy

You know it's true: those USB thumb-disk keys and removable media doodads make your personal life easier but your professional life harder. You want a way to control which hardware devices can be installed by users and which can't.

Thank you, Group Policy, for coming to the rescue.

Imagine this scenario: you allow users to have USB mice, but disallow USB Disk on Keys. You could allow CD-ROM readers, but not DVD writers. You could allow Bluetooth, but disallow PCMCIA.

You're in control, letting Group Policy do the work for you.

There are two ways to make this magic happen. One way disables the device, which is nice. But the other way restricts the driver itself from even loading. The first way uses the new Group Policy Preference Extensions' (GPEE) Devices extension.

> The GPPEs are valid for Windows XP and later. They're preinstalled in Server 2003 (when loaded), Windows 7, Windows Server 2008, and Windows Server 2008 R2.

The second way is via Group Policy's Administrative Templates. This method is valid for Windows Vista and later.

Table 12.1 will be the basis of our discussions. Here, we'll be able to see how the two Group Policy technologies compare and contrast. And when you're done reading this big section, come back to this table to make your final decision about which one to use (or, heck, maybe you'll decide to use 'em both!).

TABLE 12.1 GPPE Devices vs. Group Policy Device Installation Restriction

Feature Evaluation	GPPE Devices Extension	Device Installation Restriction
Valid for	XP+	Vista+
Mechanism	Disables the device	Prevents the driver from loading
Requirements	Machine must have Group Policy Preference Extensions	Vista+
User can avoid?	Possible: With admin rights, can re-enable	Possible: With admin rights, can avoid the Group Policy altogether, but more difficult

TABLE 12.1   GPPE Devices vs. Group Policy Device Installation Restriction *(continued)*

Feature Evaluation	GPPE Devices Extension	Device Installation Restriction
Notification of restriction	None	Pop-up balloon that doesn't always appear (not sure why)
Granularity	Works only to restrict Device Class and Device Type	Works to restrict from very specific hardware ID or generic Device IDs up to restricting the entire hardware class

Devices Extension

In Chapter 5, you learned about the Group Policy Preference Extensions (and how to install them). One of those extensions is the Devices extension. The Devices extension works for Windows XP and higher, provided the GPPE CSE is already loaded.

The Devices GPPE disables the device or port but *doesn't* prevent the driver from loading. The new Devices extension node is found by navigating to Computer Configuration ➢ Preferences ➢ Control Panel Settings ➢ Devices or User Configuration ➢ Preferences ➢ Control Panel Settings ➢ Devices. You can see the Devices Extension in Figure 12.11.

FIGURE 12.11   The Group Policy Preference Extensions have the ability to restrict devices and device classes. Here, I'm selecting a whole class to disable.

Why is it on both sides?

You'll use the Computer side when you want all users on the same machine to be affected by your edict. Use the User side when you want a specific person to be affected by your edict.

Most organizations will choose the Computer side. That way, everyone on the machine can be restricted from using, say, USB flash disks or floppy disk drives.

Deciding to Disable the Device Class or Device Type

In Figure 12.11, we can see the Select a Device Class or a Device dialog. Here you can select a root class, like **Ports (COM & LPT)**, or a specific device, like **Communication Port (COM1)**.

If you choose just the device class, only the "Device class" block gets filled in. If you choose the actual device, then both the "Device class" *and* "Device type" are populated, as seen in Figure 12.12.

FIGURE 12.12   Restricting a specific device.

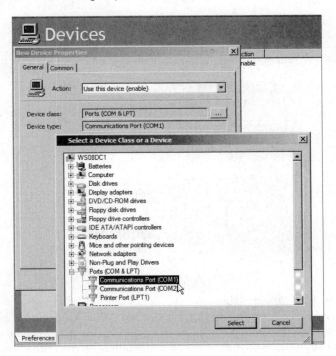

What Happens When a Device Is Restricted?

When a specific device is restricted, it is simply disabled, shown as the little down-arrow icon in Figure 12.13.

However, if you went the extra mile and disabled the class, then, usually, *all* devices within that class are restricted, as seen in Figure 12.14.

FIGURE 12.13   The Devices extension simply disables devices.

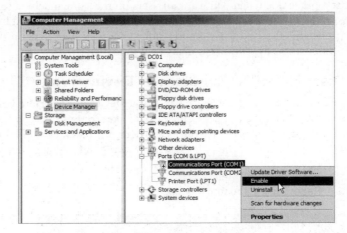

FIGURE 12.14   Disabling the whole class will disable all devices within that class.

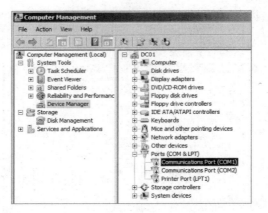

The issue is that, with proper rights, any user could right-click and re-enable the device (also seen in Figure 12.12). Now, by default, regular users (on Windows XP and later) cannot re-enable devices that are disabled like this. But because many organizations run their users as local admins, this could be easy for any admin-user to do. However, because Group Policy Preference Extensions leverage the Group Policy infrastructure, they take effect during the background refresh (about every 90 minutes or so). At that time, the device will once again be restricted.

   You cannot disable some devices. For example, on my Windows Vista machines, I was unable to disable processors. I'm pretty sure this is a "Good Thing."

Dealing with Devices That Aren't Listed

This is kind of a problem with the Devices extension: you cannot specify a piece of hardware that you don't already have on your management station.

So, while it's a snap to disable USB ports altogether, it's a lot harder to eliminate just thumb drives, or something specific like a 30GB color video iPod. In short, the easiest way to disable a device is to track one down and get it hooked into your management station. Then, you'll be able to just point to it and you're done.

Now, if you can't get a hold of the device, but you know someone who has one, you might still be in luck. That's right! Just the very act of knowing someone with the device might be able to help you get out of a jam. Instead of having to schlep that device over to your management station (or make the machine with the device a temporary management station), you can simply ask your pal to tell you what the device properties are and jam them into the XML code of the preference you created. (We covered how to edit the underlying XML code of a preference in Chapter 5.)

Table 12.2 shows what you need from the device property details and how to set them within the XML attribute.

TABLE 12.2   Device Property Details and Their Appropriate XML Attributes

XML Attribute	Device Property from Details Tab of Device Properties
deviceClass	Class long name
deviceType	Device description
deviceClassGUID	Device class GUID
deviceTypeID	Device Instance Path

The CSE has to have the deviceClassGUID and the deviceTypeID exactly as they are displayed in the device properties to correctly enable or disable the device.

Why Is There an Option to Disable and Enable?

A keen eye will spot that the Devices extension has both Disable *and* Enable.

The idea is simple: you can use GPO filtering or Group Policy Preference Extensions Item Level Targeting to decide, perhaps, who should get which hardware enabled or disabled. For instance, everyone who gets the GPO will have their USB ports disabled, except for Lab Technicians, who need USB ports enabled.

To do something like this, you might set the GPO at a high level (maybe a high-level OU or at the domain level) and then set it to Disabled. Then, lower down, say, at the **Lab Technicians** OU, set the USB ports as Enabled.

In my testing, Devices GPPE worked perfectly when I used Computer Configuration ➢ Preferences ➢ Control Panel Settings ➢ Devices. I restricted the hardware and ran the gpupdate.exe command, and my hardware was disabled. However, when I did the same thing using User Configuration ➢ Preferences ➢ Control Panel Settings ➢ Devices, and restricted the same hardware, it didn't always take effect right away.

Restricting Driver Access with Policy Settings for Windows 7

In the previous section, we talked about the Group Policy Preference Extensions and how, in using that technology, you can disable devices. That's great. But you can take it to the next level with two areas of Group Policy. There are two sections of Group Policy that we're going to talk about now to help you secure your hardware even further:

- Computer Configuration ➢ Policies ➢ Administrative Templates ➢ System ➢ Removable Storage Access (seen in Figure 12.15)

- Computer Configuration ➢ Policies ➢ Administrative Templates ➢ System ➢ Device Installation ➢ Device Installation Restriction (seen in Figure 12.16)

FIGURE 12.15 There are some predefined hardware restrictions you can leverage in Group Policy.

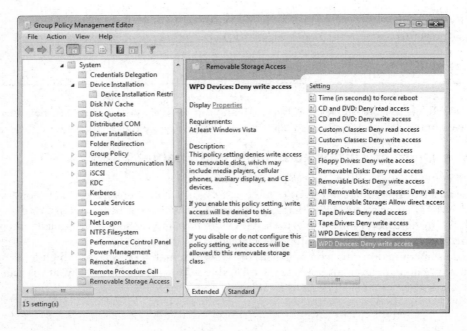

FIGURE 12.16   You can customize the kinds of hardware you want to restrict.

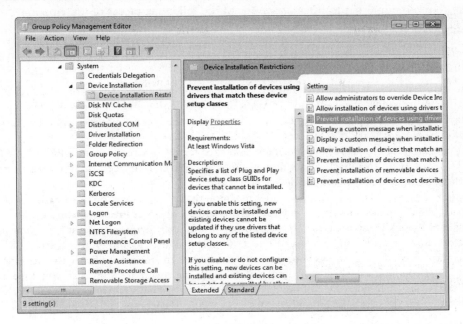

The first set (Removable Storage Access) is fairly self-explanatory. If you enable a policy setting for that kind of removable storage (CD/DVD, floppy, and so on), you can make it so that the whole device type cannot be read or written to. But it doesn't have the "super-power" the second set (Device Installation Restrictions) has.

In the first set, there is a policy setting group named **Custom Classes: Deny read access** and **Custom Classes: Deny write access**. It sounds like it has a similar ability to what we're about to explore. However, there is one difference. The Removable Storage Access policy set doesn't prevent the drivers from being installed. So, the driver for the class will be installed when the hardware is detected, but this policy prevents it from being read or written to. In the next section, when we explore the Device Installation Restrictions policy settings, we'll put the real smackdown on the driver itself.

Getting a Handle on Classes and IDs

First, you need to know what you want to restrict. You can think big or you can think small. As with the Devices extension, you can restrict a specific "class" of devices or get super-specific and restrict a single hardware type. Or you can allow only specific device classes, like USB mice.

Here's the trick: to really be effective, you're, once again, going to need to track down the hardware you'll want to restrict.

So, if you want to say "No joystick drivers can be installed on my Windows Vista machines," and "Only USB mice can be installed on my Windows 7 machines," you'll likely need to get hold of a joystick and a USB mouse. Now, this isn't always true. You can try to use the Internet to track down one of the following pieces of information:

- Hardware ID

- Compatible ID

- Device Class

But, again, it's much easier if you just have one of these devices in front of you. That way, you can introduce it to a Windows Vista or later machine and see for yourself what the Hardware ID, Compatible ID, or Device Class is. Once you know that, you'll know how to squash it (or leave it available).

In this example, we'll squash a specific sound card family: a Creative AudioPCI ES1371/ES1373. If you want to squash something else (like specific USB devices, or even USB ports), just follow along and substitute the device you want.

To do this, fire up Device Manager on a machine that already has the hardware items installed. Then, when you find the device, right-click it and select Properties and click the Details tab. By default, you'll see a "Device description." While interesting, it's not that useful. Select the Property drop-down and select "Hardware Ids," as shown in Figure 12.17.

The Hardware Ids page shows you, from top to bottom, the most specific to least specific Device ID. If you look closely at the topmost item in the Hardware Ids value list, you'll see this sound card is specifically a Rev 2 of the ES1371 soundboard. That's pretty darned specific. As you go down the list, the description becomes less specific to encompass the whole family.

FIGURE 12.17 The Details tab of the device helps you determine how to squash it.

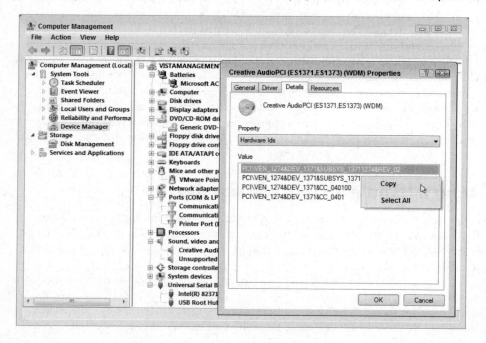

Additionally, you can change the Property setting to "Compatible Ids." These IDs also describe the hardware and are considered less specific than what you'll find in "Hardware Ids." You might choose to use the information found in "Compatible Ids" to try to corral more hardware that's similar into the "don't use" list—because it's less specific and might net you more results. The trade-off is that you might restrict something you didn't want to as you get less specific.

And, finally, the least specific category can be found by selecting Device Class from the Property drop-down. In my case, the sound card shows up as simply Media. But lots of things could be considered Media, so, again, caution should be used the less specific you go.

Once you've decided which value you want to leverage, right-click it, select Copy, and paste it into Notepad for safekeeping. Copying it directly as it's presented is important because, in the next steps, the value must be entered exactly. If there are upper- and lowercase characters in the value, they must be transferred precisely.

If you wanted to be a command-line commando instead of using the Device Manager to capture the Hardware IDs or Device Classes, check out the DevCon command-line utility at http://support.microsoft.com/kb/311272.

Microsoft has a bunch of identifiers for common classes here that may be helpful if you don't have any physical access to the device: http://go.microsoft.com/fwlink/?LinkId=52665.

Restricting or Allowing Your Hardware via Group Policy

Although we'll explore all the policy settings located in Computer Configuration ➢ Administrative Templates ➢ System ➢ Device Installation ➢ Device Installation Restriction (seen in Figure 12.18), there is really only one we'll need to complete this initial example.

Create a GPO and link it to an OU (or domain, and so on) that contains the Windows Vista and later machines you want to control. Then, edit the GPO and drive down into Computer Configuration ➢ Administrative Templates ➢ System ➢ Device Installation ➢ Device Installation Restriction ➢ **Prevent installation of devices that match any of these device IDs.** Select Enabled in the policy setting, click Show (also in the policy setting), and select Add in the Show Contents dialog box. Then, in the Add Item dialog box, paste in the information from the device you got before. All this can be seen in Figure 12.18.

There's also a switch inside this policy setting, "Also apply to matching devices that are already installed." Enabling this switch is a good idea if you want uniform restrictions. As soon as the next Group Policy update occurs, blammo! The hardware is locked out.

When you turn on a machine that has never seen the hardware device, you'll see the machine try to install the hardware device and provide pop-up balloon status information as to its progress. When completed, the goal is that the hardware is restricted, as you can see in Figure 12.19.

FIGURE 12.18   Paste the Device ID to ensure you've captured the device description exactly.

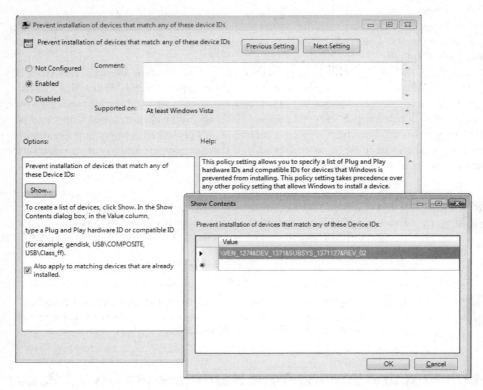

FIGURE 12.19   When implemented properly, the device driver will be prevented from installing.

Understanding the Remaining Policy Settings for Hardware Restrictions

In the example we just went through, we squashed the use of just one device. You could, if you wanted, go the opposite route, which is to restrict *all* hardware by default and allow only *some*. This can be done using the policy settings described next. Again, you can see a list of these policy settings in Figure 12.16, which shows the Computer Configuration ➤

Administrative Templates ➤ Device Installation ➤ Device Installation Restrictions branch of Group Policy.

Allow Administrators to Override Device Installation Restrictions

By default, local administrators on Windows Vista and later machines must honor the restrictions that are put in place. If you enable the **Allow administrators to override device installation restrictions** setting, local administrators can install whatever hardware they want.

Allow Installation of Devices Using Drivers that Match These Setup Classes

By entering device descriptions in this policy setting, you're expressly allowing these hardware devices as "allowed" into the system. Note that the **Allow installation of devices using drivers that match these setup classes** policy setting honors only setup classes, and not Device IDs (like those we used in the working example). You can learn more about setup classes at

```
http://msdn.microsoft.com/en-us/library/ms791134.aspx
```

Prevent Installation of Devices Using Drivers that Match These Device Setup Classes

In our earlier example, we used the Device ID to describe our hardware and enabled another policy setting, **Prevent Installation of devices that match any of these device IDs**. Note that the setting we used does not honor Class ID descriptions. To use Class ID descriptions, you need to use the **Prevent installation of devices using drivers that match these device setup classes** policy setting.

There's also a switch inside this policy setting, "Also apply to matching devices that are already installed." This is a good idea if you want uniform restrictions.

Display a Custom Message When Installation Is Prevented by Policy (Balloon Text) and Display a Custom Message When Installation Is Prevented by Policy (Balloon Title)

These are two policy settings that help you customize the message, as shown in Figure 12.19. However, I've noticed that sometimes, the custom text just fails to show up, and only the default text is shown.

Allow Installation of Devices that Match Any of These Device IDs

In our earlier example, we used the Device ID to describe our hardware. However, I also stated that the least specific way to describe our hardware is based on hardware class. It should be noted that the **Allow installation of devices that match any of these device IDs** policy setting does not honor Class ID descriptions. To use Class ID descriptions, use the policy settings **Allow installation of devices using drivers that match these device setup classes** or **Prevent installation of devices using drivers that match these device setup classes.**

This setting is best used with another setting, **Prevent installation of devices not described by other policy settings**. By preventing everything (by default), then using this setting, you can specify precisely which devices you want to allow to be installed.

Prevent Installation of Devices that Match Any of These Device IDs

In our example, **Prevent installation of devices that match any of these device IDs** is the policy setting we used to restrict a specific type of hardware based on Device IDs. If we wanted to restrict using Device Classes, we would have to leverage other specific policy settings such as **Allow installation of devices using drivers that match these device setup classes** or **Prevent installation of devices using drivers that match these device setup classes**.

Prevent Installation of Removable Devices

The **Prevent installation of removable devices** setting is a generic and quick way to restrict any hardware device that describes itself as "removable," including USB devices. I wouldn't count on this particular policy setting that often. Use the techniques described earlier to get moderately restrictive Device IDs and lock them down specifically. This setting is vague enough and there's no telling what the hardware is telling Windows about itself to be sure it's locking down what you think it is.

Prevent Installation of Devices Not Described by Other Policy Settings

The setting **Prevent installation of devices not described by other policy settings** is the catch-all policy setting that basically restricts all hardware, unless you've specifically dictated that something can install. This policy, in conjunction with the various "Allow" policies (such as **Allow installation of devices that match any of these device IDs**), can make a powerful combination you can use to allow only the hardware you want in your environment.

Time (in Seconds) to Force Reboot When Required for Policy Changes to Take Effect

The **Time (in seconds) to force reboot when required for policy changes to take effect** setting appears to be used when removing a driver would require a reboot to take effect. I didn't have a specific way of testing this, but it seems like a good idea to turn on this setting if you're about to restrict a lot of various hardware. Note this is a new policy for Windows 7 machines and will affect Windows 7 and Windows Server 2008 R2.

Assigning Printers via Group Policy

Let me guess what another of your biggest headaches is: printers, right? Wouldn't it be great if we could just zap printers down to our Windows XP, Windows Vista, and Windows 7 machines? Or, whenever Sally roams from Desktop to Desktop, she had access to the same printers?

Those are two different goals, and we're about to approach both of them here.

Ideally, you'll use the Group Policy Preference Extensions to zap printers to your users and computers. But the catch is that the Group Policy Preference Extensions client component needs to be already on your Windows XP and Windows Vista machines. Again, it's preloaded onto Windows 7 clients.

But if you have been able to get the Group Policy Preference Extensions on your target machines, let's explore how to zap printers down to your users.

Zapping Down Printers to Users and Computers (a Refresher)

We explored this subject briefly in Chapter 5, but here's a quick review.

The Printers Group Policy Preferences extension exists on both the Computer and User sides. On the Computer side, however, you can't map shared printers, but only TCP/IP and Local Printers, as you can see in Figure 12.20. On the User side, you can map all three kinds of printers, Figure 12.21 shows.

FIGURE 12.20   The Printers extension on the Computer side allows only for mapping TCP/IP and Local Printers.

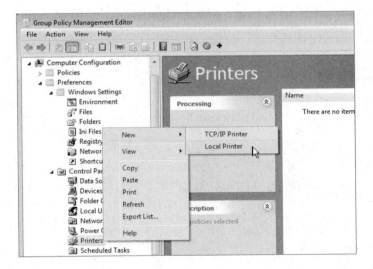

Setting up a shared printer on the User side is easy, as seen in Figure 12.22. Just set the share path to the printer share, and voilà—instant printer for the user. The bonus is that the user doesn't need to be an administrator to install the drivers that will come down from the server when this connection happens. The Group Policy engine does it on the user's behalf, so it's just done, lickety-split.

FIGURE 12.21   The Printers extension on the User side can deploy all three types of printers.

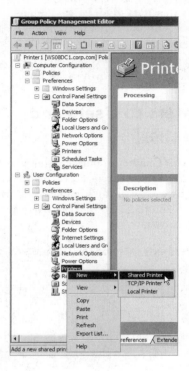

FIGURE 12.22   Shared printers are usually what most people set up.

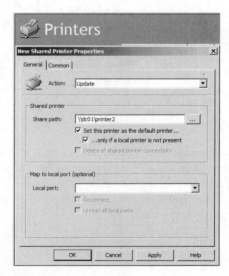

Trickier: Zapping Down Specific Printers to Users on Specific Machines

Oh, sure, you can use the Printers extension to map a specific printer to a specific user. But that means that no matter which computer a user travels to, he gets exactly the same printers.

But maybe that's not what you want. I talk with lots of people who have the same problem: how to map printers based on the computer the user is on at that moment.

Take Figure 12.23, for example. Here, you can see four zones:

- Zone 1 with Printer 1: IT computers
- Zone 2 with Printer 2: Human Resources
- Zone 3 with Printer 3: Sales
- Zone 4 with Printer 4: Marketing

FIGURE 12.23   In our sample company, we have four zones and one special shared printer requirement.

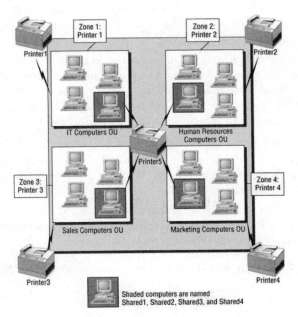

And, just for fun, I'm adding an additional challenge; a special circumstance where I have a shared computer in each zone that should not only print to the normal printer in that zone, but also map to an additional shared printer specific to the shared computers.

In Figure 12.23, our shared computer and shared printer are shaded. In these examples, the shared computers have the word "shared" in their names. This will be helpful later, as we craft our printing experience.

So the goal is that whenever anyone logs onto any computer in the zone, they get mapped to the printer for that zone.

To achieve the goal, we'll break this out into two steps:

1. Deploy the specific zone printer to all computers in the same zone.

2. Deploy the shared printer to only the shared computers in all zones.

Deploying the Same Printer to All Computers in the Zone

To accomplish our first goal, we want to make sure all computers in Human Resources get the same printer, Printer 2. You'll repeat the same procedure for other areas of your universe, but we'll just show Human Resources as an example.

We've already seen how you can't deploy Shared Printers to computers. That's a bummer, because our goal is that whenever anyone logs onto a Human Resources computer, he or she gets Printer 2.

And, natively, you can't do that. (You could do it with Group Policy Loopback in Merge mode, but you may end up getting unintended Group Policy Objects this way.)

But with a little one-two Group Policy Preference Extensions punch, we can do it without any Loopback hassle.

Punch 1: Put an environment variable on all computers in the zone   What we need is a way to tag the specific computers with a little marker, so that once we can see this marker, we can take action on it. We can use environment variables to make this little tag on specific computers, which will indicate that specific computers should use specific printers. We'll use the Group Policy Preference Environment Extension to do this for us.

Punch 2: Map Shared Printers only to users whose computers have the environment variable   Once we have the little tag on each computer, we'll use the GPPE Printers extension. We'll map shared printers to users, but only if the tag is present on the machine that specifies a printer.

Before we get started, make sure your **Human Resources** OU looks like mine does in Figure 12.24. You can see I've got **Human Resources Computers** and **Human Resources Users** within the **Human Resources** OU.

FIGURE 12.24   Make sure your Human Resources structure looks like mine.

Next, we'll create a GPO and link it over to the **Human Resources Computers** OU. We'll use the GPPE Environment extension to put a System variable on the computer called PRINTER2, and give it a value of 1 (which means true).

The idea is that if a computer in Zone 2 sees a variable with Printer2, that computer should get that printer. You can see this in Figure 12.25.

FIGURE 12.25   Use a System variable to tag computers to use specific printers.

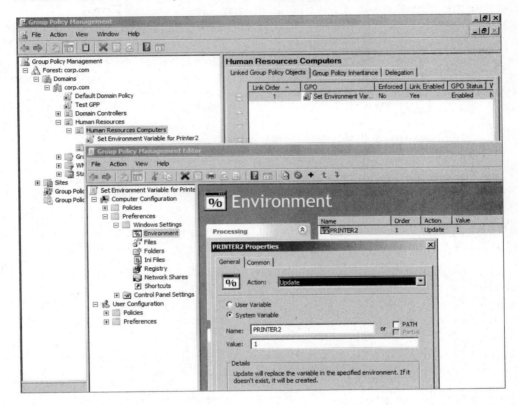

Then, create a GPO and link it to the domain level (or any higher level such that all the zones you want are covered). I'm calling my GPO "Universal Printer Map for Users." This GPO will affect all user accounts. It will use the GPPE Printers extension on the User side to map a shared printer, as seen in Figure 12.26.

Now, if we stopped here, we'd have a problem. That's because, right now, we're saying "Everyone should get \\dc01\printer2," and that's not right. What we want to say is "Everyone should get \\dc01\printer2—if they're using a computer that's tagged with the environment variable PRINTER2=1."

So, now, click the Common tab in the Printer extension properties. Then, click "Item-level targeting," as seen in Figure 12.27, and select the Targeting button to open the Targeting Editor.

FIGURE 12.26   Use the GPPE Printers extension to map a printer to everyone.

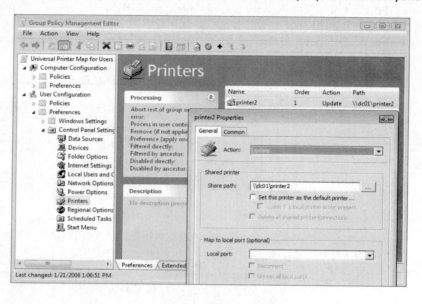

FIGURE 12.27   Use item-level targeting (ILT) to specify that the PRINTER2 environment variable must be set to 1.

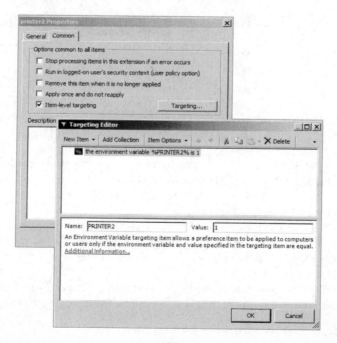

Add a New Item, select the environment variable, and specify that the PRINTER2 environment variable must be set to 1, as seen in Figure 12.27.

If all goes well, two things happen on the client system: they get the message that they should get the environment variable, and, because of that environment variable, anyone who logs onto that computer with the variable gets the printer.

Magic!

You can see this magic in Figure 12.28. The command prompt shows the environment variable PRINTER2=1, and the Printers dialog box shows the newly mapped printer based on the environment variable.

FIGURE 12.28   Based on the environment variable, anyone who uses this computer gets the printer.

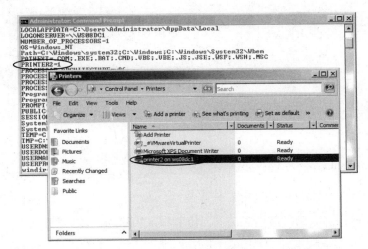

Because this "Universal Printer Map for Users" GPO is linked to the domain, it already affects every user account. And inside this GPO, you'll want to create a new preference item *for every printer*. The goal, again, is to make it such that the mapping of the printer only happens when computers have the environment variable present.

Deploying a Shared Printer to Only the Shared Computers in All Zones

In the previous example, we got everyone to use the specific printer for the computers in their zone.

However, remember that we have one special requirement: we want all the shared computers (in our examples, they're named SHARED1, SHARED2, SHARED3, and SHARED4) to use the same printer: Printer 5. So, this time, we'll use a trick in the ILT feature to specify that all computers with "shared" in the name will map to the same printer.

To do this, we'll create a GPO at the domain level called "Special Map for Public Computers" and use the Printers extension on the Users side to map \\dc01\printer5, but only when the computer name is SHARED-something.

We accomplish this by using the * indicator, as in SHARED*. You can see this in Figure 12.29.

FIGURE 12.29   You can map printers to users based on the computer name.

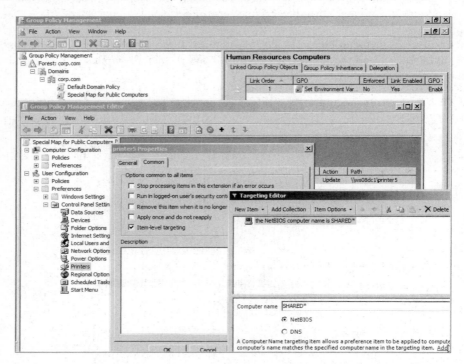

The star will evaluate to true for any computer named SHARED1, SHARED2, and so on.

Now, you've done it! You've got a universal way to ensure that people get a specific printer based on the specific computer they're logging onto. Indeed, if you were to log onto SHARED2, which is in the **Human Resources Computers** OU, you would now get two printers: you'd get Printer2 because you were in Zone 2 (from the first example), and Printer5 because you were on a shared computer, as seen in Figure 12.30.

FIGURE 12.30   Because you logged onto SHARED2, you got two printers.

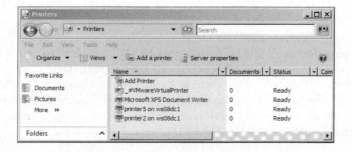

Shadow Copies (aka Previous Versions)

The idea behind Shadow Copies is awesome: preserve some number of copies of the user's precious files on the server. When the user performs a CLM (Career-Limiting Move) by deleting a file or overwriting a file with data that cannot be undone, that user can simply get that file back from a point in time. Microsoft's code name for this feature was Time Warp, and I think that pretty much says it all.

Technically, the system doesn't precisely store "copies" of a file; it preserves a "point-in-time" copy of a file—not a copy of all the bytes that compose the entire file. Sometimes, this magic is referred to as snapshots, though, technically again, it's not a direct bitwise snapshot of the file.

There are two versions of this feature:

- One works when the data is stored on a Windows Server 2003 or later machine. The clients can be Windows 2000 or later.

- The other version is built in locally to Windows Vista and later. So, if a user whacks a file on the local computer (and it wasn't ever saved on the network), you've still got the user covered.

Setting Up and Using Shadow Copies for Local Windows 7 Machines

By default, Windows Vista and later has System Protection enabled. This feature allows you to restore to a point-in-time backup if the operating system should have problems. System Protection existed in Windows XP, as well, but didn't capture the changes to data files. In Windows Vista, that's changed.

Again, System Protection is enabled, so a Windows Vista and later machine is automatically "doing its thing" and protecting the files. There isn't anything to "set up." System Protection *restore points* are created once every day and before a new driver is installed. You can also create a manual snapshot from the System Protection section of the System applet in Control Panel. Or, you can disable System Protection altogether (not recommended, though). Again, do this at Control Panel ➢ System ➢ System Protection.

When you're ready to restore a previous version of a file, you'll simply right-click over the file and select Previous Versions, as Figure 12.31 shows. In this example, you can see the Previous Versions tab shows one version of the file in a restore point cache, and the other one in from a previous backup.

Setting Up Shadow Copies on the Server

Shadow Copies work because you're making a *point-in-time* copy of the users' data files, which preserves them in case of a future calamity. The best place to do this is on the volume to which you've redirected Documents/My Documents. However, first you need to ask yourself several questions:

- How much junk, I mean, data, are my users taking up on each drive on the server?
- How much more space on this drive am I willing to cordon off to preserve previous versions of files?
- How often do I want to take a snapshot to preserve user data?

FIGURE 12.31   Windows 7's Previous Versions tab using local files.

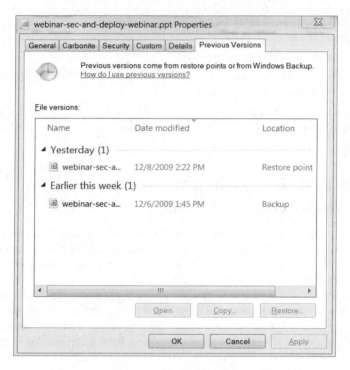

Once you answer these questions, follow these steps:

1. Right-click a drive letter on a server and choose Properties from the context menu to open the Properties dialog box, as shown in Figure 12.32.

2. Click the Shadow Copies tab, select a drive letter, and click the Settings button to open the Settings dialog box, as shown in Figure 12.33.

   Here, you can specify how much space you want to set aside for this particular volume. My recommendation is to set aside about 20–30 percent. The point of Shadow Copies isn't to keep backup copies of *all* user files forever; rather, similar to the Offline Caching mechanism, user files that get old will be flushed out of this space to make room for new files. Although Shadow Copies are a great preventive measure, they're not a substitute for general backups should the file turn out not to be available for restore.

3. In the Use Limit spin box, specify the size, and then click the Schedule button to open up the Schedule tab for the volume.

4. The Schedule tab is pretty self-explanatory. You might just wish to leave the defaults for now. When ready, click OK to confirm a changed schedule, or click Cancel to return to the Settings dialog. Click OK or Cancel again to return to the Properties tab.

FIGURE 12.32   You set the Shadow Copies characteristics on a per-volume basis.

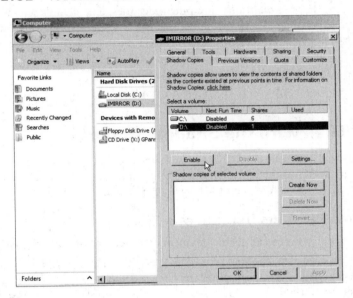

FIGURE 12.33   You can specify how much space to dedicate when files change, set a schedule to make Shadow Copies, and specify where to locate the storage area.

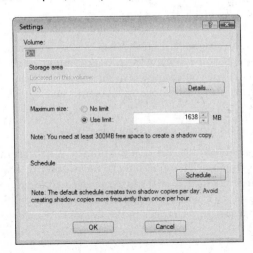

The default schedule for any enabled volume is at 7:00 a.m. and 12:00 p.m. workdays (Monday through Friday). The idea is that you'll snag points in time of the data before the workday begins, and again at the halfway point in the workday. If a user screws up and deletes a file, you've got at least two potentially restorable files from just today. If you have even more space available, you can store days or weeks of restorable data. Set the schedule however you want, but note two things:

- Shadow Copies keep a maximum of 64 previous versions of a file. Every time you take a snapshot, you're *potentially* dumping older files. The default schedule is usually pretty good for most organizations; it's estimated that it should provide about a month's worth of previous versions.

- The server will be hammered for a bit while the Shadow Copy snapshot is being made. Consequently, taking multiple snapshots during the day might not be such a hot idea. Therefore, you might want to perform fewer snapshots, say, once a day.

Restoring Files with the Shadow Copies Client

Before you can restore a file, the data must be Shadow Copied at least once, changed, and then Shadow Copied again. This process maintains a point in time of the volume—in its changed state and ready to be reverted to a previous version, or restored if it was deleted altogether.

Reverting to a Previous Version of a File

Users may inadvertently overwrite their documents with data, but you can give them the ability to revert to a previous version of the file. Ask your users to follow these steps:

1. Open the Documents folder, right-click any file, and choose Properties from the context menu to open the Properties dialog box, as shown in Figure 12.34. In Windows Vista and later, right-clicking a file in most cases will also have a "Restore previous versions" option, which takes you to the same place.

2. Click the Previous Versions tab.

3. Select the version you want, and then click one of the following:

   Open   Clicking Open (or, in pre–Windows Vista, View) launches the program associated with the file type, and you can view the file. You might be able to make temporary changes in the document, but you cannot save them back to the same place on the server as the original document. You can choose Save As and save the file somewhere else.

   Copy   You can copy the file to an alternate location. A popular location is the Desktop, but any locations that users have access to are equally valid.

   Restore   The title of this button is sort of a misnomer. When I think of the word *restore*, I think of restoring a deleted file, but the file needn't be fully deleted in order to use this option. Clicking this button will cause the selected file to revert to the previous version. Note, however, that it will overwrite the current version. So, use this Restore button with caution, because any changes in the document since a Shadow Copy was performed are deleted.

FIGURE 12.34　After at least one change is preserved, users can revert to a
point-in-time file.

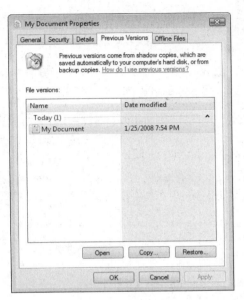

Restoring a Previous Version of a File

If a user deletes a copy of a preserved file, you or the user can restore it. Since we're using
Shadow Copies on the volume that houses our redirected My Documents/Documents, we can
leverage this magic.

On the Start Menu, locate My Documents or Documents. Then, right-click the user's My
Documents folder, choose Properties from the context menu to open the Properties dialog
box, and click the Previous Versions tab, as shown in Figure 12.34.

You'll have the same three options as before: Open, Copy, or Restore. My suggestion is to
select Open and then drag the file you need to the intended location, as shown in Figure 12.35.
Restore is quite dangerous: it will restore (replace, really) the *entire contents of the live folder*
from what's contained in the backup copy. This is not a good idea. In Windows XP, Restore
just lets you do this. In Windows Vista and later, it gets a little smarter, and UAC pops up and
asks for administrative credentials before restoring the whole shootin' match, as shown in
Figure 12.36.

Clicking Copy copies the entirety of the folder to a specific location; this is not all that useful, either, as the user might not want to restore the entirety of the point in time of the folder.

Shadow Copies completes the circle of user data protection. Without it, the only data
protection (other than normal, regularly scheduled backups) is Offline Files. Offline Files is
a good piece of technology, but, ultimately, not enough if the data on the server is deleted
or inadvertently overwritten.

FIGURE 12.35   You can restore the entire contents of the folder, or just use Open to drag and drop the file to be restored to an alternate location.

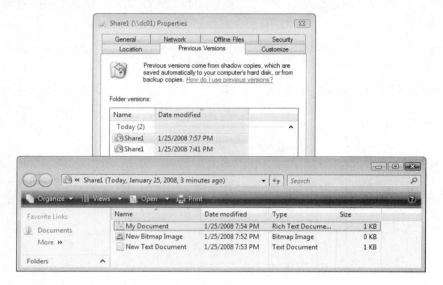

FIGURE 12.36   In Windows Vista and later, users are prevented from overwriting their entire Documents folder until admin credentials are provided.

Group Policy Settings for Shadow Copies

There are a handful of policy settings for Shadow Copies. You can see them in Figure 12.37.

FIGURE 12.37   Computer-side policy settings for Shadow Copies (also known as "Previous Versions").

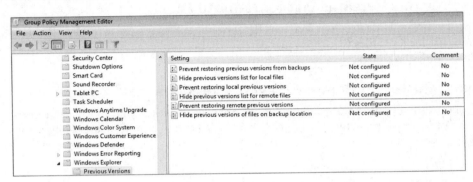

Actually, they are all listed under Shadow Copies' other name: "Previous Versions." You'll find the Computer-side entries within Computer Configuration ➢ Policies ➢ Administrative Templates ➢ Windows Components ➢ Windows Explorer ➢ Previous Versions. You'll find the User-side entries within User Configuration ➢ Policies ➢ Administrative Templates ➢ Windows Components ➢ Windows Explorer ➢ Previous Versions.

As with most policy settings, if there is conflict between the User side and the Computer side, the Computer side wins.

All settings are Windows Vista and later, even though Shadow Copies—I mean, Previous Versions—is available on Windows XP.

Prevent Restoring Previous Versions from Backups

If your users have access to locally created backups, you can enable the **Prevent restoring previous versions from backups** setting to prevent them from restoring previous versions from within those backups.

Hide Previous Versions of Files on Backup Location

The policy setting **Hide previous versions of files on backup location** removes the "Restore Previous Versions" menu item for use with backup media.

Hide Previous Versions List for Local Files

The policy setting **Hide Previous Versions list for local files** removes the "Restore Previous Versions" menu item from the context menu when you right-click over a file protected by local Shadow Copies.

Prevent Restoring Local Previous Versions

When the setting **Prevent restoring local previous versions** is enabled, the list of previous files can be seen, but the Restore button is removed. Interestingly, though, the Copy To button *is* available, and this means users *can* technically restore files—but they're restored (overwritten, really), rather than copied to another location.

Hide Previous Versions List for Remote Files

The policy setting **Hide Previous Versions list for remote files** is similar to **Hide Previous Versions list for local files** (which we just described), but applies to files leveraging network Shadow Copies on shares.

Prevent Restoring Remote Previous Versions

The policy setting **Prevent restoring remote previous versions** is similar to **Prevent restoring local previous versions** (which we just described), but applies to files leveraging network Shadow Copies on shares.

Final Thoughts for This Chapter and for the Book

The cake might be yummy, but we appreciate the frosting first.

In this chapter, we added some frosting to our already hearty, secure, and managed desktop cake. We leveraged login and startup scripts to automate user tasks. We managed Internet Explorer settings using some new techniques. We used Hardware Control to keep the bad devices off our network, and ensured that users had printers exactly when they needed them. And we made sure we could recover user's junk, I mean, files, very quickly using Shadow Copies.

I hope you enjoyed this book. It was fun to share with you some of my favorite tips, tricks, and insights into Group Policy and Desktop nirvana.

I hope you'll join me at www.GPanswers.com and explore the rest of the resources we have:

- A killer newsletter
- Constantly updated FAQ and "Tips and Tricks"
- A video series
- A community room to help get your most pressing questions answered
- And, of course, my hands-on training to take your game to the next level. You can do this with me, live and hands on, or online using my Group Policy Online University (where I'm *still* available one-on-one to help you through your toughest challenges)!

We also have some bonus chapters on GPanswers.com to round out your experience with Group Policy.

Thanks for making it to the end of the book. I hope to meet you in person at a conference or when you take one of my live training classes.

For sure, I'll see you at GPanswers.com—where *smart* Group Policy admins come to get *smarter*!

Jeremy
Moskowitz

Group Policy Tools

Obviously, the power of Group Policy is awesome, but some aspects of Group Policy and desktop management are better suited to additional tools. In this appendix, we're going to leverage a variety of tools to perform several key duties. We'll also finish discussing what the GPMC has to offer, specifically, migrating existing GPOs between domains. We'll then dive into the other free Group Policy management tools from Microsoft.

Last, we'll round up extra tools, including third-party Group Policy tools I think you'll find useful. However, note that Group Policy tool manufacturers constantly create and innovate. To that end, some manufacturers choose to show off their products on www.GPanswers.com, so be sure to check out my website's "Solutions Guide" for updated information (if available).

Securing Workstations with Templates

The Security Section of the Group Policy editor has a lot of nooks and crannies to configure. To help quickly mass-configure machines to certain security specifications, you can leverage what's known as security templates.

A security template is nothing more than a collection of security settings wrapped up in an easy-to-deploy, text-based .INF file. Once you have the .INF file locked and loaded the way you want, you can leverage Group Policy to assert your will across your enterprise.

You leverage security templates that come from many sources:

- Some templates are built into Windows. These predefined templates exist for workstations, servers, and Domain Controllers, and they range in intensity from "default security" to "highly secure."

- Note that neither Windows Vista nor Windows 7 has templates included in the box. Windows XP does, though.

- You can create your own security templates from scratch or use the predefined templates as a jumping-off point to create your own. (I don't cover this in the book. If that's interesting to you, then pick up a previous edition of the book.)

- Microsoft and other noted third parties have their own collection of security templates for your use.

Let's take a look at what predefined templates are available to us, from what sources, and what machine types they can be used on.

When we get a grip on that, we'll then use a template to lock down multiple machines at once using the broad stroke of Group Policy.

 I encourage you not to do anything with these templates until you read all the way through this section.

Incremental Security Templates

The supplied templates tighten or loosen a workstation, server, or DC (whichever the specific case may be), using the Security Configuration and Analysis MMC snap-in or the `secedit` command-line tool. (Both are described in detail later in this appendix.)

Domain Controller *.INF* Template Files

These `.INF` settings apply to Windows 2003 Domain Controllers.

securedc   Increases the security required in the Password policy and Account policy, bumps up the amount of auditing that occurs on the Domain Controller, and increases some Event log settings, such as the size. This template doesn't modify any file or Registry ACLs (access control lists).

hisecdc   Chokes off all communications with down-level machines by turning off NTLM communication. Only those machines that use NTLM v2 or Kerberos will be able to communicate with any machines to which this template is applied.

 Applying the `hisecdc.inf` template to Domain Controllers is dangerous and can prevent clients from authenticating to your Domain Controllers.

XP Professional *.INF* Template Files

These settings apply to Windows XP Professional machines.

compatws   Applications must pass certification guidelines to be considered Windows Logo–compliant. Sometimes, an older application does not follow the new rules once it's up and running. Use this template to allow some older applications (such as Office 97), which are not Windows Logo–certified, to run properly when mere mortals in the Users group run them.

This template elevates the permissions of the Users group by modifying common Registry keys, files, and folders. Often, administrators will give in and grant users who complain about incompatible applications admission into the Power Users group. Applying this template should satisfy their needs without putting them in the Power Users group. Because of this, this template removes all users and groups from the Power Users group.

You can see this behavior for yourself. As an administrator, load Word 97 (yes, old and crusty Word 97, if you can find it) with the Office 97 spelling check feature onto an NTFS volume on a Windows XP machine. Then, log back on as a regular user and, using that Word 97 installation, try to run the spelling utility. As a regular user, you cannot, because certain files must be read/writable to the installation point of Office 97 (usually under Program Files). Apply this template, and your woes disappear. The `compatws.inf` template modifies NTFS permissions on the Program Files folder so that mere mortals can modify the settings.

You can find certification guidelines for applications at www.`microsoft`.com/windowsserver2003/partners/isvs/cfw.mspx.

securews   These settings increase the security required in the Password policy and the Account policy, bump up the amount of auditing that occurs on the workstation, and increase some Event log settings such as the size. This template doesn't modify any file or Registry ACLs.

hisecws   This template turns off NTLM communication and allows only communication with other machines that are running NTLM v2 or Kerberos. NTLM v2 is available on Windows 2000 and later. Kerberos is also available on Windows 2000 machines and later. As with the `compatsw` template, all users and groups are flushed from the Power Users group. A note of caution here: the `hisecws.inf` template turns off NTLM authentication and allows communication only with other machines that are running NTLM v2 or Kerberos.

Microsoft gives you a nitty-gritty look at the provided XP templates at http://tinyurl.com/47e5u, and in Knowledge Base article 816585 (for Windows Server 2003, http://support.microsoft.com/kb/816585) and Knowledge Base article 309689 (for Windows 2000, http://support.microsoft.com/kb/309689).

Other Security Template Sources

There are several places where you locate additional templates to use on your systems.

Security Templates from Uncle Bill

There are a variety of `.inf` templates available from Microsoft you can use, depending on your situation.

Windows Server 2003 Security guide and Threats and Countermeasures guide
For Windows Server 2003, two publications that work in tandem to help administrators secure both Windows Server 2003 and Windows XP are the "Windows Server 2003 Security Guide" and "Threats and Countermeasures: Security Settings in Windows Server 2003 and Windows XP."

At last check, those documents can be found here: http://tinyurl.com/dkbu and http://tinyurl.com/ygacb8b.

The download includes several ready-to-use security templates that will go a long way to help you secure your environment. You'll find suggested templates for Domain Controllers, IIS, IAS, member servers, print servers, client systems, and more.

Security Compliance Management Toolkit templates   I touched upon the the Security Compliance Management Toolkit in Chapter 8. I described the GPOaccelerator tool, which will take the guidance in these tools and create ready-to-use GPOs for you to explore.

You can also grab .inf templates from the same download. There are some downloadable security templates (.INF files) for Windows XP, Windows Vista, Windows 7, and Windows Server 2008. Check out the following guides and links:

   http://technet.microsoft.com/en-us/library/cc677002.aspx

Security Templates from Uncle Sam

A US government agency has provided its take on some proper security templates:

National Institute of Standards and Technology   NIST has some templates to help secure Windows XP and Windows Vista:

- For XP: http://csrc.nist.gov/itsec/guidance_WinXP.html
- For Vista: http://csrc.nist.gov/itsec/guidance_vista.html
- For Windows 7: Nothing yet, but keep checking the NIST website.

Applying Security Templates with Group Policy

Group Policy's mission is to make broad-stroke enforcement a piece of cake, and this instance certainly qualifies.

Let's say you want to deploy a fictitious template, named hisecws_plus.inf, on all the computers in the **Nurses Computers** OU. To do so, follow these steps:

1. Ensure that the **Nurses Computers** OU exists. (We're making it up for the sake of example here.)

2. Move all machines to be affected by this security edict into the **Nurses Computers** OU.

3. Create a new GPO and link it to the **Nurses Computers** OU. This GPO will be used to import the settings inside the hisecws_plus.inf template you created. Give the GPO a descriptive name, such as Force hisecws_plus.inf.

Once you're editing the GPO, drill down to Computer Configuration ➢ Windows Settings ➢ Security Settings. To utilize any security .INF template, simply right-click Security Settings (as shown in Figure A.1) and choose Import Policy from the context menu.

FIGURE A.1 Drill down into the Security Settings, right-click, and then import a template.

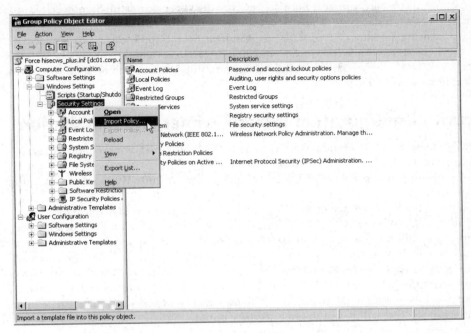

Select the policy you want to use by pointing the file requester toward the `hisecws_plus.inf` file and selecting it. You'll also notice a "Clear this Database Before Importing" check box:

- When this check box is checked, the current Security settings are replaced with those that you defined in the custom `.INF` template.

- When this check box is unchecked, only the attributes you specifically modified are changed. In other words, the state is maintained in those attributes that have no definition.

Now you are ready to reboot the machines affected by the **Nurses Computers** OU, or you can wait until the machines embrace the new security settings you specified in the GPO. Afterward, you can verify that the settings you specified in the `hisecws_plus.inf` template are indeed being reflected and locked down across all machines in the OU.

The Security Configuration Wizard

In the previous section, you learned how to leverage security templates and secure your workstations. You then linked a GPO, slurped in the security template, and secured a gaggle of workstations all in one goal.

In this section, the goal is similar.

But this time, you'll use something called the Security Configuration Wizard (SCW). I know, I know. You hate wizards. But this one is really super-powerful. So powerful, in fact, that it has its own home page at www.microsoft.com/scw. Wow!

If you're using Windows Server 2003 or Windows Server 2008, things are somewhat different. Let's start with Windows Server 2003, and then review the changes in Windows Server 2008. Note: the wizard for Windows Server 2008 R2 seems to be similar to the one for Windows Server 2008.

Security Configuration Wizard Primer and Installation

The SCW doesn't exist in Windows Server 2003 RTM. However, with Windows Server 2003/SP1 and later, it's there if you want it.

It's built into Windows Server 2008 and Windows Server 2008 R2, so there's nothing extra to add.

You'll run the SCW on one of your Windows Server machines, say, your Domain Controller. You'll tell the SCW which "roles" the Domain Controller has. For instance, perhaps, in addition to being a Domain Controller, it's a print server and a file server, and also maybe a DHCP server. Once you've told it what the machine will be used for, it will pop out a security policy that describes how to secure this Windows 2003 server. Next, you'll convert the policy into a GPO. Finally, you'll link the GPO to an OU in Active Directory, which contains the collection of Windows servers you want to secure. Hence, all servers in the OU will have the same security policy.

The true goal of the SCW is to "reduce the attack surface." That's the common phrase used when we want to stop all unused services and close up any remaining unused doors. We won't be able to go over all the ins and outs of the SCW. But we will go through a simple example and, as icing on the security cake, put a Group Policy cherry on top at the end. It'll be sweet.

One warning before we get going here: the tasks you perform with the SCW are strictly to secure your Windows servers—not your *workstations*.

The output produced by the SCW is *not* meant to secure your Windows 7, Windows Vista, Windows XP, or Windows 2000 machines. Doing so *could* render your workstations unrecoverable.

Also, it's unclear to me if you can take the output, from say, the 2003 version of the SCW and affect 2008 machines without any problems—or the 2008 version of the SCW and affect 2003 machines. For safety's sake, I recommend using only the 2003 version's output and affecting Windows Server 2003 machines. And I recommend using the Windows Server 2008 version's output and affecting only Windows Server 2008 machines.

Installing the SCW for Windows Server 2003 (SP1 and later)

As stated, the SCW is available only on Windows 2003 machines after SP1 is loaded. Once it's been loaded, the SCW's help icon should automatically appear on the Desktop. However, this does not mean that the SCW is actually installed. To install the SCW, you need to sojourn to Add/Remove Programs and specifically add it. Let's do that now. To install the SCW:

1. Log onto your Windows 2003/SP1 Domain Controller as Administrator.

2. Click Start ➤ Control Panel ➤ Add or Remove Programs.

3. Click the Add/Remove Windows Components button.

4. In the Components list, locate and select Security Configuration Wizard, as seen in Figure A.2.

FIGURE A.2   The Security Configuration Wizard's help file automatically appears on the desktop after SP1 is loaded. However, you need to specifically add in the SCW components via Add/Remove Programs.

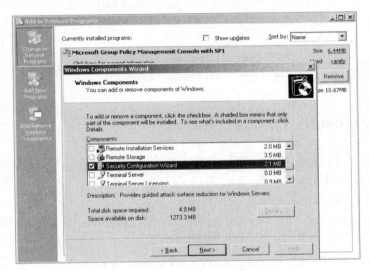

5. Click Next to load the component and close Add/Remove Programs.

   Once the SCW is loaded, you're ready to rock.

Installing the SCW for Windows Server 2008

The good news for Windows Server 2008 and Windows Server 2008 R2 fans is that the SCW is already preinstalled. All you have to do is click Start ➤ All Programs ➤ Administrative Tools and select Security Configuration Wizard, as seen in Figure A.3.

A Practical SCW Example

In this example, we'll produce an SCW policy that turns off all unnecessary services for our Domain Controller. And we'll leverage this policy for additional Domain Controllers (later) if more come aboard. To create an SCW policy, you'll run the wizard in several steps.

FIGURE A.3 The SCW is preloaded and ready to go for Windows Server 2008.

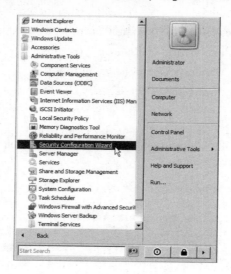

Initial SCW Kickoff

To get started with the SCW:

1. Start the SCW by clicking Start ➤ All Programs ➤ Administrative Tools ➤ Security Configuration Wizard.

2. At the first screen of the wizard, click Next.

3. At the Configuration Action screen, ensure that "Create a new security policy" is selected and click Next, as shown in Figure A.4.

FIGURE A.4 Kick off the SCW by creating a new security policy.

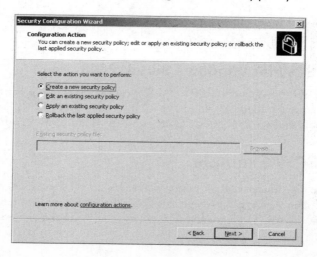

4. At the Select Server screen, ensure that the DC01 server is selected and click Next. This is the machine that we'll leverage as the baseline machine; the SCW will inspect this machine and see what's running on it so it can make some determinations about which services you might want to secure. When you click Next, the SCW will inspect this machine and try to determine what its current roles are.

5. After the SCW checks out your system, you'll receive a Processing Complete message and be given the opportunity to "View Configuration Database." The Configuration Database is a list of all possible roles the server might play. So, at this time, just click Next.

Role-Based Configuration Section

In this section, you'll have the SCW figure out what roles your server currently has installed. To inspect for roles:

1. Now, you'll be at the first screen of the Role-Based Service Configuration. This section of the wizard helps you add or remove roles this server might be playing. Again, as a Domain Controller, it might also be a print server. Click Next to continue.

2. When you do, you'll be at the Select Server Roles screen, where you are viewing a list of installed roles, as seen in Figure A.5. The SCW takes a "best guess" about what it thinks this server is already trying to do and selects those as installed roles. If you have future plans for this machine (or for others later, as you add to the OU) and want to add a role, go ahead at this point. You can select from the list presented here or use the View drop-down list and select to see all roles. Perhaps someday, you'll also use certificate services on this machine. In that case, you would need to locate Certificate Server in the list and check it. When you've selected the services you want, click Next.

FIGURE A.5   The SCW shows you the roles it thinks are currently running on your server.

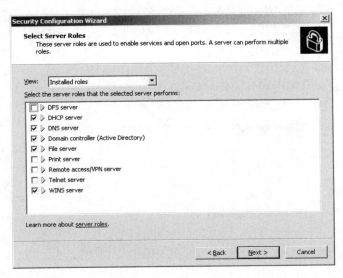

3. Now, you'll be at the Select Client Features screen. Here, you'll specify which client components your server runs. Again, by default, it chooses which components it thinks are already in use. Note that for some reason, Group Policy Administrative Client isn't selected, even though the GPMC is detected. I'm not sure why this is overlooked and unselected by default. But, in short, if you plan on running the GPMC on the servers that will get this policy, be sure to also select Group Policy Administrative Client.

4. Choose any additional features you know you are using or want to eventually use and click Next.

5. You'll be at the Select Administration and Other Options page. Like the pages before it, it makes a best guess about which options you want to use. Choose any additional features you know you are using or want to eventually use and click Next.

6. At the Select Additional Services page, the SCW looks to see if there are any services you might have also loaded. By default, those are checked to continue to run. Click Next to continue.

7. At the Handling Unspecified Services page, you're asked how to handle the services you loaded on the Windows 2008 machine. Select "Do not change the startup mode of the service" and click Next.

8. At the Confirm Service Changes page, you can see what will happen to the myriad services running on your Domain Controller. In Figure A.6, you can see that many services, currently set to Automatic, will now be configured to Disabled.

9. When you click Next, you'll proceed to the Network Configuration Section.

FIGURE A.6   The SCW will make your system less vulnerable to attack by disabling unused services.

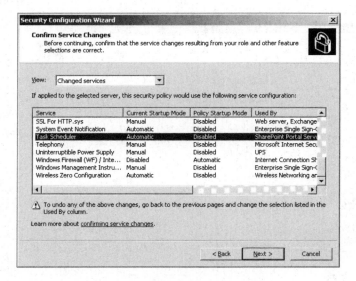

Network Security Section

In Windows Server 2003, the firewall is off by default. This means that applications and users can knock on your Windows Server 2003 servers' doors and say, "Hi. Is there anyone there who can help me?" And Windows Server 2003 always says, "Yes."

But in Windows Server 2008 and later, the firewall is on by default. This means that applications and users knock on your Windows Server 2008 servers' doors and get no response at all—ever—unless that port is open and listening.

You can decide how you want to deal with this. For Windows Server 2003, you can:

- Leave the firewall off. This is the Windows Server 2003 default configuration.

- Turn the firewall on and poke the right hole through for applications to work. This would be making Windows Server 2003 act like Windows Server 2008 and later. This approach is more work but probably a good idea.

For Windows Server 2008, you can:

- Turn off the Windows Server 2008 firewall entirely, and make Windows Server 2008 act like the older Windows Server 2003. Not a great idea, but it's the quickest, yet least secure, way to get applications to talk to your server.

- Leave the Windows Server 2008 firewall on, and poke the required holes through.

My suggestion for both Windows Server 2003 and Windows Server 2008 is to ensure the firewall is on, then poke the required holes through. And that's what this part of the wizard does (see Figure A.7).

FIGURE A.7 You can specify that a specific program have an exception to the firewall rule.

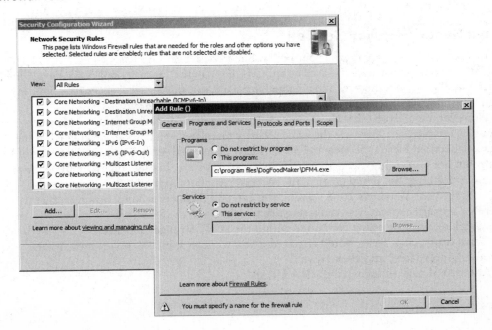

So, if you choose to continue with this section, you'll encounter the following pages (which are similar in idea to the already examined pages). That is, the wizard tries to determine what you're already doing on this system and keeps those parts enabled and available for use; it will also close off sections that it thinks are not being used. However, if you zip through this section, you're basically telling the SCW to turn on the Windows firewall for servers that this security policy will affect. That's a risky game because if you fail to open a port, your clients won't be able to access a program running on your server. So, proceed down this section with caution.

For your first tests, accept all the defaults and click Next.

Registry Settings Section

Like the previous section, this section is optional. Here, you can make decisions about SMB signing, which operating systems can connect to this server, LDAP signing, outbound and inbound authentication methods, and more.

If you're interested, read the materials on this section at `www.microsoft.com/scw`.

For our examples, we're going to skip the Registry Settings Section by selecting "Skip this section" and clicking Next.

Audit Policy Section

Again, this section is optional, and I think you'll likely want to skip it. We examined Audit policy in Chapter 8, and you've probably configured your audit policy manually and set it on the OUs containing the servers you want to audit.

Moreover, as the caveat at the end of this SCW section describes, after these settings are set, they are permanently tattooed.

For our purposes, we'll select "Skip this section" and click Next.

Save Security Policy Section

At this point, you're ready to save your policy. But it doesn't get saved as a GPO. No, no! That would be too easy! Instead, it is saved as an XML file! On the "Security policy file name" line, enter a legal path on this server and a name for the file, say, `c:\OurSecureDCPolicy.xml`. In the Description field, enter something useful as well, as seen in Figure A.8.

However, before you click Next, note that you can also, optionally, choose "Include Security Templates." These are the same security templates you could have created in the previous section. Here's the idea: the SCW is easy to use and lets you manipulate a lot of stuff, but not everything. Security templates are hard to use, but let you manipulate (just about) everything. So, if you created any security templates that additionally increased security for your Windows 2003 servers, you can add them here. Note, however, that if there's a settings conflict between a security template and the SCW, the "winner" will be the template, not the setting contained within the SCW. Strange, but true.

When ready, click Next. You'll be asked if you want to apply the policy now or later. Choose "Apply later" and click Next.

At the final page of the wizard, click Finish.

FIGURE A.8 Here, you can add additional security templates or just save your SCW policy as an XML file.

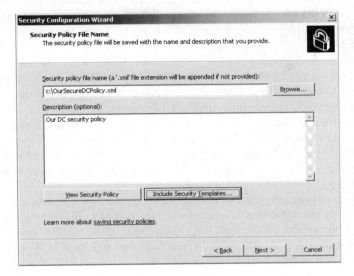

Converting Your SCW Policy to a GPO

At this point, you've got a nice XML file that you, well, can't do a lot with in its current form. However, the goal is to convert this XML file to a bona fide GPO that you can then link to an OU of your choosing. In this case, you will link it to your **Domain Controllers** OU.

You can covert the GPO with the `scwcmd.exe` command. The syntax of the command line is as follows:

```
scwcmd transform /p:name_of_xml_file_ /g:name_of_GPO_we_want_to_create
```

So, because you saved the XML file as `c:\OurSecureDCPolicy.xml`, and you arbitrarily call the GPO "OurSecureDCGPO," the syntax will be:

```
scwcmd transform /p:c:\ourSecureDCPolicy.xml /g:OurSecureDCGPO
```

Once the command is performed, you should get a "Command completed successfully" message. A GPO is now created with the name you've provided after the /g (in this case, OurSecureDCGPO).

WARNING IIS configuration that is defined in the SCW policy is not parlayed into a transformed GPO. It is lost.

Viewing and Applying Your Transformed GPO

Next, fire up the GPMC to see if the GPO you just created by transforming the XML file is there. It should be in the Group Policy Objects node but not linked to any site, domain, or OU. Note that you might have to refresh the list of GPOs in the Group Policy Objects node to see the new GPO.

When ready, link the GPO you created to the final destination. In our example, you would link the GPO to the **Domain Controllers** OU. You don't need to do this now, but you can do so if you choose. Again, the GPO will just sit there in the Group Policy Objects node swimming pool—doing nothing—unless it's linked to a GPO.

One quick warning about the GPO that is created: if you click the Settings tab in the GPMC to see the resulting GPO, you might not see anything! However, if you edit the GPO, you'll be able to see the settings that are contained within the GPO (see Figure A.9). This micro-bug appears in Windows 2003 but has been fixed in Windows 2008.

Note that if you change any settings within the GPO, the problem magically fixes itself, and then you can see the settings contained within the GPO by clicking the Settings tab. Something about editing the GPO inside the Group Policy Object Editor fixes the converted GPO and makes it viewable. Again, this is a bug that never got fixed in Windows Server 2003 but seems to be fixed in Windows Server 2008.

FIGURE A.9 The Settings tab might not show any settings from the transformed GPO. However, editing the GPO will show that the settings are indeed changed inside the GPO.

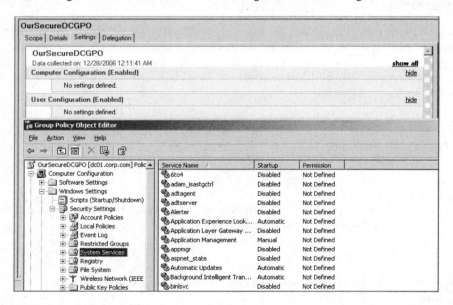

SCW Caveats

There are two additional warnings when using the SCW to create XML policies and then convert them to GPOs:

Don't use the SCW (and corresponding GPOs) to apply settings to machines other than the type you created it on   So, the SCW exists for Windows Server 2003 and Windows Server 2008. The current word from my contacts at Microsoft "is to make sure the output of a Windows Server 2003 SCW (and its GPOs) affects only Windows Server 2003 and the output of a Windows Server 2008 SCW (and its GPOs) affects only Windows Server 2008."

There might be cases where it's okay to "cross the streams" (and I'm working on getting that information to you; be sure to check www.GPanswers.com newsletters). But until then, create GPOs and link them to places that affect only the machine types you created the policy on in the first place.

But in no case should output from the SCW be used to affect and apply to Windows 7 or Windows XP systems. It's only meant for servers.

Don't expect file and Registry ACLs to be able to "roll back"   After you lay down file or Registry ACLs using GPOs, you cannot roll these settings back. They are always permanently tattooed on the target system. It doesn't matter how you lay down those file or Registry ACLs; it can be from the security templates directly or via GPOs. There's just no way for ACLs to be rolled back.

Migrating Group Policy Objects between Domains

For years, I stood in front of large audiences and recommended testing the power of GPOs in a test forest. In return, I'd get blank stares because this advice was inherently impractical. Sure, it was safe—safer than testing GPOs in production—but ultimately, my advice was doomed. How can you do the hard work in a test domain, test it, debug it, get it all right, and then lift it out of its original test lab universe and put it in production? Answer? Until the GPMC, you couldn't.

These examples will continue with our fictional multidomain environment. You can flip back to Figure 4.7 to see the relationship between our three domains: Corp.com, Widgets.corp.com, and the cross-forest trust between bigu.edu and Corp.com.

Basic Interdomain Copy and Import

Using the GPMC, you can take existing GPOs from any domain and copy them to another domain. The target domain can be a parent domain, a child domain, a cross-forest domain, or a completely foreign domain that has no trusts. Both the Copy and the Import operations transfer only the policy settings; these operations do not modify either the source or the destination links of the GPOs.

The Copy Operation

The interdomain Copy operation is meant to be used when you want to copy live GPOs from one domain to another. That is, you have two domains, connectivity between them, and appropriate rights to the GPOs. To copy the GPO, you need Read rights on the source GPO you want to copy and Write rights in the target domain.

First, you want to tweak your GPMC console so that you can see the two domains you want.

> Recall that to add new domains to the GPMC, you simply right-click Domains and choose Show Domains from the context menu to open the Show Domains dialog box. Then, simply select the domains you want to see. To add other forests, right-click Group Policy Management and choose Add Forest from the context menu to open the Add Forest dialog box. You can then enter the name of the domain in the forest.

In this first example, we'll copy a GPO from Corp.com to Widgets.corp.com. An enterprise administrator will have rights in all domains. Since we're logged in as an enterprise administrator, we have rights in both Corp.com (to read) and Widgets.corp.com (to write). Follow these steps:

1. In the Group Policy Objects container, right-click the GPO you want to copy, as shown in Figure A.10. For this example, I've chosen the "Hide Settings Tab/Restore Screen Saver Tab" GPO.

2. Adjust your view of the GPMC so that you can see the target domain. In Figure A.10, I've minimized the view of Corp.com and expanded Widgets.corp.com—especially the Group Policy Objects container.

3. Right-click the target domain's Group Policy Objects container, and choose Paste to start the Cross-Domain Copying Wizard.

4. Click Next to bypass the initial splash screen and open the "Specifying permissions" screen, shown in Figure A.11.

You can now choose to create a GPO with the default permissions or to copy the original permissions to the new GPO. The latter might be useful if you've delegated some special permissions to that GPO and don't want redo your efforts. Most of the time, however, the first option is fine. You can now zip through the rest of the wizard.

> You might see a message about migration tables. Don't fret; they're right around the corner. For this specific GPO, you won't need migration tables, so it won't be an issue.

FIGURE A.10   You can copy a GPO from the Group Policy Objects container.

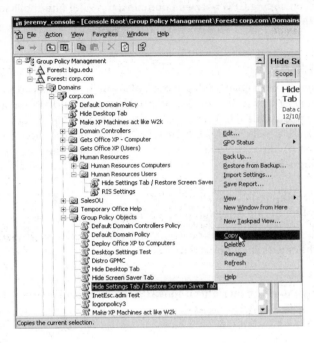

FIGURE A.11   When you paste a GPO, you can choose how to handle permissions.

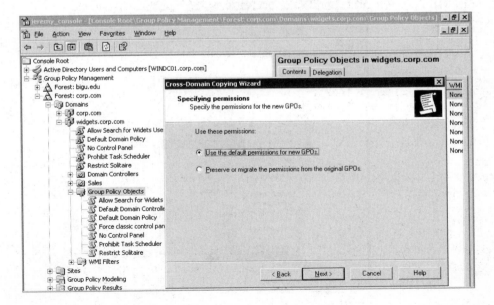

> If you copy a GPO between domains, the WMI filtering is lost because the WMI filter won't necessarily exist in the target domain.

The Import Operation

In the previous scenario, we copied a GPO from Corp.com to Widgets.corp.com. We did this when both domains were online and accessible. But if you are working on an isolated testing network, this won't be possible. How, then, do you take a GPO you created in the isolated test lab and bring it into production? First, create a backup, as described in Chapter 2. You'll then have a collection of files that you can put on a CD and take out into the real world. You can then create a brand-new GPO (or overwrite an existing GPO) and perform the import! Follow these steps:

1. Right-click the Group Policy Objects container, choose New from the context menu to open the New GPO dialog box, and in the Name Field, enter the name of a new GPO.

2. Right-click that GPO and choose Import Settings from the context menu, as shown in Figure A.12. This starts the Import Settings Wizard.

> Anyone with Edit rights on the GPO can perform an Import.

FIGURE A.12   You can import the settings and overwrite an existing GPO.

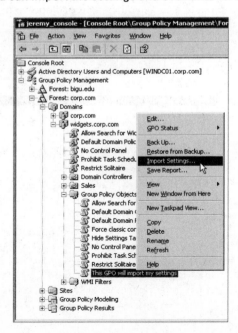

You can choose to overwrite an existing GPO, but that's just it. It's an over-write, not a merge. So, be careful!

3. The wizard then presents the Backup GPO screen, which allows you to back up the newly created GPO; however, this is unnecessary. Backing up is a safety measure should you decide to overwrite an existing GPO. You can then click Next to see the Backup Location screen.

4. In the Backup Location screen, use the Backup folder field to input the path to where your backup set is and click Next. The Source GPO screen will appear.

5. At the Source GPO screen, select the GPO from which you want to import settings, as shown in Figure A.13, and click Next.

FIGURE A.13   Select a GPO from which you want to import settings.

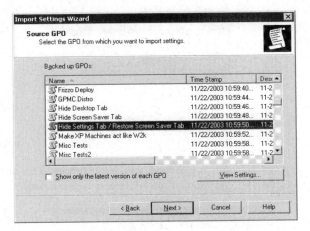

You should now be able to zip through the rest of the wizard. Ignore any references to migration tables; they're coming up next.

Copy and Import with Migration Tables

In the previous examples, we migrated the very simple GPO named "Hide Settings Tab/Restore Screen Saver Tab." That particular GPO contained only Administrative Template settings that affected the Desktop. Nothing fancy, for sure.

However, certain policy settings do perform some fancy footwork. Some GPOs can include references to security groups, such as "Allow Log on Locally." Other GPOs can include references to UNC paths, such as Folder Redirection. Indeed, an Advanced Folder Redirection policy setting contains both security group references and UNC path references. Other possibilities include Restricted Groups, Group Policy Software Installation policy settings, and pointers to scripts.

A Word about Drag and Drop

Dragging and dropping a GPO from one domain into another domain can be hazardous. For example, your intention is to copy a GPO named "Restrict Solitaire" from the GPO container in Widgets.corp.com to the **Human Resources Users** OU in Corp.com. It looks like it's going to make sense: you set up your view in the GPMC to show both domains, you can see the Group Policy Objects container in Widgets.corp.com, and you can see the **Human Resources Users** OU in Corp.com. Then, you drag and drop, and you're asked the following question:

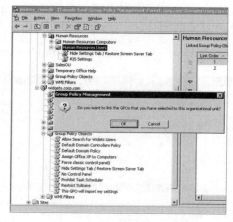

If you click OK, you're not actually copying! Indeed, you're performing a no-no! You are creating a cross-domain link to the GPO, as you can see when you click the Details tab of the GPO:

In this example, the Domain field shows that it lives in Widgets.corp.com, even though the GPO is linked to an OU in Corp.com.

Whenever a GPO is linked from across a domain, the GPO must be pulled from a Domain Controller that actually houses it. If it's across the WAN, so be it. And that could mean major slowdowns.

The moral of the story is to be sure you're copying (as described earlier) and not just linking.

When you migrate GPOs across domains, you need to take care of these references. Copying a GPO in one domain that redirects folders to the \\DC01\Data share will not likely make much sense when the GPO is used in another domain.

With that in mind, both the Copy and Import functions can leverage *migration tables*. Migration tables let you rectify both security group and UNC references that exist in a GPO when you transfer the GPO to another domain. You'll be given the opportunity to use the migration tables automatically if your Copy or Import operation detects that a policy setting needs it. After the GPO is ready to be copied or imported, you'll be notified that some adjustments are needed. It's that easy.

In the Migrating References screen of the wizard (shown in Figure A.14), you can choose two paths:

FIGURE A.14 A migration table can smooth the bumps between domains.

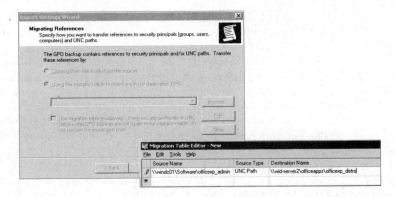

- Selecting "Copying them identically from the source" can be risky. Again, you won't know what the source is using for security groups or UNC paths. The existing security groups and UNC paths may be valid, but they may not be.

- Selecting "Using this migration table to map them in the destination GPO" gives you the opportunity to choose an existing migration table (if you have one), or you can click the New button to open the Migration Table Editor and create one on the fly.

To start, use a new blank migration table (after clicking the New button) and follow these steps:

1. If you're performing a Copy, choose Tools ➢ Populate from GPO to open the Select GPO screen; then, simply select the live GPO. If you're performing an Import, choose Tools ➢ Populate from Backup to open the Select Backup dialog box, which allows you to select a GPO from backup.

2. Choose the GPO you're copying or importing to display a list of all the references that need to be corrected.

3. In Figure A.14, you can see both the Source Name and the Destination Name fields. The Source Name field will automatically be filled in. All that's left is to enter the Destination Name UNC path for the new environment, and you're done.

4. Save the file (with a `.migtable` extension), and close the Migration Table Editor—New screen.

5. Back at the Migrating References page, simply click Browse and choose the migration table you just made.

Before clicking the Next button, you can optionally choose the check box that begins with "Use migration table exclusively." In this example, we have but one UNC reference that needs to be rectified. You might have a meaty GPO with 30 UNC paths and another 50 security principles that need to be cleared up. Perhaps you can't locate all the destination names. If you select this check box, the wizard will not proceed unless all the paths in the destination name are valid. Use this setting if you need to be sure all settings will be verified successfully.

When ready, click Next. Click Next again at the summary screen, and you're finished.

Microsoft has a detailed white paper you'll want to check out if you're planning to do a lot of this. You'll find it at

`www.microsoft.com/windowsserver2003/gpmc/migrgpo.mspx`

The only downside is that migration tables do not honor or care about anything in the Group Policy Preferences. So, if you have references in the original (source) domain, they are usually just copied through, without any possibility of translating them via a migration table. Note that Microsoft's pay product, AGPM 4.0, does have the ability to migrate between domains and includes support for Group Policy Preferences.

Wholesale Backup and Restore of Your Test Lab (or an Easy Way to Migrate to Production)

One more tip before we leave this section: when you're working in your test lab, you might find it necessary to completely demolish and rebuild your test lab for a variety of reasons. However, as noted in Chapter 2, when a GPO is restored, the links are not restored along with the GPO. Again, this is a protection mechanism for your benefit. However, as they say in the hallowed IT halls, "What you do in the test lab stays in the test lab." So, the test lab is a different animal. And, to that end, you might want to back up a whole gaggle of stuff for safekeeping:

- GPOs

- Group Policy links

- Security groups

- OUs

- Users

- Permissions on GPOs

Then, if you need to demolish your test lab and put it back in order, you'll need a way to perform a wholesale restore of all these objects. The GPMC has a built-in script that will back up all these things into one little package. Then, when you're ready, you run another script that takes the package and expands it back into these objects.

The script that does all the backup stuff is called CreateXMLFromEnvironment.vbs. The one that does all the restoring is CreateEnvironmentFromXML.vbs. Both scripts are located in C:\Program Files\GPMC\scripts (with the GPMC 1.0, and available for download for the updated GPMC at http://tinyurl.com/2quhw5). The scripts are not present by default on Windows Vista or later machines; you'll need to download them from the Scripting Center on Microsoft's website.

The other reason to use these scripts is to do a wholesale migration from the test lab into the real production environment. Personally, I'm not all that keen on a wholesale backup and restore of my test lab into the real world, but I guess if you had nothing at all in the real world, this could be a useful way to get things over lock, stock, and barrel. These scripts are a little too far-reaching for my taste, but perhaps you'll find them just the thing.

Microsoft has various documents about this script, so check out www.microsoft.com for some tips about using it. For instance, there's a Microsoft Knowledge Base article on this script at http://support.microsoft.com/kb/929397.

Microsoft Tools Roundup

As might be expected, Microsoft has a slew of tools to help you manage your Group Policy infrastructure as well as your user profiles. In this section, we'll check out the Microsoft tools and where to find them.

Group Policy Tools from Microsoft

Except for Active Directory Monitor and GPInventory, you can download the remainder of the Microsoft tools for free from the Windows 2003 Resource Kit. As of this writing, you can find what you need at:

www.microsoft.com/windowsserver2003/downloads/tools/default.mspx

under the heading "Windows Server 2003 Resource Kit Tools." After you install the Resource Kit, you'll find the tools in the \Program Files\Windows Resource Kits\Tools folder. Some of these tools are ready to use; others require additional installation.

Active Directory Monitor and GPOTOOL

These tools help to troubleshoot GPOs if the GPC and GPT get out of sync. See Chapter 7 for information.

GPMonitor—Group Policy Monitor Tool

The purpose of GPMonitor, which is shown in Figure A.15, is to perform historical analysis of what has changed between different Group Policy refresh intervals on your clients and servers. This tool requires an armload of additional installation; it unpacks to a set of files that need to stay together. You deploy the MSI (Microsoft Installer) to two locations: the clients you want to monitor and a management station that you'll use to see your results. After you unpack the MSI, you deploy the MSI file via GPSI (Group Policy Software Installation) to the clients. Additionally, this package comes with an ADM template, which you need to import into the Group Policy Management Editor. The point of the ADM file is to push the data about the client's Group Policy application to a central shared folder location.

Once your clients start pushing up the data, you can run the GPMonitorUI at your management station to see what's going on. The clients will upload their historical data every N Group Policy refreshes. (The default is every 8.) From your management station, you can then see which GPOs did or did not apply yesterday but are applying today—among other possibilities.

This tool seems to be reliable only on Windows XP and not Windows Vista and later.

FIGURE A.15 GPMonitor.

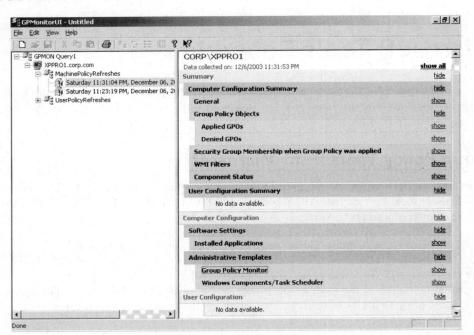

Your management station needs the GPMC loaded to display the data as seen in Figure A.15, but the clients you want to monitor do not.

GPInventory—Group Policy Inventory Tool

GPInventory is a late addition to the Windows 2003 Server Resource Kit. You must download and install it separately. To find it, search for "Group Policy Inventory" on Microsoft's website. At last check, it could be found here: `http://tinyurl.com/b38lu`.

GPInventory can reach across the network and query your clients and servers for a list of attributes you want to document in Excel or a text file. Simply point GPInventory toward a list of clients, select the attributes you want to gather, and then let it do its thing. Afterward, just save the resulting file.

In Figure A.16, I can easily find out how much memory my Windows XP clients have by selecting the WMI: Computer Memory field and documenting the RSoP (Resultant Set of Policy) status of all my clients with some of the other attributes.

FIGURE A.16   Group Policy Inventory.

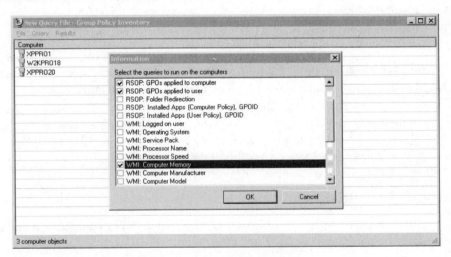

You can even change the default attributes that GPInventory will inventory for via the XML file. Read the included documentation for a how-to.

There's a great little article on GPInventory in Microsoft *TechNet Magazine*, found here: `http://tinyurl.com/2gw2ry`.

ADMX Migrator

The ADMX Migrator is actually two tools in one: an ADMX Migrator tool and an ADMX Editor tool. We discussed these tools in the section "ADMX Migrator and ADMX Editor Tools" in Chapter 6.

Group Policy Log View (GPLogView)

A new tool for Windows 7, Group Policy Log View helps you quickly view operational log results and put them in file types of your choice. We saw this tool in Chapter 7. Again, for reference, you can download it here:

```
http://go.microsoft.com/fwlink/?LinkId=75004
```

Profile Tools from Microsoft

Microsoft also has two tools to help manipulate profiles if they need a kick in the pants:

The Delprof Tool   You use this utility to bulk-delete profiles—either locally or remotely. An update is available at

```
www.microsoft.com/windowsserver2003/techinfo/reskit/tools/default.mspx
```

This is a command-line tool, so be careful; you can get in a lot of trouble in a hurry. Microsoft has a nice Knowledge Base article on this tool (315411 at http://support.microsoft.com/kb/315411) that discusses how to eliminate profiles if they are not used in, say, 30 days.

The Proquota Tool   You can use this tool to limit the size that the roaming user profile can become. This isn't a tool you can run per se. It's part of the operating system. It is invoked whenever the Limit profile size policy setting in User Configuration ➢ Policies ➢ Administrative Templates ➢ System ➢ User Profiles is set to Enabled.

Utilities and Add-Ons

There are utilities that pop up all the time to help with Group Policy management and configuration. Here are some you might find interesting:

Disable Group Policy (KillPol)   This utility temporarily stops the application of policy to help troubleshoot a system. It was originally created in 2004; you can find a new version at www.smart-x.com/.

RGPrefresh   Command Line GPO Refresh can be found here: www.gpoguy.com/Free-GPOGuy-Tools.aspx.

GPSI Viewer   This is a GUI utility for viewing and printing information on all software installation packages in a domain; you can also find it at www.gpoguy.com/Free-GPOGuy-Tools.aspx.

WMI Filter Validations utility   This is a GUI utility for testing WMI filters on a given Windows system prior to implementation; you can also find it at `www.gpoguy.com/Free-GPOGuy-Tools.aspx`.

Central Store Creator utility   This is a tool that lets you create and populate the Central Store easily; you can also find it at `www.gpoguy.com/Free-GPOGuy-Tools.aspx`.

PowerShell Cmdlets for Group Policy   These are free add-ons to PowerShell for excellent Group Policy integration (`http://sdmsoftware.com/freeware.php`). Learn more in our downloadable bonus chapter on Group Policy and PowerShell.

Specops GPUpdate   This is a Group Policy refresh utility that hooks into Active Directory Users and Computers; you can find it at `www.specopssoft.com/products/specopsgpupdate/`.

Specops Command Basic   This utility is a great way to use PowerShell scripts on your Group Policy clients: `www.specopssoft.com/powershell/`.

Specops Password Policy Basic   This utility helps tame fine-grained Password policies with a nice GUI: `http://tinyurl.com/34e3ud`.

PolicyReporter   This utility helps analyze both Windows XP and Windows 7 logs to help locate Group Policy problems: `http://tinyurl.com/2ft4nq`.

PolicyPak Design Studio   This utility helps you create a great Group Policy interface to manage and lock down your applications: `www.PolicyPak.com`.

Third-Party Vendors List

When I wrote the first edition of this book, only one or two vendors were doing interesting stuff with Group Policy. By the time I wrote the second edition of this book, I had a handful of vendors with a handful of products.

Vendors are now recognizing the power that Group Policy provides. Some vendors are adding to the management capabilities of GPOs, others help in GPO troubleshooting, and still others take the next logical step and extend Group Policy to harness even more power. By the third and fourth editions, the list just kept growing!

In this sixth edition, I'll list all the vendors I know that make third-party products. Note that names of products change, and features change all the time. To that end, it's better to simply visit a company's website to get a rundown of its current offerings.

Additionally, some vendors showcase their products on

`www.gpanswers.com/resource/solutions-guide.html`

Table A.1 lists tools that can help you in your Group Policy journey. In these tables, I provide a short description of the product.

TABLE A.1 Group Policy Management Tools

Vendor	Product	Company Website	Brief Description
Avecto	Privilege Guard	www.avecto.com	Helps you set applications to run as admins and users to run with least privilege.
AdventNet	ManageEngine ADManager Plus	www.manageengine.com/	Web-based product that simplifies Active Directory management from a central point. Has reports about Group Policy health.
BeyondTrust	Privilege Manager	www.beyondtrust.com	Helps you set applications to run as admins and users to run with least privilege.
Centrify	DirectControl	www.centrify.com	Extends Group Policy to Linux systems.
Configuresoft	Enterprise Configuration Manager	www.configuresoft.com	Centralizes and automates the labor-intensive task of planning, auditing, and monitoring changes in Group Policy objects on Windows systems deployed in large enterprise networks or web server farms.
FullArmor	Group Policy Anywhere	www.fullarmor.com	Separates Group Policy from Active Directory, allowing you to start using Group Policy today even if you are still planning for Active Directory or Group Policy.
FullArmor	PolicyPortal	www.fullarmor.com	Enforces and audits Group Policy on all machines on your network and over the Internet.
Likewise Software	Likewise Enterprise	www.likewise.com	Extends Microsoft Group Policy to Unix, Linux, and Mac.
PolicyPak Software	PolicyPak Professional	www.policypak.com	Locks down your applications with policy so users can't work around settings.

TABLE A.1 Group Policy Management Tools *(continued)*

Vendor	Product	Company Website	Brief Description
Specops Software	Special Operations Suite	www.specopssoft.com	A broad and deeply Active Directory–integrated Desktop Management suite for organizations of all sizes.
Specops Software	Specops Deploy	www.specopssoft.com	Enhances the native Group Policy Software Installation functions.
Specops Software	Specops Password Policy	www.specopssoft.com	Sets individual password requirements per OU.
Specops Software	Specops Inventory	www.specopssoft.com	Provides hardware and software inventory via Group Policy.
Specops Software	Specops Command	www.specopssoft.com	Distributed PowerShell solution that enables PowerShell deployment and execution using Group Policy.
SDM Software	GPExpert-Troubleshooting Pak	www.SDMsoftware.com	Four products (Health Reporter, Log Analyzer, Status Monitor, and Group Policy Spy) to ensure that Group Policy is functioning across your desktops and servers.
SDM Software	GPExpert Status Monitor	www.SDMsoftware.com	System tray application for desktops that helps desktop administrators find out when Group Policy is not working.
SDM Software	GPExpert Scripting Toolkit for PowerShell	www.SDMsoftware.com	Automates Group Policy management using PowerShell.

TABLE A.1   Group Policy Management Tools *(continued)*

Vendor	Product	Company Website	Brief Description
SDM Software	GPExpert Backup Manager for Group Policy	www.SDMsoftware.com	Manages the backup and recovery of GPOs and GPO links in your Active Directory environment.
Attachmate/ NetIQ	Group Policy Administrator	www.netiq.com	Provides change-management capabilities to Group Policy.
Attachmate/ NetIQ	Group Policy Guardian	www.netiq.com	Performs auditing of Group Policy changes.
Secure Vantage	Policy Controls Management Pack for MOM	www.securevantage.com	Performs auditing and discovery of Group Policy inside Microsoft MOM.
Secure Vantage	Group Policy Auditor for SCOM	www.securevantage.com	Detailed GPO attribute discovery and auditing, reporting, change alerting, and more.
ScriptLogic	Active Administrator	www.scriptlogic.com	Provides Group Policy auditing and change management.
SysPro Software	Polman	www.SysProSoft.com	A Policy Management tool; easily interprets policy settings.
Quest	GPOAdmin	www.quest.com/gpoadmin/	Provides change management capabilities to Group Policy.
Quest	Quest Authentication Services	www.quest.com/ authentication-services/	Extends Group Policy to Linux.

Index

Note to the reader: Throughout this index **boldfaced** page numbers indicate primary discussions of a topic. *Italicized* page numbers indicate illustrations.

B

H

S

U